MW00783259

PATERNOSTER BIBLICAL MONOGRAPHS

Hebrews, Christ, and the Law

The Theology of the Mosaic Law
in Hebrews 7:1-10:18

A complete listing of all titles in this series and Paternoster
Theological Monographs will be found at the close of this book.

PATERNOSTER BIBLICAL MONOGRAPHS

Hebrews, Christ, and the Law

The Theology of the Mosaic Law
in Hebrews 7:1-10:18

Barry C. Joslin

WIPF & STOCK · Eugene, Oregon

Wipf and Stock Publishers
199 W 8th Ave, Suite 3
Eugene, OR 97401

Hebrews, Christ, and the Law
The Theology of the Mosaic Law in Hebrews 7:1–10:18
By Joslin, Barry C.
Copyright©2008 Paternoster
ISBN 13: 978-1-60608-474-8
Publication date 2/18/2009
Previously published by Paternoster, 2008

Series Preface

One of the major objectives of Paternoster is to serve biblical scholarship by providing a channel for the publication of theses and other monographs of high quality at affordable prices. Paternoster stands within the broad evangelical tradition of Christianity. Our authors would describe themselves as Christians who recognise the authority of the Bible, maintain the centrality of the gospel message and assent to the classical credal statements of Christian belief. There is diversity within this constituency; advances in scholarship are possible only if there is freedom for frank debate on controversial issues and for the publication of new and sometimes provocative proposals. What is offered in this series is the best of writing by committed Christians who are concerned to develop well-founded biblical scholarship in a spirit of loyalty to the historic faith.

Series Editors

This book is dedicated to Jessica, my wonderful wife and confidant, and to our three children, Haddon Walter, Carson Douglas, and Elisabeth Sharon. You bring me inexplicable joy and are tangible blessings from the Lord God. May he "equip you with everything good that you may do his will, working in us that which is pleasing in his sight through Jesus Christ, to whom be glory forever and ever. Amen" (Hebrews 13:21).

Contents

Preface   xv
Abbreviations   xvii

Chapter 1
An Introduction to the Theology of the Mosaic Law in
Hebrews 7:1-10:18   1
Introduction   1
Thesis   2
Scope   5
Scholarly Contributions   6
  No Ongoing Validity in the New Covenant Era   8
  Ongoing Validity in the New Covenant Era   14
  Conclusion   20
Method   21

Chapter 2
The Law in Second Temple Judaism   23
Introduction   23
Old Testament Apocrypha   25
  The Wisdom of Ben Sira   27
  1 Maccabees   31
  2 Maccabees   34
  Tobit   37
  1 Baruch   39
  Conclusion   42
Old Testament Pseudepigrapha   42
  2 Baruch and 4 Ezra   43
    INTRODUCTION   43

2 BARUCH   45
4 EZRA   48
Jubilees   52
4 Maccabees   55
Conclusion   58
Josephus   59
   Introduction   59
   Josephus' Own Testimony   61
      CONCERNING THE LAW   61
      JEWS AND THE LAW   62
      JOSEPHUS' TWO SUMMARIES OF THE LAW   65
   Conclusion   66
Philo of Alexandria   67
   Introduction   67
   The Law of Moses and the Law of Nature   68
   Philo and the Patriarchs   71
   The Law and the Jewish People   72
   Conclusion   74
The Dead Sea Scrolls   74
   Introduction   74
   The Community Rule (1QS)   75
   The Damascus Document (CD)   81
   Conclusion: The Community Rule (1QS)
      and the Damascus Document (CD)   85
Conclusion   87

Chapter 3
Hebrews 7:1-10:18 and the Structure of Hebrews   91
Introduction   91
Major Issues and Approaches   92
   Donald Guthrie   95
   Leon Vaganay   97
   Ceslas Spicq   100
   Wolfgang Nauck   102
   Albert Vanhoye   104
   F. F. Bruce   109
   Harold Attridge   113

George Guthrie 116
INTRODUCTION 116
HORTATORY SECTIONS 121
EXPOSITIONAL SECTIONS 123
CONCLUSION 125
Conclusion 125

Chapter 4
Hebrews 7:1-28 – Change in the Law **132**
Introduction 132
Exegetical Overview of Hebrews 7:1-28 135
  Hebrews 7:1-10 135
    HEBREWS 7:1-3 135
    HEBREWS 7:4-10 138
  Hebrews 7:11-19 141
  Hebrews 7:20-28 154
Hebrews 7 and Νόμου Μετάθεσις 158
  Νόμος and Διαθήκη 159
  Νόμου Μετάθεσις 164
Conclusion 171

Chapter 5
Hebrews 8:1-13 – A New Covenant Blessing:
The Law Written on the Heart **173**
Introduction 173
Exegetical Overview of Hebrews 8:1-13 176
  Hebrews 8:1-6 177
  Hebrews 8:7-13 182
    PURPOSED INSUFFICIENCY 183
    VERSES 8b -12 185
    NEW COVENANT BLESSINGS 188
    VERSE 13 189
    BOTH PROMISES (8:10-12) ESSENTIAL 189
Excursus: Jeremiah 31:31-34 192
  Context of Jeremiah 31 193
  Meaning of Verse 33a 196
  The LXX's Plural Νόμους 199

Conclusion   200
Use of Jeremiah 31:31-34 (LXX 38:31-34) in Hebrews 8   200
Hebrews and the Old Testament   200
Hebrews and Jeremiah 31:31-34 (LXX 38:31-34)   204
Νόμους in Jeremiah 31:33/Hebrews 8:10   206
Conclusion   206
Νόμος in Hebrews 8:10 (10:16)   208
The Non-View   209
The No-Correspondence View   210
The Direct-Correspondence View   213
The Transformed View   216
   DIFFICULTIES WITH THE NO-CORRESPONDENCE VIEW   217
   DIFFICULTIES WITH THE DIRECT-CORRESPONDENCE VIEW 219
   PROPOSED SOLUTION: THE TRANSFORMED VIEW   220
Conclusion   222

Chapter 6
Hebrews 9:1-10:18 – The Law Possesses
a Shadow of the Good Things to Come   **224**
Introduction   224
Exegetical Overview of 9:1-10:18   226
Hebrews 9:1-10   227
Hebrews 9:11-28   230
   HEBREWS 9:11-14   230
   HEBREWS 9:15-22   233
   HEBREWS 9:23-28   236
Hebrews 10:1-18   238
   HEBREWS 10:1-4   238
   HEBREWS 10:5-10   240
   HEBREWS 10:11-14   241
   HEBREWS 10:15-18   243
The Law Possesses a Shadow   244
Εἰκών and Σκιά   245
The Tabernacle as Shadow   247
The Priests and Sacrifices as Shadow   250
Conclusion   252
Final Comments on 10:16-17   255

Exegetical and Theological Importance of Hebrews 10:16-17 255
Alterations to the Jeremiah Text: 8:8b-12 and 10:15-17 257
Conclusion 260
Conclusion 260

Chapter 7
Conclusion 263
Introduction and Summary 263
Contemporary Issues and Further Research Possibilities 268
A Personal Word 270

Appendix 1
Jewish Law-Obedience in the Second Temple Period 271

Appendix 2
Evidence from Judith and Wisdom of Solomon 274

Appendix 3
Evidence from Psalms of Solomon and
Testament of the Twelve Patriarchs 276

Appendix 4
Further Evidence from Josephus for Jewish
Obedience to the Law 279

Appendix 5
Leon Vaganay's Structural Outline of Hebrews 281

Appendix 6
Albert Vanhoye's Structural Outline of Hebrews 282

Appendix 7
George Guthrie's Structural Assessment of Hebrews 284

Appendix 8
Text-Critical Matters for Hebrews 7:1-10:18 286

Appendix 9
A Comparison of Hebrews 8:8b-12 and 10:15-17   **291**

Bibliography   **293**

Index of Scripture and Extrabiblical Literature   **319**

Index of Modern Authors   **331**

PREFACE

Several years ago as a Master's student at Dallas Theological Seminary, I became interested in Hebrews simply because it was an enigma to me, and because I knew nothing about it aside from a few well-known memory verses. The challenge of such professors as Dr. Dan Wallace, Dr. Darrell Bock, Dr. Howard Hendricks, and my pastor Rev. Rex Blankenship to investigate every book of the Bible resonated in my mind. Therefore I set out studying this enigmatic "epistolary sermon" on a daily basis for a period of over two years. Yet the more I studied and read, the more questions began to surface. However, writing a work on Hebrews never entered my mind at the time. Yet delving into this "word of exhortation" has proven to be a stimulating and worshipful experience.

This book is in large measure my doctoral dissertation, and I am extremely thankful to the exemplary professors of my supervising committee, Dr. Tom Schreiner, Dr. John Polhill, and Dr. Bill Cook. I appreciate and esteem the careful scholarship of these three gentlemen, and their encouragement both in academics as well as local church life in recent years has been greatly appreciated. Their interaction with my thesis led to the elimination or buttressing of weaknesses in my argumentation. As such, all remaining weaknesses are my own.

I am profoundly grateful to Dr. Schreiner for his interaction with and close supervision of my work, and his pastoral care for each of his doctoral students says much about him as a Christian gentleman. His careful interaction with my exegetical and theological arguments was of immense benefit, and the reader will find his suggestions on many of these pages. The same should be said for my own pastor, Dr. Bill Cook, who so graciously joined this committee at a time when his supervision was needed. I would also like to thank Dr. George H. Guthrie of Union University, whose careful efforts in Hebrews and personal encouragement have been invaluable. His work in Hebrews has inspired much of my own. Thanks are also due to Dr. Gary Cockerill of Wesley Biblical Seminary, whose scholarship and piety have proven to challenge me both academically and personally. Further, I wish to note the faithful service of Brian Lambert, Ben Stritesky, and especially my Garrett Fellow, Ben Montoya; these Christian brothers spent numerous hours reading and proofing the manuscript, as well as performing formatting and indexing duties with professionalism and care. Their Christ-centered service is seen on every page.

The lifelong impact of godly parents is incalculable. My own parents, Joe and Sharon Joslin, pointed me towards Christ from my earliest years, and their support made the writing of this work possible. My friendship with my parents is a treasured one, which made the loss of my mother to cancer during doctoral studies almost overwhelming. I anxiously await the day when I will see her again. My father continues to encourage me on an almost daily basis, and his friendship is irreplaceable. I am thankful to the Lord that he has brought companionship to my father in the form of my step mother, Sherry. I am indebted to her for her many prayers and encouragement.

Further, I would be remiss were I not to express gratitude to my paternal grandfather, the Rev. John Douglas Joslin. His decades of faithfulness and perseverance under enormous trials have served as a model of the endurance that is so explicit in Hebrews. Though he has become part of the "great cloud of witnesses," his absence is regularly felt.

My parents-in-law have been very supportive during these years that I have been a doctoral student, professor, and a husband to their daughter. I will always be thankful to Ralph and Barbara Neumann for their continued encouragement to our family and for raising their precious daughter in the fear of the Lord. I am thankful to be a part of the Neumann family.

Finally, my beloved wife, Jessica, is the greatest gift to me from the Lord (Prov 18:22; 19:14) aside from the gift of Himself. Her constant support proved to be needed refreshment during the long days of research and writing. Her willingness to work a corporate job while I pursued my studies and research is what enabled me to accomplish this task in a reasonable amount of time. Her warmth, prudence, and beauty have made me the envy of many men. Sweetie, I love you. Finally, to our sons, Haddon Walter and Carson Douglas, and our daughter, Elisabeth Sharon, you have added untold joy to our lives. May the Lord be pleased to draw each of you to Himself and to use you greatly in His kingdom.

Barry Clyde Joslin
Louisville, Kentucky
Autumn 2008

Abbreviations

ABD	*Anchor Bible Dictionary*
ALGHJ	Arbeiten zur Literatur und Geschichte des hellenistischen Judentums
AsTJ	*Asbury Theological Journal*
BDAG	Bauer, W., F. W. Danker, W. F. Arndt, and F. W. Gingrich. *Greek-English Lexicon of the New Testament and Other Early Christian Literature*. 3rd ed.
BEATAJ	Beiträge zur Erforschung des Alten Testaments und des antiken Judentums
BGBE	Beiträge zur Geschichte der biblischen Exegese
Bib	*Biblica*
BibSac	*Bibliotheca Sacra*
BJS	Brown Judaic Studies
BK	Biblische Konfrontationen
BNTC	Black's New Testament Commentary
BSC	Bible Study Commentary
BU	Biblische Untersuchungen
BZ	*Biblische Zeitschrift*
BZNW	Beihefte zur Zeitschrift für die neutestamentliche Wissenschaft und die Kunde der älteren Kirche
CBC	Cambridge Bible Commentary
CBQ	*Catholic Biblical Quarterly*
CBQMS	Catholic Biblical Quarterly Monograph Series
CBR	*Currents in Biblical Research*
CJAS	Christianity and Judaism in Antiquity Series
CJT	*Canadian Journal of Theology*
ConNT	Coniectanea Neotestamentica
ConcJourn	*Concordia Journal*
CQS	Companion to the Qumran Scrolls
CR	*Currents in Research*
CRINT	Compendia Rerum Iudaicarum ad Novum Testamentum
CTJ	*Calvin Theological Journal*
DSD	*Dead Sea Discoveries*

ECS	Epworth Commentary Series
EKKNT	Evangelisch-Katholischer Kommentar zum Neuen Testament
EvQ	*Evangelical Quarterly*
EvRTh	*Evangelical Review of Theology*
FRLANT	Forschungen zur Religion und Literatur des Alten und Neuen Testaments
GNC	Good News Commentary
GOTR	*Greek Orthodox Theological Review*
GTJ	*Grace Theological Journal*
HeyJ	*Heythrop Journal*
HKAT	Hanndkommentar zum Alten Testament
HNT	Handbuch zum Neuen Testament
IBS	*Irish Biblical Studies*
ICC	International Critical Commentary
JBL	*Journal of Biblical Literature*
JBLMS	Journal of Biblical Literature Monograph Series
JETS	*Journal of the Evangelical Theological Society*
JJS	*Journal of Jewish Studies*
JQR	*Jewish Quarterly Review*
JSJ	*Journal for the Study of Judaism in the Persian, Hellenistic and Roman Period*
JSNT	*Journal for the Study of the New Testament*
JSNTSup	Journal for the Study of the New Testament: Supplement Series
JSPSup	Journal for the Study of the Pseudepigrapha Supplement Series
JTS	*Journal of Theological Studies*
KEKNT	Kritisch-exegetischer Kommentar über das Neue Testament
KNT	Kommentar zum Neuen Testament
LCL	Loeb Classical Library
LEC	Library of Early Christianity
LSJ	Liddell, H. G., R. Scott, H. S. Jones, *A Greek-English Lexicon*. 9th ed. with revised supplement
MelT	*Melita Theologica*
MT	Masoretic Text
NA^{27}	*Novum Testamentum Graece*, Nestle-Aland, 27th ed.
NAC	New American Commentary
NCS	Newport Commentary Series
Neot	*Neotestamentica*
NIBC	New International Biblical Commentary
NICNT	New International Commentary on the New Testament
NIDNTT	*New International Dictionary of New Testament Theology*

NIGTC	New International Greek Testament Commentary
NIVAC	NIV Application Commentary
NKZ	Neue kirchliche Zeitschrift
NovT	*Novum Testamentum*
NovTSup	Novum Testamentum Supplement Series
NSBT	New Studies in Biblical Theology
NTS	*New Testament Studies*
OTP	*Old Testament Pseudepigrapha*
PatS	Patristica Sorbonensia
PBTM	Paternoster Biblical and Theological Monographs
QR	*Quarterly Review*
RB	*Revue Biblique*
RevExp	*Review and Expositor*
RevQ	*Revue de Qumran*
RSPT	*Revue des Sciences Philosophiques et Théologiques*
RTR	*Reformed Theological Review*
SBJT	*Southern Baptist Journal of Theology*
SBLDS	Society of Biblical Literature Dissertation Series
SBLMS	Society of Biblical Literature Monograph Series
SBT	Studies in Biblical Theology
ScandJTh	*Scandinavian Journal of Theology*
ScEs	*Science et Esprit*
SCJ	Studies in Christianity and Judaism
SEÅ	*Svensk Exegetisk Årsbok*
SNTSMS	Society for New Testament Studies Monograph Series
SR	*Studies in Religion/Sciences Religieuses*
SubBi	Subsidia Biblica
SUNT	Studien zur Umwelt des Neuen Testaments
SWJT	*Southwestern Journal of Theology*
TBBB	Theologie Bonner Biblische Beiträge
TDNT	*Theological Dictionary of the New Testament*
THNT	Theologischer Handkommentar zum Neuen Testament
TJ	*Trinity Journal*
TNTC	Tyndale New Testament Commentary
TynBul	*Tyndale Bulletin*
VT	*Vetus Testamentum*
WBC	Word Biblical Commentary
WTJ	*Westminster Theological Journal*
WUNT	Wissenschaftliche Untersuchungen zum Neuen Testament
ZAW	*Zeitschrift für die alttestamentliche Wissenschaft*
ZBKNT	Zürcher Bibelkommentare New Testament
ZNW	*Zeitschrift für die neutestamentliche Wissenschaft und die Kunde der älteren Kirche*
ZTK	*Zeitschrift für Theologie und Kirche*

CHAPTER 1

An Introduction to the Theology of the Mosaic Law in Hebrews 7:1-10:18

Introduction

In a 1994 article, J. C. McCullough likens Hebrews to a "Cinderella story." Though in the history of NT studies this enigmatic "word of exhortation" has been relegated to obscurity and "locked away upstairs" as it were, it now has been summoned to "come down to the ball."[1] The lack of attention to Hebrews is due in no small part to its content and complex argumentation. Indeed, Donald Hagner notes that it is "one of the most difficult books of the NT, perhaps second only to Revelation."[2] Its heavy dependence on the OT also adds a feeling of unfamiliarity to most, and at times it can be difficult to follow the writer's thought.[3] Add to this the fact that Hebrews is anonymously written, its provenance unknown, its specific audience unknown, and its exact date unknown, and it is no wonder that Hebrews has garnered so little attention in the history of the Christian Church. It is not surprising that some have asked, "Why bother with Hebrews?"[4]

Fortunately, there is much in this epistle that far outweighs the effort that is necessary for discovery. The present study seeks to add a needed component to the ongoing study of Hebrews. Study of the theology of Hebrews has increased in recent years, yet there remains considerable work to do in this particular area of NT studies. Specifically, the following study focuses on the issue of the theology of the Mosaic law in Hebrews 7:1-10:18. Surveys of bibliographies in commentaries, dictionaries, important monographs on Hebrews as well as computerized searches have yielded only a small amount of work that specifically addresses the Mosaic law in Hebrews.[5] This study seeks to be a

---

[1]J. C. McCullough, "Hebrews in Recent Scholarship," *IBS* 16 (1994): 66.

[2]D. A. Hagner, "Interpreting the Epistle to the Hebrews," in *The Literature and Meaning of Scripture*, ed. M. A. Inch and C. H. Bullock (Grand Rapids: Baker, 1981), 217.

[3]Ibid.

[4]This is the question at the center of the article by Marie Isaacs, "Why Bother with Hebrews?" *HeyJ* 43 (2002): 60-72.

[5]Though there has been considerable work done on the related matter of "covenant" in Hebrews, especially with reference to Heb 8. It should be noted at the outset that this monograph proceeds along the stream of interpretive thought that considers διαθήκη and νόμος to be related but not synonymous concepts in Hebrews. See chapter 4 below.

helpful study of fresh research and thought that focuses on this particular issue. To date, this writer has found no single detailed monograph dedicated to the issue of the Mosaic law in Hebrews, yet this is not due to the fact that Hebrews has nothing to say on the matter. Indeed, the writer of Hebrews speaks often of the law, particularly in the central section of 7:1-10:18. Thus, a study of this nature seems more than warranted.

Thesis

Broadly speaking, the argumentation in the following chapters seeks to answer the following question in the following chapters: "What is the theology of the Mosaic law in Hebrews 7:1-10:18?" The present writer seeks to demonstrate that in Hebrews 7:1-10:18 the author understands the law in both negative and positive terms. In a negative sense, it is a weak and insufficient means for putting away sin, yet in a positive sense Christ has transformed and fulfilled the law, and as such it is written on the minds and hearts of the New Covenant (hereafter NC) people. This claim is substantiated in the writer's argument for a new and eternal priesthood (7:1-28), a new and eternal covenant (8:1-13), which is founded upon a new and eternal sacrifice (9:1-10:18).

In brief, *the work of Christ has transformed the law, and this transformation involves both its internalization and fulfillment in the NC; the law has forever been affected Christologically.* This is demonstrated exegetically in chapters 4, 5, and 6. Chapter 4 (7:1-28) argues that the writer of Hebrews envisions a "change in the law" in the sense of "transformation." Chapter 5 (8:1-13) argues from Hebrews 8 that the νόμους internalized in the heart is the law that has been transformed in the NC. Chapter 6 (9:1-10:18) focuses on the matter of Christ's fulfillment of the cultus which foreshadowed the good things that have come now that the NC has been inaugurated by the eternal high priest, Jesus Christ. Thus, when taken as a whole, what the writer of Hebrews envisions for the law in the NC is its transformation. It is now viewed through the lens of Christ, and as such there is transformation that involves fulfillment and internalization. There are continuous and discontinuous aspects of the law, and this continuity and discontinuity turns on the hinge of Christ.

The commandments (and particularly the cultic regulations) are insufficient for attaining perfection (τελείωσις), which is tied to unfettered access to God and the inward cleansing of the conscience. Further, for the writer of Hebrews, the law and its requirements were never designed to atone permanently for sins, and thus to seek atonement on this basis in the present eschatological (i.e. Christological) age is to set oneself over against God. The new revelation in the son (1:2) has dramatic effects, not the least of which concerns the law. This is a critical theological point that Hebrews conveys, given that it is likely that Hebrews' original audience consisted of second generation (2:3-4) Jewish Christians who "had been nurtured intellectually and spiritually in the

Hellenistic synagogue,"[6] and who were contemplating a return to Judaism.[7] This return would involve a return to the old Levitical priesthood, the Old Covenant (hereafter OC), and the animal sacrifices.

Thus, for the writer of Hebrews, the argument he makes about the Mosaic law would likely have had tremendous and immediate significance for his readers/hearers.[8] To return to the OC administration would be to set oneself up against God, against Christ, to trample underfoot his blood, and to deny the final revelation of God in his son (1:1-4). Thus, a tremendous eschatological shift has occurred in the coming of Christ.

Therefore there are two sides to the Mosaic law for the writer of Hebrews.

---

[6]William L. Lane, *Hebrews*, WBC, vol. 47a (Nashville: Thomas Nelson, 1991), liv.

[7]For a detailed description of Hebrews' audience as well as the various proposals that have been offered, see the critical introductions to Hebrews by Lane, *Hebrews*, 1:li-lix; idem, "Hebrews," in *Dictionary of the Later New Testament and Its Developments*, ed. Ralph P. Martin and Peter H. Davids (Downers Grove, IL: Intervarsity, 1997), 444-47; Paul Ellingworth, *The Epistle to the Hebrews: A Commentary on the Greek Text*, NIGTC (Grand Rapids: Eerdmans, 1993), 21-29; Harold Attridge, *The Epistle to the Hebrews*, Hermeneia (Philadelphia: Fortress, 1989), 9-13; Philip E. Hughes, *A Commentary on the Epistle to the Hebrews* (Grand Rapids: Eerdmans, 1977), 10-19; F. F. Bruce, *The Epistle to the Hebrews*, rev. ed., NICNT (Grand Rapids: Eerdmans, 1990), 3-10; Donald Guthrie, *The Letter to the Hebrews*, TNTC (Grand Rapids: Eerdmans, 1983), 22-25; idem, *New Testament Introduction*, 4th rev. ed. (Downers Grove, IL: Intervarsity, 1990), 682-87; Craig R. Koester, *Hebrews*, AB, vol. 36 (New York: Doubleday, 2001), 64-79; George W. Buchanan, *To the Hebrews*, AB, vol. 36 (Garden City NY: Doubleday, 1981), 267; Paul Feine and Johannes Behm, *Introduction to the New Testament*, ed. W. G. Kümmel, 14th rev. ed., trans. A. J. Mattill Jr. (Nashville: Abingdon, 1965), 279-81; Barnabas Lindars, *The Theology of the Letter to the Hebrews* (New York: Cambridge, 1991), 4-15; Andrew Trotter, *Interpreting the Book of Hebrews* (Grand Rapids: Baker, 1997), 28-33; Ceslas Spicq, *L'Épitre aux Hébreux* (Paris: Gabalda, 1952), 1:220-52; and Hans-Friedrich Weiß, *Der Brief and die Hebräer*, KEKNT 15 (Göttingen: Vandenhoeck & Ruprecht, 1991), 61-76.

[8]Numerous scholars have labeled Hebrews as a sermon. They cite 13:22 in which the letter is referred to as a "word of exhortation" (τοῦ λόγου τῆς παρακλήσεως). The understanding here is that Hebrews is first and foremost meant to be *heard* by a Greek-speaking audience; it is a sermon in written form. There are other reasons for suggesting that it be heard more so than read which support the idea. The author's use of rhetoric, hook words, inclusio, and a penchant for making use of alliteration (which comes to the fore when the alliterated words are *heard*) point toward an intention for Hebrews to be heard. Lane notes that this phrase (τοῦ λόγου τῆς παρακλήσεως) "appears to have been an idiomatic designation for the homily or edifying discourse that followed the public reading from the designated portions of Scripture in the Hellenistic synagogues" (Lane, *Hebrews*, 2:568). See also the work of F. V. Filson, *'Yesterday': A Study of Hebrews in the Light of Chapter 13*, SBT 2:4 (Naperville, IL: Allenson, 1967); William L. Lane, "Hebrews: A Sermon in Search of a Setting," *SWJT* 28 (1985): 13-18.

On the one hand he can note that it has been transformed (7:12).[9] Yet at the same time, the writer of Hebrews does not suggest that the law itself (the OC's regulations) in toto has been abrogated. It will be argued below that such a view is too simplistic. The law as revelation from the God who does not change has not been brushed aside,[10] but has been fulfilled and transformed by the

----

[9]The debated terms in 7:12 are μετάθεσις and the verb form μετατίθημι. There is little consensus regarding their precise meanings. As such, they receive substantial attention in chapter 4 below. However, brief lexical comments are warranted here. The verb form is also found in 11:5 in which the writer states, "By faith Enoch was *taken up*." Many will argue on the basis of 11:5 that the priesthood and the law (in 7:12) have been completely removed ("taken up" in this same sense), now ceasing to exist and no longer having any bearing in the NC. However, this argument rests on two unproven presuppositions: first, that this indeed is the meaning of 11:5, and second, that the writer of Hebrews means the same thing in each instance. Yet this is arguably false. This assertion may be contested on two grounds. First, the lexical evidence does not demand such an assertion. Second, regardless of how one defines the term, Enoch did not cease to exist. Enoch did not cease to exist and neither does the priesthood and the law. The priesthood still exists—Christ is the high priest forever (Ps 110:4), yet there is a new order. Priesthood has indeed *changed*, but has not been *removed* (see chapter 4, below).

Concerning the verb μετατίθημι, BDAG states the following meaning for its use in 7:12: "to effect a change in state or condition, *to change, to alter*...'when the priesthood has changed, i.e. passed on to another Hb 7:12" (Walter Bauer, *A Greek-English Lexicon of the New Testament and Other Early Christian Literature*, rev. and ed. Frederick William Danker, ed. and trans. William F. Arndt and F. Wilbur Gingrich [BDAG], 3rd ed. [Chicago: University of Chicago Press, 2000], s.v. "μετατίθημι").

Regarding the noun form μετάθεσις, it will be argued below that in 7:12 the meaning is not that the law has been simply annulled in full, but rather has been *changed/transformed*. There is still priesthood, and there is still law, yet both have been radically altered in the person and work of Christ, and the meaning of this "transformation" is central to the present thesis. BDAG cites Heb 7:12 and defines μετάθεσις rightly as "transformation." LSJ supports this sense of "change" as well, "a change of position, a transposition" (Henry George Liddell and Robert Scott, *A Greek-English Lexicon*, rev. and aug. Sir Henry Stuart Jones, [LSJ] 9th ed. [Oxford: Clarendon Press: 1996], s.v. "μετάθεσις"). It is true that lexical considerations alone do not solve the matter of interpretation here, but given such lexical considerations, there is certainly both evidence and warrant for the claim made here, and enough to suggest a viable interpretation of 7:12 that does not simply relegate the law to obsolescence. See chapter 4 below.

[10]This question, viz., how revelation from a changeless God can be outmoded by God's new work in Christ, stands at the center of Graham Hughes' influential 1979 monograph, *Hebrews and Hermeneutics: The Epistle to the Hebrews as a New Testament Example of Biblical Interpretation*, SNTSMS 36 (Cambridge: University Press), 1979. This monograph is derived from his 1971 University of Cambridge dissertation. He writes, "The question that has preoccupied him [the writer of Hebrews] more deeply than any other, we shall argue, has been that of saying how we may conceive the Word of God as being subject to historical processes and yet remaining,

Christ event and is internalized in every member of the NC people (a transformation of content as well as location). The Mosaic law has been "transposed into a higher key" in light of Christ's work in the present age. This will be explained in detail.

As such, the Mosaic law still has a place in the NC people, though clearly not in the same role and capacity as under the OC. There is continuity in the midst of discontinuity, and as such Hebrews' theology of the law is complex.[11] Whereas under the OC the members were under the law, in the NC the law is now *in* God's people. The law that is internalized in the NC people is the "Christologized law," i.e., the law that has been transformed by the work of Christ. The "Christologized law" is the law when viewed through the lens of Christ. The internalization of the law, an essential "better promise" (8:6) of the NC, accomplishes obedience and renewed hearts in the covenant people. Therefore it can be said that in a new and real fashion, "I will be their God and they will be my people" (8:10). All aspects of the law are now viewed through the lens of Christ and his salvific work in these "last days" (1:2). Stated again, the present thesis is as follows: *the work of Christ has transformed the law, and this transformation involves both its internalization and fulfillment in the NC; the law has forever been affected Christologically.*

Scope

The scope of this study must be limited if it is to be helpful in the broader arena of Hebrews scholarship. Since thirteen of the fourteen occurrences of νόμος in Hebrews are found in the great expositional center of 7:1-10:18[12] (though the

---

recognizably, God's Word" (3). Hughes argues that the writer of Hebrews was faced with a great conundrum: How does one work out the old and the new revelation given by God, with both old and new remaining God's Word, yet now some of which has become obsolete? (28-29). Cf. Ernest C. Reisinger, *The Law and the Gospel* (Phillipsburg, NJ: P & R Publishing, 1997), 146-48.

[11]What is put forward here to be complex Lehne has suggested to be inconsistent (Susanne Lehne, *The New Covenant in Hebrews*, JSNTSS 44 [Sheffield: JSOT Press, 1990], 26).

[12]Specifically, νόμος is found at 7:5, 12, 16, 19, 28 (twice); 8:4, 10 (plural); 9:19, 22; 10:1, 8, 16 (plural). The only other occurrence is close by at 10:28 (which clearly refers to specific laws that are broken, and not simply "law" in a generic sense. When specific laws were broken under the OC ("set aside the law of Moses"), specific penalties were implemented for the specific offense. Thus 10:28 appears to support the point that νόμος refers to specific laws, and not merely "instruction" or "God's will" in a generic sense (see Attridge, et al.), or even less "covenant." There is a concrete reference to νόμος, viz., the Mosaic law. When the writer of Hebrews refers to νόμος, he has the law given to Moses in view at least in a broad sense, and quite often in the narrow sense of *specific* Mosaic laws (such as those specific to the Levitical cultus).

In addition, the verb νομοθετέω occurs in 7:11 and 8:6, and will receive due consideration in the exegesis of chapters 4 and 5.

idea of the law can be found outside of this section, such as 2:1-4), the present study focuses on this central section of Hebrews. One can reasonably posit that the theology of the Mosaic law in Hebrews can adequately be understood by focusing on these chapters, given the attention it receives in 7:1-10:18. To be sure, even this amount of detailed exegetical and theological study (87 total verses) could be seen as far too much for one monograph. However, the method of the present study allows for this, as not every verse in 7:1-10:18 will receive equal treatment.[13]

The necessity for such a study is easy to understand given the lack of attention that this issue has received. McCullough has observed that Hebrews has received little focus when compared to other aspects of NT studies, yet in recent decades the enigmatic epistle has received an increasing amount of attention.[14] It is the present writer's desire to argue that the epistle to the Hebrews has a voice on the important issue of the law. A detailed exegetical study that specifically seeks to hear the voice of Hebrews on the matter of the Mosaic law in 7:1-10:18 would be a helpful contribution both to NT scholarship as well as the Church.

Scholarly Contributions

As discussed above, very little has been written that specifically addresses the matter of Hebrews and the law, despite scouring bibliographies in various dictionaries, commentaries, other related monographs, essays, computerized searches of World Cat, ATLA, and the Dissertation Abstracts databases, etc. Specific computer searches have in fact produced very little.[15] Numerous searches were performed and literally thousands of hits were analyzed in the available databases. Yet as far as this writer has been able to ascertain, no dissertation, thesis, or monograph has been written on this subject as it has been articulated here. What exists is numerous critical commentaries, related monographs, and a small collection of relevant essays and articles.

---

[13]The most important passages are 7:11-19, 8:6-13, 10:1-4, and 10:16-18. Chapters 4, 5, and 6 concentrate on these texts in detail.

[14]McCullough, "Hebrews in Recent Scholarship," 66. Idem, "Hebrews in Recent Scholarship (Part 2)," *IBS* 16 (June 1994): 108-20. See also G. Guthrie (George H. Guthrie, "Hebrews in Its First-Century Contexts: Recent Research," in *The Face of New Testament Studies*, ed. Scot McKnight and Grant Osborne [Grand Rapids: Baker, 2004], 414-43), who also comments on the low volume of research on Hebrews, yet notes the growing attention that is currently being given to the epistle.

[15]The related topic of "covenant," as suspected, produces numerous hits, and the theme of covenant is at the forefront in Heb 8. The themes of law and covenant and how they relate will be discussed in chapters 4, 5, and 6. While there is significant overlap in the two terms, it is overly simplistic to read διαθήκη and νόμος merely as synonyms as some scholars do (see below). They are certainly related, yet Hebrews does not use them as if there were no distinction in these two critical concepts.

What follows below is a representative sample of the research and scholarship from some of the most important and oft-cited works of the past century. Given the lack of monographs on the specific subject, it should be noticed that the best sources for research are the better commentaries and monographs on related matters.[16] The most useful and most available

---

[16]In addition, there are a small number of theologies of Hebrews that have been written in the past century. Many of the older authors regard Hebrews as Pauline, and thus their discussions are inevitably skewed in the direction of Romans and Galatians. Others are more interested in comparing Hebrews' theology to Pauline theology. Yet even then, most speak of the law in Hebrews in very vague and general terms.

One of the oldest theologies (and still occasionally cited today) is that of Ménégoz (Eugène Ménégoz, *La Théologie de L' Épitre aux Hébreux* [Paris: Librarie Fischbacher, 1894]; see esp. 157-66). His work focuses on introductory matters of Hebrews, as well as possible origins of the author's theology. His main contribution is seen in his discussions on Christ, sacrifice, faith, law, and eschatology. His treatment of the law is brief, comprising nine pages, in which he notes that the writer of Hebrews did not fail to note the abolition of the law. He writes, "Une des conséquences de l'œuvre rédemptrice du Christ, telle que la conçoit L'Épitre aux Hébreux, est l'abolition du régime de la loi Mosaique. L'auteur ne pouvait négliger d'attirer l'attention de ses lecteurs sur ce point" (157). Ménégoz's discussion is quite brief, and there is no discussion given to the meaning of 8:10 and 10:16. Ménégoz does mention the familiar distinction of "moral law," defining it as the "immutable command of God." See also the work of E. F. Scott, *The epistle to the Hebrews: Its Doctrine and Significance* (Edinburgh: T & T Clark, 1923).

Note also the 1899 work of Milligan (George Milligan, *The Theology of the Epistle to the Hebrews*, [Edinburgh: T & T Clark, 1899]). Milligan's main interests are the critical introductory matters of the epistle and Hebrews' Christology (especially Christ's high priestly functions). He spends less than one page on the issue of the Mosaic law (200), and there the brief discussion lies under the general heading of "Relation to Paulinism."

The year 1913 saw the publication of Nairne's helpful work (Alexander Nairne, *The Epistle of Priesthood: Studies in the Epistle to the Hebrews* [Edinburgh: T & T Clark, 1913]). Nairne views Hebrews as having Philonic tendencies and says little with regard to the law. The final one-third of his book is a brief exposition of Hebrews, in which he gives cursory attention to the issue of the Mosaic law when it arises in the text. (Note for example his brevity when discussing 7:11-12 [Nairne, *The Epistle of Priesthood*, 348-49].) Also, on 8:6-13 he is silent on the matter of the law being written on the hearts.

Also note the 1956 work by Vos (Geerhardus Vos, *The Teaching of the Epistle to the Hebrews* [Grand Rapids: Eerdmans, 1956]). While he has no discussion on the law, he has a chapter on the issue of the meaning of διαθήκη in Hebrews (27-48), in which he argues that in 9:16-17 the term should be translated as "testament." While an important issue in Heb 9, it is tangential at best to this proposed study.

Finally, the recent work of Lindars (Barnabas Lindars, *The Theology of the Letter to the Hebrews* [New York: Cambridge, 1991]) should be mentioned as well. Though brief, Lindars offers a unique perspective on the setting of the epistle, especially the situation of the original audience. Yet though this little volume is valuable merit,

contributions have come by means of the better commentaries and monographs written in the past 150 years of Hebrews scholarship.

Having previewed the points that this book seeks to establish, we will now turn to the views of past and present scholars who have articulated some kind of understanding of Hebrews and the law. In the broadest sense, Hebrews scholars can be broken into two large categories regarding the matter of the law: (1) No ongoing validity of the law in the NC era, or (2) ongoing validity of the law in the NC era.[17] What follows is a delineation of scholars who hold one of these two views.[18]

No Ongoing Validity in the New Covenant Era

First is the two-volume work of Franz Delitzsch.[19] For Delitzsch the whole law is abrogated and this includes all aspects of the law. On Hebrews 7:12 he writes

---

Lindars' statements on the law are quite general, such as "the Law as the revealed will of God will be internalised in mutual knowledge and understanding" (81). Again, lack of precise meaning and the presence of such generalities is the impetus for the present study.

[17]While such general categories are useful here, the present study cannot easily be placed in either of these two categories unless certain terms such as "validity" are explained. This writer will argue that the law is no longer valid in many ways such as the matters of sacrifice and how and when one approaches the divine presence. There is discontinuity. NC believers today are not "under" the law's commands in the same sense of the OC. In this sense the present thesis could fall into the first category. Yet there is also continuity, it will be argued. The laws that are internalized in the NC do correspond to those written on stone tablets. Therefore in this sense, the present study would fall under the second category. The thesis is not an either/or regarding the divine commandments. This is the wrong question. The present study puts forward a paradigm for viewing the NC people and their relation to the immutable law of God in light of Christ's work. He becomes the paradigm. Thus the terms used here such as "Christologized law," "transformed law," "the law viewed through the lens of Christ," and "the law transposed into a higher key" all mean the same thing. There is continuity as well as discontinuity, and Christ is the "set of lenses" through which the NC people should presently view the law. Such leads to obedience from the heart, now that the "Christologized law" has been internally written on the hearts and minds of God's people.

[18]Within these two broad categories (ongoing validity, no ongoing validity of the Mosaic laws) are various scholars that equate νόμος and διαθήκη, viewing them more or less as synonyms in Hebrews while others maintain a distinction, and for this latter group, the two terms represent related ideas. Other scholars are ambiguous on this issue. Specific points of view will be seen more directly in the exegesis of 7:1-10:18 in chapters 4, 5, and 6. It is hoped that the present study will shed light on these specific areas of the theology of Hebrews in order that future studies might perhaps be more specific where at present there exists ambiguity.

[19]Franz Delitzsch, *Commentary on the Epistle to the Hebrews*, 2 vols., trans. Thomas L. Kingsbury (Grand Rapids: Eerdmans, 1952).

that the change in the law is "an essential change," and regarding the difficult term μετάθεσις he argues that it refers to the "actual transference of the priesthood from one tribe to another."[20] The change here is not simply the ceremonial/cultic aspects of the law, but "the political and moral is included along with it...a change of the priesthood affects and transforms not only the outward legal order of things, but also the ethical relation to God thereby constituted, in its various bearings."[21] Delitzsch lacks comment on the matter of the law being written on the hearts in 8:10 and 10:16, and in his comments on 10:17 he equates νόμος with the whole of the OT,[22] a claim that will be contested in later chapters.

Ceslas Spicq's two-volume work on Hebrews (*L'Épître aux Hébreux*) was and is still one of the most influential scholarly works on Hebrews. The strength of Spicq's work affected Hebrews studies for a large portion of the mid to late twentieth century, and his work should still be consulted today even though many of his conclusions have been disproved.[23] Regarding the issue of the law, Spicq offers a brief excursus in which he argues that since the priesthood has been abrogated, the law on which the priesthood rests has been removed.[24] He argues that the "destinies" of the law and the Levitical priesthood are bound up in one another, so that what happens to one happens to the other.[25]

In his 1964 commentary, Hugh Montefiore compares Hebrews to Paul, suggesting that both authors seek to "get behind the law to the period before it was given" in order to argue for its complete abrogation.[26] Hebrews,

---

[20]Ibid., 1:352.

[21]Ibid.

[22]Ibid., 2:165.

[23]One of Spicq's most memorable conclusions was that Hebrews was greatly influenced by Philonic thought. Indeed, a large portion of volume 1 (which consists entirely of introductory matters) argues for this thesis. However, the 1970 dissertation of Ronald Williamson (Ronald Williamson, *Philo and the Epistle to the Hebrews*, ALGHJ [Leiden: E. J. Brill, 1970]) soundly defeated Spicq's thesis, and as a result Spicq's influence in this regard has been greatly diminished.

[24]Spicq, *L'Épître aux Hébreux*, 2:225. However, this conclusion rests on a particular view of the debated phrase ὁ λαὸς γὰρ ἐπ' αὐτῆς νενομοθέτηται found in 7:11, as well as the whole of 7:12. See chapter 4 below.

[25]Spicq writes, "si bien que Loi et Sacerdoce ont les mêmes caractéres, et que leurs destinées sont liées: Le sort de la Loi dépend de celui du sacerdoce; la disparition de l'ancien sacerdoce entraîne l'abrogation de la Loi; le nouveau sacerdoce fonde une alliance nouvelle" (Spicq, *L'Épître aux Hébreux*, 2:225). As will be argued, this view of Hebrews and the law is a bit simplistic.

[26]Hugh Montefiore, *A Commentary on the Epistle to the Hebrews* (New York: Harper and Row, 1964), 123. Montefiore equates law and covenant, and on the basis of 8:13 concludes that the law will soon disappear (124; cp. 142). Yet in his comments on 8:10 he writes that the laws are internalized. This is a bit ambiguous, since the same term

Montefiore argues, makes use of Melchizedek (7:1-10) for such a point. Christ's priestly rank could not have been abrogated by the giving of the Levitical law, and Hebrews cites Psalm 110:4 to demonstrate this point as well as to counter such a suggestion since the oath in the Psalm was given *after* the giving of the law. Regarding the law's change in 7:12, Montefiore seems to argue for a disappearance of the law, citing 8:13, and consequently equate it with the OC. In his comments on 8:10, he states that the laws that were once written on stone will now be engraved upon the hearts, yet for Montefiore, the inward writing of the law promised by Jeremiah is merely the "promise of a new inward relationship with God."[27] Regarding the shadow in the law (10:1), Montefiore, like many others, offers little by way of explanation. Further, he asserts that the "good things to come" are "not to be identified with the Christian dispensation which has superseded the abrogated law," but rather that the law's shadow pointed to the good things that will come at the consummation of the age.[28]

Harold Attridge posits a similar perspective. Attridge argues that the change of law in view is the "disappearance" of the Mosaic law.[29] He states in his comments on 7:18, "The argument in this section is now summarized with a focus not on the priesthood, but on the law. With the inauguration of Christ's priesthood comes not simply an amendment of the law, but its definitive 'abrogation' (ἀθέτησις)."[30] In a brief excursus on the topic of "Hebrews, Paul, and the Law," Attridge argues against the continuing religious validity of the Torah.[31] This point is made with even more clarity in his comments on 8:10, in which he views the νόμους that are to be written on the hearts "not in an interiorization of Torah but in the cleansing of the conscience and in true

---

(νόμος) is used in both 7:12 and 8:10 (plural). He does not clarify what appears to be an ambiguity, i.e., how can νόμος disappear while νόμους is written on the NC heart?

[27]Ibid., 141, 171. This aspect is partially correct, but this oversimplifies what Hebrews teaches with regard to God's promises in Jeremiah's prophecy. See chapters 5 and 6 below.

[28]Ibid., 165. Part of what is driving this conclusion is his conclusion on the textual variant in 9:11. See chapter 6 below.

[29]Attridge, *The Epistle to the Hebrews*, 200-01. See also the recent work of Schenck (Kenneth Schenck, *Understanding the Book of Hebrews: The Story Behind the Sermon* [Louisville: John Knox, 2003]), who seems to be following Attridge verbatim on his view of the law in Hebrews (esp. pp. 13-14). Isaacs' recent contribution seems to fall along these same lines, given that she equates the laws of God of Heb 8:10 to a vague notion of "the internalization of the will of God" (Marie E. Isaacs, *Reading Hebrews and James: A Literary and Theological Commentary* [Macon, GA: Smyth & Helwys, 2002], 109). Regrettably, Isaacs is silent on the important issues in 7:11-19, and bewilderingly vague on 10:1.

[30]Attridge, *The Epistle to the Hebrews*, 203.

[31]Ibid., 204-05.

spiritual worship."[32] Finally, in his comments on 10:16, Attridge fully redefines the "writing of the law upon the hearts." He states, "It is clear that the law written on the heart is not the old fleshly Law that has been superseded, but the 'law' of willing obedience that Christ embodied."[33] Here Attridge's clarity is to be commended;[34] when speaking of these matters he does not do so with the ambiguity of scholars in previous generations.

In his 2001 Anchor Bible commentary on Hebrews, Craig Koester views νόμος and διαθήκη as virtual synonyms.[35] Therefore, for Koester, when the covenant is replaced, so is the law. Yet such a view is to over-read texts such as 7:12. Further, he rightly resists any sort of division of the Mosaic law. Given that the law prescribes rules for the priesthood, and the priesthood deals with ethical sins as well as other regulations, it is misguided to "neatly separate" the laws governing priesthood from the laws governing ethical/moral behavior.[36]

---

[32]Ibid., 227. This view is discussed in detail in chapter 5.

[33]Ibid., 281.

[34]Attridge is clear in that he directly takes issue with those who hold views similar to those of P. E. Hughes (discussed below) and others who maintain an ongoing validity of the law in any sense, yet he is still vague in that he redefines "law" in a very generic sense, which then introduces ambiguity and/or confusion. As noted, he interprets νόμους in 8:10/10:16 in an abstract sense. For Attridge, νόμος has been severed from its OT referent and should now be seen in an abstract, nonspecific sense. Though the writer of Hebrews does not elaborate as to precisely *which* laws are to be inscribed, "laws inscribed upon the hearts" should not be understood *independently* from those laws objectively revealed in the OT. It will be argued in chapter 5 that the Jeremiah text should not be seen as a nonspecific "word picture" in which the language is seen as metaphorically describing "laws" in an abstract sense.

Similarly, Gerd Schunack (*Der Hebräerbrief* [Zürich: Theologischer Verlag, 2002], 143) states unequivocally, "Ausgeschlossen ist eine neue, positive Bedeutung des Gesetzes." Schunack views the law as primarily cultic, and does not comment on the meaning of the Jeremiah text in Heb 8:10. On the meaning of νόμους in 8:10 he is silent. Commenting on 10:16, Schunack asserts that while a new and positive meaning of the law is impossible, the laws of God in the hearts of his people is still a gift ("die Gabe seiner Gesetze in ihre Herzen"). He does not speculate as to the contents of this new order/decree of God ("neuen Verfügung Gottes"), other than to say that its content could indeed remain wholly without meaning ("So könnte dieser Inhalt in der Tat ganz ohne Bedeutung bleiben.").

[35]Unlike most commentators, Koester includes a brief discussion on the matter of the law in Hebrews (Koester, *Hebrews*, 114-15), yet is compelled to fill the space with comparisons to Paul. See also Lehne, *New Covenant*, 75.

[36]Koester, *Hebrews*, 114. Presumably, Koester would have a similar view on the "civil matters" of the Mosaic law, though he does not specifically comment on this point. This writer agrees with Koester's resistance to subdivide the law. What is put forward here is hoped to be a better way of looking at the law, viz., its being transformed in the person and work of Christ. As such, for example, what has been traditionally regarded as the "ceremonial laws" are no longer to be practiced due to their being ended in Christ. The

On the matter of 8:10/10:16, Koester simply restates the text with little comment other than to raise a unique question: Does the idea of "God's law written on the hearts"[37] violate freedom of the human will?[38] He describes this aspect of the NC in vague terms as God overcoming the unfaithfulness of the human heart, and sees the νόμους of Jeremiah's oracle not as the Mosaic law, but rather as a way of describing the action of God in his working in the human heart that leads to a completeness of obedience and not an internalization.[39] Koester (commenting on 10:1) does argue that the law had a positive role in that it "foreshadowed the new order that Christ inaugurated."[40]

Finally, worth noting at this point are the works of Susanne Lehne[41] and Frank Thielman.[42] First, Lehne asks the following question, "Was Jeremiah's prophecy simply forgotten or was there something too ambiguous or disturbing in its content to allow for an appropriation by Jewish groups before the first century CE?"[43] She rightly avers that aside from the Qumran community, there is virtual silence on the matter of the NC both before and after the time of

---

end result is similar in many ways, yet does not face the task of having to relegate each of the Mosaic laws into one of three categories. Koester is correct in his assertion that such a task is sometimes impossible.

[37]A critical concept that Koester does not adequately explain.

[38]Koester, *Hebrews*, 391.

[39]Ibid., 386. Koester unequivocally denies that internalization is what the writer of Hebrews (and presumably Jeremiah as well) had in mind in the NC texts of Heb 8 and 10 (386-87). He notes that while some have argued for some kind of internalization of law/covenant, this view is to be eschewed in favor of an emphasis on "complete obedience" (386). However such a dichotomy is unwarranted. An internalization of the laws of God (νόμους μου) by the work of God in Christ *brings about* this completeness of obedience (the view taken here), and therefore to force a choice between these two views is unnecessary.

Koester's view parallels that of Attridge, Schenk, and Isaacs in many ways, who view νόμους in 8:10/10:16 not to be the actual laws that God gave to Israel. Rather, without explanation these scholars have reinterpreted νόμους to mean something figurative and other than specific (non-figurative) commands of God. These writers feel compelled to keep the term within quotation marks (i.e., "laws"). See for example Koester, *Hebrews*, 386; Attridge, *Hebrews*, 205.

[40]Koester, *Hebrews*, 115. Cf. Erich Gräßer (*An die Hebräer*, EKKNT [Zürich: Neukirchen, 1993], 2:51). Gräßer is compelled to discuss Hebrews' use of the law in light of Paul (see esp. 2:49-52). See also Weiß, *Der Brief*, 403-07; Attridge, *Hebrews*, 204-05. While such discussions are profitable, and even expected in light of the Pauline emphasis on law, such comparisons as those of Weiß, Gräßer, and Attridge are not within the scope of this study, and can lead to the danger of reading Hebrews' view of the law through Pauline lenses.

[41]Lehne's monograph will receive greater attention in chapter 4 below.

[42]Frank Thielman, *The Law and the New Testament: The Question of Continuity* (New York: Crossroad, 1999), 111-34, esp. 119-26, 130-32.

[43]Lehne, *New Covenant*, 35.

Hebrews in broader Judaism. Though not suggesting that there are literary connections between Hebrews and Qumran, Lehne notes that it is striking that such an issue as the NC only appears in these two communities. She notes the obvious exception of the Dead Sea Scrolls, in which are several references to the NC. Yet there is a clear distinction between the employment of the NC theme in the DSS and in Hebrews; foremost is the Qumran community's unwillingness to reject or speak negatively about the law. Lehne argues that Hebrews "subsumes the law under the rubric of cult,"[44] and effectively the law is thus rejected. Lehne views Hebrews as having only a very negative view of the law, and asserts that Hebrews' own statements about the law are "not altogether consistent."[45] Additionally, the idea of "newness" is much less radical in the DSS than in Hebrews. Whereas the DSS envisions a return to Torah, according to Lehne the same can hardly be said of Hebrews.[46]

In his 1999 book *The Law and the New Testament*, Frank Thielman views law and covenant as synonyms, and asserts that the law stands in contrast to the "better covenant" spoken of in Hebrews 8:6.[47] He then argues for the abrogation of the Mosaic law in the sense of its regulative authority for NC believers,[48] given that the law (seemingly in its entirety) is a "fleshly commandment,"[49] and understands the writer of Hebrews to point towards "the passing away of the law's regulative authority."[50] For Thielman, the Mosaic law has been fully superseded,[51] and states that in the NC, there is a "new law

---

[44]Ibid., 26; citing the work of Windisch (Hans Windisch, *Der Hebräerbrief*, HNT 14 [Tübingen: J. C. B. Mohr, 1931], 66).

[45]Lehne, *New Covenant*, 26. The present study seeks to demonstrate that while the writer's statements about the law are complex, they are not inconsistent.

[46]Ibid., 35.

[47]Thielman, *The Law and the New Testament*, 121.

[48]Note the blanket statement, "Nothing could be clearer from the argument of Hebrews that the author believed the Mosaic law to be obsolete" (Thielman, *The Law and the New Testament*, 130). Keep in mind that for Thielman, "covenant" equals "law," and if law is thereby equated with covenant, then few would argue that the covenant/law has been rendered obsolete. See also his statement, "The entire law is obsolete, moreover, and not simply the portion of the law that regulates priesthood and the sacrifices" (131).

[49]Ibid., 121.

[50]Ibid. Thielman offers no explanation of the meaning of 7:12. Concerning the law's "regulative authority," in one sense the present writer would agree with Thielman. The NC believer does not relate to the law in the same manner as in the OC.

[51]He writes, "Levitical priesthood and Mosaic law go together, and both have given way to the superior priesthood and the 'better covenant' of Jesus" (Thielman, *The Law in the New Testament*, 122). This is one of the main features of Thielman's essay, and he sees little to no distinction between "law" and "covenant." This poses a question that this monograph seeks to answer by arguing that while law and covenant are related, they are not synonyms. As such, the covenantal administration has changed from OC to NC, while the law (covenantal commands) have been transposed into a higher key due to the person and work of Christ.

entirely."[52] He does not, however, attempt to describe what this new law is in the NC, and is content to note that OC law has been replaced by a NC law. Thielman defines the writing of the laws upon the hearts as an "inward renewal," with no reference to any specific laws.[53] It follows then for Thielman that there is now a new law entirely for the NC, but there is no conjecture or suggestion as to what this "new law" might be.[54] On the question of the "shadow" in 10:1, he states that the law in its entirety was a temporary shadow of the redemptive work in Christ, who is the "good things to come."[55]

Given the representative sampling of scholars listed above, it is clear that many maintain the view of the law in Hebrews that argues for no ongoing validity in the NC. What follows below are the comments of other scholars who hold an opposite view. For these, there is greater continuity between OC and NC regarding the place and ongoing function of the Mosaic law.

Ongoing Validity in the New Covenant Era

Philip E. Hughes' work on Hebrews has proven to be a significant exegetical and theological contribution to Hebrews studies.[56] Concerning the matter of the law, his work represents a more Reformed understanding of the law, and in particular the familiar three-part division of the law (civil, ceremonial, moral). In his comments on 7:11-12, he argues that the law has been given "on the basis of the priesthood," and that the change brought about by this new priesthood "presupposes a new disposition of law."[57] Regarding this new

---

[52]Thielman, *The Law and the New Testament*, 130. What is important for the present study is that Thielman views νόμους in the Jer 31 text as having no continuity with the νόμος of the OC law. See Thielman, *The Law and the New Testament*, 129-32.

[53]Ibid., 122-23. Here Thielman seems to define the writing of God's laws upon the hearts as "purification of conscience." See also p. 125 where the promised inward writing of the law is defined by Thielman as "inward renewal." This is much like that found in Attridge et al. See also Rudolph Smend and Ulrich Luz, *Gesetz* (Stuttgart: Biblische Konfrontationen, 1981), 114. Their comments on 8:10 offer support to Thielman at this point, "Die Weissagung Jeremias, daß Gott seine...werde, wird zwar als Teil der Weissagung vom Neuen Bund zitiert (8:10), aber gerade nicht ausgelegt."

[54]He writes, "The change in priesthood has required...a different law entirely (7:12)" (Thielman, *The Law and the New Testament*, 131). This is a bit confusing, given that on pp. 122-23 and 125 Thielman seems to understand the NC "law" in 8:10/10:16 as "inward cleansing."

[55]Ibid. Both of these points are debatable, given that the text of 10:1 does not state that the law in its entirety was the shadow (see ch. 6), and while Christ is certainly to be included in the "good things to come," it is highly questionable whether this is all of what the writer of Hebrews has in mind. Specifically, the "good things" consist of the NC's "better promises" (8:6) and all that the promises entail.

[56]Philip E. Hughes, *A Commentary on the Epistle to the Hebrews* (Grand Rapids: Eerdmans, 1977).

[57]Hughes, *Hebrews*, 256.

disposition, Hughes states that the law has only been set aside "insofar as its prescriptions for the regulation of the old priesthood and its ministry are concerned."[58] Thus for Hughes, the ceremonial/priestly aspects of the law have been abrogated,[59] and the law that will be written on the hearts is the law that was formerly external and engraved on tablets of stone, viz., the Mosaic law.[60]

F. F. Bruce concludes that like Paul, Hebrews argues that the "law was a temporary dispensation...valid only until Christ came to inaugurate the age of perfection,"[61] and like the priesthood, the law was a temporary provision.[62] Yet here Bruce uses "law" to define an era, rather than the content of the OC regulations. When Bruce discusses the meaning of νόμους in the context of the Jeremiah 31 passage, he clearly sees a role for the Mosaic law in the hearts of the NC people.[63] There he notes that under the Old Covenant, the law was memorized in obedience to the command of God (Deut 6:6-9), but rote memorization is not the kind of internalization that Jeremiah 31 means. According to Bruce, the NC promise is that this law (that was formerly memorized, viz., the Mosaic laws) will be internalized by an act of the Spirit, but he does not argue for a change in content of this internalized law. Rather, Bruce understands this to refer to the same laws that were formerly memorized.[64] Further, this new action by God yields new hearts (citing Ezek 36:26-28) since human hearts are inadequate and defective. Bruce argues that the law itself was good; the problem was the nature of the people.[65] On the

---

[58]Ibid.

[59]Ibid., 257.

[60]Ibid., 300.

[61]Bruce, *The Epistle to the Hebrews*, 167.

[62]Ibid., 166.

[63]Ibid., 190. Cf. 189, 248. See also Harald Hegermann's comments on 8:10 (*Der Brief an die Hebräer*, THNT 16 [Berlin: Evangelische Verlagsanstalt, 1988], 169). Hegermann is nonspecific as to the exact nature of the phrase in 8:10, "διδοὺς νόμους μου εἰς τὴν διάνοιαν αὐτῶν καὶ ἐπὶ καρδίας αὐτῶν ἐπιγράψω αὐτούς," other than to say that the godly requirements will be internalized, thus accomplishing in the NC what was impossible under the old. However, Hegermann seems to come close to saying that what was written on stone tablets in the OC (i.e., the Mosaic law) is now written on the hearts of those in the NC. He is clear in saying that the end result of this work of God is obedience to God; the NC people will not turn away from him (citing Jer 32:40). Though this writer does not wish to press Hegermann beyond what he has written, he apparently sees a close correspondence between what was formerly external and what is now internal in the NC. If so, then his view can be seen to be in concert with the basic tenets of this monograph. See also George Guthrie, *Hebrews*, NIVAC (Grand Rapids: Zondervan, 1988), 280-95.

[64]Bruce, *Hebrews*, 190.

[65]Ibid. Note also the comments of Harrisville (Roy A. Harrisville, *The Concept of Newness in the New Testament* [Minneapolis: Augsburg, 1960], 48-49). See chapter 5 for a treatment of Heb 8:8 and how the debated text-critical issue with αὐτούς/αὐτοῖς should be grammatically and syntactically understood.

issue of the law as a "shadow" (10:1), Bruce suggests that the writer of
Hebrews specifically and only has in mind the cultic laws that regulated
priesthood and sacrifice. These have, in the present age, found their substance
in Christ.[66]

Paul Ellingworth[67] asserts that for the writer of Hebrews, the cultic aspects
are the essence of the Mosaic law, and the change spoken of in 7:12 does not
refer to a removal of the law altogether, but rather should be understood more
neutrally in the sense of a change or alteration in the law,[68] though he does not
explain or posit the nature of such a change (as such he might belong in the first
grouping of scholars). He states that the writer of Hebrews "indicates a change,
not merely in particular laws, but of the entire legal system, understood as
essentially cultic."[69] Like other scholars,[70] Ellingworth is disappointingly silent

---

[66]Bruce, *Hebrews*, 235.

[67]Given his limited amount of discussion, it is possible that Ellingworth resists
categorization. Though he states that the law has not been removed altogether
(commenting on 7:12), he does not discuss its usage in the NC. Thus, one is led to
wonder what Ellingworth means exactly when he says that the law has not been
removed altogether in the coming of Christ and the NC. Commenting on the two uses of
Jer 31:33, Ellingworth is unclear given what he argues in 7:12. On 8:10 he writes that
the NC will be written on the hearts, and on 10:16 he writes that the law will be
internalized. If 10:16 is taken with his comments on 7:12, his meaning would be quite
clear. Yet taken with his view of 8:10, a certain lack of clarity is present, mostly due to a
lack of discussion on the meaning of the law in Hebrews. It is this kind of uncertainty
that the present study hopes to clarify.

[68]Ellingworth, *The Epistle to the Hebrews*, 374.

[69]Ibid. For a similar notion, see Hans von Campenhausen, *The Formation of the
Christian Bible*, trans. J. A. Baker (Philadelphia: Fortress, 1972), 69-70. Von
Campenhausen argues that the notion of "law" in Hebrews only refers to the cultic
elements, and not the whole corpus of God's commandments (69), yet he notes that
these cultic arrangements pointed to Christ in shadow form, and references Heb 10:1.

[70]Ellingworth's treatment of 8:10 and 10:16 is quite similar to that of H-F Weiß, who
also has little comment on the meaning of these verses. Weiß (rightly) notes that the
writer of Hebrews views the Jeremiah passage Christologically, "Obwohl der Autor des
Hebr die Verheißung von Jer 31 selbst-verständlich in einer christologischen
Perspektive liest" (Weiß, *Der Brief*, 446), but does not discuss the meaning of the
internalization of the laws/law ("die Verinnerlichung des Gesetzes").

Interestingly, H-F Weiß as well as Erich Gräßer view the writer's discussion of law
as only academic and hypothetical. Weiß has a brief excursus ("Das ‚Gesetz' im
Hebräerbrief," 403-07), in which he develops this idea and contrasts this view with that
of Paul. Weiß argues that though Paul fought against Judaizers of his day, the writer of
Hebrews does not feel compelled to write about the law in the same manner. There are
no Judaizing opponents to which Hebrews is specifically addressed, Weiß maintains,
and therefore such discussions about the law on the part of the writer of Hebrews are
merely theoretical and academic. He writes, "Eher theoretisch bzw. 'akademisch' wird
hier—im Hebr—das Thema des Gesetzes erörtert, als Stilmittel gleichsam zur
Entfaltung der eigenen christologisch-soteriologischen Position des Autors im Sinne der

on the meaning of 8:10 and 10:16, offering little discussion other than to state that the NC will be inscribed on the hearts of God's people (8:10),[71] and that there will be an "inward writing of the Law" in the NC (10:16).[72]

The impact of William Lane's 1991 two-volume commentary is still being felt in Hebrews studies. Regarding the issue of the law, he rightly argues that the statements made about the law in Hebrews are not to be seen in a pejorative sense, nor are they an anti-Jewish polemic.[73] The statements about the law's inabilities and the change in the law are deductions from the author's meditation on the biblical text—the results of the inspired writer's own biblical exegesis. Concerning the Jeremiah text, Lane's comments are worth noting. He writes, "Although the Old Covenant was to be superseded and invalidated, it receives recognition as shadow and example. God will do something new, which implies discontinuity, but between the old and new there will be genuine continuity."[74] The discontinuity was built into the old revelation, and the writer of Hebrews argues on the basis of his own exegesis of those OT texts (see 8:13a, for example).

For Lane, the Torah will be implanted on the hearts *without* a change in

---

Einmaligkeit und Endgültigkeit des neuen Priesterinstituts gegenüber der 'Schwäche und Nutzlosigkeit' des die alte Kultordnung konstituierenden Gesetzes" (403-04). See also Gräßer (*An Die Hebräer*, 2:51), who cites Weiß at this point. Koester rightly disagrees with the suggestion of Weiß and Gräßer, observing that "Given the importance of the Levitical priesthood for Jewish identity, it seems likely that Heb 7:11-19 deals with live issues" (Koester, *Hebrews*, 357). Note too the work of Lindars (*Theology of the Epistle to the Hebrews*, 4-15), who presents an interesting argument for the present circumstances of the original audience. Though in this writer's view Lindars is unconvincing in the end, his suggestions concerning the reason Hebrews was written are indeed noteworthy and are in significant contrast to the views of Weiß and Gräßer.

[71]Ellingworth, *Hebrews*, 417. This kind of language is confusing, given the fact that the text does not say that the NC will be inscribed on the hearts of God's people, but rather that in the making of a NC, God will inscribe His *law* (lit. laws/νόμους) upon their hearts. This is an important distinction that is infrequently made.

In contrast, note the clarity of Leonhard Goppelt, *New Testament Theology*, ed. Jürgen Roloff, trans. John E. Alsup (Grand Rapids: Eerdmans, 1982), 2:255-57. Goppelt (rightly) makes a clear distinction between NC, OC, and the Mosaic law. However, Goppelt maintains that the Mosaic law has been "suspended" in the NC (2:256). Like Koester (cf. Ellingworth), Goppelt has no comment on the meaning of 8:10/10:16 where one promise of the NC is "διδοὺς νόμους μου εἰς τὴν διάνοιαν αὐτῶν καὶ ἐπὶ καρδίας αὐτῶν ἐπιγράψω αὐτούς." Regardless of this fact, it is noteworthy that Goppelt presupposes one of the basic tenets of this thesis, viz., that while covenant and law are related, they are distinct and should be discussed as such. Goppelt's discussion of the law in Hebrews makes it clear that the writer of Hebrews does in fact not use covenant and law interchangeably.

[72]Ellingworth, *Hebrews*, 514.

[73]Lane, *Hebrews*, 1:cxxxi.

[74]Ibid., 1:cxxxii.

content,[75] and thus not replaced. Rather, for Lane the newness of the NC is in the new *manner* of presenting God's law, and not newness of content.[76] The Levitical institutions in the law have been fulfilled and superseded by the priestly mediation of Christ. The priesthood, the NC, and the sacrifice of Christ are part of the "good things" to which the law pointed in shadow form (10:1).[77]

As somewhat of an addendum, the works of Erich Gräßer and Christoph Levin should be given attention.[78] Specifically commenting on the newness of

---

[75]However, Lane perhaps does not go far enough in his explanation of this NC phenomenon. In addition, such a statement leaves multiple questions unanswered when placed alongside exegesis of 7:11-19, even though on the surface this writer would agree with Lane that the content has not been *replaced*. The law has been changed in some sense, though the nature of this change is one of the chief questions asked here. It is not an unaltered Mosaic law that is written on the hearts, but rather one that has been *radically* altered by the work of Christ. This does not invalidate the law, but rather "transposes it into a higher key." There is still priesthood, covenant, and sacrifice in the new era, and there is still the presence of the law, though its *location* has now been forever changed, as well as the *manner* of its presentation (formerly on stone tablets, now on the hearts). Whereas the law was in the ark which was in the tabernacle and later the temple, its locus now is in the hearts and minds of NC believers by and through the work of God in the Christ event (see also James M. Hamilton, Jr., "He is With You and He Will Be in You: The Spirit, the Believer, and the Glorification of Jesus" [Ph.D diss., The Southern Baptist Theological Seminary, 2003], 51-57). The law is to be seen now as eminently Christological. In short, the internalized law has undergone a change as part of the present eschatological shift and movement of salvation history.

The point of the internalization of the law is that now the people of God will obey from the heart in a way that they did not under the OC, having the law written internally in a way that was not part of the OC. Logically then, internalization should therefore mean even greater faithfulness and obedience to the commands of God. Thus, in order to maintain the position of the law's being internalized without a change in content, it seems that Lane would then have to argue that *all* aspects of the law are now internalized (even the cultic aspects), and as a result are to be obeyed in an even greater capacity than when they were merely external. Yet this position seems hardly tenable in light of the argument of Heb 7-10, and a point that Lane himself disagrees with elsewhere (from a close reading of Lane, one could argue that he might in fact agree with this understanding).

Helpfully, Lane does not redefine νόμους in the Jeremiah text to mean "laws" in a figurative sense, disconnected from their OT context. Rather, the writer of Hebrews interprets the words of Jeremiah Christologically; his hermeneutic is Christological. Therefore, the internalized Mosaic law is not a one-to-one identical twin of the law given to Moses; it is the law given to Moses now interpreted and viewed in light of Christ. It is the law in a "higher key."

[76]Lane, *Hebrews*, 1:209.

[77]Ibid., 1:cxxxiii-iv.

[78]See Gräßer, *An die Hebräer*, 2: 37-38; 46-47; 50-51; 101-03; idem, *Der Alte Bund im Neuen* (Tübingen: Mohr, 1985), 109; Christoph Levin, *Die Verheissung des neuen Bundes in ihrem theologiegeschichtliche Zusammenhang ausgelegt*, FRLANT 137

the NC prophecy of Jeremiah 31,[79] Gräßer writes that Jeremiah 31:31-34 indicates that there will be a different method of "Torah manifestation" (Tora-Offenbarung) in the NC. He cites favorably and heavily from the study of Levin at this point, who compares the different manifestations of the Torah in the OC and NC.[80] Levin notes that in the OC, the Torah for Israel was external and learned only by great effort, "Jetzt ist die Tora für Israel ein Äußeres, auf Leder geschrieben und unter Mühen zu lernen." Not even the most perfect obedience could overcome the distance from God. All possible joy in God's law was threatened by the possibility of "missing the law."[81]

In the NC, such fear and distance is overcome by God himself when the Torah is internalized.[82] At that point, all deficiency of obedience and knowledge of God will come to an end. Levin writes, "Dann aber wird die Tora für Israel das Innerste sein, von Gott auf die Herzen geschrieben. Die Kluft zwischen Gottes Gebot und dem Wollen des menschlichen Herzen wird von Gott selbst geschlossen werden."[83]

In short, Gräßer and Levin understand the NC prophecy in Jeremiah 31 to refer to an internalization of the Torah, which has continuity with the (previously external) Mosaic law itself. It is the "internalized Torah," the law

---

(Göttingen: Vandenhoeck & Ruprecht, 1985), 264. However, Levin views the canonical form of Jer 31:31-34 as a post-exilic construction. He views it as a more pedestrian oracle, and not the high point of the prophet's theology (257-64). Rather, Levin understands the verses to be stating a scribe's dream for an ideal of future torah piety, where there will be flawless memorizing of what is taught. For Levin, Jer 31:31-34 is the utopian dream of the teacher in post-exilic Judaism.

[79]The question of "newness" brings to mind the oft-cited work of Harrisville (Harrisville, *Concept of Newness*, esp. 47-57), who rightly argues that in Hebrews, the newness of the NC describes what is "qualitatively different from the way in which God ordered His relation to men in the past, a supreme and final arrangement between God and His community, never to be supplanted or surpassed" (47). Also, Harrisville presupposes a distinction between the OC itself and the law that governed it (56). This is precisely the way that these concepts are understood in the present study.

In contrast, Harrisville's view of the newness of the NC in Hebrews is directly opposed by Walter C. Kaiser in his 1972 article, "The Old Promise and the New Covenant: Jer 31:31-34," *JETS* 15 (1972): 11-23. Kaiser argues that the NC is actually a "renewed" covenant and not "new" in the sense that Harrisville has described. He argues that Jer 31 is an extension and fulfillment of the OC, rather than a fully *new* covenant, per se. Kaiser's view, as well as others who have followed his thinking such as Fischer (John Fischer, "Covenant, Fulfillment and Judaism in Hebrews," *ERT* 13 [1989]: 175-87), is further addressed in chapter 5.

[80]Levin, *Die Verheissung*, 263-64.

[81]He writes, "Jetzt ist alle Freude an Gottes Gesetz bedroht durch die Möglichkeit, das Gesetz zu verfehlen" (Levin, *Die Verheissung*, 264).

[82]Gräßer agrees, *An die Hebräer*, 2:101-02.

[83]Levin, *Die Verheissung*, 264.

that was formerly external, now made internal by an act of God.[84] Gräßer comments, "die in Herz und Sinn geschriebene, also nicht äußerlich bleibende, sondern verinnerliche Tora, wodurch die Sehnsucht nach einem unzerstörbaren (eschatolo-gischen) Gottesverhältnis gestillt wird."[85] When the law was merely external, all joy of God's law was threatened by the possibility of transgressing his law. The end result of such an action is a new people in whom obedience is accomplished by the act of God himself.[86]

However, when commenting on the important matter of how the writer of Hebrews actually uses Jeremiah 31, Gräßer argues that the continuity between OC, NC, and the law, present in Jeremiah 31, in is in fact absent in Hebrews, and that for Hebrews the law has been annulled in the NC.[87] His interpretation is colored by his assumption that the writer of Hebrews' background of thought is the cosmic dualism of Philo and Hellenistic Judaism,[88] and as such notions of continuity are impossible from a philosophic standpoint. For Gräßer, the law belongs to the earthly and not the heavenly realm.[89] Thus, there is an apparent disconnect between the original meaning of Jeremiah 31:31-34 and how Hebrews understands it.[90]

Conclusion

The problem one encounters in doing research on Hebrews and the law is that it is often difficult to categorize various scholars regarding their views on the law, and to do so with great precision, even though certain tendencies can be seen in the above representative sample of current scholarship. There are essentially three questions asked here that become the focus of chapters 4, 5, and 6. First, "What does it mean for the writer of Hebrews that the law has changed?" (7:12). Second, "What does it mean for the law(s) to be written on the minds and hearts if/since it has been changed?" (8:10/10:16). Finally, "What does it mean that the 'law has a shadow'?" (10:1). Surely there are other questions that could be raised, but these three get at the heart of the theology of the law in Hebrews 7:1-10:18, and are therefore the focus of the present work. These are

---

[84]Specifically, "ins Herz geschriebenen Gesetz" (Gräßer, *An die Hebräer*, 2:101 n. 45). Note Levin, *Die Verheissung*, 264.

[85]Gräßer, *An die Hebräer*, 2:101.

[86]Levin writes, "Dann [i.e., "after these days" in the NC] wird alle Unzulänglichkeit der Erkenntnis und des Gehorsams ein Ende finden.... Keiner wird mehr den anderen lehren: 'Erkennt Jahweh,' keiner wird sich mehr rühmen müssen: 'Deine Tora habe ich im Herzen!' keiner wird mehr über der Tora brüten Tag und Nacht, in ungestillter Sehnsucht, sondern sie werden durch Gottes eschatologische Heilstat alle, 'von ihrem Kleinsten bis zu ihrem Größten,' die Tora im Herz tragen, werden unmittelbar sein zu dem offenbaren, seinem Volk Israel gnädigen Gott" (Levin, *Die Verheissung*, 264).

[87]Gräßer, *An die Hebräer*, 2:37-38; 46-47; 101-03.

[88]Ibid., 2:51; idem, *Der Alte Bund im Neuen*, 109.

[89]Gräßer, *An die Hebräer*, 2:47.

[90]The matter of Hebrews' use of the OT will be addressed in ch. 5.

the primary questions that this writer seeks to answer as a means to answering the broader question stated at the outset, "What is the writer's view of the law as seen in Hebrews 7:1-10:18?"

This monograph should be loosely understood as building on and advancing the view maintained by the second collection of scholars. What is meant here by "validity in the NC era" is encapsulated in the idea that the law is now internalized, and thus not abrogated in toto. Yet what is not meant, in any sense, is that the NC believer is under obligation to keep the law as prescribed under the OC as if Christ had never come and God had never spoken in the son. Rather, the requirements of the Mosaic laws have been transformed and fulfilled in the work of Christ. In this sense, there is some continuity with the first view. In short, the question, "Does the Mosaic law have validity in NC believers?" is not the right question, though this has been how the discussion has been framed in the past. This study maintains that the law of God is no longer *over* the covenant people of God, but rather is *within* all of the NC people of God, and it is in this sense that it is still "ongoing" or "valid." It is *not* ongoing in the sense of how one approaches God or how one deals with sin. In this sense the "shadow" has found its "form." In the following chapters, this writer proposes to advance the discussion by raising and answering the three more pointed questions listed above concerning the law in Hebrews.

Method

The answer to these questions in the following chapters come through a fresh exegesis of the text with the aim at producing a clear theological understanding of Hebrews and the Mosaic law built upon detailed exegetical study. This study proceeds along the following lines.

Chapter 2 addresses the broad issue of the law in Second Temple Judaism by focusing on how the law was understood in non-biblical writings of the period. The important matter of how other biblical authors viewed the law (such as Paul, Matthew, or James) is not part of the question in chapter 2. In addition, this chapter does not seek to draw original conclusions. Rather, it presents an important piece of the puzzle by answering the question as to how the Mosaic law was understood in Second Temple Judaism. It provides a relevant context in which to discuss the more specific question of how the writer of Hebrews presents the same topic.

Having addressed the cultural and theological backdrop of the issue in chapter 2, chapter 3 is devoted to placing 7:1-10:18 in its literary context. This involves interaction with the most influential and most recent efforts that have been written on the structure of Hebrews in the past century. The important and varied contributions of Albert Vanhoye, Leon Vaganay, Ceslas Spicq, Wolfgang Nauck, Donald Guthrie, Harold Attridge, F. F. Bruce, and George Guthrie are presented and discussed. The goal of chapter 3 is not necessarily to argue for a specific literary and structural approach (though conclusions and preferences are clearly articulated), but rather to recognize the varied approaches and to articulate an argument for how 7:1-10:18 fits into the overall organization of Hebrews.

Chapter 4 centers on Hebrews 7:1-28, and specifically the question, "What does it mean for the writer of Hebrews that the law has changed?" It first overviews the movement of Hebrews 7 in three sections: vv. 1-10, 11-19, and 20-28. This is followed by a focus on 7:12. Fundamentally, the matter of νόμου μετάθεσις is essential for ascertaining the writer's view of the law and is therefore the focus of the second movement of the chapter. This culminates with a discussion of the findings concerning the present writer's view of the law.

Chapter 5 centers on Hebrews 8:1-13, with the topic of the law and the NC taking center stage. Here the question is asked, "What does it mean for the law(s) to be written on the minds and hearts if/since it has been changed?" Since Christ is the priest of the NC (8:1-6), what then does it mean that the law will be written on the minds and hearts in this NC that he inaugurates? First is an exegetical overview of 8:1-13 in two parts (8:1-6; 8:7-13) that sets up a general framework within which more specific matters may be discussed. Second, given the centrality of Jeremiah 31 (LXX 38) to Hebrews 8, an excursus concerning Jeremiah 31:31-34 and its context is warranted. Third, this excursus is followed by another on the topic of the writer's use of the OT. Fourth is a discussion of the central text of 8:10 (as well as the parallel passage of 10:16) as understood by current Hebrews scholars, as well as the matter of νόμος/νόμους in this central text. This is followed by this writer's own view of the text, which, as will be seen, is a modification of one of the prevailing scholarly views. A conclusion follows.

Chapter 6 addresses the specific matter of the law's having a shadow (10:1). Building on the exegetical conclusions of the previous chapters, the question asked is, "What does it mean that the 'law has a shadow'?" The chapter proceeds in three movements. First is an overview of the contents and flow of 9:1-10:18 divided into three main sections: 9:1-10, 9:11-28, and 10:1-18. This is followed by the meaning of the law's "having a shadow." Third is a theological consideration of the role of the NC blessings as well as further comments on the repetition of Jeremiah 31 in 10:16-17. This is then followed by a conclusion.

The seventh and final chapter summarizes and concludes the argument carried through these chapters. Here, the various points of the preceding investigation are tied together, offering to the reader a clearer picture of the Mosaic law as it is understood by the writer of Hebrews. As noted at the outset, the fundamental purpose of this monograph is to advance NT scholarship, and more importantly, advance the Church's understanding of this intricate "word of exhortation," the epistle to the Hebrews.

CHAPTER 2

The Law in Second Temple Judaism

Introduction

The following survey of the law in the thought of Second Temple Judaism is intended to uncover the theological context of the present larger discussion, and must by its very nature be succinct.[1] To be sure, there are numerous avenues down which this chapter could meander given the magnitude of the issue. Yet given such temptations and other matters available for study, this chapter must maintain a focus on essential questions. First, "When Jewish writers of this period wrote of the law, what did they mean and to what did they refer?" Second, "What was their view of the law?" Even though these questions are broad, the intent here is in fact to paint with broad strokes, and therefore demonstrate an overall picture of what likely came to mind for a first-century Jew when the idea of the law was considered.[2]

It would be naïve to think that such a theologically significant term as תּוֹרָה/ νόμος would mean one and only one thing in the Judaism of the Second Temple period. Therefore, this writer does not conclude that νόμος means exactly the same thing in every circumstance in the literature under discussion for the present chapter.[3] However, one may safely speak of certain tendencies

---

[1]Even though the present chapter is lengthy, what is presented here is in fact a succinct discussion of the issue.

[2]One could perhaps run the risk of being *so* broad so as to say *nothing*. But the purpose of this chapter is not to advance the discussion of law in first-century Judaism, but rather to paint a broad backdrop as to the general thoughts and attitudes regarding the law in this particular period. Thus, a smaller amount of accepted literature provides ample material for such an endeavor. This is important to the present study on the theology of Hebrews since it will put the discussion of the law in Hebrews in a broader religious context. To this end the method and purpose of the present chapter fit within and contribute to the overall thesis of the present work.

[3]In an influential article from the 1930s, C. H. Dodd argued that LXX translators mistakenly translated תּוֹרָה with νόμος (C. H. Dodd, *The Bible and the Greeks* [London: Hodder & Stoughton, 1935], 25-41). In the process of translation there is rarely such a thing as a clear one-to-one equivalent for significant theological and sociological terms such as תּוֹרָה and νόμος. The issue is whether or not LXX translators were wrong, reflecting an error common to Hellenistic Judaism as Dodd alleges. This view was commonly held for much of the twentieth century (see Solomon Schechter, *Some*

within the religious writings examined below. Again, the goal of this chapter is to discover a broad understanding of what was meant by "law," and what the general attitude or feeling was toward the law in the relevant literature.

Continuing with matters of scope, it is necessary to limit this study to those texts that most clearly and demonstrably represent this period of Jewish history. This chapter will focus on a representative sample of five of the most important and relevant Jewish works from the period: the OT Apocrypha, OT Pseudepigrapha, Josephus, Philo, and the Dead Sea Scrolls. These were chosen since they represent several strands of Jewish thought during the Second Temple period, and are largely accepted as being relevant to the discussion.

Aspects of Rabbinic Theology [New York: Macmillan, 1923]; Samuel Sandmel, *The Genius of Paul*, 3ʳᵈ ed. [Philadelphia: Fortress, 1979]; Alan F. Segal, "Torah and *Nomos* in Recent Scholarly Discussion," *SR* 13.1 [1984]:19-27), but there are those who presently argue that νόμος is an adequate translation of תּוֹרָה, and that νόμος had a broader meaning than Dodd and Schechter allowed (see Joseph Blenkinsopp, *Wisdom and Law in the Old Testament and in Early Judaism* [Oxford: University Press, 1984]; Stephen Westerholm, "Torah, Nomos, and Law: A Question of Meaning,'" *SR* 15.3 [1986]: 327-36). For a discussion of the history of the debate, see Peter Richardson and Stephen Westerholm, eds., *Law in Religious Communities in the Roman Period: The Debate over* Torah *and* Nomos *in Post-Biblical Judaism and Early Christianity*, SCJ 4 (Ontario: Wilfrid Laurier University Press, 1991).

Dodd argues that Hellenistic Judaism mistranslated תּוֹרָה, and in doing so skewed the understanding of תּוֹרָה to support a legalistic view of the OT. Yet Martin Hengel has demonstrated that the sharp distinction between Palestinian and Diaspora Judaism is inadequate. See his *Judaism and Hellenism: Studies in Their Encounter in Palestine During the Early Hellenistic Period*, 2ⁿᵈ ed, trans. John Bowden (Minneapolis: Fortress, 1981). See also W. D. Davies, *Paul and Rabbinic Judaism: Some Rabbinic Elements in Pauline Theology*, 4ᵗʰ ed. (Philadelphia: Fortress, 1980), xxiii, who notes that the discussions regarding Palestinian vs. Diaspora Judaism have demonstrated that a strict dichotomy of the two is overly simplistic and mistaken. Such a distinction "was to ignore the unmistakable interpenetration of the two cultures both outside and inside Palestine" (xxiii).

However, Samuel Sandmel (*The Genius of Paul*, 3ʳᵈ ed. [Philadelphia: Fortress, 1979]), maintains a distinction between Palestinian Jews and Greek Jews and argues that each would have understood תּוֹרָה *differently*. For Palestinian Jews, תּוֹרָה would have meant more than simply "law," which is how Greek Jews understood the concept of תּוֹרָה. Sandmel argues, "Greek Jews focused their attention on Judaism as though it was both in essence and as a totality *law* and nothing but *law*" (46, emphasis his). He adds, "Greek Jews nowhere raised the question of whether Torah really means *nomos*, law! And whenever they defended their Jewish convictions, it was always on the premise, startling to modern Jewish students, that *nomos* did adequately translate *Torah*" (47). Adding to this he states, "The Graeco-Jewish equation of Torah and law was picked up and propagated by the church fathers" (48) and the result is that within Protestantism since the 1870s, Judaism has come to be identified with legalism and regarded with condescension (48).

Old Testament Apocrypha

The apocryphal books of the OT[4] provide several insights into the Jewish mind of this time period regarding how "law" was understood. In an early twentieth century work, Ralph Marcus concluded,

> Whatever influence may have been exerted upon...Judaism..., the great theological ideas which are most prominent in...Judaism, such as the belief in the oneness and uniqueness of God, in his moral attributes, in the necessity and efficacy of repentance, in the divine origin and preexistence of scripture—these ideas as they are expressed in the apocryphal literature are seen to be a natural development of the religious teachings which are recorded in the Old Testament.[5]

Marcus comes to the same conclusions that E. P. Sanders and others eventually would: broadly speaking, the average Jew did indeed seek to adhere to the commandments of the law.[6] Yet he is quick to point out that in the Apocrypha, even scrupulous fulfillment of the cultic laws "was not considered sufficient in itself to form the sum of the religious duties of the people."[7] Marcus maintains that the consistent teaching of the apocryphal works is that the commandments of the law must be and were expected to be kept.[8]

---

[4]Unless otherwise noted, translations of apocryphal works are those of the RSV.

[5]Ralph Marcus, *Law in the Apocrypha*, Columbia University Oriental Studies 26 (New York: Columbia University Press, 1927), 113.

[6]E. P. Sanders, "Law in Judaism of the New Testament Period," in *ABD*, ed. David Noel Freedman (New York: Doubleday, 1992), 256-63. Sanders' research points to the conclusion that the commandments were largely followed by the common Jew of the first century. See also A. I. Baumgarten, "The Torah as a Public Document in Judaism," *SR* 14.1 (1985): 17-24, who concludes, "the conviction that all Jews should know and observe the Torah was an ideal widely held" (18). See also E. P. Sanders, *Judaism: Practice and Belief 63 BCE-66CE* (Philadelphia: Trinity Press International, 1992), 47-51; 119-45; 190-240, esp. 191-92; idem, *Jewish Law From Jesus to the Mishnah: Five Studies* (Philadelphia: Trinity Press International, 1990), 255-308; W. D. Davies, *Jewish and Pauline Studies* (Philadelphia: Fortress, 1984), 3-26; Jacob Neusner, *Reading and Believing: Ancient Judaism and Contemporary Gullibility*, BJS 113 (Atlanta: Scholars Press, 1986), 54-56; Eduard Lohse, *The New Testament Environment*, trans. John. E. Steely (Nashville: Abingdon, 1976), 80; and David M. Rhoads, *Israel in Revolution 6-74 C.E.: A Political History Based on the Writings of Josephus* (Philadelphia: Fortress, 1976), 33. For more discussion, see Appendix 1.

[7]Marcus, *Law in the Apocrypha*, 113.

[8]Ibid. Marcus concludes that in the Apocrypha the Pentateuch came to be referred to simply as "the Book of the Law" (114). Marcus maintains the view of his day held by Schechter and Dodd that νόμος is an inadequate translation of תּוֹרָה (43). This is true of another important work published the same year as Marcus' dissertation, that of George Foote Moore (*Judaism in the First Centuries of the Christian Era: The Age of the Tannaim* [Cambridge: Harvard University Press, 1927], 1:263). What is interesting is

In more recent works that consider the writings of the Apocrypha, conflicting views of the law (and in particular the *role* of the law in broader Judaism) are presented. In his influential work, *Paul and Palestinian Judaism*, E. P. Sanders argues that apocryphal texts such as Sirach articulate his well-received "pattern of religion," viz., covenantal nomism.[9] Though he does not discuss all of the apocryphal writings, he consistently acknowledges that the law played a significant role in the life of Second Temple Judaism, not the least of which was the desire of broader Judaism to keep the law of Moses. For Sanders, such law-keeping is significant, since those who obey the law remain in the covenant. Thus, for Sanders, law-keeping in the Apocrypha (and in the whole of Second Temple Judaism) maintains one's covenant status. Stated simply, works of the law do not earn salvation, they maintain one's covenant status.[10]

The role of "works of the law" in Second Temple Judaism's soteriological framework is only tangential to the purposes here (though certainly not unimportant), and thus will not receive a full-orbed discussion. However, what is important, and what can be gleaned from the current debate, is the *emphasis* on the law itself in the Second Temple period. Whether one asserts that law-keeping does not earn salvation in the theology of this period (Sanders), or that law-keeping is in fact meritorious[11] is not the specific question at hand. What is

---

that Marcus, Moore, Dodd and Schechter, and even at times W. D. Davies not only are stating the same ideas as one another, but do in fact use almost *identical wording* to articulate this idea. Davies is slightly different in that while he recognizes that תּוֹרָה /νόμος can have the broader meaning argued for by Schechter et al., it *normally* has a *more narrow sense*. It is in this sense that Davies bridges the gap between the first and second halves of the twentieth century.

[9]In E. P. Sanders' *Paul and Palestinian Judaism: A Comparison of Patterns of Religion* (Philadelphia: Fortress, 1977), Sirach is the only apocryphal book that receives attention from Sanders. In the present chapter, it is argued (tangentially) that his views of the law in Second Temple Judaism are not always helpful and are subject to debate (especially given the contributions of other scholars such as Mark Elliott and Simon Gathercole, noted below). In subsequent works, Sanders treats (at least in some measure) other works of the Apocrypha such as Judith, Tobit, 1, 2, 3, 4 Maccabees, and the Wisdom of Solomon. See E. P. Sanders, *Jewish Law from Jesus to the Mishnah* (Philadelphia: Trinity Press, 1990); idem, *Judaism*.

[10]Sanders, *Paul and Palestinian Judaism*, 542; cf. 329-33; 346, passim. This is Sanders' conclusion, but it has been significantly criticized in more recent works. As a way of understanding the Judaism of the era, the present writer finds covenantal nomism unpersuasive.

[11]See the recent works of Simon J. Gathercole, *Where is Boasting? Early Jewish Soteriology and Paul's Response in Romans 1-5* (Grand Rapids: Eerdmans, 2002); Mark A. Elliott, *The Survivors of Israel: A Reconsideration of the Theology of Pre-Christian Judaism* (Grand Rapids: Eerdmans, 2000); D. A. Carson, Peter T. O'Brien, and Mark A. Seifrid, eds., *Justification and Variegated Nomism*, vol. 1, *The Complexities of Second*

important for the present thesis is that both sides of this larger issue agree that there was a significant interest in keeping the law, the written Mosaic Torah, in the centuries prior to and encompassing the NT era. The *motive* for law-keeping, whether to stay in the covenant or to merit salvation, is not the specific question with which this chapter is concerned. What is important at this point is how the law was viewed in the literature. This chapter enters into the greater debate on the matters of soteriology and eschatology of Second Temple Judaism insofar as it is necessary.

The apocryphal books that are most relevant here are Sirach (The Wisdom of Ben Sira),[12] 1 and 2 Maccabees, Tobit, and Baruch.[13] To be sure, some of these writings are more important than others.

The Wisdom of Ben Sira

The Wisdom of Ben Sira (Sirach)[14] was likely written in Hebrew sometime in the late second century BC by Joshua/Jesus ben Sira, and some fifty years later translated into Greek by his grandson,[15] and its similarities to other Jewish wisdom literature are widely noted.[16] Di Lella argues that the central chapter of this work is chapter 24 ("the law book of Moses") and argues that the theme of Sirach is "wisdom, which is identified with the law, can be achieved only by

---

Temple Judaism (Grand Rapids: Baker, 2001); and Mark A. Seifrid, *Justification by Faith: The Origin and Development of a Central Pauline Theme*, NovTSup 68 (New York: E. J. Brill, 1992). Though these works have various theses, what they have in common is a rethinking and reconsideration of Sanders' fundamental conclusions. Each weighs the primary literary sources of Second Temple Judaism and concludes that Sanders' expressed "pattern of religion" for the period is at best insufficient and even problematic.

[12]Also known as Ecclesiasticus, its Latin name, which means simply "church book." See Craig A. Evans, *Noncanonical Writings and New Testament Interpretation* (Peabody, MA: Hendrickson, 1992), 13.

[13]To this list Judith and the Wisdom of Solomon could likely be added. See Appendix 2.

[14]The term νόμος is found in twenty-seven verses, yet this varies slightly depending on textual witnesses. These do not include such phrases such as "to keep his ways," and the "commandments of the Lord" that are frequent in Sirach and are, in their specific contexts, most likely references to the commands of the Mosaic law. These will be considered as they arise in the literature, since the concept of "law" may be present even when the term (νόμος) is not.

[15]Evans, *Noncanonical Writings*, 13.

[16]Ibid. See also the excellent introduction by Patrick W. Skehan and Alexander A. Di Lella in *The Wisdom of Ben Sira: A New Translation with Notes*, AB, vol. 39 (New York: Double Day, 1987), 3-92. Skehan and Di Lella observe the similarities with Sir 24 and Prov 8:22, especially in the personification and preexistence of wisdom (76). DeSilva also gives an excellent introduction and summary in his recent work (David DeSilva, *Introducing the Apocrypha: Message, Context, and Significance* [Grand Rapids: Baker, 2002], 153-97).

the one who fears God and keeps the commandments,"[17] and that the Mosaic law is fundamental to Ben Sira. For the author, the law is the most important part of the curriculum he teaches, and therefore insists on the observance of the commandments of the law.[18] In Ben Sira's own words, "The whole of wisdom is fear of the Lord; complete wisdom is the fulfillment of the law."[19] J. Sanders avers, "Ben Sira was surely Torah-devout. He was very familiar with the Mosaic Torah, and he was convinced both that it was for Israel's benefit and that Jews should live by it."[20] Ben Sira was first and foremost a scholar of the Mosaic law, and his teaching is clearly indebted to the Torah.[21] The ideas of wisdom and the fear of God are paramount for Ben Sira, and are found dozens of times throughout the work.

But wisdom is only to be had by those who keep the commandments of the law, and "law," for Ben Sira, is the book written by the man Moses to the people of Israel.[22] Ben Sira writes in 1:26, "If you desire wisdom, keep the commandments, and the Lord will bestow her upon you," and in 15:1, "He who fears the Lord will do this; he who is practiced in the law will come to Wisdom." The words of 38:34 are noteworthy as well, which speak of the person "who devotes himself to the fear of God and to the study of the law of

---

[17]Skehan and Di Lella, *Ben Sira*, 76. See also DeSilva, *Introducing*, 153, 187-89. DeSilva concludes that rewards and punishments for Ben Sira are directly tied to one's obedience of or neglect of the law and its wisdom (191).

[18]Joseph Blenkinsopp, *Wisdom and Law in the Old Testament and in Early Judaism* (Oxford: University Press, 1984), 141.

[19]Sir 19:20. Unless otherwise noted, the English citations from Sirach are those found in Skehan and Di Lella. J. Sanders adds that the "fear of the Lord" idea present in the introduction of Ben Sira is akin to "keeping the Mosaic Torah" (Jack Sanders, "When Sacred Canopies Collide: The Reception of the Torah of Moses in the Wisdom Literature of the Second-Temple Period," *JSJ* 32 [2001]: 123).

[20]J. Sanders, "Sacred Canopies," 125. Sanders also notes that in Ben Sira (as well as in the DSS), there is an elevation of Torah (128). He notes Sir 18:4, 9 in which the law is described as an "imperishable light" and that the people "with one accord agreed to the divine law." Here the clear reference is to the Mosaic commands of the Pentateuch, and as in other wisdom literature of the period, is associated with wisdom. "Love is the keeping of her (wisdom's) laws" (128).

[21]Markus Bockmuehl, *Jewish Law in Gentile Churches: Halakhah and the Beginning of Christian Public Ethics* (Edinburgh: T & T Clark, 2000), 98. He also points out, "The pursuit of wisdom must in the first instance be concerned with Torah." See also Di Lella, who in his comments on Sir 38:24-39:11 writes, "Fear of the Lord and devotion to the Law are indispensable; without them the scribe can in no way be considered wise" (Di Lella, *Wisdom of Ben Sira*, 451).

[22]Donald E. Gowan, "Wisdom," in *Justification and Variegated Nomism*, vol. 1, *The Complexities of Second Temple Judaism*, ed. D. A. Carson, Peter T. O'Brien, and Mark A. Seifrid (Grand Rapids: Baker, 2001), 219.

the Most High."[23]

Keeping the law is not to be seen as an impossible task, but rather is looked upon favorably in 23:27, "Nothing is better than the fear of the Lord, nothing sweeter than obeying his commandments." In fact, those that "fear the Lord and seek to please him" are "filled with his law."[24] This is based on the Deuteronomic equation that to fear God is to love him and is to keep his commandments.[25] In contrast, Ben Sira denounces those who do not obey the law in 41:8, "Woe to you, O wicked people, who forsake the law of the Most High." In Sirach there is reward or punishment in this life, depending on if one is obedient to the commandments.[26]

One of the unique features of Sirach is the oft-cited equation of wisdom and the law (Torah) of God. In a context in which wisdom is praised and wisdom speaks, Sirach 24:23 appears to equate wisdom with the written law of Moses. In 24:22, the voice of wisdom (who is speaking) says, "Whoever obeys me will not be put to shame, and those who work with me will not sin."[27] The author proceeds in verse 23, "All this [what has been said of and by wisdom] is the book of the Most High's covenant, the law which Moses enjoined us as a heritage for the community of Jacob."[28] Blenkinsopp notes, "The novel element in Ben Sira's thinking is seen in the second part of the poem (of chapter 24) in which he identifies this preexistent, immortal Wisdom with Torah."[29] J.

---

[23]Cf. Sir 32:15, "Whoever studies the law masters it, but the reckless is caught in its snare."

[24]Sir 2:16, "οἱ φοβούμενοι κύριον ζητήσουσιν εὐδοκίαν αὐτοῦ καὶ οἱ ἀγαπῶντες αὐτὸν ἐμπλησθήσονται τοῦ νόμου." See also Johannes Marböck, "Gesetz und Weisheit: zum Verständnis des Gesetzes bei Jesus ben Sira," *BZ* 20 (1976): 1-21, who discusses 17:11-14, in which the commandments of the law are seen as a gift of God. This is in keeping with the idea that the law was not a burden.

[25]Skehan and Di Lella, *Ben Sira*, 79. See Deut 10:12-13; 30:16. Di Lella writes here, "Accordingly, Ben Sira teaches that believers must love and fear God, must walk in his ways and keep the commandments of the Law.... One can now see more clearly why in 24:23a the Law and wisdom are identified."

[26]Gowan, "Wisdom," 218.

[27]ὁ ὑπακούων μου οὐκ αἰσχυνθήσεται καὶ οἱ ἐργαζόμενοι ἐν ἐμοὶ οὐχ ἁμαρτήσουσιν.

[28]ταῦτα πάντα βίβλος διαθήκης θεοῦ ὑψίστου νόμον ὃν ἐνετείλατο ἡμῖν Μωυσῆς κληρονομίαν συναγωγαῖς Ιακωβ. One must grammatically provide the equative verb here.

[29]Blenkinsopp, *Wisdom and Law*, 143. Blenkinsopp argues that Ben Sira assimilates Torah/law with the eternal principle of wisdom in Sir 24, but does so modeling wisdom on the goddess Isis (143), a point that is given no support. Torah becomes "the divine principle of order" (144). This idea of identifying wisdom with Isis and Isis' behavior is also found in Udo Schwenk-Bressler, *Sapientia Salomonis als ein Beispiel frühjüdischer Textauslegung*, BEATAJ 32 (Frankfurt: Peter Lang, 1993), 103. See also Martin Hengel, *Judaism and Hellenism*, 158; cf. Di Lella, *Ben Sira*, 332.

Sanders agrees, even stating that Ben Sira seems to be "preoccupied" with presenting Torah in light of wisdom, with wisdom quite often overshadowing Torah, although he points out that "Ben Sira does insist on the observance of the commandments."[30]

For Ben Sira, the commandments were given to Moses by the hand of God and are the "law of life and understanding" that are to be taught to Jacob (45:4-5), and it is the teaching and observance of the law that brings about true wisdom (one could even call it "Torah-Wisdom") in the people of God. In 24:28a, Ben Sira states, "the first human" (Adam), "never knew wisdom fully," given that he lived and died before the Torah was given to Moses. "The Torah, which *is* wisdom, was not yet revealed...Israel's wisdom, her Torah, is so inexhaustible and profound that not even 'the [human] law' on earth could 'succeed in fathoming her' (v. 28b)."[31] Though there are great mysteries yet to be solved, there is no mystery in how people should live; "that has been fully revealed in the Torah."[32] Gowan therefore finds that the wisdom Ben Sira seeks to teach is in full accord with the Torah (see 51:13-30).

Finally, though there seems to be no works-salvation schema in Sirach according to Gowan, such acts of obedience to the law are on the same level as offering sacrifices to God.[33] In 35:1-5, the "one who keeps/treasures the law presents offerings in abundance." This is explained as heeding the commandments, returning kindness, giving alms, keeping from wickedness, and forsaking unrighteousness. In this context (35:4), Sirach warns not to appear before the Lord *without* such an offering, "for all that you offer is in fulfillment of the commandment" (35:5). The following verses make clear the acceptability of such offerings of obedience, "The offering of the righteous enriches the altar, and its pleasing odor rises before the Most High. The sacrifice of the righteous is acceptable, and it will never be forgotten."[34] Thus for Sirach, obedience to the law is pleasing to God.[35]

Obedience to the law is also rewarded by God in Sirach. Reward or punishment according to one's deeds is clearly seen (sickness or health [28:1; 30:14-20], a good wife [25:8], or a long life [3:1, 6]).[36] The conclusion of Sirach demonstrates this "reward-for-deeds" doctrine as well, "Do your work in good time, and in his own time God will give you your reward" (51:30). What

---

[30]J. Sanders, "Sacred Canopies," 124.

[31]Di Lella, *Ben Sira*, 337.

[32]Gowan, "Wisdom," 219.

[33]Ibid.

[34]Ibid., 220.

[35]Büchler asserts that God does take note of the sinful acts of individuals, yet only remembers them when that individual seeks to do wrong to his neighbor. See A. Büchler, "Ben Sira's Conception of Sin and Atonement," *JQR* 14 (1923-24): 55.

[36]Gathercole, *Where Is Boasting?*, 38.

is left to uncertainty, however, is the question of *when* reward or punishment will be granted. Yet it seems likely that Sirach envisioned such recompense to be in this life. "Deeds" are acts of obedience to the law of Moses.

In sum, Sirach is relevant to the present study. First, for Sirach, the law was the written Pentateuch and in particular its commandments that were to be obeyed by his readers. Fundamentally, obedience to the law is seen in how one relates to and worships God (35:1-5) and how one relates to one's neighbor (17:14). Second, such obedience will be rewarded. Third, there is no specific emphasis on any certain aspect of the law such as the cultic requirements, since various commands of the law are mentioned such as fasting, purity laws, almsgiving, prayer, and love of one's neighbor (see 34:20-26). Rather, the law seems to be viewed as an entity to be obeyed in all its parts. Fourth, it is clear that the law of Moses is venerated in Sirach as having been sent by God through Moses. Fifth, in keeping with this observation, the Torah itself was not only the source of true wisdom, but even is equal to wisdom in chapter 24. God has granted to his people Israel his wisdom in written form, and the law is a divine gift (17:11-14). At times the author appears in awe of the Torah as the wisdom of God (51:25-26). Sixth, there is inherent (and even absolute) authority in the law—a logical conclusion given its divine origin and the author's urgings to obedience. Seventh, this high view of the Mosaic law reflects not only its value to the people of Israel, but also the significant role that the commandments played in the life of the pious Jew. Finally, wisdom, fear of the Lord, and obedience to the law are naturally connected.[37]

1 Maccabees

The works of 1 and 2 Maccabees tell of events surrounding the Jewish revolt against Antiochus IV Epiphanes in 167-164 BC. In his commentary introduction, Goldstein informs the reader that there had been a long period of stability and security for the Jewish people, even though in subjection to Persia and the Hellenistic kings. During this time pious Jews had little or nothing to fear so long as they kept the Lord's commandments. However, such obedience to the Lord's commands became punishable under the rule of Antiochus. Goldstein soberly states, "No harsher trial ever tested the monotheistic faith of the Jews."[38] The revolt was due to the zeal for keeping the commandments of the Lord in the face of a ruler who demanded the opposite.

Regarding the matter of the law, 1 Maccabees has much to contribute. Over half of the occurrences of νόμος in 1 Maccabees are found in the first two

---

[37]See especially Gowan, "Wisdom," 218.
[38]Jonathan A. Goldstein, *1 Maccabees: A New Translation with Introduction and Commentary*, Anchor Bible, vol. 41 (Garden City, NY: Doubleday, 1976), 3.

chapters.[39] It seems clear that the writer and those of whom he writes maintain a high view of the specific commandments of Moses. Their zeal for the law is the reason for the penalties imposed by Antiochus. He wanted Jews to disregard the restrictions of the Torah of Moses in favor of Greek practices, such as the educational institution of the gymnasium (1:10-15).[40] In 167 BC Antiochus decreed that the Jews cease from observing the Torah and ordered the Jewish people to violate the law's commands (1:54-57).[41] Those found keeping the law (or even having a copy of the law) were killed and the copies of the law burned (1:56). Women were killed for circumcising their male infants according to the law, and the circumcised infants were hung from their mothers' necks (1:60-61). Many others died because they would not profane the covenant by breaking the food laws (1:62-63).

Thus, a dilemma surfaced regarding the law. On the one hand, it was felt that Jews were bound to obey the Torah, yet they were also bound to obey the authorities. This tension is clear in 1 Maccabees 2. Mattathias the priest is confronted with the agent of the king who commands him to offer sacrifice on the altar to the king. Mattathias refuses and kills the king's agent along with a fellow Jew who had attempted to make the sacrifice to the king, and he destroys the altar (2:17-25). In 2:26 Mattathias "burned with zeal for the law" (ἐζήλωσεν τῷ νόμῳ) in doing so. As a result, Mattathias cries out for all who are zealous for the law to follow him (2:27).

Zeal for the law, especially Sabbath laws, is pronounced in 2:29-38. In these verses the king's army kills one thousand men, women, and children when they refuse to fight on the Sabbath and profane the law of the Sabbath (2:34, 37-38).[42] From this point Mattathias teaches that one could in fact fight on the

---

[39]B. Renaud, "La Loi et les Lois dans les Livres des Maccabées," *RB* 68 (1961): 39. Specifically, fourteen occurrences out of a total twenty-seven.

[40]Goldstein, *1 Maccabees*, 4. E. P. Sanders notes that the building of a gymnasium "brought into social prominence a crucial difference between Jew and Greek" given that young men typically exercised in the nude (E. P. Sanders, *Judaism Practice and Belief*, 17). The issue of circumcision came to the fore. He states that there is evidence for at least some young Jewish males undergoing a surgery to "remove the marks of circumcision" (ibid). Those that did were seen to have abandoned the holy covenant (1 Macc 1:14).

[41]Cf. E. P. Sanders, *Judaism Practice and Belief*, 17-20.

[42]Such Pietists were called the (H)Asidaeans and "formed an identifiable group or association committed to the strict observance of the law and counting among their number those whose task it was to interpret it" (Blenkinsopp, *Wisdom and Law*, 124). See also Goldstein, *1 Maccabees*, 6-7. There is some question as to whether these (H)Asidaeans are related to the Essenes mentioned by Josephus and Philo, or whether they were precursors of the Pharisees.

Sabbath if attacked on the Sabbath (2:41).[43] The author adds, "Then there united with them a company of Hasideans, mighty warriors of Israel, all who offered themselves willingly for the law" (πᾶς ὁ ἑκουσιαζόμενος τῷ νόμῳ). In this context, νόμος is a reference to the commands of the law—the Mosaic legislation, and specifically the laws pertaining to the Sabbath. The second chapter draws clear distinctions between those who obey the commands of the law and are thus seen to be righteous, and those who do not. The Pietists "saved the law from the hand of the Gentiles" (2:48), and as he died, Mattathias charged his sons to "grow strong in the law" (2:64), to join themselves with "all who observe the law" (2:67), and to "give heed to the command of the law" (2:68).[44] Gathercole concludes, "The personal motivation for Torah observance in 1 Maccabees is the reward of glory and honor."[45] On this matter Mattathias is clear, "My children, be courageous and grow strong in the law, for by it you will gain honor" (2:64).[46]

This zeal for the law does not end with the death of Mattathias the priest (2:70). Adherence to the commands of the Mosaic law mark the rest of 1 Maccabees. In 3:48, the "book of the law" is searched and consulted regarding idolatry. In 3:56 Judas acts according to the law (κατὰ τὸν νόμον) in keeping with Deuteronomy 20:1-9.[47] In 1 Maccabees 4:42 Judas appoints priests who are "lovers of the Torah" in his efforts to purify and restore the temple. In 4:47 this group of undefiled priests seek to construct a new altar in keeping with the law (Exod 20:25; Deut 27:6), and to offer sacrifices according to the law in 4:53[48] (see also 10:14; 13:4, 48; 14:14, 29; 15:21).

Thus it is clear that zeal for the law marked the Jews of this period according to the record of 1 Maccabees. Specifically, there is a focus on Sabbath laws and prohibitions against idolatry, while other specific commands such as burnt and drink offerings, the festivals, food regulations, idolatry and circumcision are also mentioned (1:44-64). Segal avers, "nomos is normally

---

[43]E. P. Sanders ("Law in Judaism," 256) states that this rule was observed in 63 B.C.E. by the followers of Aristoblus II, but by 66 C.E. the Jews saw fit to attack *on* the Sabbath in the beginning of the war against Rome. Such an attack was seen by Josephus to be an abandonment of religion (*Wars* 2.19.2.§518). See also E. P. Sanders, *Judaism Practice and Belief*, 18, 26, 209; idem, *Jewish Law from Jesus to the Mishnah*, 7.

[44]The Torah (νόμος) here is the *written* Torah. See 1 Macc 1:56; 3:48.

[45]Gathercole, *Where Is Boasting?*, 52.

[46]This statement by Mattathias helps to lead Gathercole to a particular conclusion, viz., that there is a strong reward theology in 1 Maccabees (Gathercole, *Where Is Boasting?*, 52). This is important to the present study in that for Gathercole, one is rewarded for obeying the commands of the Mosaic legislation.

[47]Goldstein, *1 Maccabees*, 263. See also Exod 18:21.

[48]Goldstein sees a reference to Exod 29:38-42 (Goldstein, *1 Maccabees*, 286). See also John R. Bartlett, *1 Maccabees*, Guides to Apocrypha and Pseudepigrapha (Sheffield: Sheffield Academic, 1998), 73-74.

used to denote the Jewish religious law," i.e., the Mosaic commands, "as well as the Pentateuch itself."[49] Renaud agrees, and maintains that νόμος most often refers to the Mosaic legislation in both 1 and 2 Maccabees.[50] One sees a particular focus on laws pertaining to the Sabbath and idol worship in 1 Maccabees, likely due to the specific situation. Other commands, such as the food and purity laws, come into focus in 2 Maccabees.

2 Maccabees

The witness of 2 Maccabees is similar to that of 1 Maccabees with much the same reverence for the law as discovered in 1 Maccabees. It opens with a letter presumably sent to the Jews in Egypt, which, among other things, requests that God "give you all a heart to revere Him and to do His will...may He open your heart to His Torah and to His commandments."[51] In 2:2 the prophet Jeremiah is said to have commanded those going into exile to take with them the fire from the altar as well as the book of the law itself, here the Pentateuch.[52] After giving them the law Jeremiah is said to exhort his readers "not to let the νόμος depart from their hearts" in 2:3. What seems to be clear is that the specific referent for νόμος is the written commandment of the law of Moses.[53]

In 2 Maccabees 2:19-32, the writer notes that Judas Maccabaeus and his brothers "reestablished the laws that were on the point of being abolished" (2:22a). This is a reference to the events of 1 Maccabees, and this reestablishment was accomplished "because the Lord in the fullness of His grace became merciful to them" (2:22b). The laws of 2:22a are the commands found in the Pentateuch and are presumably those referred to in the previous discussion of 1 Maccabees.[54] In 3:1, Onias the high priest is said to have strictly enforced the laws due to his hatred of wickedness, and he, along with a great number of the people, cry out to God to preserve the honor and purity of the

---

[49]Alan F. Segal, "Torah and *Nomos* in Recent Scholarly Discussion," *SR* 13.1 (1984): 21-22.

[50]Renaud, "La Loi et Les Lois," 39.

[51]2 Macc 1:3-4. The translation is that of Goldstein (Jonathan A. Goldstein, *2 Maccabees-A New Translation with Introduction and Commentary* [Garden City, NY: Doubleday, 1983], 137). Goldstein notes that the existence of such a prayer here may indicate that the Jews in Egypt had been "less than perfect in obeying God and his commandments" (142).

[52]Segal, "Torah and *Nomos*," 21-22.

[53]See Goldstein, *2 Maccabees*, 183.

[54]Such were the laws attacked by Antiochus. In 1 Maccabees the emphasis was on the law as a whole, with special emphasis on the Sabbath and idol worship, likely due to the historical context. In addition, Arenhoevel argues that the law is even more pronounced in 2 Maccabees than in 1 Maccabees (Diego Arenhoevel, *Die Theokratie nach dem 1. und 2. Makkabäerbuch* [Mainz: Matthias-Grünewald-Verlag, 1967], 129-31). See also Renaud, "La Loi et Les Lois," 39-67.

temple. Therefore in 4:2 Onias is referred to as a "defender of the laws."[55] In 5:15, Menelaus (a Jewish traitor) escorts Antiochus into the most holy place in direct violation of the law. The author notes that in doing so Menelaus had betrayed "the laws and his country." In addition, the author specifically notes in 5:16 the pollution and uncleanness of Antiochus as he "seized the sacred vessels" (5:16). The specific laws that were broken all find their place in the Mosaic legislation regarding the holy place. Thus, when the priest is noted for his zeal for the law (3:1; 4:2 etc.), it seems clear that he is regarded as a defender of those that govern purity and the holy place.

In 2 Maccabees 6:1 Antiochus sends a senator to compel the Jews "to depart from their ancestral laws and to cease living by the laws of God." This is important for two reasons. First, it suggests that at least a majority of the Jews (or at least enough to warrant such a visit) were living according to the law, and second, it has been demonstrated that the laws in view are those articulated in the Pentateuch. This seems to be the case in 6:5 as well, "The altar was covered with abominable offerings that were forbidden by the laws."[56] Further, 6:18-31 records the account of Eleazar's martyrdom where he chooses to "die a beautiful death" (6:28) since he refuses to eat foods forbidden by the Mosaic law. Immediately before he is tortured he states that he dies eagerly and willingly "in the defense of our revered and sacred laws."

While there are other examples in 2 Maccabees, this section will conclude with the well-known account of chapter 7 in which seven brothers and their mother are tortured and killed for refusing to obey the decree of Antiochus. Under the penalty of torture and death, all seven sons and their mother are arrested and killed for not eating the meat of pagan sacrifices (7:42). The words of a spokesman are recorded in 7:2 that states that they are "ready to die rather than violate the laws of our forefathers." For his commitment to the Torah, this spokesman was scalped, his tongue was cut out, his hands and feet were cut off; then he was burned while still alive (7:3-5). The second brother died saying, "The King of the universe will resurrect us, who die for the sake of His laws" (7:9). The third also claims that he is being killed "for the sake of His laws" (7:11), and so also the fourth, fifth, sixth, and seventh (7:13-40). Before he is killed, the seventh son states, "I refuse to obey the king's command; I heed the

---

[55]On this phrase see also 1 Macc 2:26-27, 50, 58. Note 2 Macc 4:11, where Jason the Oniad is said to have overthrown the civic institutions of the Torah, and introduced new practices that were contrary to the law, such as a gymnasium (4:12). On this text Goldstein sees a clear reference to specific Pentateuchal commands (Goldstein, *2 Maccabees*, 227).

[56]There is a likely parallel in 1 Macc 1:44-64, in which specific Mosaic laws (such as the burnt offerings, laws of cleanness, the Sabbath etc.) were commanded to cease. There the people were urged to forget the Torah and to violate all of its commandments (1 Macc 1:49).

command of the Torah given through Moses to our forefathers.... I, following my brothers' example, give up my body and soul for the sake of the laws of our forefathers" (7:30, 37). It is clear that the narrator holds the same view of the martyrs, noting that such a death leaves them undefiled (7:40). He writes in 7:40, "So he died in his integrity, putting his whole trust in the Lord."[57]

There are several notable points that issue from this account. First, the text does not suggest that the martyrs were Jewish leaders or organizers of a rebellion. The account simply states in 7:1, "At that time seven brothers, too, with their mother were arrested." These are depicted as pious Jews who understood the laws of the Mosaic legislation to be more important than their own lives. Obedience to God's laws meant death at the hand of Antiochus. Second, the laws of Moses are known by and practiced by the common pious Jew. Third, νόμος in this account is a reference to the commands of "the Torah given through Moses" (7:30). Fourth, there is a sense of both realized and deferred eschatology in this account.[58] Gathercole states that the opponents are judged in this life, and Harrington asserts that the martyrs die full of confidence that they will be vindicated by God for their law-keeping and as a result of such will live with him after death.[59]

Therefore νόμος in both 1 and 2 Maccabees is a reference to the written Mosaic legislation, and is highly revered and honored. It is the word and command of the God of Israel as given through the hand of his servant Moses, and obedience is preferred even to the point of death.[60] Specifically, one discovers in 2 Maccabees that such obedience and martyrdom is found in the life of priests and *nameless* Jews who suffer horrific deaths due to their allegiance to the law of Moses. Such is seen in the lives of both priests and people alike (women included) when the purity of the holy place becomes threatened (3:3-40). It seems likely that the martyrdom stories are meant to challenge the readers to have the same kind of devotion to the law. In 2 Maccabees there is a particular emphasis on obedience to the sacrificial and cultic laws, the food laws, circumcision, and the honor and purity of the holy

---

[57]Translation from the RSV.

[58]Gathercole, *Where Is Boasting?*, 54-56; 75. See also J. Tromp, "Taxo, the Messenger of the Lord," *JSJ* 21 (1990): 209.

[59]D. J. Harrington, *Invitation to the Apocrypha* (Grand Rapids: Eerdmans, 1999), 149. Harrington contends that for 2 Macc the full reward for obedience to the law is deferred until the afterlife.

[60]In his comments on the historicity of this account, Goldstein agrees that such torture of this magnitude certainly could have occurred under Antiochus (Goldstein, *2 Maccabees*, 292). For additional references that support these conclusions, see also 2 Macc 8:21, 36; 10:26; 11:31; 12:40; 13:10, 14; 15:9. In 15:9 the reference to the law is made more explicit in that it is juxtaposed to the prophets, leading one to the same conclusions suggested above by Goldstein and Segal.

place.[61] These emphases should be understood in light of the fact that these particular laws were under attack. There is allegiance to the law, and the deaths of Eleazar the scribe, the mother, and her seven sons are said to honor the law,[62] which is said to receive eschatological remuneration. Obedience is the basis for the recompense.[63] Overall, there is a clear emphasis on obeying and honoring the whole, and not merely obedience to certain laws.

Tobit

Though νόμος appears only five times in Tobit,[64] the authority of the Mosaic Pentateuch is seen throughout the work,[65] and νόμος is either referred to as "the law of Moses" (1:8; 6:13; 7:13, 14) or "the book of Moses" (7:11-13). In his comments Fitzmyer notes that the entire account "tells of the life and conduct of Tobit, his fidelity to the Mosaic law and the Jewish way of life."[66] In his comments on the theology of the prayers offered up by Tobias and Sarah, Moore notes the centrality of the law.[67] P. R. Davies states that in Tobit (as well as other didactic stories) the nation is guided by its "constitution," which for Israel is the "laws of the God who chose it."[68] Obedience to the laws of God revealed through Moses guarantees safety and their survival as a nation.

---

[61]Joseph Hellerman, "Purity and Nationalism in Second Temple Literature: 1-2 Maccabees and *Jubilees*," *JETS* 46 (2003): 401-22. Hellerman identifies four symbols that "reflect authorial preoccupation" in the writings of 1-2 Maccabees and *Jubilees*: the importance of male circumcision, the distinction between sacred and profane places, times, and foods. These distinctives serve to highlight a further and more fundamental distinction, viz., the distinction between sacred and profane *peoples*. Thus, for Hellerman, law-keeping serves to mark out Jews from Gentiles.

[62]See 2 Macc 6:23, where it is written that Eleazar will not violate the "holy God-given law" to eat swine's flesh. See also 7:2, 9, 11, 23, passim.

[63]Gathercole, *Where Is Boasting?*, 54. Note also Nickelsburg, who states that the martyrs of 2 Maccabees (particularly the seven brothers) face death due to their obedience to the Torah and are vindicated because of their obedience to the Torah (George W. E. Nickelsburg, *Resurrection, Immortality, Eternal Life* [Cambridge, MA: Harvard University Press, 1972], 96). See 2 Macc 7:2, 9, 11, 23, 30, 37.

[64]1:8; 6:13; 7:13, 14; 14:9. The exact text of the original Tobit is still being reconstructed by scholars. This is relevant for 14:9, given that not all MSS contain the particular phrase that refers to law-keeping. See Joseph A. Fitzmyer, *Tobit*, Commentaries on Early Jewish Literature (New York: Walter de Gruyter, 2003), and Carey A. Moore, *Tobit: A New Translation with Introduction and Commentary*, AB, vol. 40a (New York: Double Day, 1996) for current discussions regarding the actual text of Tobit. See also Harrington, *Invitation*, 10-13; DeSilva, *Introducing*, 63-74.

[65]Joseph Fitzmyer notes the underlying authority of the Pentateuch that particularly marked this era (Fitzmyer, *Tobit*, 51). See also DeSilva, *Introducing*, 76-77.

[66]Ibid., 91. Cf. 105.

[67]Moore, *Tobit*, 30.

[68]P. R. Davies, "Didactic Stories," 104.

Fidelity to the law of Moses is seen as early as 1:3 and is made explicit in 1:6 in which Tobit goes to Jerusalem "as was prescribed in a standing decree for all Israel." Fitzmyer suggests that the likely referent here is Exodus 23:14-17.[69] Tobit 1:8 is the first mention of νόμος where the referent is explicitly the "law of Moses" that sets forth a particular decree that Tobit intends to follow (Deut 14:28-29),[70] having learned the law of Moses from his grandmother Deborah.[71] In 1:16-17 Tobit describes his charitable acts to be in keeping with the law. Tobit 6:12-13 alludes to Deuteronomy 25:5-10 when the angel tells Tobiah to marry Sarah due to his hereditary right to her. Sarah was to inherit her father's estate since she had no brothers, and according to Numbers 36:5-12 should marry within her own tribe, which she does by marrying Tobiah.[72]

In Tobit 7:12-14[73] there is another appeal to the "law and the ordinance written in the Book of Moses."[74] In 7:1-17 Tobiah arrives at the home of Raguel in order to marry his daughter Sarah. Again, an appeal to the law of Moses is made to Tobiah—it commands him to marry Sarah. The authority of the written commands of the Mosaic law is explicit, and there is an expectation for Tobiah to obey. The words of the law are identified as the very ordinance of heaven by Raguel, who asserts in 7:11 that heaven itself has decreed that Tobiah take Sarah as his wife.

It is also noteworthy that when such appeals are made in Tobit, it appears to be to the *written* law of Moses.[75] In the story of Tobit, his piety results from his

---

[69]Fitzmyer, *Tobit*, 107.

[70]Johannes Gamberoni, "Das 'Gesetz des Mose' im Buch Tobias," in *Studien zum Pentateuch*, ed. G. Braulik (Vienna: Herder, 1977), 227-42. Gamberoni makes the interesting suggestion that in Tobit the "law of Moses" should be more broadly interpreted than as shorthand for the Pentateuch. He maintains that burying the dead and almsgiving are not emphasized in the Pentateuch, though such righteous acts are stressed in Tobit. However, one does see such examples of these righteous acts in the narrative portions of the Pentateuch, such as Abraham's burying of Sarah and the care for the bones of Joseph. Further, Gamberoni observes the presence of the law even when not explicitly mentioned, such as in 3:15, 17.

[71]Moore, *Tobit*, 31, 110.

[72]Fitzmyer, *Tobit*, 212.

[73]Or 7:11-13, depending on versification.

[74]Fitzmyer, *Tobit*, 223.

[75]The final appearance of νόμος is found in 14:9, in which Tobit, on his deathbed, charges his son and grandsons with his final instructions (Fitzmyer, *Tobit*, 323), in which he charges them to "keep the law and the commandments" (τήρησον τὸν νόμον καὶ τὰ προστάγματα). Moore and Fitzmyer do not comment on the phrase, perhaps due to the questions of its authenticity given that it is not found in all versions of Tobit. It would, however, be in keeping with the rest of the story and would fit nicely here in Tobit's final instructions, but the question of its authenticity is presently unanswered from the extant MSS.

obedience to the specific commands of the Mosaic law, such as burying the dead according to the dictates of the law, and the insistence that Tobit's son marry a fellow Israelite. P. R. Davies observes a focus on fasting, praying, and giving to the poor, yet suggests the possibility that the piety of the characters has perhaps been overplayed.[76]

The observations in Tobit parallel those of 1 and 2 Maccabees, viz., that there is a reverence for the written law of Moses and thus an assumption that those who are pious live in obedience to it be they a scribe, a priest, or a "common" Jew. As was the case of 1 and 2 Maccabees and Sirach, in Tobit νόμος is likely a general referent to the Mosaic law[77] itself as a whole, though *specific* Pentateuchal commands are referred to such as Deuteronomy 25 and Numbers 36 noted above.[78] For Tobit the law is applicable to everyday life, and it is in particular circumstances as those described in Tobit one sees the law lived out and applied to life. Even if P. R. Davies is correct, and the writer of Tobit stresses piety of the main character to the "point of absurdity,"[79] obedience to the written Mosaic law is still upheld as the ideal to which the readers should ascribe.

1 Baruch

Baruch consists of two parts that were brought together sometime in the first century BC.[80] It is one of several works attributed to Baruch, Jeremiah's secretary, and claims to address the Jewish people in the Babylonian captivity (1:1-14). Baruch calls the Jewish leaders together to hear the book's reading in 582 BC.[81] Νόμος occurs only four times[82] and in the first three occurrences, the written law of Moses is clearly in view.

The first two occurrences are located in the prayer that comprises 1:15-3:8,

---

[76]P. R. Davies, "Didactic Stories," 111-12. Davies stresses the importance of obedience to the Jewish law (112), which he asserts that in some ways has been equated with wisdom, though "torah" is not precisely equal to "Mosaic law" in Davies' understanding. However, he concludes that the Mosaic law is in fact an authoritative *expression* of divine wisdom to which the Jewish people are to be obedient (103).

[77]Contra Gamberoni, "Das 'Gesetz des Mose' im Buch Tobias," 227-42. Except for Tob 14:9, each usage of νόμος is modified by the genitive Μωσῆς or Μωυσῆς. One cannot be more specific than this from the evidence in Tobit. Νόμος either refers to the *commands* of the Pentateuch, or possibly the Pentateuch as a whole. However, it is not clear whether the author would have made such a distinction. What was commanded in the Pentateuch was to be obeyed in the life of the people of Israel.

[78]DeSilva, *Introducing*, 76-78.

[79]P. R. Davies, "Didactic Stories," 111.

[80]Evans, *Noncanonical Writings*, 13-14. "1 Baruch" is also known simply as "Baruch."

[81]G. W. E. Nickelsburg, "The Bible Rewritten and Expanded," in *Jewish Writings of the Second Temple Period*, ed. Michael E. Stone (Philadelphia: Fortress, 1984), 140.

[82]Νόμος is found in Bar 2:2, 28; 4:1, 12.

which consists of a "corporate confession of sins and a petition that God will withdraw his wrath and return the exiles to their homeland."[83] In 2:2 the author states, "Under the whole heaven there has not been done the like of what he has done in Jerusalem, in accordance with the threats that were written in the law of Moses" (κατὰ τὰ γεγραμμένα ἐν τῷ νόμῳ Μωυσῆ). Similarly in 2:28, "as you spoke by your servant Moses on the day when you commanded him to write your law [γράψαι τὸν νόμον σου] in the presence of the people of Israel." Here, νόμος specifically refers to the covenantal stipulations/commandments, and not the Pentateuch as a whole, or even less, "instruction" in a generic sense.

The third use of νόμος in Baruch is found in the wisdom poem of 3:9-4:4, and is arguably in the tradition of Sirach 24.[84] Commenting on 4:1, Gathercole rightly avers that the writer equates Torah with wisdom and that νόμος is explicitly the written commandments of the Mosaic law.[85] The writer speaks of wisdom and knowledge (3:9-37) and connects the two to the law of Moses in 4:1. It reads, "She [wisdom] is the book of the commandments of God, the law that endures forever. All who hold her fast will live, and those who forsake her will die." Sanders notes the meaning of 4:1 is simply that "Torah is paramount and that one should derive all wisdom from there," and not from the wisdom tradition itself; the Mosaic Torah/law is primary.[86] Gowan agrees but adds an important comment, "The law is by no means a burden, but is a gift of grace, the source of life for Israel."[87] This point is unambiguous in the author's mind, and 4:4 states, "Happy are we, O Israel, for we know what is pleasing to God."[88] To live in obedience to νόμος is to demonstrate wisdom and knowledge and is thus regarded as a blessing. Dunn argues that the idea of "live" in 4:1 (πάντες οἱ κρατοῦντες αὐτῆς εἰς ζωήν) should not be seen as eschatological, but rather that life lived in obedience to the law will be blessed and increased.[89] Far from being an unbearable burden, the writer regards the nation to be happy in light of the gift of the law. The law reveals what is pleasing to God; νόμος reveals the will of God for his people. In addition, the writer knows that such a gift has been given only to Israel (3:15-23; 27-28, 31, 36), and that having the law is an advantage over all other peoples (4:3).

---

[83]Nickelsburg, "The Bible Rewritten," 140.

[84]Ibid., 141. Also, both attribute life to those who keep the commands of Torah. See Gowan, "Wisdom," 223; Gathercole, *Where Is Boasting?*, 41.

[85]Gathercole, *Where Is Boasting?*, 41.

[86]J. Sanders, "Sacred Canopies," 125-26.

[87]Gowan, "Wisdom," 223.

[88]The text reads, "μακάριοί ἐσμεν Ισραηλ ὅτι τὰ ἀρεστὰ τῷ θεῷ ἡμῖν γνωστά ἐστιν." The author is happy/blessed (μακάριος) to know what pleases God, viz., obedience to the law's commandments. Cf. Deut 30:11-14.

[89]Gathercole agrees (*Where Is Boasting?*, 41). See also James D. G. Dunn, *The Theology of Paul the Apostle* (Grand Rapids: Eerdmans, 1998), 152-53.

The final use of νόμος is found in 4:5-5:9 in what Nickelsburg calls the "Zion poem."[90] In this poem the author admonishes the readers to take courage since God has not forgotten his people. The personified city of Jerusalem speaks to the exiles in 4:12-13, "Let no one rejoice over me, a widow and bereaved of many; I was left desolate because of the sins of my children, because they turned away from the law of God (ἐξέκλιναν ἐκ νόμου θεοῦ). They had no regard for his statutes; they did not walk in the ways of God's commandments." Obedience to the Mosaic law brings blessing and disobedience brings cursing. Gathercole asserts that the law is the "means to righteousness and life," and that "the theological discourse of Baruch...is thoroughly Deuteronomic."[91]

For Baruch, the promise of life is held out to those who follow the law,[92] and "those who hold fast to Torah will have their life increased, presumably with longevity and prosperity."[93] To obey the commandments of the law is to live in peace forever with "length of days and light for the eyes" (3:13-14). Death comes to those (even Israel) who "forsake the fountain of wisdom" (3:12), which is specifically defined as the commands of the Book of the law of Moses (4:1).

In conclusion, Baruch does not add significant information to what has already been discovered, yet is important since it reinforces important points. First, νόμος is understood as the written words from the hand of Moses, and second, that the written law is seen to be the essence of revealed wisdom from God to his people. Those who obey it find life, and those who do not are subject to the curses detailed within it. Reward and death are individualistic and nationalistic in Baruch as well, based upon obedience or disobedience to the revealed will of God in the law (1:15-22; 2:1-10; 4:1-5).[94] Thirdly, "Baruch" calls out to all of Israel, and summons his readers to live according to the law. Curses are brought upon them because of their disobedience, but blessings and life are for those who will walk in the wisdom and the knowledge of God revealed to Israel alone in the Mosaic law. Again, the law is venerated and has a divine origin and thus inherent authority. There is no specific focus in Baruch on any certain aspect or any certain set of commands, other than the promises

---

[90]Nickelsburg, "The Bible Rewritten," 140.

[91]Gathercole, *Where Is Boasting?*, 41. Cf. Deut 27-30. Recall Bar 2:2.

[92]Gowan, "Wisdom," 223. Cf. Lev 18:5; Deut 4:1; Ezek 20:11; Neh 9:29.

[93]Gathercole, *Where Is Boasting?*, 41.

[94]The prayer in Bar 1:15-22 details the curses that have befallen the *nation*, and prays that the Lord will have mercy on his people as a whole, but the final verse of the confession (1:22) denotes why judgment upon the nation came about, viz., *each one* pursued other gods and did evil (καὶ ᾠχόμεθα ἕκαστος ἐν διανοίᾳ καρδίας αὐτοῦ τῆς πονηρᾶς ἐργάζεσθαι θεοῖς ἑτέροις ποιῆσαι τὰ κακὰ κατ᾽ ὀφθαλμοὺς κυρίου θεοῦ ἡμῶν).

made to Israel regarding blessing and cursing. Rather, the law as a whole is
exalted and the people as a whole are summoned to return to full obedience to
the law. This is doubly true given that Israel is blessed among all nations for
having and knowing what pleases God (4:4).

Conclusion

If the threads of evidence from the apocryphal books are drawn together, one
may safely make a few points. First, when one encounters νόμος in the
apocryphal literature above, the referent is overwhelmingly to the Torah of
Moses, the Pentateuch, or the commandments written therein by Moses.
Second, in numerous cases the written Mosaic law is the explicit referent,
whether by referring to specific laws from the Pentateuch itself and/or the
phrase "written in the book/law of Moses." Third, the law is viewed as having
divine authority and origin. Fourth, the Jewish people as a whole (and not
merely the leaders) typically attempted to obey the law of Moses (even if at
times it meant death), and/or were summoned to do so by individual writers or
characters. Fifth, the law of Moses is from God and is at times associated with
and even equated with wisdom, and therefore should play a significant role in
the daily lives of pious Jews.[95] Finally, at times there is a focus on *specific*
laws, such as cultic, food, and purity laws (1 and 2 Maccabees) or laws
concerning marriage and inheritance (Tobit). Such foci stem from the narrative
events—which of the specific commands are applicable to the situation? One
could easily assert that from the zeal for law-obedience seen above, it would
not matter which specific command is in view, since there seems to be an
inclination simply to keep the law—the whole law and not just specific
commands. Specific commands are mentioned (food laws, purity etc.) because
of the specific context, and it is not as though there was a zeal for obedience for
one aspect of the law with disregard for other aspects. Finally, more often than
not, νόμος either points to the Mosaic legislation as a whole, or the Pentateuch
(yet even here the commands found in the Pentateuch are not far from view).
Yet it is clear that νόμος demands piety and morality from the people of Israel;
they are to live in accordance with its wisdom and ethic.

Old Testament Pseudepigrapha

The following section asks the same question of the Pseudepigrapha as was
asked of the Apocrypha. It aims to search the relevant Pseudepigraphical
literature in order to procure an understanding of how the law was perceived as
well as ascertain what is meant by νόμος or at minimum establish a range of

---

[95]It is not assumed here that *all* Jews without exception were considered pious (law-
keeping). However, one may also not assume that *no* Jews without exception were
considered pious.

meaning for the term. The works most relevant here are the apocalypses of *2 Baruch* and *4 Ezra, Jubilees,* and *4 Maccabees.*[96]

2 Baruch and 4 Ezra

INTRODUCTION

These two works are often treated together, given their similarities.[97] They can roughly be dated towards the latter part of the first century of the common era,[98] having been written in response to the fall of Jerusalem in 70 C.E. Both are apocalyptic, and claim to address the people of Israel after the conquest of Jerusalem in 586 B.C.E. It is quite plausible that the emphasis on the law in these two works is due to a desire to comfort the Jewish people in light of the horror of 70 C.E.,[99] and that law-keeping insures the reward of eternal life for those who have kept the law. Desjardins writes that their literary apocalyptic framework reflects upon this experience, and that "present suffering is due to peak soon in the end time and then terminate with the inauguration of the messianic kingdom, which will be followed by the judgment day and the

---

[96]To this section could be added brief notes from the *Psalms of Solomon* and *Testament of the Twelve Patriarchs.* See Appendix 3.

[97]See for example the studies of Michel Desjardins, "Law in *2 Baruch* and *4 Ezra,*" *SR* 14 (1985): 25-37; Michael Knowles, "Moses, the Law, and the Unity of *4 Ezra,*" *NovT* 31 (1989): 257-74; Shannon Burkes, "'Life' Redefined: Wisdom and Law in Fourth Ezra and Second Baruch," *CBQ* 63 (2001): 55-71; Geert Hallbäck, "The Fall of Zion and the Revelation of the Law: An Interpretation of *4 Ezra,*" *ScandJTh* 2 (1992): 263-92; Wolfgang Harnisch, *Verhängnis und Verheißung der Geschichte: Untersuchungen zum Zeit- und Geschichtsverständnis im 4. Buch Esra und un der syr. Baruchapokalypse* (Göttingen: Vandenhoeck & Ruprecht, 1969), 11-12; Michael E. Stone, "Apocalyptic Literature," in *Jewish Writings of the Second Temple Period,* ed. Michael E. Stone (Philadelphia: Fortress, 1984), 408-14; George W. E. Nickelsburg, *Jewish Literature Between the Bible and the Mishnah* (Philadelphia: Fortress, 1981), 280-94; A. F. J. Klijn, "2 Baruch," in *OTP,* ed. James H. Charlesworth (New York: Doubleday, 1983), 1:616-17; E. P. Sanders, *Paul and Palestinian Judaism,* 427; 417-18; Richard Bauckham, "Apocalypses," in *Justification and Variegated Nomism,* vol. 1, *The Complexities of Second Temple Judaism,* ed. D. A. Carson, Peter T. O'Brien, and Mark A. Seifrid (Grand Rapids: Baker, 2001), 175-82; Gathercole, *Where Is Boasting?,* 136-42; and Elliott, *Survivors of Israel,* 136-40; 270-72.

[98]Desjardins, "Law in *2 Baruch* and *4 Ezra,*" 25; Evans, *Noncanonical Writings,* 25-26. Evans suggests an early second century date for *2 Baruch.* See also Klijn, "2 Baruch," 617.

[99]Desjardins plausibly suggests that a focus on the law and keeping it served to sustain some communities after the destruction of the Temple ("Law in *2 Baruch* and *4 Ezra,*" 37). He suggests a date sometime soon after 70 C.E. It was a time of darkness (77:14), but regardless of the suffering and present circumstances, the law would abide, "sustaining those who look to it" (77:16).

introduction of the new age where salvation or damnation awaits everyone."[100]

Both documents have a distinct emphasis on the law, yet there are slight differences. *Second Baruch* is more optimistic about the present suffering and assures salvation for those who have kept the law, while *4 Ezra* is far more pessimistic regarding even the possibility of keeping the law. *Fourth Ezra* embraces a legalistic perfectionism,[101] but *2 Baruch* softens this notion to a certain degree. While emphasizing that God's mercy is available, the authors stress the need for human achievement in obedience to the Mosaic law, and salvation is dependent on obedience in both works.[102] Yet the righteous are not sinless, and God's mercy plays a much greater role in *2 Baruch* than in *4 Ezra*. However, as Bauckham avers, mercy is only for those who follow the law and who have a store of good works, while "those who reject the Law have cut themselves off from mercy."[103] He is critical of Sanders' contrast between *2 Baruch* and *4 Ezra*, and states that is more accurate to suggest that "God grants mercy on the righteous *because of their good works*,"[104] rather than simply to say, "God grants mercy on the righteous."[105] There is therefore a decisive role that the law plays in the theology (specifically the soteriology and eschatology) of each.

---

[100]Ibid.

[101]Even E. P. Sanders acknowledges this, yet states that *4 Ezra* is "not a particularly good representative of Judaism" (Sanders, *Paul and Palestinian Judaism*, 427). It is not a good example, Sanders concludes, since it is so clearly legalistic, and such a merit-based soteriology contradicts his covenantal nomism. This seems to be a bit circular in his argument for his detailed "pattern of religion," and fails to adequately explain the "clear legalism" here. Köberle agrees that *4 Ezra* is legalistic and states that in *4 Ezra* belief in grace and mercy are, in fact, flatly denied (Justus Köberle, Sünde und Gnade im religiösen Leben des Volkes Israel bis auf Christum [Munchen: C. Beck, 1905], 657).

[102]Bauckham, "Apocalypses," 182; see also D. A. Carson, "Summaries and Conclusions," in *Justification and Variegated Nomism*, vol. 1, *The Complexities of Second Temple Judaism*, ed. D. A. Carson, Peter T. O'Brien, and Mark A. Seifrid (Grand Rapids: Baker, 2001), 519.

[103]Bauckham, "Apocalypses," 181.

[104]Ibid., 182; emphasis his. Bauckham asserts that this does not equate to a simple merit theology, since God's grace is seen in his giving of the covenant and the commandments of the law to begin with. Yet again, salvation *is* "dependent on adherence to God and his Law" (182), and God grants mercy *"because of their good works"* (183). See also D. A. Carson, *Divine Sovereignty and Human Responsibility* (London: Marshall, Morgan, and Scott, 1981), 68-69. Commenting on these texts, and contrasting Sanders' covenantal nomism, Carson concludes that in these writings, "[Grace] is a kind response to merit."

[105]Sanders, *Paul and Palestinian Judaism*, 421.

2 BARUCH[106]

The point of *2 Baruch* is to exhort the people to keep the law since God has not abandoned his covenant with Israel, and that God's mercy awaits those who keep the law.[107] Commenting on 19:1-3, Elliott observes that *2 Baruch* expresses a "conditional and individual basis of judgment."[108] This particular text urges the people to keep the law so that they might receive the benefit of the covenant promises since God has not forsaken his covenant with them. Salvation is possible for Gentiles as well as Jews, but only for those who either remain faithful to the law (Jews), or for those who enter the covenant by subjecting themselves to the law and who live according to it (i.e., Gentiles).[109] This is the Israel that will be saved. It is therefore a more inclusive covenantalism than what is seen in *4 Ezra*, yet they are in harmony on the matter of the individual: to participate in salvation, he must faithfully keep the law.[110]

Since the references to the law in *2 Baruch* are numerous, it should suffice to mention several representative texts. In chapters 41-42 the writer considers both apostates and proselytes, and demonstrates "the notion of salvation as the reward for the good works of the righteous does not imply a nice calculation of

---

[106]Unless otherwise noted, translations from *2 Baruch* are those of A. F. J. Klijn, "2 Baruch," in *OTP*, ed. James H. Charlesworth (New York: Doubleday, 1983), 1:615-52.

[107]Bauckham, "Apocalypses," 176, 182.

[108]Elliott, *Survivors of Israel*, 271.

[109]Bauckham, "Apocalypses," 179. Chapters 41-42 of *2 Baruch* are significant, since "getting in" to the covenant is volitional on the part of the proselyte who willingly subjects himself to the yoke of the law. It is not by birth or national election (i.e., Sanders). At least for the proselyte, "getting in" and "staying in" are profoundly legalistic in that the proselyte must subject himself to the law and keep it if there is to be any soteriological or eschatological hope. To be sure, Sanders acknowledges *4 Ezra* as an "exception" (Sanders, *Paul and Palestinian Judaism*, 418, 422), but the same is true in *2 Baruch* (which Sanders does not mention). This reason, in part, has led many to question the covenantal nomism of Sanders and the "pattern of religion" that he avers is present in Second Temple Judaism. See for example the works of Gathercole (*Where Is Boasting?*), Elliott (*The Survivors of Israel*), and Carson, O'Brien, and Seifrid, (*Justification and Variegated Nomism*), each of which is cited throughout this chapter. Each raises significant questions as to Sanders' reading of the literature.

Gathercole criticizes Sanders' lack of discussion of *2 Baruch*, noting that had he discussed it, he would have had to explain why *4 Ezra* is *not* the only exception to his covenantal nomism, and that *2 Baruch* would require an "important modification of Sanders' thesis" (Gathercole, *Where Is Boasting?*, 139). Bauckham also criticizes Sanders for not including *2 Enoch* (another exception to Sanders' thesis), which he considers to be an exception to covenantal nomism at least on the level of *4 Ezra*, and likely *more so* (Bauckham, "Apocalypses," 156). As such, Sanders' covenantal nomism is open to question.

[110]Bauckham, "Apocalypses," 179.

merit and reward, but it does make salvation dependent on adherence to God and his Law."[111] Apostates are those who have "separated themselves from your statutes and who have cast away your law" (41:1, 3). In contrast, proselytes are those who take on "the yoke of the law." In the final judgment, the proselyte's former disobedience to the law will not be counted against him, while the apostate's former obedience to the law will not count for him.

In *2 Bar* 48:22, "your law is with us...we keep your statutes," and as a result those who follow it do not stumble.[112] In 48:27 God is the speaker who says, "my law demands its right." The expectation is that these demands must and will be followed fully—the judgment on Jerusalem indicates what will come of those who do not.[113] In 48:24 the law is likened to wisdom (cp. Sir 24) and states, "law is among us and will help us...that excellent wisdom...will support us."

In *2 Bar* 46:1-5, the people learn that Baruch will go away soon, and they respond with fear that when he is gone there will be no one to guide them and teach them the law of God and its wisdom. They understand that the only way to life and not death is through the law. Baruch responds by telling them that the law will abide forever, and that after he is gone there will be other shepherds who will guide them in its truth. "Israel will not be in want of a wise man.... But only prepare your heart so that you obey the law, and be subject to those who are wise and understanding with fear" (46:4-5). Burkes comments, "the way to life exists apart from these circumstances" of the destruction of Jerusalem.[114] The way to life (the law) is unaffected by such situations, for Baruch describes the Torah as "the eternal law which exists forever" (59:2; 85:3).

This brings to mind an important point regarding the law in *2 Baruch*, namely its function in soteriology and eschatology.[115] Stated simply, one must follow the law if one is to be declared righteous and rewarded with eternal life. For *2 Baruch*, law-keeping is necessary if one is to obtain mercy, since "God has mercy on the righteous *because of their good works*."[116] Desjardins summarizes this recurring theme when he writes, "One's attitude to the Law is *the determining factor* in guaranteeing salvation or punishment in the coming age."[117] Likewise, blessings are promised to those who keep the law, while destruction is assured for those who do not (84:1-6). *Second Baruch* 84:2 cites

---

[111]Ibid., 182.

[112]Burkes, "'Life' Redefined," 64.

[113]The author, in his reflection on 586 B.C.E., states that Israel was not punished as fully as she perhaps should have been (see *2 Bar* 77).

[114]Burkes, "'Life' Redefined," 66.

[115]Desjardins, "Law in *2 Baruch* and *4 Ezra*," 27.

[116]Bauckham, "Apocalypses," 182, emphasis his. See *2 Bar* 14:11; 24:1; 44:14.

[117]Ibid., 28, emphasis added. See also *2 Bar* 32:1, 42, 44; 54:13-14; 57:1-2; 84:2-11.

Deuteronomy 33:19-20 in which Moses assures blessings for obedience to the law and judgment for disregarding it.[118] Klijn states, "Those who live according to the Law will be gathered together (78:7), will take part in the resurrection of the dead, and will enjoy life on a new earth (30:1-2)."[119] He adds, "Only the Law, which is known to Israel alone, *is efficacious.*"[120] The author also states succinctly in 38:2, "Your law is life" (cf. 45:2; 46:3), and in chapter 57 this is defined as the promise of life that the law provides to those who keep it and who are faithful and thus righteous.[121]

Further, in *2 Baruch* there is a fundamental distinction common to the apocalyptic literature: there are the righteous, and there are the sinners/wicked. The primary distinction between the two is whether there is acceptance or rejection of God's law.[122] Gathercole agrees and observes the two groups that are consistently contrasted in *2 Baruch*: those who have sinned, and those who have proved themselves to be righteous (see 21:9, 11; 24:1).[123] This comes to a head in chapter 51, where those who have proven themselves to be righteous on account of the law are promised significant advantages (51:3). Citing 51:7 Gathercole states, "Miracles, however, will appear at their own time to *those who are saved because of their works,* and for whom the Law is now a hope and intelligence, expectation and wisdom and trust."[124] The law is a "hope" that casts an eye towards eschatological judgment.

Finally, what is arguably in view by νόμος here is the written law of Moses. Burkes argues that νόμος is equal to the Torah of Moses and specifically the

---

[118]This is a helpful text, in that "law" and "commandments" are used almost interchangeably, both of which are attributed to Moses.

[119]Klijn, "*2 Baruch*," 618.

[120]Ibid., 619, emphasis added.

[121]See Desjardins, "Law in *2 Baruch* and *4 Ezra*," 29-30. Desjardins makes a valid point that the law is not only relevant for the life to come, but also for the present life. This is seen in the example(s) of the fate of Jerusalem. See *2 Bar* 54:15-19 where man is able to determine his course regardless of Adam's sin. Obedience to the law results in benefits on earth, but especially for the imminent messianic kingdom (28). See also 29:2; 32:1. Klijn makes the same observation, "Darkness is the result of Adam's sin (18:2). Everyone is free to choose between light and darkness (54:15, 19; 85:7). He who chooses to live according to the law [in this life] will receive eternal life (32:1; 38:1; 48:22; 51:3, 4-7; 54:15), the good things (44:7), and grace and truth (44:14)" (Klijn, "*2 Baruch*," 618-19).

[122]Bauckham, "Apocalypses," 180. See *2 Bar* 54:14, 17; 48:40; 51:4; 42:4; 44:3; 54:5; 66:1; 75:7; 14:5; 54:4; 38:4; 14:11; 24:1; 57:2.

[123]Gathercole, *Where Is Boasting?*, 140.

[124]Ibid., emphasis his. Gathercole adds the following note, "Unsurprisingly, Sanders does not mention this text" (140 n. 15). See also *2 Bar* 41:6 which states that those who have abandoned the law will face eschatological judgment in "that last time," and will "be judged as the scale indicates."

commands.[125] Desjardins agrees. He states that in *2 Baruch*, "Moses is the Lawgiver and is the key figure, aside from the seer himself. It is the written Law of Moses that is key."[126] Gathercole concludes similarly—for *2 Baruch*, νόμος is the Torah of Moses that is to be obeyed if one is to be righteous and thus saved at the eschaton.[127] Elliott confirms that the written Torah of Moses is in view, but offers the suggestion that what is to be obeyed is not *only* the written Torah of Moses, but also some interpretation of the law.[128] Bauckham is more restrictive than Elliott in his view of νόμος, and concludes that in *2 Baruch* νόμος specifically refers to the commandments of God given to Moses at Sinai.[129] The present writer concludes that for *2 Baruch* νόμος is the written Mosaic law and must be obeyed if one is to avoid judgment both in this life, and the life to come. The law, as a whole, simply *must* be obeyed.

4 EZRA

As noted above, *4 Ezra* is quite similar to *2 Baruch* in many ways, and there is a good bit of overlap between the two works regarding their theology of the law.[130] Given 14:21-22, in which Ezra laments that the law had been burned in the fall of Jerusalem, and asks to *write another copy of it*, it seems to be a correct summation that in *4 Ezra* (like *2 Baruch*), "law" refers to the written Torah of Moses, and specifically its commands.[131] Further, 7:72 states that the people had received "the commandments...the law," which they did not keep. This should be read in light of 9:26-37, which extols the abiding glory of the Mosaic law, "which does not perish but remains in its glory" (9:37).[132]

Metzger avers that the theological outlook regarding humanity and free will is basically pessimistic in *4 Ezra*, and that "sin is conceived as consisting essentially in unfaithfulness to the Law (9:36), resulting in alienation and estrangement from God."[133] This alienation marks the majority of all of

---

[125]Burkes, "'Life' Redefined," 60. In addition he sees *2 Bar* 85:3-5 as a summary of the book's theme: the exiled people assert that all they have is God and the law. If they obey his commands, they will receive back what was lost.

[126]Desjardins, "Law in *2 Baruch* and *4 Ezra*," 28.

[127]Gathercole, *Where Is Boasting?*, 140.

[128]Elliott, *Survivors of Israel*, 139. Cf. Eckhard J. Schnabel, *Law and Wisdom from Ben Sira to Paul: A Tradition Historical Enquiry Into the Relation of Law, Wisdom, and Ethics* (Tübingen: J. C. B. Mohr, 1985), 157-58.

[129]Bauckham, "Apocalypses," 178-81.

[130]The translation used here is that of Bruce Metzger, "The Fourth Book of Ezra," in *OTP*, ed. James Charlesworth (New York: Doubleday, 1983), 1:517-59.

[131]Burkes, "'Life' Redefined," 60.

[132]This idea of the eternality of the law is also present in *2 Baruch*.

[133]Metzger, "The Fourth Book of Ezra," 521. This pessimism is noted by most scholars. See for example the discussion of Hallbäck who argues that "Ezra" is pessimistic

humanity. In keeping with the general pessimism towards humanity, Ezra is told in 8:3, "Many have been created, but few will be saved."[134] For *4 Ezra* this salvation comes by obedience to the law. Whereas there is some mention of grace in *2 Baruch*, in *4 Ezra* human achievement takes center stage while God's grace is marginalized. There is here an emphasis on "meriting salvation by works of obedience to the Law."[135]

One of the features that marks the seer is his pessimism. Hallbäck states that according to *4 Ezra*, "The salvation or damnation in the afterlife is decided in this life, and the criterion is the obedience to God's Law."[136] Such obedience brings eschatological reward for those who perfectly keep the law.[137] The issue of the law and life is no longer national, but individual, and even though the law is directed towards all the people, its commandments must be individually kept.[138] This is to be understood in light of the fact that the seer believes that every individual is descended from Adam and therefore has inherited Adam's evil heart (3:21-22). After Adam, God gave the law to Moses, but it was unable to root out the sin in the evil heart of man (3:22-26).[139] The angel Uriel agrees with Ezra that keeping the law is very difficult, and in fact only a few do keep it "such that they can be considered righteous."[140] Yet even though keeping the law is so difficult, those who do not keep it will not be given mercy in the end and have only themselves to blame. Sanders notes concerning *4 Ezra*, "[I]t is better for transgressors to perish than for *the glory of the law* to be besmirched by having mercy on them."[141] Rather than finding comfort, Ezra's pessimism is confirmed while his appeals for mercy upon those who transgress the law are denied.[142]

What is clear is the relationship between life and the law: if one neglects the law in this life, then one forfeits his or her own life as a result. This is the free

---

regarding the law vs. the evil condition of the human heart (Hallbäck, "The Fall of Zion," 285).

[134]This is in contrast to the less pessimistic view of *2 Baruch* discussed above.

[135]Bauckham, "Apocalypses," 174.

[136]Hallbäck, "The Fall of Zion," 279.

[137]Bauckham, "Apocalypses," 173-74.

[138]Hallbäck, "The Fall of Zion," 285. See also the older work by Robert A. Bartels, "Law and Sin in Fourth Esdras and St. Paul," *Lutheran Quarterly* 1 (1949): 319-29, who compares *4 Ezra* to Paul. He comments on *4 Ezra*, that though "...none have lived up to God's demands in the Law, he reveals no hatred for it. On the contrary, he upholds the Law with the same devotional reverence that appears in the rest of the apocalyptic writings" (323). Bartels cites 7:20, "Let many perish who are now living, rather than the law of God which is set before them be disregarded!"

[139]Desjardins, "Law in *2 Baruch* and *4 Ezra*," 34.

[140]Bauckham, "Apocalypses," 165.

[141]Sanders, *Paul and Palestinian Judaism*, 416; emphasis added.

[142]Ibid.

choice of the individual, and each is responsible for his own actions regarding the law.[143] Elliott concurs, pointing to numerous statements in *4 Ezra* chapter 7 that affirm this statement. He summarizes, "life and death are contingent on faithful fulfillment of certain requirements placed on each individual."[144] This loss of life (due to disobedience) begins in the present life since rejection of the law leads not just to death, but also to a "dying in this life." Few will actually be seen to have lived righteously, viz., in strict obedience to the law, given the strength of sin in the heart of man. Even though the individual had both understanding and the law, most individuals simply *cannot* follow it in such a manner so as to be righteous (7:72).[145] Consequently, in 7:19-25 the angel says to a distraught Ezra that all who disregard the law will perish; those who have not followed the law have "no store of good works" (8:36). Thus, if man does not obey the law in this life, there is no hope for salvation in the age to come. Stated simply, in *4 Ezra* "the role of the righteous is to keep God's law."[146]

However, in spite of the sin in the heart of man, those who do keep the ways of the Most High will see "the glory of him who receives them" (7:91). Those that obey are granted this eschatological reward since they have "laboriously served the Most High, and withstood danger every hour that they might keep the law of the lawgiver perfectly" (7:88-89). This point is reinforced in 7:96 when the angel explains that those who managed to overcome their internal evil are given immortality,[147] and Desjardins concludes that it is in this aspect that following the law is oriented to the future in *4 Ezra*.[148] Those who choose to obey the law are granted eternal life.[149] However, Ezra comes to find out that

---

[143]Burkes, "'Life' Redefined," 58. See also E. P. Sanders, *Paul and Palestinian Judaism*, 414.

[144]Elliott, *Survivors of Israel*, 270. See *4 Ezra* 7:21-24, 45-48, 105, 127-31.

[145]Burkes, "'Life' Redefined," 59.

[146]Bauckham, "Apocalypses," 165.

[147]E. P. Sanders, *Paul and Palestinian Judaism*, 414. Sanders suggests that the pessimistic view of the angel is actually that of the original author (Sanders, *Paul and Palestinian Judaism*, 416).

[148]Desjardins, "Law in *2 Baruch* and *4 Ezra*," 34. He adds, "The author pleads with his audience to obey the Law in order to be granted salvation in the world to come." This is man's part of the covenantal agreement (31). "The confident, declarative tone of *2 Baruch* is replaced by a succession of 'whys' which seriously call into question the justice of God and the efficacy of the Law" due to the intense suffering of the people. In the end Desjardins observes that for the seer, God's justice is unquestioned (31).

[149]Bauckham, "Apocalypses," 167. Thus, there is a correlation between law, wisdom, and (eternal) life (Burkes, "'Life' Redefined," 60). See also Bruce W. Longenecker, *2 Esdras* (Sheffield: Sheffield Academic Press, 1995), 30. Longenecker observes throughout *4 Ezra* a "policy of legalistic perfectionism in which salvation is bestowed upon those who are obedient to the law without fault" (30). He too observes Sanders'

this remnant will in fact be a multitude, thus fulfilling the promises made to Abraham (Gen 17:4). Though there will be a righteous remnant, keeping the law so as to be considered righteous demands "very considerable determination and effort."[150] Sanders calls this "legalism gone mad" and claims that such is what happens when covenantal nomism collapses.[151]

Thus, the view of the seer is that of salvation by works of obedience to the law (for "Ezra" as well as "Baruch"), coupled with a pessimistic view that only a very few will be saved (7:60-61). Works of obedience to the law are stored up with God (7:77; 8:32-33, 36), for which they will be rewarded (8:33; 7:35, 83, 98; 8:39). The language of "works" is common, yet so also is the language of "faith." But according to Bauckham, "faith" in *4 Ezra* is faithfulness in keeping the law.[152] He notes that human achievement takes center stage while God's grace is marginalized, and that there is an emphasis on "meriting salvation by works of obedience to the Law."[153] In Ezra's final address, he tells the people that they are being punished by God for not keeping the law, and that they are to renew their efforts in the difficult task of keeping the law (14:29-34) in order that they may find God's mercy after death.

In conclusion, the Mosaic law is revered and considered to be the standard one must meet for salvation. This aspect of the merit of law-keeping is a significant feature in *4 Ezra*. The law is heralded and exalted as the way to salvation, and there appears to be no specific focus on any particular type of law or commandment.[154] Like *2 Baruch*, if one is righteous then he keeps the whole law, though in *4 Ezra* this marginalizes any notion of grace. In *4 Ezra* (as well as *2 Baruch*) νόμος is a reference to the written law of Moses. The law is viewed with unwavering respect given its divine origin, even to the point of despair. The trouble is not with the law and its demands, but rather with the sinfulness and inability of man—yet he is still commanded to keep it. The commandments of the entire Mosaic law must be strictly obeyed if one is to receive soteriological and eschatological reward.

---

discussion and apparent discomfort with the merit based soteriology of *4 Ezra* (30-32). Cf. Gathercole, *Where Is Boasting?*, 136-37.

[150] Bauckham, "Apocalypses," 167. See also *4 Ezra* 7:94; 6:32; 7:89. Bauckham adds, "Undoubtedly the result is a strong emphasis on the need to merit eschatological reward by difficult obedience to the Law" (173).

[151] Sanders, *Paul and Palestinian Judaism*, 409.

[152] Bauckham, "Apocalypses," 171. However, what is absent is a weighing of good versus evil deeds in order to see if one is considered righteous or not. What is present is two ends of the spectrum: the righteous who perfectly keep the law, and the apostates who despise God and his commandments (172).

[153] Ibid., 174.

[154] Additionally, Seifrid observes a nationalistic aspect regarding the law and *4 Ezra*. For *4 Ezra*, "Israel's identity is bound up with its keeping the Law" (Seifrid, *Justification by Faith*, 134).

Jubilees

The book of *Jubilees* purports to have been received by Moses at Mt. Sinai (1:1-4), and is written as if the speaker is God himself.[155] It is a retelling of Genesis and the first half of Exodus that largely follows the biblical storyline.[156] Its purpose is "to call the Jewish reader to a more faithful obedience to the law."[157] Regarding the law, Hafemann notes, "In *Jubilees*, it is the law itself which is being commented upon and enlarged."[158] Hafemann concludes that, "the law" is a reference for the Pentateuch as a whole in *Jubilees*.[159]

There is a distinct emphasis on the law in *Jubilees*, as well as an insistence that the patriarchs from the time of Noah practiced those parts of the Torah that had been revealed to them before being codified at Sinai.[160] Wintermute writes that the author is greatly concerned that his readers strictly obey the law of Moses, and that there are great blessings to be had from a renewed fidelity to the law.[161]

This emphasis on the law can be seen in the author's view of the law's authority and perpetuity. Regarding its authority, the author proves the law's authority by giving various examples of the punishment incurred by those who did not keep it. For example, in 7:20-39, Noah commands his sons to bless God the creator, honor their father and mother, love their neighbor, and preserve themselves from "fornication and pollution and from all injustice." The references to the law are clear. He goes on to state that due to a violation of

---

[155]The translations cited here, unless noted, are from O. S. Wintermute, "Jubilees," in *OTP*, ed. James Charlesworth (New York: Doubleday, 1983), 2:35-142.

[156]James C. Vander Kam, *The Book of Jubilees* (Sheffield : Sheffield Academic, 2001), 11; see also John C. Endres, *Biblical Interpretation in the Book of Jubilees*, CBQMS 18 (Washington: Catholic Biblical Association, 1987), 226.

[157]Evans, *Noncanonical Writings*, 31.

[158]Hafemann, "Moses in the Apocrypha and Pseudepigrapha," 90. Cf. Sanders, *Paul and Palestinian Judaism*, 362-82.

[159]Hafemann, "Moses in the Apocrypha and Pseudepigrapha," 90; see Jub 6:22. This is the view of Wintermute ("Jubilees," 2:38), as well as George J. Brooke ("Torah in the Qumran Scrolls," in *Bibel in jüdischer und christlicher Tradition: Festschrift für Johann Maier zum 60. Geburtstag*, ed. Helmut Merklein, Karlheinz Müller and Günter Stemberger, TBBB 88 [Frankfurt: Anton Hain, 1993], 97). Though not solely concerned with *Jubilees*, Brooke has a section on *Jubilees* and the Torah, and is focused on Torah "in the strict sense" of the Pentateuch itself.

[160]See VanderKam, *Jubilees*, 11-13. For a summary of the author's theology, see VanderKam, *Jubilees*, 120-34. See also his essay, "The Origins and Purposes of the Book of Jubilees," in *Studies in the Book of Jubilees*, ed. Matthias Albani, Jörg Frey, and Armin Lange (Tübingen: Mohr Siebeck, 1997), 3-24. Interestingly, Endres concludes that E. P. Sanders is correct in his assertion that the author of *Jubilees* was a "covenantal nomist" (Endres, *Biblical Interpretation*, 228; see also 226-27).

[161]Wintermute, "Jubilees," 2:38.

these commandments (particularly fornication, pollution, and injustice) God judged the earth with the flood (7:21).

Regarding its perpetuity, the commands of the law were present in the days of Noah (though not in completed form). Noah himself kept that which was "ordained and written in the heavenly tablets" (6:17) and was blessed for it. Such practices as the feast of Shevuot (first fruits) were to be practiced forever (6:20-21).[162] *Jubilees* 1:26-27 assumes the ongoing validity of the law, given that the writer identifies the Mosaic law as something given by the hand of God to his people through the direct mediation of angels to be a testimony forever (cf. Heb 2:1-4; Gal 3:19).

Righteousness itself, according to the author of *Jubilees*, is defined by keeping the law's commandments (7:34; 20:2-13), and is seen in the writer's emphasis on the examples of the righteous: Noah, Abraham, Jacob, Joseph, and Moses. For those who obey the law there is blessing (17:17-18; 18:14-19; 20:9-10; 40:8-11), and for those who disregard it there is judgment and death (7:20-25; 16:5-9; 20:6-8; 30:9; 39:6). Wickedness before the Lord is described as abandoning the laws and ordinances in 23:16-21. Finally, in 23:26, repentance from such wickedness is defined as a return to the law's commands, which is called the "way of righteousness."

As Gathercole asserts, "Again, as in the Maccabean texts, there is a reward of greatness and righteousness for deeds. In *Jubilees*, righteousness is not merely a category of status but is contingent upon behavior and describes a person's obedience."[163] By his citations of such passages as *Jubilees* 30:17-23 one understands that Gathercole specifically has in mind obedience to the commands of the Torah.[164] He comments on 30:21-22, "The hope is that Israelites will obey the commandments and in the end be recorded as 'friends of God.' *This points to an understanding of the relationship with God that is promised in the future and that depends upon (of course, covenantal) obedience*

---

[162]Davies notes the timelessness of the law in *Jubilees* (W. D. Davies, *Torah in the Messianic Age*, 7 n. 5). Other commands were present for the author before the fall of man, such as the laws of purification after childbirth (3:8). There is also an element of the law's *eternality* in a certain sense, given that the law is written on "heavenly tablets." VanderKam, "Origins and Purpose," 18. For example, see *Jub* 3:31; 6:17; 30:10; 33:10-15.

[163]Gathercole, *Where Is Boasting?*, 60. Cf. Hellerman, who argues that the writer of *Jubilees* was "preoccupied" with several symbols of the socio-political identity of the Jews. There are four: (1) the importance of male circumcision, (2) the distinction between sacred and profane places, (3) the distinction between sacred and profane times, and (4) the distinction between sacred and profane foods (Hellerman, "Purity and Nationalism in Second Temple Literature," 401, 412-21).

[164]Gathercole, *Where Is Boasting?*, 60-61.

to the Law."[165] To be a friend of God, one must be part of the covenant people who, for the writer of *Jubilees*, are strictly Jewish. Thus, salvation is *only* for the Jews, and cannot be offered to Gentiles.[166]

In conclusion, first, the author of *Jubilees* maintains a high view of the law, and if VanderKam and Hafemann are correct, the written Torah of Moses (the Pentateuch) is the specific reference in mind when speaking of the law.[167] On occasion νόμος clearly refers to *specific* commandments revealed to Moses at Sinai, and not the Pentateuch as a whole. This is demonstrated by the listing of various and specific laws[168] as well as from the author's treatment of the sin of Reuben in *Jubilees* 33. *After* the law was given, there was knowledge of the sin of incest, and the writer dubs incest an "eternal sin" for which there is no atonement. Indeed, for *Jubilees* a person loses his place in the covenant when a

---

[165]Ibid., 62; emphasis his. He adds that such is not a covenantal nomistic view of "staying in" the covenant, as Sanders would argue. Rather, according to Gathercole it "is a verdict given subsequent to obedience" to the commandments of the law (ibid.).

[166]If this reading of *Jubilees* is correct, then Sanders' reading of *Jubilees* may not be too far off the mark. Enns agrees with Sanders that for the writer of *Jubilees*, salvation is based on election, and thus cannot be offered to Gentiles (Peter Enns, "Expansions of Scripture," in *Justification and Variegated Nomism*, vol. 1, *The Complexities of Second Temple Judaism*, ed. D. A. Carson, Peter T. O'Brien, and Mark A. Seifrid [Grand Rapids: Baker, 2001], 94-96).

The role of the law in *Jubilees* is essential, and there is significant disagreement between Enns and Sanders on this point. Sanders states that loyalty to the covenant (i.e., obedience to the law) is actually one aspect forming the basis of salvation (Sanders, *Paul and Palestinian Judaism*, 367). Sanders writes, "Obedience is the *condition* of salvation...but not its cause.... Obedience *preserves* salvation" (371). Enns is quick to note that this seems to contradict what Sanders has said elsewhere, but stops short of actually accusing Sanders of self-contradiction. He writes, "It seems that the whole thrust of Sanders' argument is that the 'basis of salvation' is *only* 'membership in the covenant' (i.e., election) and not 'loyalty to it,' which is obedience" (Enns, "Expansions of Scripture," 95). Enns concludes, "It might be less confusing to say that *election* is by grace and *salvation* is by obedience" (98). Staying in the covenant is by individual work although "getting in" is by birth. Thus Enns is critical of Sanders, in that for Sanders, getting in the covenant is by God's grace, while covenantal status can be forfeited if one is not obedient to the law. Salvation is therefore accomplished by "staying in" since "getting in" is by birth. Therefore for *Jubilees* the focus is on individual obedience to the law (98).

[167]Hafemann, "Moses in the Apocrypha and Pseudepigrapha," 90; VanderKam, *Jubilees*, 11-13; idem, "The Origins and Purposes of the Book of Jubilees," 3-24.

[168]See Sanders, *Paul and Palestinian Judaism*, 364-65. *Jubilees* lists several specific commands that the pious Jew was responsible for keeping. These include keeping the Sabbath (2:18), covering nakedness (3:31), ritual cleaning after childbirth (3:8-11), abstaining from meat with blood (6:10), keeping the Feast of Weeks (6:17), keeping the Feast of Tabernacles (16:29), and not committing incest (33:10).

"sin unto death" is committed. Yet in the case of Reuben, mercy is extended in spite of his incest. Since Reuben sinned before the giving of the law, it is possible for him to receive mercy (33:16). Yet for the readers of *Jubilees*, no such mercy exists since they have the law. They cannot sin in ignorance.[169]

Second, the writer of *Jubilees* views the Torah as immutable.[170] Third, the author clearly maintains the common righteousness/unrighteousness distinction, based upon whether one obeys the commandments or not. Fourth, *Jubilees* is unique, given that there is an explicit emphasis on the existence of (and obedience/disobedience to) specific commands prior to Sinai. Finally, in keeping with the last point, *Jubilees* sees in the (pre-Sinai) patriarchs visible examples of those who kept the law and were considered righteous, and are therefore to be emulated. There were laws already revealed to the patriarchs that were later codified by Moses, but this in no way downplays the significance of the Mosaic legislation since it was the first time that laws and stipulations had been codified for the nation as a whole. The author makes the claim that "The entire law was carefully practiced by the patriarchs,"[171] and thus for *Jubilees*, all Jewish readers are responsible to keep the commandments.

4 Maccabees

Fourth Maccabees was written in Greek during the first century AD, likely prior to the destruction of Jerusalem,[172] and has nothing to do with the Maccabean period.[173] Instead, the work is a philosophical one that seeks to demonstrate that Judaism is the true religion. The discussion centers on the matter of whether religious reason, attained by obedience to the Torah of Moses, is sovereign over one's emotions.[174] Fourth Maccabees relies on the

---

[169]Enns, "Expansions of Scripture," 96.

[170]Nickelsburg, *Jewish Literature*, 75.

[171]Elliott, *Survivors of Israel*, 255. See *Jub* 21:4-20. For those who do not obey the covenant stipulations, they have no part in covenant life (265). Elliott states that the writer of *Jubilees* is primarily individualistic regarding the covenant. Individuals must obey the laws of the covenant if they are to remain in the covenant (264-65). This is quite similar to Enns' and Sanders' conclusions from *Jubilees*.

[172]Hugh Anderson, "4 Maccabees," in *OTP*, ed. James Charlesworth (New York: Doubleday, 1983), 2:531-64. The translations cited here are those of Anderson.

[173]Evans, *Noncanonical Writings*, 36-37. It derived its name from its reference in 4 Macc 6:18-7:20 to the account of the seven sons and their mother who were martyred during the Maccabean period.

[174]This is clear from the outset of 4 Macc, and is often repeated. See 1:7, 9, 13, 19, 30; 2:6, 24; 7:16; 13:1; 16:1; 18:2. P. R. Davies agrees with this assessment. He observes that the author of 4 Maccabees defines wisdom to be that knowledge acquired from the law of Judaism. Should one live in obedience to the Mosaic law, then they will be just, wise, and temperate (P. R. Davies, "Didactic Stories," 125). He adds the point that for 4

martyrdom accounts found in 2 Maccabees 6-7 (see above) to prove the
aforementioned thesis. For the author, these martyrs from the Maccabean
period ruled their emotions by means of fidelity to the law of Moses, and
illustrate his thesis. Rumination on these accounts comprises the majority of the
book (see 5:1-17:6).

Νόμος is used forty times in 4 Maccabees, with a clear and identifiable
referent in six of those occurrences, according to Redditt.[175] First, in 1:34 the
referent is to the dietary regulations of Leviticus 11:1-31. Second, νόμος is
used twice in 2:5-6 which cites commandment of Exodus 20:17 and receives
commentary.[176] Third, in 2:9 there is a reference to Leviticus 19:9-10 (cf.
23:22; Deut 24:19-21). Fourth, there is a parallel between obedience to the law
and Moses in 9:1-2. Finally, νόμος is used in the technical sense of "law and
the prophets" in 18:10.[177] There are approximately thirty-four other referents,
and Redditt asserts that these other occurrences refer to the first five books of
the Hebrew Bible; in 4 Maccabees, νόμος points to actual commandments of
the written Mosaic law. Such references function "to inspire not simply pious
behavior, but rational living."[178] Anderson avers that "The chief aim of the
writer of 4 Maccabees is to advocate fidelity to the Law and to demonstrate that
the hope of fulfilling the Greek ideal of virtue resides only in obedience to the
Law of Judaism."[179] Martyrdom due to fidelity to the law of God is beneficial,

---

Maccabees, obedience to the law is the essence of personal virtue. Akin to Aristeas,
there is an impulse to equate the Jewish law with the reason in Greek philosophy (126).

[175]Paul L. Redditt, "The Concept of Nomos in 4 Maccabees," *CBQ* 45 (1983): 250-51.

[176]In Redditt's list, 2:5-6 apparently account for two of the six total references. Again,
for the author, obedience to the law is purely reasonable and right. In addition, though
Redditt does not comment on it, 2:8 seems to be another clear referent to the specific
commandments of the Pentateuch. It says, "As soon as a man conducts himself
according to the law (τῷ νόμῳ πολιτευόμενος), then even if he be avaricious, he
reverses his own natural tendency and lends to the needy without interest, canceling the
debt with the coming of the seven-year period." The author here apparently refers to
Deut 15:7-11; 23:19-20; Lev 25:35-55.

[177]Redditt rightly notes the questions surrounding the authenticity of 18:6-19, but
includes it since the authenticity question is not proven, and due to his desire to be
comprehensive (Redditt, "The Concept of Nomos in 4 Maccabees," 251).

[178]Ibid., 249-50.

[179]Anderson, "4 Maccabees," 532. Gilbert agrees almost verbatim (M. Gilbert, "Wisdom
Literature," in *Jewish Writings of the Second Temple Period*, ed. Michael E. Stone
[Philadelphia: Fortress, 1984], 318). In addition, Redditt argues that though the writer
utilizes Greek philosophical terms in his discussion, his Judaism overwhelms and
subsumes the Greek thought. All is subject to the divine law, the Pentateuch (Redditt,
"Concept of Nomos," 249-70). See also Nickelsburg, *Jewish Literature*, 226; P. R.
Davies, "Didactic Stories," 126.

since it procures eternal life (15:2; 17:18) and immortality.[180] According to Nickelsburg and Stone, such martyrdom accounts of 4 Maccabees illustrate *the commonly held attitude* of Hellenistic Judaism toward the law. "All virtues come from the observance of the law.... The observance of the Torah is thus the true philosophical life."[181] For the writer, true piety, and all of the desired virtues of the Greek world, can be attained by adherence to the law of Moses.[182]

Gathercole argues that in 4 Maccabees, as in 1 and 2 Maccabees, there is a vested interest to demonstrate the maintenance of Israel's law within the community.[183] There is a strong and unified testimony here that assumes and presupposes that the people did indeed keep the law.[184] Further, having the law and keeping the law are virtually inseparable.[185] In 5:16 the law is called divine and the author, in his address to Antiochus, comments that there is "no compulsion more powerful than our obedience to the law." In addition, Gathercole cites 4:24 in which the author writes that Antiochus Epiphanes "had not been able in any way to put an end to the people's observance of the law."[186] This presupposition is found elsewhere throughout 4 Maccabees (see 5:29; 7:9; 9:2; 12:11, 14; 15:9-10; 18:4).

Thus, from the evidence listed above one can make the following conclusions. First, the written Pentateuch (and specifically its commands) is the referent for νόμος. Second, the law is divine (see 5:16, 18; 6:21; 9:15; 11:27; 13:22), having come from God (5:25). Third, the author clearly maintains a

---

[180]Gilbert, "Wisdom Literature," 318. Evans and Anderson both note that martyrdom is a substitutionary atonement for the author of 4 Macc (Evans, *Noncanonical Writings*, 37; Anderson, "4 Maccabees," 539). Fourth Macc 17:1 reads, "καὶ τὸν τύραννον τιμωρηθῆναι καὶ τὴν πατρίδα καθαρισθῆναι ὥσπερ ἀντίψυχον γεγονότας τῆς τοῦ ἔθνους ἁμαρτία." P. R. Davies makes the same observation concerning Eleazar's speech in 6:27-29 (P. R. Davies, "Didactic Stories," 128-29).

Martyrdom accounts in 4 Maccabees serve to illustrate the main thesis cited above. See George W. E. Nickelsburg and Michael E. Stone, *Faith and Piety in Early Judaism: Texts and Documents* (Philadelphia: Fortress, 1983), 106. See also Redditt, "The Concept of Nomos in Fourth Maccabees," 249. P. R. Davies comes to the same conclusion. He states that in 4 Maccabees obedience to the Mosaic law is stressed, and martyrdom is the ultimate expression of the "supremacy of reason/law over passions" (P. R. Davies, "Didactic Stories," 125-26).

[181]Nickelsburg and Stone, *Faith and Piety*, 107.

[182]Anderson, "4 Maccabees," 538. Observe the account of 4 Macc 6, in which Eleazar the priest is tormented and martyred for his refusal to break the dietary laws. For the author, such martyrdom is due to strict law-keeping. Davies also notes the possibility of such a death having an atoning value. See P. R. Davies, "Didactic Stories," 128-29.

[183]Gathercole, *Where Is Boasting?*, 186.

[184]Ibid. See also P. R. Davies, "Didactic Stories," 125-29.

[185]Gathercole, *Where Is Boasting?*, 171-72.

[186]Ibid. His translation.

high view of the written law, citing it verbatim at times. Fourth, since 4 Maccabees draws heavily from the accounts of 1 and 2 Maccabees, it is no surprise to see specific laws mentioned and upheld, such as those pertaining to dietary regulations.[187] Fifth, the law is seen to be the rule of life for those who are considered righteous, and thus the ethics of the law play a significant role. Sixth, there is an underlying assumption that the people did in fact observe the Torah on some considerable level. Righteous living is the same as living in obedience to the law's commands. Finally, sound reason finds its root in the Torah, and this wisdom is the education/instruction of the law (1:17a).

Conclusion

From the Pseudepigraphical evidence, one comes to several conclusions. First, there was a high view of the law[188] in each of the works, especially regarding its authority over the life of the Jew. Second, the law itself as well as its authority is seen to be perpetual. Third, in each case, the overwhelming referent was to the Pentateuch and specifically its commands written by Moses.[189] Fourth, if one was to be considered righteous, then one had to live according to the Mosaic commandments. Fifth, blessing (and even eternal life in some sense) was granted to those who maintained fidelity to the law.[190] Sixth, the

---

[187]See also 4 Macc 2:8, which appears to be an appeal to Deut 15:7-11, 23:19-20 and/or Lev 25:35-55 regarding the lending of money to the needy without interest, and canceling debts in the seventh year.

[188]Though opinions on man's ability to keep it varied (in the case of *2 Baruch* and *4 Ezra*). Still, any pessimism is not directed towards the law (in *4 Ezra*) but towards man and his inability. Even when there was pessimism regarding law-keeping, the law itself was extolled.

[189]Thus Blenkinsopp's conclusion seems to be justified. He notes that referencing the first five books as Torah can be seen clearly, starting in the second century B.C.E. (Blenkinsopp, *Wisdom and Law*, 75).

[190]Regarding the ongoing discussion of law in the Second Temple period, one notes the distinct differences between E. P. Sanders' *Paul and Palestinian Judaism*, and the work of scholars such as Simon J. Gathercole (*Where Is Boasting?*), and Mark A. Elliott (*Survivors of Israel*). Each of these scholars has been mentioned throughout this chapter and significantly contribute to the current debate. The Pseudepigraphal evidence brought forward here is best explained by Gathercole, viz., that this period is permeated by the notion of a final judgment on the basis of works (contra Sanders, *Paul and Palestinian Judaism*, 418-24, who concludes that obedience keeps one in the covenant rather than earning one judgment or reward at the eschaton). In fact, the first four chapters of Gathercole's work (*Where Is Boasting?*, 37-160) focus on the single theme of the role of obedience in final vindication at the eschaton (37). With reference to the Apocryphal and Pseudepigraphal evidence Gathercole concludes, "These texts still point to the reward of life for obedience" (90), which means obedience to the written law of Moses. The "life" that is assured for faithful law-obedience is at times blessing and reward in the present life, or at times in the reception of eternal life. Gathercole writes, "We have

corollary to this last statement is true as well: *infidelity* to the law brings great punishment. Finally, there is an emphasis on individual accountability towards the law's commands; the Deuteronomic blessings and curses are applied to the individual at times.

Josephus

Introduction

As one might expect, the references to νόμος in the collective writings of Josephus are numerous. Though there are many aspects of this discussion that are debated among Josephus scholars, such intramural debates do not derail the broader purposes here.[191] This section seeks to discover how Josephus used νόμος, what he meant by it, and what his views were towards it. However, this

---

seen clear evidence that obedience is a vital *basis* for receiving eternal life" (90, emphasis added).

Elliott's chief dissent with Sanders regarding his own reading of the writings of the Second Temple period is that scholarship should no longer refer to a unified idea of a nationalistic election within Judaism. Rather, Elliott asserts that what is frequent in this literature is a "remnant theology," viz., smaller groups within Second Temple Judaism who thought of themselves as the elect in opposition to other groups in Israel (Elliott, *Survivors of Israel*, 242). He describes it as fundamentally a *"protest movement...that...expressed* itself in *nonnationalistic* terms" (241). Such groups saw themselves as the purists, the conservatives, or perhaps even the traditionalists (242). He takes direct aim at Sanders' conclusions when he determines that one can no longer state that some writings were more "representative" than others of the Judaism of the period (contra Sanders, *Paul and Palestinian Judaism*, 418, 420, 422-24, passim). Elliott strongly asserts, "This essentially nonnationalistic view is too *important* a voice in Judaism for scholars to go on referring to nationalistic voices as if *they* were the only significant ones, particularly, one might add, in the context of prolegomena to the study of the New Testament" (Elliott, *Survivors of Israel*, 243, emphasis his).

What is helpful for the present study is one particular point of agreement, viz., that the law's commands were to be and largely were followed by the Jew of the period (even if the motivations for obedience are still a matter of significant debate). This was an expectation and presupposition of Jewish life in this period. Where these scholars differ—the specific *role* of obedience to the law (either getting in [merit] or staying in [covenantal nomism])—is not the specific question asked here, though it is not irrelevant, to be sure.

[191]Scholars tend to fall into two main categories when engaging in discussion of Josephus. There are those that have a generally positive view towards Josephus' writings (that they are a credible witness) and those that view his writings with great suspicion and doubt. For a survey, see P. Bilde *Flavius Josephus Between Jerusalem and Rome. His Life, His Works, and Their Importance*, JSPSup 2 (Sheffield: JSOT Press, 1988), 123-71. The translations are from the Loeb Classical Library, unless otherwise noted.

section is different from the last two in at least two ways. First, the writings
under discussion are from a single author. Second, the materials researched
here are dated much closer to the time of the composition of Hebrews. This
section consists of four parts. It begins with a brief introduction on the matter
of νόμος in Josephus. Second, it addresses Josephus' personal testimony
concerning his own practice of the law. Third, is the consideration of what
Josephus says concerning the Jewish people and their practice of the law.
Fourth is the consideration of the two summaries of the law found in
Antiquities 3.224-86; 4.190-301 and *Against Apion* 2.190-217. It is fitting to
turn to Josephus at this point of the discussion. Sanders' comment is
noteworthy, "The principal source for the history of the period, and for its
social, political, and religious issues, is the work of the Jewish author,
Josephus."[192]

Blenkinsopp asserts that in the writings of Josephus, the references to νόμος
are shorthand references for the Pentateuch.[193] This is affirmed by Gathercole,
who concludes that for Josephus, the "Torah" is the Mosaic legislation.[194] W.
D. Davies seems to agree. He states that the names given to the OT varied
("law and the prophets," or "law, prophets, and the writings"), but that νόμος
usually referred to the Mosaic law and its commands. He writes, "The
fundamental section of the Old Testament was the Mosaic law..., the Decalogue
as such was given prominence."[195] Though the Decalogue was given
prominence, Davies notes that it was not to be regarded as exclusively *the*
Torah. In first-century Judaism, when the term "law" is found, "it is difficult
not to think of the Pentateuch, as a whole, as constituting the Mosaic law: it
was called Torah, even in its non-legal aspects."[196] Sanders echoes these
conclusions when he writes that while *any part* of divine revelation could
rightly be called "law," what was usually meant by both תּוֹרָה and νόμος was
the "commandments and prohibitions which are observable, or for the scrolls
on which they are written down."[197] He observes that when Josephus

---

[192]E. P. Sanders, *Judaism Practice and Belief*, 5. Given that this is what Sanders
believes about the importance of Josephus, it is striking that *Paul and Palestinian
Judaism* has no discussion of Josephus whatsoever, and only refers to his writings three
times. Spilsbury makes this observation as well (Paul Spilsbury, "Josephus," in
Justification and Variegated Nomism, vol. 1, *The Complexities of Second Temple
Judaism*, ed. D. A. Carson, Peter T. O'Brien, and Mark A. Seifrid [Grand Rapids:
Baker, 2001], 241).
[193]Blenkinsopp, *Wisdom and Law*, 75.
[194]Gathercole, *Where Is Boasting?*, 147.
[195]W. D. Davies, "The Law in First Century Judaism," 91.
[196]Ibid.
[197]Sanders, "Law in Judaism of the NT Period," 255. See also W. Gutbrod, "νόμος," in
TDNT, ed. Gerhard Kittel, ed. and trans. Geoffrey W. Bromily (Grand Rapids:
Eerdmans, 1967), 4:1050. "In Josephus νόμος is normally used to denote the Jewish

summarizes the "laws and the constitution" in *Antiquities* 4.8.3. §194, he speaks specifically of commandments. This is noteworthy, in that it asserts that though νόμος in first-century Judaism *could* have a broad semantic range, it *usually* referred to OT commandments of the written Mosaic law in a narrow sense. In keeping with this point, Sanders (cf. Gutbrod) observes that it seems quite clear that in Josephus (as well as the whole of first-century Judaism) νόμος normally took on this special and more narrow sense of commands and prohibitions, and particularly those within the Pentateuch.[198]

Josephus' Own Testimony

CONCERNING THE LAW

Stated succinctly, Josephus portrayed himself as one who kept the law in all its requirements. He believed the Mosaic law to have come directly from God and thus it held inherent authority,[199] and presents himself and the Jewish people as having kept the law even down to its minutiae.[200] In *Life* 135 Josephus declares his own fidelity to the law, and Feldman comments that Josephus does so in order to express his own piety.[201] He claims that he himself had kept the laws of Torah from his youth.

Josephus also tells his readers that he had been highly trained in the law. Feldman writes, "That Josephus was well acquainted with all aspects of the Law may be seen in his extensive summary of Halakhah in Books 3 and 4 of

---

religious Law." He adds, "The basis of the significance and authority of the Law lies in its divine origin, which Josephus firmly accepts" (1051).

[198]Sanders, "Law in Judaism of the NT Period," 255. Segal also argues for this point (Segal, "Torah and *Nomos* in Recent Scholarly Discussion," 21-22). Spilsbury echoes this and asserts that the Jews saw themselves to be blessed because they were connected to the lawgiver Moses, and had been given the law by the ruler of the universe through him (Spilsbury, "Josephus," 258).

[199]See *Antiquities* Preface 3; *Against Apion* 2.18.

[200]See for example Josephus *Against Apion* 2.82, in *Josephus* 1:326, trans. H. St. J. Thackeray, LCL. "Throughout our history we have kept the same laws, to which we are eternally faithful."

[201]Louis H. Feldman, "Torah and Greek Culture in Josephus," *Torah U-Maddah Journal* 7 (1997): 45. Feldman specifies that what is meant is the written Torah. One particular example perhaps demonstrates Josephus' fidelity towards the written Torah. During the intertestamental period, defending oneself in case of direct attack came to be seen as permitted on the Sabbath, when at one time it was not (*Jub* 50:12). After a rout of a group of pietists who would not fight on the Sabbath (when the Jews were fighting for independence from Seleucid rule), this interpretation of the law was changed by common agreement. See Josephus, *Jewish Wars* 2.19.2.§518); Sanders, "Law in Judaism of the NT Period," 256-57.

his *Antiquities*."[202] In *Life* 9, Josephus boasts that as a young boy of fourteen, the leading men of Jerusalem would regularly come to him and ask his thoughts concerning specific laws and thus, "he regarded himself as eminently well qualified to comment on the legal code."[203] Further, Josephus reveals that even his companions viewed his own comprehension of the law to outweigh theirs.[204]

JEWS AND THE LAW

Throughout his writing, Josephus testifies to the Jewish adherence and fidelity to the law of Moses. Spilsbury begins with a datum: "God's relationship with the Jews in Josephus' writings is founded upon Jewish observance of the Law of Moses."[205] This proposition is woven into the fabric of each of Josephus' major works, and there are several texts that demonstrate this fundamental point. In *Against Apion* 2.174, Josephus states that all matters of life are clearly articulated in the law, which "left nothing, however insignificant, to the discretion and caprice of the individual.... For ignorance he (Moses) left no pretext."[206] Concerning this text Spilsbury states that the law is for Josephus a "standard and rule" and is a "father and master" for those who live under it.[207] Elsewhere in *Against Apion*, work should be abandoned once a week to hear the law read and to obtain an accurate understanding of it.[208] Josephus writes, "He appointed the law to be the most excellent and necessary form of instruction, ordaining...that every week men should desert their occupations and assemble to listen to the law and to obtain a thorough and accurate knowledge of it."[209] In addition, possession and performance are linked. This assertion underlies the whole of *Against Apion* 2.174-78 and "creates...both a wonderful unanimity among the Jewish people and a common way of life."[210]

---

[202]Feldman, "Torah and Greek Culture," 45.

[203]Louis H. Feldman, "Use, Authority and Exegesis of Mikra in the Writings of Josephus," in *Mikra: Text, Translation, Reading and Interpretation on the Hebrew Bible in Ancient Judaism and Early Christianity*, ed. Martin J. Mulder, CRINT 2.1 (Philadelphia: Fortress Press, 1988), 507.

[204]Josephus *Antiquities*, 20:263; *Life*, 198. See Feldman, "Use, Authority and Exegesis of Mikra," 507.

[205]Spilsbury, "Josephus," 247.

[206]Josephus *Against Apion* 2.174, in *Josephus* 1:362-63, trans. H. St. J. Thackeray, LCL.

[207]Spilsbury, "Josephus," 258. Spilsbury essentially concludes that Josephus argues for a strict (and glad) adherence to the Mosaic code.

[208]See Geza Vermes, "A Summary of the Law by Flavius Josephus," *NovT* 24 (1982): 291.

[209]Josephus *Against Apion* 2.175, in *Josephus* 1:362-63, trans. H. St. J. Thackeray, LCL. See also *Against Apion* 2.178, 257.

[210]Gathercole, *Where Is Boasting?*, 172; see also 171. Gathercole adds that for Josephus, "transgressors in the Jewish nation are few" (172). See also E. Kamlah, "Frömmigkeit

In *Jewish Antiquities* 4.209-210 Josephus similarly notes that the reason for the public reading the law is for memorization. He argues in *Against Apion* 2.181 (cf. 179, 283) that such common knowledge of the law by the public reading and subsequent memorization underlies an inherent unity within the Jewish people. He writes of his fellow Jews, "With us all act alike, all profess the same doctrine about God, one which is in harmony without law and affirms that all things are under his eye."[211] There are numerous other references that could be cited on this point, but the most oft-cited statement of the Jewish apologist concerning the fidelity of the Jewish people towards the law of Moses is found in *Against Apion* 2.178. He writes,

> But, should anyone of our nation be questioned about the laws (νόμους), he would repeat them all more readily than his own name. The result, then, of our thorough grounding in the laws come from the first dawn of intelligence [i.e., as a child] is that we have them, as it were, engraven on our souls.[212]

This idea is not just present in *Against Apion*. Spilsbury's essay begins with a discussion of Josephus' *Antiquities* in which he asserts the following:

> The Law in the *Antiquities* is the gift of God. It is the means by which God governs his people and, Josephus argues, it is obeyed by the Jews in every detail. The Law is inherently good and it causes the Jews to be the most generous, hospitable and charitable of people. It is also profoundly rational and in keeping with the natural laws of the universe. As such it reflects not only its divine origin, but the extreme piety and sagacity of the lawgiver, Moses. Further, in Josephus' view, piety is explicitly linked to observance of the Law, and law-observance results naturally in God's favor.[213]

Jews who would read *Antiquities* would know that mere ethnic descent is not sufficient for Jewish identity. Ethnic descent without detailed observance of the law is anathema for Josephus. In fact, to be a descendent of Abraham and not to obey the law is far worse. Hence, "clearly, the Law is at the heart of Israel's relationship with God."[214]

However, such a high view of all Jews (as portrayed in *Against Apion* 2.178)

---

und Tugend: Die Gesetzesapologie des Josephus in c Ap 2,145-295," in *Josephus-Studien: Untersuchungen zu Josephus, dem antiken Judentum und dem Neuen Testament*, ed. Betz, Haacker, and Hengel (Göttingen: Vandenhoeck & Ruprecht, 1974), 220-32.

[211]Josephus *Against Apion* 2.181, in *Josephus*, 1:364-65, trans. H. St. J. Thackeray, LCL. See also 2.179-80.

[212]Josephus *Against Apion* 2.178, in *Josephus*, 1:364-65, trans. H. St. J. Thackeray, LCL.

[213]Spilsbury, "Josephus," 248.

[214]Ibid., 251.

is not to be met without a bit of critical discernment. As an apologist, it is understandable that Josephus has perhaps overstated his case concerning the nation's fidelity to their divinely given law. Yet despite some probable exaggeration, Baumgarten concludes that Josephus "saw knowledge of Jewish law by all Jews as one of the distinctive aspects of Judaism."[215] He argues that despite the overstatement, the average Jew considered the Torah to be public and thus *lived out* in public.[216] In fact, their lives gave credibility to such statements concerning fidelity to the law. Baumgarten notes, "they accepted the ideal of knowledge and practice (of the Law), believing that they ought to know the law as thoroughly as possible and observe its commandments as carefully as they could."[217] In short, the law is the source of piety for the Jew; by obeying its commands one is pious.[218] According to Josephus, the average Jew was careful to observe (at least) the main laws of Judaism. This seems tenable from the citations noted above. However, this writer does not suggest that all of Josephus' statements about his fellow Jews be read woodenly and without a critical eye.[219]

Finally, law-keeping has eschatological results. Gathercole concludes that for Josephus, "the destiny of each person is determined, when this time comes, by their obedience to the Torah. Those who receive new life at the eschaton are those who live according to the commandments."[220] Vermes agrees, noting that for the pious Jew there is reward in the future life for those who have obeyed

---

[215]A. I. Baumgarten, "The Torah as a Public Document in Judaism," *SR* 14.1 (1985): 18. Spilsbury has opted to read Josephus on his own terms, and thus maintains a positive view of Josephus even in light of what might be a bit of overstatement in *Against Apion* 2.178. The present researcher does not read Josephus with great amounts of suspicion, but neither does he read texts such as *Against Apion* 2.178 without a modicum of reservation. Any hint of reservation seems to be missing in Spilsbury's essay, though this writer is in significant agreement with his conclusions regarding Josephus and the Mosaic law.

[216]This is the main thesis of Baumgarten's article. The Torah was public because its demands could be *seen* in the lives of the Jewish people.

[217]Baumgarten, "Torah as a Public Document," 22. In his concluding remarks, Baumgarten states emphatically, "the conviction that all Jews should know and observe the Torah was an ideal widely held" (24). If indeed such statements about the piety and law-keeping of the Jewish people were patently false, such a wild claim could have been easily struck down by even the casual reader of Josephus in the ancient world.

[218]Vermes, "A Summary," 291. For Vermes, νόμος in Josephus equals the Mosaic law and eschatological reward is for those who so obey the Mosaic commands that they are ready to be martyred for them (301).

[219]For one further line of evidence that reinforces this point, see Appendix 4.

[220]Gathercole, *Where Is Boasting?*, 147.

the Mosaic law.[221] Ultimately, Jews who live their lives in unswerving obedience to the law of Moses will have peace and blessing in the age to come. [222] This is the point Josephus makes in *Against Apion* 2.217-19, where he writes, "Each individual...is firmly persuaded that to those who observe the laws and, if they must needs die for them, willingly meet death, God has granted a renewed existence and in the revolution of the ages the gift of a better life."[223] This text goes on to state that Josephus is aware that there are many who have indeed died for the law. He continues, "Many...have on many occasions ere now preferred to brave all manner of suffering rather than to utter a single word against the Law."[224] Vermes comments that eschatological reward is for those "who remain so firmly attached to the commandments that, like the many martyrs of past ages, they are prepared to die for them."[225] Again, this idea of dying rather than deny the law is a feature common to the period. Finally, in *Antiquities* it is clear that Josephus sees God as the one who rewards virtue and punishes the wicked.[226]

JOSEPHUS' TWO SUMMARIES OF THE LAW

On two separate occasions Josephus includes summaries of the law. These summaries are found in *Antiquities* 3.90-286; 4.190-301 and *Against Apion* 2.164-219. Such summaries were in fact tangential to Josephus' overall purpose of recording Jewish history.[227] Thus, it follows that the very presence of such summaries is a strong indicator of how seriously and personally Josephus took the Torah laws.[228] The presence of such summaries is notable given that Josephus stated clearly in *Antiquities* 3.223 that he intended to write a further

---

[221]Vermes, "A Summary," 291. Eschatological reward in the future life for those who are the faithful observers of the law is seen in *Antiquities* 4.218-19.

[222]Spilsbury, "Josephus," 258. See also Josephus, *Wars*, 3.374.

[223]Josephus *Against Apion* 2.217-219, in *Josephus*, 1:380, trans. H. St. J. Thackeray, LCL.

[224]Ibid.

[225]Vermes, "A Summary," 301. See also Louis H. Feldman, *Josephus's Interpretation of the Bible*, (Los Angeles: University of California Press, 1998), 421.

[226]Carson, *Divine Sovereignty*, 110. Gathercole argues that obedience and disobedience are actually the *basis* for which one receives (or does not receive) eschatological reward. He writes, "When the resurrection comes, those who have been obedient to the Torah will be rewarded with a new and better life" (Gathercole, *Where Is Boasting?*, 144-45). For further evidence, see Josephus *Jewish Wars* 3.374-75; *Against Apion* 2.217-18.

[227]Feldman, "Torah and Greek Culture in Josephus," 47.

[228]Sanders' comments are helpful here. He argues that when Josephus summarized the "laws and the constitution" in *Antiquities*, he speaks specifically of commandments (Sanders, "Law in the NT Period," 255). Feldman adds, "The very fact, we may suggest, that Josephus summarizes the Mosaic code at such length...shows how important law was for him" (Feldman, *Josephus's Interpretation*, 399).

and separate work about the laws of the Torah themselves. Feldman argues that in doing so Josephus seeks to both elevate Moses and to defend the specific laws of the Torah as the highest standard of ethics.[229] Vermes agrees with Feldman, concluding that Josephus' summaries of the Mosaic law are "probably the earliest Jewish theological synthesis. Its primary aim was manifestly to impress on educated Graeco-Roman readers the outstanding excellence of Judaism."[230]

Vermes summarizes and observes the oft-mentioned fact that Josephus begins with the Ten Commandments and from there proceeds to discuss the Mosaic institution of the Tabernacle and cultus (etc.).[231] The shorter summary found in *Against Apion* is seen to be Josephus' answer to the distortions published by Apollonius Molon. It is significant that Josephus answers such accusations by a "demonstration that the Mosaic Law, faithfully practiced by the Jews, has nothing in common with Apollonius' description of Judaism."[232] Vermes concludes by stating that this later work is not an abridgement of *Antiquities* and is not dependent on it in any way.[233]

Conclusion

First, νόμος is chiefly a referent to the Pentateuch and specifically its commandments in Josephus. Second, it seems evident that the apologist had a high regard for the law, and that in his own writings he states that he was both highly trained in the Mosaic law and that he kept the Mosaic commandments. Third, law-keeping visibly characterized a pious Jew; to be a true Jew one must obey the law of Moses. Even if one reads Josephus' words with a skeptical eye (admitting the possibility and even likelihood of overstatement for apologetic purposes), it seems correct that from a reading of *Against Apion* the Jewish people as a whole held the law in high regard and practiced it to a certain (and

---

[229]Feldman, "Torah and Greek Culture in Josephus," 47. Yigael Yadin notes that there are similarities between Josephus' classification of the laws and those found in the Temple Scroll of Qumran (Yigael Yadin, *The Temple Scroll* [Jerusalem: Ben Zvi, 1983], 1:62, 93-4, 305).

[230]Vermes, "A Summary," 301-02.

[231]Ibid., 290.

[232]Ibid., 291.

[233]Ibid. The rest of Vermes' article (see pp. 301-03) describes the specific laws and how Josephus articulates them with regard to the Mosaic legislation. Vermes does not go into the matter of oral vs. written Torah, since for Vermes, it is always about the written Torah of Moses. What Josephus comments on and summarizes are actual *written* laws. However, note Josephus' commendation for the people to pray twice daily (*Antiquities* 4.212). This was not a specified Pentateuchal practice, but could have been a "tradition" harkening back to Josephus' Pharisaism. Regardless, he does not treat such a practice here nor refer to it as νόμος.

possibly significant) extent.[234] This is likely given that certain Jewish practices in obedience to the law were quite visible and well-known to the Romans. Fourth, obedience to the law yielded eschatological reward.[235] Fifth, dying for the law is acceptable and honorable for Josephus. Finally, the two summaries of the Mosaic law found in *Antiquities* and *Against Apion* demonstrate the fact that for Josephus, the written law of Moses is both the highest standard of ethics and central to the life of first-century Judaism.

Philo of Alexandria

Introduction

Like Josephus, Philo is an apologist writing a defense of Judaism to the Greek-speaking world. In Philo's writings, νόμος takes on a broader meaning, though not substantially different from that of Josephus.[236] For instance, like Josephus, νόμος can refer to the laws of nations,[237] as well as the written law of Moses and the Pentateuch itself.[238] Philo is broader than Josephus in his use of νόμος, in that he is also concerned with the Greek idea of the law of nature. In general, however, νόμος is typically a referent for the "Torah of the Palestinians,"[239] and specifically the commands of the Pentateuch.[240] It is this νόμος that is the nucleus of Philo's spiritual life. The law of Moses is eternal and divine, having come from God himself, and is the essence of true virtue for mankind. Indeed, it can be assumed that in a qualified sense according to Philo, the Jews both

---

[234]Spilsbury observes that if the Jews were to be blessed (both in the present life and eschatologically) then they were to conform their lives to the day-to-day requirements of the law. This would therefore highlight the ethical concerns of the law since such law-keeping was visible and external (Spilsbury, "Josephus," 259). What is absent from Josephus is the notion of an internalization of the law into the minds and hearts of the people of God such as is found in Heb 8 and 10. Rather, he seems to be more concerned with how one *appears* to be keeping the law—i.e., to be a follower of the Mosaic law and thus a true Jew will have tangible and visible results. Quite simply, for Josephus, the Jews lived according to the law and as such this was reflective in day-to-day life.

[235]See especially Josephus, *Against Apion* 2.182-83. "This conviction...explains why the Jews are so famous for their willingness to die rather than disobey the Law" (Spilsbury, "Josephus," 257). See also Gathercole, *Where Is Boasting?*, 144-47.

[236]Gutbrod, "νόμος," 1052.

[237]Philo *On Joseph* 63, in *Philo*, 6:172-73, trans. F. H. Colson, LCL.

[238]Philo *On Abraham* 1, in *Philo*, 6:4-5, trans. F. H. Colson, LCL. Here Philo states that the sacred laws have been written down in five books, the first of which is Genesis.

[239]Gutbrod, "νόμος," 1052. See also Sandmel, *The Genius of Paul*, 46-47.

[240]For E. P. Sanders it seems clear that "law" normally took on a special and more narrow sense of commands and prohibitions, and particularly those in the Pentateuch. This law is equal to the will of God (Sanders, "Law in Judaism of the NT Period," 255).

knew and practiced the law of Moses.[241]

The Law of Moses and the Law of Nature

Philo wrote to a Greek audience for whom νόμος had a range of meaning, and as such there was room for him to take advantage of such ambiguity. Segal argues, "Philo, the diaspora Jew par excellence, knew of the ambiguity in the term for nomos and endeavored to persuade his Hellenistic colleagues of the real meaning of the term."[242] What he means is that Philo sought to prove that the highest laws of nature and wisdom are the same as the laws practiced and followed by the Jews, and that such laws are perfectly rational.[243] In this manner, Philo is unique. Segal clarifies, "Only a law which was revealed by God, who is the creator of nature, can be in accordance with nature in the true sense of the term, for such a law, being the work of God, is like nature itself-universal, eternal, and immutable."[244] Philo contends that the written law of

---

[241]This is very similar to Josephus. By "qualified sense" what is meant is that the modern reader of Philo must understand that Philo is writing an apology, and that in his efforts to paint Judaism as the true and divinely given religion, Philo may (like Josephus) be guilty of overstatement. Concerning the obedience of the Jewish people to the law, Baumgarten argues, "Philo stressed the expertise of Jews in matters concerning their ancestral laws" (Baumgarten, "Torah as a Public Document," 17). See Philo *Special Legislation* 2.62; *Life of Moses* 2.216; *Hypothetica* 7.12, 14 where this point is explicit.

[242]Segal, "Torah and *Nomos*," 24.

[243]See for example Philo's discussion of the practice of circumcision in *Special Legislation* 1.1-10, where Philo argues for the rationality of the practice of circumcision. It is to be practiced because it is hygienic (it prevents disease in 1.4), and on the other hand, it is a symbol of a heart that has been "circumcised" (1.5). Here Philo's allegorical exegesis is clearly seen. One should note, however, that even though Philo allegorizes such laws, it is not at the expense of the literal interpretation (he does, after all, advocate the literal practice of circumcision), and in *Migration of Abraham* 89 he makes it clear that the literal sense of the law must be followed. See also Philo's condemnation of adultery and prostitution. On the basis of the Mosaic law he calls for the death penalty (*Special Legislation* 3.51; *Hypothetica* 7.1).

David Hay agrees concluding that Philo does not simply resort to allegory, but more often "interprets the laws on a literal level indicating that they are to be obeyed in the realm of the external world" (David Hay, "Philo," in *Justification and Variegated Nomism*, vol. 1, *The Complexities of Second Temple Judaism*, ed. D. A. Carson, Peter T. O'Brien, and Mark A. Seifrid [Grand Rapids: Baker, 2001], 375). This of course does not deny the practice of allegorizing to Philo. Rather, Philo sees himself in a rather elite group of interpreters who accept both the literal as well as allegorical exegesis (Hay, "Philo," 378). Idem, "Putting Extremism in Context: The Case of Philo, *De Migratione* 89-93," *Studia Philonica Annual* 9 (1997): 126-42.

[244]Segal, "Torah and *Nomos*," 26.

Moses is in accordance with nature, and is "law" in the true sense.[245]

For Philo, God created nature to operate by following a set of ordered rules, "operations which are invariably carried out under ordinances and laws which God laid down in His universe as unalterable."[246] Philo writes that there is an eternal "law engraved in the nature of the universe which lays down this truth."[247] In *Special Legislation* 2.13 he makes his connection clear between the "law of our ancestors" and the laws evident within nature. He avers, "Justice and every virtue are commanded by the law of our ancestors and by a statute established of old, and what else are laws and statutes but the sacred words of Nature?"[248] But what is the content of the law of nature? Philo tries to define it and concludes that this law can be attained by the proper use of one's reason.[249]

Bockmuehl agrees that the created order reveals much. He writes, "The natural order, perceived in creation, calls for certain orderly patterns of human behaviour, which are also in keeping with the Law of God."[250] Borgen concludes, *"The particular ordinances of the Jewish Law coincide with the universal cosmic principles. Thus to Philo universal and general principles do not undercut or cancel the specific ordinances or events of the Mosaic Law."*[251] It is argued here that Goodenough is in error when he maintains that Philo regards the written law of Moses to be secondary to the law of Nature.[252] Borgen is again helpful. He contends that when Philo speaks of the harmony of the two laws (*On the Creation* 3), that the written law of Moses cannot be

---

[245]Ibid., 26-27. See also Gutbrod, "νόμος," 1053.

[246]Philo *On the Creation* 61, in *Philo* 1:46-47, trans. G. H. Whitaker, LCL.

[247]Philo *On Drunkenness* 141, in *Philo*, 3:392-93, trans. F. H. Colson, LCL.

[248]Philo *Special Legislation* 2.13, in *Philo* 7:312-15, trans. F. H. Colson, LCL.

[249]Philo *On The Decalogue* 132. In the opening of *On The Decalogue*, Philo states that he intends to comment on and describe accurately the particular written laws that Moses gave at Sinai (Philo *On the Decalogue* 1.1, in *Philo* 7:6-7, trans. F. H. Colson, LCL). Here the connection between the unwritten law of nature and the written law of Moses is particularly explicit.

[250]Bockmuehl, *Jewish Law in Gentile Churches*, 102. According to Bockmuehl, there is no conflict between what God has revealed in his creation and what he commanded the people at Sinai.

[251]Peder Borgen, *Philo of Alexandria: An Exegete for His Time*, NovTSup 86 (New York: Brill, 1997), 147 (emphasis his); see also 144-48. See also his "Heavenly Ascent in Philo," in *The Pseudepigrapha and Early Biblical Interpretation*, ed. James H. Charlesworth and Craig A. Evans, JSPSup 14 (Sheffield: Sheffield Press, 1993), 268.

[252]E. R. Goodenough, *By Light, Light: The Mystic Gospel of Hellenistic Judaism* (New Haven, CT: Yale University Press, 1935), 88-94. See also Samuel Sandmel who also concludes that the written law was "at best a copy, and thereby inescapably secondary" (Samuel Sandmel, *Philo's Place in Judaism: A Study of Conceptions of Abraham in Jewish Literature* [New York: Ktav Publishing House, 1971], 197).

surpassed by the law of Nature.[253] What must be said of Goodenough (and Sandmel) is that such a conclusion is his own deduction and is, according to this writer's reading of the data, in conflict with the actual words of Philo.[254]

Further, there are occasions when one is unsure whether Philo refers to an "oral law" or to the law of nature when he speaks of an "unwritten law." Martens persuasively argues that the unwritten law of which Philo speaks is the law of nature itself and thus not an oral law in any sense.[255] He notes that this "explicit connection between the true law of nature and the unwritten law is not made in any other Greek source."[256] Along this same line of thought, Myre has argued that the written law is in fact a *copy* of the unwritten law of nature.[257] Though the law of nature existed in time before the written law of Moses, in Philo's mind this does not denigrate the written law of Moses.

Goodenough has argued that the Greek mind could counter that since the Jewish law of Moses is a written law, it is therefore secondary to the transcendent law of nature. He argues that for Philo, the written law of Moses is to be transcended and ultimately superfluous.[258] But Martens (et al.) rightly disagrees, stating that for Philo the written law of Moses is the only law that people will ever need, and "it is the best written law by far...he could not imagine a better written law."[259] According to Martens, "Philo seems to be arguing against the Graeco-Roman view that there is no true representation here on earth of the law of nature."[260] When Philo speaks of the laws of Moses as a copy, he does *not* intend to denigrate and minimize the written laws of Moses (contra Goodenough and Sandmel). This is a mistaken assumption that

---

[253]Borgen, *Philo of Alexandria*, 148; contra Goodenough, *By Light, Light*, 89-90.

[254]The logic of such a deduction seems to be that since Philo sees the law of Nature as coming before the law of Moses that the written copy is at best secondary. Such a conclusion seems to go beyond the limits of the data. For further treatment, see Valentin Nikiprowetzky, *Commentaire de l'Ecriture chez Philon d'Alexandrie*, ALGHJ 11 (Leiden: E. J. Brill, 1977), 117-31. See also Hay, "Philo," 375.

[255]John W. Martens, "Philo and the 'Higher' Law," *SBL 1991 Seminar Papers* 30, ed. Eugene H. Lovering, Jr. (Atlanta: Scholars, 1991), 313-14. Hay also finds no reason to assert that Philo refers to an oral law (Hay, "Philo," 376).

[256]Martens, "Philo and the 'Higher' Law," 314. Given the wealth of research present in his article, one is apt to believe that Martens has indeed searched most if not all of Greek literature in order to make such a statement. Gutbrod too notes the connection when he writes, "The decisive concern for Philo in his discussion of the Law is to show the agreement between the OT Law and the cosmic order in reason and nature at large" (Gutbrod, "νόμος," 1053).

[257]Andre Myre, "La Loi de la Nature et la Loi Mosaique selon Philon d' Alexandrie," *ScEs* 28.2 (1976): 168.

[258]Goodenough, *By Light, Light*, 73-96.

[259]Martens, "Philo and the 'Higher' Law," 316.

[260]Ibid., 317.

is not in keeping with the whole of Philo. It was the transcendent God who created nature who gave the written law, and thus the law is not secondary. In no way could Philo "admit that the Mosaic law was only a shadowy sketch of true law. God gave the law to Moses; God also created the world and with it the law of nature."[261] Thus, the two were in perfect agreement and harmony, and without contradiction. The present writer agrees with Martens, Hay, Nikiprowetzky, and Borgen who conclude that Philo unified the natural law and the Mosaic law, yet in no way see the written law of Moses as secondary in Philo. For Philo, there are no higher laws that "are not intimately connected to the written, Mosaic law."[262]

This point is due to the fact that for Philo, the written law of Moses and the law of nature are both from the same eternal creator. Bockmuehl agrees with Martens and states, "God and his creation never ultimately speak with two distinct voices.... God's voice is clearly heard both in creation and in the Torah, and the two are fundamentally related."[263] In the Hebrew mind, any "natural law" is not distinct from the truth of Torah. In his teaching on Moses, Philo writes that the laws of Moses are "firm, unshaken, immovable, stamped, as it were, with the seals of nature herself," and that those laws "remain secure from the day when they were first enacted to now, and we may hope that they will remain for all future ages as though immortal."[264] Both laws have one and the same content.[265]

Philo and the Patriarchs

Philo also paints an idealized picture of the patriarchs. He states that they embodied the law and intuitively obeyed the Torah before it was written by Moses.[266] In short, the patriarchs lived according to true virtue since the written law codified what was known to be both true and virtuous. In his concluding statements on Abraham, Philo writes that the patriarch "obeyed the law...himself a law and an unwritten statute."[267] The patriarchs of the nation lived lives in happy obedience to the law, having discerned the law by use of

---

[261]Ibid.
[262]Ibid., 319. See also Adele Reinhartz, "The Meaning of Nomos in Philo's Exposition of the Law," *SR* 15.3 (1986): 344. Reinhartz notes that one of many reasons why the Mosaic law is superior to all other law codes is "the content of the theological doctrine or philosophy present in the Mosaic law" (341). See Philo *On the Creation* 170-72.
[263]Bockmuehl, *Jewish Law*, 89.
[264]Philo *Life of Moses* 2.14, in *Philo* 6:456-57, trans. F. H. Colson, LCL.
[265]Bockmuehl, *Jewish Law*, 108. See Philo *On the Creation* 3.
[266]See Philo *On Abraham* 3, 5, 6; *Life of Moses* 2.14; *Every Good Man is Free* 62; *On the Virtues* 134.
[267]Philo *On Abraham* 276, in *Philo* 6:134-35, trans. F. H. Colson, LCL. On the matter of patriarchs being unwritten laws themselves, see Martens, "Philo and the 'Higher' Law," 313.

their reason. Sandmel is likely correct when he concludes that Philo's desire is to persuade the reader to be like the patriarchs.[268]

The Law and the Jewish People

Finally, like Josephus, Philo expected the Jewish people to obey the law. For instance, *On Joseph* 42 states, "We children of the Hebrews follow laws and customs which are especially our own."[269] Likewise, there is punishment for those that disregard the law. Philo writes, "Disobedience to the law, for all its short-lived seductiveness, recoils upon the disobedient."[270] But Philo does not suggest that everyone in Israel is fully obedient to the law, and in *Special Legislation* 1.154 observes that there are those that do in fact disobey it. Obedience is praised while disobedience is punished. Following the "law of life" means following the Mosaic law, and this leads to a life that is characterized by virtue.[271] For Philo, scripture (primarily the Pentateuch) is the lens through which he sees the world.[272] The Pentateuch is perfect in its teaching and expression, and is in no substantial conflict with the best of the world's philosophy.[273] Therefore the Mosaic law is more than just law; it teaches about true virtue, and is thus superior as a law code and is thus to be obeyed. Even so, Reinhart argues that the specific laws are not necessarily the main point—virtue is the point.[274] Yet for Philo obedience to the specific commands of the Mosaic law *is* the path to virtue. Obedience to the law of Moses is something that the Jewish people are trained in from their earliest years,[275] and is obligatory for the Jewish people.[276]

---

[268]Sandmel, *Philo's Place*, 197.

[269]Philo *On Joseph* 42, in *Philo* 6:162-63, trans. F. H. Colson, LCL.

[270]Philo *Special Legislation* 1.155, in *Philo* 7:186-87, trans. F. H. Colson, LCL.

[271]See Philo *Life of Moses* 2.13; *On Abraham* 4, 5, 6. This is one among many examples where the fusion of the Jewish law with the quality of "virtue" in the Greek mind is made clear. This is perhaps the greatest of contributions of Philo, viz., his defense (*apologia*) for the Jewish faith to the Greek world. Martens notes that in doing so, Philo extends Judaism to the world in Greek dress. Far from a subverter of the faith, he is, indeed a protector" (Martens, "Philo and the 'Higher' Law," 322).

[272]Hay, "Philo," 362. There are 536 occurrences of νόμος in Philo and according to Hay, this is Philo's standard term for the Mosaic legislation (373). Hay summarizes, "Philo is persuaded that all of the specific commandments of Moses have permanent validity...though he was aware of problems of applying them in his own time" (Ibid.). See also David Dawson, *Allegorical Readers and Cultural Revision in Ancient Alexandria* (Berkeley: University of California Press, 1992), 125-26.

[273]Hay, "Philo," 362.

[274]Reinhart, "The Meaning of Nomos in Philo's Exposition of the Law," 345.

[275]See Philo *On the Embassy to Gaius* 210. E. P. Sanders ("Law in Judaism in the NT Period," 257-59) argues this point from Philo's writings. Cohen professes that for Philo, the Mosaic laws were to be obeyed first and foremost on a literal level (Naomi G.

In addition, Martens notes that one practical suggestion for Philo's adamant defense of the Mosaic law was the good of the community. If the Greek idea of a transcendent law of nature were seen to render the Mosaic written law secondary, then "there was a real risk of people abandoning the Mosaic Law in favor of a non-nationalistic Jewish Law."[277] If this suggestion is correct, then one can see a two-fold apology in Philo: one to the Greek, and one to the Jew. Yet to both audiences the message is the same, viz., the Mosaic law is the highest of all forms of law and is superior to all other forms.[278] It is rational and reasonable, and should be obeyed resulting in righteousness and true virtue. The Mosaic law is for all humanity, and all of its commands are meant to be obeyed without selecting which were to be followed rather than others.[279]

Finally, Philo has given us what could be argued to be his own summary of the law in *Special Legislation* 2.63. Echoing Deuteronomy 6:5 and Leviticus 19:18, Philo argues that in the Mosaic law there are two main ideas (δύο κεφάλαια) that rise above all the rest, the first being one's conduct towards God shown in piety and holiness (εὐσεβίας καὶ ὁσιότητος), and one's conduct towards one's neighbor ruled by the rules of humanity and justice (φιλανθρωπίας καὶ δικαιοσύνης). Sanders observes that Philo discusses two sets of five commandments each, one set oriented to God, and the other to neighbor.[280] For Philo then, the Jewish people were to keep the law of Moses, demonstrating lives of virtue towards both God and neighbor.[281]

Cohen, *Philo Judaeus: His Universe of Discourse* [New York: Peter Lang, 1995], 286-87). Cohen says of Philo, "We are justified in concluding that there is every reason to look upon Philo as a distinguished representative of the contemporary Alexandrian version of 'normative Judaism'" (287). One essential point of her research is that Philo regarded obedience to the law on the literal level to be rudimentary.

[276]Hay, "Philo," 378-79. Sanders comments on Philo's pilgrimage to Jerusalem (*Special Laws*, 1.141-4) and that Philo "emphasized not only his own devotion but that of the Palestinians. He contrasted the taxes paid by compulsion in the rest of the Graeco-Roman world with those that supported the Jerusalem temple, which were paid 'gladly and cheerfully,' and which were so abundant that even the poorest priests were 'exceedingly well-to-do" (E. P. Sanders, *Judaism*, 52). He adds that Philo goes on to describe the sacrificial system in "loving detail, emphasizing its spiritual and ethical value" (ibid.). See Philo, *Special Laws*, 1.76; 66-345.

[277]Martens, "Philo and the 'Higher Law,'" 320.

[278]Peder Borgen, "Philo of Alexandria," in *Jewish Writings of the Second Temple Period*, ed. Michael E. Stone (Philadelphia: Fortress, 1984), 233.

[279]Hay, "Philo," 374-75. See Philo, *Special Legislation* 4.143.

[280]E. P. Sanders, *Judaism*, 193-94. See Philo, *Who is Heir of Divine Things* 168-73.

[281]E. P. Sanders, *Judaism*, 192-95. In addition, in his discussion of νόμος in Philo, Gutbrod notes that for Philo the Decalogue is the "sum of the whole Law, and the basis of all else" (Gutbrod, "νόμος," 1054).

Conclusion

Philo has produced a vision of law that was unique in the Graeco-Roman world. First, in his apology to the Greek world he tied all forms of law to the written code of Moses, and argued that the law of Moses was superior over them all. Indeed, all forms of "higher law" are bound tightly to the Mosaic law.[282] The deity who gave the law of Moses is responsible for the law of nature, and therefore there is no tension between the two; they are in fact one and the same. Second, unique to Philo is his argument to the Greek world that the patriarchs of Judaism completely followed this "higher law" before its being written down by Moses. These men were themselves a living embodiment of the law (and thus virtue). Third, there is a high view of the written law of Moses in Philo's writings. Fourth, all Jewish people were to follow it and obey it: obedience brings blessing, and disobedience brings judgment. Finally, Philo is a bit more elastic in his use of νόμος than some of the other literature examined in the present study. However, the Mosaic law written in the Pentateuch is the chief referent for νόμος, and whenever Philo spoke of other laws (such as the law codes of other nations or the law of nature), the idea of the Mosaic law was never far from his mind. Again, Philo tied *all* forms of law to the Mosaic law.

The Dead Sea Scrolls

Introduction

The final strand of evidence comes from the writings of the Qumran community.[283] Generally speaking, there is significant agreement among Qumran scholars that the community saw itself as the true remnant of Israel and people of God who have a new covenant and the correct understanding of the written Mosaic Torah/law.[284] The following is a discussion of two of the

---

[282]Martens, "Philo and the 'Higher Law,'" 321.

[283]Unless noted, all translations of the DSS are those of Florentino García Martinez and Eibert J. C. Tigchelaar, eds, *The Dead Sea Scrolls Study Edition*, 2 vols. (Leiden: Brill, 2000).

[284]See Nickelsburg, *Jewish Literature*, 122-60; Devorah Dimant, "Qumran Sectarian Literature," in *Jewish Writings of the Second Temple Period*, ed. Michael Stone (Philadelphia: Fortress, 1984), 483-550; E. P. Sanders, *Paul and Palestinian Judaism*, 239-57; Joseph Blenkinsopp, *Wisdom and Law*, 107-29; Wayne McCready, "A Second Torah at Qumran?" *SR* 14.1 (1985): 5-16; Sidnie White Crawford, "Lady Wisdom and Dame Folly at Qumran," *DSD* 5 (1993): 355-65; Jack Sanders, "Sacred Canopies," 126-27; Johannes A. Huntjens, "Contrasting Notions of Covenant and Law in the Texts from Qumran," *RevQ* 8.3 (1974): 361-80; Philip R. Davies, "Who Can Join the 'Damascus Covenant'?" *JJS* 46 (1995): 134-42; Bockmuehl, *Jewish Law*, 104; W. D. Davies, *Torah in the Messianic Age*, 45-47 (especially regarding his notes on the Damascus Document); Moore, *Judaism in the First Centuries of the Christian Era*, 1:271.

most significant documents from the Qumran sect[s], the *Community Rule* (1QS), and the *Damascus Document* (CD).[285] These two important documents sufficiently answer the present question regarding the understanding and status of law (תּוֹרָה) at Qumran.

The Community Rule (1QS)

The discussion of the Torah/law in 1QS should begin with a lengthy citation from the document itself: 1QS 5:7-11.[286] In speaking of the "rule for the men of

---

Huntjens is most interested in the eschatological underpinnings of the community. He argues that "Torah obedience and faith in eschatological mysteries" existed side by side "without...conflict" (Huntjens, "Contrasting Notions," 379). He lists the following excerpts to parlay his point: 1QS 10:25; 9:23-26; 1QS 1:1ff; 1 QpHab. 8:1-3, 10-11, 18; 1QH 16, 6, 7, 13, 15. He concludes, "The whole object of their intensive legalism and searching of the Torah was to be ready for the eschaton" (380). For Huntjens, the Torah referred to at Qumran is indeed the written Torah of Moses, i.e. the Pentateuch. It is distinct from the prophets and the rest of the Jewish Scripture (380). Contra Fabry (Heinz-Josef Fabry, "Der Begriff 'Tora' in der Tempelrolle," *RevQ* 18.1 [1997]: 63-72) who attempts to demonstrate from 4QMMT that the term "torah" was not yet an explicit reference to the Mosaic Pentateuch, and that the *Temple Scroll* understands itself to actually be the canonical Torah (63). This thesis has not been widely supported.

[285]One could add to this list 11Q Temple, 4QMMT, or excerpts from the biblical commentaries found at Qumran such as 1QpHab (esp. on Hab 2:4 where "living by faith" is understood to mean observance of the Torah and faith in the "Teacher of Righteousness"). There is also the familiar connection between those who are wise and those who follow תּוֹרָה in 4Q525 2:3-4; the adherence to the written code concerning mixed clothing fibers in 4Q418 103:6-9; or 4Q419 1:1-2 that states, "which you will do in accordance with all the prece[pts...] to you by the hand of Moses." J. Sanders cautiously suggests that this citation perhaps points to an even closer adherence to the Mosaic Torah than even what was discovered in Sirach (J. Sanders, "Sacred Canopies," 127).

Geza Vermes summarizes the Qumran outlook on the Mosaic law and its commands when he cites from 1QpHab 7:9, "If it (the end) tarries, wait for it, for it shall surely come and shall not be late (Hab. 2:3)–Interpreted, this concerns the men of truth who keep the Law, whose hands shall not slacken in the service of truth when the final age is prolonged" (Geza Vermes, *The Dead Sea Scrolls-Qumran in Perspective* [London: William Collins and Sons, 1977], 214). Gathercole echoes this finding and singles out 1QpHab 8:1, which speaks of "those who do Torah" (Gathercole, *Where Is Boasting?*, 95).

[286]The Community Rule document is likely a compilation of several writings which were collected over time, thus forming the present document. Though much could be said regarding the various strata of 1QS, it is beyond the scope of the present chapter. For a discussion of the development of 1QS see Jérôme Murphy-O'Conner, "La genèse littéraire de la Regle de la Communauté," *RB* 76 (1969): 528-49; Claus-Hunno Hunzinger, "Beobachtung zur Erwicklung der Disziplinarordnung der Gemeinde von Qumran," in *Qumran-Probleme*, ed. Hans Bardtke, Deutsche Akademie der

the Community who freely volunteer to convert from all evil" (and thereby join the Community, 5:1-2), the document states,

> These are the regulations of their behaviour concerning all these decrees when they are enrolled in the Community. Whoever enters the council of the Community enters the covenant of God in the presence of all who freely volunteer. He shall swear with a binding oath to revert to the Law of Moses, according to all that he commanded, with whole heart and whole soul, in compliance with all that has been revealed of it to the sons of Zadok, the priests who keep the covenant and interpret his will and to the multitude of the men of their covenant who freely volunteer together for this truth and to walk according to his will. He should swear by the covenant to be segregated from all the men of injustice who walk along the path of wickedness. For they are not included in his covenant since they have neither sought nor examined his decrees in order to know the hidden matters in which they err.

Citing this text, Blenkinsopp argues that the written code of the Pentateuch was the basis for all rules and law of the Qumran community. Though the whole of the Pentateuch was the usual referent of תּוֹרָה in 1QS, there was, however, a specific emphasis on the commands found within the Pentateuch itself.[287] In fact, Blenkinsopp repeatedly emphasizes that the "law" that was followed was in fact the *written law*, which in the Second Temple period specifically came to refer to the Pentateuch.[288]

What is notable in 1QS 5:1-2 is that the Qumranites freely bound themselves to the written commands of the law of Moses and thereby became part of this "new covenant" community.[289] The Mosaic law was to be followed and strictly obeyed by all members of the Qumran sect. In fact, should one member break one of the commandments of the law of Moses, even by carelessness, that member was banished from the community council and would not be associated with by any other of the "men of holiness."[290] However, if the

---

Wissenschaften Zu Berlin 42 (Berlin: Akademie, 1963), 231-45. Jean Pouilly, "Evolution de la legislation pénale dans la communauté de Qumrân," *RB* 82 (1975): 522-51; Christoph Dohmen, "Zur Gründung der Gemeinde von Qumran (1QS 8-9)," *RevQ* 11.1 (1982): 81-96; Nickelsburg, *Jewish Literature*, 133.

[287]Blenkinsopp, *Wisdom and Law*, 120, 128. See also Nickelsburg, *Jewish Literature*, 133-37.

[288]Blenkinsopp, *Wisdom and Law*, 109-27. See also Westerholm, *Law in Religious Communities*, 48.

[289]To be part of the "new covenant" community, one pledged himself to keep the law of the OC. Thus, the covenant is not new, but is either a renewal or displacement of the covenant with Israel. As seen elsewhere in the literature, covenant and law are related, but not synonymous. One enters into the covenant, and pledges himself to obey the commands of the law. See also 1QS 8:5-17.

[290]1QS 8:20-23.

individual broke a law through oversight, he could be reinstated, but only after two years of perfect conduct.[291] What is frequently noted in 1QS 5:7-11 is the statement found in 5:8-9, which states that the members of the community bound themselves to the written law of Moses, but also they must live "in compliance with all that has been revealed of it to the sons of Zadok, the priests." The community had the written law of Moses, and believed that they had also received the proper *interpretation* of the law as well. The text of 1QS 8:10-12 mandates that those who are to become priests in the community must first spend two full years in perfect adherence to the Torah, which is "the law which was commanded through the hand of Moses" (1QS 8:15). To the priests of the community (the "sons of Zadok") has been revealed the *halakhoth* that require obedience if one is to belong to the community and the covenant. It must be noted that though the community members are to follow the Torah-understanding set forth by the sons of Zadok, these *halakhoth* are not contrary to the written law of Moses. This is not surprising in any way, since such a view can be found within *any* religious community, ancient or modern.[292] Blenkinsopp is likely correct when

---

[291] 1QS 8:24-26.

[292] Geza Vermes agrees and points to the example of Ezra and Nehemiah in Israel's history, when "Ezra and his colleagues, the ancient scribes of Israel, 'read from the book of the Law...made its sense plain and gave instruction in what was read" (Vermes, *Dead Sea Scrolls*, 166). Vermes points out the significant parallels between the Torah-interpretation of ancient Israel and the Torah-interpretation of the Qumran sect.

With this in mind, one must take issue with McCready's analysis (McCready, "A Second Torah," 5-16). Broadly speaking, McCready is correct in his observation based on a study of 1QS and CD that the Qumran Community did interpret the law of Moses and that these interpretations were to be followed. Yet based on 1:3-4:9 he argues for a "second-phase Torah," and based on texts such as 1QS 1:1-3a and 5:7-12, argues that the interpretation of the community was to be obeyed as much as the inherited Torah of Moses if one was to be considered clean. McCready is mainly correct in his assertions, though he seems to read such texts as these as though the community's interpretations/applications of the law of Moses were actually in *contrast* to the law of Moses, and this does not follow from the evidence he attempts to marshal. He writes, "The Mosaic Torah was the starting point for religious claims but the activity and presence of Qumran made the Torah understandable and complete" (8). However, he adds that the community added to and subtracted from the Mosaic Torah when necessary in light of new revelation from God in favor of the Torah "rightly understood" (14). Again, if this is the case he has not proven his thesis from the supplied evidence. He goes on to argue that such new revelations/interpretations of Torah were often more authoritative than Moses' Torah (14), and thus there was "a Torah" at Qumran (the Pentateuch) and there was "the Torah" (i.e., the community library). (Here he reticently follows Ben Zion Wacholder, *The Dawn of Qumran: The Sectarian Torah and the Teacher of Righteousness* [Cincinnati: Hebrew Union College Press, 1983].) He concludes his article by noting that even though the Mosaic Torah has a chronological

he notes, "Their lives were governed by a strict interpretation of the laws, especially the laws of purity, in addition to which they cherished their own esoteric teachings which they were bound by the most solemn oaths not to disclose."[293] This much is clear even from a cursory reading of the documents. Yet it must be reiterated that such Torah-interpretations are not unexpected in a zealous religious group that sees itself as the remnant of Israel living in the end times awaiting the Messianic Age dedicated to living in complete obedience to the written law of Moses. Given that they were displaced from Jerusalem, such interpretations are not only understandable, but expected.

In addition, such interpretations and explanations of the Mosaic law were necessary given that the six hundred and thirteen positive and negative commandments in the law do not provide for all the problems that the Qumran community encountered. This is especially true for those situations that arose in the centuries following the enactment of biblical legislation.[294] Regarding the interpretations of the Torah followed by the community, it is clear that some of these interpretations were at times stricter than even that of the Pharisees.[295] Elliott agrees with this summation, observing at Qumran a heightened attention to law-keeping. He asserts, "At Qumran the heightening of the authority of the Hebrew Scriptures was accompanied by what is referred to as the 'radicalization of Torah obedience,' an intense attempt to fulfill every jot and tittle of the Law."[296] The community alone possessed the true interpretations of the Scriptures.

Gathercole is enlightening on this point, affirming the central role of the Mosaic law at Qumran. He argues from 1QS for the law's centrality to the life of the community. His main focus is on how obedience to the law effects final vindication and judgment. Language of eschatological reward for the righteous (those who are obedient to the Torah and its interpretation) and recompense for

---

priority over the community interpretations/applications, "community membership must ultimately rest with an allegiance to the Qumran library" (McCready, "A Second Torah," 15). The issue here is that he offers no specific examples to support this particular claim (that the interpretations were actually *more* authoritative than the Torah law itself).

[293]Blenkinsopp, *Wisdom and Law*, 126-27. Here one can see the importance of the Mosaic laws in addition to the community's own teachings and rules.

[294]Vermes, *Dead Sea Scrolls*, 165-66; contra McCready.

[295]For example the Pharisees would allow an animal to be pulled out of a pit on the Sabbath (Matt 12:11), while the community forbade it (see CD 11:13-14). See also the Qumran prohibition against an uncle marrying his niece. This was licit in Pharisaic and rabbinic Judaism (such a tradition survives in the Talmud [bYebamoth 62b]), but seen to be fornication in the Qumran sect (CD 5:7-9). Vermes, *Dead Sea Srolls*, 166-67.

[296]Elliott, *Survivors of Israel*, 120.

the wicked is frequent in the Qumran literature.[297] Sanders is to be eschewed at this point, who seeks to draw a distinction between final salvation and rewards for the righteous.[298] Yet as Gathercole concludes, "1QS 4 shows that final salvation *is* the reward."[299]

Further, the *Community Rule* affirms that the Mosaic Torah was studied communally. In 1QS 6:6-8 the Torah is defined specifically as the written book of the law, which was studied as a group. While "searching the Torah...specific commandments (*mishpatim*) emerge from this study and then [were] shared and decided upon in the community."[300] These are the rules that govern the day-to-day internal life of the sect (1QS 6:24b-7:25). Yet Huntjens is likely correct when he points out that the community saw itself as recipients of revelation from God that was in addition to the Mosaic law. "The 'revealed things' are the laws which are stated in the Torah [of Moses] in clear terms or which have been gradually clarified by the sect so that they can be stated in unequivocal terms as established maxims to be followed."[301] Such things are revealed to the community by God through a careful searching of the Torah of Moses and all that is revealed in it.[302] He concludes, "To be obedient to the new covenant is to follow the rules and regulations which have been laid down by the sect as a result of its exegetical decisions."[303] Thus, one must obey the written Mosaic

---

[297]Gathercole, *Where Is Boasting?*, 97. See 1QS 10:18; 1QS 3-4; 1QSb 2:23. Perhaps one of the most telling citations for Gathercole comes from 4QMMT (C 23-25), which Gathercole cites on several occasions. It reads, "Remember the kings of Israel and contemplate their deeds: whoever among them feared the Torah was delivered from troubles; and these were seekers of the Torah whose transgressions were forgiven. Think of David who was a man of righteous deeds and who was therefore delivered from many troubles and was forgiven" (233).

[298]E. P. Sanders, *Paul and Palestinian Judaism*, 318-21.

[299]Gathercole, *Where Is Boasting?*, 97 (emphasis his).

[300]Huntjens, "Contrasting Notions," 365.

[301]Ibid., 368. This is the basic thrust of McCready's article as well, "A Second Torah at Qumran." He argues that the primary reference of תּוֹרָה was the Mosaic law, but on a secondary level can at times refer to the instructional writings of the community (5-6; see discussion above). Blenkinsopp is a bit more reserved in his conclusions than McCready, and asserts that the community interpretations of the Mosaic law were not *more* authoritative than the Torah of Moses itself (contra McCready), since they were all *based* on it (Blenkinsopp, *Wisdom and Law*, 125-27).

[302]Note 1QS 5:8; 1QS 8:15; 1QS 9:1ff.; 1QS 13:19.

[303]Huntjens, "Contrasting Notions," 378. The end purpose of such legalistic obedience is to prepare the community for the eschaton. He adds that at Qumran, covenant and Torah/law are not the same. One is in the covenant so long as he or she obeys the laws of the Torah and the community (368). Bockmuehl writes that the covenant spoken of in 1QS is a defining characteristic of the sect, and "has become more particularly the sect's own exclusive alliance devoted to Torah observance" (Markus Bockmuehl, "1QS and Salvation at Qumran," in *Justification and Variegated Nomism*, vol. 1, *The Complexities*

law as well as specific community applications based on the law.

One must be careful when reading 1QS (along with the other Qumran documents) not to set the written Mosaic Torah over against such community rules and interpretations based on the Torah, as if the two are in conflict (contra McCready). The community venerated the law of Moses, and did not see itself as denigrating the written revelation of the law or its innate authority given that the law of Moses was their guide.[304] They did, however, as seen in 1QS, see themselves as the true remnant of Israel who were separate from Gentiles and the remainder of the Jewish people. According to Bockmuehl, they were members of the sectarian community whose defining characteristic was the idea of covenant, *"over against* the nation (and of course the nations) at large" (emphasis his).[305] Elliott notes that at Qumran there existed an expressed desire

---

of Second Temple Judaism, ed. D. A. Carson, Peter T. O'Brien, and Mark A. Seifrid [Grand Rapids: Baker, 2001], 389).

[304]To be sure, the newly revealed secrets of the Qumran community were given by the Zadokite priests who controlled the exegesis of the Mosaic law by which such secrets are now revealed. This is part of what distinguishes this covenant community from the Mosaic covenant community, most of which were destroyed due to their lack of obedience (E. P. Sanders, *Paul and Palestinian Judaism,* 241-42). If one was to be found righteous and pure, then it required a physical separation from the rest of the Jewish people, and a pledging of oneself to the law of Moses and to the Qumran community. The community then set themselves to prepare for the coming eschaton and the judgment of the righteous and the wicked. See also E. P. Sanders, "Law in Judaism of the NT Period," 261.

[305]Bockmuehl, "1QS and Salvation at Qumran," 389. Whether or not the covenant of the Qumran community was understood as a renewal or replacement is not the central question being asked here, yet it is related. See Bockmuehl, "1QS and Salvation at Qumran," 390-92, who argues for renewal. For the perspective that the new covenant had displaced the covenant with Israel, see Seifrid, *Justification by Faith,* 88-90.

Elliott argues that the fact that there is a mention of a "new covenant" in the DSS indicates their dynamic view of covenant (that "covenant" was not a static idea not subject to alteration). Whatever the "new covenant" of Damascus, the Mosaic covenant appeared to possess continuing validity for the Qumran Community (Elliott, *Survivors of Israel,* 253). He adds that the evidence is best read in terms of a covenant that is distinctly new "rather than being merely a restatement or even a renewal of the Mosaic covenant" (257). Elliott qualifies this statement slightly (256-57), not wanting to rule out the possibility that there may be some overlap with earlier covenants. See also Annie Jaubert, *La notion d' alliance dans le Judaïsme aux abords de l'ère chrétienne,* PatS 6 (Paris: Éditions du Seuil, 1963), 216-17; 222, and Jürgen Becker, *Das Heil Gottes. Heils- und Sündenbegriffe in den Qumrantexten und im Neuen Testament,* SUNT 3 (Göttingen, Vandenhoeck & Ruprecht, 1964), 65. Becker writes, "Der Lehrer der Gerechtigkeit kann diesen Bund sogar als seinen Bund bezeichnen. Doch lassen sich diese Aussagen nicht so verstehen, als sei hier ein neuer Bund, ein anderer als der Väterbund gemeint, vielmehr kann vom Bund auch ganz allgemein so gesprochen

to define the covenant participants by defining themselves over against other groups in Israel, as well as articulating the necessity to keep certain vital laws, adding additional stipulations, and adherence to the calendar.[306] They alone had the true revelation of the Torah as well as the correct interpretation of it. Their task was to align themselves with the law while awaiting the final judgment of the impending eschaton.[307]

Thus, in 1QS the Torah is the written law of Moses, and was to be strictly obeyed without reservation if one was to be in the "new covenant" community. All ties with outsiders, even fellow Jews, had to be severed since they stand outside of the covenant (1QS 5:10-11). They were required to "obey the Torah, following the 'revealed' *halahkoth* which are set down by the (Zadokite) priests of the Community."[308] Over and above all sociological factors is the "*theological* factor of the need to obey Torah in order to be vindicated and rewarded on the last day. This theological matrix has been demonstrated in abundance."[309]

The Damascus Document (CD)

Much of what was seen in the above discussion of the *Community Rule* (1QS) is also present in the *Damascus Document* (CD).[310] The *Damascus Document* is comprised of two clearly defined parts.[311] It contains (1) admonitions based on

---

werden, daß deutlich wird, daß Israel den von Gottes Seite her noch bestehenden Bund gebrochen hat und nicht mehr in ihm wandelt, die neue Heilsgemeinde aber wieder in ihm steht." What both Jaubert and Becker suggest is that what is in view at Qumran is a second *phase* of the Mosaic covenant.

[306]Elliott, *Survivors of Israel*, 250. For the significance of the calendar at Qumran, see also 151-52; 159-61.

[307]For example see 1QS 4:2-14. One's eschatological reward or judgment was based upon one's obedience. Nickelsburg (*Jewish Literature*, 135-36) observes that eternal rewards and punishments are "closely paralleled in the eschatological sections of apocalyptic writings." See also Dimant, "Qumran Sectarian Literature," 498; Gathercole, *Where Is Boasting?*, 95-100; 108-11.

[308]Nickelsburg, *Jewish Literature*, 134.

[309]Gathercole, *Where Is Boasting?*, 110. He concludes, "Final judgment on the basis of works [obedience to the law] permeates Jewish theology, Qumran included" (111).

[310]First discovered by Solomon Schechter in 1910, the Damascus Document is dated approximately to the middle of the first century B.C.E. (Vermes, *Dead Sea Scrolls*, 48-49). For a brief overview of the history of research and the state of the discussion up to 1992, see Joseph M. Baumgarten, "The Laws of the *Damascus Document* in Current Research," in *The Damascus Document Reconsidered*, ed. Magen Broshi (Jerusalem: Israel Exploration Society, 1992), 51-62.

[311]See Nickelsburg, *Jewish Literature*, 123-24; Charlotte Hempel, *The Damascus Texts*, CQS 1 (Sheffield: Academic Press, 2000), 26-27. For a concise description of these two parts, see the helpful article by J. M. Baumgarten (J. M. Baumgarten, "Damascus

history, and (2) specific commandments for the community life.[312] Indeed, as
Davies asserts, the righteousness demanded by the written Mosaic Torah is in
no way different from that which was commanded in the *Community Rule*.[313]
Gathercole likewise asserts that CD (along with 1QS and 4QMMT)
fundamentally teaches that the Mosaic law must be obeyed.[314] Like 1QS, the
community understood itself to be the true covenant people. They alone had the
correct understanding of Torah.[315] In their own self-definition, this is what set
them apart from other sectarian/remnant groups.[316]

: The *Damascus Document* begins by denouncing the opponents of the
Teacher of Righteousness. As CD 1:18-2:1 states, this is because the opponents
"sought easy interpretations, chose illusions, scrutinised loopholes, chose the
handsome neck, acquitted the guilty and sentenced the just...their soul
abominated all those who walk in perfection...and kindled was the wrath of

---

Document," in *Encyclopedia of the Dead Sea Scrolls*, ed. Lawrence H. Schiffman and
James C. VanderKam [Oxford: University Press, 2000], 1:166-70).

[312]Baumgarten writes, "Admonition in CD is primarily that of an introduction to the
laws" (Baumgarten, "The Laws of the *Damascus Document*," 52). He adds, "The
Admonition, which repeatedly calls for adherence to the proper interpretation of the
Law, is thus to be viewed as essentially an introduction to a corpus of Torah
interpretation and sectarian rulings" (55). See pp. 53-55.

It is important to emphasize that it is the written as opposed to an oral law that is
revered and followed at Qumran. In a separate essay he notes, "It is hardly accidental
that in the Qumran corpus of laws, now augmented by Cave 4 materials, there is never
any mention of authoritative tradents from the past" (J. M. Baumgarten, "Sadducean
Elements in Qumran Law," in *The Community of the Renewed Covenant: The Notre
Dame Symposium on the Dead Sea Scrolls*, ed. Eugene Ulrich and James Vanderkam,
CJAS 10 [Notre Dame, IN: University of Notre Dame Press, 1994], 33). Given the
community's desire to separate from the Jerusalem form of "compromised" Judaism and
to practice true religion, this is no surprise. Such "traditions of the elders" would have
been met with suspicion in a community who desired to be separate from Jerusalem's
form of Judaism. See also Blenkinsopp, *Wisdom and Law*, 107-29. See also Dimant,
"Qumran Sectarian Literature," 490-91; Nickelsburg, *Jewish Literature*, 123; Vermes,
Dead Sea Scrolls, 49-50.

[313]W. D. Davies, *Torah in the Messianic Age*, 47-48. He concludes that there would be
no denigration of the Mosaic Torah in the Messianic Age (in which the Qumranites saw
themselves), rather, the commandments would be "better studied and better observed
than ever before; and this was indubitably the common belief" (48).

[314]Gathercole, *Where Is Boasting?*, 97, 99-102. He adds that it must be obeyed if one
expects to receive salvation at the eschaton.

[315]Nickelsburg, *Jewish Literature*, 123. It is important to note that the community saw
its specific interpretations and applications of the Mosaic Torah as coming from God
himself (CD-B 19:1-6).

[316]Dimant, "Qumran Sectarian Literature," 490-91; Nickelsburg, *Jewish Literature*, 123;
Vermes, *Dead Sea Scrolls*, 49-50; Elliott, *Survivors of Israel*, 250.

God." The opponent of the community is labeled "the scoffer" (CD 1:14), and such an enemy of the community is set in contrast to the remnant. The righteous are those few "who remained steadfast in God's precepts" (CD 3:12), to whom God establishes his covenant, and to whom he reveals "hidden matters in which all Israel had gone astray" (CD 3:14).[317] The secret will of God has been revealed to the remnant, and its author is clear in his command for the people to obey.[318] In addition, other hidden matters concerning the feasts and sabbaths are now revealed, along with what "man must do in order to live by them" (CD 3:14-16).

This passage (CD 3:14-16) likely alludes to Leviticus 18:5. Elliott observes that the writer has gone well beyond the sense of the Deuteronomic idea of earthly recompense and has attributed "spiritual and timeless significance" to the term "life" in the phrase.[319] What is being granted is *eternal life* for those who obey the Torah and the community's authoritative interpretations. The text seems to assert that life will be granted to those who live in obedience to the law and to the regulations of the community. Gathercole contends that what is in view here is not *regulation* (to live "by them"), but rather a promise. "The contrast is not obedience-disobedience (living by them or not living by them) but rather life or not life (reward-punishment)."[320] The context supports such an interpretation, given that CD 3:20 appears to explain the term "life" of CD 3:14-16. It reads, "Those who remained steadfast in it will acquire eternal life, and all the glory of Adam is for them." One clearly sees the centrality of the law and obedience to it and to the community interpretation. If Elliott and Gathercole are correct (contra Sanders), the stakes could not be higher: eschatological salvation is granted *only* to those who are obedient to the law.

Further, this group believed that they had received the proper interpretation of the Torah (akin to 1QS), and therefore were to keep its commands (CD 3:14). This "proper interpretation of Torah" is described in CD 6:3-4 as "digging a well." "The well is the law, and those who dug it are the converts of Israel." Nickelsburg writes, "When the majority in Israel strays this group remains faithful."[321] This remnant in Israel (as they saw themselves)[322] dug deep into the waters of the Torah, and thus "whoever spurns them (the

---

[317]Note especially Elliott, *Survivors of Israel*, 133.

[318]Gathercole, *Where Is Boasting?*, 100.

[319]Elliott, *Survivors of Israel*, 117-18. See also Gathercole, *Where Is Boasting?*, 100-02.

[320]Gathercole, *Where Is Boasting?*, 101. See also 4QD[a]. He argues that if doing the commandments brings life, then martyrdom does not achieve such a goal. In short, the "reference is to life in the age to come" (102). Contra Sanders (*Paul and Palestinian Judaism*, 295) whose only comment is to read this text through the lens of his covenantal nomism, with no comment on 3:20. Gathercole is thus critical, "Sanders has again set up the question to get the desired answer" (*Where Is Boasting?*, 102).

[321]Nickelsburg, *Jewish Literature*, 124.

[322]Elliott, *Survivors of Israel*, 116-17.

stipulations of the law) will not live" (CD 3:17).

As seen in the preceding discussion of 1QS, CD affirms the same kind of radical adherence to the written Mosaic law and the community's strict interpretations. The community, which saw itself as living in the age of wickedness, must "take care to act in accordance with the exact interpretation of the law" (CD 6:14). The text states explicit laws in 6:15-21 that must be fully carried out by every member, and are part of the specific laws and communal rules that comprise the second aspect of the contents of CD.[323] Such laws include: abstaining from wealth which defiles, stealing from the poor or from widows, murdering orphans, keeping the Sabbath, keeping the festivals and the day of fasting, loving one's brother, and strengthening the hand of the poor.[324] From this list one can see that such commands as these are anchored in the Mosaic law. This was a community committed to the law of Moses, and to applying its "just stipulations and truthful paths" to the daily life of the covenant community (CD 3:15). This section of the document (CD 6:11-7:10) reiterates the point that the covenant community is summoned to their responsibility to live according to the Torah and the community's strict understanding of it, and if they were to receive blessing and not judgment, then such obedience was mandatory. Many of the specific rules listed here find their basis in the Holiness Code of Leviticus 17-26, which promises for those who despise these matters that God will "empty over them the punishment of the wicked" when he "visits the earth" (CD 7:9).[325]

Finally, CD goes on to speak of those who are now former members due to their turning their backs on the law and thus the community and God (CD-B 19:33b-20:1a), of the temporary expulsion of disobedient members who are cursed by the assembly (CD-B 20:1b-8a), and of the condemnation of those members who have fully turned their backs on the covenant community (CD-B 20:8b-13a). Some of the harshest judgment language has been reserved for this

---

[323]The body of laws can be broken down into two further categories, (1) interpretations of religious laws, and (2) specific regulations in the community. Some are based on exegesis of specific Torah texts, such as the prohibition against polygamy and the marriage union of an uncle to his niece. However, many of the laws given in this section of CD are not stated alongside specific OT references. This is similar in practice to the Mishnah, but are listed under specific topic headings such as water purification (CD 10:10), the Sabbath (CD 10:14), and the oath of a woman (CD 16:10). Qumran scholarship still debates significant aspects of the contents and placements of the laws, both religious and communal.

[324]For additional regulations such as those that govern purification-atonement at Qumran, see Elliott, *Survivors of Israel*, 163-66; Lawrence H. Schiffman, *Sectarian Law in the Dead Sea Scrolls: Courts, Testimony, and the Penal Code*, BJS 33 (Chico, CA: Scholars Press, 1983), 216.

[325]Nickelsburg, *Jewish Literature*, 125. See especially CD 7:4b-6a.See also CD-B 19:29-35. Cf. 1QS 6:24-7:25; Elliott, *Survivors of Israel*, 63; 269 n. 61.

last group. They have idols in their "stubborn hearts" (9b-10a), and "for them there shall be *no part* in the house of the law" (10b).[326] Turning aside from the community meant a turning aside from the Torah and thus there was little hope for such individuals. As such, there is no other place where one might turn having left the community; eschatological judgment awaits all who apostatize. In summary, such texts make it clear that the Qumranites saw themselves as the lone remnant preserved by God; they alone have the Torah and its interpretation.

Conclusion: The Community Rule (1QS) and the Damascus Document (CD)

In conclusion, it seems clear that both 1QS and CD assert a high view of the written Mosaic Torah and the community's strict interpretation of it. Its understanding of Torah and the community's view of itself led to an exclusivist soteriology. Elliott concludes, "A more transparent exposition of a soteriology that is fundamentally exclusivist could hardly be imagined than what we have seen in the Community Rule and the Damascus Document."[327] At this point several broad conclusions can be drawn from the preceding research.

First, "Torah" is most often equal to the written Torah of Moses, i.e., the Pentateuch. Huntjens rightly argues that it is distinct from the prophets and the rest of the Scripture in the minds of the Qumranites.[328] Blenkinsopp, too, has concluded that the Torah at Qumran was indeed the Pentateuch, and specifically its laws.[329] However, one cannot maintain that the term תּוֹרָה at Qumran *only* served as a referent to the written Mosaic law with absolute certainty. The present research has had to be broad and thus not exhaustive, researching only two of the largest and most significant documents, 1QS and CD.[330] Therefore this writer cannot say one way or another that in *every* use of תּוֹרָה in the Qumran library, the written law was the intended referent. With qualification, however, it may be stated that תּוֹרָה generally refers to the written law of Moses as Huntjens maintains. But given the community's understanding

---

[326]The exclusivity of the group is nowhere more clearly seen than in this phrase, התורה בבית. The community saw itself as the only one to properly revere, understand, and follow the Mosaic law.

[327]Elliott, *Survivors of Israel*, 118. He adds that what is a stake is the eternal destiny of the individual based upon individual choice and not upon national election (contra E. P. Sanders).

[328]Huntjens, "Contrasting Notions," 380. Huntjens' conclusions are based on a more detailed study than the two significant documents addressed here. It is significant that he has concluded that the referent is the *written* law of Moses.

[329]Blenkinsopp, *Wisdom and Law*, 128.

[330]However, this writer proposes that other documents such as 11QTemple and 4QMMT would complement the present conclusions.

that they alone held the proper interpretation of the Mosaic law, it seems possible and even likely that at times תּוֹרָה included more than what was written by Moses (but never *less*), encapsulating community interpretation as well as what was written "by the hand of Moses."

Second, this community was clearly devoted to the study of the written law and to its observance.[331] In fact, "the Qumran community apparently attached greater importance to the strict observance of the Mosaic law than did their contemporary Jewish colleagues in Judea."[332]

Third, the community held to a strict interpretation of the written law.[333] However, since the law's commands do not extend to every aspect of Jewish life, there needed to be an authoritative interpretation and application of the individual laws if the pious Jew of the elect remnant community was to be truly pious according to the Torah.

Fourth, the community saw themselves as the *only group* properly following the Mosaic Torah.[334] They saw themselves as following the law of the Most High—the wise guide for all human conduct for the Qumran community.[335]

Fifth, with these broad deductions in mind, one may conclude that for the Qumranites the Torah of Moses was clearly elevated to an elite status. To be part of the community, to be part of the remnant, to be part of the righteous ones, and to be seen as the true people of God, one must pledge himself or herself fully to the Mosaic Torah and to the community. They saw their commitment to be distinct from the rest of the Jews in Judea—their own commitment to the commands of the Mosaic law as a community/remnant

---

[331]Vermes contends, "their paramount aim was to pledge themselves to observe its precepts with absolute faithfulness," and "all the Jews in the inter-Testamental era...agreed that true piety entails obedience to the Law" (Vermes, *The Dead Sea Scrolls*, 165). See also Fitzmyer, *The Dead Sea Scrolls*, 35; 1QS 8:14-16.

[332]Fitzmyer, *The Dead Sea Scrolls*, 252. This conclusion is based on Fitzmyer's analysis of 4QMMT, but the same conclusion is warranted from a study of 1QS and CD. For instance, based on 1QS alone, Nickelsburg comes to the same conclusion (Nickelsburg, *Jewish Literature*, 134).

[333]Vermes writes, "Without an authentic interpretation it was not possible properly to understand the Torah" (Vermes, *The Dead Sea Scrolls*, 165). See 4QBeat where such obedience is extolled.

[334]This parallels the overall thesis of Elliott's *Survivors of Israel*. The idea of a national election is not sufficient for understanding Judaism during the Second Temple period given the number of dissident groups (such as the Qumranites). These groups each thought of themselves as the elect, the remnant, who alone will ultimately experience salvation and therefore vindication for their sectarianism. See, for example, pp. 115-18, 250; passim.

[335]Fitzmyer, *The Dead Sea Scrolls*, 116. Note the connection to wisdom. See also Bockmuehl, "1QS and Salvation at Qumran," 386.

eclipsed their fellow Jews.[336] The law of Moses was the foundation and starting point for all of life in the community.

Finally, the community not only venerated the law of Moses, but also sought to interpret it. They viewed themselves as living in the last days awaiting the eschaton. Such Torah interpretation played no small part in the life of the community as they sought to be righteous in the moments preceding the coming judgment. As Gathercole and Elliott have observed, obedience to the law led to life in the eschaton whereas disobedience led to judgment.

Conclusion

Conclusions here must be broadly stated, recognizing that there are certain nuances that have not been brought out in the preceding discussion. Drawing together the major strands of thought from the Apocrypha, Pseudepigrapha, Josephus, Philo, and two of the most important Qumran Scrolls leads to a theological backdrop for considering the theology of the Mosaic law in Hebrews 7:1-10:18.

Perhaps the following conclusions are *too* broad and conservative, but more restrictive conclusions are not fitting given the nature of the present study. One can see that several of the specific conclusions overlap one another. In general, each of the following conclusions is true of each of the five bodies of literature under investigation.

First, there is a high view and high regard for the law of Moses, defined as the written commands given to the people of Israel at Sinai. In none of the literature was there discovered to be a single denigration of the commandments, the νόμος, given to the people of Israel by the hand of Moses. Indeed, the law of Moses has an elite status in the Judaism of the Second Temple period.

Second, νόμος overwhelmingly refers to the written law of Moses, the Pentateuch. More specifically, there is a tendency for νόμος specifically to mean the commandments found in the Pentateuch, those given at Sinai, and not merely the five books of Moses as a whole.[337] This specificity is seen in the fact that many of the documents cite or clearly allude to specific written commandments in the law when referring to νόμος. This too is in keeping with our thesis relating to Hebrews, namely that when the writer speaks of νόμος, he is essentially speaking of specific commands found within the OC legislation,

---

[336]On the matter of various sects (one of which would be the Qumranites) viewing themselves as dissidents from the nation of Israel as a whole, see Elliott, *Survivors of Israel*, 187-243. For Elliott election for salvation is not nationalistic at its root (178-79).

[337]Though there are, to be sure, occasions when the Pentateuch is the referent for νόμος in the literature, as indicated above. Also recall Philo, in which it could refer to the laws of nature or of nations. Yet, Philo tied *all* forms of law to the Mosaic law.

and not necessarily the covenant itself.[338]

Third, it is clear that the Mosaic law held inherent authority in the literature discussed above. This is due to the fact that the common belief that God himself had authored and given the law to/through Moses. In each of the documents under examination this assumption is quite often made explicit. The commandments were divinely authoritative in and of themselves, and were thus to be obeyed. They were God's people to whom had been given this specific body of commands. An apology for the law was discovered in Philo and Josephus, yet even in such apologies one finds that the Mosaic law was authoritative in the life of the average Jew. This is not to suggest that all Jews were pious and law-keeping without exception, but there seems to be no reason to assume that Philo and Josephus purposefully misled their audiences when speaking of the importance and authority of the commands of the law in the life of the average Jew. There is the possibility (or probability) of some amount of exaggeration in the apologists, but it is unwarranted to dismiss their testimony out of hand. Thus the commands of the Mosaic law were in fact authoritative in Second Temple Judaism. The written law of Moses is the highest ethic and is central to life.

This leads to an obvious fourth conclusion. Speaking in broad terms, the Jewish laity was not unconcerned with the matters of the Mosaic law. It was not simply the Jewish leadership that was expected to follow the commandments and observe them, but this was also the expectation for the whole of the people. Recall that in 1 and 2 Maccabees, some died for their keeping specific laws, Philo and Josephus concur, and one could not even enter the Qumran community without pledging an oath to observe fully the Mosaic law. To be sure, one cannot argue that every Jew was pious according to the law, but neither can the argument be sustained that the average Jew was ignorant and unconcerned with the practice of the Mosaic law. The evidence does not support such a conclusion. All were expected to obey, even if some chose not to do so.

Fifth, Jewish piety of the period was directly connected with the law. If one was pious, then he kept the commands of the law. Blessings were expected for the righteous (i.e., those that kept the law), and infidelity to the law of the Lord was expected to bring judgment. This judgment was also clearly defined as *individual* judgment, specifically in the Apocrypha, Pseudepigrapha, and in 1QS and CD. In these groups of writings individual accountability is explicit.

---

[338]Given that the DSS are in Hebrew and not Greek, the term תּוֹרָה was determined to have the same basic and fundamental referent(s) as νόμος in the other literature under investigation. However, תּוֹרָה could at times refer to the interpretations and applications of the Mosaic commands, along with the commands themselves. It is noteworthy that the research did not discover that the referent of תּוֹרָה excluded the Mosaic laws, though sometimes it included interpretation and application.

Sixth, a common refrain was that the law of Moses was associated with and even equated with wisdom. While not a major theme throughout the literature, it deserves mention. This point is not unexpected. Given that the law was from God who is understood in Judaism as being all-wise, this is a logical corollary that receives some emphasis in the literature.

Finally, it should be noted that no identifiable parallels to Hebrews regarding the cessation of the practice of certain laws were discovered. The writer of Hebrews clearly sees that certain commands of the Mosaic law are no longer to be kept in light of the Christ event. On the contrary, the point made in the literature discussed here is that the law was to be fully obeyed in all of its parts. Thus, when the writer of Hebrews argues that God has given further revelation in the son (Heb 1:1-2) and that pious Jews are no longer to bring the blood of animals in keeping with the law of Moses (Heb 9), he is firmly at odds with the broader testimony of Second Temple Judaism.[339] This perhaps helps to explain some of the difficulties with the Jewish Christians who were struggling with what God had, on the one hand, legislated in the past, yet on the other, had now revealed in the "time of reformation" (Heb 9:10). Indeed such a struggle is understandable to a degree.

Yet the research suggests that there are similarities between the writer of Hebrews and the view of the law held by Second Temple Judaism. Themes such as the veneration of the Mosaic law, the recognition of its authority, and the confession that it has come from God are found in both Hebrews and Second Temple Judaism. Further, there are many individuals listed in the *exempla* of Hebrews 11 who followed the law (clearly, "by faith") and are seen to be righteous in God's sight. They had faith in God who gave the law (Heb 11:1-3, 6), and therefore obeyed it. Some even did so to the point of torture and death (Heb 11:36-39), which is paralleled at points in the literature discussed above. Some perhaps might try to suggest that because νόμος is not mentioned in Hebrews 11, then it is illegitimate to make such a parallel. However, unless one is ready to admit that Hebrews had a completely different concept of the patriarchs, Moses, David, Samuel and the prophets (etc.) than the rest of Judaism, then severing obedience to the law from faith is erroneous. The issue is that their faith was demonstrated by obedience.

Such examples of obedient faith serve as examples to be followed by the audience of Hebrews. Yet clearly, now that Christ has come, obedience to God takes on a different look. The law has been transformed in light of Christ's coming, and specifically how the people of God relate to the law. Those who desire to be obedient to God are not to live as if there has been no change at all. For instance, in light of Christ's work it would be *wrong* to offer up the blood

---

[339]Even the Qumranites, who could or would not bring sacrifices to the temple, did not suggest an abrogation of this cultic rite. Rather, they sought to reinterpret it in light of their present historical context.

of bulls and goats as prescribed by the law of Moses. Formerly, they responded either in obedience and faith (Heb 11), or disobedience and faithlessness (Heb 3-4), but now with the law internalized and engraved upon the hearts of all who are in the NC (Heb 8, 10), the obedience that God desires and rightfully demands is assured for his NC believers.

Further, it will be demonstrated in chapters four, five and six below that what is meant in Hebrews by νόμος (as well as the plural form νόμους) parallels the usage of νόμος in the Second Temple period. When the term is used by the writer of Hebrews it is the written commands of the law of Moses that are fundamentally in view. Specific commands may be in view, or the collection of Moses' laws as a whole.

In the next chapter, the present study will give focused attention to the actual structure of Hebrews itself, and will seek to identify how Hebrews 7:1-10:18 fits within the epistle, structurally and contextually speaking.

CHAPTER 3

Hebrews 7:1-10:18
and the Structure of Hebrews

Introduction

The following chapter focuses on the specific matter of the literary structure of Hebrews.[1] Numerous proposals for the structure and various divisions of Hebrews have been suggested in recent decades, and the present task will be to survey and summarize the proposals that have had the most significant influence in this area. Those discussed in the present chapter are Donald Guthrie, Leon Vaganay, Ceslas Spicq, Wolfgang Nauck, Albert Vanhoye, F. F. Bruce, Harold Attridge, and George Guthrie.[2]

The impetus for the present chapter is clear, and Guthrie states the importance of such a study in the form of a question. He asks, "If a scholar is confused, uncertain, or incorrect in evaluating the structure of an author's discourse, is that scholar not destined to flounder at points when presenting propositions concerning the author's intended meanings in the various sections of that discourse?"[3] How one views the ebb and flow of the author's train of thought and progression of certain themes affects exegesis. Thus, the discussion is necessary and warranted despite the fact that there is nothing that resembles a consensus in modern Hebrews studies. Aune notes that even with the rise of modern linguistic and literary-critical techniques, the issue of the structure of

---

[1]A shorter and slightly less technical version of this chapter was published as Barry C. Joslin, "Can Hebrews Be Structured? An Assessment of Eight Approaches," *CBR* 6.1 (2007): pp. 99-129.

[2]The groundwork for this discussion stands on the shoulders of scholarship dating from Aquinas. See Thomas Aquinas, *In Omnes S. Pauli Apostoli Epistolas Commentaria* (Taurini: Petri Marietti, 1917), 2:287-88. Observe Vanhoye's comments on the influence of Aquinas (Albert Vanhoye, *La structure littéraire de L'Épître aux Hébreux* [Paris: Desclée de Brouwer, 1963, 13-14]. Other notable contributions prior to the twentieth century come from J. Calvin, H. Zwingli, H. Bullinger, N. Hemingsen, J. Bengel, and H. von Soden. Though new approaches to the study of the structure of Hebrews have come about in recent decades, such approaches benefit from the work of these and others.

[3]George H. Guthrie, *The Structure of Hebrews: A Text-Linguistic Analysis* (Grand Rapids: Baker, 1998), xvii. Guthrie's work here is essentially his 1991 Ph.D. dissertation, originally published in 1994 (NovTSupp 73 [Leiden: E. J. Brill, 1994]).

Hebrews is still very much an unsolved problem.[4] Additionally, such a topic is not an easy one. Black states flatly, "Some writers would like to think (or give the impression) that the outlining of Hebrews is a rapid, simple process. The real problem is, of course, far more complex, bewildering, and time-consuming."[5] The present chapter therefore proceeds with an eye to such words of caution.

Major Issues and Approaches

Koester has recognized that two proposals have dominated the discussion of the structure of Hebrews in the latter half of the twentieth century.[6] Broadly speaking, most proposals fall into one of these two approaches. The first is a five-part division akin to that of Vanhoye, and the second is a three-part division similar to that of Nauck. Research into the scholarship of the past sixty years demonstrates the truth of Koester's summary.[7] However, as one might expect there are many variations on these two approaches to the structure of Hebrews.[8]

---

[4]David Aune, *The New Testament in its Literary Environment*, LEC 8 (Philadelphia: Westminster, 1987), 213.

[5]David Alan Black, "The Problem of the Literary Structure of Hebrews: An Evaluation and a Proposal," *GTJ* 7 (1986): 176.

[6]Craig Koester, "The Epistle to the Hebrews in Recent Study," *CR* 2 (1994): 123-45.

[7]Though there are variants on these two approaches, most recent approaches can be seen as "limbs of a tree" that can easily be traced back to the "trunk" of either Vanhoye or Nauck. (There is, however, the more traditional, quasi-Pauline two division outline, represented here by Donald Guthrie [below], which has few adherents and stands on its own quite apart from Nauck and Vanhoye). Koester echoes the statements of Aune and Black concerning the lack of consensus. See Koester, "Epistle to the Hebrews," 125; D. A. Black, "Literary Structure," 163-64.

[8]One cannot wade too far into discussions of structure without realizing that other issues overlap such discussions, such as the matter of the genre of Hebrews. How one decides whether it is an epistle, a homily, or a "word of exhortation" will affect his or her understanding of the structure. See Floyd Filson, *"Yesterday" A Study of Hebrews in Light of Chapter 13*, SBT 4 (Naperville, IL: Alec R. Allenson, 1967), 16-26. Filson argues that 13:22 (τοῦ λόγου τῆς παρακλήσεως) is the key to the literary structure of the entire epistle. For Filson, this "word of exhortation" is the best way to understand the purpose of writing. The main point of Hebrews therefore is to exhort, and thus the sections of exhortatory material should be given special consideration and not relegated to an excursus from the "main point." For Filson, the exhortation *is* the main point.

Along similar lines, Barnabas Lindars is representative of those who prefer to see Hebrews in light of ancient rhetorical speech forms. In a 1989 article (Barnabas Lindars, "The Rhetorical Structure of Hebrews," *NTS* 35 [1989]: 382-406) he argued that the classical tradition accepted three main types of rhetoric: epideictic, deliberative, and forensic (383). He concludes that only the deliberative type can make sense of the

A key question surrounds the place of 4:14-16 and 10:19-25. The tripartite approach of Nauck divides the book at these points, resulting in three large sections. These two passages are seen to be parallel and the main point to consider when outlining the book. Those who do not favor the tripartite arrangement either acknowledge the significance of these texts,[9] or make little of them.[10]

Another fundamental issue is the matter of *form* versus *content*. The debate centers on this question: "Does one make content or literary form the central concern when considering the structure of Hebrews?" How one answers this question greatly affects one's view of the outline and flow of Hebrews. Nauck, Bruce, and Donald Guthrie give more weight to the former, while Vaganay, Spicq, Vanhoye, and Attridge clearly opt for the latter. George Guthrie has offered a more eclectic approach.[11]

---

rhetoric of Hebrews, and such a rhetorical strand can be traced back to Stephen in Acts 6 (404). In ancient literature this type of rhetoric was often found in political arguments in which a piece of legislation was presented and argued, the sole purpose of which was to persuade the hearers to accept it. Lindars suggests that this would fit the sustained argument of Hebrews (383). He concludes with great certainty that once Hebrews is seen from this angle, "*every detail* of the letter will be found to fall into place" (383). Lindars' conclusions are based on a presupposition that Hebrews indeed must be a rhetorical speech in one of the three classical forms, yet he offers no explanation for such a presupposition. He views the composition of Hebrews entirely from the point of view of its intended effect on the readers (384), and finds that the climax of the argument is not to be found in the central section of the book (7:1-10:18), but rather in 10:19-12:29. His view of Hebrews as a deliberative speech has not found wide support.

[9]See for example F. F. Bruce, *Epistle to the Hebrews*, rev. ed., NICNT (Grand Rapids: Eerdmans, 1990), vii-x; idem, "The Structure and Argument of Hebrews," *SWJT* 28 (1985): 6, 7-8, 10.

[10]See for example Vanhoye, "Discussions sur la structure de l'Épître Hébreux," *Bib* 55 (1974): 349-80, Ceslas Spicq, *L'Épître aux Hébreux* (Paris: Gabalda, 1952), 1:32-34, and Attridge, *The Epistle to the Hebrews* (Hermeneia. Philadelphia: Fortress, 1989), 17-18, who argue that 4:14-16 is not a significant turn in the movement of the book.

[11]However, it is clear that George Guthrie's approach lies closer to that of the Vaganay-Vanhoye school than that of Nauck, though he does find fault with the Vaganay-Vanhoye school. Guthrie rightly criticizes Vanhoye for either ignoring or looking past the clear structural parallel that exists between 4:14-16 and 10:19-25 (and thus violating Vanhoye's own methodology). See Guthrie, *The Structure of Hebrews*, 117.

G. Guthrie has identified several distinct proposals to the structure of Hebrews (*The Structure of Hebrews*, 23-41). In his own history of research he has classified five approaches. First is the "Agnostic Approach" that asks, "How can a discourse which shifts back and forth from genre to genre and topic to topic, repeating previously discussed material, be depicted in a step-by-step structure?" (25). Moffatt falls into this category and is skeptical that there is any identifiable outline for the epistle (James

With such introductory matters now illuminated, the chapter now turns to the specific offerings of several important scholars who have emerged as the major players in the matter of the structure of Hebrews.[12] First to be considered

---

Moffatt, *A Critical Commentary on the Epistle to the Hebrews*, ICC [Edinburgh: T. & T. Clark, 1924; reprint 1952], xxiii-xxiv).

Second is what Guthrie calls the "Conceptual/Thematic Analysis." This centers its outline of Hebrews on one or more of the central concepts or themes found in the text, and is more "content-centered." This type of approach has been the most popular, and scholars such as Donald Guthrie and F. F. Bruce (discussed below) take such a view (see also P. E. Hughes, *A Commentary on the Epistle to the Hebrews* [Grand Rapids: Eerdmans, 1977], ix-x; 2-4). Such themes as the "Superiority of Christ" dominate the discussion. The essential difficulty with such an approach is its subjectivity.

The third category is "Rhetorical Criticism." This approach seeks to identify the structure of Hebrews by comparing it to what is known about ancient forms of rhetoric. Several attempts have been made to see Hebrews in such a rhetorico-critical light (see the comments concerning Lindars, above). Koester adopts this approach in his 2001 commentary (Craig Koester, *Hebrews*, AB 36a [New York: Doubleday, 2001], 84-86).

Fourth is the approach of "Literary Analysis." Since the mid twentieth century, this approach has received much attention and has persuaded numerous scholars. It focuses on literary cues in the text such as hook-words, the use of the inclusio, chiasmus, and other features. It has become popular because research has shown that such literary features were in fact utilized by the writer of Hebrews. Also germane to this approach is the point often made concerning the shifts in genre *within* Hebrews (see below). Nauck and Vanhoye are two scholars most associated with this approach. Most of the discussion of the structure of Hebrews in recent decades has centered around some kind of literary analysis, and there is still significant disagreement over such matters as the role of 4:14-16 and 10:19-25 in the discussion. An advantage of this method is that it tends to be more objective than some of the older suggestions, and decisions are made more on the basis of clues found within the text itself (though no approach is purely objective). The disadvantage of this approach is that it can tend towards downplaying the content of the epistle, a point for which Swetnam persuasively argues in making his critique of Vanhoye (James Swetnam, "Form and Content in Hebrews 1-6," *Bib* 53 [1972]: 369).

The fifth and final approach is "Linguistic Analysis," and is a relatively new method of analyzing the structure of Hebrews. The first to propose such an approach was Dussaut in 1981 (Louis Dussaut, *Synopse structurelle de l'Épître aux Hébreux*, [Paris: Éditions du Cerf, 1981]), who attempted to show that his fourteen sections were unified in structure and concept. Dussaut was followed by Linda Neeley ("A Discourse Analysis of Hebrews," in *Occasional Papers in Translation and Linguistics* 3-4 [1987]: 1-146) who utilized discourse analysis. George H. Guthrie has taken this a step further and offers a more eclectic approach, which he calls a "Text-Linguistic Analysis" (discussed below).

[12]The present chapter focuses on the advances in the twentieth and early twenty-first centuries. For a concise discussion of previous centuries and the work of those such as Aquinas, Bullinger, Hemingsen, and Bengel, see G. Guthrie, *Structure of Hebrews*, 3-8.

is the contribution of Donald Guthrie who will be followed by Leon Vaganay, Ceslas Spicq, Wolfgang Nauck, Albert Vanhoye, F. F. Bruce, Harold Attridge, and George Guthrie.

Donald Guthrie

Donald Guthrie divides Hebrews in a quasi-Pauline two-fold structure of doctrinal instruction followed by application (1:1-10:18 [doctrinal instruction] 10:19-13:17 [application]).[13] This layout has not received a great deal of support among modern Hebrews scholars, often characterized as simplistic and not in keeping with the flow of the epistle's argument. Yet it does enjoy the attestation of the history of the church and is often called the "traditional approach" to the epistle's structure.[14] D. Guthrie argues that his approach to the structure "culminates in the doctrinal exposition of Christ as the eternal high priest."[15] Indeed, such a two-fold division can boast in its simplicity, and given that Hebrews was for so long associated with the apostle Paul, such a traditional division between one section of doctrine followed by a section of application can be persuasive. Guthrie's presentation is quite thematic, with each division of the doctrinal section of Hebrews (1:1-10:18) being described with the traditional "superiority" nomenclature.[16]

Yet many scholars who take this approach do observe application in the first part of Hebrews as well as doctrine in the second, thus making such a position more difficult to embrace. This separation of the kerygma and parenesis is perhaps this approach's greatest difficulty, and the criticism for such a proposal is common. D. Guthrie himself notes that the author "punctuates his doctrinal argument with direct moral exhortations."[17] For example, in his comments on the section entitled "Superiority to Angels (1:4-2:18)," he notes the warning of 2:1-4, regarding it merely to be a digression.[18] In his discussion of Hebrews 3, Guthrie acknowledges that the writer of Hebrews exhorts his readers not to be as the OT Israelites, but again does not see such exhortations as contributions to matters of structure.[19]

D. A. Black criticizes such a juxtaposition of kerygma and parenesis. Given

---

[13]Donald Guthrie, *New Testament Introduction*, rev. ed. (Downers Grove, IL: Intervarsity, 1990), 668-721, esp. 717-21. His outline in brief can be found in Donald Guthrie, *Hebrews*, TNTC 15 (Grand Rapids: Eerdmans, 1983), 58-59.

[14]Black, "Literary Structure," 164-66.

[15]D. Guthrie, *New Testament Introduction*, 717.

[16]Simon Kistemaker seems to imply a two-part approach similar to Donald Guthrie in his outline when he labels 10:19-12:29 as "Jesus' Work Is Applied by the Believer." See Simon Kistemaker, *Hebrews*, NTC (Grand Rapids: Baker, 1984), 18.

[17]D. Guthrie, *New Testament Introduction*, 714.

[18]Ibid., 717.

[19]Ibid., 718.

the number of exhortations found within Guthrie's doctrinal section, it seems difficult not to regard them as playing a more significant role in the question of structure, and not simply a digression from the kerygma. He writes, "Such basically hortatory passages as 2:1-4; 3:7-4:11; 4:14-16; and 5:11-6:12 incline the careful student of Hebrews to regard these passages as integral to the main purpose of the author."[20] Such sections are too numerous and weighty to be considered excursuses by the writer of Hebrews. Black continues, "To label them 'digressions' or 'inserted warnings' is to beg the question of the author's purpose in including them in this part of his writing with such frequency."[21]

Numerous scholars have expressed dissatisfaction with the traditional division such as Hans Windisch, who resists the idea that such "interruptions in the argument" are merely excursuses.[22] Werner Georg Kümmel, too, notes the difficulty of such a two-part division, and suggests that such sections are actually the point to which the exposition is driving. He writes,

> Der Aufbau des Hb. ist dadurch gekennzeichnet, daß ohne jede briefliche Einleitung sofort die Darlegungen beginnen, denen ein mahnender Teil nicht erst am Schluß des ‚Briefes', wie in den moisten Plsbr.n, folgt, sondern die immer wieder durch Paränesen (2,1-4 ; 3,7-4,11; 4:14-16; 5,11-6,12; 10,19-39; 12,1-13,7) unterbrochen werden, die offensichtlich der eigentliche Zielpunkt der ganzen Ausführungen sind.[23]

Wolfgang Nauck agrees that the kerygma and parenesis are too interwoven to be kept so distinct.[24] Otto Michel views the parenetic sections as the high point of the theological/doctrinal sections and states, "Die Spitze des theologischen Gedankens liegt in den paränetischen Teilen."[25] Michel understands such exhortations to prepare the community for persecution and tribulation. Such emphasis on the hortatory sections has led Filson to argue that 13:22 should be the focus and starting point when asking questions about the structure of Hebrews.[26]

Although Donald Guthrie's two-part division of Hebrews has enjoyed

---

[20]Black, "Literary Structure," 166; see also 177.

[21]Black, "Literary Structure," 166.

[22]Hans Windisch, *Der Hebräerbrief*, HNT 14 (Tübingen: J. C. B. Mohr, 1931), 8.

[23]Werner Georg Kümmel, *Einleitung in das neue Testament* (Heidelberg: Quelle & Meyer, 1963), 281.

[24]Wolfgang Nauck, "Zum Aufbau des Hebräerbriefes," in *Judentum-Urchristentum-Kirche: Festschrift für Joachim Jeremias*, BZNW 26, ed. W. Eltester (Berlin: Töpelmann, 1960), 202-03.

[25]Otto Michel, *Der Brief and die Hebräer*, KEKNT (Göttingen: Vandenhoeck & Ruprecht, 1966), 27.

[26]Filson, *"Yesterday"*, 16-26. Filson's point is that Hebrews reveals that his work is specifically a "word of *exhortation*."

acceptance throughout the history of the Church, twentieth century scholarship has generally eschewed this approach in favor of more recent proposals, though there are some who still maintain this view.[27] The present writer sees such a structure as too simple; it does not do justice to the epistle's intricacy. This approach at times seems to be forced, especially given the doctrinal significance of material in the second part of Donald Guthrie's outline and the presence of so much parenesis in the first. Further, such a proposal fails to consider the literary and rhetorical devices that have clearly been utilized by the writer of Hebrews.[28] This view is a bit dated, and better and more persuasive proposals have emerged in recent generations of scholarship such as those discussed below, beginning with Leon Vaganay.

Leon Vaganay

Leon Vaganay's 1940 essay, "La Plan de L'Épître aux Hébreux," has been highly influential in this area of Hebrews studies.[29] Michel has noted its importance in the ongoing discussion,[30] and George Guthrie suggests that Vaganay's essay is "the beginning of the modern literary discussions on the structure of Hebrews."[31] Indeed, many recent commentaries and studies trace their work back to Vaganay.

Building on the 1902 work of Thien,[32] Vaganay identified the presence of the "mot-crochet" (hook-word) in Hebrews. Such a literary device is used to "hook" sections of material together and was fairly common in the ancient world. The presence of this device led Vaganay to move beyond Thien to see a specific section in Hebrews 1 and 2, the whole of which Thien had dubbed as

---

[27]See for example Homer Kent, *The Epistle to the Hebrews* (Grand Rapids: Baker, 1972) 11, and the NT introduction of Edmond Hiebert, *An Introduction to the New Testament* (Chicago: Moody, 1977, 3:92-100).

[28]D. A. Black, "The Literary Structure," 168.

[29]Leon Vaganay, "La Plan de L'Épître aux Hébreux," in *Memorial Lagrange*, ed. L. –H. Vincent (Paris: J. Gabalda et Cie, 1940), 269-77.

[30]Michel, *Der Brief*, 29. Michel is quick to note how Vaganay influenced the future of the question of the structure of Hebrews. He writes, "Hier ist zunächst die Untersuchung von L. Vaganay...zu nennen, die zwar zunächst wenig Aufsehen erregte, aber doch in der Folgezeit von Wichtigkeit wurde."

[31]G. Guthrie, *The Structure of Hebrews*, 11-12.

[32]F. Thien, "Analyse de L'Épître aux Hébreux," *RB* 11 (1902): 74-86. Thien understood Heb 1-2 to be the introduction, with 13 being the conclusion. He divided the remainder of the epistle as follows: 3:1-5:10; (5:11-6:20 is a digression of sorts for hortatory purposes); 7:1-10:39, and 11:1-12:29. Such divisions were based on an announcement of two themes, which would then be developed in inverse order. Thien is to be credited with making the observation that that writer of Hebrews typically announces his themes before developing them in inverse order, a point that Vanhoye later utilizes in his own schema.

the introduction.[33] Vaganay suggested that in fact only 1:1-4 serve as the introduction, given that the term ἀγγέλων is seen in both 1:4 and 1:5. For Vaganay, this meant that instead of one section, there were two that were "hooked" together via the term ἀγγέλων.[34] This section ends at 2:18 where the term ἀρχιερεύς is found in v.17, "hooked" to 3:1 where ἀρχιερεύς also appears. According to Vaganay this section extends to 5:10, where the readers are first introduced to the term Μελχισέδεκ, also present in 5:11.[35] Vaganay acknowledges that 5:11-6:20 represents a hiatus in the argument, and that it resumes at 6:20/7:1 with the reiteration of the term Μελχισέδεκ.[36] The first section of the third theme begins in 7:1, with the discussion of Μελχισέδεκ, and the whole of Hebrews 7 is seen to be a unit that concludes with the theme for the next section (τετελειωμένον),[37] a reprise of 5:9. Hebrews 8:1–9:28 is the second section of the third theme and ends by announcing the theme to the third section (εἰς σωτηρίαν). Hebrews 10:1-39 comprises the third section of the third theme, which concludes with the hook-word πίστις, the topic of the fourth theme. This fourth theme (11:1-12:13) is made up of two sections (mirroring the second theme's two sections), the first concerning faith (11:1-12:2), and the second concerning perseverance (12:3-13).[38] The theme for 12:3-13 (ὑπομονή), having been first announced at 10:36-39, is reiterated in 12:1-2, in keeping with the author's pattern. Vaganay's fifth and final theme has a single section (mirroring the first theme), is concerned with peace and holiness in the life of the believer (12:14-13:21),[39] and is joined via the hook-words "τῆς ἁγιότητος αὐτοῦ...εἰρηνικόν" (12:10-11) and "εἰρήνην...καὶ τὸν

---

[33]Thien, "Analyse," 76.

[34]Vaganay, "La Plan," 271. The hook-words connect the five main themes which are made up of 1, 2, 3, 2, 1, sections, respectively. The main ideas that will be discussed in the subsequent themes are announced ahead of time toward the close of the previous theme. For a helpful visual layout of Vaganay's structure, see Vanhoye, *La structure litteraire*, (1963), 26-27. To reiterate, the *themes* (five total) are connected via the "mot-crochet," while the main points in each of the five themes are announced ahead of time, and then reiterated just prior to their being taken up in the epistle.

[35]Vaganay, "La Plan," 273. This pattern continues throughout the epistle. See especially pp. 273-77. Additionally, he argues that Heb 5:9-10 announces the three themes of the lengthy center section, τελειωθεις, ἅιτιος σωτηρίας αἰωνίου, and ἀρχιερεὺς κατὰ τὴν τάξιν Μελχισέδεκ.

[36]Actually, Vaganay refers to 5:11-6:20 as a "preamble," the use of which is in keeping with the rules of ancient rhetoric. He writes, "Avant d'aborder la première section de ce theme capital, l'auteur se met en frais d'un préambule conçu suivant les règles de la rhétorique" (Vaganay, "La Plan," 273).

[37]Vaganay divides Heb 7 as follows: vv. 1-3; 4-10; 11-25; 26-28. See also Vanhoye, *La structure littéraire*, 25-27.

[38]Vaganay, "La Plan," 275.

[39]Ibid., 276.

ἁγιασμὸν" (12:14). He suggests that 13:22-25 is the conclusion and final exhortations (παρακαλῶ δὲ ὑμᾶς).[40]

As one can see, this pattern of hook words extends throughout the epistle and serves to divide it into a symmetrical arrangement of five themes, each with its own sections, bordered by the introduction of 1:1-4 and the conclusion of 13:22-25.[41]

It should be noted that one of the most significant advantages to this approach is its perceived objectivity. The presence of hook words and other literary-rhetorical devices is demonstrable and less subjective, though their significance can and has been questioned. This is unlike some of the thematic approaches to the structure of Hebrews. Although the hook word can be objectively identified and is on the surface of the text, the question remains as to whether such literary devices were intended by the author to mark out the *formal divisions* of the text.

To be sure, Vaganay's observations have been monumental in discussions of the structure of Hebrews. However, not all scholars have been swayed by the discovery of the hook-word. Michel is a bit skeptical of utilizing it as a *basis* for such divisions. He concludes his discussion of Vaganay by asking, "Ist das Stichwortverfahren in unserem Brief allein ausschlaggebend oder muß es durch andere Gesichtspunkte ergänzt werden?"[42] Perhaps the greatest shortcoming in this approach is its reliance upon literary analysis for the formal divisions of the epistle, while consideration of content is pushed to the side. These are two very different approaches to the deciphering of *any* text's structure. Bligh noted in 1964 that there is great doubt "as to whether a division based on purely literary criteria will reveal the conceptual structures of the epistle."[43] Swetnam expressed similar concerns as to this method in 1972.[44] More recently, Ellingworth averred that some choice must be made, and that the scholar must be willing to accept the shortcomings of either approach. Though Ellingworth follows the Vaganay-Vanhoye school in his commentary he notes, "The disadvantage of this decision is that the titles of sections and subsections inevitably refer to the content."[45]

Despite these criticisms, most Hebrews scholars are quick to acknowledge

---

[40]Ibid.

[41]See Appendix 5 for Vaganay's structural analysis.

[42]Michel, *Der Brief*, 28.

[43]John Bligh, "The Structure of Hebrews," *HeyJ* 5 (1964): 175. Bligh is pessimistic as to the possibility of there ever being a reconciliation of these two methodologically-diverse approaches.

[44]Swetnam, "Form and Content in Hebrews 1-6," 368-69. To be precise, Swetnam leveled this criticism specifically at Vanhoye, but Vanhoye stands on the shoulders of Vaganay's literary analysis.

[45]Paul Ellingworth, *The Epistle to the Hebrews*, NIGTC (Grand Rapids: Eerdmans, 1993), 58.

the contribution that Vaganay has made to the present discussion. His identification of the hook-word and his application of Thien's "announcement of the theme" have made his work influential to this day. The value of his contributions is demonstrated in that they were adapted by one of the most influential commentators of the mid twentieth century, the French scholar Ceslas Spicq.

Ceslas Spicq

At the time of its publication, Spicq's 1952 two-volume commentary was perhaps the most important critical commentary that had been printed to date. Though he did not attempt to make new inroads into the matter of Hebrews' structure, Spicq's position on the matter must be included given his importance in the history of Hebrews studies; few rival the impact of Ceslas Spicq. While perhaps some of his arguments concerning critical introductory matters have been disproved,[46] Spicq's is an important voice in Hebrews studies and must be considered here on the matter of structure.

Spicq divides Hebrews into four main divisions, bordered by an introduction (1:1-4) and an appendix (13:1-19). Following Vaganay he notes the hook-word[47] τῶν ἀγγέλων at 1:4/1:5, and states that the epistle's main themes are announced in the introduction and are developed in the four main sections of Hebrews. He labels the first theme (1:5–2:18) "Le Fils de Dieu incarné est Roi de l'univers,"[48] and breaks this large block into two smaller sections with the exhortation at 2:1-4 dividing them. Hebrews 3:1–5:10 makes up the second of four main themes. Spicq identifies the second as "Jésus, grand Prêtre fidèle et compatissant," which are the two main points developed in these chapters. Like Vaganay, he sees three hook-words in 5:9 that are the main theological points of 7:1-10:18,[49] although he disagrees with Vaganay that this section should extend all the way to 10:39.[50] This center section is Spicq's third main division, which he titles, "L'authentique sacerdoce de Jésus-Christ." The third theme is divided into three smaller units, 7:1-28, 8:1-9:28, and 10:1-18. Here he argues that Christ is the eternal and unique high priest, that Christ is the priest of the

---

[46]For example, in his commentary Spicq maintains that the work of Philo held significant weight for the writer of Hebrews (Spicq, *L'Épître aux Hébreux*, 1:39-91), a point that has been largely eschewed in recent decades. See especially the lengthy work of Ronald Williamson, *Philo and the Epistle to the Hebrews* (Leiden: E. J. Brill, 1970), who addresses this matter specifically and demonstrates that such a conclusion is ill-founded.

[47]Though Spicq at times calls them "key words" ("mots clefs") rather than "hook-words" ("mots-crochets").

[48]"The incarnate Son of God is King of the Universe" (author's translation). Spicq, *L'Épître aux Hébreux*, 1:34.

[49]Ibid., 1:35.

[50]Ibid., 1:36 n. 2.

NC who officiates in a heavenly temple in the presence of God, and that Christ is the author of eternal salvation.[51]

The fourth main theme is found in 10:19–12:29 ("la foi persévérante"). Spicq finds the concept of persevering faith to be the overarching idea in this fourth and final topic, but not as a doctrinal teaching, *but as a practical application of the previous doctrinal discussion.* One must note Spicq's comments regarding all that follows 10:18, "L'argumentation doctrinale est terminé: le Christ roi-prêtre éternel et céleste a abrogé l'ancienne Alliance et son sacerdoce. Il reste à en tirer les applications practiques détaillées."[52] He essentially identifies 10:19 and following as the "practical application" of the doctrine presented in 1:1-10:18. Therefore Spicq partially belongs to the traditional approach (as seen in D. Guthrie, above), and partially to the more literary-rhetorical approach made popular by the work of Vaganay. Combining the traditional approach to the structure of Hebrews with clear influence from Vaganay makes Spicq unique. Such is the reason for including him here: his approach can essentially be labeled a "transitional" view.

As one can see, Spicq is heavily influenced by the schema of Vaganay. However, one notable difference is that Spicq's fourth theme (10:19-12:29) combines portions of Vaganay's third and fifth themes (5:11-10:39, 11:1-12:13).[53] Additionally, whereas Vaganay viewed 12:14-13:21 as a fifth theme, Spicq views 13:1-19 merely as an appendix (thus violating Vaganay's symmetry), and 13:20-25 as an epilogue. He writes, "Cet appendice est complété par un epilogue, comportant voeux et salutations, conformes à l'usage épistolaire."[54] Yet this may partially be explained by his understanding of Hebrews to be divided into two even larger divisions, one dogmatic and the other moral, a division which clearly demonstrates a lingering influence of the traditional approach. He writes, "Ce n'est pas une partie morale qui s'ajoute à la partie dogmatique, mais la mise en oeuvre des données de foi qui ont été élaborées: comment concevoir la vie chrétienne en function du sacerdoce du Christ?"[55] For Spicq, this is the practical/moral question taken up in 10:19-12:29.

In many ways, the criticisms of Donald Guthrie's "traditional approach" are applicable to Spicq. Recall the words of critics such as Kümmel, who noted how unconvincing such a dogmatic–moral division is in light of more recent research.[56] Hebrews does not easily break down into two such easily-defined sections, and the chief criticism is simply that there is ample exhortation found

---

[51]Ibid., 1:35-36.
[52]Ibid., 1:36.
[53]George Guthrie notes this as well. See his *Structure of Hebrews*, 13 n. 32.
[54]Spicq, *L'Épître aux Hébreux*, 1:37.
[55]Ibid., 1:36.
[56]W. G. Kümmel, *Einleitung in das neue Testament*, 281.

where there should be dogmatic material. Additionally, one is curious as to why the whole of chapter 13 is considered an appendix, when its content is in keeping with the "detailed practical application" that Spicq discusses in 10:19-12:29.[57] In light of this observation, one could suggest that Spicq might not have held to the authenticity of chapter 13, however, this is not the case.[58] He observes the practical nature of 13:1-19, stating that the writer of Hebrews moves from the more general to the more specific—practical matters for the individual in the specific community.[59]

Though not fully persuaded by the whole of Spicq's approach, the present writer affirms Spicq's conclusion that 7:1–10:18 is distinctly doctrinal, which is in keeping with the current thesis. However, for reasons cited below, his grouping of 8:1–9:28 as a unit is not to be preferred. Moreover his dogmatic-moral division at 10:18 is unsatisfying to the whole of the epistle. Perhaps Spicq's greatest weakness is his suppression of the parenetic material found throughout the epistle. In contrast, the parenetic material and its role in the structure of Hebrews was the central emphasis for an influential scholar who wrote in 1960, to whom the chapter now turns.

Wolfgang Nauck

Nauck introduced his influential tripartite scheme in his 1960 essay, "Zum Aufbau des Hebräerbriefs."[60] Many scholars who were unconvinced by Vaganay found Nauck's proposal more satisfying. In this short essay Nauck sought to compare the proposals of Spicq and Michel[61] and found himself to be much closer to Michel's divisions than those of Spicq (who was greatly influenced by Vaganay). Michel had argued for three major sections, with major breaks coming after 4:13 and 10:18. In some ways, Nauck's proposal is a variation of the older, traditional two-part outline,[62] yet Nauck's variation is that he in no way sought to differentiate between the kerygmatic and parenetic elements, as they were far too intermingled.

Nauck argues that Hebrews is framed around the hortatory blocks of material that form three major movements, and such is essential to his proposal. He suggests that 1:1-4:13 is the first main section and an integrated unit, which

---

[57]Spicq, *L'Épître aux Hébreux*, 1:36.

[58]Ceslas Spicq, "L'authenticitié du chapitre XIII de L'épître aux Hébreux," *ConNT* 11 (1947): 226-36.

[59]He writes, "Descendant de plus du général au particulier, et s'adressant exclusivement à une communauté donnée, Hebrews ajoute un Post-scriptum pour determiner rapidement quelques règles de vie pratique" (Spicq, *L'Épître aux Hébreux*, 1:37).

[60]Nauck, "Zum Aufbau des Hebräerbriefes," 199-206.

[61]Specifically, Nauck compared Spicq's structure to the fifth edition of Michel's commentary, which was published in 1960.

[62]D. A. Black, "The Literary Structure," 166.

concludes with the exhortation in 4:11-13, "therefore let us be diligent." For Nauck, each of the three major sections begins and ends with parallel texts. For instance, Nauck contends that this first section begins with a "logos-hymn" in 1:2b-3 and ends with a "sophia-hymn" in 4:12-13. Hebrews 4:14–10:31 is the second major movement, and there should be no break at 10:18 (as per Michel). Nauck notes the similarities of 4:14-16 and 10:19-25, and lists five possible parallels in the Greek text between 4:14-16 and 10:19-25.[63] Most notably, this section begins and concludes with, "therefore since...let us draw near." Nauck further modifies Michel by extending the second major movement to include the warning passage of 10:26-31. The third and concluding section is 10:32-13:17 (13:18-25 are a postscript) and is marked out by parallel exhortations to "remember" in 10:32 and 13:7 (ἀναμιμνήσκεσθε and μνημονεύετε respectively), which are followed by "die Konsequenzen" in 10:35ff. and 13:9ff.[64] Since this section is framed by similar exhortations, it marks the final movement of Hebrews.[65]

At the time of his publication in 1960, Nauck represented a fundamental difference in philosophy of how Hebrews' structure should be understood. He criticized Spicq's divisions for two reasons. First, he disagreed with Spicq's approach, opting instead to divide the epistle along the lines of the major exhortations in Hebrews (following Michel), and therefore not dividing the text along more linguistic or theological lines as others had in the past. Yet Nauck alters the structure of Michel by asserting that the end of the second section should be 10:31. Second, he is not persuaded by Spicq's usage of hook-words (or any literary device), refusing to agree that they should be considered in matters of structure.[66] Although he notes, "Spicqs Argumentation ist bestechend,"[67] he concludes that the hook-words that Spicq utilizes are little more than a rhetorical device, and not a structural device.

This approach was adopted by Michel in the sixth edition of his commentary, and was followed soon after by Kümmel.[68] Lane notes that the

---

[63]Nauck, "Zum Aufbau des Hebräerbriefs," 203-04.

[64]Ibid., 204-05; cf. Jukka Thurén, *Das Lobopfer der Hebräer: Studien zum Aufbau und Anliegen von Hebräerbrief 13* (Åbo, Finland: Åbo Akademi, 1973), 30-32.

[65]Nauck, "Zum Aufbau des Hebräerbriefs," 204-05.

[66]Ibid., 201. Again, this is the line of demarcation for matters of structure. What role do literary-rhetorical devices play in questions of structure, if any? Note Vanhoye's comments on the work of both Spicq and Nauck in the second edition of his fundamental 1963 work, Albert Vanhoye, *La structure littéraire de l'Épître aux Hébreux*, 2nd ed (Paris: Desclée de Brouwer, 1976), 30-32.

[67]Nauck, "Zum Aufbau des Hebräerbriefes," 200.

[68]In more recent years, Weiß has adopted a three-part schema that is quite close to that of Nauck, with two alterations. First, while maintaining a tripartite division, Weiß sees a break at 10:18. Second, Weiß continues the final section all the way to 13:25 (see Hans-Friedrich Weiß, *Der Brief an die Hebräer*, 15th ed., KEKNT, vol. 13 [Göttingen:

strength of this approach is that it recognizes the "primacy of parenesis," although he places more weight on rhetorical and literary devices in the text.[69] Nauck's approach is tempting for those who are not convinced of either a thematic-oriented structure or by proposals such as those of Vaganay/Spicq/Vanhoye. For those who prefer this structure, the parallels and similarly-worded paragraphs of 4:14-16 and 10:19-25 are compelling, and are seen to mark out the central section of Hebrews. Though this approach is often praised for its simplicity, it may also be criticized for the same reason. Attridge rightly states that such a division does not account for the intricacies of the structure, and that Nauck's view "does little to illuminate the complex interrelationships of sections within the text."[70] Further, there is distinct disagreement among those who follow a three-part schema concerning the placement of 10:19-39. Some end section two at 10:18, some at verse 25, some at verse 31, and still others at verse 39.[71] Additionally, Nauck's assessment of the "logos-hymn" in 1:2b-3 and the "sophia-hymn" in 4:12-13 is far from a compelling parallel and seems to be a distinct weakness in this phase of his argument.

In spite of such criticisms, Nauck's approach has enjoyed significant acceptance, especially for those who are persuaded neither by the traditional approach nor the proposals of Vaganay/Spicq. However, Nauck's structure is in contrast to perhaps the most influential scholar in this discussion, to whom the discussion will now turn.

Albert Vanhoye

Any discussion of the structure of Hebrews must take into account the influential French scholar Albert Vanhoye. Regardless of whether one agrees with him, few can dispute the significance of Vanhoye's contribution to the discussion in recent decades. He has shown himself to be flexible in his argumentation, altering his outline of Hebrews in places in response to the ongoing discussion. Though there have been a few modifications from his early work, the bulk of his original argument remains intact.

Vanhoye's work, *La structure littéraire de l'Épître aux Hébreux*, has been heralded as "the most influential and debated work ever written on the structure

---

Vandenhoeck & Ruprecht, 1991], 8-9; 42-51). See also Hans Zimmerman, *Das Bekenntnis der Hoffnung: Tradition und Redaktion im Hebräerbrief*, (Köln: Peter Hanstein Verlag, 1977), 18-24.
[69]William L. Lane, *Hebrews 1-8*, WBC, vol. 47a (Nashville: Thomas Nelson, 1991), lxxxviii.
[70]Attridge, *Hebrews*, 15.
[71]Ibid., 15 n. 125, 126.

of Hebrews."[72] His great contribution is seen in his synthesis of several strands of thought into one sustained discussion and thesis regarding the structure of Hebrews. Vanhoye freely acknowledges his indebtedness to several scholars before him.[73] He was heavily influenced by Vaganay and his recognition of the "mot-crochet," as well as the contributions of von Soden, Gyllenberg, and Thien, among others.[74]

Vanhoye developed Vaganay's contribution (and that of Gyllenberg, von Soden, Descamps, and Thien) and greatly expanded it to include five literary devices found in the epistle.[75] First, *l'annonce du sujet* which precedes and prepares the reader for what is to come. Second, *les mots-crochets*, which mark the end of one section and are repeated again at the beginning of the next

---

[72]G. Guthrie, *Structure of Hebrews*, 14. Likewise, in his comments on Vanhoye, David A. Black feels that Vanhoye's thesis is the "point of departure" for any discussion of structure. He writes, "Vanhoye envisages a reconstruction totally unlike anything we have seen before, yet one which results in a relatively coherent and self-authenticating structure" (D. A. Black, "Literary Structure," 171). Black continues, "The great merit of Vanhoye's treatment is that it shows concretely how an understanding of structural linguistics can serve the expositor" (174).

Over the past forty years Vanhoye has published several articles as well as a second edition of his original work that take into account his interaction with other scholars, yet his basic approach has not been radically altered from the first edition of his work (for example, see Albert Vanhoye, "Discussions sur la structure de l'Épître aux Hébreux," *Bib* 55 [1974]: 349-80). He acknowledges that there were slight changes in his general outline, but far from radically changing his outline, such modifications actually *confirm* his original 1963 outline. In the second edition of his work, he concludes the first and seminal chapter, "Quelques changements ont été introduits dans ce chapitre. Ils ne modifient pas le dessin général de la structure, mais au contraire le conferment" (Vanhoye, *La structure littéraire*, [1976], 52). See also Vanhoye, "Literarische Struktur und theologische Botschaft des Hebräerbriefs (1. Teil)," *Studien für die Neue Testament Umwelt* 4 (1979): 119-47; idem, "Literarische Struktur und theologische Botschaft des Hebräerbriefs (2. Teil)," *Studien für die Neue Testament Umwelt* 5 (1980): 18-49. A careful study of these more recent articles reveals that in fact his original outline has hardly been altered at all, and even then, the alterations are not to the specific divisions of the text.

[73]Vanhoye, *La structure littéraire*, (1963), 24-32. The influence of von Soden, Gyllnberg, and Thien is clear as well (16-23). See below.

[74]Hermann von Soden, writing in the first decade of the twentieth century, suggested that much could be gained by analyzing Hebrews along the lines of ancient Greek literary/rhetorical properties. See Hermann von Soden, *Urchristliche Literaturgeschichte: die Schriften des Neuen Testaments* (Berlin: Dunker, 1905), 127-28. Some fifty years after von Soden, Rafael Gyllenberg emphasized the switch between genres in Hebrews, and argued that such a switch was in fact the main point around which the epistle should be organized. See Gyllenberg, "Die Komposition des Hebräerbriefs," *SEÅ* 22-23 (1957-58): 137-47.

[75]Vanhoye, *La structure littéraire*, (1963), 37.

section, thus "hooking" the two sections together by means of vocabulary. The third device Vanhoye discusses is that of *genre*, specifically the shift that frequently occurs between sections of exposition and parenetic material. The fourth device is that of *les terms caractéristiques*, which are terms that are found several times within a given section of material, thus making that section distinct. The fifth and final literary device is Hebrews' use of the *inclusio*, a term or statement found both at the beginning and end of a given section, thus "bracketing" that pericope.

To be sure, Vanhoye did not discover each of these five devices. Rather, he brought the work of several of his forebears together and added to their work, thereby significantly advancing the discussion. For example, Vanhoye acknowledges von Soden's suggestion that the structure of Hebrews could be illumined by the aid of rules of Greek rhetoric.[76] His reliance upon Gyllenberg (and previously Büchsel) is well noted, as well as Thien and Vaganay. Likewise, the French scholar Descamps had previously made the observation concerning certain terms that were characteristic in one section of Hebrews or another.[77] Vanhoye should be credited with the significant work that he did regarding the usage of the inclusio as a rhetorical device in Hebrews,[78] as well as with introducing the problem of the structure of Hebrews as crucial to understanding the message of Hebrews.

One other fascinating characteristic of his structure is the symmetry Vanhoye asserts in the structure of Hebrews.[79] He heaps praise upon the writer of Hebrews for his extraordinary talent, a "true man of letters," and states that there is form and purpose for every phrase and word in the epistle; nothing is left to chance. At the outset of his influential work he writes,

> On reconnaît en cette épître l'œuvre d'un véritable homme de letters, dont le talent peu ordinaire a été mis en valeur par une excellente formation. Rien, dans ces pages ne semble laissé au hazard; au contraire, choix des mots, rythme et construction des phrases, agencement des divers themes, tout paraît dominé par la recherche d'un équilibre harmonieux, où de subtiles variations viennent estomper une symétrie savamment calculée.[80]

His admiration for the author's literary abilities led Vanhoye to argue for a perfect chiastic structure of Hebrews that pivots at 8:1-9:28 on the sacrifice of

---

[76]Ibid., 16-17.

[77]Albert Descamps called attention to the writer's use of characteristic terms. See his two-part article, "La structure de l'Épître aux Hébreux," *Revue Diocésaine de Tournai* 9 (1954): 251-58; 333-38.

[78]For a list of inclusions according to Vanhoye, see *La structure littéraire*, (1963), 222-23.

[79]Ibid., 60-64.

[80]Ibid., 11.

Christ. "Now Christ" (Χριστὸς δὲ) found in 9:11 is *literally* the very center of the entire structure of Hebrews, according to Vanhoye.[81] It is the central point of the central section, and is both preceded and followed by five and a half sections (152 and 146 verses, respectively). If one counts the five verses at the very end (the epistolary conclusion) then the number changes to 152 verses before and 151 after.[82] Vanhoye perhaps overemphasizes the "extraordinary nature" of this point. Regarding such mastery and literary perfection, Vanhoye writes that the writer of Hebrews "did not feel that the importance of his message dispensed him from care in giving it form."[83] Vanhoye makes much of this symmetry: parts one and five have one section, while parts two and four have two sections each, and part three has three sections. It is the second part of the third section in which the pivot point of the epistle can be found, Hebrews 9:11.

Though Vanhoye's work has been highly influential in Hebrews studies, it has been met with criticism since its publication. Black notes that one outstanding difficulty of Vanhoye's approach is "his method...makes several unwarranted deletions to secure perfect symmetry."[84] Black also states that Vanhoye dismisses 13:19 and 13:22-25 as later additions to Hebrews, an argument that has been overturned by the compelling studies by Spicq and Filson.[85] Kuss likewise finds fault with the perfect symmetry of Vanhoye's arrangement, and suggests that such an arrangement says more about the determination of the modern scholar than about the structure of Hebrews. He writes,

> Der jeweilige Aufweis einer durchsystematisierten Gliederung aber gibt eher von der Entschlossenheit und dem konstruierenden Scharfsinn der betreffenden Ausleger Zeugnis als von der wirklich einleuchtenden Planmäßigkeit einer bis in die Einzelheiten berechneten und gar an strenge Regeln gebundenen artifiziellen Komposition des unbekannten Autors.[86]

Swetnam questions the legitimacy of an approach that puts so much emphasis on literary devices and so little emphasis on content. He is critical of the suggestion that part five of Hebrews (12:14-13:18) is eschatological, as Vanhoye concludes. Swetnam asks, "can one give to 12, 14 – 13, 18 an

---

[81]Albert Vanhoye, *Structure and Message of the Epistle to the Hebrews*, Subsidia Biblica 12, trans. J. Swetnam (Rome: Editrice Pontifico Istituto Biblico, 1989), 36.

[82]Obviously versification is a later addition to the NT. These numbers are listed for the modern reader, and indicate, according to Vanhoye, the symmetry of the epistle.

[83]Vanhoye, *Structure and Message*, 32. For Vanhoye's structure of Hebrews, see Appendix 6.

[84]D. A. Black, "Literary Structure," 175.

[85]Spicq, "L'authenticité du chapitre XIII," 226-36; Filson, *"Yesterday,"* 15-16.

[86]Otto Kuss, *Der Brief and die Hebräer* (Regensberg: Friedrich Pustet, 1966), 14.

eschatological coloring and to deny it to 11, 1-40 which seems equally to be
aimed at a future goal (cf. 11, 40)?"[87] Further, he doubts the parallels of
sections one and five, and questions the placement of 5:11–6:20 before the
central section, and states that such a decision is "formally anomalous:
exhortation normally follows exposition."[88] In the end, Swetnam, one of
Vanhoye's most outspoken critics, considers this approach to be overly
complex and one that disregards content. He opts for a combination of formal
factors and content to illumine a coherent structure.[89]

Further, P. E. Hughes[90] and W. G. Kümmel[91] have criticized this approach,
though they have not offered any alternative or interaction. Additionally,
George Guthrie has observed at least one major flaw in this approach: Vanhoye
seems to have overlooked one of the biggest parallels in Hebrews, the parallels
that exist in 4:14-16 and 10:19-23.[92] This is one of the major questions one
must confront when studying the structure of Hebrews, of which Nauck's
approach makes much.[93] Likewise, Craig Koester does not follow Vanhoye's
approach, and comments that "it seems unlikely that Hebrews as a whole is
structured in a concentric manner."[94] For Koester (also Swetnam) it is not
evident that parts one and five deal with eschatology, while two and four center
on ecclesiology. Finally, Koester questions whether or not priesthood is in fact
the central theme. His reason for doing so comes from his conclusion that
Hebrews is a speech, and in the ancient forms of rhetoric, the main point came
at the beginning and end of the speech for a better rhetorical effect, and not in
the middle of the speech.[95]

---

[87]James Swetnam, "Form and Content in Hebrews 7-13," *Bib* 55 (1974): 345.

[88]Ibid., 345-46. He adds that this one factor alone would destroy Vanhoye's symmetry
and makes "his whole structure suspect" (346). Swetnam is not all negative concerning
Vanhoye. He notes that there is much that is correct in Vanhoye's conclusions, such as
seeing 7:1-28 as a complete unit, the fact the 8:1 begins a new division, and that 10:19
begins an exhortation (346). Swetnam's greatest criticism is that Vanhoye has perhaps
overemphasized form and underemphasized content.

[89]Swetnam, "Form and Content in Hebrews 7-13," 348.

[90]P. E. Hughes, *Hebrews*, 2. Hughes simply states, "Vanhoye in his detailed study seems
to me to err on the side of overstatement and to tend to find more stylistic symmetries
and literary subtleties than are really present." This is akin to Kuss and Swetnam.

[91]W. G. Kümmel, *Einleitung in das neue Testament*, 281. Kümmel's disagreement is
more fundamental, viz., he views the book to revolve around the parenetic sections (cf.
Michel, Kuss, and Nauck) and therefore does not agree with the literary approach of the
Vaganay-Vanhoye school.

[92]G. Guthrie, *Structure of Hebrews*, 79.

[93]Nauck, "Zum Aufbau des Hebräerbriefs," 200-03. See above.

[94]Koester, *Hebrews*, 83.

[95]Ibid., 83-86. For his part, Koester's outline is itself difficult to accept, given that he
sees significant breaks in the text at 2:9 and 12:27, while not seeing significant breaks at

Yet from the first publication of Vanhoye's work there have been numerous scholars who have found his basic premises compelling. For instance, one year after the publication of *La structure littéraire de l'Épître aux Hébreux*, Montefiore accepted Vanhoye's outline, using it as the basis for his 1964 commentary. He writes of Vanhoye, "His plan carries conviction because the structure he proposes appears to have been worked out by our author as rigorously as the logic of his Epistle."[96] Likewise, Buchanan basically adopted Vanhoye's divisions with no discussion in 1972.[97] Harold Attridge,[98] Bénétreau,[99] Ellingworth,[100] and Lane[101] also generally follow the approach of Vanhoye with only slight alterations. The more recent work of Dussaut greatly relies on Vanhoye, and still argues for the concentric nature of the epistle centering around the term Χριστὸς in 9:11.[102] Though by no means amounting to a consensus, the influence of Vanhoye in more recent decades should be noted. However, as Koester observes, questions still remain.[103]

F. F. Bruce

F. F. Bruce has proposed a content-centered approach for the structure of Hebrews.[104] He notes that the epistle is a carefully crafted work of literature that has a "concentric symmetry and an elaborate inclusio."[105] He favorably cites the studies of Vaganay and Vanhoye, and it seems clear that he has been influenced

---

4:14 and 10:19. Again, Koester has concluded that Hebrews is an ancient rhetorical speech, and his outline reflects such a conclusion (I. Exordium, II. Proposition, III. Arguments, IV. Peroration, V. Epistolary Postscript). The present writer doed not find this structure to be very helpful to the present discussion, since it is far from proven that Hebrews has been crafted along the lines and rules of ancient rhetoric, though it does include rhetorical devices.

[96]Hugh Montefiore, *A Commentary on the Epistle to the Hebrews*, BNTC (London: Adam & Charles Black, 1964), 31.

[97]George W. Buchanan, *To the Hebrews*, AB 36 (Garden City, NY: Doubleday, 1972), 1-2.

[98]See below.

[99]Samuel Bénétreau, *L'Épître aux Hébreux* (Vaux-sur-Seine: Edifac, 1989-90), 1:31-33.

[100]Ellingworth, *Hebrews*, 58. Ellingworth acknowledges the fact that there are difficulties in Vanhoye's approach, yet adopts it for his commentary. See his comments on p. 58.

[101]Lane, *Hebrews*, viii–ix; lxxxiv–xcviii.

[102]Note his comments regarding Vanhoye (Dussaut, *Synopse structurelle*, 3-4). Concerning 9:11, Dussaut writes, "Nous sommes ainsi arrivé au coeur meme de l'Epître. 'Le Christ...' ce Nom-fonction qui ouvre la huitième Section est placé en plein coeur de l'Epître" (72-73).

[103]Koester, *Hebrews*, 83.

[104]F. F. Bruce, *Hebrews*, vii – x; idem, "The Structure and Argument of Hebrews," *SWJT* 28 (1985): 6-12.

[105]Bruce, "Structure and Argument," 6.

by some of their divisions of the text. He sees Hebrews to be arguing a
"superiority" motif, and such is reflected from the outset of his discussion. In
addition, the climax of Hebrews is the three-fold "Let us" hortatory
subjunctives of 10:19-25, which, for Bruce is the climax to which the entire
epistle builds. He writes, "The preceding argument leads up, stage by stage, to
this exhortation, and what comes after reinforces it."[106]

Bruce finds eight distinct sections in Hebrews, each one given a title that
reflects the content within that section. The first section, "I. The Finality of
Christianity (1:1-2:18)" centers on the matter of the son's superiority to the
angels. The second section is "II. The Rest that Remains for the People of God
(3:1-4:13)."[107] Jesus is superior to Moses in 3:1-6 and is over the household of
God. This is connected to 3:7-19, which is a clear admonition to beware of
unbelief. Those in the household of Christ (1-6) are to continue in their faith (7-
19). Rather than rebelling as those in the wilderness, believers are admonished
to enter into the Sabbath rest of God (4:1-13).

Bruce sees a hard break at this point, and identifies his third section as
"Christ the High Priest (4:14-6:20)" which is comprised of six subsections:
4:14-16, 5:1-10, 5:11-14, 6:1-8, 6:9-12 and 6:13-20.[108] Most of this third
section is given to admonition and warning (5:11-6:8), and an encouragement
to persevere (6:9-12) based upon God's sure promise (6:13-20).

Section four is the whole of chapter 7, which most scholars acknowledge to
be an independent unit.[109] Bruce simply titles his fourth section, "The Order of
Melchizedek," with three distinct divisions, 7:1-10 ("The Greatness of
Melchizedek"), 7:11-14 ("The Imperfection of Aaronic Priesthood"), and 7:15-
28 ("Superiority of the Melchizedek Priesthood").[110]

---

[106]Ibid.

[107]Again the question arises as to the placement of 4:14-16. Does it go with the rest of
Heb 4, or does it go with what comes in Heb 5? Bruce (cf. Nauck) views it as an
introduction to what follows, while Vaganay, Vanhoye, Spicq, and Attridge place it in
the middle of the second major movement of the book, and therefore do not see 4:14-16
as a dividing point in the structure. George Guthrie offers a helpful answer to this
question. See below for his treatment.

[108]In this third section, it is difficult to understand Bruce's title ("Christ the High Priest")
when only the first third actually deals with anything relating to Christ as high priest,
and given the fact that the topic of the high priest is more directly taken up in Heb 7. As
Bruce himself notes, the bulk of this section contains an exhortation and warning—
content whose connection to "Christ the High Priest" is not spelled out by Bruce, nor is
it easily seen by this writer.

[109]See for example Steve Stanley, "The Structure of Hebrews from Three Perspectives,"
TynBul 45 (1994): 260, and James Swetnam, "The Structure of Hebrews: A Fresh
Look," *MelT* 41 (1990): 39.

[110]Again, note the "superiority" motif here that Bruce favors. Additionally, the division
after 7:14 is most peculiar and emphasizes the weakness of this approach. There is

The fifth section of Bruce's structure of Hebrews comprises 8:1-10:18 ("Covenant, Sanctuary, and Sacrifice"), and consists of eight subsections: 8:1-7, 8:8-13, 9:1-10, 9:11-14, 9:15-22, 9:23-28, 10:1-10 and 10:11-18. This doctrinally-heavy section drives towards the climax of the epistle, found in the sixth main section of Hebrews, "Call to Worship and Persevering Faith" (10:19-12:29), which consists of eight smaller sections. Bruce writes that the sustained exhortation of 10:19-25 "might well have formed the conclusion of the homily, had not our author judged it wise to expand and apply in greater detail the points made here, for the further encouragement and strengthening of his readers."[111] In saying this Bruce comes close to the traditional view.

Finally, section seven of Bruce's outline consists of 13:1-21 ("Concluding Exhortation and Prayer") and is composed of "ethical injunctions" (13:1-8), a note about "the true sacrifices" (13:9-16), and "obedience and prayer" (13:17-21). Part eight is the postscript (13:22-25).

As noted previously, one significant shortcoming of this approach is its subjectivity. Should another scholar give a different heading to a particular section, it would inevitably affect the thematic exposition of the text. Second, this approach does not distinguish any change in genre, and as it has been noted before, the movement from kerygma to parenesis is important for the structure of Hebrews. Such movement has significant effects on one's understanding of Hebrews itself.[112] What Bruce does not do is explain why he has made the divisions that he has in the text. It seems that he has made such decisions based upon his own understanding of changes of subject, or changes of direction in the flow of the argument of Hebrews. Attridge rightly notes that such a method does little to illumine the function of the various sections.[113] In short, we are left wondering *why* he has defined the structure in the manner that he has. Short of a footnote in the revised edition of his commentary,[114] there is very little from the pen of Bruce that lets his readers know what he thinks regarding matters of

---

nothing in the Greek text itself to indicate any sort of division between vv. 14 and 15, and in the mind of this writer, no shift in topic either. This highlights the subjectivity of the content approach: there is a division here because Bruce, the commentator, senses one. That said, one would be naïve to assert that there is *any* approach that is *entirely* objective. The words of Stanley ought be heeded (Stanley, "The Structure of Hebrews," 256-57). Similarly, Ellingworth notes the difficulty of maintaining this "better than/superior" approach to the structure of Hebrews in light of the fact that the term in question (κρείσσων-κρειττων) is absent from 1:4-6:9 (Ellingworth, *Hebrews*, 52).
[111]Bruce, *Hebrews*, 249.
[112]G. Guthrie, *Structure of Hebrews*, 28.
[113]Attridge, *Hebrews*, 14.
[114]Bruce, *Hebrews*, xxii n. 1. In this brief note, F. F. Bruce merely notes that the structure of Hebrews has been the topic of study in recent decades. He notes that specific scholars have addressed the issue, yet there is no interaction with the various scholars he lists.

structure. Indeed, Black seems to be correct in his criticism of Bruce's "patchwork approach," in which there seems to be "no overriding theory of structure."[115] Black also notes that this approach is "unwilling to accept the traditional model and is in apparent opposition to those engaged in refined literary analyses of Hebrews."[116] In the end one is led to conclude that Bruce does not see matters of structure to be significant, in contrast to the majority of current Hebrews scholars.

Likewise, Ellingworth sees several difficulties to this approach, such as the tendency to press the structure into a form or pattern that may not be found in the text. Secondly, seeing similarities with the "traditional approach" of D. Guthrie, he observes a tendency to read modern concepts and distinctions, such as Guthrie's divisions between social, private, and religious life, into the text of Hebrews.[117] He is also cautious regarding the tendency of the content-centered approach to "over-sharpen the gradual transitions which are a notable feature of Hebrews."[118]

With criticisms noted, the position here is not that Bruce offers nothing to the current discussion. Rather, this writer agrees with Bruce concerning several of his large divisions. For instance, there should be a break of some kind after 2:18, 4:13, 6:20, 7:28, 10:18, and 12:29. However, the question arises as to how one should describe such breaks. Are they major breaks in the flow of the writer's argument? This is what Bruce would seem to suggest, as each marks the end of major sections in his outline.

In the end, this approach attempts to be descriptive of the work's content, with no expressed criteria for its various divisions and subdivisions. In seeking to be completely inductive regarding divisions of the various sections, it is not very helpful to the current discussion. Perhaps Black's label of Bruce's as the

---

[115]Black, "Literary Structure," 163; cf. 175-76.

[116]Ibid., 175. By "traditional" Black is referring to the approach of D. Guthrie et al., described above. Secondly, Black uses the word "apparent" because Bruce simply does not say. Bruce does not interact with any discussion of structure. Whether Bruce is actually in *opposition* to the approach of literary analysis is an argument from silence. However, Bruce's silence on the matter is marked. It is perhaps striking and telling that twenty-six years elapsed between Vanhoye's *La structure littéraire* and Bruce's 1990 revision of his commentary, and twenty-two years between Vanhoye and Bruce's 1986 article, "The Structure and Argument of Hebrews," yet there is no mention of Vanhoye's influential work. It seems safe to suggest that for Bruce, discussions regarding structure are of little importance.

[117]Ellingworth, *Hebrews*, 52.

[118]Ibid., 52-53. For example, Bruce sees a major break at 11:1, yet such does not acknowledge that the topic of discussion throughout Heb 11 (faith) is carefully established at the end of Heb 10.

"patchwork approach" is warranted.[119]

Harold Attridge

Attridge's conclusions as to the structure of Hebrews largely follow those of the Vaganay-Vanhoye school of thought, and his own thoughts on matters of structure and the purpose of articulating such matters are set forth clearly in the commentary's introduction.[120] He observes that an analysis of the structure of a work "should serve the more important function of articulating the system of internal relations of the parts of the discourse,"[121] and rightly notes that the problem lies not with the delineation of the smaller units of material (the paragraph level), but rather with the delineation and relationship of the larger units. He criticizes the approaches of Spicq and Bruce when he writes,

> Structural analyses are, however, notoriously subjective, and what is articulated is often simply the critic's prejudices or perceptions of thematic coherence.... Thematically oriented...construals do little to indicate the function of the various sections of the text and often skew the interpretation of the text as primarily a dogmatic work.[122]

He also criticizes the tripartite scheme of Nauck for its inability to articulate the relationships of the various sections in the text.[123]

After briefly surveying the major approaches, Attridge finds himself compelled by the "purely formal criteria" set forth by Vanhoye,[124] though he does not embrace all of Vanhoye's conclusions without reservation and criticism.[125] Attridge attempts to bind together the "static organizational principles" as well as the "dynamic developmental features" in his own analysis.

---

[119]Lest this writer be regarded as being too critical of F. F. Bruce, it must be stated that though his approach to the structure of Hebrews is not helpful to the particular discussion of structure, his commentary is quite helpful. The criticism here lies in the matter of putting the parts *together*, which is where this writer avers that Bruce has fallen short. Ellingworth may be more on target when he suggests that surface structure analysis, such as that of Vanhoye and Dussaut may in fact reveal certain features that could be a complement to the content-centered approach of Bruce. Though these two approaches are quite different, they may in fact, in time, prove to be complementary (Ellingworth, *Hebrews*, 55).

[120]Attridge, *Hebrews*, 19.

[121]This is a bit ironic given Swetnam's criticism of Attridge. See his remarks below.

[122]Attridge, *Hebrews*, 14.

[123]Ibid., 15.

[124]Ibid.

[125]Harold Attridge, "The Uses of Antithesis in Hebrews 8-10," *HTR* 79 (1986): 1-9. Attridge criticizes Vanhoye for being "forced" and "artificial" at times.

Though there are differences with Vanhoye in the smaller sections of his structural assessment, he lists five major sections that all but directly correspond to those offered by Vanhoye. After an exordium in 1:1-4, which Attridge describes as an "elaborate and carefully composed rhetorical exordium that poetically encapsulates the major doctrinal affirmations of the text," the first major section begins with 1:5 and concludes with 2:18. The second major movement, 3:1-5:10, centers on the two major epithets announced at the conclusion of the first, "Christ Faithful and Merciful."[126] It is in 5:6 that Psalm 110 is cited, the implications of which will be explored in the following section. The third major division (5:11-10:25) is simply entitled, "The Difficult Discourse," whose first subsection is the lengthy parenesis in 5:11-6:20 after which exposition resumes in 7:1. A distinct difference between Attridge and Vanhoye is Attridge's decision to conclude this lengthy central section at 10:25, rather than at 10:39 as per Vanhoye. Thus it is clear that Attridge is not as concerned with concentricity as Vanhoye. This section of the epistle is broken into three further parts, 7:1-28, 8:1-10:18, and concludes with 10:19-25, a "Parenetic Application" of what has been previously argued. The fourth major section (10:26-12:13) therefore begins with parenesis (10:26-38),[127] followed by an encomium on faith (11:1-40) and a homily on faithful obedience (12:1-13). The fifth and final movement is parenetic in nature (12:14-13:21) and consists of two halves, 12:18-29 and 13:1-21. The final verses (13:20-25) mirror the introductory exordium, and contain a benediction and various greetings.

James Swetnam states that Attridge's 1989 Hebrews commentary represents a "major event in New Testament scholarship"[128] and in particular in the study of Hebrews. Indeed, Swetnam heaps praise upon this publication, putting it on the same level of importance as those commentaries by Spicq, Michel, and Moffatt.[129] However, Swetnam expresses significant disappointment in the structure that Attridge has adopted. Since Attridge has adopted a structure so similar to that of Vanhoye, he finds himself facing many of the same criticisms as Vanhoye (noted above). However, though Attridge prefers the Vaganay-Vanhoye school over that of Nauck, he concludes that such tripartite schemes cannot be ignored. He observes the close relationship between the first and second movements as the third and fourth movements. He rightly adds, "The first two develop...the major features of the text's Christological position and...introduce a key parenetic theme," while the final two sections of Hebrews

---

[126]One can see here a fundamental disagreement with those who see a break at 4:14-16. He refers to 4:14-16 as a "resumptive paragraph" (Attridge, *Hebrews*, 17).

[127]Heb 10:39 seems to have dropped out of Attridge's outline. See Attridge, *Hebrews*, 19.

[128]Swetnam, "A Fresh Look," 25.

[129]Ibid.

"are both primarily parenetic and are involved with applications of and inferences from the preceding doctrinal exposition."[130]

What is clear from Attridge's proposed analysis is that he has not merely adopted an outline without first considering the options available to him. Though he does not attempt a fresh undertaking, it is apparent that his conclusions, though based on the divisions of Vanhoye, do not leave the other prevailing options unconsidered. Indeed, one sees that he acknowledges the strengths of both the tripartite and other schemes.

Yet there are criticisms that can be leveled against Attridge specifically. Swetnam states, "In this structure the epistle comes through as being ill-focused and its author not clear about what he was driving at."[131] He states that a key difficulty in Attridge's proposed structure is its fragmentation of the structure into so many parts. He writes, "one has to have recourse to an outline to know just where one is. Form is obscuring content, not enhancing it."[132] Whereas the skill and vigor of the writer of Hebrews should produce clarity of form, Swetnam states that Attridge has actually created "fuzziness" that does not mark the epistle. Further, Attridge leaves several questions lingering with the reader such as, "What then is the author of Hebrews really up to? What is he saying? What does he expect his audience to do?"[133] In the end, Swetnam gives Attridge a "vote of no confidence."[134]

Swetnam is perhaps guilty of overstatement at times in his criticism of Attridge, given that as one encounters Hebrews he realizes that no simple account of its structure will suffice. In fact, Attridge is quite succinct on pages 17-19 of his commentary, in which he summarizes his own understanding of the ebb and flow of the epistle. This writer personally finds many aspects of Attridge's approach quite persuasive. That said, perhaps the text-linguistic approach of George Guthrie stands at the front of the line among current explanations of Hebrews' structure. Guthrie's "eclectic" approach to the current question is quite compelling, and to this we now turn our attention.

---

[130]Attridge, *Hebrews*, 19.

[131]Swetnam, "A Fresh Look," 26.

[132]Ibid., 25 n. 2. One will recognize a similar complaint from Swetnam regarding Vanhoye.

[133]Ibid., 26.

[134]Ibid. This statement is not in the least softened by Swetnam's admission that he gives himself the same "vote of no confidence." The present writer feels that Swetnam is overly harsh in his criticisms at this point – criticisms that go back two decades to his interactions with Vanhoye.

George Guthrie

INTRODUCTION

In his 1991 dissertation, George Guthrie offered an advance in the discussion of the structure of Hebrews by making use of text-linguistic analysis, a relatively new discipline in its application to biblical studies.[135] Text-linguistic analysis is concerned with how larger units of material fit together. In this discipline, Guthrie writes that the "critic seeks to understand the relationships between sections of an author's discourse....[and] is based upon an assumption that written texts begin with the author's conception of the theme which he wants to communicate."[136] To this he adds, "This theme is then expressed and developed by the author's language choices—individual words, grammar, and style— which give meaning and structure to the 'cola' which make up his 'paragraphs.'"[137] This demonstrates the importance of seeing and understanding the relationships between constituent paragraphs if one desires to understand the whole of the main discourse. This, as one can see, is directly applicable to one of the most important features of the structure of Hebrews: the interweaving of exposition and parenesis, or in Guthrie's terms, "expository and hortatory."[138]

---

[135]For Guthrie's complete structural assessment, see Appendix 7.

[136]Guthrie, *Structure of Hebrews*, 46.

[137]Ibid.

[138]Recall that the recognition of a shift in genre within Hebrews was articulated by Büchsel, Gyllenberg and Vanhoye. However, this approach has not been wholly embraced by Cynthia Westfall, *A Discourse Analysis of the Letter to the Hebrews: The Relationship between Form and Meaning*, LNTS 297 (London: T&T Clark-Continuum, 2005), 18-20. Westfall finds Guthrie's outline, which visualizes the exposition and exhortatory material running side-by-side to be "not a coherent mental representation of the discourse" (20). Westfall continues, "The assertion of discontinuity between the exposition and exhortation is reminiscent of F. C. Synge who questioned the integrity of the entire discourse" (ibid.). However, Guthrie himself nowhere questions the integrity of the discourse. On the contrary, Guthrie states that the discourse is woven together (as a unity) with the two threads of exhortation and exposition forming one coherent work. Westfall adds that rather than help readers of Hebrews visualize the structure of the book, "Guthrie's structural representation comes from a confusion of central and support material, and the result is a lack of coherence and cohesion" (ibid.). Westfall's statement is certainly not true for all readers of Guthrie's work, and the present writer concludes that Guthrie's structure does in fact yield a helpful visualization. Further, his structural layout has been an asset to my own students who use it.

Westfall also faults Guthrie for suggesting that the writer of Hebrews put forward a piece of writing that has no parallels in the ancient culture. She states, "Guthrie cannot locate a discourse pattern with two backbones in the sociocultural milieu of Hellenistic literature" (*Discourse Analysis*, 20). Yet Westfall states that many of the *rhetorical elements* of which Guthrie writes are indeed found in the cultural milieu of Hebrews.

Guthrie has made at least two major contributions to the ongoing discussion of structure. First, he has demonstrated that there are no fewer than nine devices in Hebrews that connect the various units of material and bring about the transitions in the discourse. Second, he notes the distinct function of the kerygma/exposition and parenesis/exhortation. His structural outline of Hebrews is unique from other scholars before him, placing a distinct and *visible* emphasis on the two genres, so that one can see the actual interweaving of the two.[139] Indeed, in his outline of the structure one clearly sees the benefit of placing these distinct units side by side. In doing so, he proposes two major semantic discourse notions: expository and hortatory. He rightly observes that Hebrews shifts back and forth between exposition and exhortation, observing that these two lines move in concert with one another as the epistle progresses.[140] Guthrie notes Nauck's influence on his own conclusions when he

---

The present writer wonders if it is as necessary to "locate a discourse pattern with two backbones" as Westfall seems to demand in order for Guthrie's approach to be valid. Again, what Westfall seems to have the most difficulty with is the very point that the present writer has found the most helpful: Guthrie's depiction of exhortation and exposition. Westfall's dissatisfaction seems a bit ill-founded given that the writer of Hebrews does in fact move from one genre to the other. Guthrie's outline merely depicts this.

In the end, Westfall seems to find Guthrie's analysis more confusing than helpful. If Guthrie's assessment were truly this confusing then there would be implications for the original hearers of this word of exhortation. In short, Westfall seems to suggest that if Guthrie is correct, then the original audience would have been more confused by what they heard than helped. However, Guthrie acknowledges that the hearers would not have had to catch every twist and turn in the discourse in order to benefit despite the dual structure of Hebrews that that he puts forward (Guthrie, *Structure of Hebrews*, 146-47). What would have been clear to the original listeners is the shift back and forth from exposition to exhortation; the original audience would not have had to grasp all of the subtle rhetorical nuances in order for the epistle to have its intended effect. Turning the tables a bit, the present writer would argue that since Westfall does not delineate between the two genres in her analysis of Hebrews, she has unfortunately disregarded a major concern with respect to the structure of the epistle that the writer of Hebrews intended. The present writer avers that any proposed structure of Hebrews that does not take into account the shift in genre will be at a decided disadvantage.

[139]In his comments, Lane notes, "It is Guthrie's contention that in an outline of Hebrews it is necessary to distinguish sharply between exposition and exhortation, since each genre is assigned a distinctive function. His outline reflects his understanding of the relationship between alternating genres, based on a text-linguistic analysis" (Lane, *Hebrews*, 1:xcvi). In fact, this sharp distinction is seen in the final chapter of Guthrie's work, in which he argues that expositional and hortatory units must be considered separately, at least initially. See Guthrie, *Structure of Hebrews*, 112-16.

[140]For a practical illustration, see his 1998 Hebrews commentary (George H. Guthrie, *The NIV Application Commentary: Hebrews* [Grand Rapids: Zondervan, 1998], 28).

writes, "When these two genres are held too far apart and the important hortatory passages are lost in an expositionally oriented outline, the overall purpose of Hebrews is skewed."[141]

What makes Guthrie's proposal unique is that he relates to both of the major approaches represented by the work of Nauck and Vanhoye. He argues that emphasis ought to be placed on the hortatory sections of Hebrews with regard to its structure, similar to Nauck, yet with modifications. Likewise, Guthrie draws much from Vanhoye's approach, though not without criticism.[142] Commenting on his own work Guthrie writes,

> I offered an eclectic approach combining identification of techniques highlighted by earlier literary approaches, identification of types of transition techniques, and various other linguistic methods in a discourse analysis of the text. I challenged Vanhoye...at...numerous points, preeminently his lack of attention to a prominent *inclusio* at 4:14-16 and 10:19-25. However, both Vanhoye's work and mine make clear that the use of techniques such as *inclusio* and hook-words...plays a significant role in marking the structure of Hebrews.[143]

In his analysis of the structure of Hebrews, Guthrie brings to the surface hook-words, distant hook-words, three types of hooked key words, overlapping constituents, parallel introductions, inclusio, change in genre, direct intermediary transitions, and woven intermediary transitions, building on the work of the Vaganay-Vanhoye school of thought.[144] He has identified specific rhetorical tools of transition on the surface-level of the text, which are more objective and useful for identifying transitions than that of the thematic approach of others such as Bruce. It is the view of this writer that this is one of the strongest benefits to this kind of approach.[145]

In his arrangement Guthrie separately outlines the expositional and hortatory

---

[141]G. Guthrie, *Structure of Hebrews*, 115. Contra Westfall, *Discourse Analysis*, 18-20.

[142]G. Guthrie, *Structure of Hebrews*, 35.

[143]George H. Guthrie, "Hebrews in its First-Century Contexts: Recent Research," in *The Face of New Testament Studies*, ed. S. McKnight and G. Osborne (Grand Rapids: Baker, 2004). 424. For a concise summary of Guthrie's text-linguistic approach, see Lane, *Hebrews*, 1:xc-xcviii. Lane laments the fact that Guthrie's study was completed only after his own commentary on Hebrews had been completed. However, Lane was able to include an addendum that discusses and briefly interacts with Guthrie's work.

[144]Each of these components and their usage in Hebrews is the focus of chapters 4, 5, and 6 of Guthrie's work.

[145]This brings to mind the criticism of Nauck, Kümmel, and Michel, who suggest that it is not the expositional portions that are the center, but the exhortations (see above). Hence they typically see significant breaks after 4:13 and 10:18/31. Nauck argued that the parallel passages of 4:14-16 and 10:19-31 framed three major sections of the epistle. See Nauck, "Zum Aufbau des Hebräerbriefes," 203-06. Therefore 5:1-10:18 form a expository unit. However, the bulk of 5:11-6:20 is clearly exhortation.

materials.[146] After the introduction of 1:1-4, the first major section of exposition comprises 1:5-2:18 (excluding 2:1-4, which is exhortation) and is titled, "The Position of the Son in Relation to the Angels." This is made up of two main subpoints, "The Son Superior to the Angels" (1:5-14), and "The Son Lower Than the Angels (i.e., among men) to Suffer for the Sons" (2:10-18).[147] The intervening section of 2:5-9 (based on Ps. 8:1-2) serves as a transition between these two points that Guthrie titles, "The Superior Son for a Time Became Positionally Lower Than the Angels."[148]

The second and most significant block of exposition comprises the bulk of 4:14-10:25, "The Position of the Son, Our High Priest, in Relation to the Earthly Sacrificial System."[149] This main section consists of a significant inclusio at 4:14-16 ("We Have a Sinless High Priest Who Has Gone into Heaven") and 10:19-25 ("We Have a Great High Priest Who Takes Us into Heaven").[150] Within this second section there are two main subsections, tied together with a "direct intermediary transition" at 8:1-2 ("We Have Such a High Priest Who Is a Minister in Heaven").[151] The first subsection consists of 5:1-10, where the subject matter concerning Melchizedek and his priesthood is introduced, and 7:1-28 ("The Appointment of the Son as a Superior High Priest") where this new priesthood is explained as having already been spoken

---

[146]See fig. 28 in Guthrie, *Structure of Hebrews*, 117.

[147]Guthrie suggests that there is a connection of at least four points between 2:10 and 17-18 (G. Guthrie, *Structure of Hebrews*, 77-78). First, the terms ἔπρεπεν-ὤφειλεν in vv. 10 and 17 correspond to one another in that they both present an aspect of the incarnation. Second, both passages refer to the Son's "development" in that he is "perfected" and he "becomes." Third, in both passages Jesus comes as an aid to "sons" and "brothers." Fourth, "suffering" is found in 2:10 and 18 (παθημάτων-πέπονθεν).

However, instead of calling this an inclusio, Westfall suggests that it would be better to see v. 10 as a topic-opening sentence of the sub-unit, and vv. 17-18 are topic-closing, since the intervening sentences all have similar bonds (*Discourse Analysis*, 100-110). Yet the idea of topic-opening and closing is not foreign to the practice of the inclusio. See G. Guthrie, *Structure of Hebrews*, 15.

[148]Contrast Neeley, "Discourse Analysis," 66, who sees 2:1-19 as a unit.

[149]It should be noted that unlike Nauck ("Zum Aufbau des Hebräerbriefes," 201-03), Guthrie's methodology allows him to *visually* separate the hortatory material of 5:11-6:20 in his structure.

[150]This is a significant critique of Vanhoye's work, who seemingly overlooked the inclusio at 4:14-16 and 10:19-25. This critique is established by Guthrie, *The Structure of Hebrews*, 79-82.

[151]The debate over where exactly 8:1-2 "fits" might well be solved. Guthrie persuasively describes this as having elements of what has come before as well as after, and describes it as a "direct intermediary transition" (G. Guthrie, *The Structure of Hebrews*, 105-08). It is because of the fact that these verses have elements of both 7:1-28 *and* 8:3-10:18 that has made 8:1-2 difficult to place. Noting their transitory nature from one topic and section to another is quite helpful.

of in the OT (Genesis 14 and Ps 110).[152] The second subsection consists of 8:3-
10:18 ("The Superior Offering of the Appointed High Priest"),[153] in which the
more excellent ministry of the heavenly high priest is articulated (8:3-6),
followed by the new and eternal priest's new and eternal covenant (8:7-13), and
the priest's superior NC offering (9:1-10:18). Hebrews 10:19-25 forms an
inclusio with 4:14-16 and functions as the closing of the large center section of
Hebrews.[154]

---

[152]This is the point of the important article by G. B. Caird, "The Exegetical Method of
the Epistle to the Hebrews," *CJT* 5 (1959): 44-51.

[153]Though grammatically 8:3 is connected to 8:2 simply by γὰρ, 7:1-28 and 8:1-13 are
"hinged" by the direct intermediary transition of 8:1-2. Thus it may be difficult to speak
of 8:3 as the beginning of this section when there is no significant grammatical break
between 8:2 and 8:3. Guthrie visually isolates 8:1-2 in his outline, though contextually it
is connected with 8:3-13 and 7:1-28. What is noteworthy is that for Guthrie, the
transition of 8:1-2 is more than a movement in the expositional argument; it indicates
spatial movement of the Son from the realm of earth to the realm of heaven. For further
discussion of this spatial aspect, see Guthrie, *The Structure of Hebrews*, 121-24.

[154]Westfall notes the parallelism between these collections of subjunctives (three each),
though she begins at 4:11 and not 4:14. She asserts, "The central section of Hebrews
(4:11-10:25) develops the topic of Jesus' high priesthood that was introduced in 2:17
and deactivated after 3:1. The section lies between the two parallel units of three
hortatory subjunctives in 4:11-16 and 10:19-25" (Westfall, *Discourse Analysis*, 140; cf.
133-39). She avers that her central section is similar to George W. Buchanan's fourth
section: 5:1-10:39 (Buchanan, *To the Hebrews*, 1) and to Neeley's 'Paragraph 2' in
4:14-10:18 (Neeley, "Discourse Analysis," 33-35).

The reason Westfall begins the section at 4:11 and not 4:14 is that she sees 4:11 as
beginning a summary. Noting the difficulty in the demarcation of the beginning of this
section she writes, "It is generally recognized that the topic of Jesus' high priesthood is
reactivated in 4:14, so that a major structural shift is often placed in the middle of the
hortatory subjunctive span in 4:11-16" (Westfall, *Discourse Analysis*, 140). Yet this
writer argues that the presence of the subjunctive in 4:11 (σπουδάσωμεν) should *not* be
seen as beginning the summary which concludes this section. Rather, it is the logical
conclusion for what has been explicitly argued in 4:1-10, viz., the κατάπαυσις of God.
Westfall is unique in her decision at this point, and this represents another distinction
between her analysis and that of Guthrie's with respect to the divisions of that text, and
what data should guide such decisions. The subjunctive in 4:11 is not on the same level
as those in 4:14-16, and should not be included. Rather, 4:14-16 recapitulates what was
begun in 2:17-18; 4:11 brings 4:10 to a close and should not be so grouped with vv. 14-
16. Westfall rightly observes the influence of Vanhoye, who labels 4:14 as a conclusion
of 3:1-4:14 as well as an inclusion, on such scholars G. Guthrie and Lane (140 n. 3). Cp.
Vanhoye, *Structure and Message*, 25-26, 40, 86; Guthrie (*Structure of Hebrews*, 78);
and Lane (*Hebrews*, 1:96-97).

Further, Westfall criticizes Guthrie for not giving the conjunctions their just due in
terms of divisions in the text. One such example will suffice. As stated above, Guthrie
asserts a shift in genre at Hebrews 3:1 from exposition to hortatory. Westfall disagrees

HORTATORY SECTIONS

Separately, Guthrie identifies the hortatory sections as well.[155] He notes that the epistle opens with an exordium in 1:1-4 in which key elements are introduced. The warning of 2:1-4 is the first of several emphatic, pastoral warnings. The whole of 3:1-4:13[156] is then considered in four sections: Hebrews 3:1-6 is understood as hortatory,[157] encouraging the "house of God" to be faithful as Christ was faithful; 3:7-19 centers on the failures of the wilderness generation, the nexus of which is the testimony of Ps 95:7-11; Hebrews 4:3-11[158] offers the promise of rest for those who endure, in contrast to those just mentioned from the wilderness generation; 4:12-13 offers another warning to the effect that none can hide from the word of God. Guthrie rightly notes, "Just as the promise of rest still stands, so does the 'oath' of anger and judgment for those who follow the example of disobedience provided by those who fell in the wilderness."[159] The next hortatory section begins at 5:11-6:3,[160] (which is part

---

based upon what the writer of Hebrews had begun in 2:14-18 (Westfall, *Discourse Analysis*, 111-15). She claims Guthrie is mistaken, stating that "he misses the semantic weight of inferential conjunctions such as ὅθεν" (111, n. 89). In contrast, Guthrie maintains that the inferential conjunction ὅθεν introduces a point that the author wishes to drive home via the shift to hortatory (Guthrie, *Structure of Hebrews*, 65-66, 128).

[155]G. Guthrie, *Structure of Hebrews*, 127-34.

[156]G. Guthrie concludes that there is an inclusio that opens at 3:1 and closes at 4:14 (G. Guthrie, *Structure of Hebrews*, 78; see also Vanhoye, *La structure littéraire*, 1964:54). Westfall is uncertain (Westfall, *Discourse Analysis*, 140 n. 109).

[157]As noted above, Westfall fails to see a shift in genre from exposition to hortatory at 3:1. See Westfall, *Discourse Analysis*, 111-15; cp. G. Guthrie, *Structure of Hebrews*, 65-66; 128.

Again, one of the central differences between Guthrie and Westfall is the question of a shift in genre back and forth from exposition to exhortation. Westfall disagrees, yet for the present writer, does not adequately explain these shifts. For example, Westfall downplays any such shift at 5:10/5:11 (Westfall, *Discourse Analysis*, 140-51), though numerous scholars do in fact see a distinct shift at this point (such as Vanhoye, Lane, and Attridge). See discussion on 5:10/5:11 below.

[158]Heb 4:1-2 is an intermediary transition that hinges together what comes before and after. See also the discussion above concerning 8:1-2. There is, however, a grammatical break at 4:1 that is more obvious than at 8:1. The transitional 4:1-2 begins with φοβηθῶμεν οὖν, while 8:1-2 begins by Κεφάλαιον δὲ ἐπὶ τοῖς λεγομένοις.

[159]G. Guthrie, *Structure of Hebrews*, 130.

[160]Attridge identifies 5:11-6:3 as an "introductory exhortation" (Attridge, *Epistle to the Hebrews*, 156). Concerning the whole of 5:11-6:20, Lane states, "Although it is commonly recognized that 5:11-6:20 forms a literary unit within the structure of Hebrews, there has been no general agreement concerning its character or logical scheme" (Lane, *Hebrews*, 1:133).

of a larger section of hortatory, 5:11-6:20)[161] in which the hearers are berated
for their spiritual immaturity. The warning of 6:4-8 is quite harsh, and Guthrie
views this section as a warning to those who have experienced the Christian
faith in some sense, viz., there is no other place to go for salvation.[162] After
such a harsh warning, there is mitigation in 6:9-12, in which the author
expresses his confidence in his audience.[163]

After the large central section of exposition (7:1-10:18)[164] that concludes

---

[161]This is a difficult issue regarding the structure of Hebrews. On the matter of 5:11-6:20
Lane notes, "It is commonly recognized that 5:11-6:20 forms a literary unit within the
structure of Hebrews" (Lane, *Hebrews*, 1:133). Westfall recognizes the difficulty when
she notes, "Most scholars are agreed that there is a high level shift in 5:11 to a separate
section that splits the discussion of Jesus' high priesthood in two parts in 5:1-10 and 7:1-
10:18. Therefore, most find problems with the general placement of chapters 5 and 6"
(Westfall, *Discourse Analysis*, 140-41). See for example Neely, who does not include
5:11-6:20 in her summary because she sees it as a digression (Neely, "Discourse
Analysis of Hebrews," 33). Westfall suggests a different reading is needed, and alleges
that seeing 5:11-6:20 as Lane, Guthrie, Bruce, Buchanan, deSilva, Koester and Michel
do amounts to referring to this section as a disorganized digression (Westfall, *Discourse
Analysis*, 141). Therefore according to Westfall, "There appears to be a consensus
among scholars concerning 5:11-6:20 that infers a lack of coherence (or at least
disorganization) in the discourse" (ibid.). Yet this is a bit overstated since this writer
does not find such a charge of "disorganization" or "lack of coherence" to be the
consensus at all.

This writer disputes the notion that the writer of Hebrews is disorganized or lacking
coherence in this part of his discourse. This is one reason why Guthrie's view is helpful.
In his analysis, the digression of 5:11-6:20 is purposeful and pastoral—it is meant to
exhort the readers to open their ears and minds to the gravity of the situation at hand.
There is no discontinuity in the argument, and rhetorically the beginning and end of this
section is joined by an inclusio to close out the exhortation and prepare them for the
difficult topic of the Melchizedekian priesthood (G. Guthrie, *Structure of Hebrews*, 71,
100).

[162]In his 1998 commentary on Hebrews, Guthrie interprets this warning as being to those
persons who have been a part of the Christian community in some sense, yet have never
experienced true saving faith. As such, what is described in this warning is not the loss
of salvation (G. Guthrie, *Hebrews*, 228-32).

[163]For Guthrie, Heb 6:13-20 is a transition back to the exposition introduced at 5:1-10.

[164]Contra Westfall, who sees 6:13-7:3 as a unit (Westfall, *Discourse Analysis*, 152-69).
According to present research, this division seems to be unique to Westfall. At this point
of her work she is silent as to the mention of Melchizedek in 6:20 other than to call it a
"reactivation." Nothing is mentioned at this point regarding the term "Melchizedek"
being a hook word as Vanhoye, Lane, and G. Guthrie (et al.) maintain, to speak nothing
of the shift from first person plural to third singular at 6:19-20 and 7:1ff. She confesses
that her understanding is controversial and writes, "The cohesion patterns in the second
unit in 6:1-7:3 are not as controversial, except for the placement of 6:9-12 together with
6:13-7:3, and the inclusion of 7:1-3 in the unit" (184). She is correct in asserting, "The

with the closing/overlap of 10:19-25, Guthrie argues that the balance of Hebrews is exhortation. After the overlap of 10:19-25, the author warns his readers again in 10:26-31 with words similar to that of 6:4-8. Hebrews 10:32-39 sets the stage for the *exempla* of 11:1-40 by reminding them of how they endured at first, and that they should continue in this perseverance like those who have gone before them (11:1-40). This unit of material is bracketed by an inclusio (11:1-2 and 11:39-40) and is designed to give overwhelming proof that endurance is to be preferred even in the face of difficulties.

After the *exempla* list of 11:1-40, the example *par excellence* is Jesus in 12:1-2. Therefore, they should endure discipline as sons of God (12:3-17), and are reminded of the blessings of the NC in 12:18-25. A final warning is issued in 12:25-29, since there is no escape for those that reject the word of God. Guthrie's outline of Hebrews concludes with practical exhortations (13:1-19), a benediction (13:20-21), and a closing (13:22-25).

By grouping the hortatory units together, one sees a significant amount of reiteration of key motifs in order to persuade the audience to endure. This is done by warning, by encouraging, and by giving examples (both good and bad). This is a significant aid in understanding the larger and more pastoral purposes for the epistle to the Hebrews, challenging them to right action.[165]

EXPOSITIONAL SECTIONS

Guthrie understands the logical flow of the exposition as follows. In 1:5-14, the son is superior to the angels. Yet in 2:5-9 and 2:10-18 the son becomes spatially lower than the angels by coming to earth as a man to dwell and to suffer among men, the purpose of which is to deliver men from sin. On the basis of his identification with humanity, in 5:1-10 and 7:1-28, the son is taken from among men and is appointed to be the high priest announced in Psalm 110:4. Therefore, because of his appointment to the role of eternal high priest, Christ is then able to offer a superior offering in heaven. This is the substance of 8:3-10:18. This is, in a thumbnail sketch, the logical flow of the exposition in Hebrews.[166] What is essential to the present study is 7:1-10:18, in which Jesus is appointed as the eternal high priest of the Melchizedekian order in 7:1-28,[167] who inaugurates a new and eternal covenant (8:1-13). This is based on the new

---

primary issue concerning 6:1-7:3 is the challenge to its coherence and cohesion in the surrounding co-text" (184-85).

[165]See Guthrie's discussion on the cohesion and function of the hortatory units (G. Guthrie, *Structure of Hebrews*, 134-39).

[166]Ibid., 124-27.

[167]The idea of which was mentioned in 5:1-10, but the writer of Hebrews leaves the matter of Melchizedek for 7:1-28 in order to exhort his audience in 5:11-6:20. In 6:20, Melchizedek is reintroduced and the idea is expounded through the texts of Gen 14 and Ps 110 in 7:1-28.

and eternal sacrifice of his blood and is carried out by Christ the high priest himself, the eternal mediator between God and man who offers a superior offering under the NC (9:1-10:18).

This heart of the expositional section (7:1-10:18) is part of a larger unit that opens at 4:14-16 and closes at 10:19-25. These two passages "represent the most striking use of *inclusio* in the book of Hebrews."[168] Guthrie somewhat modifies the parallels listed by Nauck that form the major inclusio of 4:14-16 and 10:19-23, which was missed by Vanhoye. Guthrie notes the following parallels:

4:14	10:19
Ἔχοντες οὖν	Ἔχοντες οὖν
4:14	10:23
ἀρχιερέα μέγαν	ἱερέα μέγαν
4:14	10:20
διεληλυθότα τοὺς οὐρανούς	διὰ τοῦ καταπετάσματος
4:14	10:19
Ἰησοῦν	Ἰησοῦ
4:14	10:21
τὸν υἱὸν τοῦ θεοῦ	οἶκον τοῦ θεοῦ
4:14	10:23
κρατῶμεν τῆς ὁμολογίας	κατέχωμεν τὴν ὁμολογίαν
4:16	10:22
προσερχώμεθα μετὰ παρρησίας	προσερχώμεθα μετὰ
4:16	10:19
παρρησίας	παρρησίαν

After noting such parallels that mark this sizable inclusio Guthrie states, "The *inclusio* formed by the extensive parallels at Hebrews 4:14-16 and 10:19-23 must be considered as a potentially important indicator of structural dynamics in the book...[4:14-16 and 10:19-23] have been clearly shown to be the opening and closing of a major *inclusio*."[169]

---

[168]Guthrie, *Structure of Hebrews*, 79; see also Nauck, "Zum Aufbau des Hebräerbriefs," 200-03. Nauck finds the following parallels, and the parallels are striking: 4:14 (Ἔχοντες οὖν ἀρχιερέα μέγαν) parallels 10:19 and 21 (Ἔχοντες οὖν...ἱερέα μέγαν); 4:14 (διεληλυθότα τοὺς οὐρανούς) parallels 10:20 (διὰ τοῦ καταπετάσματος); 4:14 (Ἰησοῦν τὸν υἱὸν τοῦ θεοῦ) parallels 10:19 (ἐν τῷ αἵματι Ἰησοῦ,); 4:14 (κρατῶμεν τῆς ὁμολογίας) parallels 10:23 (κατέχωμεν τὴν ὁμολογίαν); and 4:16 (προσερχώμεθα...μετὰ παρρησίας) finds a parallel in 10:22 (προσερχώμεθα μετὰ ἀληθινῆς καρδίας). Nauck extends the passage to 10:31, which Guthrie notes is unwarranted, given that parallels are not found after 10:23.

[169]Guthrie, *Structure of Hebrews*, 80-81.

CONCLUSION

Guthrie acknowledges that keeping hortatory and exposition visually distinct does not make for a pretty outline, but it does offer a beneficial tool for seeing how Hebrews flows between kerygma and parenesis. He concludes, "[I]t serves to highlight the functions of the individual units within the broader discourse,"[170] and in doing so one is not forced to place the hortatory sections under the expositional units. Although his outline may be complex, this is not to be unexpected given that Hebrews is such a complex work of literature. Given the intricacy of the epistle and the author's abilities,[171] one ought to be suspicious of overly simplistic outlines of the work. Guthrie may be correct when he wonders if part of the difficulty of outlining Hebrews stems from the fact that it was originally designed to be heard—designed to make a significant rhetorical impact on those who would hear.[172] This writer concludes that Guthrie has made a substantial contribution, and that his treatment of the text is currently the most satisfying approach. He has taken the best of the two most influential approaches, those of Nauck and Vanhoye, and has produced a coherent, though not simplistic, outline of the structure of Hebrews.

Conclusion

Given the attraction to the work of George Guthrie, this chapter concludes with this writer's understanding of how 7:1-10:18 fits into the overall structure. By way of reminder, the present study focuses on what Gräßer categorizes as the "Hauptteil" of the work,[173] and Lane argues, "The writer devotes 7:1-10:18 to an exposition of distinctive features of the high priestly office of the Son."[174] The lengthy central section of Hebrews is exposition with no exhortation. None of the scholars cited above dispute this assertion. This section of Hebrews stands as the great doctrinal center section of the epistle in which the author describes how the priesthood, covenant, and sacrifice have changed in light of the person and work of Christ. These eighty-seven verses serve as the theological basis for the lengthy exhortative material that follows, as shown in George Guthrie's treatment. This section is the *indicative* that serves as the basis for the following *imperative* (even if the imperative is implied as in 11:1-40, *"Imitate these faithful saints of old"*).

---

[170]Ibid., 145.
[171]Recall the praise of Vanhoye, "On reconnaît en cette épître l'œuvre d'un véritable homme de lettres, dont le talent peu ordinaire a été mis en valeur par une excellente formation" (Vanhoye, *La structure littéraire*, [1963], 11).
[172]Guthrie, *Structure of Hebrews*, 146.
[173]Erich Gräßer, *An die Hebräer*, EKKNT (Zürich: Neukirchen, 1993), 1:29.
[174]Lane, *Hebrews*, 2:257.

It is clear that 7:1-28 stands as a unit,[175] broken into two major sections, vv. 1-10 and 11-28, and a cursory reading of major scholarly works confirm this. Following Vanhoye, Guthrie notes an inclusio at 7:1 and 7:10 in the idea that Melchizedek "met Abraham" (συναντάω).[176] In addition, an inclusio is present at 7:11 and 28, marked by the parallel ideas of perfection (τελείωσις), priesthood (ἱερωσύνης), and law (νενομοθέτηται). This writer agrees with Vanhoye as to his smaller divisions of chapter 7,[177] who sees a minor break after verse 19. The first ten verses center on Melchizedek and are highlighted by a discussion of Genesis 14:17-20. At 7:11 there is a shift towards the priesthood and the law that opens an inclusio that closes at 7:19. The terms τελείωσις-ἐτελείωσεν in verses 11 and 19 establish the inclusio and are the warrant for the conclusion to break up the larger unit, 7:11-28, into two smaller units, 11-19 and 20-28.[178]

With the structure of 7:1-28 identified, the question arises concerning how

---

[175]See most commentaries; see also Stanley, "The Structure of Hebrews," 260; Swetnam, "The Structure of Hebrews: A Fresh Look," 39; idem, "Form and Content in Hebrews 7-13," 334. Contra Westfall, *Discourse Analysis*, 152-69; 169-87.

Notably, one sees how the hook-word "Melchizedek" returns the discussion to Melchizedek and his unique priesthood, an idea stated in 5:6 but abandoned at 5:10 in favor of a change in genre to exhortation. In 6:20, the term Melchizedek "hooks" the hortatory section (which ends at 6:20) with the exposition of 7:1-28. See G. Guthrie, *Structure of Hebrews*, 97-99. Thus, it is easy to recognize the shift in genre from exposition to exhortation and then back to exhortation in 7:1-10:18.

[176]Guthrie, *Structure of Hebrews*, 84; Vanhoye, "Literarische Struktur (1. Teil)," 139.

[177]Vanhoye, *La structure litteraire*, (1976), 129-36.

[178]See also Lane (*Hebrews*, 1:184-86), who notes this break after v. 19. He avers that in 7:18-19 the argument begun at 7:11 is brought to a close (1:184). This is supported by Gräßer, *Der Brief*, 2:ix, 52; H-F Weiß, *Der Brief*, 8, 407; Bruce, *Hebrews*, 170; Ellingworth, *Hebrews*, 369; and Attridge, *Hebrews*, 199. This makes good sense, given that the writer of Hebrews shifts his exposition from the second line of Ps 110:4 regarding Melchizedek to the first line regarding Christ's eternal priesthood. Several scholars see an additional minor break after 7:25, with vv. 26-28 forming a conclusion. George Guthrie agrees, and demonstrates that 7:26-28 close an inclusio begun in 5:1-3 (G. Guthrie, *Structure of Hebrews*, 82, 84-85). Additionally, Westfall concludes that 7:11-19 is an identifiable sub-unit of material (Westfall, *Discourse Analysis*, 172-74).

Further research has shown that there is an inclusio that opens in 7:20-21 and closes at 7:28, thereby further marking these verses as an identifiable subunit of 7:1-28. The inclusions in these verses are ἱερεῖς (7:20) and ἀρχιερεῖς (7:28); εἰς τὸν αἰῶνα (7:21) and εἰς τὸν αἰῶνα (7:28); ὁρκωμοσίας (7:20) and ὁρκωμοσίας (7:28). These parallels were discovered during research and were confirmed by George Guthrie via email correspondence in April 2005. To these Guthrie added λέγοντος (7:20) and ὁ λόγος (7:28; the parallel of "speaking" and "the word"), as well as the use of μετά in 7:21 and 28.

the structure of 8:1-10:18 should be understood.[179] In the broadest sense, this is a large unit of exposition followed by exhortation in 10:19-25. This is quite easily proven. First there is no parenesis in the whole of 8:1-10:18 (nor in 7:1-28). Second, there is an inclusio that opens at 8:3 (after the direct intermediary transition of 8:1-2)[180] and closes at 10:18. In 8:3 the writer of Hebrews states the necessity for Christ the high priest to have something to offer (ὅθεν ἀναγκαῖον ἔχειν τι καὶ τοῦτον ὃ προσενέγκῃ), while at the close of this expository section in 10:18 he notes that there is no longer any offering needed since the goal of forgiveness has been attained through the work of the eternal high priest (ὅπου δὲ ἄφεσις τούτων, οὐκέτι προσφορὰ περὶ ἁμαρτίας). Thus the need to have something to offer is raised in 8:3 (προσενέγκῃ), and is concluded in 10:18 by way of contrast (οὐκέτι προσφορά).[181]

In addition, there is a much larger inclusio at 8:8-12 and 10:15-17, opening with the quotation of Jeremiah 31:31-34 (LXX 38:31-34) in 8:8-12 and closing with a restatement of the OT text in 10:15-17 in summary form.[182] The biblical citation itself serves as a literary marker as to the overall structure of this larger literary unit, as well as determining what the main point of this section concerns: the inauguration of the NC. Finally, the grammar itself displays such a shift in the structure. From 8:1-10:18 there are only indicative verbs in the third person. This sudden shift to hortatory subjunctive verbs in the first person plural in 10:19ff. (προσερχώμεθα, κατέχωμεν, κατανοῶμεν) indicates a change in the movement of the epistle.[183] Exhortation has resumed, based upon the theological instruction concerning the eternal Melchizedekian priesthood of Christ (7:1-28), the new and eternal covenant (8:1-13), and the new and eternal sacrifice (9:1-10:18).[184] This proves to be a major break in the structure of Hebrews both in genre and in context. Therefore, this study of Hebrews concludes at 10:18.

---

[179]Westfall breaks the main central section at 8:1 as well (Westfall, *Discourse Analysis*, 188-96).

[180]Guthrie, *Structure of Hebrews*, 84-85; 106-09.

[181]Ibid., 85. Guthrie adds, "Thus Heb. 10:18 offers a fitting closure to the *inclusio* opened at 8:3."

[182]Ibid., 84-85. This writer disagrees with Westfall that the citation from Jeremiah 31 is merely a proof-text that is present only to note that there is in fact a NC (Westfall, *Discourse Analysis*, 196). See below, chapters 5 and 6. See also Barry C. Joslin, "Christ Bore the Sins of Many: Substitution and the Atonement in Hebrews," *The Southern Baptist Journal of Theology*, 11:2 (2007): 83-88.

[183]Also note the use of the inferential conjunction οὖν in 10:19.

[184]Though we speak of 7:1-10:18 in three phases, we do not imply that the content of these three sections are not interrelated. Rather, what we see in the exposition is a focus on the Melchizedekian high priest in Heb 7, a focus on the inauguration of the NC in Heb 8, and a focus on (and building up to) the function of the new high priest as he offers himself as the new and eternal one-time sacrifice in 9:1-10:18.

Further, Hebrews 8:7-13 is a smaller unit of material, bracketed by the inclusio at vv. 7 and 13 (πρώτη//πρώτην), which refers to the first (πρῶτος) covenant made at Sinai. Importantly, after 8:13 there is a shift in the argument beginning at 9:1 to the specific regulations of the first covenant, opening an inclusio that closes at 9:10 (δικαιώματα//δικαιώματα). These are the only two uses of the term δικαίωμα in Hebrews, and these "statements containing the word bracket a description of those regulations as set forth in the Torah."[185] In 9:1ff. the writer of Hebrews explains just how the NC has been inaugurated. For him, the idea of covenant and forgiveness of sin necessitates blood and purgation in order for covenant inauguration and cleansing to occur. Therefore, 9:1-10:18 are seen to be the writer of Hebrews' explanation of Jeremiah 31.[186] As will be demonstrated below in chapter 6, the presence of the NC and its "better promises" (8:6, 10-12; cf. 10:16-17) that have come (9:11, 10:1) are explained by means of the Day of Atonement imagery and the covenant-inauguration ritual. Via the atoning work of Christ, the NC has arrived and has been inaugurated with its essential and promised blessings.

In 9:1-10, he describes the regulations of the OC in order to establish a platform from which he argues that Christ has fulfilled and superseded those regulations. A slight break after 8:13 is therefore demonstrable by way of context/argumentation, by literary features (one inclusio closes at 8:13 [πρῶτος], another opens at 9:1 [δικαίωμα]), and by grammatical considerations (the new section begun at 9:1 begins with μὲν οὖν).[187] For these reasons 8:1-13 is the focus of chapter 5 of this study, with 9:1-10:18 under examination in chapter 6.

Therefore, 8:1-13 is an identifiable subunit of material,[188] and 9:1-10:18

---

[185]G. Guthrie, *Structure of Hebrews*, 86.

[186]For a fuller explanation, see Barry C. Joslin, "Christ Bore the Sins of Many: Substitution and the Atonement in Hebrews," *SBJT* 11:2 (2007): 74-103. Christ's blood both atones for sins and inaugurates the NC.

[187]Westfall agrees with this position (Westfall, *Discourse Analysis*, 196-97). She contends with Attridge and Ellingworth concerning the force of μὲν οὖν at 9:1 (Attridge, *Hebrews*, 231; Ellingworth, *Hebrews*, 420). They understand μὲν οὖν to resume the theme of covenant from 8:7, yet 8:13 explicitly deals with the first covenant. In 9:1 the specific point of the *regulations* of the first covenant is taken up, and it is therefore difficult to argue for a resumptive force for μὲν οὖν. Westfall rightly cites the lexicon of Louw and Nida, which asserts that this is a discourse marker of "considerable emphasis" (J. P. Louw and E. A. Nida, *Greek-English Lexicon of the New Testament: Based on Semantic Domains* [New York: United Bible Societies, 1989], 1:811-12). Contra Spicq, *L'Épître aux Hébreux*, 2:247, who writes, "οὖν ne conclut rien, et marque peut-être une pause de dictée, en tout cas une reprise des idées précédemment exposées."

[188]To be precise, this thesis follows George Guthrie's view that 8:1-2 is actually a direct intermediary transition between Heb 7 and 8. Since it is a transition, we may refer to

another unit, though quite clearly not severed from what was argued in 7:1-28 and especially 8:1-13 (Guthrie rightly views 8:3-10:18 as one larger unit, and all of these smaller sections are part of the larger 7:1-10:18). Hebrews 8:7-13 announces the NC, and 9:1 begins the author's argument as to the better offering of Christ and his inauguration of the NC, a discussion that continues until the close of the central section's exposition at 10:18. Additionally, there is continuity between 8:13 and 9:1 with the implied term διαθήκη in most English translations of 9:1. What occurs at 9:1 is a movement forward in the theological discussion to the matter of just *how* this Melchizedekian priest (7:1-28) who has inaugurated the NC (8:1-13) offers himself as the once-for-all covenant sacrifice for sin in the heavenly tabernacle according to the will of God (9:1-10:18). The "seams" that connect these smaller units are not abrupt. Rather, the units are masterfully connected to one another by the various conventions utilized by the writer of Hebrews.

Concerning 9:1 Lane writes, "The thematic introductory sentence in 9:1 announces the exposition of two subjects, namely, regulations for cultic worship and the earthly tabernacle," and notes that in keeping with the author's style, they are developed in inverse order.[189] These are then contrasted with the argument of 9:11-28. The conclusion and summary of the whole of 7:1-10:18 (and particularly 8:1-10:18) is found in 10:1-18 joined to the preceding material with γάρ, which indicates supporting material.[190] Hebrews 10:1-4 is connected to the whole of 9:1-28 in that it states that all of the sacrifices prescribed by the law were ineffective, and thus the law was unable to perfect, having only a shadow of what was to come in Christ.

Although one speaks of 10:1-18 as a conclusion to the doctrinal argument, Lane is correct when he asserts that we should in no way "obscure the continuity in argument in 9:1-10:18."[191] Attridge is similar, though where this writer sees 9:1-10:18 as a large unit, he sees this section proceeding only to 10:10, with 10:11-18 as a conclusion.[192] In reality there is no real tension on this point, given that most, if not all, scholars see a conclusion to the doctrinal argument at this point of Hebrews 10. However, this writer observes the four

---

8:1-13 for pragmatic reasons, and shall do so henceforth, yet it is maintained that 8:1-2 has a larger function in 8:1-10:18. It serves to introduce the main ideas that unfold in 8:3-10:18 as Guthrie avers.

[189]Lane, *Hebrews*, 2:217. Rightly, Lane appears to give significant weight to the contextual shift, but also notes the grammatical break (μὲν οὖν); see also Westfall, *Discourse Analysis*, 197. Contra Attridge, *Hebrews*, 231, Ellingworth, *Hebrews*, 420, and Spicq, *L'Épître aux Hébreux*, 2:247.

[190]Westfall notes, "The shift to the new sub-unit in 10:1-18 is virtually unmarked by particles or grammatical forms. The sub-unit is joined with γάρ indicating support material" (Westfall, *Discourse Analysis*, 220).

[191]Lane, *Hebrews*, 2:258.

[192]Attridge, *Hebrews*, 19.

inclusions at 10:1 and 14,[193] and also suggests that the grammar of 10:11 does not indicate a concluding statement or significant break from the previous verse, as Attridge maintains.[194] Ergo, there is no true disparity on this particular issue, though on this point this writer would offer a dissenting voice to Attridge's view on both grammatical and literary bases.

Based on the study of the structure of Hebrews outlined above, chapters 4, 5, and 6 proceed along the following lines: chapter 4 (7:1-28) focuses on the question of the "change of the law" since the high priest of the order of Melchizedek has come; chapter 5 (8:1-13)[195] centers on the question, "Since Christ is the priest of the NC, what does it mean that the law (lit. "laws") will be written on the minds and hearts in this NC that he inaugurates?" Christ has inaugurated the NC, and one of its key features is the internalization of the law. Chapter 6 (9:1-10:18) addresses the specific matter of the law's having a shadow (10:1) in the cultus of what was to come in Christ. The work of Christ as eternal high priest, having offered an eternal sacrifice, brings to light matters concerning the law that were once shadows. The structure of each of the next three chapters closely follows the divisions set forth by George Guthrie and Lane, which are quite similar and largely proceed from the Vaganay-Vanhoye school of thought discussed above. Yet, it is George Guthrie who stands on the shoulders of both Vanhoye and Nauck, and this writer considers his eclectic approach to the structure of Hebrews quite persuasive with only a few points of modification.

In conclusion, the importance of the structure of Hebrews for any serious exegetical inquiry into the epistle to the Hebrews must be emphasized. Exegetical questions cannot be adequately answered without a knowledge of where one is in the epistle's structure and flow of thought. This has been the

---

[193]According to Guthrie, there are four sets of contrasts opened at 10:1 and closed at 10:14 (*Structure of Hebrews*, 87). First, ταῖς αὐταῖς θυσίαις parallels μιᾷ...προσφορᾷ; second, προσφέρουσιν εἰς τὸ διηνεκὲς parallels [τετελείωκεν] εἰς τὸ διηνεκὲς; third, οὐδέποτε δύναται...τελειῶσαι parallels τετελείωκεν; and fourth, τοὺς προσερχομένους parallels τοὺς ἁγιαζομένους.

[194]Attridge, *Hebrews*, 19. Cf. Westfall, who criticizes Guthrie concerning the four inclusios in vv. 1 and 14 (Westfall, *Discourse Analysis*, 222).

[195]Heb 8:1-2 is a direct intermediary transition, yet it does not deserved to be isolated from the discussion of 8:1-13 since these two verses comprise a transition into 8:3-13. By distinguishing 8:1-2 as a transition it is not suggested that it should be severed from the discussion of 8:3-13. On the contrary, 8:1-2 serve as a segue into Heb 8 and the whole of 8:3-10:18. This is Guthrie's point concerning 8:1-2. Yet 8:1-2 also looks back to the appointment of the Melchizedekian high priest, the topic of 7:1-28. This is the difficulty in placing 8:1-2. It belongs in some sense with chapter 4 *and* chapter 5 of the present study. No scholars interacted with in this study discuss 8:1-2 with 7:1-28, but rather include these verses in their comments on Heb 8. Therefore, this study will do the same.

thrust of the present chapter. Examining the structure of Hebrews answers questions related to exegesis, such as the unity of 7:1-28, the place of 8:1-2, the flow of 8:1-10:18, the point that 10:1-18 is not to be separated from 9:1-28, and the question of where the conclusion to this section is located (10:11-18? 10:15-18?) are but a few important examples. The matter of structure is also important when deciphering between the NT's indicative as the basis for the imperative.[196]

In addition, various rhetorical and structural devices employed by the writer of Hebrews significantly aid in the quest for ascertaining the structure of his word of exhortation. For instance, the inclusio is a very helpful tool in knowing both where a section may begin and end literarily, as well as understanding the opening and closing of argumentation. This is particularly helpful for the writer of Hebrews, whose rhetorical abilities are significant. As such, this writer is persuaded that the literary analysis offered by the school of thought represented by Vaganay, Vanhoye and especially Guthrie (with his inclusion of Nauck) is preferable. Guthrie's visual representation of how the writer of Hebrews moves between both exposition and exhortation is a helpful contribution to the present study of the epistle.

By understanding the structure of Hebrews, one is certainly more likely to be able to understand the meaning of Hebrews. Identifying 7:1-10:18 as a unit of doctrinal exposition, and identifying the major and minor breaks within this section puts one on a more solid footing for proceeding with the exegetical and theological task—taken up in the subsequent chapters.

---

[196]On a side note, this writer's own thoughts have been piqued as to how George Guthrie's proposal could affect the ongoing discussion of the warning passages. For example, it could be demonstrated that Hebrews describes a NC believer as one who has had 1) *the laws of God internalized* (inscribed on his or her mind and heart for the purpose of covenant obedience from the heart), and 2) *has had all his or her sins forgiven* (past and future, "I will remember their sins and lawless deeds no more"). This much seems clear from the "indicative" of 8:1-10:18. If this is the case, then what are the implications for the exhortative warning passages (the "imperative")? If the indicative describes the NC working of God (note all of the divine "I's") as forgiving all of one's "sins and lawless deeds" (10:17), then is it truly possible for the NC believer to fall away? This is an entertaining and interesting theological question that, to my mind, has not yet been fully explored and poses an interesting suggestion for future study of how the book's genres and theology intersect.

CHAPTER 4

Hebrews 7:1-28 – Change in the Law

Introduction

This chapter focuses on Hebrews 7:1-28, and seeks to discover what these verses reveal as to how the writer of Hebrews views the law of Moses. Though the present study is focused on the law, it should be stated here that the main issue for the writer of Hebrews in 7:1-28 (as well as 7:1-10:18) is not the law, but priesthood.[1] In these central chapters of Hebrews, the author focuses his attention on the thesis that Jesus is the new and eternal high priest of a different kind. His priestly order, his covenant, and his sacrifice are all unique to his priesthood. The notion of Christ as priest was introduced as far back as 1:3b when the writer speaks of Christ's making purification for sins.[2] This is cultic/priestly language and is a prefatory statement for the priesthood of Christ in Hebrews as a whole. Yet in 7:1-10:18, the writer of Hebrews explains the ministry of this new priest, and why his ministry is different and superior to the ministry of the Aaronic priests that had served God and his people up to this point in redemptive history. A shift has occurred, and the law of Judaism has been affected—its cultus and what it had pointed to has been fulfilled in the work of Christ, the eternal Melchizedekian high priest (see esp. 9:1-10:18).

Thus, priesthood is the central issue (8:1). However, one cannot speak of the

---

[1]This has been the long-standing view of the central section of Hebrews. For a concise summary of other proposals for the doctrinal center of Hebrews as a whole offered in the history of Hebrews study, see David J. MacLeod, "The Doctrinal Center of the Book of Hebrews," *BibSac* 146 (1989): 291-300. MacLeod lists a dozen different views of the doctrinal center of Hebrews under the headings of "Proposals Stressing Theology" (seven) and "Proposals Stressing Parenesis" (five). For a more in-depth study, see MacLeod's dissertation, "The Theology of the Epistle to the Hebrews: Introduction, Prolegomena, and Doctrinal Center" (Th.D. diss., Dallas Theological Seminary, 1987); see also Joy D. Tetley, "The Priesthood of Christ as the Controlling Theme of the Epistle to the Hebrews" (Ph.D. diss., University of Durham, 1987); Alexander Nairne, *The Epistle of Priesthood* (Edinburgh: T. & T. Clark, 1913).

[2]Harold Attridge, "New Covenant Christology in an Early Christian Homily," *QR* 8 (1988): 93. For an explicit discussion on Hebrews' theology of the atonement, see Barry Joslin, "Christ Bore the Sins of Many: Substitution and the Atonement in Hebrews," *SBJT* 11:2 (2007): 74-103.

priesthood, its covenant, and its sacrifice without speaking of the law. This is a significant issue for the writer of Hebrews, and as he focuses his considerable abilities on the matter of priesthood he necessarily must speak of the law. This is important for the original audience, who are likely second generation Jewish Christians.[3] If this suggestion concerning audience is correct (as a majority of scholarship asserts), then one must pause to consider the gravity of the situation before them. Put simply, what they have known about their religion and its practices, and what they have been explicitly commanded to do with regards to sin and sacrifice for centuries have all changed in light of Christ. To follow the same priesthood and to sacrifice animals for sin is now to go against the work of God and not to hear his speaking in the son. Thus the writer of Hebrews must make a forceful theological argument built upon the OT for the legitimacy of this new priest and his ministry. Their relationship to the law has changed in light of the Messiah's work, and they must trust that the work of the new and eternal high priest is sufficient. The law that prescribed the priesthood and the sacrifices has changed. This matter of the "change in the law" (7:12) is the primary question upon which the present chapter focuses.

More specifically, the present chapter seeks to answer how νόμου μετάθεσις in 7:12 should be understood. It is argued here that what the writer of Hebrews means in 7:12 is that the law has been "transformed" in light of the Christ event. What is meant by "transformation" is simply this: the "transformed law" is the result of what occurs when Christ intersects the law. There are radical changes that occur in both the priesthood and the law that involve both discontinuity and continuity, and the best term that encompasses such changes is "transformation" (μετάθεσις). This involves the cessation of the Levitical priesthood due to its fulfillment in Christ. In Hebrews 7, it becomes evident that νόμου μετάθεσις involves cancellation of the priestly lineage requirement since a new priesthood has been declared by God in the oracle of Psalm 110:4. This cancellation necessitates the cessation of the Levitical priesthood and its cultus due to Christ's fulfillment of what it foreshadowed (which anticipates Heb 9 and 10). This is due to the fact that priesthood as a divine office has been overtaken and filled up by the new Melchizedekian priesthood of Christ. For the category of priesthood, such a change involves fulfillment and escalation whereby the Levitical order is announced to be concluded in light of the new Melchizedekian priesthood. What the Levitical priesthood pointed to in all of its duties prefigured the eternal Melchizedekian priesthood of Christ. Here is a new priesthood whose

---

[3]See above, chapter 1. See also Barnabas Lindars, "Hebrews and the Second Temple," in *Templum Amicitiae*, ed. William Horbury, JSNTSS 48 (Sheffield: Academic Press, 1991), 413-17. This does not deny the possibility that the audience could have been a mix of Jews and Gentiles. Rather, the point here is that the audience likely had a strong Jewish element.

high priest lacks no sufficiency in his priestly office, his covenant, or his sacrifice.

For the law, there is fulfillment and escalation as well. Christ has fulfilled the law, and therefore it no longer remains an external set of regulations for the covenant people that cannot perfect.[4] Yet as will be demonstrated in chapter 5, the writer of Hebrews maintains that in the NC, one of the "better promises" is the internalization of the law: what was external and on tablets of stones and scrolls has now been internalized, thereby producing obedience from renewed hearts in the people. In Hebrews 8, it is the law as viewed through the lens of Christ that is internalized—Christ becomes the interpretive principle and set of lenses through and by which the law must now be viewed in these eschatological "latter days." This is the meaning of the phrase used here, "Christologized law." When viewed in this manner, there are distinct elements of discontinuity (cessation of the Levitical priesthood in Heb 7) and continuity (the "Christologized law" is internalized in the people in Heb 8).

In short, the thesis argued for in the following chapters is this: *the law has been transformed in Christ, and this transformation involves both its internalization and its fulfillment in the New Covenant.* The meaning of each aspect of this statement is the burden of chapters 4, 5, and 6.

In chapter 3 it was concluded that Hebrews 7:1-28 can be divided into two main sections (1-10; 11-28), with 11-28 being further broken down into two subsections (11-19; 20-28). Hebrews 7:1-10 reintroduces Melchizedek, who was mentioned first in 5:6 by means of Psalm 110:4. The author's explanation concerning Melchizedek would have to wait, however, since 5:11-6:20 is an excursus for exhortational purposes. In 6:20 the name Melchizedek is restated; the writer of Hebrews has accomplished his pastoral purposes for the moment (5:11-6:20) and thus begins his explanation of this enigmatic priest-king. Thus, 6:20 and 7:1 form a "seam" that ties the exhortation of 5:11-6:20 to the following exposition and functions as a transition and a return to the topic of Melchizedek.

The present chapter will first overview the movement of Hebrews 7 in three sections: verses 1-10, 11-19, and 20-28. This will be followed by a focus on 7:12. Fundamentally, the matter of νόμου μετάθεσις is essential for

---

[4]It should be noted that Hebrews does not separate the law into tidy divisions, such as moral, civil, and ceremonial, despite how helpful these categories might be at times. Scholars who have argued in the past that Hebrews cancels the ceremonial law fail to make a convincing case that that part of the law is the *only* aspect that is affected. Truly, the *whole* law is transformed, not just the ceremonial. That being said, since the ceremonial law is *so greatly* affected, it is easy to see why many have argued this way. What is asserted here is that such a view (1) separates the law arbitrarily, and (2) does not account for the fullness of the law's transformation. It is not just a transformation of its content, but also a transformation of its location.

ascertaining the writer's view of the law and is therefore the focus of the second movement of the present chapter. This will culminate with a discussion of the findings concerning the present writer's view of the law.

Exegetical Overview of 7:1-28

Hebrews 7:1-10

The form of 7:1-10 resembles the practice of homiletical midrash in which the exposition of the Scripture itself forms the structure of the ensuing discussion.[5] The writer of Hebrews first notes the meeting of Abraham and Melchizedek in verse 1, followed by the blessing and the tithe in verse 2. Verse 3 describes Melchizedek as one who appears to be eternal. Verses 4-10 investigate the significance of the Melchizedek/Abraham meeting in reverse order: the tithe is explored first in verse 4, followed by the blessing in verse 6 and the meeting in verse 10. The argument concerning the superiority of the Melchizedekian priesthood is based on the author's reflection on Genesis 14:17-20.[6]

HEBREWS 7:1-3

Before the writer of Hebrews can make the connection between the priesthood of Melchizedek and Christ, he must first remind his readers of this enigmatic figure. Drawing from the only other mention of Melchizedek besides Psalm 110:4, he describes his meeting with Abraham when Abraham was returning from the slaughter of the kings in Genesis 14. Hebrews is only concerned with Melchizedek insofar as much as he relates to Christ,[7] and receives attention

---

[5]J. A. Fitzmyer, "'Now This Melchizedek'... (Heb 7:1)." *CBQ* 25 (1963): 305; cf. William L. Lane, *Hebrews 1-8*, WBC, vol. 47a (Nashville: Thomas Nelson, 1991), 158-59; J. W. Thompson, *The Beginnings of Christian Philosophy: The Epistle to the Hebrews*, CBQMS 13 (Washington: Catholic Biblical Association, 1982), 116-17; J. C. McCullough, "Hebrews and the Old Testament" (Ph.D. diss., Queen's University, 1971), 457-65.

[6]Some have considered Gen 14:17-20 to be an interpolation. For a detailed discussion, see J. A. Emerton, "The Riddle of Genesis 14," *VT* 21 (1971): 403-39; Harold Attridge, *The Epistle to the Hebrews*, Hermeneia (Philadelphia: Fortress, 1989), 187; John G. Gammie, "Loci of the Melchizedek Tradition of Genesis 14:18-20," *JBL* 90 (1971): 385-96; Gordon J. Wenham, *Genesis 1-15*, WBC, vol. 1, (Waco, TX: Word, 1987), 319; Robert H. Smith, "Abram and Melchizedek," *ZAW* 77 (1965): 129-53.

[7]Ellingworth is perhaps asking the wrong question when he wonders how Melchizedek and Christ relate. It seems clear that both are superior to Abraham, but how do they relate to one another? (Paul Ellingworth, "'Like the Son of God': Form and Content in Hebrews 7, 1-10." *Bib* 64 [1983]: 255-62.) Melchizedek and the Gen 14 account are only mentioned insofar as they support the main point that Christ is of a new eternal priesthood as promised in Psalm 110:4. Ellingworth asks how these two *persons* (Melchizedek and Christ) relate to one another, when the thrust of the passage is not on

simply because his priestly office and this meeting with Abraham supply evidence for the writer's main thesis, viz., that there is a new priesthood that is superior to the old.

The Genesis 14 account unveils Melchizedek to be a "priest of God Most High" (Gen 14:18), which provides the connection to Psalm 110:4 that will soon take center stage after the relevant points have been drawn from Genesis. Before Hebrews can explain the importance of the Psalm he must first paint the background that this new priesthood was actually prefigured before the Levitical priesthood. Additionally, the writer's exegesis of Genesis 14:17-20 draws as much from the silence of Scripture as from what is expressed by the actual words and is, as Attridge notes, "tantalizingly restrained."[8]

First, who is Melchizedek? The author paraphrases the Genesis account in 7:1-2a: He was King of Salem and a priest of God Most High who met Abraham, received tithes from him, and blessed him. This is merely the subject matter of the Genesis text. In verses 2b-3 the writer of Hebrews articulates why Melchizedek is important for his argument about Christ's priesthood: first of all,[9] he was "king of righteousness" and "king of Salem/peace."[10] The writer of Hebrews makes these conclusions based on the etymology of the name Melchizedek.[11]

Verse 3 has been called the "crux interpretum," and has been difficult in the history of Hebrews interpretation.[12] The problem is simply that the writer of

---

personhood and preeminence in that realm, but rather on priesthood. The emphasis is on the Melchizedekian vs. Aaronic *priesthoods* (i.e., office), and not on the individuals themselves. Yet if one must answer the question Ellingworth posits, then the answer is surely that these two individuals are not on the same level, for all discussion of Melchizedek (be it his person or his office) vanishes after 7:10. See also Paul Kobelski, Melchizedek and Melchireša[c], CBQMS 10 (Washington: Catholic Biblical Association, 1981), 117. Additionally, Hanson's suggestion that Melchizedek was Christ preincarnate is speculative and doubtful (Anthony T. Hanson, *Jesus Christ in the Old Testament*, [London: SPCK, 1965], 70-71).

[8]Attridge, *Hebrews*, 187.

[9]Πρῶτον μὲν in v. 2b begins the writer's exegesis. The expected δὲ comes in v. 2c.

[10]Salem is regularly identified either with Jerusalem or the ancient site of Shechem. See Lane, *Hebrews*, 1:164. For more detailed discussion on the etymology, see J. A. Fitzmyer, "Now This Melchizedek," 305-21.

[11]The MT of Gen 14:18 makes this clear (וּמַלְכִּי־צֶדֶק מֶלֶךְ שָׁלֵם). Hebrews 7:2b-c reads βασιλεὺς δικαιοσύνης ἔπειτα δὲ καὶ βασιλεὺς Σαλήμ, ὅ ἐστιν βασιλεὺς εἰρήνης.

[12]For a historical consideration of Heb 7:3, see Bruce Demarest, "Hebrews 7:3: A *Crux Interpretum* Historically Considered," *EvQ* 49 (1977): 141-62. Demarest refers to John Owen who, in the 17th century, asserted that there are as many interpretations of this verse as there are interpreters (142). After tracing the history of interpretation, Demarest concludes, "It is safer to conclude that the statements in vs. 3 were stimulated by the Messianic prophecy of Psalm 110:4. Since the full significance of the Psalm-text was

Hebrews makes four assertions about Melchizedek that do not arise from and are not self-evident from a reading of the Genesis text. The four assertions are (1) Melchizedek is without father (ἀπάτωρ), (2) without mother (ἀμήτωρ), (3) without genealogy (ἀγενεαλόγητος), and (4) without beginning of days or end of life (μήτε ἀρχὴν ἡμερῶν μήτε ζωῆς τέλος ἔχων).[13] Regarding these assertions it seems best to conclude that the writer develops "the essentially Jewish notion that Melchizedek is representative of no priestly ancestry, and that for all of his greatness the non-Levitical priest bears a scandalous relation to the Mosaic Law."[14] The point seems to be that whereas Levitical priests had to have a certain genealogy, Melchizedek had none, yet was a "priest of the Most High God." The OT text makes no mention of Melchizedek's ancestry and therefore the writer of Hebrews exploits this silence in order to make a contrast between his priesthood and that of the Levites. Lane is helpful when he notes that Melchizedek was not qualified for a Levitical priestly ministry, yet was a priest nonetheless, implying that his priesthood was not established by any hereditary process (cf. 7:16).[15] This, of course, is one of the writer of Hebrews' main points as priesthood relates to Christ.

Because of these features, Melchizedek is likened to the son of God in verse 3c (ἀφωμοιωμένος δὲ τῷ υἱῷ τοῦ θεοῦ, μένει ἱερεὺς εἰς τὸ διηνεκές).[16] The main idea is the perpetuity of the Melchizedekian priesthood,[17] and the purpose for such an argument from Genesis 14 is to clarify what is meant by

---

not immediately clear, the writer, whose mind was steeped in the OT, turned to Gen. 14:17 ff. to discover what the Psalmist intended by the words, 'priest forever after the order of Melchizedek'" (161). For a more detailed account of the history of interpretation of 7:1-10, see Bruce Demarest, *A History of Interpretation of Hebrews 7,1-10 from the Reformation to the Present*, BGBE 19 (Tübingen: J. C. B. Mohr, 1976).

[13]The purpose here is not to detail all discussions regarding Heb 7:3. For a detailed treatment in summary form, see Demarest, "A *Crux Interpretum*," 141-62; Lane, *Hebrews*, 1:164-67; Attridge, *Hebrews*, 189-95; Kobelski, *Melchizedek*, 119-27. For a discussion of Melchizedek and typology, see C. L. Bird, "Typological Interpretation within the Old Testament: Melchizedekian Typology," *ConcJourn* 26 (2000): 36-52.

[14]Lane, *Hebrews*, 1:165. See also Gareth L. Cockerill, "The Melchizedek Christology in Heb 7:1-28," (Th.D. diss., Union Theological Seminary, 1976), 38-41.

[15]Lane, *Hebrews*, 1:166. See also Attridge, *Hebrews*, 190.

[16]Spicq likens Melchizedek to a mirror, in that the author found reflected in him an aspect essential to the person and priestly work of Christ. He writes, "L'Épître aux Hébreux s'est servie de la figure biblique de Melchisédech comme d'un miroir. En Melchisédech, en effet, elle a trouvé reflété un aspect essentiel de la personne et de l'œuvre de Jésus-Christ: la souveraine grandeur de son sacerdoce" (Ceslas Spicq, *L'Épître aux Hébreux*, [Paris: Gabalda, 1952], 2:184).

[17]Friedrich Schröger, *Der Verfasser des Hebraerbriefes*, BU 4 (Regensburg: F. Pustet, 1968), 133; Otto Michel, *Der Brief and die Hebräer*, KEKNT (Göttingen: Vandenhoeck & Ruprecht, 1966), 263; Attridge, *Hebrews*, 191.

"according to the order of Melchizedek" in Psalm 110:4.[18] Eternality is the focal point and ties Genesis 14 to Psalm 110.[19] Thus it is clear that there is another priestly order, one that is perpetual and significantly different than the OC priesthood.[20]

In the record of Genesis 14, the writer finds a fitting type of Christ. Bruce notes that in each detail, written and unwritten, the writer of Hebrews finds and explores a correspondence to Christ, the new high priest.[21] Christ's eternality as well as his priesthood is actually what Melchizedek's was only typically. By looking at Melchizedek through Christ, Hebrews finds significant correspondence to Christ in the enigmatic priest. It is in these respects that he resembles and prefigures Christ. The connection between the two is typological and not allegorical.[22]

Thus, with Genesis 14 serving as a backdrop for Psalm 110:4, the writer of Hebrews argues in 7:11-28 that Christ is an eternal high priest from this new priestly order and thus the priesthood has changed. There is still priesthood, but the priesthood of Christ is altogether better: since the order of Melchizedek is an eternal order of priest, it is a better priesthood that that of the Levites.[23] Precisely *why* the Melchizedekian priesthood is superior to the Levitical is the thrust of 7:4-10.

HEBREWS 7:4-10

Whereas 7:1-3 mentions the meeting, the blessing, and the tithe, 7:4-10 addresses these three matters in reverse order. For Hebrews, if it can be shown that Melchizedek is superior to Abraham, then the priesthood that would come

---

[18]Attridge, *Hebrews*, 191. See also Hans Windisch, *Der Hebräerbrief*, HNT 14 (Tübingen: J. C. B. Mohr, 1931), 61-62; Ernst Käsemann, *The Wandering People of God* (Minneapolis: Augsburg, 1984), 208; Michel, *Der Brief*, 262-63.

[19]David Hay, *Glory at the Right Hand: Psalm 110 in Early Christianity*, SBLMS 18 (Nashville: Abingdon, 1973), 147; Craig Koester, *Hebrews*, AB, vol. 36a (New York: Doubleday, 2001), 346-47. Koester rightly observes that the technique used to tie these two texts together is *gezerah sawah*, in which a single word common to each text allows them to be read together (347). See also George Guthrie, *The Structure of Hebrews* (Grand Rapids: Baker, 1994), 67, 108, 125, 126, 141.

[20]Lane writes, "The most obvious source for the notion of perpetuity of Melchizedek's priesthood in v. 3 is the writer's confidence in the eternal priesthood of Christ" (Lane, *Hebrews*, 1:167). See also Cockerill, "Melchizedek Christology," 484-93.

[21]F. F. Bruce, *The Epistle to the Hebrews*, rev. ed., NICNT (Grand Rapids: Eerdmans, 1990), 160.

[22]P. E. Hughes, *A Commentary on the Epistle to the Hebrews* (Grand Rapids: Eerdmans, 1977), 247-48.

[23]Not only is perpetuity of the office an advantage to the Melchizedekian priesthood, but this new priest also inaugurates a better and eternal covenant (13:20) with the better and eternal sacrifice (9:1-10:14). This is broadly the framework of 7:1-10:18.

from Abraham would be inferior to Melchizedek and his priesthood. Therefore the writer of Hebrews seeks to prove that Melchizedek is in fact superior in this peculiar meeting with Abraham.

First, Abraham pays Melchizedek a tithe from the spoils of war. Though the LXX is ambiguous about who paid who in Genesis 14:20b, Hebrews is not.[24] The reading from the LXX (ἔδωκεν) is replaced with ἐμέρισεν in 7:2, and 7:4 employs the tithe as evidence for Melchizedek's superiority over Abraham. Though Abraham is the patriarch, exalted in status in the history of Israel, he is subordinate to Melchizedek to whom he gave the spoils. On the one hand (μὲν), the Levite priests have a command to collect tithes, but on the other hand (δὲ), the one who has no genealogy collected a tithe from Abraham.[25] Though the law gave a command for the Levitical priests to receive tithes (Num 18:21-32), here they paid tithes to Melchizedek, in a sense, by still being "in the loins" of their father Abraham (ἐν τῇ ὀσφύι).[26] Demarest asserts that ἀγενεαλόγητος "emphasizes his complete disassociation from the legal priestly regime...[and] adumbrates the Messianic priest who was descended from the non-sacerdotal tribe of Judah."[27] The issue of priestly tribe is brought to the forefront in 7:13-14. Put simply, "if the lack of a Levitical genealogy did not prevent Melchizedek from collecting a tithe from Abraham, it cannot disqualify Jesus from serving as priest."[28]

Second, though Abraham had the promises (v. 6b; cf. 6:14), Melchizedek blessed him, and Hebrews concludes that "the lesser is blessed by the greater" (v. 7). Hebrews can say that Melchizedek is greater than Abraham because he receives a tithe, and thus is the superior of the two when the blessing is given. Even though Abraham had an exalted status as the one to whom had been given promises by God, Melchizedek is still the greater for having received tithes and blessing the patriarch.[29]

---

[24]Attridge, *Hebrews*, 188, cf. 188 n. 27. Jewish tradition made this explicit as well. See Josephus, *Antiquities*, 1:181; 1QapGen xxii.17. See Fitzmyer ("Now this Melchizedek," 318), who concludes that in the Genesis text it was actually Melchizedek who as a vassal paid tithes to Abram. Yet for Hebrews, Fitzmyer acknowledges that Melchizedek received tithes from Abram, thus demonstrating the greatness of Melchizedek (319).

[25]The term γενεαλογούμενος is a NT hapax legomena. It is only used in the LXX once as well at 1 Chr 5:1.

[26]Note that νόμος clearly refers to a specific Pentateuchal command in v. 5. This is the first occurrence of the term in Hebrews (though ἀνομία is found in 1:9; cf. 10:17). Lane observes that the LXX distinction between νόμος and ἐντολή is maintained in Hebrews, which is clear in 7:5 (Lane, *Hebrews*, 1:168). The point concerning the law here seems to be that Melchizedek did not need a command in order to receive tithes. See also Cockerill, "Melchizedek Christology," 67-68; 105-07.

[27]Demarest, *A History of Interpretation*, 134.

[28]Koester, *Hebrews*, 351.

[29]Paul Ellingworth, *The Epistle to the Hebrews*, NIGTC (Grand Rapids: Eerdmans,

Verse 8 sets up the additional comparison that both Melchizedek and Levitical priests received tithes, but Melchizedek has no end to his priesthood unlike those appointed by the law. Grammatically, the distinction is quite sharp between the two (καὶ ὧδε μὲν...ἐκεῖ δὲ). The contrast is between men who die (ἀποθνῄσκοντες ἄνθρωποι) and the one of whom it is witnessed that he still lives (μαρτυρούμενος ὅτι ζῇ).[30] Hughes observes that this distinction (life and death) is the sharpest of the contrasts and is the fundamental cause for the impermanence of the Levitical structure. He writes, "It is this which necessitates the clumsy mechanics of hereditary succession for its survival and validity."[31] Verse 8b refers back to the initial argument in verse 3 that Melchizedek has no beginning or end.[32] Demarest writes, "The silence of the record invests Melchizedek with an intransmissible and hence continuous priesthood which symbolically portrays the unbounded perpetuity of the priesthood of Christ."[33] In short, given the silence of Scripture, the writer of Hebrews affirms Melchizedek's priesthood to be free from all temporal limitations, and thus free to apply such a promise of Psalm 110:4 to Christ and his priesthood. The argument here foreshadows the contrast between Christ and the Levitical priests.

Verses 9 and 10 complete the discussion of Melchizedek and begin to transition from Abraham to the Levitical priesthood, the subject of 7:11-14.[34] The writer of Hebrews draws a significant exegetical implication from the account of Melchizedek, asserting that the Melchizedekian priesthood is greater than the Levitical priesthood since Melchizedek was paid tithes by all of the Levitical priests who were "still in the loins of Abraham." The ones who *collect* tithes, according to OC legislation (v. 5), are said to have *paid* tithes. The exegesis is perhaps "playful,"[35] and given the phrase "ὡς ἔπος εἰπεῖν," the writer of Hebrews perhaps acknowledges his creativity.[36] He recognizes that the

---

1993), 365. Ellingworth observes a gnomic present in v. 7 (εὐλογεῖται), and states the principle that a less prominent individual receives the blessing of a more prominent individual (366). See also Lane, *Hebrews*, 1:169.

[30]See John Dunnill, *Covenant and Sacrifice in the Letter to the Hebrews*, SNTSMS 75 (Cambridge: University Press, 1992), 166.

[31]Graham Hughes, *Hebrews and Hermeneutics*, SNTSMS 36 (Cambridge: University Press, 1979), 15.

[32]Attridge, *Hebrews*, 196; Lane, *Hebrews*, 1:170.

[33]Demarest, *A History of Interpretation*, 136. Demarest adds, "The priest who stands forth in Scripture in the power of life administers a priesthood which is absolute and inviolable" (ibid.). See also Schröger, *Der Verfasser*, 143.

[34]Ellingworth, *Hebrews*, 368.

[35]Attridge, *Hebrews*, 197.

[36]Ibid. See also Lane, *Hebrews*, 1:170; Cockerill, "Melchizedek Christology," 23-24, 78; Heinrich Zimmerman, *Das Bekenntnis der Hoffnung* (Köln: Peter Hanstein, 1977), 150-51.

statement is not literally true, yet Levi is corporately identified here with the patriarch Abraham, and thus it can be said that Levi paid "through Abraham" (δι''Αβραάμ). This solidarity with Abraham means for Hebrews that "Levi was fully represented in Abraham's action,"[37] and thus the subordination of Abraham/Levi to Melchizedek/Christ has a clear basis in the historical narrative of the Genesis account. Verse 10 concludes the section by giving the grounds for which the assertion from 9b may be sustained. For Hebrews, the actions of Abraham can be said to represent his offspring including all ensuing Levitical priests. In one stroke, the whole of the Levitical priesthood is subordinated to that of Melchizedek.[38]

Hebrews 7:1-10 forms the exegetical and logical basis on which the rest of the chapter rests,[39] therefore adequate space has been given to summarizing these essential verses. The following section explains verses 11-19 (in which the argument moves from Melchizedek to the Levitical high priests) and 20-28 (which moves from the Levitical high priest to Christ). Verses 11-19 are essential to the present study in that they focus attention on the physical requirement of the priesthood. Most importantly, it is here where one finds the radical notion of νόμου μετάθεσις.

Hebrews 7:11-19

This central section of chapter 7 is framed by an inclusio in verses 11 (τελείωσις) and 19 (ἐτελείωσεν).[40] The main topic is that of the priesthood and not the law, though the two are closely related as 7:12 makes clear.[41] Since the writer of Hebrews has argued that there is another priesthood, he now proceeds to articulate the implications of such a claim.[42] Melchizedek has faded from the discussion, thus demonstrating that the Genesis 14 narrative serves only as a stepping stone to get where the writer of Hebrews wishes to go, theologically speaking. There is another priesthood, and this other priestly order is superior to the Levitical order. This is the main point for all of 7:1-

[37]Lane, *Hebrews*, 1:170.
[38]Hughes, *Hebrews and Hermeneutics*, 16.
[39]Erich Gräßer, *An die Hebräer*, EKKNT (Zürich: Neukirchen, 1993), 2:34.
[40]See Albert Vanhoye, *La structure littéraire de L'Épître aux Hébreux* (Paris: Desclée de Brouwer, 1963), 129; Attridge, *Hebrews*, 199; Lane, *Hebrews*, 1:178; Ellingworth, *Hebrews*, 370; Gräßer, *An die Hebräer*, 2:34-35; Hans-Friedrich Weiß, *Der Brief an die Hebräer*, 15th ed., KEKNT, vol. 13 (Göttingen: Vandenhoeck & Ruprecht, 1991), 395.
[41]Albert Vanhoye, *Old Testament Priests and the New Priest According to the New Testament*, trans. J. Bernard Orchard (Petersham, MA: St. Bede's Publications, 1986), 164; David Peterson, *Hebrews and Perfection: An Examination of the Concept of Perfection in the "Epistle to the Hebrews,"* SNTSMS 47 (Cambridge: Cambridge University Press, 1982), 108. Michel states the matter succinctly, "Am Schicksal des Priestertums hängt nach Hebr das Schicksal des Gesetzes" (Michel, *Der Brief*, 270).
[42]Gräßer, *An die Hebräer*, 2:35.

10:18 and the foundation for such a claim has been established by the writer by reading Psalm 110:4 and Genesis 14.[43]

Verse 11 introduces the new point concerning the Levitical priesthood: its temporality and inability to bring about perfection. As Gräßer observes, this was quite the opposite of Jewish thought, which saw the Levitical priesthood as a never-ending order.[44] This change of priesthood was forecast in Psalm 110:4, which was declared subsequently to the giving of the law and the ordination of the Aaronic priesthood (7:28). Had the old priesthood been effective to bring about perfection, there would be no need for another order of priests (or another covenant or sacrifice for that matter). Now, the writer of Hebrews declares, the change of priesthood has arrived in the person of Jesus Christ. Priesthood has passed from Levi to Christ, from many priests to one. In so doing, the Levitical priesthood has been cancelled and overtaken; in the coming of Christ, there has been a radical and permanent transformation.[45] Priesthood has been transformed in that it has been transformed from Levitical to Melchizedekian.

The central issue with the priesthood of the OC is its inadequacy to bring about perfection (τελείωσις).[46] Attridge correctly notes that "perfection" language in Hebrews is complex, "and does not simply reproduce any of the various perfectionist ideals of the first century."[47] Perfection connotes the notion of completion, and is not merely a moral or cultic ideal. Rather, for Hebrews it is linked to the removal of sin,[48] and thus access and relation to God in the NC that Christ inaugurates. There is an eschatological dimension to the

---

[43]Psalm 110:4 is primary in these verses. Contra Fitzmyer ("Now This Melchizedek," 305-06), who asserts that the whole of Heb 7 is a midrash on Gen 14:18-20, and that Ps 110:4 is secondary. Yet this cannot be the case, as the Genesis text plays no role in 7:11-28, and the Psalm text has already been announced prior to Heb 7 (5:6; 6:20) and plays a major role in 11-28. See Sidney G. Sowers, *The Hermeneutics of Philo and Hebrews: A Comparison of the Interpretation of the Old Testament in Philo Judaeus and the Epistle to the Hebrews* (Richmond: Knox, 1965), 123-24; Lane, *Hebrews*, 1:177; Cockerill, "Melchizedek Christology," 16-18; Attridge, *Hebrews*, 199; Gräßer, *An die Hebräer*, 34.

[44]Gräßer, *An die Hebräer*, 2:35-36. See *Jubilees* 13:25.

[45]The most important of which is how those in the covenant relate to God, the covenant maker. This new priesthood has brought with it a new and sufficient sacrifice. Once it was made in the inauguration of the NC, unhindered access to God was then granted to all covenant people since the covenant sacrifice eternally atoned for sin. (For a detailed treatment of the idea of "approach" and "drawing near" in Hebrews, see the work of John M. Scholer, *Proleptic Priests*, JSNTSS 49 [Sheffield: Sheffield Academic Press, 1991]; 82-207.) In addition, the transformed νόμος is written on the minds and hearts of the covenant people, enabling them to keep the covenant and obey God (see chapter 5 below).

[46]The matter of τελείωσις in Hebrews has garnered significant discussion. For a detailed treatment, see especially Peterson, *Perfection*. See chapter 6 below.

[47]Attridge, *Hebrews*, 86.

[48]Peterson, *Perfection*, 108-12; 128-30. This is the particular thrust of Heb 9.

idea, in that there is the fulfillment of NC promises that alter the manner in which God and man forever relate.[49] There are aspects that are involved in the present as well, in that this becomes the present reality for those whose consciences have been cleansed (10:14). Yet it also goes beyond the present age to the new Jerusalem (12:18-24). This is the thrust of the author's chief and most consistent complaint about the priesthood and the law itself—its inherent insufficiency and inability to atone for sin and to sanctify.[50]

The parenthetical note in 7:11b has been a difficult one for translators and commentators alike. The unusual term νενομοθέτηται should be translated "for the people received regulations concerning it [the Levitical priesthood]."[51] This makes the most sense and is in keeping with other first-century usage.[52] This anticipates the logical corollary in verse 12, that when there is a change in priesthood, there must therefore be a change in the regulations that govern it.

There must be a change in the law in 7:12 (νόμου μετάθεσις) if the author's argument is to carry any weight with his readers. If the law prescribed a certain regulation for the priesthood, and yet there is a new priesthood that does not conform to that regulation, then that regulation must no longer be in force due to Christ's new priesthood. This point is reinforced by the argument concerning lineage in verses 13-14: Jesus is from Judah, whereas Levitical priests must, by definition, be from the tribe of Levi. He is not a priest on the basis of a specific earthly/human requirement of a certain lineage, but rather is declared a priest on the basis of an indestructible life (7:16). More will be said below concerning νόμου μετάθεσις, but here it may be stated that while the

---

[49]Koester, *Hebrews*, 122-25; Lane, *Hebrews*, 1:181.

[50]See Heb 9:9, 13, 14, 28; 10:1-4, 10, 14.

[51]For a list of grammatical possibilities for the prepositional phrase ἐπ' αὐτῆς νενομοθέτηται, see Koester, *Hebrews*, 353; and Lane, *Hebrews*, 1:174. For the translation here see Koester and Lane, also Frank Thielman, *The Law and the New Testament: The Question of Continuity* (New York: Crossroad, 1999), 133 n. 19; Vanhoye, *Old Testament Priests*, 161; Weiß, *Der Brief*, 395. Weiß rightly notes, " ἐπ' αὐτῆς here not—as ἐπί with genitive might point to—in the sense of 'on this basis' (the levitical priesthood) 'the people received the law' but exactly the reverse: 'about that' (concerning the levitical priesthood) 'the people received legal instructions'" (author's translation).

[52]So Lane, *Hebrews*, 1:173-74; Koester, *Hebrews*, 353; Weiß, *Der Brief*, 392; see Philo, *Special Laws*, 2.35; 1.235; Josephus, *Against Apion*, 2.276; cf. Walter Bauer, *A Greek-English Lexicon of the New Testament and Other Early Christian Literature*, rev. and ed. Frederick William Danker, ed. and trans. William F. Arndt and F. Wilbur Gingrich [BDAG], 3rd ed. (Chicago: University of Chicago Press, 2000), s.v. "νομοθετέω." G. Hughes writes, "The priesthood owes its existence...to the Law" (Hughes, *Hebrews and Hermeneutics*, 18, see also 15). Contra Michel, *Der Brief*, 269; James Moffatt, *A Critical and Exegetical Commentary on the Epistle to the Hebrews*, ICC (Edinburgh: T & T Clark, 1924; reprint 1952), 96.

new priesthood renders the old obsolete, the change of the priesthood did not abrogate priesthood; there is still the office of priesthood (with its actions of intercession, sacrifice, mediation, representation etc.). Likewise, νόμου μετάθεσις does not abrogate the law, for there is still law. Verse 12 is axiomatic.

Yet "priesthood" as a category has been transformed by the presence and work of the new eternal high priest.[53] In practical terms, this transformation involves the cessation of the OC priesthood and the inauguration of a new order. The Melchizedekian order is a new priestly order, though it performs the same fundamental functions as the Levitical priesthood. Thus the parallels between old and new priesthoods should not be downplayed. At the same time, the functions of mediation, sacrifice, and intercession have found their fulfillment in the new priesthood. They pointed to, in outline form, what Christ has presently fulfilled (10:1). There is still priesthood (in the form of the Melchizedekian priesthood) and there is still law (in the form of the internalized "Christologized law"; see 8:10 and 10:16).[54] The law has been radically altered in the coming of Christ the high priest, and this transformation involves both its fulfillment and internalization in the NC (see chapter 5, below). Since the category of priesthood has been "Christologically transposed," so has the law.

The point of verse 11 is that the earthly priesthood could not make the people perfect. Verse 12 announces a change in the priesthood and law, and verses 13-14 establish the point that Jesus was from the tribe of Judah, about which nothing is said concerning priests. Christ as the new high priest is one of a different kind (ἕτερον ἱερέα) who belongs to another tribe (φυλῆς ἑτέρας μετέσχηκεν).[55] Christ lacks the legal conditions made explicit in the law.[56] Therefore, since Jesus is the priest foretold in Psalm 110:4, it verifies that a drastic change has occurred in the priesthood. Christ has fulfilled what the OT priesthood lacked and merely pointed to, and his priesthood is based upon the oath of God (Ps 110:4) and not on a specific genealogical requirement. There is a new order of priest.

Verses 15-17 give a positive comparison of Jesus to Melchizedek, in contrast to the negative (he is not from Levi) in verses 13-14.[57] What is "very

---

[53]Koester makes an excellent observation that for Hebrews there can only be one priesthood at a time. This is unlike Greco-Roman society. If a Melchizedekian order had been inaugurated, then there must be the change in the priesthood from Levitical to Melchizedekian. This idea of a singular priesthood is particularly Jewish (Koester, *Hebrews*, 359).

[54]Contra Gräßer, *An die Hebräer*, 2:38-39.

[55]On the perfect, see Spicq, *L'Épître aux Hébreux*, 2:192.

[56]Cockerill, "Melchizedek Christology," 92-93.

[57]Gräßer, *An die Hebräer*, 2:44; Ellingworth, *Hebrews*, 377.

evident" (κατάδηλόν) for the writer of Hebrews is that the Levitical order has been overtaken by the Melchizedekian since there is a new priest who does not meet the Levitical genealogical requirement. Since this is the case, then that lineage requirement can no longer be imposed.[58] The apodosis ("it is clearer still") begins in verse 15a (preceding the protasis given in verse 15b), and is completed by the two relative clauses in verse 16. This grammatical disjunction (dividing the apodosis) is purposeful, Lane argues, since it puts off the resolution until the rhetorically powerful comment of verse 16b ("power of an indestructible life") which is reinforced by the Psalm 110:4 citation in verse 17.[59]

The relative pronoun in verse 16a points back to ἱερεὺς ἕτερος in 15b. Jesus, who is the "other priest," has become a priest not like those of the Levitical priesthood, i.e., by a regulation that prescribed a specific physical requirement concerning lineage and tribe, but according to the "power of an indestructible life." Jesus, who was raised from the dead, was not subject to the temporal limits of the Levitical priests, each of whom died (7:23-24). Based upon a life that is indestructible, his priesthood is far superior to those priests procured by the requirement of physical descent.[60] His priesthood "was endowed by virtue of his resurrection and exaltation to the heavenly world, where he was formally installed in his office as high priest."[61] This qualification is essential if Psalm 110:4 is to be applied to Christ.[62]

Negatively, Jesus has become a high priest "not on the basis of a law of physical requirement" (οὐ κατὰ νόμον ἐντολῆς σαρκίνης). Grammatically, δύναμις stands semantically in opposition to νόμος, and ζωῆς ἀκαταλύτου stands semantically in opposition to ἐντολή σαρκίνης, and Gräßer states that the last pair of genitives are interpreting genitives to the first.[63] What is in view is the specific physical requirement given in the Mosaic law that all priests are

---

[58]"Cessation due to fulfillment" is a significant feature of what is meant here by "Christologized law."

[59]Lane, *Hebrews*, 183; see also Gräßer, *An die Hebräer*, 2:44. It is important to note that the writer of Hebrews substitutes "order of Melchizedek" in Ps 110:4 with "likeness of Melchizedek" in 7:15b. The similarities between Christ and Melchizedek are deeper than merely order of priesthood. This change of terminology points to one in the "'likeness' or 'type' of Melchizedek, not to an ongoing order of priests" (Koester, *Hebrews*, 355). Lane asserts, "The promise was fulfilled in Christ who *is* actually what Melchizedek *was* symbolically" (*Hebrews*, 1:183). See also P. E. Hughes, *Hebrews*, 264; Gerd Schunack, *Der Hebräerbrief*, ZBKNT 14 (Zürich: Theologischer Verlag, 2002), 95.

[60]Vanhoye, *Old Testament Priests*, 162.

[61]Lane, *Hebrews*, 184; Bruce, *Hebrews*, 169.

[62]Hay, *Glory at the Right Hand*, 145-47; Spicq, *L'Épître aux Hébreux*, 2:210.

[63]Gräßer, *An die Hebräer*, 2:44.

to be from a mother who was an Israelite and a father who was a priest.[64] There was no such requirement that Jesus met in his ordination to the Melchizedekian priesthood; he became a priest due to the "power of an indestructible life" instead.[65] The writer of Hebrews asserts that this requirement (ἐντολή) was external only—having to do with one's physical lineage from Levi. Lane, Schrenk, and Cockerill each contend that the writer of Hebrews, in keeping with the LXX, maintains a distinction between ἐντολή and νόμος, in which ἐντολή denotes a specific commandment and νόμος refers to the collection of commandments (see 7:5).[66] This is likely the case in 7:16 (and 7:18), where the meaning is the *specific* requirement regarding priestly lineage. Lane writes, "The 'former commandment' has primary reference to the *particular* ordinance regulating the priesthood in v 16...this previous, transitory ordinance based on physical descent has been abrogated."[67] Such abrogation of this requirement helps to explain what is meant by νόμου μετάθεσις in 7:12.[68] Since there is a new high priest who is clearly from a different order, the requirement governing genealogical descent has ceased due to Christ's new and eternal priesthood. Since there is a new high priest who does not die, there is no more need for imperfect priests who were sinners themselves. Thus, what is "set aside" in 7:18 is the "law of physical requirement," and *not* the law as a whole.

Further, the phrase νόμον ἐντολῆς σαρκίνης in verse 16 should not be understood as connoting a Pauline sense of "flesh" to the lineage requirement.[69]

---

[64]Ellingworth agrees (Ellingworth, *Hebrews*, 381). See also Peterson, *Perfection*, 128; Lane, *Hebrews*, 1:185.

[65]On this verse, see Bruce Demarest, "Priest After the Order of Melchizedek. A History of Interpretation of Hebrews 7 from the Era of the Reformation to the Present" (Ph.D. diss., University of Manchester, 1973), 337-38. Demarest argues that the phrase δύναμιν ζωῆς ἀκαταλύτου pertains to the resurrection and ascension of Christ. See also Bruce, *Hebrews*, 169; Michel, *Der Brief*, 272-73.

[66]Lane, *Hebrews*, 1:168. See for example Exod 16:18; 24:12; Josh 22:5; Sir 35:24; 45:5; Dan 3:30; *T. Benj.* 10:3-4; *T. Dan.* 5:1. See also Gottlob Schrenk, "ἐντολή," in *TDNT*, ed. G. Kittel, trans. G. W. Bromily (Grand Rapids: Eerdmans, 1964), 2:546. Concerning these verses (Heb 7:5, 16, 18), Schrenk states, "The ἐντολή is the individual ordinance and the νόμος is the sum of the ἐντολαί." Cockerill agrees, (Cockerill, "Melchizedek Christology," 105-06). See also Schunack, *Der Hebräerbrief*, 95.

[67]Lane, *Hebrews*, 1:185; emphasis added.

[68]See the helpful treatment of Bayes, who essentially follows this same line of thought (Jonathan F. Bayes, *The Weakness of the Law: God's Law and the Christian in New Testament Perspective* [Carlisle, England: Paternoster Press, 2000], 177-78, 188-89).

[69]Contra Attridge, *Hebrews*, 202; see also George Wesley Buchanan, *To the Hebrews*, AB, vol. 36 (Garden City, NY: Doubleday, 1972), 125. Attridge and Buchanan ascribe a Pauline sense of "fleshy" to the term σαρκίνης, and Buchanan avers that the term puts the requirement into the category of things that were "ethically bad" (Buchanan, *Hebrews*, 125). This is rightly rejected by Hurst (*The Epistle to the Hebrews: Its Background of Thought*, SNTSMS 65 [Cambridge: University Press, 1990], 73), who

The term denotes physical descent, and should be seen in parallel with 7:11 (οὐ κατὰ τὴν τάξιν᾽Ααρὼν λέγεσθαι).[70] The priesthood and the law were given by God to the OC people and thus were not "bad,'' in the pejorative sense that relegates the law to the realm of the ethically sinful, or evil.[71] Disparaging or

---

asserts that σαρκίνης simply means "natural" or "human" in this context. Agreeing with Hurst, Lane notes that the main thrust is not to make a pejorative comment about the law as a whole, but rather to point out the fact that Jesus does not meet the lineage requirement (Lane, *Hebrews*, 1:185). Thus, νόμος is not seen here by Hebrews in the kind of derogatory manner that Attridge and Buchanan ascribe. The stipulation that priests always descended from Aaron was a command that was only concerned with lineage/physical descent, and not in the Pauline sense of "sinful flesh." Hebrews does not ascribe any kind of sinfulness to the requirement. It is "fleshy" in that it deals with physical matters of genealogy (who one's parents are). Note the RSV rendering, "not according to a legal requirement concerning physical descent." Montefiore is helpful when he asserts, "This use of flesh is free from the Pauline overtones of sin, but it does convey something of the transitoriness and earthbound nature of the commandment" (Hugh Montefiore, *A Commentary on the Epistle to the Hebrews* (New York: Harper and Row, 1964), 125). See also Michel, *Der Brief*, 272; Bruce, *Hebrews*, 169; Lane, *Hebrews*, 183-84; George H. Guthrie, *Hebrews*, NIVAC (Grand Rapids: Zondervan, 1998), 266-67. Contra Attridge, who compares the usage here to 1 Cor 3:3 (*Hebrews*, 202); contra Thompson, *Beginnings*, 123; Gräßer, *An die Hebräer*, 2:45.

[70]Cockerill, "Melchizedek Christology," 108.

[71]Ellingworth affirms this reading of the text when he states, "Here the context shows that the author is suggesting, not that the law is evil or 'ethically bad,' but that it lacks the power to give people τελείωσις (v. 11; cf. v. 19a) or access to God (v. 19b)" (Ellingworth, *Hebrews*, 379). "Weakness" does not necessarily infer "sinfulness" or some sense of "ethical shortcoming." See also Moises Silva, "Perfection and Eschatology in Hebrews," *WTJ* 39 (1976): 68. This is in keeping with the present study that in Hebrews the law in Christ has been fulfilled and internalized in the NC people. The law was insufficient and external on its own and thus lacked the power to perfect the people, yet it was from God for the good of his covenant people (see Gerhard von Rad, *Old Testament Theology*, vol. 1, trans. D. M. G. Stalker [New York: HarperCollins, 1965], 190-203; esp. 193-96), and still has a positive application in the NC, though how the covenant people relate to it has forever been altered for their good.

However, this does not deny *any* pejorative sense, since even referring to the Levitical priesthood and the law as "weak" and "ineffective to perfect" can be understood in a pejorative manner. For Hebrews, the priesthood was limited and insufficient, and the commandments, being merely external, could not bring the people to completion. It is argued in the following chapter that in fact the laws are fulfilled and internalized in the NC, and thus are not "bad" in and of themselves. The problem was not as much with the commandments as with the people's inability to obey them, a problem that the NC solves.

Yet what is denied here is disparagement in the sense of accusing the law to be worthless, evil, or ethically bad. Ellingworth perhaps goes too far in suggesting that the law "failed in its essential purpose" (*Hebrews*, 379; see also Gräßer, *An die Hebräer*,

belittling the priesthood and law as sinful or evil does not seem to be the writer's focus. Rather, his disposition toward the law and the priesthood seems to be more pointedly that they were *insufficient* (7:11, 19) and thus a change must occur (7:12) if τελείωσις is to be attained by the covenant people. The law could neither bring the worshipper near to God nor perfect him. As Bayes observes, the law was weak because it failed to produce nearness to God that comes from a cleansed conscience. He argues that the writer of Hebrews clarifies and qualifies the specific feature of its weakness in 7:19: that the law could not cleanse the conscience, specifically. It could not remove sins and purge the worshipper.[72]

By building his Christological argument on the foundation of the very institutions of the OC, Hebrews argues in 7:1-10:18 that the old priesthood, its

---

2:38), if what he means is that the law was designed to forgive sins and to make perfect. Yet, the law did *not* fail in its divinely-given purpose. Rather, its purpose was to articulate the will of God for the covenant people and to be a shadow of the reality that would come in Christ (and thus point to Christ). In *this* sense the law has not failed (see Bruce, *Hebrews*, 169, who seems to agree with this point by acknowledging that that a significant change was *inevitable* due to the limits of the OC cultus). The law was designed to be lacking on its own and to point forward to a future reality. This is the purpose of such texts as Ps 110 and Jer 31 that point to and promise something else that will come (a new and eternal priest and a new and eternal covenant, respectively; see G. B. Caird, "The Exegetical Method of the Epistle to the Hebrews," *CJT* 5 [1959]: 44-51). It is not as though God was forced to come up with a different plan since the first was apparently not working out.

Thus one must be both careful and clear when arguing that the priesthood and law have "failed," and the term "failure" must be carefully defined lest one imply failure to the one who gave the law and ordained the priesthood as some scholars have clearly done. (For how does one separate God's person from his divine word and revelation? To reject his word is to reject his person.) Were the law in toto a failure, then the writer of Hebrews would have little to build his case on given that his argument regarding Christ (whose priesthood, covenant, and sacrifice are all eternal) completes and fills out what the OC cultus pointed towards, hand in glove. Silva rightly asserts that the law was *meant* to be insufficient ("Perfection and Eschatology," 68), and thus point to Christ who would fill up what was lacking regarding sin, sacrifice, atonement, the priesthood, and covenant. To suggest that they failed their purpose makes the Christ event look like a divine "Plan B." Thielman agrees here and adds the point that God's purposes were never frustrated in the OC (Thielman, *The Law and the New Testament*, 125). See also Koester (*Hebrews*, 359), who is better, "Hebrews...contends that God did not *complete* his purposes through the Levitical priesthood" (emphasis added). See also Dunnill, *Covenant and Sacrifice*, 229.

[72]Bayes, *Weakness*, 181-82. Bayes rightly asserts that this does not mean for Hebrews that the whole law was worthless (see also 204-05). See chapter 6 below on 9:9, 14, and 10:1).

covenant and sacrifice were shadows pointing to the reality of Christ.[73] Thus, to argue that the writer of Hebrews disparages the law and its priesthood as "ethically bad" and "a failure" is perhaps either to go beyond the text or at minimum to raise questions as to the *divine* purpose for the law and priesthood.[74] Additionally, Schunack rightly avers that without those institutions, there would be no framework to describe what Christ has done.[75] To be sure, the Levitical priesthood and its institutions were insufficient to bring about forgiveness and access to God. Therefore, a new order of priest has come, made explicit in 7:17.

Verses 18-19 complete the central unit of Hebrews 7, and consist of a μέν-δέ grammatical construction that is interrupted by a parenthetical comment in verse 19a. The point in these verses is that the former commandment (ἐντολή)

---

[73]This idea of "fulfillment" versus "abrogation" is near the center of Graham Hughes' influential dissertation, published as *Hebrews and Hermeneutics: The Epistle to the Hebrews as a New Testament Example of Biblical Interpretation*, SNTSMS 36 (Cambridge: University Press, 1979). Commenting on Hughes' work, George Guthrie observes, "For Hughes the historical frames of the Old Testament text are distinct from, but correspond to, the historical framework inherent in the interpretive program of the early church. The connection between the two are [sic] not discernable by mere historical scrutiny" (George Guthrie, "Hebrews in Its First-Century Contexts," in *The Face of New Testament Studies*, ed. S. McKnight and G. Osborne [Grand Rapids: Baker, 2004], 435; contra Susanne Lehne, *The New Covenant in Hebrews*, JSNTSS 44 [Sheffield: Journal for the Study of the Old Testament, 1990], 95). Yet, the OT forms "grant permission" to the NT interpreter certain meanings that only now, in light of new revelation in the coming of Christ, may be found. Thus, Hughes calls this approach a "hermeneutic of permission" (Hughes, *Hebrews and Hermeneutics*, 63-64). Stated simply, what grants them continuity and thus what draws them together is the fact that God's is the voice that speaks consistently through both. Therefore there is genuine continuity in the interpretation of the OT text. Hughes notes that within the OT texts there is an inherent expectation for something future that the writer of Hebrews recognizes.

[74]In a private interview conducted with OT scholar Daniel Block in March 2004, Block patently asserted that the OC and the law were not "bad" in *any* sense, but rather were "gifts from God" since "no other people on earth had this treasure besides Israel." See also Childs, *Biblical Theology of the Old and New Testaments*, 247, 539, 548; E. A. C. Pretorius, "Διαθήκη in the Epistle to the Hebrews," *Neot* 5 (1971): 38-39; Jon D. Levenson, *Sinai and Zion: An Entry into the Jewish Bible* (Chicago: Winston Press, 1985), 50; W. D. Davies, *Torah in the Messianic Age*, JBLMS 7 (Philadelphia: Society of Biblical Literature, 1952), 26; and Thielman, *The Law and the New Testament*, 125. Dunnill is excellent on this point when he asserts that "any understanding or appreciation of the new covenant must begin from the recognition of the goodness of the world as created by God and the *graciousness* and *power* of the old covenant made with Israel" (Dunnill, *Covenant and Sacrifice*, 230; emphasis added).

[75]Schunack, *Der Hebräerbrief*, 96.

regarding lineage and descent has been annulled (ἀθέτησις)[76] and is no longer useful since a new order of priest has been declared by Psalm 110:4. In context, verse 16 specifies exactly what is in view in verse 18, viz., νόμον ἐντολῆς σαρκίνης ("a law of physical requirement").[77] Therefore in this new order of

---

[76]BDAG, s.v. "ἀθέτησις." BDAG defines ἀθέτησις as a legal term, here the legal annulment of a commandment. Its placement in verse 18 is emphatic, emphasizing to what degree the law has changed (7:12) and enhancing and explaining the meaning of νόμου μετάθεσις rather than redefining it.

[77]Again, the whole law in its entirety is not in view at this point. On this verse, see Grant R. Osborne, "The Christ of Hebrews and Other Religions," *JETS* 46.2 (2003): 262. See also Koester, *Hebrews*, 356; contra Windisch, *Der Hebräerbrief*, 66; G. Schrenk, "ἐντολή," in *TDNT*, 2:546. In the view of this writer, this is where fresh thought and discussion is needed. Exegetically, the writer's point is that the specific ἐντολή has been annulled since there is a new priest who is such not on the basis of that particular ἐντολή. Since Christ, who is from Judah, is a high priest, then that ἐντολή can logically no longer be employed (7:18). Yet many have wanted to see the annulment of the law in its entirety in this verse. It is proposed here that such an extrapolation goes beyond the writer's intentions. It is too simplistic to argue that the law in toto has been nullified and declared useless (see for example Moffat, *Hebrews*, 96).

Note the work of Peterson (*Perfection*, 111), who agrees with this exegesis of 7:16, yet extrapolates 7:16 (with no discussion) to assert that the *whole* law had been declared "invalid, nullified, set aside." Peterson's conclusions seem to stem from a decision that for the writer of Hebrews law = cult, which goes back at least to Hans Windisch. Windisch asserts that for the writer of Hebrews, "law" is equal to "cultus," and submits that for Hebrews there is nothing more to the law than cult (Windisch, *Der Hebräerbrief*, 66). While the cultus is certainly in focus (this is *expected* since the overall main point is the priesthood), Windisch is perhaps guilty of overstatement. This is likewise the view of Lehne who also follows Windisch (Lehne, *New Covenant in Hebrews*, 26). In short, the outworking of such a view is problematic: if law = cult, and since there is no more cult, then in 8:10 and 10:16 law (νόμος) has no content and thus must be redefined as "instruction" or "God's will" in a generic sense with little or no identifiable meaning (as Attridge, Lehne, and Thielman et al., but see Lane, *Hebrews*, 1:209). This is the logical conclusion to the assumption of those who see the law as merely the cultus. It is perhaps more precise to say that in his discussion of the law, the writer of Hebrews focuses on the cultus since his main point is that of the changing of the priesthood, which includes covenant and sacrifice.

Therefore, a nullification of the law in toto is not the specific meaning of vv. 16 or 18, since what is specifically in view is the lineage requirement for priests (the requirement for a priest had to change or 8:1 is nonsensical). Therefore language such as "nullification of the law due to its failure" is to be eschewed in favor of more exegetically and theologically precise statements such as "transformation and fulfillment of the law in light of Christ" as argued here. It is clear from Heb 7:1-10:18 that Christ has filled up and filled out what was lacking in the OC priesthood by his own priestly ministry of a new order.

priest there is the introduction of a better hope (7:19b).[78] The parenthetical comment of verse 19a ("for the law made nothing perfect") explains precisely *why* there is annulment of the commandment governing lineage. The law could not perfect because it was always *external*, dealing with *external* matters and regulations (such as lineage requirements) and was not in the hearts of the people. It was "over" the people, and not "in" the people. What it needed was to be *internalized* in the hearts (8:10, 10:16) in order to bring about an inward transformation and renewal of the heart that is so closely tied to the writer of Hebrews' concept of perfection. This is accomplished via the new Melchizedekian priesthood and work of Christ.

Again, what is "weak and no longer useful" (7:18) is the commandment (ἐντολή) regarding priestly lineage, and the grammar allows for no other viable option concerning the adjectives ἀσθενὲς and ἀνωφελές, since διὰ τὸ αὐτῆς must refer to ἐντολῆς first mentioned in 7:16. The meaning of ἐντολή in verse 18 is explained in verse 16 (see above) and here the writer of Hebrews announces the fact that such a requirement is no longer valid since Christ had no such qualification, being from Judah.[79] Stated simply, there is no longer a νόμον ἐντολῆς σαρκίνης since there is a new priest who does not fit that description (i.e., from Levi). Such an external regulation was weak and ineffective since it appointed priests who were mortal and subject to death (7:23), who were sinful themselves (7:27), and whose sacrifices were ineffective as opposed to Christ's (7:27). Now the "better hope" has arrived in the new priest (7:19b), who will inaugurate a better covenant, and offer a better sacrifice in the heavenly temple. Now all NC people can draw near to God (ἐγγίζομεν τῷ θεῷ), something that only the Levitical priest was allowed to do.[80] The νόμου μετάθεσις of 7:12 is described positively here as the introduction of the new and better hope.[81]

Further, if this particular ἐντολή is no longer valid, then the Levitical priesthood has given way to a new priesthood ordained by something else, namely, the word of the oath in Psalm 110. The "better hope" (7:19b) is the new Melchizedekian priesthood, with all of its facets and better promises that accompany the covenant it inaugurates. "Better hope" stands in grammatical contrast to ἐντολή in verse 18, which regulated the Levitical lineage of the old priesthood. Weiß is surely correct in his assertion that the introduction of the

---

[78]Gräßer, *An die Hebräer*, 2:46.
[79]Koester, *Hebrews*, 356; Peterson, *Perfection*, 110; Michel, *Der Brief*, 272; Bruce, *Hebrews*, 169.
[80]In the LXX, this expression is used of priests who enter the sanctuary (Exod 3:5; Lev 10:3) as well as more generally as a worshipper approaches God through prayer (Ps 31:6; 33:19; 144:18; Hos 12:6; Zeph 3:2; Jdt 8:27). See Cockerill, "Melchizedek Christology," 118-20; Lane, *Hebrews*, 186.
[81]Lane, *Hebrews*, 1:185.

new priest *effects* the annulment of the ἐντολή of 7:16, 18.[82] The entrance of the new priest necessitated the change, and thus the change did not come first. In other words, the writer argues "backwards," from what presently *is* (there is a new priest) to what *must be* (therefore the Levitical priesthood must no longer exist).

In conclusion, the law was unable to perfect or bring anything to its completion since the law itself was weak. The covenant people did not need the imperfect shadows; they needed the reality—Christ. He is able to perfect and complete what the law could not in its externality. The law and its priesthood cannot bring about what is most necessary for the covenant people as they relate to God, viz., forgiveness of sins and a renewed heart for obedience (this is the burden of 9:1-10:18 and the promise of Jer 31). Christ has done so, and has filled up what was lacking in the insufficiency of the old order.

In the argument of 7:11-19 the writer does not appear to be saying that the law in toto is "no longer useful," and fully annulled in an absolute sense (i.e., complete discontinuity).[83] This seems to go beyond the bounds of the author's

---

[82]Weiß, *Der Brief*, 401. See also Vanhoye, *Old Testament Priests*, 148.

[83]If so, then such a conclusion presents several problems, especially with regard to the Jeremiah prophecy in Heb 8. Scholars such as Attridge and Theilman maintain this conclusion in 7:18-19 (Attridge, *Hebrews*, 202-05; Thielman, *The Law and the New Testament*, 121, 131), which in turns forces them to conclude that νόμος inscribed on the hearts and minds in 8:10 and 10:16 means in a generic sense that "instruction" or "God's will" is written internally with no explanation as to what this might mean (Attridge, *Hebrews*, 227), which is distinct from how Hebrews typically uses νόμος (as the sum of the Mosaic ἐντολαί, see Lane, *Hebrews*, 1:168; G. Schrenk, "ἐντολή," in *TDNT*, 2:546; Cockerill, "Melchizedek Christology," 105-06; Schunack, *Der Hebräerbrief*, 95). Such a conclusion empties νόμος of meaning. Rather, this transformation involves the cessation of Levitical priests and the cultus because Christ has become the high priest of the eternal covenant (13:20) whose sacrifices are not shadowy and insufficient, but are effective. Again, it is better to speak of "fulfillment" and "transformation" rather than "abrogation" and "failure."

Part of what is driving Gräßer's exegesis is an underlying presupposition concerning the background of Hebrews thought. He sees Hebrews in a dualistic framework of "earthly" vs. "heavenly" (Gräßer, *An die Hebräer*, 2:48) following the Platonic/gnostic approach to Hebrews articulated in Käsemann's *Das wandernde Gottesvolk*, to which he acknowledges his indebtedness. Hurst has noted this view (as well as its significant shortcomings) in his influential monograph (*The Epistle to the Hebrews: Its Background of Thought*), and makes a convincing case against a Gnostic background (see esp. 70-75). He notes that for Käsemann and Gräßer, "*Auctor* and gnosticism view this world as essentially evil and hostile, with salvation consisting essentially in an escape to the 'heavenly' realm of Light and Spirit" (70). Hurst states flatly, "That Hebrews has a fundamentally dualistic outlook appears to run counter to the evidence" (73), and suggests that the "time may be ripe" to bring such a discussion concerning a gnostic or even pre-gnostic background in Hebrews to a close (74). Hengel agrees (Martin Hengel,

intention for 7:11-19. The main point is that another (and superior) priest has arisen from a different order, and thus the old priestly order has been replaced. There is a new priesthood whose existence replaces the Levitical priesthood. Therefore, since the law specified a regulation regarding who was eligible to be a priest, the regulation (ἐντολή) is no longer in effect. Here at the close of this section he asserts that the ἐντολή concerning priestly lineage has been annulled. Thus, "change in the law" involves at least the cessation of the priestly lineage requirements. This regulation only provided for weak priests, thus the law can be said to be unable to perfect since the priests it set forth were weak and insufficient. Ellingworth agrees when he notes that ἐντολή in verse 18 should be understood as the *particular* command concerning lineage given that it stands as a counterpart to Psalm 110:4.[84]

Yet by implication more is meant at this point than the cessation of the specific regulation regarding priestly lineage. If the command that establishes the Aaronic order is no longer valid, then there is no longer a Levitical order. By logical implication, therefore, the cultus that the old order performs can no longer be carried out. Though the writer of Hebrews does not explicitly make this point in 7:11-19 (saving it for 9:1-10:18), this implication is valid here. In Hebrews 9-10 the focus is specifically on how Christ, the eternal high priest, has made full atonement for the sins of those in both the OC and NC by both becoming and offering the eternal sacrifice. He fulfills what the cultus pointed to (10:1). The whole Levitical cultus has ceased since it has been fulfilled in Christ.[85] This point particularly comes into focus in 9:1-10:18.

The Son of God, trans. J. Bowden [Philadelphia: Fortress, 1976], 33, n. 66) hoping that such "gnostic fever" will completely disappear from NT studies as a whole.

Further, Graham Hughes also reacts strongly to Gräßer's approach (*Hebrews and Hermeneutics*, 137-42). Hurst and Hughes are persuasive. The view maintained here is that Hebrews better reflects the framework of apocalyptic Judaism rather than a philosophical framework akin to Plato, Philo, or gnostic thought. Such a view of Hebrews is not new, and has a significant number of growing adherents in recent decades. (For an excellent overview, see George H. Guthrie, "Hebrews in its First-Century Contexts: Recent Research," in *The Face of New Testament Studies*, ed. S. McKnight and G. Osborne [Grand Rapids: Baker, 2004], 425-30).

Since this is Gräßer's philosophic understanding of Hebrews, he seems to cast everything into one of two specific categories, and as such there can be little room for continuity regarding the law, or room for a "transformation" of the law, and only its absolute cancellation in all aspects. Gräßer maintains that Hebrews' discussion regarding the law is purely theoretical, and Koester rightly disagrees with Gräßer on this point. He avers, "Given the importance of the Levitical priesthood for Jewish identity, it seems likely that Heb 7:11-19 deals with live issues" (Koester, *Hebrews*, 357; cf. Donald Guthrie, *Hebrews*, TNTC 15 [Grand Rapids: Eerdmans, 1983], 161).

[84]Ellingworth, *Hebrews*, 381; also Peterson, *Perfection*, 128.
[85]See chapter 6 below. Again, this helps to explain what is meant by νόμου μετάθεσις.

Hebrews 7:20-28

Hebrews 7:20-28 explains the first half of Psalm 110:4—that Jesus is a priest forever.[86] Priesthood has changed, and the promised priesthood is the "better hope" by which the people of God may all now draw near.[87] There is still priesthood, but it is no longer Levitical; it is Melchizedekian and thus eternal and superior by being based on the "word of the oath" in Psalm 110:4a. Yet, as Ellingworth observes, Melchizedek has been left behind, even to the point of omitting the reference to his name when quoting Psalm 110:4.[88] The emphasis is now solely on Jesus Christ and his eternal priesthood. This is the thrust of 7:20-28.[89]

Hebrews 7:20-22 is a single lengthy sentence interrupted by a parenthesis (20b-21) whose main point is to contrast the appointment of Levitical priests to the priesthood versus the priesthood of Christ. The Levitical priesthood is not based upon an oath from God (7:21), but rather upon a legal requirement based on lineage (7:13-14, 16). This ἐντολή is no longer valid since Jesus is from Judah, and since his appointment is derived from the declaration of Psalm 110:4a.[90] The Levitical priesthood has no such oath. Further, there is a two-fold assurance given that this new priesthood is superior and perpetual. The Lord

---

Christ has fulfilled the sacrificial system as the new priest, and thus the regulations that manage external matters of sin and purity have found their end in Christ. It is only in his fulfillment of the law that it may now be transformed and internalized in the NC people.

[86]Koester, *Hebrews*, 358; Bruce, *Hebrews*, 170. Lane observes that the "pastoral implications of the conclusion reached in vv 18-19 are more fully drawn out in 7:20-25" (*Hebrews*, 1:186).

[87]G. Hughes, *Hebrews and Hermeneutics*, 22.

[88]Ellingworth, *Hebrews*, 382. There are several MSS that include the last line (ℵ², A, D, ψ, 1739, 1881, 𝔐, vg^mss, sy bo^pt, Eusebius), but the addition is likely an assimilation to 7:17 (see also 5:6). See also Bruce Metzger, *The Textual Commentary on the Greek New Testament*, 2nd ed. (Stuttgart: Biblia-Druck, 1994), 597. Metzger and committee give the *txt* reading their highest rating concluding, "many scribes would have felt the temptation to add the phrase here (from ver. 17)."

[89]Ellingworth observes the repetition of the prepositional phrase εἰς τὸν αἰῶνα, found in 7:21, 24, and 28 (*Hebrews*, 382). Structurally, this section is bound together by the inclusions ὁρκωμοσίας, ἱερεῖς/ἀρχιερεῖς, and εἰς τὸν αἰῶνα in vv. 20-21 and 28, as well as the concept of speaking in vv. 21 (λέγοντος) and 28 (ὁ λόγος). For these last two parallels the writer is indebted to George Guthrie, who drew attention to them during the writing process of this thesis.

[90]Hughes notes that the oath confirms the new priesthood as over against the old Levitical priesthood (G. Hughes, *Hebrews and Hermeneutics*, 21). See also Dunnill, *Covenant and Sacrifice*, 236. Dunnill rightly notes that Scripture has implicit authority; they are authoritative utterances (246). Lehne observes that every aspect of Ps 110:4 has been stressed in the epistle: the oath (7:20-21, 28), Christ as priest (5:6, 10; 7:28), the permanence of his priesthood (7:24, 28; see 7:3, 16), and the order of Melchizedek (7:11, 17) (Lehne, *New Covenant in Hebrews*, 29).

has sworn (ὤμοσεν)[91] and will not change his mind (μεταμεληθήσεται).[92] These terms taken together assure the fact that this new priest is affirmed by God himself, and that the priesthood is eternal.

Verse 22 is the first occurrence of the term διαθήκη in Hebrews, where it is said that Jesus is the κρείττονος διαθήκης ἔγγυος. The introduction of Jesus as the "guarantor" of a "better covenant" prefaces the larger discussion regarding covenant, which comes into focus in Hebrews 8. Here the language of 7:22 mirrors 8:6 regarding the covenant, and this sudden introduction to the concept of διαθήκη is both downplayed and purposeful. Ellingworth writes, "Διαθήκη is introduced here in such a smooth and unemphatic way that the significance of the concept is not immediately apparent."[93] The term διαθήκη recalls LXX usage, denoting the idea of "sovereign arrangement."[94] It is through this new arrangement that sin will be "remembered no more," and the νόμους "will be written on the minds and hearts" (8:10-12; 10:16-18), and thus such an arrangement is rightly a κρείττονος διαθήκης.[95]

The identification of Jesus as the ἔγγυος of the better covenant is a more specialized term than what is found in 8:6 (μεσίτης). Here, ἔγγυος refers to one who acts as a surety, or "assurance for the fulfillment of something."[96]

---

[91]Cf. Heb 6:13, 16 where God could swear by no one greater, he swore by himself. See G. Hughes, *Hebrews and Hermeneutics*, 20-23.

[92]BDAG, s.v. "μεταμέλομαι." BDAG rightly notes that there is no focus on a lack of regret in this usage. Hebrews 7:21 is the only occasion in the NT where God is the subject.

[93]Ellingworth, *Hebrews*, 385. See also Osborne, "The Christ of Hebrews," 263.

[94]BDAG, s.v. "διαθήκη;" Lane, *Hebrews*, 1:187-88. Moffatt refers to διαθήκη in Hebrews as the "order of religious fellowship" (Moffatt, *Hebrews*, 99). See also Johannes Behm, "διαθήκη," in *TDNT*, ed. G. Kittel, trans. G. W. Bromiley (Grand Rapids: Eerdmans, 1964), 2:132. Behm defines διαθήκη in Hebrews as "a 'disposition' of God, which reveals to men His will, and especially his saving will, or it is the order thereby established as a divine institution." He adds that the source of the author's theology of διαθήκη is Jer 31:31-34. See also Ceslas Spicq, ("La théologie des deux Alliances dans l'épître aux Hébreux," *RSPT* 22 [1949]: 15-30), who defines διαθήκη in Hebrews as a free act of the love of God (23). Note George E. Mendenhall and Gary A. Herion, "Covenant," in *ABD*, ed. David Noel Freedman (New York: Doubleday, 1992), 1:1179-1202. See also von Rad, who defines covenant as a beneficial arrangement that establishes a relationship of the two covenant partners to one another (G. von Rad, *Old Testament Theology*, 1:311). See 1:190-203 for the importance of laws within the covenant context.

[95]Dunnill, *Covenant and Sacrifice*, 229.

[96]BDAG, s.v. "ἔγγυος." Cf. Sir 29:15; 2 Macc 10:28. See Herbert Preisker, "ἔγγυος," in *TDNT*, ed. G. Kittel, trans. G. W. Bromiley (Grand Rapids: Eerdmans, 1964), 2:329. Preisker writes, "Like the rest of the NT, [Hebrews] speaks of the present possession of the gifts and powers of the kingdom of God (12:12ff.). Yet salvation finds fulfillment or completion only in the future (4:1; 6:11 f.; 9:15; 10:36)." The promises of God need

Jesus is therefore the surety for God's promise[97] and the readers may rest assured that the promises of the better covenant are guaranteed. Though not synonymous, both titles (μεσίτης and ἔγγυος) function analogously to assure the addressees of the effectiveness of Christ's work.[98] Reflecting on this verse, Loader states simply, "Die Wirklichkeit des neuen Bundes und seine Wirksamkeit ist durch Jesus ermöglicht."[99]

Verses 23-25 involve a contrast via the writer's familiar use of the μὲν...δέ construction. These verses advance the argument that Jesus' priesthood is better, given that the Levitical priests, being many, could not continue in their duties since they were mortal (v. 23). In contrast (v. 24), because he remains forever[100] (διὰ τὸ μένειν αὐτὸν εἰς τὸν αἰῶνα), his priesthood abides forever as well. Again, the writer's main concern in these verses is to demonstrate that Jesus is a priest εἰς τὸν αἰῶνα.

Since Christ is one and the Levitical priests are many, this is one of the main contrasts that the writer of Hebrews wishes to put forward. The many died, Christ does not. The grammatical contrast in the chiastic structure of verses 23-24 (διὰ τὸ θανάτῳ κωλύεσθαι παραμένειν· ὁ δὲ διὰ τὸ μένειν αὐτὸν εἰς τὸν αἰῶνα) emphasizes this temporal aspect of the numerous priests in contrast to the permanence of the one.[101] Michel points out that "many" in Hebrews carries the idea of imperfection,[102] and it is clear that the many priests and their many sacrifices were insufficient (7:27).

Verse 25 is the writer's deduction (ὅθεν)[103] based upon verses 23-24. The logical deduction is soteriological. Since Christ's office is eternal, Hebrews concludes that he is also "able to save forever those who approach God through him." Τοὺς προσερχομένους recalls verse 19, ἐγγίζομεν, and δύναται recalls δύναμιν ζωῆς ἀκαταλύτου in verse 16. The verb σῴζω is only used twice in Hebrews, 7:25 and 5:7. In 5:7 it is used to speak of Christ crying out to God, the "one able to save" (τὸν δυνάμενον σῴζειν αὐτὸν) whereas here Christ, by virtue of his exalted office as eternal high priest, is the one "able to save" (σῴζειν...δύναται). Thus, Jesus is able to bring salvation, as well as be the avenue through which his people approach God.

---

assurances of their fulfillment, notes Preisker, and for Hebrews Jesus himself is the Guarantor. See also, Lehne, *New Covenant in Hebrews*, 102.

[97]Attridge, *Hebrews*, 209. See also G. Hughes, *Hebrews and Hermeneutics*, 20-23.

[98]Lehne, *New Covenant in Hebrews*, 102. See also Gräßer who asserts that these titles do not refer to any one particular function of Jesus, but rather point to the entirety of Christ's work (Erich Gräßer, *Der Alte Bund im Neuen* [Tübingen: Mohr, 1985], 103).

[99]Loader, *Sohn und Hoherpriester*, 249.

[100]Attridge suggests that the usage of μένειν might reflect a traditional Christological acclamation, akin to John 8:35 and 12:34 (Attridge, *Hebrews*, 209).

[101]Lane, *Hebrews*, 1:189.

[102]Michel, *Der Brief*, 276.

[103]This is typical of Hebrews. See 2:17, 3:1, 8:3, 9:18, and 11:19.

While verses 26-28 conclude the immediate paragraph (20-28), they also conclude the chapter and bring to a close the discussion of Melchizedek that began as far back as 5:1-10 (especially note the parallels with 5:1-3). In 7:1-25 the writer of Hebrews demonstrates that Melchizedek is superior to Abraham and thus the line of priests from Abraham, that the priesthood has changed in light of the application of the oath of Psalm 110:4 to Jesus, and that the new priestly order of Melchizedek is superior to the old Levitical priesthood since it is eternal, singular, and has a better covenant. The author "now describes the perfection of Jesus' high priesthood and...his self-offering (vv. 26-28)."[104] In doing so the stage is set for chapters 8-10 which describe the NC work of Christ in the heavenly tabernacle and its present and abiding effects.[105] The final paragraph of Hebrews 7 articulates the character of Jesus, as well as his achievement and high priest status.

The author describes Jesus as a high priest who is ὅσιος, ἄκακος, and ἀμίαντος, three terms that are cultic in nature and denote devotion, innocence, and cultic purity.[106] In short, they assert the sinlessness of Christ, the new Melchizedekian high priest.[107] Jesus has assumed a place higher than the heavens where he, as high priest, accomplishes his priestly duties, being "separate from sinners" in the sense that he has ascended into the heavenly tabernacle having "direct, unhindered access to God."[108] This anticipates the explanation of his work to be detailed in 9:1-10:18. In contrast to the Levitical priests who not only repeatedly had to offer sacrifices for the people as well as themselves, 7:27 notes that Jesus has no such need. This is based on the fact that he himself is without sin (7:26), and that he offered himself willingly (cf. 10:5-10). Cockerill notes the logical progression between verses 26 and 27. He writes, "Being the kind of High Priest described in verse 26, He was able to make the sacrifice described in verse 27."[109] Such is one of the more significant distinctives of the new high priest. Whereas sacrifices under the OC were

---

[104]Moffatt, *Hebrews*, 129.

[105]Cockerill, "Melchizedek Christology," 27-29, 148, 260. These closing verses have a dual function in that they conclude the present chapter, yet also introduce concepts that will only be fully explained in Heb 8-10.

[106]Michel states, "die wohl alle drei kultisch priesterlich verstanden werden wollen" (*Der Brief*, 279). See also Ps 12:1; 18:26; 25:21; 32:6; 79:1-2; 132:9, 16; 149:1-2; Prov 1:22; and 2 Macc 14:26; 15:34; see also Josephus, *Jewish Wars*, 6.99; Philo, *On Flight*, 118; *Special Laws*, 1.113. See Ellingworth, *Hebrews*, 393-94; Isaacs, *Sacred Space*, 115-16.

[107]Spicq rightly concludes, "Ces trois termes experiment les qualities cultuelles habilitant le prêtre à remplir validement ses fonctions...le grand prêtre des chrétiens possède une perfection intérieure, religieuse et morale, consommée, due à sa personnalité divine" (Spicq, *L'Épître aux Hébreux*, 2:201).

[108]Cockerill, "Melchizedek Christology," 171.

[109]Ibid., 172.

offered daily (καθ' ἡμέραν; see 5:3) and were numerous (θυσίας), Christ presented the singular offering of himself (ἑαυτὸν ἀνενέγκας) only once (ἐφάπαξ).[110] Again, the comparison between the two priesthoods demonstrates the better priesthood of Christ.

Chapter 7 therefore concludes with a final comparison and contrast between the old and new priesthoods and functions as a summary of the chapter. The main contrast in verse 28 is between how the law (ὁ νόμος) appoints priests (via family lineage) and the word of the oath (ὁ λόγος τῆς ὁρκωμοσίας). This alludes to Psalm 110:4, which announced the presence of the new priestly order.[111] As seen in 7:16 the law specified that priests descend from the tribe of Levi, yet Jesus was from Judah (7:13-14). Yet in the coming of Christ, the new priesthood (prefigured in Melchizedek) announced in Psalm 110:4 effectively renders the Levitical priesthood no longer necessary, since there can only be one priesthood at a time. The new high priest will not die, and thus his office has no end (7:24). He is a son (υἱὸν)[112] who is perfect (τετελειωμένον)[113] and eternal (εἰς τὸν αἰῶνα). The Levitical priesthood failed to supply salvation and full access to God for the covenant people. The law only appointed priests who could offer insufficient sacrifices, and could never bring about τελείωσις in the people. Thus, a radical change was necessary due to the insufficiency of these repeated appointments. The work of Christ, the Melchizedekian high priest, brings such a change both to the priesthood and the law.

Ascertaining the logical flow of Hebrews 7 is necessary in order to place the ensuing discussion in its exegetical context. Specifically, the idea of νόμου μετάθεσις in 7:12 is the focus for the remainder of the present chapter.

Hebrews 7 and Νόμου Μετάθεσις

It is clear that for the writer of Hebrews the Mosaic law was insufficient. It could not bring about perfection due to its externality and the shadowy cult that its many sinful priests legislated. Yet the question is whether the writer of Hebrews envisioned an abrogation and full nullification of the law when he penned νόμου μετάθεσις in 7:12. Is it in keeping with the writer of Hebrews

---

[110]Ellingworth states that though ἐφάπαξ can have both theological and legal connotations in Hebrews, here the former is more in view than the latter (*Hebrews*, 396).

[111]Weiß, *Der Brief*, 426-27.

[112]"Son" recalls 1:2, where Christ is the preexistent son through whom God has spoken in the present age. See Gräßer, *An die Hebräer*, 2:72. See also 1:5, 8; 3:6; 4:14; 5:5, 8; 6:6; 7:3.

[113]The perfect tense of the participle is noteworthy, since it signifies the permanent and lasting state of Christ's perfection, which is linked to his exaltation. See Attridge, *Hebrews*, 215; F. B. Meyer, *The Way into the Holiest* (Grand Rapids: Zondervan, 1950), 90, 95; Raymond Brown, *Christ above All* (Downers Grove, IL: Intervarsity, 1982), 137. See also Weiß, *Der Brief*, 427.

to argue that the law is "useless"[114] and that in its entirety has been "abrogated,"[115] "annulled,"[116] or "cancelled/ reversed,"[117] "made obsolete"[118] in light of the coming of the new priesthood of Christ? Or has something else occurred, something more textured and complex that is characterized by "transformation" or "transposition"[119] in light of Christ? Is it possible that the law is viewed through the lens of Christ and that the writer's view is less about "abrogation and annulment in full" and more about "fulfillment and transformation in full" as described at the outset of this chapter? While the entire question cannot be answered based solely on Hebrews 7, the present thesis argues for the latter. Further arguments for this view are made in subsequent chapters of this work.

Νόμος and Διαθήκη

One of the issues that clouds the entire discussion is the matter of the close relationship between νόμος and διαθήκη in Hebrews. If one concludes that these two terms are virtual synonyms, as some suggest,[120] then one will conclude that the law (= covenant) has been cancelled and abrogated in its entirety, since Hebrews 8 is so clear that there is a *new* διαθήκη. Yet this leads to unnecessary creativity when attempting to explain 8:10 (and 10:16), and what Jeremiah could have meant when he prophesied the NC and its promise to write the νόμους on the hearts and minds of the NC people.[121]

---

[114]Moffatt, *Hebrews*, 98; Weiß, *Der Brief*, 400-01.

[115]Attridge, *Hebrews*, 201, 203; Koester, *Hebrews*, 351.

[116]Gräßer, *An die Hebräer*, 2:38, 47; Weiß, *Der Brief*, 400-01.

[117]Schunack, *Der Hebräerbrief*, 96.

[118]Thielman, *The Law and the New Testament*, 130.

[119]For example see Ellingworth, *Hebrews*, 374. Ellingworth is notable here, in that he concludes that a total removal of the law is not in view in 7:12.

[120]Such as Attridge (*Hebrews*, 203, esp. n. 72, where διαθήκη is clearly in view), and Thielman (*The Law and the New Testament*, 111). These are singled out since they advocate synonymy for νόμος and διαθήκη. See also Montefiore, *Hebrews*, 124; Lehne, *New Covenant and Hebrews*, 75; Gräßer, *Der Alte Bund im Neuen*, 99. Bayes seems to use the terms interchangeably, and this leads him to argue that the law has been terminated and abolished, yet has an ongoing status (Bayes, *Weakness*, 190). This is confusing at best. When making such statements, he repeatedly qualifies νόμος in the way that the term διαθήκη is used here.

[121]Among recent commentators, Ellingworth offers a more detailed treatment and definition of διαθήκη in Hebrews (Ellingworth, *Hebrews*, 386-88). He cites a "working definition" of διαθήκη in Hebrews from Spicq, "a free manifestation of divine love, institutionalized as an 'economy' whose stability and consummation are guaranteed by a cultic ratification, the sacrificial death of Christ, and whose aim is to make men live in communion with God, to impart to them the treasure of grace and the heavenly inheritance" (388). See Spicq, "La théologie des deux Alliances," 23.

Rather, the view of νόμος and διαθήκη understood in the present study strives for a greater precision, though is by no means novel.[122] In brief, what is meant by "distinction" is not that διαθήκη and νόμος are two radically different things, but that the former is the "disposition of God," or "arrangement" God makes in his relation to his people, and the latter is the stipulations and requirements of that "arrangement." This definition of covenant is assigned to διαθήκη for example by Behm.[123] In a more recent study of the OT idea of בְּרִית, Gordon McConville echoes this definition when he defines בְּרִית more specifically as a "treaty, agreement, alliance, or covenant."[124] McConville notes that in the OT the idea of covenant is essentially conceived as relational, between individuals or more importantly between God and his people. Further, McConville observes the general point that the covenant is kept by obeying the laws or stipulations of the covenant.[125] Under a discussion of the Mosaic covenant he adds that the covenant people are obligated to keep the laws of the covenant, i.e. its specific stipulations. Further, he avers that Israel's life is regulated by the specific laws God gives when making the covenant with Israel. What is relevant here is that nowhere in the essay does McConville attempt to argue for a distinction between the terms. He *assumes* that they are distinct and not synonymous, though clearly related to one another in that specific laws regulate life within the covenant.[126] Again, what is meant in the present thesis is no different from McConville.

A number of other works make the same point.[127] For example, in the

---

Mathias Rissi is helpful when he notes that the meaning of διαθήκη in Hebrews becomes clear when one considers that both the readers and the author speak of a new covenant with reference to Jer 31 (8:8-12; 10:16-17). He asserts that this means that God orders the relationship to him in a new way in the NC: "He will put his law in their heart," giving the covenant people the "freedom and potential of joyful obedience." For Rissi, law and covenant are related, but not synonyms. See Mathias Rissi, *Die Theologie des Hebräerbriefes* (Tübingen: J. C. B. Mohr, 1987), 122.

[122]The 1989 work of Fred A. Malone is important at this point given that Malone too maintains this distinction in Hebrews between νόμος and διαθήκη. In doing so, his work is quite clear. See Fred A. Malone, "A Critical Evaluation of the Use of Jeremiah 31:31-34 in the Letter to the Hebrews," (Ph.D. diss., Southwestern Baptist Theological Seminary, 1989).

[123]Behm, "διαθήκη," in *TDNT*, 2:132.

[124]Gordon J. McConville, "בְּרִית," in *NIDOTTE*, ed. Willem A. VanGemeren (Grand Rapids: Zondervan, 1997), 1:746-54. In addition, διαθήκη is the term most frequently chosen by the LXX translators to express the idea of בְּרִית.

[125]McConville, "בְּרִית," in *NIDOTTE*, 1:749.

[126]He lists numerous OT texts that support this point. See McConville, "בְּרִית," in *NIDOTTE*, 1:749.

[127]This is also how the noted Hebrews scholar Albert Vanhoye understands the two terms when he plainly states, "In the Bible, the Law is presented as the Law of the Covenant, which regulates the life of the people of God" (Vanhoye, *Old Testament*

treatment of διαθήκη by Guhrt,[128] this same distinction between law and covenant is made. The διαθήκη is the broader "agreement" made between two parties such as between two friends (1 Sam 18:3), between two rulers (Gen 21:22-24; 26:26-29; 1 Kgs 5:12; 20:34), two tribes (Josh 15:9) between Israel and its slaves (Jer 34:8 ff.), between a king and his subjects (2 Kgs 11:4; 1 Sam 11:1; 2 Sam 3:12-13), between YHWH and others such as Noah (Gen 6:18),

---

Priests, 165), and this distinction is maintained throughout *Old Testament Priests*. See also Brevard S. Childs, *Biblical Theology of the Old and New Testaments: Theological Reflection on the Christian Bible* (Minneapolis: Fortress: 1992), 133-34, whose articulation of law and covenant is the same as is argued here, viz., that they belong closely together but are not synonyms. Law is the stipulations of the covenant which are to be obeyed. For Childs, covenant loyalty means keeping the laws which were the written standards which regulated the community (137, 539; see also W. Zimmerli, *The Law and Prophets: A Study of the Meaning of the Old Testament*, trans. R. E. Clements [Oxford: Basil Blackwell, 1965], 46-60). See also George E. Mendenhall, *Law and Covenant in Israel and the Ancient Near East* (Pittsburgh: Biblical Colloquium, 1955) who, building on the thoughts of Alt and Wellhausen (with which he does not always agree), Mendenhall defines covenant in terms of relationship (5), and law as the stipulations of the covenant. He writes, "the people entered into covenant...to keep the commandments of the Lord" (47; see also 5, 13-17, 49). Concerning the Decalogue he asserts, "[The] Decalogue was simply the stipulation of the obligations to the deity which the community accepted as binding" (5). See also Pretorius ("Διαθήκη in the Epistle to the Hebrews," 39), in which "law" is simply defined as "rules" of the covenant that God makes with the people. See also Ernest W. Nicholson, *God and His People: Covenant Theology in the Old Testament* (Oxford: Clarendon Press, 1986), 210-15, who writes, "the covenant entailed the solemn submission of Israel to Yahweh's will expressed in his commandments" (212). See also Levenson, *Sinai and Zion*, 48-50; O. Palmer Robertson, *The Christ of the Covenants* (Phillipsburg, NJ: Presbyterian and Reformed, 1980), 167-99.

In listing such works the intent is not to be exhaustive, but rather to demonstrate the idea that such a distinction between νόμος and διαθήκη is not new or novel in any sense, but rather is common in the discussion of these two terms. There is, more often than not, little or no explanation for the decision to view νόμος and διαθήκη as synonyms in Hebrews, and in the writer's view clouds the exegesis and theological assertions of these texts. Yet others, such as Marie Isaacs, *Sacred Space: An Approach to the Theology of the Epistle to the Hebrews*, JSNTSS 73 (Sheffield: Academic Press, 1992), maintain this distinction between νόμος and διαθήκη in Hebrews, and as a result her arguments are far more lucid.

[128]Joachim Guhrt, "Covenant," "διαθήκη," in *NIDNTT*, ed. Colin Brown (Grand Rapids: Zondervan, 1975), 1:365-72. See also H. –H. Esser, "Law," "νόμος," in *NIDNTT*, ed. Colin Brown (Grand Rapids: Zondervan, 1975), 2:438-51; esp. 441-48. In this related article, Esser argues that in the time of Jesus, law was "an absolute in itself and was independent of the covenant" (441). While one may or may not agree with this statement what is important here is that for Esser the two terms are clearly not synonymous.

Abraham (Gen 17; see also 2 Kgs 13:23), and David (2 Sam 7; see also Jer 33:21).[129] Regarding the NC of Jeremiah 31:31-34 Guhrt defines διαθήκη as God's "disposition" in the sense of "arrangement." In addition he discusses "law" in terms of instructions and regulations for life in the covenant.[130] Simply, as one reads each of these texts it becomes difficult to see how law and covenant could be synonyms.[131]

In addition to the OT texts cited in the articles above, this distinction between law and covenant is evident in texts such as Exodus 24:1-8, where the people affirm their covenant with God by agreeing to obey the specific laws. The law is what one obeyed (it was "the law and commandment written for their instruction" [24:12]) if the people agreed to and entered into the covenantal arrangement (Exod 24:3). See also Joshua 8:32, 34.

To be sure, these terms are closely related (breaking a law can be described

---

[129]Guhrt, "Covenant," in *NIDNTT*, 1:365-66.

[130]Ibid., 1:367. Importantly, there is an editor's note by Colin Brown that specifically addresses the NC of Jeremiah 31. The point of the editorial note is that in the NC, the law [not synonymous with covenant] is *not* abolished. Brown's comments favor the overall point being argued here. "For Jeremiah, this relationship is to be realized not by setting aside the law but by a more personal application of it" (1:368). See also Weiß, *Der Brief*, 413-14.

[131]The same conclusions can be drawn from similar essays. See Jack R. Lundbom, "New Covenant," in *ABD*, ed. David Noel Freedman (New York: Doubleday, 1992), 4:1098-94; Mendenhall and Herion, "Covenant," 1:1179-1202. See especially Samuel Greengus, "Law: Biblical and ANE Law," in *ABD*, ed. David Noel Freedman (New York: Doubleday, 1992), 1:242-54, where he notes the connection with covenant. Greengus observes that a biblical covenant was an agreement made between God, the sovereign Lord, and Israel, his subject people. When the covenant was made, specific commandments and stipulations were laid upon the covenant people to obey (1:245). Greengus adds, "The occasions of making and renewing the covenant became in fact settings for revealing and restating some or all of the laws (2 Kgs 23:1-3; Jer 34:8-22; Ezra 9-10; Neh 9-13)" (1:245). Greengus demonstrates the relationship between law and covenant as OT concepts, and clearly delineates the two. E. P. Sanders authored the second part of this lengthy article ("Law: Law and Judaism of the NT Period," in *ABD*, ed. David Noel Freedman [New York: Doubleday, 1992], 1:254-65), in which he argues that νόμος is defined in this period as "specific commandments...both the Heb and Gk terms were especially used for commandments and prohibitions which were observable" (1:255). In keeping with his conclusions elsewhere (see chapter 2 above), Sanders concludes that "law" should be understood within the theological context of election, grace, and covenant (1:264).

See also Peter Richardson and Stephen Westerholm, eds., *Law in Religious Communities in the Roman Period: The Debate Over Torah and Nomos in Post-Biblical Judaism and Early Christianity*, SCJ 4 (Ontario: Wilfrid Laurier University Press, 1991), passim; Lindars, "Hebrews and the Second Temple," 414, 416, 432; von Rad, *Old Testament Theology*, 1:190-203.

as transgressing the covenant, and obeying the law is what it means to keep the covenant), but there is a subtle distinction that can be made, and *is* in fact made in broader NT studies as well as in Hebrews studies.[132] To cite but one example, in the writings of E. P. Sanders[133] one enters the covenant (the larger agreement/relationship) and remains in the covenant by keeping the law (specific requirements), according to Sanders' covenantal nomism. This is all that is meant by "subtle distinction" in the present study of Hebrews and is in concert with the findings of chapter 2, above.

The preceding point illumines the fact that synonymy between law and covenant is by no means the conclusion of broader OT and NT scholarship. Therefore it seems best to conclude that the burden of proof lies with Hebrews scholars who argue (or presume) that διαθήκη and νόμος are interchangeable or in some way synonymous. Since the text and theology of Hebrews makes good sense when understood as articulated here, then it seems best to read νόμος and διαθήκη in Hebrews as related, but not synonymous terms. In addition, this affords the opportunity for a generally consistent meaning of νόμος (a body of commandments to be obeyed).[134] Therefore it is logical to suggest that though the OC has been superseded by the NC, there is the possibility of continuity between νόμος in both covenants.[135]

More importantly, this is indeed the language Hebrews uses when speaking of the two terms. When speaking of διαθήκη the author uses terms such as "a better covenant" (7:22; 8:6), "eternal covenant" (13:20), "first and second

---

[132]See Vanhoye, *Old Testament Priests* (cited above); see also Barnabas Lindars, *Theology of the Letter to the Hebrews* (Cambridge: University Press, 1991).

[133]See for example E. P. Sanders, *Paul and Palestinian Judaism: A Comparison of Patterns of Religion* (Philadelphia: Fortress, 1977); idem, *Jewish Law from Jesus to the Mishnah: Five Studies* (Philadelphia: Trinity Press International, 1990); idem, *Judaism: Practice and Belief 63 BCE-66CE* (Philadelphia: Trinity Press International, 1992). Again, the point is not to be exhaustive, but rather to demonstrate adequately the point. For recent examples in Hebrews studies, see Isaacs, *Sacred Space*, 115-26; G. Hughes, *Hebrews and Hermeneutics*, 16.

[134]See G. Schrenk, "ἐντολή," in *TDNT*, 2:546; Lane, *Hebrews*, 1:168; Cockerill, "Melchizedek Christology,"105-06; Schunack, *Der Hebräerbrief*, 95. This is also largely in keeping with the findings of νόμος in the Second Temple period from chapter 2 above.

[135]Recall from chapter 2 of the present study that νόμος is consistently a referent for the Pentateuch and more precisely the commands within the Pentateuch. This is precisely the point here. This makes sense in the present context given that in 7:5 and 16, what is referred to is a specific commandment, and in 7:12 and 19a the body of commandments (the law) is the referent. The theme of "covenant," as the broader arrangement between God and his people, becomes the focus in Heb 8. There the writer of Hebrews asserts that a new arrangement (covenant) has been made that replaces the old, and that in the NC there is still νόμος (8:10; 10:16).

covenant" (8:7, 13; 9:1, 16, 18; 10:9), "new covenant" (8:8, 13; 9:15),[136] of the OC's "obsolescence," "growing old," and "close to disappearing" (8:13), "inauguration" of the new (9:18), the "taking away of the first (covenant)" in order that the second (new) covenant may be "established" (10:9). Yet when speaking of νόμος the writer of Hebrews speaks of the "change of the law," the law's "inability to perfect" (7:19; 10:2), and laws (νόμους) being "inwardly written" in the NC (8:10; 10:16). In short, the writer of Hebrews does not use the same terms to describe νόμος as he does to describe διαθήκη.

Finally, the assertion that the law is a collection of ἐντολαι (and not synonymous with διαθήκη) is reinforced by the oft-repeated phrase, "according to the law" (κατὰ τὸν νόμον), meaning something was done that was commanded by a specific command in the law (7:5, 16; 8:4; 9:19, 22; 10:8; cf. 7:28).[137] This further reinforces the point that νόμος for Hebrews is a set of requirements given for the people to obey and follow as part of the overarching covenantal arrangement between God and his people. Thus, given the evidence here from specialized studies, broader NT studies, Hebrews studies, and from the text of Hebrews itself, it is more likely that διαθήκη and νόμος should be seen as related but not synonymous terms. If this is a correct nuance of the terms, then there is reason to suggest that while the overarching relational arrangement between God and his people (διαθήκη) has been replaced, the covenant regulations (νόμος) have been transformed (μετάθεσις) and internalized. Both διαθήκη and νόμος have been affected by the coming of Christ, but not in identical fashion. While it is impossible to speak of one and not think of the other, it is possible to speak of one and not mean the other.

Νόμου Μετάθεσις

In the exegesis of Hebrews 7:1-28 above, it was demonstrated that though some might suggest that νόμου μετάθεσις in 7:12 might have the sense of "change" in a broad sense, it surely means that the law has been "abrogated/cancelled" in full. Yet it is asserted here that such a conclusion is not required by the text nor is it the best way of understanding these verses.[138] Scholars such as Lane, Schrenk, and Cockerill (et al.), acknowledge that the primary meaning for verses 16, 18-19 is the cancellation of the particular legal requirement (ἐντολή) which governs bodily descent for priests.[139] The specific command (ἐντολή)

---

[136]See also 12:24. Lehne makes a similar observation, that terms for "new" are reserved only for διαθήκη (Lehne, *New Covenant in Hebrews*, 53). See also Pretorius, "Διαθήκη in the Epistle to the Hebrews," 47-48.

[137]The law's specific commands/regulations are in view in 9:1 as well, especially when read with 10:8.

[138]See too Bayes concerning νόμου μετάθεσις in 7:12 (Bayes, *Weakness*, 191).

[139]See Lane, *Hebrews*, 1:165, 168; G. Schrenk, "ἐντολή," in *TDNT*, 2:546; Cockerill, "Melchizedek Christology," 105-08. See also Schunack, *Der Hebräerbrief*, 95; G.

refers to lineage requirements for the priesthood and not the whole law, which is comprised of the ἐντολαί. This requirement is specifically in view in verses 13-14,[140] where the readers are reminded that Jesus was not from the priestly tribe, but rather from Judah, about which nothing had been commanded regarding priests. If Psalm 110:4 predicts that there will be a new priestly Melchizedekian order, then it stands to reason that if Jesus is a priest, then the priestly requirement has been set aside.[141] Such a requirement is weak (v. 18, ἀσθενὲς) and no longer useful,[142] providing for priests who themselves were weak (v. 28, ἀσθένειαν). Therefore, what is annulled is the requirement of bodily descent.[143]

If this is what the writer of Hebrews has in mind for ἀθέτησις in 7:18, then it would be faulty to ascribe ἀθέτησις to the law as a whole, and therefore

---

Hughes, *Hebrews and Hermeneutics*, 17.

[140]See Lindars, "Hebrews and the Second Temple," 425.

[141]One additional observation merits mentioning here. The writer of Hebrews reasons "backwards" *from* the reality of Christ the high priest *to* the text of the OT in order to explain what must have happened to law and priesthood in light of Christ. He looks backwards and biblically reasons through the realities of what Christ has accomplished. In short, he sees the OC requirements and its institutions through the lens of the coming of the new and eternal high priest, and this concerns the law and all of its commandments. In light of this new priesthood, certain changes must have occurred to the law, he reasons. Viewed through the lens of Christ, the law and the institutions that it regulated makes perfect sense. It was insufficient and external, only providing for weak priests and insufficient sacrifices that could not assuage guilt nor the cleansing of the conscience (9:9-10, 14; 10:2, 4; see Lindars, "Hebrews and the Second Temple," 425-27). It is suggested here that it pointed to Christ, and has been "Christologized" by his coming, and therefore in this significant change the law has been fulfilled in the work of Christ. The NC people no longer have Levitical priests and no longer offer sacrifices since the priesthood and cult have found their end in Christ. Thus, the people no longer relate to these commandments as they once did. This is akin to W. D. Davies' "Christified law" in his essay, "The Moral Teaching of the Early Church," in *The Use of the Old Testament in the New and Other Essays: Studies in Honor of William Franklin Stinespring*, ed. James A. Efrid (Durham, NC: Duke University Press, 1972), 317.

[142]Lane makes the point that in 7:18, the weakness "inheres not in the law or its purpose, but in the people upon whom it depends for its accomplishment" (Lane, *Hebrews*, 1:185; see also Bayes, *Weakness*, 192-93).

[143]Weiß, *Der Brief*, 401; Vanhoye, *Old Testament Priests*, 148. See Cockerill ("Melchizedek Christology," 107-08), who writes, "The main emphasis seems to be on the physical descent of the priests...the context supports the emphasis on physical descent.... Clearly, the emphasis is on the aspect of descent." See also Isaacs (*Sacred Space*, 116), who writes, "It is therefore the Psalm which claims that the law pertaining to Levitical priesthood was demonstrably weak (7:18), since that priesthood failed to gain access to the true holy of holies.... This is what our author means when he says 'the law made nothing perfect' (7:19)." Contra Gräßer, *An die Hebräer*, 2:38.

would be more helpful to explore the idea of transformation and what that means for the priesthood and the law rather than abrogation. It is unnecessary to read 7:12 as being controlled by 7:18-19. It is better to suggest that 7:12 states the main idea at the outset of the section, and 7:18-19 develop what is meant by 7:12, viz., that the transformation of the law entails an essential element of cessation. This avoids the lexical conundrum that what μετάθεσις "really means" is ἀθέτησις. Further, since priesthood and law are so intertwined in the axiomatic statement in 7:12, how logical is it to conclude that priesthood is changed from Levitical to Melchizedekian, while law has been cancelled in full?

In addition, "transformation, alteration, transposition" is in fact the meaning of μετάθεσις in both its noun and verb forms.[144] This is true in the secondary literature as well.[145] Priesthood has been transformed (7:11-12a), changing from

---

[144]See BDAG, s.v. "μετάθεσις." On the verb μετατίθημι BDAG cites Heb 7:12, "to effect a change in state or condition, to change, to alter... 'when the priesthood has changed, i.e. passed on to another Hb 7:12," s.v. "μετατίθημι." LSJ supports this sense of "change" as well, "a change of position, a transposition" (Henry George Liddell and Robert Scott, A Greek-English Lexicon, rev. and aug. Sir Henry Stuart Jones, [LSJ] 9th ed. [Oxford: Clarendon Press: 1996], s.v. "μετάθεσις"; "μετατίθημι"). LSJ never suggests "remove," for either the noun or verb forms, but cites numerous examples for the sense of "alteration," "transposition," and "amendment." Christian Maurer ("μετατίθημι," "μετάθεσις," in TDNT, ed. G. Kittel, trans. G. W. Bromiley [Grand Rapids: Eerdmans, 1972], 8:161) finds this to be the case for both noun and verb forms in LXX and NT usage, citing Jude 4 ("transforming God's grace into licence") as well as the "translation" of Enoch in Heb 11:5 and the "alteration" of the law in 7:12. See also G. Hughes, Hebrews and Hermeneutics, 17. Note that even when the verb has the sense of "remove" (such as Enoch in Heb 11:5), the idea of "nullification" is not present. Rather, the idea is removal in the sense of transference, such as Enoch who was transferred to another place.

[145]This meaning of "alteration," "transformation," or "transposition" is found in several examples of secondary literature. See for example Philo (On Abraham, 18, in Philo, 6:12-13, trans. F. H. Colson, LCL), who writes of Enoch who was "transferred" (using both the noun and verb forms in On Abraham, 17-19), "ἡ γὰρ μετάθεσις τροπὴν ἐμφαίνει καὶ μεταβολήν, πρὸς δὲ τὸ βέλτιον ἡ μεταβολή, διότι προμηθείᾳ γίνεται θεοῦ," which is translated, "For (the idea of) transference implies turning and changing, and the change is to the better because it is brought about by the forethought of God." See also Josephus, Jewish Antiquities, 18.57, in Josephus, 9:44-45, trans. L. H. Feldman, LCL.

In the sense of the "alteration" of Abraham's name, see Philo (On Abraham, 81) where μετάθεσις is linked by καὶ to the term ὑπαλλαγή, which also carries the idea of "change" as a noun and "change gradually, change a little, exchange, alter" in its verb form (LSJ, s.v. "ὑπαλλαγή;" see also Josephus, Against Apion, 1.285-86, in Josephus, 1:278-79, trans. H. St. J. Thackeray, LCL). See also On the Giants 66 (in Philo, 2:478-79, trans. F. H. Colson, LCL), where Philo writes of a "change and alteration of

Levitical to Melchizedekian. There is still priesthood, though what is known of it has been escalated and transposed into a higher (Christological) key. In like manner, the law has been changed, and one aspect of this change is the cancellation of the lineage requirement (though further aspects are revealed in subsequent chapters). Stating it this way places 7:18 alongside 7:12 and serves to explain an important aspect as to what νόμου μετάθεσις means. Reading Hebrews in this manner allows the writer's language of 7:12 to have its full force, and does not necessitate usurping the usual meaning of μετάθεσις.[146]

To argue for a Christological transformation of the law is, to be sure, a more complex theological undertaking than simply to say that law (and therefore priesthood) are completely abrogated. Yet this actually avoids difficulties later on when explaining Hebrews 8:10 and 10:16 (where νόμους is written on the minds and hearts), since if νόμος has been annulled, then νόμος in Hebrews 8 would therefore be required to mean something quite different than νόμος in Hebrews 7 (see chapter 5 below). Retaining the idea of "transposition" or "change" in a more neutral sense[147] allows νόμος in the NC text to have some

---

purpose" (μεταβολὴ καὶ μετάθεσις). It is useful in this example that μετάθεσις is linked by καὶ to μεταβολὴ which carries the meaning of "transfer, transition" (LSJ, s.v. "μεταβολεύς"). For "change" in the sense of "distortion," see Josephus, *Against Apion*, 2.26, in *Josephus*, 1:302-03, trans. H. St. J. Thackeray, LCL. Thucydides, too, uses μετάθεσις in the sense of "alteration" or "transformation." He writes, "Δίκαιον γὰρ εἶναι πᾶσι τοῖς ξυμμάχοις γεγράφθαι τὴν μετάθεσιν" ("For it would have been just, they thought, that the clause should have given the power to alter the articles to all the allies"). In *Histories*, Polybius uses μετάθεσις repeatedly to refer to "changing sides" in the sense of "going over to the Romans." (For example, see Polybius, *Histories*, 18.6.7, in *Polybius: the Histories*, 5:96-97, trans. W. R. Paton, LCL; see also Polybius, *Histories*, 5.86.8). Polybius also uses μετάθεσις to refer to the "change" or "alteration" or "transformation" of Genthius' attitude in *Histories*, 29.11.3. See also *Letter of Aristeas* 160 which notes the "change" or "transformation" of men that comes from meditating on the works of God (R. J. H. Shutt, "Letter of Aristeas," in *OTP*, ed. James Charlesworth [New York: Doubleday, 1983], 2:23).

In short, the lexical evidence supports the definition of μετάθεσις as meaning "change, transformation, alteration" and not simply "cancellation, abrogation."

[146]In addition, Enoch was not "cancelled" or "abrogated" in Heb 11:5 (πίστει ᾽Ενὼχ μετετέθη). Enoch did not cease to exist, but was rather transformed and transferred (presumably to heaven?) due to his faith. In this sense he was "removed from one place and put in another place." Such an idea is consistent with the present argument. One vital aspect of the νόμου μετάθεσις is the law's change of location. What was formerly external is now internal in the NC people.

[147]Ellingworth, *Hebrews*, 374. See also Lane (*Hebrews*, 2:482) who avers that in 7:12 μετάθεσις is used with the nuance of a "change or alteration in condition or status." However, neither Ellingworth nor Lane explores the nature of such a transformation of the law. While this writer agrees with their assertions concerning the law in 7:12, such a discussion as to the nature of this transformation seeks to advance the discussion of the

correspondence to νόμος in the old,[148] though clearly not without a significant amount of μετάθεσις. In short, for the writer of Hebrews, μετάθεσις involves a strong element of cancellation, but "cancellation, abrogation" is inadequate by itself. As such, "transformation" is a better term that allows for a broader understanding of how the author sees Christ affecting the law. "Transformation" allows for greater contour and texture, and sanctions a measure of continuity as well as discontinuity.

Further, the assertion that the law has been transformed and not fully cancelled is latent in several works written in recent decades. Besides the assertions of Ellingworth and Lane who affirm the more neutral sense of νόμου μετάθεσις in 7:12, a few monographs have posited the same question asked here, though none have undertaken a serious theological inquiry and can only be found in seminal form.

First, in *Covenant and Sacrifice in the Epistle to the Hebrews*, John Dunnill asserts that 7:12 denotes a "major change in the law."[149] For Dunnill this major change results in the "fulfillment and abolition at one stroke of the expiatory cultus" and "the day of the Renewal of the Covenant, in which the age-old covenantal traditions, symbols, paraeneses and promises are *transformed* into realties of the new age...(and) is the day of the new priesthood...'after the order of Melchizedek'."[150] Thus for Dunnill, the coming of Christ has effected a great change in the law which involves, negatively, the abolition of the OC sacrifices, and positively, fulfillment due to transformation of the covenant symbols in the new eschatological age. Further, Dunnill refuses to ascribe a negative view of the law and OC to the writer of Hebrews. His emphasis is not on nullification. He writes, "When Hebrews casts doubt on the efficacy of the old covenant, calling it weak, its sacrifices incapable of removing sin...its criticism does not amount to dismissal."[151] He adds, "A tactic more representative of the book, though, is to praise the new covenant and its agents, expressing moderate criticism of the old through the use of comparative formulae."[152]

Second, in *The New Covenant in Hebrews*, Susanne Lehne postulates the question, "If priesthood and law are so intimately connected, as posited in 7:11-

---

law in Hebrews. This study seeks to make such an advancement.

[148]Lundbom, "New Covenant," in *ABD*, 4:1089; Lane, *Hebrews*, 1:209. Lane argues that in the NC, the content of the law has not changed, but rather only the new manner of presenting the law, i.e., on hearts and minds. This is akin to the view of Christoph Levin, *Die Verheißung des neuen Bundes* (Göttingen: Vandenhoeck & Ruprecht, 1985), 264, who asserts that for Jeremiah 31:31-34, there is no new law in the promised NC, but rather the change in is the manner of Torah-revelation—on the hearts and minds of men. Levin is further discussed in chapter 5.

[149]Dunnill, *Covenant and Sacrifice*, 256-57.

[150]Ibid.

[151]Ibid., 229.

[152]Ibid.

12, could it then be that Heb. envisages a new Law in the order of the Son?"[153] However, though Lehne notes a level of continuity, given that both new and old orders have covenant, priesthood, and bloody sacrifice, she does not entertain the idea that her own question raises regarding the law. Rather, Lehne attributes such continuity of concepts between the old and new orders to the writer of Hebrews, even though the idea of a new covenant comes from the canonical text of Jeremiah and the notion of a different priest comes from the Psalmist, and thus not from the author of Hebrews. Rather than creating such continuity via his own "genius,"[154] the present writer asserts that Hebrews utilizes such categories from his reading and understanding of the OT. Still, the fact that Lehne raises the question here regarding a "new law" in the NC is relevant.

Third, in *Sacred Space*, Marie Isaacs also ponders the question regarding the law in light of Christ's work in the NC age.[155] Her treatment of the NC prophecy from Jeremiah, though brief, asserts that the law (commands of the covenant) will be written on the hearts and will lead to "radical Torah obedience" in the NC.[156] This is in contrast with recent scholars such as Attridge, Lehne, and Thielman, in that νόμος in the NC is reduced to an idea of relationship and a clean conscience,[157] a generic sense of "inward renewal,"[158] or an undefined and generic sense of "God's will."[159] While inward renewal and clean conscience are part of the idea, there is more to be considered; in this new relationship with God, with him as their God and them as his people, νόμος has been written on their hearts.[160]

---

[153]Lehne, *New Covenant and Hebrews*, 26.

[154]Ibid., 27, 100.

[155]Isaacs, *Sacred Space*, 115-19.

[156]Isaacs, *Sacred Space*, 119.

[157]See Attridge (*Hebrews*, 227), who writes that νόμοι written on the minds and hearts is not "an interiorization of the Torah, but a cleansing of the conscience and in true spiritual worship" (contra Levin, *Die Verheißung des neuen Bundes*, 264). Though this writer agrees that the NC entails the cleansing of the conscience, the current study suggests that this is not an either/or proposition.

[158]Thielman, *The Law and the New Testament*, 125; Lehne, *New Covenant in Hebrews*, 115.

[159]Gräßer should also be mentioned here, in that he passes over the meaning of the Jeremiah text's promise of an inward writing of the law. He states that the only reason the writer of Hebrews quotes the entirety of the NC promise from Jer 31 is in order to establish the point of something "new" and thus the statement of 8:13 (Gräßer, *An die Hebräer*, 2:101; see also 99). Though he makes no comment, he does seem to cite approvingly from Christoph Levin (Levin, *Die Verheißung des neuen Bundes*, 264), though for Gräßer, the promise of an internalized law is unimportant.

[160]One wonders whether there is an unconscious resistance in the minds of some scholars to include νόμος in *any* sense in the New Covenant, despite its presence in the Jeremiah text. By redefining νόμος in such generic terms, it becomes νόμος in name only—empty of most or all of its usual meaning.

Where Isaacs is helpful is in the question she asks whether there will be a new law in light of the new priesthood. She wonders aloud if in the NC there is a new law, a "Law of Christ" for Hebrews.[161] Keeping in mind that for Isaacs, νόμος is the sum of the covenant stipulations, then her question is similar to the one posed here. It is imperative to note that based on her study of Hebrews, Isaacs assumes that that there is law of some kind in the NC,[162] yet she does not pursue this question since it is not part of her overall purpose. The thesis advanced here is that there is indeed νόμος in the NC, and that it is not an entirely new law in terms of its content, but rather is the law of Moses that has undergone μετάθεσις in light of the Christ event.[163]

This thesis also helps to explain the meaning of the insufficiency of the priesthood (7:11) and of the law (7:19). Being insufficient to bring about τελείωσις, μετάθεσις of the priesthood and the law was necessary. Because of the weakness of the priesthood that was regulated by the law, "nothing was brought to its appointed end."[164] The law was weak and imperfect, appointing priests who were weak and imperfect, offering sacrifices that could not atone for sin, within a weak covenant that was not eternal (ct. 13:20).[165] The sacrifices were time-bound and in need of repetition,[166] therefore a significant μετάθεσις must take place.

It is essential to note that transformation and thus perfection are only available since Christ has effected such changes in his person and work. Thus any idea of τελείωσις or μετάθεσις must be tied to Christ. Only the new priest, appointed by the oath of Psalm 110:4, could fulfill the inadequacies of the old order and assign a positive role for the (fulfilled and internalized) law in the NC. Though the covenant, the priesthood, the law, and the sacrifices were insufficient, they all pointed to and find their fulfillment in Christ for the writer of Hebrews. There is a new arrangement in which obedience is assured due to the internalization of the laws of God,[167] forgiveness of sins, a new priesthood, and a new sacrifice. All of that which was insufficient was designed to be

---

[161]Isaacs, *Sacred Space*, 116.

[162]Contra Lehne, *New Covenant in Hebrews*, 26.

[163]Isaacs' suggestion for "a new Law—that of Christ" (*Sacred Space*, 116) is not far from what is offered here. This writer is comfortable with the term "law of Christ" for Hebrews if what is meant is both continuity and discontinuity with the laws given by Moses, i.e., the Mosaic commandments viewed through the lens of Christ's work. Such a view also expresses a certain amount of continuity between Hebrews and Jeremiah, since it is unlikely that what Jeremiah meant in his NC prophecy was an abrogation of the תּוֹרָה. Quite the opposite. Rather than a contraction of meaning, there is expansion (Christologically) of Jeremiah's meaning. See chapter 5 below.

[164]Kögel, "De Begriff τελειοῦν," 60.

[165]Michel, *Der Brief*, 273; Peterson, *Perfection*, 187.

[166]Lindars, "Hebrews and the Second Temple," 426, 428.

[167]Isaacs, *Sacred Space*, 119; Levin, *Die Verheißung des neuen Bundes*, 264.

insufficient, in order to point to Christ who would bring about τελείωσις.[168]

Conclusion

Therefore, this chapter has sought to establish a foundation on which to make several statements about Hebrews and the law. First, what 7:12 means is that the law has been transformed. Specifically for Hebrews 7, when Christ and the law intersect, radical changes occur that involve, in part, the cessation of the Levitical priesthood. Given the presence of the new Melchizedekian priest, the Levitical priesthood has ceased. The singular priesthood of Christ overtakes and annuls the ministry of the many and fulfills what the office of priesthood aimed to be (cf. 9:1-10:18). Priesthood as a divine office has been overtaken and filled up by the new Melchizedekian priesthood of Christ.

Second, in Hebrews 7 there is dissatisfaction with the externality and weakness of the law and what it produces (an imperfect people). Before the coming of the new high priest the law was insufficient to perfect. It provided for a priesthood that could only do so much given its weaknesses. One detects a latent desire for something better that will come via the positive aspect seen in 8:10 and 10:16.

Third, μετάθεσις contains a strong element of cessation to go along with the primary element of transformation. The Levitical priesthood (and by implication its sacrificial system) has been fulfilled and has ended in Christ. The Levitical priesthood (and thus its sacrifices) have concluded because what they pointed to has arrived.[169] There is an important distinction between "abrogation" and "transformation," and "transformation" better characterizes the writer's overall understanding, better expressing the contours of what has taken place with regards to the law. Since Christ is the new high priest, the commands that regulated the priesthood are no longer to be kept. To keep them would assert that the Christ event did not fulfill the old priesthood's cultic duties. Such commandments within the law have been cancelled,[170] and the

---

[168]Dunnill, *Covenant and Sacrifice*, 229; Peterson, *Perfection*, 145; Michel, *Der Brief*, 330; Lane, *Hebrews*, 186; Bruce, *Hebrews*, 234-35; Silva, "Perfection and Eschatology in Hebrews," 60-71; Pretorius, "Διαθήκη in the Epistle to the Hebrews," 40; G. L. Cockerill, "Between Sinai and Zion: The Biblical Theology of Hebrews" (paper presented at the annual meeting of the Evangelical Theological Society, Philadelphia, PA, 16-18 November 1995), 5.

[169]Dunnill, *Covenant and Sacrifice*, 229. This point comes into full focus in 9:1-10:18. See also G. Guthrie who, though not speaking specifically about the matter of the law, comments: "The author...interprets with new-covenant eyes, seeing in Christ the fulfillment of what obviously is left undone in the former era" (George Guthrie, "Hebrews in its First-Century Contexts," 437). See chapter 6 below.

[170]Though it might still be possible that there is some degree of obedience even to the cultic commands when NC believers bring their "sacrifices" as described in Heb 13.

accent falls on their fulfillment rather than mere abrogation due to their insufficiency and worthlessness. One expresses a negative connotation while the other does not. The law's insufficiency and weakness is such when it is seen on its own and not in terms of Christ's work. Such weakness is due to the people and not to the character of the law itself.

Fourth, the writer of Hebrews does not view the law only negatively, though the accent in Hebrews 7 is more negative. When dealing with external matters of lineage requirements and the Levitical priesthood, there is an incompleteness and dissatisfaction rooted in the inability to produce perfection. Hebrews can, on the one hand, be critical of the law's inabilities to perfect the people (negative), yet on the other hand state that in the NC the law is transformed (positive), which entails its fulfillment and (in Heb 8) its internalization.

Fifth, apart from Christ, the law was external and insufficient to perfect God's people, even though it was given to them as a divine gift. In Christ, it has been transformed, with the emphasis in Hebrews 7 falling on cessation of the Levitical priesthood due to the presence of the Melchizedekian priest. Yet the axiomatic statement of 7:12 prompts the reader to the reality that more will be said concerning the law. In Christ's new and eternal covenantal arrangement, the law will play a role that heretofore had only been an unattainable ideal. The theme of perfection is linked only to the NC, in which νόμος plays a role in the changed hearts and cleansed consciences as the "Christologized law."

Finally, if the law has been transformed in such a manner, then it opens the door to the likelihood of the law's playing a role in the NC believer such as its being implanted within the NC believer, which guarantees obedience and knowledge of God (8:10-12; 10:16-17). This is the concern of the following chapter, to which the discussion will now turn.

CHAPTER 5

Hebrews 8:1-13 - A New Covenant Blessing: The Law Written on the Heart

Introduction

The task of the present chapter is to answer the logical question concerning νόμος in the Jeremiah citation of Hebrews 8. Specifically, how can the law, which cannot bring about the perfection of God's people (7:19), be understood as a blessing of the NC (8:10; see also 10:16)? Are such ideas as law and blessing diametrically opposed? If the charge is true that the writer of Hebrews is only negative when he speaks of the law, then perhaps Lehne is correct when she asserts that the writer of Hebrews is "perhaps not altogether consistent" in his statements concerning the law.[1]

Building on the conclusions of the previous chapter, the point of the present chapter is to join together the concepts of νόμου μετάθεσις in Hebrews 7:12 with the NC promise of Jeremiah 31:31-34 (LXX 38:31-34), "διδοὺς νόμους μου εἰς τὴν διάνοιαν αὐτῶν καὶ ἐπὶ καρδίας αὐτῶν ἐπιγράψω αὐτούς," viz., the inward writing of νόμους[2] upon the hearts and minds of the NC people. This chapter seeks to demonstrate the compatibility of a transformed law with the inward writing of the law, and to suggest a plausible connection between the transformed law of Heb 7:12 and the NC blessing of Heb 8:10 (see also 10:16).

Specifically, it will be argued that when the law is viewed through the lens of Christ, it is transformed (recall the term "Christologized law") and it is in this transformation that it is internalized in the NC people by God the covenant-maker. It is no longer seen as an external set of regulations, but has become internal as a blessing of God. The law, as the will of God, has been "put into their minds and engraved on their hearts," and this internalization brings about covenant obedience in the people. Heretofore, God's people had primarily been

---

[1] Susanne Lehne, *The New Covenant in Hebrews*, JSNTSS 44 (Sheffield: JSOT Press, 1990), 26. Lehne rightly notes that in the theology of Hebrews the "category of Law is in many ways the most difficult one to assess" (99). The question posed at the outset of this chapter brings into focus the difficulty.

[2] The matter of the plural form of νόμος is explained below.

marked by disobedience to God,[3] and now "in these latter days" God undertakes a new covenantal arrangement that insures the obedience of the people to the law from the heart. Such a view of the law entails the fulfillment of the law by Christ and the obedience of his people as a result of his work and the "better promises" of his NC. What is internally written on the heart has significant continuity with what was formerly written on tablets of stone, viz., the law.

As a set of external commands over the people the law was never designed to have the power and capacity to perfect the people or permanently forgive sins. Therefore, the people consistently sinned and rebelled against God. The specifically "negative" comments concerning the law's weakness speak to its role and operation before the coming of the son and the accomplishment of his NC work. In the former days it could not perfect the people; now in the NC it has been transformed and has become an internal blessing. How the people of God relate to the law has changed significantly in the present "time of reformation" (9:10), in that now it is no longer "over them," but now it is "in them." Thus God has granted further revelation and completion in his son (1:1-2).[4] There has been a significant step forward in salvation history in the coming of Christ.

In Hebrews 8, the law is positively applied to the NC people. It pointed to Christ in expectation, and in Christ it has been fulfilled. In so doing it is internalized and thus is a "better promise" for the NC people of God. Thus, an "either/or" view of the law (as either only positive or only negative) is too simplistic. The writer of Hebrews can speak of the law's inabilities to bring about perfection and the limits of its cultic requirements and at the same time affirm with Jeremiah that in the NC there is a positive value ascribed to the law. These positive statements occur when the law is seen in relation to Christ; Christ is the interpretive and hermeneutical key.[5] He has fulfilled the law, and only in its fulfillment can the blessing of its being inwardly written on hearts and minds be possible. This internalization insures that the NC people would be

---

[3]See especially 3:7-4:13; 8:8-9.

[4]Concerning the prologue, Graham Hughes rightly surmises that it "is the hermeneutical key to the whole theology of the two covenants" (Graham Hughes, *Hebrews and Hermeneutics: The Epistle to the Hebrews as a New Testament Example of Biblical Interpretation*, SNTSMS 36 [Cambridge: University Press, 1979], 47). What he means is that there is continuity across the covenants due to the fact that it is the same voice of God that speaks in both.

[5]Otfried Hofius, "Biblische Theologie im Lichte des Hebräerbriefes," in *New Directions in Biblical Theology*, ed. Sigfred Pederson, NovTSup 76 (Leiden: E. J. Brill, 1994), 112-13; 124. Hofius rightly contends that for the writer of Hebrews, Christ is the interpretive key to understanding the OT.

faithful to God, the covenant-maker.[6]

Additionally, in light of the final revelation of God in the son, the suggestion is put forward here that what is internalized is not merely a one-to-one replication of the Mosaic laws without change, as many suggest. Rather, μετάθεσις has occurred when Christ intersects the law. The view put forward here thus makes an advancement on a popular view of 8:10 (10:16) that will be spelled out in the following pages. There is, to be sure, correspondence between what was formerly written on stone and what is now written on the hearts. For Hebrews, Christ has fulfilled the law in these latter days, and therefore it is not left unaffected; its internalization must be understood in light of the eschatological truth of expectation and fulfillment. This changes the manner in which the NC believer is related to the law. The law has been *transformed* and this transformation involves both its *internalization* and *fulfillment* in the NC.[7] The law that is written on the hearts and minds of NC believers (the "Christologized law") takes into account the effect that Christ has had on how the covenant people now relate to the law. Therefore there is both discontinuity as well as continuity.[8] Further, if there is νόμος in the NC, and this νόμος corresponds to the OC νόμος, then it will not do to argue that νόμος simply has been cancelled in toto.[9] Some other explanation must be given.

---

[6]Peterson notes the importance of the inward writing of the law in 8:10 and 10:16, and convincingly argues that this promise is intricately tied to the perfection of the NC people and the cleansing of the conscience (9:10, 14; 10:22 etc). Such a work of God produces the inward cleansing of the heart and conscience. See David Peterson, *Hebrews and Perfection: An Examination of the Concept of Perfection in the "Epistle to the Hebrews,"* SNTSMS 47 (Cambridge: Cambridge University Press, 1982), 132-40.

[7]Such a conclusion is in keeping with the writer's hermeneutic, and how he sees self-professed limitations in the OC to be fulfilled in the person and work of Christ. The new revelation in the son fills out the shortcomings of the old so that there is one revelation of God across the ages. For an articulation of this hermeneutical approach to the OT, see especially G. B. Caird, "The Exegetical Method of the Epistle to the Hebrews," *CJT* 5 (1959): 44-51; Graham Hughes (*Hebrews and Hermeneutics*, passim); R. T. France, "The Writer of Hebrews as a Biblical Expositor," *TynBul* 47 (1996): 245-76; J. Walters, "The Rhetorical Arrangement of Hebrews," *AsTJ* 51 (1996): 59-70.

[8]See Marie D'Angelo, *Moses in the Letter to the Hebrews*, SBLDS 42 (Missoula, MT: Scholars, 1979), 256. D'Angelo concludes that Hebrews' view of the law stresses the continuity between the two covenants. She asserts that this continuity is found in the midst of discontinuity, given that in the OC the law was unable to bring about perfection (τελείωσις) of the covenant people, yet was preparatory for the better promises to come. She contrasts this to Paul, who stresses the *discontinuity* between the two covenants. The present writer is not convinced that Paul and Hebrews are so far apart in their theology of the law.

[9]As will be seen below, the answer put forward by many Hebrews scholars is to argue that νόμος in Heb 8:10 (and 10:16) means something quite different than νόμος in Heb 7, such as a generic idea of "God's will" with no link to the commandments of the law.

One caveat needs to be repeated: law is not the writer's chief concern. Thus, what is addressed in the present study is secondary to his main concerns in 7:1-10:18, viz., there is a new and eternal priest who inaugurates a new and eternal covenant based on better promises by offering a new and eternal sacrifice. The readers' relation to God has been transformed in the work of Christ, by means of his "indestructible life" as well as his sacrificial death. But given that one cannot consider the covenant apart from discussing the law, one finds that the writer of Hebrews is not silent on the matter of the law. What is said concerning νόμος is the concern here, and in 8:10 (10:16) the writer of Hebrews reveals an important aspect concerning his theology of νόμος. Given the likelihood that the original audience consisted of a high percentage of converted Jews, this matter of the law would not have been irrelevant when discussing the notion of a new covenant.[10] Indeed, the Jeremiah text concerning the internalized νόμος would have likely significantly resonated with such an audience.

The present chapter will proceed along the following lines. First an exegetical overview of 8:1-13[11] sets up a general framework within which more specific matters may be discussed. Second, given the centrality of the Jeremiah 31 (LXX 38) text to Hebrews 8, an excursus concerning Jeremiah 31:31-34 and its context is warranted. This will be followed by a discussion of the writer's use of the OT. Fourth will be a presentation of the views of how 8:10 is understood by current Hebrews scholars. This is followed by this writer's view of the text, which, as will be seen, is a modification of one of the prevailing scholarly views. A conclusion will follow.

Exegetical Overview of Hebrews 8:1-13

Verses 1-6 center on the ministry (λειτουργός) of the new heavenly high priest in the heavenly tabernacle, while verses 7-13 center on the new covenantal

---

Others have suggested (without explanation) that νόμος = διαθήκη, and thus there is a New Covenant/law in which the covenant = law is internalized. See pp. 159-64 above.

[10]For example at Qumran, the notion of the NC is clearly seen, yet it consists of greater obedience to the law of Moses (and the community's strict interpretations). At Qumran, the NC was seen chiefly in terms of the Old, anticipating the return of the OC sacrifice and ideals. See above, chapter two. See also, J. C. McCullough, "Hebrews and the Old Testament" (Ph.D. diss., Queen's University, 1971), 318-20.

[11]The Greek text used here is NA[27]/UBS[4], which, according to Metzger consists of two variants significant enough to note in his reference work, though other variants are discussed below as well. See Bruce Metzger, *A Textual Commentary on the Greek New Testament*, 2nd ed. (Stuttgart: Biblia-Druck, 1994) 597. The two are 8:8 and 8:11. For 8:8, see Appendix 8. For a succinct analysis of the textual variants in these verses, see William Lane, *Hebrews*, vol. WBC 47a (Nashville: Thomas Nelson, 1991), 199-202. For an exhaustive analysis, see McCullough, "Hebrews and the Old Testament," 48-68.

arrangement (διαθήκην καινήν) that Christ the new high priest inaugurates.[12] Each is superior to their former counterparts: there is a better priest who has a better ministry, who mediates a better covenant in a better sanctuary.

Hebrews 8:1-6

Verses 1-2 hinge the conclusion of Hebrews 7 and introduce Hebrews 8.[13] These verses mark a transition by pointing back to what has been said concerning the new high priesthood of Christ in 7:26-28, and also introduce the primary themes to be taken up in 8:3-10:1-18.[14] The "main point"[15] that the writer of Hebrews seeks to make is that there is such a high priest who is unlike the priests of the OC. He not only is such a high priest at the right hand of God, but his ministry is carried out in the heavenly sanctuary and is thus effective, thereby contrasting with the old priesthood which could not remove sin.

This new priesthood is unlike the old, in that the Levitical priests only served a shadow of the heavenly sanctuary in which Christ now ministers. There is a correspondence to that heavenly sanctuary and ministry, but the OC priests serve an imperfect system. That Christ now serves at the "right hand of the throne of the Majesty in the heavens,"[16] is essential to the logic of verses 1-

---

[12]Otto Michel, *Der Brief and die Hebräer*, KEKNT (Göttingen: Vandenhoeck & Ruprecht, 1966), 286. See too Malone who rightly notes, "Jer 31:31-34 bounds the entire argument of Heb. 8:1-10:18 by its unique double use in 8:8-12 and 10:16-17" (Fred A. Malone, "A Critical Evaluation of the Use of Jeremiah 31:31-34 in the Letter to the Hebrews" [Ph.D. diss., Southwestern Baptist Theological Seminary, 1989], 174).

[13]See above, chapter 3.

[14]George H. Guthrie, *The Structure of Hebrews: A Text-Linguistic Analysis* (Grand Rapids: Baker, 1998), 105-08. It is because of the fact that these verses have elements of both 7:1-28 and 8:3-10:18 that has, at times, made 8:1-2 difficult to place. Noting their transitory nature from one topic and section to another is helpful.

[15]The term κεφάλαιον refers to "the main point" or "the main thing." See Walter Bauer, *A Greek-English Lexicon of the New Testament and Other Early Christian Literature*, rev. and ed. Frederick William Danker, ed. and trans. William F. Arndt and F. Wilbur Gingrich [BDAG], 3rd ed. (Chicago: University of Chicago Press, 2000), s.v. "κεφάλαιον." See also Erich Gräßer, *Der Alte Bund im Neuen* (Tübingen: Mohr, 1985), 99; B. F. Westcott, *The Epistle to the Hebrews*, 2nd ed. (Grand Rapids: Eerdmans, 1950), 212; Harold Attridge, *The Epistle to the Hebrews*, Hermeneia (Philadelphia: Fortress, 1989), 217; Albert Vanhoye, *Old Testament Priests and the New Priest According to the New Testament*, trans. J. Bernard Orchard (Petersham, MA: St. Bede's Publications, 1986), 173. For a slightly different translation, note Lane's "crowning affirmation." Such is a "crowning affirmation" in that "Christ exercises his ministry in the heavenly sanctuary is the 'crowning affirmation' to the foregoing argument" (Lane, *Hebrews*, 1:200); see also Ronald Williamson, *Philo and the Epistle to the Hebrews* (Leiden: E. J. Brill, 1970), 123-29.

[16]This allusion to Psalm 110:1 has a distinct purpose here, according to Hay. Christ's service as the exalted high priest is not on earth, but in the heavens (David Hay, *Glory at*

6, given that if he were on earth (v. 4), he would not be a priest, since there already are earthly priests.[17]

In verse 2 this new high priest is described as the ministering priest in the heavenly sanctuary, which is the true tabernacle.[18] The heavenly sanctuary is the locus of his service, and such was "pitched" by God and not man, indicating its eternality and effective value. P. E. Hughes rightly concludes that the "true tent" is the heavenly sanctuary that contains the presence of God.[19] This is in contrast to that which Moses built (v. 5), and such a contrast plays into the hands of the writer of Hebrews who focuses his attention on the passing away of the old in favor of the new. The OC institutions foreshadowed what was to come in Christ (10:1), whose ministry and service is the eschatological reality foreshadowed in the old.[20]

Verse 3 expresses the logical connection between priesthood and sacrifice for the writer of Hebrews. The theme of sacrifice runs through Hebrews 9 and

---

the Right Hand: Psalm 110 in Early Christianity, SBLMS 18 [Nashville: Abingdon, 1973], 87, 151). He notes that the Psalm text is "a crucial foundation stone for the two-sanctuary reasoning adumbrated...in chapters 8-10" (87).

[17]Gourgues rightly avers the importance of Ps 110 in these verses given that the announcement of the psalm is the scriptural basis for the assertions of the new priesthood and its service in heaven (Michel Gourgues, *A la Droite de Dieu: Résurrection de Jésus et actualisation du psaume 110:1 dans le Nouveau Testament* [Paris: J. Gabalda, 1978], 110-19). See also Hay, *Glory at the Right Hand*, 87.

[18]There is some disagreement over the phrase τῶν ἁγίων...καὶ τῆς σκηνῆς τῆς ἀληθινῆς. Specifically, does Hebrews mean to speak of two divisions of the tabernacle (inner and outer sanctuary), or is the καὶ epexegetical, as it is rendered here? For the former, see Samuel Bénétreau, *L'èpître aux Hébreux* (Vaux-sur-Seine: Edifac, 1989-90), 2:52; Attridge, *Hebrews*, 218; Otfried Hofius, *Der Vorhang vor dem Thron Gottes* (Tübingen, Mohr, 1972), 59-60; and William Loader, *Sohn und Hoherpriester*, WMANT 53 (Neukirchen: Neukirchener, 1981), 163. For the view that the καὶ is best understood as epexegetical, see Ceslas Spicq, *L'Épître aux Hébreux* (Paris: Gabalda, 1953), 2:234; Michel, *Der Brief and die Hebräer*, 288; Lane, *Hebrews*, 1:201; P. E. Hughes, *A Commentary on the Epistle to the Hebrews* (Grand Rapids: Eerdmans, 1977), 281 n. 54; 289; and Peterson, *Perfection*, 130-31. Lane is correct to observe that there is little agreement as to the theological significance of a division here by those who argue against the epexegetical use of καὶ.

[19]See the lengthy discussion of P. E. Hughes (*Hebrews*, 283-90). He offers a nice discussion of the options concerning the translation of 8:2. Osborne agrees with Hughes' conclusions (Grant R. Osborne, "The Christ of Hebrews and Other Religions," *JETS* 46.2 (2003): 262.

[20]See Aelred Cody, *Heavenly Sanctuary and Liturgy* (St. Meinrad, IN: Grail Publications, 1960), 9-46. Cody's main point is that "the idea of a heavenly sanctuary is Semitic in origin, and flows from the Semitic ideas of heaven and of the holy places on earth" (9), and thus it is not Platonic/Philonic. He argues that any search for a background to a "heavenly sanctuary" must begin in the OT.

10, and is significantly developed at that point. In the logic of verses 3-4, it is mandatory for a priest to offer a sacrifice, and Christ is no different (see 5:1). His heavenly session is precisely what enables him to make these offerings, since if he were on earth, he would not offer sacrifices since he would not be a priest to begin with. Additionally, there would be no need for his offering gifts and sacrifices, since there are already those who do such according to the law.[21] Attridge is correct that the writer establishes a principle based upon what he ascertains from Christ's exaltation and high priesthood, and then draws conclusions from this principle.[22] Thus Hebrews reasons "backwards" from what *is* true to what *must be* true, making logical deductions concerning the old order based upon newly revealed facts and a better understanding in light of the new revelation "in the last days" (1:1-2).[23] Priesthood as an institution is still extant (now perfected in Christ's priesthood), and therefore Christ the high priest must offer sacrifices, though exactly what he will offer is not mentioned at this point (though see 7:27).[24]

Verse 5 has garnered no small amount of attention given its "copy" (ὑπόδειγμα)[25] and "shadow" (σκιά) designations versus the "heavenly things" (τῶν ἐπουρανίων). In the writer's logic, the Levitical priests serve a "copy" in the sense of an imperfect sketch or "rough reminiscence"[26] of the original that Moses was shown on the mountain.[27] Though it is but a shadow, the service

---

[21]This usage of νόμος (κατὰ νόμον) is in keeping with the view maintained in this thesis, that νόμος is in its most fundamental sense the collection of Mosaic commandments that were to be obeyed by the covenant people. Here the writer has in view the specific commands that detail the priestly duties. Verse 5 could easily be read as "according to the *commands* of the law." Here it is shortened to simply, "according to the law." See also 7:5; 9:19, 22; 10:8. Heb 10:1 should be read similarly—as a body of commandments from God. Cf. chapter 2 above.

[22]Attridge, *Hebrews*, 218.

[23]Such argumentation is reminiscent of 7:13-16: Since Christ *is* a high priest, the genealogical requirement *must* be cancelled due to Christ's more perfect priesthood. As Westcott notes, there can not be two divinely appointed priesthoods at the same time. They cannot coexist (Westcott, *Hebrews*, 216).

[24]Harold Attridge, "The Uses of Antithesis in Hebrews 8-10," *HTR* 79 (1986): 3.

[25]ὑπόδειγμα and σκιά are virtually synonymous here. See Paul Ellingworth, *The Epistle to the Hebrews*, NIGTC (Grand Rapids: Eerdmans, 1993), 406; James Moffatt, *A Critical and Exegetical Commentary on the Epistle to the Hebrews*, ICC (Edinburgh: T & T Clark, 1924; reprint 1952), 105; Peterson, *Perfection*, 131.

[26]E. Kenneth Lee, "Words Denoting 'Pattern' in the New Testament," *NTS* 8 (1962): 168-69. Lee avers that the purpose for such a ὑπόδειγμα is largely pedagogical, in that the "shadowy suggestion" trains the mind "to appreciate eventually the reality of the heavenly truths themselves" (168).

[27]The writer of Hebrews quotes Exod 25:40 with slight changes. First, it is likely that Hebrews adds πάντα. Regarding the second variation, it is almost certain that he changes the tense of the participle from perfect (δεδειγμένον) to the aorist (δειχθέντα).

offered in the earthly tabernacle resembles the true tabernacle so as to point beyond itself to the heavenly reality; the earthly tabernacle and its worship pointed to and anticipated something greater.

The cultus was purposed for a time, but now it is no longer to be practiced since Christ has fulfilled the cult in his priesthood and sacrifice. In this manner, the argument of chapters 9 and 10 is anticipated. Additionally, though the language of verse 5 resembles Platonic dualism as mediated through Philo, Lane is correct in asserting that the similarities are superficial and merely verbal.[28] It seems best to conclude that while the writer of Hebrews felt the freedom to utilize terminology familiar to Alexandrian Platonism, he was not compelled to conform to the philosophical baggage that accompanied it. Thus, the point of the comparison between old and new institutions in Hebrews is temporal (first and second temporality), and not Platonic (higher vs. lower dualism), despite the "higher" nature of the "heavenly realities."[29] The "copies"

It is possible that πάντα is either borrowed from Exod 15:9 (Paul Ellingworth, *The Epistle to the Hebrews*, NIGTC [Grand Rapids: Eerdmans, 1993], 407) or was added by the writer of Hebrews in order to include the whole context of Exod 25-31 (D'Angelo, *Moses in the Letter to the Hebrews*, 205-22). Ellingworth suggests the reason for the change in verb tense is due to a shift in temporal perspective (Ellingworth, *Hebrews*, 407). For further discussion see also the works of Thomas (Kenneth J. Thomas, "The Old Testament Citations in Hebrews," *NTS* 11 [1965]: 303-25), and J. C. McCullough (McCullough, "Hebrews and the Old Testament," 120-22, 315-17).

[28]Lane, *Hebrews*, 1:207. McCullough comes to the same conclusions and notes that any similarities between Hebrews and Philo or the Qumran sectaries are merely superficial ("Hebrews and the Old Testament," 479). See also Peterson, *Perfection*, 131, and especially the work of Williamson (*Philo and the Epistle to the Hebrews*, 557) who has all but lain to rest the notion of a direct influence of Philo on the writer of Hebrews. On 8:5 in particular, see David J. MacLeod, "The Cleansing of the True Tabernacle," *BibSac* 152 (1995): 60-71. MacLeod overviews major interpretive options concerning the "true tabernacle."

[29]See Shinya Nomoto, "Herkunft und Struktur der Hohenpriestervorstellung im Hebräerbrief," *NovT* 10 (1968): 10-25, esp. 17-19; and Roy A. Harrisville, *The Concept of Newness in the New Testament* (Minneapolis: Augsburg, 1960), 50-51. Harrisville concludes that the issue is not one of Platonic forms and particulars or the "real" vs. the "ideal," but rather, "two divine dispensations, the one earthly and provisional, the other heavenly and final" (50-51). Christ is the union between the two, "and that union is historical event, and its benefits are guaranteed within the historical framework" (ibid.). See also Barnabas Lindars, "Hebrews and the Second Temple," in *Temple Amicitiae: Essays in the Second Temple Presented to Ernst Bammel*, ed. William Horbury, JSNTSS 48 (Sheffield: JSOT, 1991), 428.

The matter of Philonic or gnostic influence on Hebrews has received significant attention, especially in the twentieth century. Numerous suggestions have been offered regarding Hebrews' background of thought. The most influential suggestions have been proposals of a strong Philonic or gnostic influence, and more recently and convincingly, apocalyptic Judaism.

A gnostic backdrop was argued by Käsemann originally in 1939 in his *Das wandernde Gottesvolk* (Ernst Käsemann, *Das wandernde Gottesvolk* [Göttingen: Vandenhoeck & Ruprecht, 1939]), and his influence can be felt in German scholarship to this day (for instance, see the writings of Erich Gräßer, who casts Heb 8 in terms of "cosmic dualism" [*Der Alte Bund im Neuen*, 109]). Concerning such dualism, Lincoln Hurst writes, "For Käsemann and Grässer, *Auctor* and gnosticism view this world as essentially evil and hostile, with salvation consisting essentially in an escape to the 'heavenly' realm of Light and Spirit" (L. D. Hurst, *The Epistle to the Hebrews: Its Background of Thought*, SNTSMS 65 [Cambridge: University Press, 1990], 70). The research of Laansma (Jon Laansma, *'I Will Give You Rest': The 'Rest' Motif in the New Testament with Special Reference to Mt. 11 and Heb. 3-4*, WUNT 98 [Tübingen, Mohr Seibeck, 1997]) and especially Hurst has cast into serious doubt the contention that there is any real connection to gnosticism in Hebrews' background of thought (see esp. Hurst's discussion and conclusions regarding Hebrews and a gnostic background, *Epistle to the Hebrews*, 67-75). Hengel is critical of scholars who would assert *any* gnostic influence in any part of the NT (Martin Hengel, *The Son of God: the Origin of Christology and the History of Jewish-Hellenistic Religion*, trans. John Bowden [Philadelphia: Fortress, 1976], 33 n. 66).

Ceslas Spicq was perhaps the most prominent advocate for a Philonic backdrop, and this point is argued in the first volume of his Hebrews commentary (Ceslas Spicq, *L'Épître aux Hébreux*, 2 vols. [Paris: Gabalda, 1952-53]). This view was so influential that it achieved an almost universal consensus in his day. Yet in the decades following, his position began to be questioned and reassessed, and subsequent scholarship has chipped away at this thesis until sufficiently eroded. Specifically, it was Williamson's work (*Philo and the Epistle to the Hebrews*; see also Richard P. C. Hanson, *Allegory and Event* [London: SCM Press, 1959]) that is to be credited for casting into serious doubt Spicq's conclusions regarding Philonic influence. In fact, Guthrie has gone so far to say that Williamson *dismantled* Spicq's research (George H. Guthrie, "Hebrews in Its First-Century Contexts: Recent Research," in *The Face of New Testament Studies*, ed. McKnight and Osborne [Grand Rapids: Baker, 2004], 428).

In his 1956 essay, Barrett combated the idea of a Philonic/Platonic background (C. K. Barrett, "The Eschatology of the Epistle to the Hebrews," in *The Background of the New Testament and Its Eschatology*, ed. W. D. Davies and D. Daube [Cambridge: University Press, 1956], 363-93). Barrett argues for a backdrop of Jewish apocalyptic thought, while still maintaining some elements of Philonic thought. As Hurst succinctly notes, "The works of Hanson, Barrett, and Williamson *ended* any thoroughgoing forms of Platonic/Philonic approach to Hebrews" (Hurst, *Epistle to the Hebrews*, 41, emphasis added). See also L. D. Hurst, "Eschatology and 'Platonism' in the Epistle to the Hebrews," *SBL Seminar Papers* 23 (1984): 41-74.

As a result of the landmark works of Barrett, Hanson, and Williamson, the scholarly tide has turned in favor of a background of thought rooted in Jewish apocalyptic. G. Guthrie notes that Jewish apocalyptic is "highly spatial, focusing on the distinctions between the heavenly and earthly realms," yet is highly temporal as well (G. Guthrie, "Hebrews in its First-Century Contexts," 429). Note especially Hurst, *Epistle to the*

(ὑπόδειγμα) and shadows (σκιά) pointed forward in the vein of Jewish apocalyptic.[30] The author's orientation is not dualistic, but eschatological, "drawing temporal contrasts between the past and present eras,"[31] which introduces a "dramatic temporal and historical aspect into the contrast developed in 8:1-5.... The contrast developed is...a historical situation in the past and one that succeeded it *in time*."[32]

Verse 6 asserts that Christ's more excellent ministry has now begun in the heavenly tabernacle. Though a logical connective to verses 4-5, the νυνὶ δέ also reinforces the temporal aspects of the comparisons made in this pericope.[33] The perfect tense of τέτυχεν also indicates that this ministry has begun and is ongoing for the writer. Further, Christ is the mediator (μεσίτης)[34] of a better covenant (κρείττονός διαθήκης), which involves the better promises (κρείττοσιν ἐπαγγελίαις) articulated in the passage from Jeremiah.[35] The repetition of "better" (κρείττων) points to the superiority of the NC.

Hebrews 8:7-13

Structurally, these verses are framed by the term πρῶτος in verses 7 and 13. The content of the quotation roughly divides between verses 9 and 10. Verses

---

Hebrews, 21-42, 131-33. He concludes, "The apocalyptic tradition, in particular, supplies at several points a cogent Jewish alternative for ideas which were previously considered Platonic or gnostic" (133), and suggests that apocalyptic Judaism as a background is the direction scholarship should take (131). For further research concerning Hebrews' background of thought, see Koester's 1994 article (Craig Koester, "The Epistle to the Hebrews in Recent Study," *CR* 2 [1994]: 123-45), and more recently Guthrie's 2004 essay (G. Guthrie, "Hebrews in its First-Century Contexts: Recent Research," 425-29).

[30]See Heb 9:1-10:18, where specifically the tabernacle, priesthood, and sacrifices come into focus as pointing beyond themselves to that which they anticipated. See chapter 6, below.

[31]George H. Guthrie, *Hebrews*, NIVAC (Grand Rapids: Zondervan, 1998), 280 n. 5. See also Lane, *Hebrews*, 205; Ellingworth, *Hebrews*, 408; Peterson, *Perfection*, 131. Contra Attridge, *Hebrews*, 219.

[32]Lane, *Hebrews*, 1:207 (emphasis his). He adds, "During the former situation...there was no entrance into the real, heavenly presence of God.... The celestial sanctuary became the scene of an effective priesthood only from the moment of Christ's exaltation...the ministry of the Levitical priests...was antecedent to the ministry exercised in the heavenly sanctuary."

[33]Ellingworth, *Hebrews*, 408-09.

[34]The term μεσίτης is always used with διαθήκη (see also 9:15; 12:24. Cf. 7:22). Ellingworth is helpful: "Both here and in 7:20-22, Jesus' status in relation to the new covenant is not arbitrary or accidental; it is by divine appointment attested in scripture" (Ellingworth, *Hebrews*, 409).

[35]Hugh Montefiore, *The Epistle to the Hebrews*, BNTC (London: Adam & Charles Black, 1964), 139.

8-9 refer to the OC people who were disobedient to the Lord (the exodus generation is specifically named), and verses 10-12 denote the specific blessings that accompany the NC.[36]

In addition to contrasting the earthly, the writer of Hebrews begins a new paragraph addressing the matter of the second (δευτέρας) covenant in 8:7. Christ has inaugurated a new arrangement between God and his people, one that is marked by the "better promises" of 8:6. He does so by citing Jeremiah 31:31-34 (LXX 38:31-34) in its entirety, and makes the point that the first covenant was an insufficient arrangement. The covenant people were not true to the first covenant, therefore, God announced a second as a unilateral act of mercy.[37] The NC people are thus contrasted to those described in 3:7-4:6 who incur God's anger and wrath, and who have unbelieving, evil hearts (3:12).

PURPOSED INSUFFICIENCY

The inadequacy of the first covenant espoused in verse 7 centers on the inabilities of its sacrificial system to deal with sin[38] and in the "rebellious hearts" and "stiff necks" of the people (recall 3:7-4:13 and the indictment of Ps 95).[39] The criticism here comes from God, the speaker.[40] This is significant given that he was responsible for making the first covenant. God, the covenant-maker, established a covenant which he knew to be anticipatory and limited in its abilities. He knew that it would be insufficient and that its sacrificial system would ultimately not be acceptable to him in order to take away sin (9:1-10:18).

---

[36]For a text-critical note on 8:8, see Appendix 8.

[37]It should be observed that the way in which Hebrews speaks of the covenant here as πρῶτος and δεύτερος further reflects a Jewish apocalyptic understanding of time. See Oscar Cullmann, *Christ and Time: the Primitive Christian Conception of Time and History*, trans. Floyd V. Filson (Philadelphia: Westminster, 1950), 54; G. Hughes, *Hebrews and Hermeneutics*, 45. Contra Erich Gräßer, *An die Hebräer*, EKKNT (Zürich: Neukirchen, 1993), 2:96.

[38]William Manson, *The Epistle to the Hebrews: An Historical and Theological Reconsideration* (London: Hodder & Stoughton, 1951), 128.

[39]Weiß points out that the writer of Hebrews uses the Jeremiah text first and foremost to register a complaint concerning the fathers of old. See Hans-Friedrich Weiß, *Der Brief an die Hebräer*, 15th ed., KEKNT 13 (Göttingen: Vandenhoeck & Ruprecht, 1991), 446. It is no coincidence that the same generation appears earlier in Heb 3-4. See also David DeSilva, *Perseverance in Gratitude: A Socio-Rhetorical Commentary on the Epistle "to the Hebrews"* (Grand Rapids: Eerdmans, 2000), 285, and Ellingworth (*Hebrews*, 411).

[40]Hebrews has a tendency to cite the OT with God (or even Christ or the Holy Spirit) as the speaker as he has here in v. 8, using a form of λέγει rather than γέγραπται. See 1:5, 6, 7, 13; 4:3, 4, 7; 5:6; 6:14; 7:21; 8:13; 10:30; 12:26, etc. See George H. Guthrie, "Hebrews' Use of the Old Testament: Recent Trends in Research," *CBR* 1 (2003): 274. Though not Chalcedonian, there is an implied trinitarianism in Hebrews since Father, Son and Spirit each are said to speak (λέγει) the divine and powerful word.

Therefore one must pause and make the assertion that God had, in this manner, *always* planned for a NC that would be superior to the old, and one that would consist of the blessings both to take away sin as well as to make obedience a hallmark of the NC people.[41] Thus 8:7 reinforces the point that the first covenant was not a failure, but was insufficient due to its *built-in insufficiencies* that anticipated a new arrangement. Therefore it fulfilled its divinely-ordained anticipatory purpose.[42] The new arrangement is unveiled in verses 8-12.[43] God's

---

[41]See William Lane, *Call to Commitment: Responding to the Message of Hebrews* (Nashville: Thomas Nelson, 1985), 129-37. The inward writing of the law is what produces obedience out of "heart devotion" to God. Such obedience is wrought in the NC by God himself (137). On the matter of Heb 8:10 producing obedience there is significant consensus. Note Deut 30:14.

[42]See Caird, "The Exegetical Method of the Epistle to the Hebrews," 44-51. Harrisville is worth quoting at length on this point. Concerning Heb 8:8-12 he asserts, "On this passage most commentators remark that the breaking of the old covenant by an unfaithful people occasioned the establishment of the new. Such an interpretation, however, is not only contrary to the Biblical concept of the faithfulness of God but also to the idea of the covenant itself....God remains faithful to His covenant even though man's unfaithfulness to that covenant results in his being cut off from his people. It is nowhere stated in the Old Testament that if His people remain unfaithful to it, God will destroy His covenant.... It is the *blessing* of the covenant which is conditioned.... Hence it is only from the human side that the covenant may be broken.... Jeremiah's promise of the new covenant, therefore, is not occasioned by the breaking of the old by an unfaithful people, but is rather an announcement that the divine purpose and plan will have its further unfolding in the form of a new covenant. The old covenant was unable to make the law inward and to mediate pardon, for it was only an *intermediate step toward the unfolding of the divine purpose*.... Both covenants have their origin in and are an expression of the one divine will—herein lies the continuity between them. Nevertheless, both are not equivalent manifestations of that will...the first covenant acquires its provisional character and necessitates the establishment of a new covenant. Apart from a total view of God's activity...the new covenant is [in danger of being] *reduced to a mere compensation for the frustration of the divine will*" (Harrisville, *The Concept of Newness*, 48-50; emphasis added).

[43]Such a view taken here and affirmed by Harrisville (see also Lane, *Hebrews*, 1:209) seems quite opposed by Lehne (see also Gräßer, *Der Alte Bund im Neuen*, 107-08; Rudolph Smend and Ulrich Luz, *Gesetz*, BK 1015 [Stüttgart: Kohlhammer, 1981], 114). Lehne's main thesis is that the writer of Hebrews uses cultic categories simply in deference to his original audience's frame of mind. Thus, Lehne would not affirm that such categories have a divine pedagogical purpose that were always anticipatory of the sacrifice of Christ (See Lehne, *New Covenant in Hebrews*, 16-17; 58; passim). Such are mere metaphors, and are the writer's "creative reinterpretation" (119). According to Lehne, covenant and newness are merely ideas in the mind of the author that address the needs of the original recipients. Though helpful at many points, her treatment of the NC in Hebrews (chapter 5) is quite brief and is hampered by her view that the writer of Hebrews employed Middle-Platonic categories (97, 122, passim), disagreeing (without

redemptive purposes were not exhausted in the OC, and new action would be taken by God on behalf of his people.[44] This is highlighted in verses 10-12, where God announces what *he* will do in the new arrangement.

VERSES 8b-12

These verses fully cite Jeremiah 31:31-34 (LXX 38:31-34) with only a few alterations.[45] In the Jeremiah text, God announces through his prophet that a new arrangement will replace the old at some point in the unspecified "coming

---

substantive discussion) with the conclusions of G. Hughes (*Hebrews and Hermeneutics*, 45, 63-66, passim). The work of Hurst (*Epistle to the Hebrews: Its Background of Thought*) was published the same year as Lehne's monograph; as such there was likely no interaction with it. This is confirmed by a perusal of her author's index, in which Hurst is absent. Yet there is also no mention of Hurst's important 1984 essay, "Eschatology and 'Platonism' in the Epistle to the Hebrews," *SBL Seminar Papers* 23 (1984): 41-74.

Given such conclusions as to the philosophical background of the writer of Hebrews, it comes as no surprise that Lehne finds no place for νόμος in the NC in any sense. In fact, Heb 8:10 is only mentioned on one page of her monograph (Lehne, *New Covenant in Hebrews*, 115). Her only comment is that this verse refers to a changed heart with no further explanation. Whatever "changed heart" means for Lehne, νόμος plays no part, regardless of its presence in 8:10 and 10:16.

[44]Westcott notes that in the NC, "God comes to man as giving and not requiring" (Westcott, *Hebrews*, 220). He adds, "The feeling of dissatisfaction, want, prompted to a diligent inquiry; and to this the words addressed to Jeremiah—the prophet of the national overthrow and exile—bear witness."

[45]McCullough examines the question concerning the OT citations in Hebrews, and in particular asks what the author's attitude is toward his OT text (J. C. McCullough, "The Old Testament Quotations in Hebrews," *NTS* 26 [1980]: 363-79, esp. 364-67). McCullough concludes that the writer of Hebrews stays very close to his Vorlage, and only departed deliberately two or three times due to stylistic reasons (378-79). For a more detailed account of the modifications made to the Jeremiah text, see McCullough's dissertation, "Hebrews and the Old Testament," 48-68; Thomas, "Old Testament Citations," 303-25; esp. 310-13; Friedrich Schröger, *Der Verfasser des Hebraerbriefes*, BU 4 (Regensburg: F. Pustet, 1968), 162-68.

Thomas finds four alterations in the Jer 31 text cited here and in 10:16-17. They are: (1) πρὸς αὐτούς for τῷ οἴκῳ 'Ισραήλ, (2) ἐπὶ καρδίας αὐτῶν καὶ ἐπὶ τὴν διάνοιαν αὐτῶν for εἰς τὴν διάνοιαν αὐτῶν καὶ ἐπὶ καρδίας αὐτῶν, (3) the addition of καὶ τῶν ἀνομιῶν αὐτῶν, and (4) μνησθήσομαι for μνησθῶ (Thomas, "Old Testament Citations," 310). Regarding alteration 2, Thomas avers that the purpose is to bring together νόμους and καρδίας. Citing Kistemaker, Thomas notes, "this exchange is due to the importance of the words 'law' and 'heart' in the earlier part of the discourse.... With the putting of the laws on our hearts, we have a new confidence and a new hope, as indicated in the following discussion in x. 19-25" (ibid., 311). See Simon J. Kistemaker, *The Psalm Citations in the Epistle to the Hebrews* (Amsterdam: Van Soest, 1961), 129.

days." Though Jeremiah specifically addresses Israel and Judah, it becomes clear that Hebrews sees the prophecy's fulfillment in the eschatological days of the present time,[46] and that it is applicable to more than simply the Jewish nation, though clearly they are not excluded.[47] This is especially clear in 10:15-17, when the NC blessings are repeated at the close of 8:1-10:18. There the citation is freer and the NC blessings are summarized and applied "to us" (ἡμῖν).[48]

God specifically declares that he will effect (συντελέσω)[49] this new arrangement and it will be unlike the old (8:9). The divine complaint against the people recalls 3:7-4:13, noting God's critique of the those who were led out of Egypt only to rebel against him in the wilderness. They did not continue in the covenant and God "disregarded them" (κἀγὼ ἠμέλησα αὐτῶν).[50] The NC remedies the faults and insufficiencies of the people. The connection back to the former generation is specific in verses 8b-9.

What exactly 8:10 means by διδοὺς νόμους μου εἰς τὴν διάνοιαν αὐτῶν καὶ ἐπὶ καρδίας αὐτῶν ἐπιγράψω αὐτούς is discussed in detail below, but most scholars would agree with the following. First, what is accomplished by God's "giving" and "inscribing" applies to each covenant

---

[46]For a more detailed articulation of the prophecy to Israel and Judah applies to the NT believer, see Malone, "Critical Evaluation," 155-275.

[47]See Homer Kent Jr., "The New Covenant and the Church," *GTJ* 6.2 (1985): 289-98; Bruce A. Ware, "The New Covenant and the People(s) of God," in *Dispensationalism, Israel and the Church: the Search for Definition*, ed. Craig A. Blaising and Darrell L. Bock (Grand Rapids: Zondervan, 1992), 68-97.

[48]Koester agrees and observes that the Jeremiah text is for all who are of "God's house" (3:6), and not merely the houses of Israel and Judah (Craig Koester, *Hebrews*, AB, vol. 36a [New York: Doubleday, 2001], 389). He adds, "In announcing that God has promised a new covenant to 'the house of Israel,' the author in effect tells the listeners that God has promised a new covenant 'to you.'" See also F. F. Bruce, *The Epistle to the Hebrews*, rev. ed., NICNT (Grand Rapids: Eerdmans, 1990), 194; O. Palmer Robertson, *The Christ of the Covenants* (Phillipsburg, NJ: Presbyterian and Reformed, 1980), 43.

[49]The usage of συντελέσω over the LXX's διαθήσομαι could be a significant alteration on the part of the author, or merely a stylistic change. The writer has demonstrated his affinity for the τέλος/τελέω word group, and Thomas argues that the writer deliberately chose such a term to demonstrate that this new arrangement will not be broken (Thomas, "Old Testament Citations," 310). He asserts that συντελέσω in the context of διαθήκη has the meaning of a covenant that is not broken (see Jer 41:18). He writes, "It may be concluded that the author deliberately used these verbs as in Jer. xli in order to make clear the difference between the two covenants" (ibid.). See Attridge, *Hebrews*, 227; Ellingworth, *Hebrews*, 416; Schröger, *Der Verfasser*, 164 n. 1; Malone, "Critical Evaluation," 182. But see McCullough ("Old Testament Quotations," 366) who posits that the term could have already been in his Vorlage.

[50]The MT reads בָם בָּעַלְתִּי וְאָנֹכִי, "though I was their husband/master." Hebrews follows the LXX reading, καὶ ἐγὼ ἠμέλησα αὐτῶν.

member. Second, what it produces is a heart that is inclined to God the covenant maker in a new way, and this entails an inward renewal unlike the OC. Finally, such divine actions produce obedience.[51] Most would agree with these fundamental assertions. The issue of contention is the meaning of νόμους, why it is plural in the LXX (in place of the MT singular תּוֹרָה), and the question of what is to be said for the place of νόμος in the NC. Suffice to say there is little consensus on this point.[52]

However, by way of anticipation, a few remarks should be made. First, on a most basic level, whatever νόμος means in this context, it is seen as a *blessing* of the NC. The very fact that νόμος is found in the NC passage from Jeremiah accounts for the varied interpretations of its meaning.[53] Second, simply by way

---

[51]An opportunity for further research arises here. If the purpose of the internalization of the divine law is obedience, and such a divine act is accomplished in each NC member, then what (if any) bearing does this have on the current discussion concerning perseverance in Hebrews? Further, what is not in view is the notion that NC people no longer ever sin. Such a suggestion goes beyond the bounds of sound exegesis.

[52]There is also little *discussion* on this point, a matter that makes substantive discussion here difficult. A perusal of the literature produces confusion, as νόμος is either *redefined* only for 8:10 and 10:16, or it is a *referent* to the actual OC laws. It is hoped that the present study will be a stimulus for further research, either to reinforce or rebut the present conclusions. Malone is to be recognized for his contribution to the meaning of 8:10 in his 1989 dissertation on the passage, and his conclusions are found below. With the fact of so little consensus in mind, this writer concurs with a truism from Attridge when he warns that "[t]his portion of Hebrews [chapters 8-10] is replete with exegetical difficulties" ("Use of Antithesis," 1). Nowhere is this more true than in matters concerning the law. Recall Lehne's assertion as well, viz., that in Hebrews the category of law is perhaps the most difficult one to assess (Lehne, *New Covenant in Hebrews*, 99).

[53]There are three broad categories that can be delineated. Though discussed at length below, a brief illustration of the tension can be mentioned here. While recognizing the existence of νόμος in the NC promise, Gerd Schunack asserts that whatever it means, "Ausgeschlossen ist eine neue, positive Bedeutung des Gesetzes." He does not speculate as to the contents of this new order/decree of God, other than to say that its content could indeed remain *wholly without meaning*, "So könnte dieser Inhalt in der Tat ganz ohne Bedeutung bleiben" (Gerd Schunack, *Der Hebräerbrief* [Zürich: Theologischer Verlag, 2002], 143).

Note also Gräßer (*An die Hebräer*, 2:102-03), who is only negative concerning the law (recall that he views Heb 8 in cosmic dualistic terms (idem, *Der Alte Bund im Neuen*, 109), and sees any discussion of the law in Hebrews merely as theoretical), yet cites positively (and at length) the work of Levin (Christoph Levin, *Die Verheissung des neuen Bundes in ihrem theologiegeschichtliche Zusammenhang ausgelegt*, FRLANT 137 [Göttingen: Vandenhoeck & Ruprecht, 1985], 263-64). In his extensive study on Jer 31:31-34, Levin writes that the NC promise of νόμος on the heart cannot be anything other than the Torah. What is therefore promised is a new kind of "Torah-revelation," in that what was formerly written on stone and animal skins and learned via much effort is

of observation, νόμος is one part (even a central part) of διαθήκη in this context.[54] Confusion is the result when they are viewed as synonyms. If they were synonymous, then they would be logically interchangeable, yet Hebrews never refers to a καινός νόμος, or ἀ πρῶτος νόμος, δεύτερος νόμος or a κρείττων νόμος, while consistently applying such adjectives *only* to διαθήκη. The writer speaks of new, first, second, and better covenants, with νόμος being the divine commandments that are kept by the people in the covenantal arrangement, and in Hebrews νόμος is part of *both* the OC and NC. What exactly is meant by its presence in the new arrangement has been variously interpreted.

NEW COVENANT BLESSINGS

Verses 10-12 dictate the characteristics of the new arrangement between God and his people. The divine blessing of the "inwardly inscribed law" (8:10) yields a universal knowledge of the Lord (8:11). This is combined with the divine blessing of forgiveness of sins due to the mercy of God (8:12). Additionally, Malone avers that the knowledge of the Lord in 8:11 refers to the instruction taught by God for *entering* the covenant; it does not eliminate the need for teachers. Simply, all NC members know God,[55] a claim that could not be asserted by the OC people (see 3:7-4:13[56]). Verse 12 is fairly straightforward

---

now on the heart as a gift of God. However positive an assessment of νόμος Levin might appear to have, it must be understood that Levin views the canonical form of Jer 31:31-34 as a post-exilic construction and as a more pedestrian oracle; it is not the high point of the prophet Jeremiah's theology (257-64). Rather, Levin (of whom Gräßer approves) understands the verses to be stating a scribe's dream for an ideal of future torah piety, where there will be *flawless memorizing* of what is taught. For Levin, Jer 31:31-34 is the utopian dream of the teacher in post-exilic Judaism.

[54]Lane argues that the internalization of the law is central to the NC promise (Lane, *Hebrews*, 1:209). Whatever νόμος means, it cannot mean covenant here. One is *in* the covenant, and *obeys* commandments (however one defines "commandments"). It is imprecise to say that God will internalize the covenant; what is internalized is the laws/commandments/νόμους of God so that obedience to the covenant (and thus God) is the result. In the LXX (which arguably informs the writer of Hebrews), בְּרִית is consistently translated by διαθήκη, and תּוֹרָה is translated by νόμος the vast majority of times (between 250-300 times out of roughly 320 uses of תּוֹרָה). The burden of proof, therefore, is on those that would maintain that these terms are synonymous, and LXX usage does not point to this conclusion.

[55]Malone, "Critical Evaluation," 189. See also Ellingworth, *Hebrews*, 414.

[56]Yet also note the many who *were* obedient in the OT cited in the *exempla* list of Heb 11. There is continuity between the NC people and the OC faithful in Heb 11, not the OC people as a whole. The difference is faith that perseveres and heeds the divine word. Those in Heb 3-4 did not believe and thus disobeyed (3:19; 4:2, 6) while the NC people both hear and *believe* (4:2). Thus the enduring faith exhibited in the NC people serves to

in its meaning—that in the NC there is forgiveness and a "divine forgetting" of transgressions, indicating that the covenant member is in right relation to God and his covenant via an act of divine mercy. The repetition of sacrifices in the OC all but guaranteed that sins *were* remembered by both God and people, yet 8:12 assures that sins and misdeeds are "erased from God's memory."[57] How such a blessing is made possible in the NC is explored in the subsequent exposition: the NC blessings of God that verses 10-12 assure via his mercy (ἵλεως ἔσομαι) are demonstrated and explained in 9:1-10:18.

VERSE 13

The concluding verse of Hebrews 8 underscores the replacement of the old arrangement by the new, and such is a sovereign act of God.[58] The writer emphasizes the fact that when the Lord foretells an arrangement that is καινὴν (in 8:8),[59] the πρώτην is logically declared "old" and "worn out."[60] The two arrangements cannot coexist, thus the mere mention of the term "new" renders the first "old" and no longer useful as an arrangement between God and his people. Something new has happened; Christ has inaugurated the NC of which Jeremiah spoke. Hebrews views the OC as having reached its limits, and in light of the Christ event, it is rendered παλαιούμενον καὶ γηράσκον ἐγγὺς ἀφανισμοῦ.[61]

BOTH PROMISES (8:10-12) ESSENTIAL

The blessings of the NC stated in 8:10-12 are essential and integral one to the other. The NC blessing of the knowledge of the Lord via his writing his νόμους on the "inward parts" is not separated from the blessing of forgiveness of sins. Rather, forgiveness of sins and the engraving of νόμους on the "inward parts"

---

connect them to the OC *faithful*, listed in Heb 11. These are, according to Hebrews, the inhabitants of "God's house" (3:6) and the new Jerusalem (12:22-24).

[57]Malone, "Critical Evaluation," 190.

[58]Lehne, *New Covenant in Hebrews*, 122, 98.

[59]The adjectives καινός and νέος (see Heb 12:24) are reserved exclusively for διαθήκη.

[60]BDAG, s.v. "παλαιόω." See also Heinrich Seesemann, "παλαιόω," in *TDNT*, ed. G. Kittel, trans. G. W. Bromiley (Grand Rapids: Eerdmans, 1972), 5:720. See also Heb 1:11.

[61]See Gen 18:13; Ps 37:25 (LXX 36:25) and John 21:18 where the term γηράσκω is used to refer to physical aging. See BDAG, s.v. "ἀφανισμός," defines ἀφανισμός as "the condition of being no longer visible" in the sense of "destruction." Here the OC is seen as near destruction or disappearing (ἐγγὺς ἀφανισμοῦ). Ellingworth notes that in the terms alone there is not sufficient warrant to say whether or not the old cultus has already disappeared (Ellingworth, *Hebrews*, 419).

are part of the *single* act of entering into the NC.[62] Therefore they should not be
discussed as if they are not tethered one to the other in the writer's theology.
Νόμους on the "inward parts" is bound up with being forgiven. The theological
dimension of forgiveness in the NC, which is based on the work of the new
high priest (which is the central interest in the exposition of 9:1-10:18),[63] is not
divorced from the reality of a perfect and cleansed conscience (9:10, 14), the
"good things to come" (9:11; 10:1), and a sincere and cleansed heart (10:22)[64]
in the present "time of reformation" (9:10).

In his 1989 dissertation Malone establishes the point that in Hebrews there is
more to forgiveness than cleansing alone. "Forgiveness always presupposes a
positive consecration to God through obedience,"[65] which for Malone means
the law (specifically the Decalogue) has been inscribed on the heart. They are
tied together as the better promises of the NC (8:6). One cannot be considered
separately from the other, as if only the promise of forgiveness was relevant
and could be emancipated from the promise of the internalized law.[66]
Forgiveness *and* νόμους on the heart together is what makes the NC people
unlike the rebellious wilderness generation described in 3:7-4:13.

Ellingworth is helpful (and corrective) in noting that such an extensive
quotation of Jeremiah 31 is not given merely as a proof-text whose sole purpose
is to assert that there is something "new" without further comment, in contrast
to Gräßer. Rather, Hebrews asserts that "the new covenant is a new act of God,

---

[62]Contra Gräßer (*An die Hebräer*, 2:99-101), who finds no purpose for the Jeremiah text
other than to prove that something new has occurred, and maintains that the blessings
are irrelevant until 10:15. This is opposed to the view taken here (see also Peterson,
Perfection, 132-40; Kistemaker, *Psalm Citations*, 127-32; Malone, "Critical
Evaluation," 175, 193; France, "Biblical Expositor," 259; Richard N. Longenecker,
Biblical Exegesis in the Apostolic Period, 2nd ed. [Grand Rapids: Eerdmans, 1999], 155-
65), *that the NC promises underlie the whole of 9:1-10:18*. For instance, to speak of a
clean conscience (9:10, 14—the climax of 9:1-10 and 11-14) is to speak of the renewal
and change in the innermost being that God promised in 8:10. See also 10:14, 22. See
chapter 6, below.

[63]Spicq, *L'Épître aux Hébreux*, 2:244.

[64]See Peterson, *Perfection*, 132-40. This is in contrast to the "evil and unbelieving
hearts" of 3:10, 12. Ellingworth (*Hebrews*, 411) and DeSilva (*Perseverance*, 285)
concur. Note also Gunnar Östborn, *Torah in the Old Testament*, trans. Cedric Hentschel
(Lund: Hakan Ohlssons Koktryckeri, 1945), 151. Östborn maintains this connection
between obedience and forgiveness when he writes, "This dispensation of *tora* [on the
heart] takes place *in conjunction with* an act of forgiveness on the part of Yahweh"
(emphasis added). Thus they cannot be severed from one another so as to speak only
about one blessing without any reference to the other.

[65]Malone, "Critical Evaluation," 193. He adds, "Forgiveness of sins is tightly bound to
the renewed heart on which has been written the Law of God" (175).

[66]Contra Lehne, *New Covenant in Hebrews*, 27.

to which scripture bears witness."[67] Similarly, Peterson asserts that the promises of 8:10-12 are not irrelevant to the author's mind in the least, and they do in fact play a role in what follows. Though there is a heightened emphasis on the latter promise to forgive sins (8:12; 10:17), it is not isolated from the work on men's hearts that is promised in 8:10-11 (10:16), and *both* aspects underlie the subsequent exposition.[68] In fact, Peterson (rightly) notes the importance of the promise of 8:10 in the author's theology of perfection, and asserts the importance of the author's repetition of this promise at the conclusion of the exposition in 10:16-17.[69] It may therefore be argued that Jeremiah 31:33 is the OT underpinning of all NC obedience for Hebrews. The precise connection between the two main blessings of the NC is this: the

---

[67]Ellingworth, *Hebrews*, 417-18. Contra Schunack (*Der Hebräerbrief*, 143); Weiß (*Der Brief*, 446); Rolf Rendtorff ("Was ist neu am neuen Bund [Jer 31]?" in *Lernen in Jerusalem—Lernen mit Israel*, ed. Martin Stöhr, Veröffentlichungen aus dem Institut Kirche und Judentum 20 [Berlin: Institut Kirche und Judentum, 1993], 34); and Gräßer (*An die Hebräer*, 2:101), who maintain the view that essentially these verses (esp. 9-12) have no meaning for the writer of Hebrews, and are irrelevant to the discussion. This writer asserts that such a view is shortsighted. God's inward writing of his νόμους (changing the heart) and forgiveness of sins are in fact part of the subsequent discussion. The two blessings of vv. 10-12 underlie the exposition of 9:1-10:18 and explain the fulfillment of Jeremiah's prophecy. See France, "Biblical Expositor," 259, 264-65.

Essentially, Gräßer is mistaken when he asserts the writer of Hebrews had only one reason (lit. "one goal") for quoting the entirety of the Jeremiah citation, viz., to reach the statement made in v. 13. For Gräßer, the only relevance Jeremiah has is his point in 31:31, that something "new" was to occur (Gräßer, *An die Hebräer*, 2:101). Yet if it is irrelevant to the writer, why bother making such a lengthy quotation, and why make any changes (stylistic or otherwise) if there is only a single word relevant for the writer of Hebrews is καινός? To this writer, such a view is an incredible assertion. Why alter and repeat in summary form the two essential promises of the NC in 10:15-17 if they truly are as irrelevant as Gräßer describes?

[68]In contrast to Gräßer, it is contended here that what immediately follows in 9:1-10:18 is the author's exposition of the Jeremiah text which emphasizes the forgiveness of sins and the inward change promised in 8:10-12. Yet Gräßer argues that not even forgiveness is elaborated upon, and is emphasized no earlier than 10:17. This is almost word for word the view of Frey (Jörg Frey, "Die alte und die neue διαθήκη nach dem Hebräerbrief," in *Bund und Tora*, ed. Avemarie and Lichtenberger [Tübingen, J. C. B. Mohr, 1996], 278) and Schunack (*Der Hebräerbrief*, 112). Schunack goes so far as to assert that the Jeremiah text does not even have a key exegetical role in Hebrews (cf. Weiß, *Der Brief*, 446). This contrasts the view that is persuasively put forward by Caird, "Exegetical Method," 47-51; France, "Biblical Expositor," 259, 264-65; and Walters, "Rhetorical Arrangement," 59-70. Cf. Longenecker, *Biblical Exegesis*, 155-65.

[69]Peterson, *Perfection*, 135. E. McKnight also notes that the repetition of the Jeremiah text in summary fashion (10:16-17) makes it clear that both of the "better promises" of the NC are "foremost in the author's mind" (Edgar V. McKnight, *Hebrews-James* [Macon, GA: Smyth & Helwys, 2004], 186).

fulfillment of 8:10-11 (Jer 31:33-34a) is made possible by the fulfillment of
8:12 (Jer 31:34b),[70] which is a tangible demonstration of God's declaration of
his mercy (ἵλεως ἔσομαι). The NC promises point to a radical new
relationship with God, one that is marked by forgiveness and cleansing (8:12),
which is tethered to obedience due to the gift of the νόμους in the heart and
mind (8:10), which results in knowing God (8:11).

The lengthy quotation from Jeremiah therefore prepares the readers for the
following discussion in 9:1-10:18. The writer of Hebrews Christologically
interprets Jeremiah in what follows, even though it was not necessarily
Christological in its original setting. This reflects the writer's view of the OT.
Given that it is the same voice speaking across the ages, there is no
contradiction between Hebrews and Jeremiah.[71] Rather, Jeremiah's prophecy
only comes into its full meaning when it is read Christologically.[72] D. Guthrie
writes, "Looking at the passage from the threshold of the Christian era, he sees
more in the words than it was possible for Jeremiah to see."[73] There is
correspondence and expansion, and not contrast between the two biblical
writers.

Such is the present writer's understanding of Hebrews 8. Given the
centrality of the Jeremiah text, an excursus is warranted that specifically
addresses the original context and setting of this passage from Jeremiah.

Excursus: Jeremiah 31:31-34

This excursus addresses the question concerning the OT meaning of Jeremiah
31:31-34, and verse 33 in particular. In addition, the question is asked, "How
would the readers/hearers of Jeremiah have understood the meaning of תּוֹרָה[74]
'on the heart,' and would it have been understood to be a blessing?"

---

[70]Peterson agrees, (*Perfection*, 135-36).

[71]Caird, "Exegetical Method," 46. See also G. Hughes, *Hebrews and Hermeneutics*, 127,
passim; France, "Biblical Expositor," 245-76; Longenecker, *Biblical Exegesis*, 140-65;
and Walters, "Rhetorical Arrangement," 59-70.

[72]Commenting on the lengthy quotation Ellingworth avers, "its full significance can only
be seen in light of Christ's sacrifice, which forms the substance of the new covenant"
(Ellingworth, *Hebrews*, 418). It also forms the substance of 9:1-10:14.

[73]Donald Guthrie, *Hebrews*, TNTC 15 (Grand Rapids: Eerdmans, 1983), 178.

[74]The matter of the LXX translation of singular תּוֹרָה with the plural νόμους is
addressed below.

Context of Jeremiah 31[75]

The prophet's call was for the people to return to the Lord God, which is defined in Jeremiah 7:23 as, "Obey my voice, and I will be your God, and you shall be my people; and walk only in the way that I command you, so that it may be well with you." Note Jeremiah 9:12 as well, "The Lord said, 'because they have forsaken My law (תּוֹרָה / νόμος) which I set before them, and have not obeyed My voice nor walked according to it.'"[76] While Jeremiah 11:6 summons the people to covenant obedience, 7:24 is typical of the response, "they did not obey or incline their ear, but walked in their own counsels and in the stubbornness of their evil heart." In spite of the revival during the reign of Josiah, in which the people pledged themselves to obey the commandments and keep the covenant (see 2 Kgs 23:3), Jeremiah is clear that such resolve will not last. The central matter was disobedience to the commands of the law. This is Jeremiah's most basic problem.[77]

That the issue was one of disobedience arising from evil hearts is clear in texts such as Jeremiah 3:10, 17; 4:4, 14, 18; 5:23-24; 7:24; 9:14, 26; 11:8; 12:11; 16:12; 17:1,[78] 5, 9; 18:12; 22:17; 23:17, and 26-27. The "heart" is

---

[75]Though there are numerous critical issues surrounding the book of Jeremiah such as date, unity, authorship, etc., such questions are not immediately in view here. The present writer proceeds from the standpoint that the book of Jeremiah tells of the prophecies and events of the prophet Jeremiah, who likely wrote much or all of the material, born close to 643 B.C.E., and who served the prophetic office in the late seventh and early sixth century. Jeremiah prophesied to Judah before the fall of Jerusalem and the beginning of the Babylonian captivity, which came as a result of generations of disobedience to Yahweh, the covenant God of Israel.

Additionally, though the authorship of Jer 31:31-34 is debated, there is no reason to deny that it goes back to Jeremiah. On this matter Thompson concludes, "We accept the view that apart from some editorial reworking the passage goes back to Jeremiah. It may not preserve his *ipsissima verba*, but it would be strange indeed if Jeremiah's remarkable theological insights did not lead him through to this point" (J. A. Thompson, *The Book of Jeremiah*, NICOT [Grand Rapids: Eerdmans, 1980], 580). See also John Bright, *Jeremiah*, AB (Garden City, NY: Doubleday, 1965), 287. Bright asserts that the authenticity of the pericope "ought never to have been questioned," and that it represents the high point of the prophet's theology. See also W. D. Davies, *Torah in the Messianic Age and/or the Age to Come*, JBLMS 7 (Philadelphia: Society of Biblical Literature, 1952), 13-15. Davies notes that the consensus of scholarship (in 1952) favored the authenticity of the passage. Contra Duhm (Bernhard Duhm, *Das Buch Jeremia*, HKAT [Tübingen and Leipzig: J. C. B. Mohr, 1901], 255), who asserts that these verses are merely the emanations of an idealistic post-exilic scribe. Cf. Levin, *Die Verheissung*, 257-64.

[76]See also 11:10; 16:11, passim.

[77]J. Gordon McConville, "Jeremiah: Prophet and Book," *TynBul* 42 (1991): 93.

[78]Coppens notes the parallels between Jer 17:1 to Jer 31:33 (J. Coppens, "La nouvelle alliance en Jérémie 31, 31-34," *CBQ* 25 [1963]: 14). Jeremiah 17:1 is significant in that

therefore a central issue in Jeremiah, and it is no surprise to discover that any new work of Yahweh on behalf of the people would address the central concern of the heart.[79] It is Yahweh who knows, tries and searches the heart of man (11:20; 17:10; 20:12), yet it is wicked and deceitful (13:22; 17:9).[80] Such texts lay the groundwork for the Book of Consolation in chapters 30-33. In spite of their rebellious hearts, Yahweh purposed to give the people a heart to know him and to return to him in 24:7 (וְנָתַתִּי לָהֶם לֵב לָדַעַת אֹתִי). Such a text clearly brings to mind the NC promise of 31:33, and is an assurance that the issue of the people's disobedient hearts would be remedied by God himself. Whereas disobedience to his law is found in the hearts of the people and on which *sin had been written* (17:1), God had promised to make a new arrangement in 31:31-34 that would involve an *inward writing of the law* that would lead to the obedience of his covenant people.

The background to the NC pericope is the covenant made at Sinai in Exodus 19:1-24:11.[81] Jeremiah declares that a spiritual dilemma faced the covenant people. Since the time of Moses, the people had demonstrated that they were incapable of obedience to the stipulations of the covenant.[82] Such disobedience to the laws had brought about the covenant curses, and there was little hope for change which led Jeremiah to ask, "Can the Ethiopian change his skin or a leopard his spots?" (13:23). Certainly not, and in the same way there was little promise for Israel to change her disobedient ways unless the Lord accomplished a new work.[83] The central problem to the covenant people had always been their disobedience to the laws given them at Sinai.[84] Thus a new arrangement was needed and promised to insure obedience from the heart.[85]

---

it says that the sin of Judah is "engraved on the tablet of their heart." Citing this verse F. B. Huey avers, "Before God can fill human hearts with his law, he must remove the sin that is written there" (F. B. Huey, Jr. *Jeremiah, Lamentations*, NAC, vol. 16 [Nashville: Broadman Press, 1993], 286).

[79]Van Groningen notes that "heart" is placed first in the phrase (Jer 31:33) thereby emphasizing it as the central factor (Gerard Van Groningen, *Messianic Revelation in the Old Testament* [Grand Rapids: Baker, 1990], 722).

[80]Though speaking of a previous generation of people, Hebrews uses similar language to describe the rebellious generation in 3:7-4:13.

[81]Thompson, *Jeremiah*, 580; Ernest W. Nicholson, *The Book of the Prophet Jeremiah: Chapters 26-52*, CBC (Cambridge: University Press, 1975), 70.

[82]Nicholson, *Jeremiah 26-52*, 70-71.

[83]Coppens, "La nouvelle alliance," 16-20.

[84]Paul R. House, *Old Testament Theology* (Downers Grove, IL: Intervarsity, 1998), 319. House identifies the broken stipulations here specifically as the written law of Moses.

[85]Thompson, *Jeremiah*, 580-81; Walter Brueggemann, *To Build, To Plant: A Commentary on Jeremiah 26-52* (Grand Rapids: Eerdmans, 1991), 71.

Something *new* must be done.[86]

Thus Yahweh announces that he will unilaterally make this new covenantal arrangement.[87] It is he who will bring about a radical change in the innermost being of the people. Thus, von Rad observes that "a new man, a man who is able to obey perfectly because of a miraculous change of his nature" is the outcome of such a unilateral work of God.[88] God's instructions to his people had always been merciful and gracious, yet had consistently been rejected by all but a faithful remnant in her history (cf. Heb 11).[89] The NC insures that all covenant people will obey the Lord, and as such there will be no further need for subsequent covenants, since this covenant will never cease.[90]

---

[86]For the position that what is described by Jeremiah is not *new*, but rather a *renewal* of the Mosaic covenant, see Walter Kaiser, "The Old Promise and the New Covenant: Jer 31:31-34," *JETS* 15 (1972): 11-23; idem, *Toward an Old Testament Theology* (Grand Rapids: Zondervan, 1978), 231-35; 268-69; John Fischer, "Covenant, Fulfillment and Judaism in Hebrews," *EvRTh* 13 (1989): 175-87 (who cites heavily from Kaiser); Gräßer, *Der Alte Bund im Neuen*, 67-68 nn. 284, 290; Van Groningen, *Messianic Revelation*, 721-22.

In contrast, F. B. Huey persuasively argues against the idea that what is in view is merely a "renewal" of the OC, despite the continuity and parallels between the two. He posits, "Does this understanding, however, do justice to the declared discontinuity between the new and Mosaic covenants ('not...like the covenant I made with their forefathers...when I led them out of Egypt')?" (Huey, *Jeremiah*, 280-81 n. 50). Note also the phrase "not anymore" in v. 34 (see also 30:8; 31:12, 40). See also Davies, *Torah in the Messianic Age*, 16; Gerald Keown, Pamela J. Scalise, and Thomas G. Smothers, *Jeremiah 26-52*, WBC, vol. 27 (Dallas: Word, 1995), 130-31. Likewise Nicholson writes, "In short, formally the 'new covenant' follows the same pattern of, and has the same goal as, the covenant which Israel's infidelity has annulled. What is different is that in a new act of grace Yahweh is so to transform the will of Israel that it will henceforth spontaneously live as his people" (E. Nicholson, *God and His People*, 212).

[87]House, *Old Testament Theology*, 319; see also R. Clements, *Old Testament Theology: A Fresh Approach* (Atlanta: John Knox Press, 1978), 103. Huey rightly notes the five "I will" assertions made by Yahweh in the text (Huey, *Jeremiah*, 284).

[88]Gerhard von Rad, *Old Testament Theology*, vol. 2, trans. D. M. G. Stalker (Edinburgh: Oliver and Boyd, 1965), 213-14; see 213-17; see also John L. Mackay, *Jeremiah* (Fern, Ross-shire: Mentor, 2004), 2:236. McComiskey writes, "The primary reason for the abrogation of the old covenant was the failure of the people to receive the law into their hearts. It is precisely this weakness that the new covenant overcomes because it promises a new heart, a responsive attitude to God's law" (T. E. McComiskey, *The Covenants of Promise: A Theology of the Old Testament Covenants* [Grand Rapids: Baker, 1985], 85). On the content of תּוֹרָה in verse 33, he concludes that it can be no other than the Mosaic legislation (84).

[89]House, *Old Testament Theology*, 319.

[90]Ibid.; see also Huey, *Jeremiah*, 285.

Meaning of Verse 33a

The question posed at the outset of this excursus concerns verse 33a, and what is meant by the "law on the heart" for Jeremiah. Specifically, what is the meaning of תּוֹרָה in the phrase, נָתַתִּי אֶת־תּוֹרָתִי בְּקִרְבָּם וְעַל־לִבָּם אֶכְתֲּבֶנָּה?

There is significant agreement that Jeremiah 31:33 refers to the laws of the Mosaic covenant, the commandments given at Sinai, and that these will be inscribed into the "innermost parts" of the NC people.[91] "God's law" and "My law" in Jeremiah are consistent references to the laws of God given to the people via Moses, and it is this against which the people rebelled.[92] Yet in the NC, there would be a unilateral act of God that would insure that the people would obey the laws of the Sinai covenant. Keown, Scalise, and Smothers are representative when they maintain that in Jeremiah, תּוֹרָה "usually refers to the revelation of God's will and way in the form of commandments, statutes, and words that must be heeded (6:19; 9:13-14; 16:11; 26:4; 32:33; 44:10, 23)."[93] Specifically, they conclude that for Jeremiah 31:33 there is no indication "that the content of the law, God's will revealed in commandment, statute, and ordinance, will be altered in the new covenant." They observe that Jeremiah's audience is knowledgeable of the covenant laws and of the fact that stone tablets are breakable (Exod 32:19; Deut 9:17), and that scrolls can be lost (2 Kgs 22:8) or even destroyed (Jer 36:23; 51:63). But, in the NC, these media are bypassed.[94]

Likewise, for Nicholson, תּוֹרָה in verse 33a amounts to the stipulations of the Mosaic covenant;[95] for Paul House verse 33 refers to the written law of Moses;[96] G. von Rad observes that תּוֹרָה here is "Jahweh's will as expressed in law," and there is no change of content in the NC.[97] Carroll likewise concludes

---

[91]See Ware, "New Covenant," 75-79, 80. Ware joins Jer 31 to Ezek 36 and asserts that "his Spirit indwells those covenant participants, making his law a very part of their inner life" (77). Here "law" is the Mosaic law. See also Moshe Weinfeld, "Jeremiah and the Spiritual Metamorphosis of Israel," *ZAW* 88 (1976): 28, 32.

[92]McComiskey, *Covenants of Promise*, 84-85. McComiskey remarks, "Although it is possible that the prophet used the word *torah* in the more general sense of the will of God, without reference to the Mosaic law, it is highly unlikely" (84). He adds, "The covenant context of the passage would certainly lead Jeremiah's hearers to think in terms of the Mosaic legislation, and Jeremiah used the term *torah* to refer to the statutes of the Mosaic covenant in *every one of its occurrences* in his prophecy" (84-85; emphasis added).

[93]Keown, Scalise, and Smothers, *Jeremiah 26-52*, 134.

[94]Ibid., 133.

[95]Nicholson, *Jeremiah 26-52*, 70.

[96]House, *Old Testament Theology*, 319.

[97]G. von Rad, *Old Testament Theology*, 2:213.

that what is meant is the "stipulations and content of the divine torah."[98] To this list others could be added such as Brueggemann, Levin, Davies, Östborn, Lundbom, McKane, Mackay, Kaiser, Hyatt, Brown, Rendtorff, Smend and Luz, Huey, Ware, and Weinfeld.[99]

---

[98]Robert P. Carroll, *From Chaos to Covenant: Uses of Prophecy in the Book of Jeremiah* (London: SCM Press, 1981), 218; 222.

[99]See Brueggemann, *To Build, to Plant*, 71; Levin, *Die Verheissung*, 257-64; esp. 264; W. D. Davies, *Torah in the Messianic Age*, 13-28; Östborn, *Torah in the Old Testament*, 151, passim. See also Jack Lundbom, "New Covenant," in *ABD*, ed. David Noel Freedman (New York: Doubleday, 1992), 4:1089. It is interesting that in Lundbom's essay, when discussing the Jeremiah text, he asserts "tora remains in the New Covenant" (1089), yet in his discussion of the text in Hebrews, he makes no mention of this whatsoever (1092). See also William McKane, *A Critical and Exegetical Commentary on Jeremiah*, ICC (Edinburgh: T & T Clark, 1996), 2:825. McKane concludes that what is in view corresponds to what was formerly written on tablets of stone. He offers the suggestion that what is in view is simply the Decalogue (820, 25). However, he is very attracted to Duhm's hypothesis that what is envisioned here is more pedestrian, stating the author's hope for future torah piety, where there will be flawless memorizing of what is taught. This is similar to Levin. Also note Mackay, *Jeremiah*, 2:236-37. Mackay observes that what is meant is the law formerly written on stone tablets, i.e., what was formerly "put before them." On this phrase (נָתַתִּי לִפְנֵיהֶם) being used of the law "set before" the people, see Jer 9:13 (9:12 MT); Deut 4:8; 11:32; 1 Kgs 9:6. Mackay observes that "rather than (the written law) being put before them, God undertakes to make an inner copy of it" (2:237). See also Walter Kaiser, *Toward an Old Testament Theology* (Grand Rapids: Zondervan, 1978), 231-35. Kaiser emphasizes continuity, stating that between the OC and NC there is the same covenant-making God, the same law ("My torah"...not a different one than Sinai), same divine fellowship ("I will be your God"), same "seed" and "people," and the same forgiveness (233). See too J. Philip Hyatt, "Torah in the Book of Jeremiah," *JBL* 60 (1941): 381-96, esp. 394-95. Hyatt suggests that what might be in view is simply the ethical requirements of the Decalogue. He also asserts that תּוֹרָה was much more of an important concept to the redactors of Jeremiah, and not so much to the prophet himself, since Hyatt only finds five true uses of the term that go back to the prophet (395). See also the editorial note by Colin Brown in the article "Covenant" by J. Guhrt in *NIDNTT* (J. Guhrt, "Covenant," in *NIDNTT*, ed. Colin Brown [Grand Rapids: Zondervan, 1975], 1:368). Brown notes the essential continuity between the covenants. "Jeremiah does not speak of the abolition of the law...this relationship is to be realized not by setting aside the law but by a more personal application of it." Also note Rolf Rendtorff, "Was ist neu am neuen Bund (Jer 31)?," 27. Rendtorff states that for Christian readers it is an important discovery when they understand that Jeremiah does not envision a new covenantal arrangement without torah, but a covenant in which the torah is even more firmly anchored in the person. Therefore, the keeping of the torah is guaranteed by God himself. He adds that what this means is that there is no prophetic contradiction or even rebellion against the law and no vision of a future without torah which has to be followed and fulfilled. He rightly criticizes Gräßer for his view of absolute discontinuity between the covenants, accusing

Additionally, most scholars observe that the concept of "law on the heart" was a common concept in the OT, citing such passages as Deuteronomy 6:6; 10:16; 11:18 (cf. 17:19-20); 30:5, 6, 11-14; 32:45-46;[100] Joshua 22:5 (cf. 1:8); Psalm 1:2; 37:31; 40:8; and Isaiah 51:7. In speaking directly to the Psalm texts, and especially Deuteronomy 6, 11, and 30, Davies notes, "In all these passages the Torah, i.e., the written code of laws, can be regarded as having been so much impressed upon 'Israel' that it can be said to be upon or in their hearts."[101]

For the present study it is helpful to note the point of Keown, Scalise, and Smothers that there is no division between God's will and his written covenant laws, but rather his will is *defined* by his commandments, statutes, and words.[102] In other words, God's will is not distinct from his written

---

him of an "eclectic approach" to the Jeremiah text and contorting the texts to fit his theological and dogmatic premises (34-35). See too Smend and Luz, *Gesetz*, 43. They write that in the NC, the individual will do naturally what the law commands since it has become part of him. This lends great assurance to the people, since they can be confident that they will not fail to keep the law. Also note Huey, *Jeremiah*, 284-85. Among commentators Huey is rare, in that he addresses (however briefly) the Jeremiah text in the NT, and notes that something has changed in the NT regarding the Mosaic law without concluding what that might be (286). See also Ware, "New Covenant," 75-79. Ware argues that the OC commands will be internalized in the NC. His joining of Jer 31 and Ezek 36 rightly leads him to the conclusion that in the NC, the "Spirit indwells those covenant participants (Ezek 36:27), making his law a very part of their inner life (Jer 31:33)" (77). For Ware, "his law" is the same as that which was written on tablets of stone, i.e., the OC laws (76, passim). It is the same law that is "carried over and maintained" (76). See also M. Weinfeld ("Jeremiah and the Spiritual Metamorphosis," 26-34) argues that Jeremiah could not have meant anything other than the divine OC law. In the NC, "the law remains as before and only the spirit of man changes" (32). For Weinfeld, the covenant undergoes a "metamorphosis" (ibid.), and "law" in Jer 31:33 is the written law of the Lord (28).

[100]Given the parallels with Deuteronomy, Nicholson asserts that the NC passage of Jeremiah was actually penned by a Deuteronomic author (Nicholson, *Jeremiah 26-52*, 71).

[101]W. D. Davies, *Torah in the Messianic Age*, 22. Davies contends that this point can also be reinforced by passages in Ezek 11:19-20 and 36:25-27. He concludes, "Now, if it be permissible to use Ezekiel in this manner...then it will also follow that the Torah of the NC will be the old Torah. This is made clear in Ezekiel 36:27f, where the 'new heart' and the 'new spirit' are expressly connected with the written statutes and judgments of Yahweh" (23). See also Carroll, *From Chaos to Covenant*, 222. The connection between Jer 31 and Ezek 36 is often made, and the present writer suggests the possibility (likelihood?) of an allusion to or an echo of Ezek 36:25-27 in Heb 10:22.

[102]Keown, Scalise, and Smothers, *Jeremiah 26-52*, 134. This view apparently runs counter the view of some Hebrews scholars such as Lehne and Attridge who seem to divorce "laws on the heart" from God's covenant laws when reading Hebrews. They

commandments in the law. Davies also contends against the vague notion of "will" or "instruction" in general as the meaning of law in verse 33, and corroborates this by his own exegetical study and by the LXX translation of תּוֹרָה with νόμους. To this matter the present chapter will briefly turn.

The LXX's Plural Νόμους

Scholars do not frequently mention the LXX rendering of the singular תּוֹרָה with the plural νόμους in Jeremiah 31:33,[103] and of the few that do, even fewer offer suggestions as to the purpose behind this unusual alteration.[104] Westcott notes that the change is remarkable.[105] However, the matter was addressed by Sheldon Blank in a focused study in 1930.[106] Blank concludes that there was no underlying reading that could account for the change from singular תּוֹרָה to plural νόμους in the LXX of Jeremiah 31:33(LXX 38:33), and that such a change is extremely rare in the LXX. The only other clear example Blank gives is found in 2 Kings 14:6 (LXX[B], where the reference is clearly to specific "laws written by Moses"), Jeremiah 26:4 (LXX[A]), and a few additional marginal scribal corrections.

This led Davies to conclude that the plural is chosen here "so as to make it clear what the reference is—it is to the many demands of the Torah."[107] This is the conclusion of Malone's research as well, who concludes that the plural form likely refers to the *specific* laws of the covenant. His findings apparently come independently of Davies, though they are virtually identical.[108] Thus, the plurality is due to a desire for specificity. There is to be no vague notion of "law" in the context. The plural makes specific what could have been seen to be

---

divide God's will from God's law, as if the two are separable. Such was certainly not the case in the OT, yet becomes the case for some in the study of Hebrews. This point is taken up below.

[103]Not even Hebrews scholars. This is a notable lacuna, given that some kind of answer must be given for the change.

[104]For example, Ellingworth notes that the plural in the LXX is different than the singular תּוֹרָה in the MT, but offers no comment (Ellingworth, *Hebrews*, 416).

[105]Westcott, *Hebrews*, 223.

[106]Sheldon H. Blank, "LXX Renderings of Old Testament Terms for Law," *Hebrew Union College Annual* 7 (1930): 259-83.

[107]Davies, *Torah in the Messianic Age*, 24.

[108]Malone, "Critical Evaluation," 186. Bayes comments on the plural as well, though without positing a suggestion for the change from singular to plural (Jonathan F. Bayes, *The Weakness of the Law: God's Law and the Christian in New Testament Perspective* [Carlisle, England: Paternoster Press, 2000], 196-97). His conclusions are in the vein of Malone and Davies though he does not cite them. For Bayes, the plural reflects its comprehensiveness (197) (contra Westcott). He asserts that the promise of Heb 8:10 refers to "the law revealed in the OT," with any other suggestion being "inadmissible" (196).

vague. The many specific laws that had been broken by the people for generations would one day be kept due to their being inscribed on the hearts and minds of the people.

Such an understanding of "laws" also fits with the covenant-making context of the passage and coincides with the findings of the previous section concerning verse 33. This is the understanding of the present writer.[109]

Conclusion

By way of conclusion, it is evident that the NC passage in Jeremiah 31 is significant in Jeremiah's theology. In the midst of the darkest of days in Israel's history, the prophet repeatedly announces God's judgment upon the people for their disobeying the commandments of God in chapters 1-29. Such disobedience is the result of hearts that are rebellious and corrupted by sin. Yet on the heels of such declarations, the Book of Consolation (chapters 30-33) highlights a new arrangement that God will make with the people in the unspecified future.

The promise of a NC announces that there would be an end to the old, and yet there would be continuity regarding the laws in both.[110] The NC that Jeremiah announces will be unlike the Old, in that the laws of the covenant will be written on their "inward parts" and the people will be granted forgiveness of their many sins. It was discovered that "law" in verse 33 refers to the will of God for the people as the commandments given to them via Moses by God. Such an act would change the very nature and heart of the NC persons, resulting in obedience. Therefore, if this is the meaning of Jeremiah 31:31-34, then the next logical question concerns how the writer of Hebrews understood Jeremiah.

Use of Jeremiah 31:31-34 (LXX 38:31-34) in Hebrews 8

Hebrews and the Old Testament

At this point the author's Christological use of the OT has already been

---

[109]Thus, any suggestion of a broad meaning of "instruction" in a vague sense, and apart from the more focused definition of actual commandments, must offer a better explanation regarding the existence of the plural. Given that Heb 8:10 and 10:16 are the only places in the NT where the plural of νόμος is found, such a rarity deserves explanation, though is seldom if ever addressed.

[110]Noting the continuity between the OC and NC, O. Palmer Robertson maintains that the substance of covenant law in each provides a basis for continuity between the two covenants. Though Robertson suggests that a broader view of תּוֹרָה might be in view in v. 33, he adds, "It will be essentially the same law of God that will be the substance of this engraving" (Robertson, *Christ of the Covenants*, 281-82). See also the conclusions of Ware, Weinfeld, Kaiser, and McComiskey, cited above.

introduced. What remains is to articulate how the writer of Hebrews utilizes the OT scriptures,[111] and to posit a hermeneutic that best explains his use and understanding of Jeremiah 31.[112] This will then be applied to the Jeremiah text and conclusions will be made.

By the usage of his introductory formulae in which God, Christ, or the Spirit is the one speaking (using a form of λέγω),[113] it is apparent that the writer of Hebrews understands the OT as having been "spoken" by God and that it was absolutely relevant to the readers in his day.[114] A cursory examination of these

---

[111]To be sure, there is no *one* specific way in which the OT is employed in every case. The writer of Hebrews used principles of exegesis that were common in his day, though in a manner that can clearly be described as "Christological." For him, the OT is in large measure anticipatory, and its meaning is only fully understood by reading it through the lens of Christ. Read in such a way the OT writer is not disregarded. Rather, for Hebrews, the focus centers on what God has said to the fathers by the prophets in the former days (1:1) and what God has said in his son in these "latter days," with the two complementing one another and the latter completing the former.

[112]For a fuller treatment of the various exegetical approaches such as proof-texting, typological approach, anthropological-existential approach, Philonic exegesis, the *sensus plenior* approach of many in Roman Catholicism, the dialogical hermeneutics of Markus Barth and other approaches, see the aforementioned works of L. D. Hurst, G. Hughes, R. Williamson, G. B. Caird, R. N. Longenecker, F. A. Malone, R. T. France as well as J. C. McCullough, "Old Testament Quotations," 157-70; G. Guthrie, "Hebrews' Use of the Old Testament," 283-91; M. Barth, "The Old Testament in Hebrews: An Essay in Biblical Hermeneutics," in *Issues in New Testament Interpretation*, ed. W. Klassen and G. F. Snyder (New York: Harper & Row, 1962), 53-78; J. Walters, "Rhetorical Arrangement," 59-70; Hofius, "Biblische Theologie," 112-13, 124; David Peterson, "God and Scripture in Hebrews," in *Trustworthiness of God*, ed. Paul Helm and Carl R. Truemann (Grand Rapids: Eerdmans, 2002), 118-38; and E. E. Ellis, *Prophecy and Hermeneutic in Early Christianity*, WUNT 18 (Tübingen: J. C. B. Mohr, 1978), 163-72.

[113]Hebrews does not utilize forms of γράφω as is common elsewhere in the NT (see Luke Timothy Johnson, "The Scriptural World of Hebrews," *Int* 57 [2003]: 237-50, esp. 239-41). The introductory formula goes back to the prologue which states that God, *after speaking* in the "former days," *spoke* in his son in these "latter days" (ὁ θεὸς λαλήσας...ἐλάλησεν). G. Guthrie finds 35 OT quotations in Hebrews and observes that in 23 of them, God is the speaker (G. Guthrie, "Hebrews' Use of the Old Testament," 274). He notes that this number fluctuates a bit among scholars, and that there is currently no agreed upon method for determining the exact number, which ranges from 29-40 (see pp. 272-75).

[114]McCullough, "Old Testament Quotations," 378-79. This is the central thesis argued in Steven K. Stanley's dissertation, "A New Covenant Hermeneutic: The Use of Scripture in Hebrews 8-10" (Ph.D. diss., University of Sheffield, 1994). Several attempts were made to procure a copy of Stanley's work during research for the present study, yet the writer has had to settle for his all too brief summary (Steven K. Stanley, "A New Covenant Hermeneutic: The Use of Scripture in Hebrews 8-10," *TynBul* 46 [1995]: 204-

texts reveals the fact that the author repeatedly views the OT as speaking of Christ. Though he uses several exegetical practices common in his day (such as dispelling confusion, reinforcement, implications, the literal sense of a word or phrase, other early rabbinical principles such as argument from lesser to greater [*qal wahomer*] and verbal analogy [*gezerah shavah*], chain quotations, example lists, typology, and homiletical midrash),[115] he is not guilty of gnostic or Philonic-allegorical exegesis,[116] nor the proof-texting as Weiß alleges.[117]

Throughout the first two-thirds of the twentieth century, there was a virtual consensus that the writer of Hebrews utilized Philonic exegetical principles when interpreting the OT, thanks in large part to the writings and influence of Spicq. Yet Barrett, Williamson, and Hurst greatly diminished the influence of this position as well as those views that argue for a gnostic approach or a background of Merkabah mysticism.[118] It is also rejected that Hebrews uses the OT in a way that abuses the original meaning of the human author. Synge is correct when he notes that the first step for the NT exegete (and of Hebrews in particular) is to note the respect for the OT author's meaning and not to violate it.[119]

Rather, the writer of Hebrews demonstrates a reverence and caution that stands in contrast to his contemporaries.[120] Based on his exhaustive research,

---

06). Stanley concludes that the "Old Covenant has been fulfilled in the New Covenant and the Christ-event, and the Old Covenant Scripture was fulfilled in the age of the New Covenant.... Therefore, filtered through the grid of 'fulfillment,' God's revelation in Scripture still has meaning, significance and authority for the readers of Hebrews as New Covenant believers" (206).

[115]Lane, *Hebrews*, 1:cxix-cxxiv.

[116]For detailed rebuttals see especially the works of Graham Hughes, Ronald Williamson and L. D. Hurst, noted at length above.

[117]Weiß, *Der Brief*, 181. This position has been persuasively assailed by Motyer in his examinations of the catena in Heb 1 (Steven Motyer, "The Psalm Quotations of Hebrews 1: A Hermeneutic-Free Zone?" *TynBul* 50 [1999]: 3-22). Motyer argues that such a proof-text approach does not adequately account for Hebrews' eschatology and his understanding of salvation history, nor does it account for the effort put forth in the writer of Hebrews' detailed exegetical arguments. Motyer therefore concludes that the writer of Hebrews, contrary to Weiß, was quite sensitive to the historical, literary, and theological contexts from the OT texts on which he built his case for Christ. See also C. H. Dodd, *According to the Scriptures* (London: Fontana Books, 1952), 126. Dodd concludes that "it is the *total context* that is in view [of the NT writer], and [total context] is the basis of the argument." This too is the conclusion of Guthrie (G. Guthrie, "Hebrews' Use of the Old Testament," 290).

[118]Barrett, "The Eschatology of the Epistle to the Hebrews," 363-93; Williamson, *Philo and the Epistle to the Hebrews*; Hurst, *The Epistle to the Hebrews: Its Background of Thought*. See n. 29 above.

[119]F. C. Synge, *Hebrews and the Scriptures* (London: SPCK, 1959), 60-64.

[120]McCullough, "Old Testament Quotations," 379.

McCullough concludes that Hebrews firmly believed that in the OT God was preparing his people for what was to come in Christ. Therefore the real inspiration for looking to the OT in this way is based solely on the fact that the writer is a NC Christian looking back at what God has spoken in the past.[121] A similar conviction leads G. Hughes to assert that the OT citations, "when brought forward from their original setting to function as Christian λόγοι are seen not as outmoded but as present forms of the Word of God, whether in theology or parenesis."[122]

The present writer has been greatly persuaded by the Caird-Longenecker-France-Walters approach, viz., that the writer of Hebrews is essentially an OT expositor who does not run roughshod over OT meaning,[123] and by the work of Graham Hughes, which complements the view of Caird-Longenecker-France-Walters.[124] Hughes argues that the OT permits the NT writer meanings that are found in light of new revelation. There is continuity between the testaments because it is the voice of God in each, and this revelation only comes into full view by looking at the OT through the lens of the person and work of Christ. There is an expressed idea of expectation in the writer's chosen OT texts, a view that complements the thesis put forward by Caird et al. OT expectation is fulfilled in Christ, yet is done so in a manner that does not nullify the older revelation. Rather, the OT revelation is fulfilled and given its fullest expression

---

[121]Ibid., 466. See also G. Hughes, *Hebrews and Hermeneutics*, 127.

[122]Hughes, *Hebrews and Hermeneutics*, 70. Interestingly, Hughes observes that the Christian faith in Hebrews has an explicit OT character. In arguing the theological basis that the OC has gone (discontinuity), the NC character of faith *looks* quite similar to the OC faithful (continuity). The connection, it is suggested here, is that the laws that have been written on the hearts in the NC have a dynamic and organic connection to the laws obeyed by the faithful men and women in the old, though now NC obedience stems from God's working in the hearts of all covenant members, and not just an exemplary remnant. See also D'Angelo, *Moses in the Letter to the Hebrews*, 256.

[123]Caird, "Exegetical Method," 44-51; Longenecker, *Biblical Exegesis*, 140-65; France, "Biblical Expositor," 245-76; and Walters, "Rhetorical Arrangement," 59-70. See also G. Hughes, *Hebrews and Hermeneutics*, 127, passim; and McCullough, "Old Testament Quotations," 157-73; 466-78. Though these scholars are not unanimous, at minimum they all share a common denominator, viz., that the writer of Hebrews actually exegetes the OT with attention paid to the original OT context.

A similar view is that of Kistemaker who asserts that four texts from the Psalms (8:4-6; 95:7-11; 110:4; 40:6-8) are the overriding texts in the epistle, and that all others are subservient to them (Simon Kistemaker, *The Psalm Citations in the Epistle to the Hebrews* [Amsterdam: Van Soest, 1961], 130-33). While Kistemaker's thesis that the writer of Hebrews is fundamentally an expositor of the OT is correct and in fundamental agreement with Caird et al., his assertion that the OT basis for Heb 8-10 is Ps 40 (and not Jer 31) has been accepted by few in Hebrews scholarship.

[124]To this list others could undoubtedly be added, but these scholars represent a specific hermeneutical school of thought concerning the OT in Hebrews.

in the light of Christ. This is particularly noticeable in the Jeremiah text, in which the OT expectation is fulfilled both by Christ and in the NC people. *There is a Christological escalation in the text*—Hebrews is not merely repeating Jeremiah "flatly," but is reading and interpreting it Christologically. It is in Christ that these OT texts come into their fulfillment and find their telic purpose in these "latter days." Though originally Jeremiah 31 was not explicitly Christological, what the prophet announced (a new covenantal arrangement) has arrived in Christ. In other words, Jeremiah is incomplete without Christ.

In his exposition of the OT, Hebrews finds that these texts only reach their fullest meaning in the NC context. Though there are forward-looking texts that are characterized by expectation, they are not each necessarily Christological in their original setting.[125] Hughes is correct to point out that such texts *"permit* an interpretive relationship between them and what happens in Jesus. But it is *not* a *necessary* relationship.... To see them in a relationship is an interpretation."[126] Thus, Hebrews 8:1-10:18 is an interpretation/exposition of Jeremiah 31:31-34, and is in continuity with the OT context. This is akin to the view of Caird et al. The continuity between the texts comes from the God who speaks himself, and this insight is brought to the text in faith: The writer of Hebrews *believes*, first and foremost, that his OT text has something to say about Christ and/or to be completed through Christ in his present eschatological context.[127] It is in this sense that "a Christian hermeneutic cannot be other than a hermeneutic of faith."[128] Thus it may be concluded with Caird-Longenecker-France-Walters and Hughes that the OT scripture is allowed to function in a new way in light of the Christ event, yet not in a way that is contrary to the old. We might use the phrase, "Christological expansion." It may mean more in the NC context, but not less; thus there is an escalation between OC text and NC interpretation/application that occurs when read Christologically by the writer of Hebrews.[129] The relationship between the two is that of promise and consummation, prophecy and escalation in its fulfillment.

Hebrews and Jeremiah 31:31-34 (LXX 38:31-34)

Though not necessarily Christological in its original setting, Jeremiah 31:31-34 is viewed this way in Hebrews. Applying the text to Christ and the NC work is an escalation of Jeremiah 31, and should be understood this way given the "latter-day" speaking and ministry of the son (1:2). The writer views the OT as

---

[125]G. Hughes, *Hebrews and Hermeneutics*, 57-58.

[126]Ibid., 104 (emphasis his).

[127]D'Angelo affirms that Christ is the "exegetical principle" of the writer of Hebrews (D'Angelo, *Moses in the Letter to the Hebrews*, 260). Similarly Hofius, "Biblische Theologie," 112-13.

[128]G. Hughes, *Hebrews and Hermeneutics*, 118.

[129]Malone, "Critical Evaluation," 187-88, 210, 216.

a consistent testimony about Christ, and therefore there is little surprise that he views Jeremiah in this fashion. Is there a usurping of Jeremiah's original intent here as Lehne alleges?[130] As argued above, no. While there are discontinuous aspects between the two authors,[131] the accent falls on continuity.[132] Matters of discontinuity between the two authors are best understood as Christological expansion and fulfillment of Jeremiah's intent, and not an abuse.[133] The precise *nature* and *manner* of fulfillment is not specified by Jeremiah (he did not know *how* God would accomplish such a promise, but simply that God *would*), yet it is argued here that he would have no complaint with the writer of Hebrews using his text in this manner. In fact, given the anticipatory nature of Jeremiah 31, it is averred here that Jeremiah's text is incomplete *until* it is read via the

---

[130]Lehne, *New Covenant in Hebrews*, 31.

[131]Such as an expansion of the promise to apply to Jew and Gentile alike, and the point that Jer 31 does not appear to be Christological in its original setting. For its application to both Jew and Gentile and the questions this poses, see Ware, "New Covenant," 84-97; Kent, "New Covenant and the Church," 89-98.

[132]Note the following parallels: (1) both affirm the NC to be eternal; (2) both affirm the result of the NC is obedience and forgiveness of sins; (3) both affirm the centrality of the heart and inner man (Jer 9:12; 7:24; 17:1, 9; Heb 3:7-19; 4:12; 9:10, 14; 10:22); (4) both affirm that God initiates the covenant; (5) both affirm that it is unilaterally accomplished by God (though in Hebrews exactly *how* this is done is unveiled); (6) all NC members will be marked by the promises; (7) both understand the background to the NC is the Sinai covenant; (8) both affirm the idea that "laws on the heart" is a blessing; (9) both see the NC being inaugurated in the "latter days;" (10) both affirm that the NC brings about a change of heart.

[133]This brings to mind the matter of typology. Malone sees typology at work in Hebrews 8, by which he means that there is "an old covenant correspondence that is escalated in the new, but the new is not merely a repetition of the old" (Malone, "Critical Evaluation," 210, passim). However, the matter of typology is a tricky one, in that there is no universally accepted rule as to what constitutes a type in Hebrews and as such no universal definition. Guthrie is correct in asserting that this is an area in Hebrews studies that is in need of further research. He generalizes that "typological hermeneutics" can most generally be defined as a correspondence in biblical history "between persons, institutions and events" (G. Guthrie, "Hebrews' Use of the Old Testament," 288, 289-90). The term is quite broad, and if defined in such a broad sense, most Hebrews scholars would acknowledge varying degrees of typology, though there would be debate on *how much* typology and exactly *what is* a type in Hebrews. Guthrie wonders if "New Covenant hermeneutic" might be more appropriate for Hebrews and the OT, "since the author of Hebrews appropriates Old Testament texts that are not specifically tied to types" (ibid.). See Leonhard Goppelt, *Typos: The Typological Interpretation of the Old Testament in the New*, trans. D. H. Madvig (Grand Rapids: Eerdmans, 1982), 161-78. In contrast, Lindars argues against typology in Hebrews (Barnabas Lindars, *Theology of the Letter to the Hebrews* [Cambridge: University Press, 1991], 53-55).

lens of Christ; there is tension and expectation until read with NC eyes.[134]

Νόμους in Jeremiah 31:33/Hebrews 8:10

The matter in question at this point is the content of νόμους in 8:10. More will be said in the following section, but the issue should be addressed along hermeneutical lines first. Combining the conclusions made from the Jeremiah context with the hermeneutical conclusions described above, this writer finds any interpretation that does not find significant correspondence between νόμους in 8:10 (or 10:16) and the written laws of Moses runs counter to the OT context and its author, and thus runs contrary to the hermeneutic of the writer of Hebrews. Thus, any definition of νόμους such as "God's will" that is not tethered to his will written in the OT laws is to be questioned. This is arguably how Hebrews consistently uses the term, and is how his audience would have likely understood it.[135]

Conclusion

The writer of Hebrews utilizes Jeremiah in a way that is sensitive to and not contrary to the original author's intent, and is eminently Christological. In speaking of a new arrangement with God's people, Jeremiah announced a coming eschatological work of God that is gracious and unconditional in which the anticipatory aspects of the old arrangement would be met and fulfilled in the new. Specifically, there is a new way of relating to God that is different from the old. Jeremiah spoke of this, but its contours are only fully felt in the light of the new.

Now it remains to apply this hermeneutic to the text of Jeremiah and specifically the meaning expressed in Hebrews. Given that the writer of

---

[134]This is not in any way meant to suggest that Jeremiah 31 is lacking in its very nature as Scripture. But when read against the whole of the canon, it raises expectations that do not rest until they are met and satisfied by the prophecy's fulfillment.

[135]Recall the conclusions of chapter 2, above. The following point should be made (though perhaps a bit guilty of being an argument from silence): If νόμος meant something different from this in 8:10 (and 10:16), then such a change from the norm would have demanded some explanation. But such as it is, the normal meaning of νόμος (as the set of laws written by Moses on tablets of stone and scrolls) fits well in the text, especially when the issue of the plural form is brought to bear on the definition. "laws on the heart" (especially given the Jeremiah context) would have meant *specific commands* that God had given to his people (plurality adds to specificity here), and any redefinition would have demanded an explanation. If it be accepted that the audience was primarily Jewish, then "laws" would have had a concrete meaning of the Mosaic commandments of God concerning how to live as his people in conformity to his will. Further, as mentioned above, "law on the heart" is a common OT concept which is always tethered to the Mosaic commandments and not a generic and isolated idea of God's will.

Hebrews does not run roughshod over the OT writers, it stands to reason that Hebrews expresses a fulfillment of the NC prophecy in a manner consistent with the original. What is described by both Jeremiah and Hebrews is *one* work of God, accomplished by God and still ongoing in the "latter days." This one promise of a new covenantal arrangement consists of several aspects that are tethered together: the internalization of the laws which produces universal knowledge of and obedience to God, and the forgiveness of sins. The result of which is that they would be his people and he their God. These encompass a single work of God inaugurated and still being accomplished in Christ.

One final concluding note is necessary to articulate at this point. Given that what is described by both Jeremiah and Hebrews is a single work of God, it is errant to attempt to divide this work as if any aspect of the overarching single work of God can be divorced from another. Specifically, it is errant only to speak of the work of forgiveness of sins (Jer 31:34; Heb 8:12; 10:17) while rendering useless the divine work of the internalized law (Jer 31:33; Heb 8:10; 10:16).[136] To be sure, it is possible to explain one aspect at a time (in which one comes to the fore), but always with the knowledge that no part is severed from another. Thus, while Hebrews expounds the aspect of forgiveness of sins with the most force in 9:1ff., the other half of the "better promises" (8:6), which is the laws upon the hearts, is never far from his mind.[137] This is why it is no surprise for him to reassert *both* of the positive aspects of the NC in 10:16-17.[138] The people have a renewed heart that knows God and his laws and have had their sins forgiven, therefore the author exhorts them on the foundation of these facts (10:19-25; esp. 22). Forgiveness of sins is granted to the individual, putting the person in a right relation with God; internalization of the laws produces obedience so that the person may *remain* in right relation to God. This is the full meaning of "I will be their God and they will be my people" (Heb 8:10). More will be said below in chapter 6, but it is important here to acknowledge the importance of each of the "better promises" assured in the NC, and to assert that Hebrews sees the importance of each—thus doing no violence to Jeremiah.

Having articulated the present writer's understanding of both the meaning of Jeremiah and the hermeneutic of the writer of Hebrews, the task of the

---

[136]Contra Schunack, *Der Hebräerbrief*, 143; Weiß, *Der Brief*, 446; Rolf Rendtorff, "Was ist neu am neuen Bund (Jer 31)?," 34; and Gräßer, *An die Hebräer*, 2:101.

[137]As mentioned previously, Peterson rightly makes the connection between this work of God in the heart and mind for obedience, and the cleansing of the conscience and heart seen in Heb 9-10 (Peterson, *Perfection*, 135-36). See also Kistemaker, *Psalm Citations*, 127-32.

[138]Peterson, "God and Scripture in Hebrews," 132; Kistemaker, *Psalm Citations*, 129. Kistemaker persuasively argues that "laws in the heart" is the point of 10:1-18. Obedience to the will of God is the underlying point of the use of Ps 40. See also Bayes, *Weakness*, 200-03.

following section is to list and evaluate the ways 8:10 (10:16) has been
understood regarding the meaning of νόμους, and to state how the present
writer understands 8:10 in light of Jeremiah's meaning viewed through the
Christological hermeneutic of Hebrews.

Νόμος in Hebrews 8:10 (10:16)

The following section describes how "law" in 8:10 (or in this case *laws*) is
currently understood in Hebrews scholarship. Given that there is precious little
discussion of the matter, such a task can be challenging. What is difficult is the
task of ascertaining just *how* particular scholars arrive at the conclusions they
do, since there is often little or no discussion. Though at times difficult, there
are a few patterns that emerge and are here noted and categorized. The purpose
here has been to categorize various scholars based upon their work. The present
writer has attempted to be very precise and fair in the organization of various
scholars into one of these views. At times this is quite difficult given some
writers' ambiguity on the matter, though three clearly-defined categories
emerge.

There are essentially three views of νόμος in Hebrews 8:10 (10:16) and can
be classified in the following manner: (1) The Non-View, (2) The No-
Correspondence view, and (3) The Direct-Correspondence view. The first
category says nothing definitive on the meaning of νόμος. The second sees
"νόμος on the heart" as a way of simply saying "inward renewal" or "the will
of God" in a manner that is discontinuous with the OC commandments of
Moses. "law on the heart" is simply a way of saying that God will work in the
heart. Some scholars suggest that God writes his will on human hearts, yet
"God's will" does not in any way refer to the Mosaic commands. The third
understands νόμος as the OC commandments that were formerly written on
stones or scrolls (either simply the Decalogue or the whole law) now written on
the heart and mind of the NC believer. The basic issue dividing these two
groups is whether νόμος in 8:10 (10:16) has *no correspondence* or *direct
correspondence* to the commandments of Moses (hence the nomenclature).
Bound up in all of this are those scholars who hold to a strong dualism (either
Jewish apocalyptic or Platonic), Philonic idealism, or a gnostic view of
Hebrews.[139] Of those scholars who *do* comment on the meaning of "laws" in
8:10, most would agree that whatever its meaning, it is a blessing for every
believer and obedience is the purpose and end product. That said, the range of
meaning for νόμος in this text could hardly be broader: from a generic or

---

[139]In short, those who maintain either a strong dualism or a gnostic view usually fall
under the second view. Recall the gnosticism of Käsemann whose most recent advocates
are Erich Gräßer and Gerd Theissen. The present writer concurs with the criticisms of
this view presented above under the discussion of Heb 8:2.

spiritualized idea of "God's will" without correspondence to the Mosaic laws, to the whole of the written law, and even to the Decalogue specifically. Each of the three views will be presented, which will be followed by the present writer's view and a conclusion.

The Non-View

Scholars in this category essentially offer little or no comment concerning the meaning of νόμος in Hebrews 8:10 (or 10:16). While it is true that all theological matters in Hebrews cannot be covered in any single work of scholarship, saying *nothing* about this aspect of the promised NC is not helpful.

Such an absence of comment is seen in works such as those of Hagner, Moffatt, Ellingworth, Gench, Gordon, Haldane, Manson, E. McKnight, and Lundbom.[140] Each of these have in common the essential fact that either they do

---

[140]See D. Hagner, *Hebrews*, GNC (San Francisco: Harper and Row, 1983), 103; idem, *Hebrews*, NIBC, vol. 14 (Peabody, MA: Hendrickson, 1990), 123; idem, *Encountering the Book of Hebrews* (Grand Rapids: Baker, 2002), 114, 131-32. Hagner is difficult to pin down, given the paucity of comments in either of these three works. Given that he might be read as belonging to any of the three views, he has been categorized as belonging to the first view. This is due to the fact that those in the next two categories make their understanding more explicit than does Hagner. See also Moffatt, *Hebrews*, 110-11. In an otherwise helpful commentary, Moffatt says not a single word as to the meaning of 8:10 and 10:16 regarding the law on the heart. In such a grammatical work as his, one might also expect some comment on the plural form of νόμος, yet there is none. See also Ellingworth, *Hebrews*, 412-16. Ellingworth's excellent commentary comes up short on two points here. First, though he mentions that the plural form of νόμος is different from the MT, he offers no comment. Second, concerning 8:10, he does not comment on its meaning other than to say that the NC is "on the hearts of God's people," but "covenant on the heart" is unclear since the text says νόμους and not διαθήκη on the heart, and besides this fact Ellingworth still does not explain what he means. His only comment is, "the last two lines of v. 10 present the new covenant as identical in form with the old" (417). By this statement Ellingworth might be asserting a certain level of continuity concerning the "laws on the hearts...I will be their God," but since this is the whole of what is said concerning the meaning, it is unclear and thus has been placed in the first category. See also his earlier (and much less extensive) work (Ellingworth, *Hebrews*, ECS [London: Epworth, 1991], 67). See also Frances Taylor Gench, *Hebrews and James* (Louisville: Westminster John Knox, 1996), 53-54; Robert P. Gordon, *Hebrews* (Sheffield: Sheffield Academic Press, 2000), 93-94; and James A. Haldane, *Notes Intended for an Exposition of the Epistle to the Hebrews*, 2nd ed., NCS (Springfield, MO: Particular Baptist Press, 1860; reprint 2002), 216-17. Haldane simply repeats the text with no explanation. See also Manson, *Hebrews*, 128. Mansons' only comment is, "They will be inwardly established in the Law," which might place him in category three, since "the law" to this point in Hebrews is the Mosaic law. On 10:16 he makes no comment. See also E. McKnight, *Hebrews-James*, 185-86. McKnight's only explanation of 8:10 is that it is an interior covenant that puts one in right relation to God.

not comment on the meaning of 8:10 (or 10:16), simply restate the text with no comment, or say so little that it becomes speculation as to how they understand 8:10.[141] The point established here is in no way meant to take away from the contributions made by the preceding writers, but rather to illustrate the point that the meaning of 8:10 is at times left either unstated or ambiguous. Several of these are shorter works, and perhaps space limitations are to blame.[142]

The No-Correspondence View

The second and third views comprise much of Hebrews scholarship. Regardless of differing views on any number of issues in Hebrews, it is possible to group these writers together based on what is said concerning their meaning of 8:10 and 10:16. Such diversity on other matters is at best tangential at this point.

Essentially, those who maintain this view see no correspondence between νόμους in 8:10 and 10:16 and the law(s) of Moses. They generally maintain significant discontinuity between the OC and NC, and whatever Hebrews means in these verses, he does not have in view the law as written by Moses. Thus, νόμους is interpreted generically as "God's will," "instruction," "new laws," or "inward renewal."[143] This is the essential difference between views 2

Thus he might belong to category 2. See also Jack Lundbom, "New Covenant," 4:1088-94. After discussing Jer 31, Lundbom's conclusions regarding Jeremiah's meaning are in concert with those presented above. Yet when he addresses the NC in Heb 8 and 10 he makes no comment at all. Therefore he is placed here.

[141]Westcott (*Hebrews*, 222-23) might belong here, given that though he mentions "new laws" in his comments on 8:10, he does not explain what he means. He says nothing on 10:16.

Harald Hegermann (*Der Brief an die Hebräer*, THNT 16 [Berlin: Evangelische Verlagsanstalt, 1988], 169) is indefinable as well. He is non-specific other than to say that the godly requirements will be internalized, thus accomplishing in the NC what was impossible under the old. However, Hegermann seems to come close to saying that these "godly requirements" are what was written on stone tablets in the OC (i.e., the Mosaic law), and are now written on the hearts of those in the NC (and thus might belong in category 3). He is quite clear in saying that the end result of this work of God is obedience to God when he writes, "So wird Gott selbst bewirken, daß die Empfänger des Neuen Bundes 'nicht von mir weichen'" (citing Jer 32:40).

Koester is ambiguous as well. In his comments on 8:10, he wrestles briefly with the question of the content of νόμους. He notes the similarities with the Decalogue in Heb 10:29 and 13:4-5, but observes that whatever the content, the cultic laws are not included (Koester, *Hebrews*, 386).

[142]But see Leon Morris' short commentary on Hebrews, which is only 137 pages in length (Leon Morris, *Hebrews*, BSC [Grand Rapids: Zondervan, 1983], 77-78). Though his is a brief work, Morris is clear on his view of 8:10 and falls into the third category.

[143]It should be noted that the idea of "inward renewal" is not isolated to view 2. Many in view 1 and all in view 3 affirm that inward renewal is an essential aspect of the NC. However, the distinction between views 2 and 3 on this matter is whether or not God's

and 3, and the confusion between them was pointed out decades ago by W. D. Davies.[144]

Among the most recent and best Hebrews scholars, Harold Attridge stands as a representative of this view. Concerning 8:10, he writes that the NC "will involve the innermost being of those with whom it is made."[145] Few would dispute this statement given that it is generally accepted that what is produced in the end is an internal change. However, Attridge adds clarity to what he means when he asserts that this new relationship with God does not consist in "an interiorization of Torah but in cleansing of the conscience and in true spiritual worship."[146] For Attridge (and most in view 2), διδοὺς νόμους μου εἰς τὴν διάνοιαν αὐτῶν καὶ ἐπὶ καρδίας αὐτῶν ἐπιγράψω αὐτούς is simply a *way of saying* that God is going to do an inward work that brings about obedience with no real connection to the laws of the OC. Thus, the promise is expressed in figurative language.[147]

Peterson and Lehne are representatives of this view as well. In his

---

internalizing of the Mosaic laws has any part of this renewal. View 2 says no; view 3 says yes, and that is the distinction. The same could be said concerning God's will/ instruction. The issue centers on the question of whether or to what extent God's will or instruction in the NC is tied to his will and instruction in the old, revealed in the Mosaic laws.

[144]In his discussion of Jer 31:33 and the content/meaning of νόμους, Davies pointed out Östborn's confusion regarding "will" in contrast to "law" in the Jeremiah passage and asserted that what *must* be in view is the Mosaic laws (W. D. Davies, *Torah in the Messianic Age*, 23-24).

[145]Attridge, *Hebrews*, 227.

[146]Ibid. Those in view 3 (as well as the present writer) would argue that there is no dichotomization between "internalization of Torah" and "cleansing of the conscience and in true spiritual worship," as Attridge does here.

[147]What is missing is the matter of how he arrives at this conclusion. There are two hermeneutical matters that need to be raised with this position. First, this definition of νόμος is in discord with Jeremiah's meaning (as well as how Hebrews has used singular νόμος), yet Attridge does not address this point. In fact, almost no discussion of Hebrews' use of the OT can be found in his commentary, a surprising lacuna in such an excellent and able work by an accomplished scholar. Second, while it is clear that the text does not mean that there is a *literal* engraving of literal organs, it is unclear how Attridge comes to view "internalization of the laws" in such a manner, i.e., merely a "way of saying" that God will renew the inward person. This is especially difficult when one recalls that this idea of the "laws on the heart" was *common* in Judaism and consistently refers to the actual commands of Moses that were to be "obeyed from the heart." How Attridge makes this jump is unclear. It is perhaps due in part to his assumption that Hebrews is written from the perspective of a modified Platonist (Attridge, *Hebrews*, 219-24). If this were indeed the writer's philosophical foundation, then any notion of law and continuity significantly fades.

writings,[148] Peterson consistently explains "laws on the hearts" as a promise
from Jeremiah fulfilled in the transformation of the hearts of God's people, a
point that most would agree with. The difference is the role of νόμος in the
transformation of the heart. What is absent is any discussion of what νόμους
means in the context of Jeremiah or Hebrews. Like Attridge, Peterson seems
content to read διδοὺς νόμους μου in a manner that has little or no contact
with νόμος in the rest of Hebrews, or in the original OT context of Jeremiah
(LXX). Likewise, Lehne offers little comment on the meaning of 8:10. In her
treatment of the NC in Hebrews she simply states that the verse refers to a
renewal of heart, without commenting on the text's use of νόμος.[149] Neither
does she comment on the plural form.

There are others that could be placed in this category as well.[150] For those in

---

[148]Peterson, *Perfection*, 134-36; idem, "God and Scripture in Hebrews," 130-33; idem,
"Prophecy of the New Covenant," 76-79.

[149]Lehne, *New Covenant in Hebrews*, 115; see also 99-100. The absence of any
discussion of νόμος in 8:10 and 10:16 appears to be based on her earlier verdict that
νόμος plays no role in the NC (27). This is akin to Frey (Jörg Frey, "Die alte und die
neue diatheke nach dem Hebräerbrief," 302).

[150]See Frank Thielman, *The Law and the New Testament: The Question of Continuity*
(New York: Crossroad, 1999), 125; R. C. H. Lenski, *The Interpretation of the Epistle to
the Hebrews and of the Epistle of James* (Columbus: Wartburg, 1937), 267; and Roger
Omanson, "A Superior Covenant: Hebrews 8:1-10:18," *RevExp* 82 (1985): 363. Grant
Osborne seems to belong here as well. See his article, "The Christ of Hebrews and Other
Religions," *JETS* 46 (2003): 263. See also Marie E. Isaacs, *Reading Hebrews and
James: A Literary and Theological Commentary* (Macon, GA: Smyth & Helwys, 2002),
109, 120. Isaacs is a bit difficult to assess on this matter, since in *Reading Hebrews and
James* she seems to be in category two, yet in her monograph (Marie E. Isaacs, *Sacred
Space: An Approach to the Theology of the Epistle to the Hebrews* [Sheffield: JSOT,
1992], 119) she interprets 8:10 as radical Torah obedience that comes from a "universal
knowledge of the Law's demands," and thus would seem to belong in category 3. See
also Smend and Luz (*Gesetz*, 43, 112-15). On the one hand, Smend and Luz affirm that
Jeremiah had in mind the actual Mosaic laws, noting that in the NC, the individual will
naturally do what the law demands (43). Yet in their brief discussion of Hebrews and the
law, no such use of the law is to be found, and for them it plays no role in the NC (112-
15). See also Gräßer (*Der Alte Bund im Neuen*, 107-09), where he (like Smend and Luz)
acknowledges that Jeremiah meant actual Mosaic laws on the heart, yet denies this in
Hebrews 8:10 and 10:16. What is involved for Gräßer is simply a renewed heart (109)
without regard for νόμος. Note the aforementioned criticisms of Gräßer by Rendtorff
("Was ist neu am neuen Bund," 34-35). Gräßer's assertion of dualism in Hebrews
perhaps will not allow him to see any continuity on this point. See also Schunack, *Der
Hebräerbrief*, 112, 143. On p. 143 he acknowledges that Jeremiah's promise directly
corresponds to the actual Mosaic laws, yet Schunack will not allow such a view of
Hebrews. He states that 8:10 and 10:16 can only mean one of two things. Either the

the "No-Correspondence view," Hebrews 8:10 (10:16) is typically a way of saying that God will renew the inner person in the NC. This in turn marks the interiority of the NC while the Mosaic laws play no role in the NC promises.

By way of critique, first is the issue of the meaning of the original OT author. Previously it was concluded that Jeremiah foretold of a new arrangement that would include the covenant laws that had been so grossly disobeyed by the people. Many in this second category affirm this reading of Jeremiah 31. If this reading is accurate, then it becomes difficult to accept the conclusion that the writer of Hebrews either did not understand Jeremiah, or that he did understand Jeremiah but betrayed his meaning by using the prophet's words in a manner inconsistent with his intent. What is largely missing by those in this category is an explanation of how Jeremiah and Hebrews intersect. How can νόμος in 8:10 (and 10:16) have no connection to what Jeremiah 31:33 originally meant, and be reinterpreted with the writer of Hebrews giving no such indication as to the change in meaning of νόμος? The law was no small thing and was central to the covenant. Thus, to empty it of its meaning without explanation or rationale is problematic.

Second, for several in category 2 there is an inconsistency and ambiguity regarding the term νόμος. Though for these scholars it may carry the idea of cultic laws, the Mosaic laws in general, or be a synonym for διαθήκη, the term is not being used consistently and there is little explanation given for a change in meaning when reading 8:10 and 10:16.

Third, there is typically no discussion of the rare plural form of νόμος in the covenant-making context of Hebrews 8. In addition, presuppositions (such as the dualism and modified Platonism of Gräßer and Attridge, et al.) are at work. This is less a critique and more of an observation, given that *all* scholars read Hebrews 8:10 and 10:16 with certain presuppositions and conclusions concerning the writer's background of thought.

The Direct-Correspondence View

This view is representative of a large number of Hebrews scholars. In general, the view states that for both Jeremiah and Hebrews what is promised in the NC is an internalization of the Mosaic commands. It seems fairly clear for this group that the writer of Hebrews sees what was formerly written on stones now to be on the hearts of those in the New Covenant. This is part of the interior nature of the NC that remakes the heart of man and produces obedience to the Lord. There is continuity between the covenants in that what is expressed in each are the same laws. This view applies the Mosaic laws to the NC heart in 8:10 with no alteration. What is distinct about view 3 is that those in this category do not dichotomize the "inward change of the heart" and the "inward

---

promise could be *without meaning or significance*, or it must be read in a way that means *simply a renewal* of the person through the cleansing of the conscience.

writing of the laws." Here, "laws" has a specific and well-known referent: the commandments given by God through Moses. For these scholars, the category of the law is clearly not inherently negative. It is used by God to accomplish his NC work in his people and as such plays some kind of role in the life of the NC believer.[151] What was formerly external and written on tablets of stones and scrolls is now internal. There is a one-to-one correspondence.

As noted above, a significant number of Hebrews scholars fit into this category. Lane is illustrative when he writes concerning 8:10, "The central affirmation of the new covenant is the pledge of the presence of the law in the hearts of believers as the gift of God.... The quality of newness intrinsic to the new covenant consists in the new manner of presenting God's law and not in newness of content."[152] In short, the internalized laws have not changed in content, but rather have changed *locations* (in the NC they are on the heart and no longer external). He crystallizes his point, asserting that what is in view is a new "manner of presenting Torah, not in newness of content," and that what is not in view is a replacement of the Torah.[153] This he finds is the high point of continuity between the covenants. Lane is also quick to tie "laws on the heart" to the grace of God that "had reached its zenith in the priestly ministry of Jesus."[154]

This is the view of 8:10 and 10:16 espoused by Vanhoye and Spicq as well. Vanhoye writes, "The prophecy [of Jeremiah] specifies that God will write his laws on their hearts (8:10); everyone knew that at Sinai they had been written on stone."[155] Vanhoye rightly emphasizes that the issue lay in the hearts of the people (in keeping with the original context of Jeremiah), given that they were unable to obey the OC laws that God had given them. Now in the NC, God intervenes and writes them into their inward parts.[156] What emerges is a transformed human heart that produces supreme obedience and love. Spicq concludes similarly that the contrast between the OC and NC is the intensity of

---

[151]Most often this matter is left unexplored, a point that will be addressed at the conclusion of this chapter.

[152]Lane, *Hebrews*, 1:209.

[153]Ibid., 1:cxxxii.

[154]Ibid., 1:cxxxiii. He adds, "There is in Hebrews a constant appeal to the normative character of the Scriptures, and more particularly of the Torah...the law delivered to Moses at Sinai" (1:cxxvi).

[155]Vanhoye, *Old Testament Priests*, 183. Vanhoye is helpful in that he allows the writer of Hebrews to note the insufficiency of the priesthood, sacrifices and the OC, yet maintain that in the NC the idea of the law is spoken of in positive terms of the promise of it being on the heart. The polemic against the law, for Vanhoye, seems to be isolated to its presence in the OC, not the New (163-85; 220-222).

[156]Vanhoye, *Old Testament Priests*, 221.

the same law written on the heart of each covenant member.[157] The interior nature of the new arrangement guarantees the covenant people against revolt by spontaneous consent to the law.

Numerous other scholars belong here such as B. Lindars, P. E. Hughes, D. DeSilva, L. Morris, G. W. Buchanan, S. Kistemaker, F. F. Bruce, and J. Calvin.[158] The common pole around which each of these turn is the assertion that what was formerly engraved on stones and disobeyed by earlier generations—the Mosaic laws—has now been "engraved" into the hearts and minds of the NC people. This involves an inward renewal of all members of the covenant community, produces obedience, and is thus quite distinct from the old arrangement (it is *new*). These laws are now a delight to fulfill as an

---

[157]Spicq, *L'Épître aux Hébreux*, 2:242. See also the detailed work of Malone, "A Critical Evaluation," 184-88.

[158]See Lindars, *Theology of Hebrews*, 47-48, 81, 89, 100. On p. 100 Lindars notes that this means that the people will do the will of God. On pp. 81 and 89 he notes that it is the law (which he defines as "the codified law") will be "internalized in mutual knowledge and understanding" which establishes a new relationship between God and people as a result of divine forgiveness of sin. See also P. E. Hughes, *Hebrews*, 300-01; DeSilva, *Perseverance*, 285. DeSilva is notable in that he observes that such a promise, "clearly resonates with his [the writer of Hebrews] interest throughout the sermon in the believers' living so as to 'please' God and to avoid what he hates (12:16-17, 28; 13:15-16, 21), fixing their hearts on God and his favor in loyal trust (3:12-13; 13:9), obeying God's commands to them (4:11), and living out the love of neighbor that is at the heart of God's law (6:9-12; 10:24-25, 32-36; 12:14; 13:1-3)." He is helpful in that he sees the writer of Hebrews contrasting the NC people with the disobedient people in Heb 3-4. "Through Jeremiah the author takes the hearers back again to the generation that God led out of Egypt...the same group of historic figures that had served so powerfully as a negative paradigm for the audience's own behavior" (ibid.). For DeSilva, the commandments of God that the disobedient generation transgressed are now internally written, thereby producing a people unlike those in Heb 3-4. See also Morris, *Hebrews*, 77-78; G. W. Buchanan, *To the Hebrews*, AB, vol. 36 (Garden City, NY: Doubleday, 1972), 139, 166; Simon J. Kistemaker, *Exposition of the Epistle to the Hebrews*, NTC (Grand Rapids: Baker, 1984), 225-27; Bruce, *Hebrews*, 189-90; John Calvin, *Commentaries on the Epistle to the Hebrews*, trans. and ed. John Owen (Grand Rapids: Eerdmans, 1949), 188-90; Montefiore, *Hebrews*, 141. Montefiore seems to be clear here on 8:10, but given his comments at 7:12 and 10:1 seems to argue for the law's abrogation (thus belonging in the previous category). Montefiore is ambiguous at this point since he equates law and covenant without defining his terms (see discussion in chapter 4 above). To this a brief comment of E. E. Ellis could be added. In his comments on Heb 8:8-12 he notes that there is little reason to see a contrast between the law on the heart and the law on the scrolls or tablets in the temple (Ellis, *Prophecy and Hermeneutic*, 183). Contra the passing suggestion of D. Guthrie, *Hebrews*, 176.

expression of grateful obedience to God who has brought this about.[159]

Generally speaking, for this group the OC defect was not so much in the laws themselves, but in the people's inability to obey them.[160] Thus what was needed was a new arrangement between God and his people, one that would make these laws an integral part of the people's constitution, being "written on the hearts and minds."[161]

A few comments on this view are in order. First, this view agrees with Jeremiah as to the centrality of the law in the NC promise, and thus in the view of this writer stands on more certain hermeneutical footing than does the No-Correspondence view. Second, there is a latent appreciation for the law as divine revelation from God, and a general hesitancy to criticize it. Rather, the more pointed criticism lies with what the laws could not do being external to the people, and thus the main fault lies with the people. Third, this position maintains a greater level of continuity between the covenants. For these reasons the Direct-Correspondence view is preferable over the No-Correspondence view by the present writer, yet not without critique, modification, and advancement. The discussion will now turn to this final point.

The Transformed View

A fourth view is put forward here by the present writer as a modification of the Direct-Correspondence view. Stated succinctly, it maintains the tie to

---

[159]P. E. Hughes adds, "[N]or is there any antithesis between law and love. Love, indeed, love of God and love of man, is the summary of the law (Lk. 10:26f.; Rom 13:8-10)" (Hughes, *Hebrews*, 301).

[160]Hughes is again helpful when he writes, "It must be understood, then, that the law is ineffective only in relation to sinful man, and that the deficiency is located in sinful man rather than in the law; for in itself, as Paul insists, the law is holy and spiritual (Rom 7:12, 14): it is, after all, *God's* law" (P. E. Hughes, *Hebrews*, 265; emphasis his). Cf. Lane, *Call to Commitment*, 117. The "weakness of the law" for Hebrews, therefore, is simply that the people were not able to keep it since it was external to them and "over" rather than "in" them. In such a state it could not produce perfection, and was transformed in the NC work of Christ.

[161]An interesting derivation of this view is put forward by Malone in his 1989 study. Malone argues that what is in view in 8:10 is specifically the Decalogue. Malone states that in the Hebrew of Jer 31:33, the verb אֶכְתֳּבֶנָּה is only used with God as its subject, "in connection with the Ten Words (Ex: 24:12; 31:18; 32:15; 34:1; Deut 4:13; 5:22; 9:10; 10:2-4). The only thing that God personally writes in the Old Testament is the Decalogue" (Malone, "Critical Evaluation," 79; see also 184-88; 194-95; 213-17). See also W. F. Lofthouse (*Jeremiah and the New Covenant* [London: SCM Press, 1925], 88-89), to whom Malone appeals for support of this assertion. In doing so he denies that any other legislation is in view, thus avoiding questions concerning the validity of specific laws, such as those that may be raised by theonomists (233-268). Concerning the issue of the Sabbath, see Malone's appendix.

Jeremiah's meaning of the actual written laws (like view 3), but advances this approach by viewing the promise of law on the heart through the lens of the Christ event, and as such there is a modification of what is actually "inwardly written." This view expands the meaning of Jeremiah in a more Christological direction, and suggests that there is transformation of the law that involves both the *fulfillment* and *internalization* of the law. Viewed Christologically, the law's requirements have been fulfilled through Christ's sinless life and sacrificial death, and it is only in Christ's fulfillment that they can be internalized in the sense promised in Jeremiah 31. They are internalized in the NC believer, which produces a people who are renewed and cleansed internally, who then spontaneously obey the commands of God (i.e., heart-obedience with which God is pleased; see 10:5-10). In this view there is nothing negative about the promise of νόμους on the heart corresponding to the OC law, and this view proposes answers to difficult questions raised with the two prevailing views.

What follows is a discussion of this proposed view in comparison and contrast to the No-Correspondence and Direct-Correspondence views. First, for those who see in this NC promise no correspondence to the Mosaic law, one important difficulty is that the intent and meaning of the OT writer is removed from the NT interpretation, thus doing violence to the original author (see below). As argued previously, this is not in keeping with the hermeneutic of the writer of Hebrews. Second, for those who maintain a direct correspondence to the Mosaic law in their interpretation of this NC promise, the question naturally arises: Do they mean that *all commandments without exception* are internally written and thus are to be obeyed? Yet all would assert that *something* has changed regarding the OC commands in that some have ended and are no longer to be kept given Christ's accomplished work. For example, if there is "no change in content" (as the Direct Correspondence view argues), then are the NC people still to obey the cultus? If the chief purpose of internalization is to produce obedience, and there is no alteration in content to what is inwardly written, then it logically follows that the NC people are to obey the OC law with no change of content (*including* keeping the cultus). This is the logical consequence, yet for reasons that are quite obvious *none* in this view would suggest this deduction to be valid. This is the logical deduction of this view, though it seems that none who maintain this view have followed through with the logical implications and deductions of this position. Therefore this writer puts forward the "Transformed View" here. It should be added that though there are significant distinctions between these popular views, there is no substantive discussion on these matters or on the differences between the views in the scholarly literature. It is hoped that the present discussion will perhaps raise the level of dialogue.

DIFFICULTIES WITH THE NO-CORRESPONDENCE VIEW

First, those in the No-Correspondence category face hermeneutical difficulties

since Hebrews does not seem to neglect the original OT meaning.[162] This would
be particularly important in the matter of the law given its centrality to Jewish
life. Concerning the matter of the author's meaning of Jeremiah 31:33b, if the
conclusions in the excursus above are correct regarding what is meant by "laws
on the heart" (as well as the conclusions regarding Hebrews' hermeneutical
sensitivity to the OT context and meaning), then one must ask why those in this
category bypass Jeremiah's meaning in only *one part of one verse*. While
affirming the author's meaning in Jeremiah 31:31-32 (a new covenant will be
made in the latter days due to the breakage of the OC), and 31:33a, 33c-34
(YHWH will be their God, universal knowledge of the Lord, forgiveness of
sin), they *deny Jeremiah's meaning of the single phrase concerning the
internalization of the laws* (31:33b). In short, there is not a consistent
hermeneutic applied to the whole of the Jeremiah text by scholars who maintain
this interpretation. Forgiveness of sin and knowledge of the Lord are
interpreted in such a way that upholds Jeremiah's intent, while the point
concerning the law is not. This is a noticeable inconsistency.

Second, there is also a lack of consistency in their usage of the term νόμος.
In every other instance it refers to something concrete (such as a specific
commandment or requirement, or even synonymous with covenant for some),
but those in this category move from the concrete to the abstract when
explaining νόμος in 8:10 (and 10:16). In the NC promise, νόμους refers to
either "God's will" or "instruction" with no identifiable connection to the actual
OT laws, or the phrase is taken only to mean "inward renewal." The question
therefore arises: In the New Covenant, what specifically are the people to obey
if all that is meant is a generic idea of 'the divine will'? Since the days of Eden,
obedience to YHWH has always consisted of definable and specific
commandments. This is part of what made OT Israel unique: they alone had the
written codification of the divine law (recall chapter 2 above).

In addition, one might suggest that the commandments of Jesus are meant by
"νόμους on the heart." But this is not persuasive since "Jesus as law-giver" is
quite foreign to this context. God the Father (YHWH) is the covenant-maker in
Hebrews, and it is *his* commandments that are to be kept.[163] Recall that the text
says that it is *God's* new covenantal arrangement and that it is *his* laws that *he*
internalizes as an expression of divine mercy (8:12). Jesus is the agent/effecter

---

[162]Recall the discussion above, pp. 200-08.

[163]This is not at all to suggest that there is a *conflict* between the will of the Father and
the Son (who is, after all, the exact representation of the Father's nature; 1:3). Rather, it
is to say that in Hebrews the roles of the Father and the Son are distinct. The text here is
Hebrews 8 and 10, and not Matthew 5-7. That said, the present writer sees no
substantive conflict between the Sermon on the Mount and Hebrews' transformation of
the law, or even the Pauline idea of "the law of Christ" (see 1 Cor 9:21) or James' "law
of our king" (James 2:8; cf. 11, 12).

of God's new work—the one *through whom* the NC comes. Jesus is the covenant-inaugurator, guarantor and mediator, but not the covenant-maker.[164] There is but one transtestamental covenant-maker, and it is God the Father. Believers (i.e., the faithful) in both the OC (which was mediated by Moses) and the NC (which is mediated by Jesus) are in covenant with God the Father, which makes them his covenant people, his "house" (see 3:6), and members of the "church of the firstborn who are enrolled in heaven" (12:22-24).

Further, interpretive suggestions such as "divine will" are far too vague, and are not even especially Jewish or Christian if severed from the law, given that "divine will" has little meaning when severed from the very thing (the laws) that was written to *express* the divine will. Such an explanation begs the question: "In the understanding of the first century author and his readers, would there have been such a chasm between 'God's will' or 'God's instruction' and the written covenant laws so that the two do not correspond?" This question becomes especially pointed when one considers Jeremiah's original meaning, and the likelihood that the original recipients of Hebrews were largely Jewish, for whom "law" meant something specific. As demonstrated in chapter 2 above, "law" meant something specific, typically the collection of the written commandments given to Moses or even the Pentateuch as a whole. What "law" and "laws" did *not* refer to in Second Temple Judaism is something ambiguous. For these reasons, the No Correspondence view fails to satisfy.

DIFFICULTIES WITH THE DIRECT CORRESPONDENCE VIEW

There are hermeneutical difficulties for the Direct-Correspondence view as well. These scholars typically acknowledge Hebrews' Christological reading of Jeremiah 31:31-34, and in light of this reading affirm at least the following Christological expansions of that text:

(1) That these are the latter days of which Jeremiah spoke (Jer 31:31)

(2) That the readers of Hebrews are "God's people" through Christ's work and are part of "God's house" (Jer 31:33c)

(3) That Christ has inaugurated the promised NC (Jer 31:33a)

(4) That the promised knowledge of the Lord has been obtained through Christ (Jer 31:34a)

(5) That through the work of Christ forgiveness has been procured (Jer 31:34b).

---

[164]This is demonstrated in the gospel accounts as well. Luke records the words of Jesus who says, "This cup is the new covenant in my blood" (Luke 22:20; cf. Matt 26:28). The New Covenant is that of God the father, mediated and inaugurated by Christ and his blood. Again, Christ is not the covenant *maker*.

Thus for those scholars in this category, these five specific aspects of Jeremiah 31 have been Christologically affected. Such a reading demonstrates Hebrews' Christological hermeneutic. For these writers there has been a Christological expansion of the Jeremiah text that does not violate the intent of the original author.

Yet while these five specific aspects of the Jeremiah text have been so affected, the specific aspect of internalized laws has *not* been affected (Jer 31:33b).[165] In other words, while allowing for a Christological expansion of most of the Jeremiah text, the point concerning "law on the heart" is left "flat." Instead, verse 33b (and thus Heb 8:10b) is read with a rather "static" hermeneutic that concludes that what is written on the hearts amounts to the OC laws without any Christological expansion, enhancement or transformation. If the law on the heart is for obedience to God, yet the promise of "laws on the heart" is read statically, then the logical conclusion is that NC believers are to practically obey the *whole* law without *any* change or alteration, which would logically include the sacrificial system (as mentioned above in brief). Therefore the question for those in this category is, "Are the NC people to obey all the laws without change?" Surely none in this category would answer in the affirmative given that Hebrews is so adamant that the cultic laws are no longer to be kept due to their fulfillment/telos in Christ. To do so would be tantamount to rejecting the work of Christ, a conclusion that none would affirm. Therefore, a simple one-to-one inward writing of the law with no transformation of content is not correct in light of what Christ has accomplished. It is argued here that one cannot read Jeremiah 31:33b correctly apart from affirming that Christ has in fact Christologically transformed and expanded *all* aspects of Jeremiah 31:31-34.

PROPOSED SOLUTION: THE TRANSFORMED VIEW

The suggestion here is that the whole of the Jeremiah text should be read through the lens of Christ's work. In so doing the promise of the "laws upon the hearts" is realized (it has been accomplished in Christ for all NC people) and yet in so doing the laws are not left unaffected. The law has been transformed in Christ (argued above in chapter 4), and this involves both its fulfillment (see chapter 6) and internalization in the NC heart (the focus of the present chapter). Such produces a cleansed heart and conscience that knows and does the will of God.

It is consistent with the writer's hermeneutic to suggest that *every* aspect of the NC promise of Jeremiah 31 has been Christologically expanded. Thus,

---

[165]Recall Lane's assertion, "The central affirmation of the new covenant is the pledge of the presence of the law in the hearts of believers as the gift of God.... The quality of newness intrinsic to the new covenant consists in the new manner of presenting God's law and not in newness of content" (Lane, *Hebrews*, 1:209; see also cxxxii-cxxxiii).

regarding "laws on the heart," there is significant correspondence to the meaning of Jeremiah, but now in light of the Christ event, this NC promise must be read Christologically. Such a reading applies the fulfilled law to the NC heart, and thus remains sensitive to Jeremiah, yet expands his meaning in light of Christ's work. If it has been fulfilled, then the NC people would no longer keep, for instance, the cultic laws, since to obey them in the present age would be to regard Christ's death as insufficient. This leads to the conclusion that *all* matters regarding sin and purity have been resolved in Christ for the writer of Hebrews.[166] Christ and his work become the lens by which the law is to be viewed in the outworking of this NC promise in the lives of his people. Therefore, the writer of Hebrews can argue both that the law is internalized, yet many laws (such as the sacrificial system and those maintaining the Levitical priesthood) are no longer to be practiced due to their completion in the person and work of Christ. The NC believer obeys what God has internalized—his law as having been transformed in the Christ event.

An important point needs to be clarified before concluding. The writer of Hebrews does not indicate that a NC believer will never sin. Such is seen clearly in 5:11-14 where the audience is chastised for their spiritual lethargy. See also 12:1-17 where the author acknowledges sin in the life of NC people that "so easily entangles." It is against sin that the believer strives (12:4). It is the very reality of sin's ongoing presence in the life of the NC believer that elicits the discipline and training of the loving heavenly father in 12:4-13 (citing Prov 3:11-12). Further, dedication to God and holiness is to be pursued by the NC believer (12:14). The imperatives and hortatory subjunctives throughout Hebrews, as well as the *exempla* list in chapter 11, each serve to push the NC believer onward in the journey to the eschatological Sabbath rest of God. Such is essentially equal, theologically speaking, to persevering in faith in Hebrews. Therefore, the writer of Hebrews does not envision a sinless people while in their sojourn towards the New Jerusalem. Rather, he envisions a changed people whose inclinations of the heart are for obedience to the inwardly-written laws of God, having been inwardly cleansed and washed with pure water (10:22). As they sojourn, they continue in their love for one another (13:1), present the Christian sacrifices of praise and thanksgiving, and perform acts of fraternal love, with which God is pleased (13:15-16). This is also a divine work, in that it is the God of peace who equips the NC people to do his will in every good thing (13:20-21). All of this is what is meant in 2:10—his "bringing many sons to glory." Far from maintaining a sinless perfection, the writer of Hebrews acknowledges the ongoing battle to persevere in faith and thus obeying the inwardly-written divine will.

---

[166]This becomes especially clear in light of 9:1-10:18. Nearness to God has been granted via perfection of the NC member due to the sacrifice of Christ. Such nearness to the divine presence *demands* purity in all its forms.

By way of conclusion, if such a view were adopted then discussions concerning the categories of "civil, ceremonial, and moral laws" might be curtailed. The question is essentially, "How do NC believers live in relation to the law of God?" This writer suggests, based on the present findings from Jeremiah and Hebrews, that the law should be read and taught through the "grid" of Christ's work. He becomes a filter of sorts when ascertaining the will of God for the NC people. Broadly speaking, therefore, such commands as those that denounce murder, or that call for the praise of the Lord God would "pass through" such a "filter," while the commands to sacrifice animals for sin or the specific purity laws (such as the food laws) would not. Exactly what this would look like in every instance cannot be ascertained from Hebrews, though it is put forward here that this is, in seminal form, the way the writer of Hebrews views how the NC believer relates to the law in light of Christ. For the NC believer, what is "written on the heart" is the OC law viewed through the lens of the NC Christ event.

Conclusion

Viewed this way there is nothing negative about the promise of "law on the heart" having significant correspondence to the OC law. What is specifically negative concerning the law is its weakness and inability to produce obedience before the coming of the son and the accomplishment of his NC work. Yet in these latter days, the law and how God's people relate to it has been transformed through Christ. As such, NC people should still look to the law as a signpost for the will of God and as a shadow that pointed to the reality to come in Christ. Such a view does justice to the original intent of Jeremiah, and acknowledges the reality of the new and transformative work of Christ described by the writer of Hebrews. For Hebrews, the law is on the hearts of the people, yet the application of such a "better promise" cannot be made without reference to the fulfillment and transformation in Christ. The law has been "Christologized," viz.—affected in all its contours by the person and work of Christ—which includes its fulfillment and its change of location. It is no longer seen as an intimidating external set of regulations, but has been internalized as a blessing of God that renews and changes the heart. It is no longer ruling over the people, but through Christ it becomes an internal blessing and delight that insures obedience. The writer of Hebrews can speak of the law's inabilities to bring about perfection and the limits of its cultic requirements (external), and at the same time affirm with Jeremiah that in the NC there is a positive value ascribed to the law (fulfilled and internalized). These positive statements and the positive affirmations of 8:10 (10:16) occur when the law is seen in relation to Christ and the NC. Christ (and his work) becomes the interpretive principle for how NC believers understand and obey the commandments of God.

Thus, Hebrews' theology of the law turns on the hinge of Christ. Apart from his work and the NC's inauguration, it is understood as insufficient since none could keep it. It could not produce perfection/completion due to the weakness of the people and the OC arrangement. Yet in the NC it is granted a positive function in that it is transformed, and this involves both its fulfillment by Christ and internalization in the believer. That which is internalized has significant correspondence to the Mosaic commandments (continuity), yet not complete correspondence due to fulfillment (discontinuity). It is the matter of fulfillment that is explicitly in view in 9:1-10:18, to which this writer now turns.

Hebrews 9:1-10:18 – The Law Possesses a Shadow of the Good Things to Come

Introduction

It has been argued in the preceding chapters that Hebrews' theology of the Mosaic law is textured and complex, consisting of both continuous and discontinuous elements. At once one is struck by the difficulty of understanding the statements regarding νόμος, highlighted in chapters 4 and 5.[1] It has been maintained that neither complete discontinuity nor complete continuity render a fair reading of Hebrews 7:1-10:18, and this study has endeavored to demonstrate that in these Christologically-centered "latter days" the law has been transformed in the Christ event, and in particular the NC believer's relation to the law. The element of "νόμος on the heart" and its connection with the Mosaic law was established in the previous chapter. It is often maintained in the literature that in the NC the Mosaic law is no longer exterior to the people, commanding purity and obedience from people who are hardened in heart and stiff-necked (3:7-4:13), but is now present in the heart of the NC people as a gift of God, rendering the heart-obedience that God desires from his people (recall both the Direct-Correspondence and Transformed views).

When the writer of Hebrews views the law through the lens of Christ, he is able to make negative statements regarding the law's inability to perfect (7:19; 10:1b), as well as assert that in the NC it will be internalized (8:10; 10:16), which denotes a positive role and function for the law in the NC. Yet this positive role can only come via the fulfillment of the law in the priestly ministry of Christ. Hebrews 9:1-10:18 further reinforces this understanding by

---

[1]Davies notes that ambiguity marked the first Christians with regard to their attitudes towards the law. He observes that at times they would recognize and assert the claims of the law, as well as reject them at other times (W. D. Davies, *Jewish and Pauline Studies* [Philadelphia: Fortress, 1984], 232). Regarding Hebrews and the law, Davies remarks that for Hebrews the law was the word of God and was still valid, and that Hebrews does not argue for a radical dismissal of the law (239). "Moreover, the ordinances of the law had a positive value. They pointed upward to what was already eternally existent in the mind of God, and forward to a real fulfillment of that after which they grope in the future" (ibid.). This idea of anticipation and fulfillment comes to the fore in Hebrews 9:1-10:18.

focusing on the aspect of fulfillment. The OC sacrificial/cultic system is the "shadow possessed by the law" (10:1) that pointed to and therefore anticipated Christ. By Christ's inauguration of the NC via the willing offering of himself (10:5-10), the NC's "better promises" (8:6) listed in 8:10-12 and 10:16-17 are realized in the cleansing from sin and the inward writing of the law that produces a life of obedient service to God (9:9, 14; 10:22 etc.).

Hebrews 8:8-13 sets the stage for 9:1-10:18 by announcing the new covenantal arrangement foretold in Jeremiah, and such an announcement is pregnant with questions that 9:1-10:18 answers. How has this new arrangement been inaugurated? If there is forgiveness of sin, what about blood and sacrifice? How does such an arrangement affect the covenant people? Why a new covenant? In announcing the NC of Jeremiah 31 in 8:8-12, Hebrews conveys something that they had already known but had heretofore not appreciated its full significance.[2] Hebrews thus explains the presence and blessings of the NC in terms of the shadowy cultus of the Old. If there is indeed a new covenantal arrangement that secures forgiveness of sins and heart-obedience, then the matter of the sacrificial system vis-à-vis Christ's work and their relationship must be addressed. The articulation of these matters is the author's task in 9:1-10:18.

The main point concerning the law in the present chapter is that the sacrificial system prescribed in it was a shadow that pointed to something better that is ultimately satisfying both to God and the people. The cultic institutions of tabernacle, priesthood, and sacrifices were designed as a shadow and parable that anticipated something greater. They were to outline and anticipate the substance that has now been revealed in Christ who has fulfilled the sacrificial system.[3] In short, the OC's means of access to God has been fulfilled and overtaken by a new and better arrangement.[4] The writer of Hebrews' essential thesis in 9:1-10:18 is that Christ has fulfilled the sacrificial system, and in filling out the shadow of the cultus he has satisfied the law's requirements for worship and its divinely-given demands for purity. In such an action there is both cleansing from sin and consecration to God for obedient service on behalf of the people. Thus, the NC blessings of the laws on the heart and forgiveness of sins have become reality in the inauguration of the NC.

---

[2]Barnabas Lindars, *Theology of the Letter to the Hebrews* (Cambridge: University Press, 1991), 81. He pointedly comments, "This is why they have not been able to see that they already possess the answer to the problem which has brought them to the verge of apostasy."

[3]Roger T. Beckwith, "Christ as Sacrifice in Paul and Hebrews," in *Sacrifice in the Bible*, ed. Roger T. Beckwith and Martin J. Selman (Grand Rapids: Baker, 1995), 135.

[4]See John Dunnill, *Covenant and Sacrifice in the Letter to the Hebrews*, SNTSMS 75 (Cambridge: University Press, 1992), 115. He writes, "Hebrews alone attempts a systematic interpretation of Christian salvation as fulfillment of the Old Testament sacrificial cultus."

The task of the present chapter is to distill and explain two main thoughts in 9:1-10:18. First and foremost is the fundamental point made in 10:1 that the law "has a shadow of the good things to come." The "shadow" (σκιὰν) is the OC sacrificial system (the focus of 9:1-28), and serves to point to what would come in the ministry of Christ. Therefore, such a declaration has both negative and positive features. Negatively, the sacrificial system cannot bring forgiveness nor put one in a right relationship to God due to the impurity of sin. Positively, the cultus serves a pedagogical purpose in that it prefigures and outlines the realities that are now present in the ministry of Christ. Second, in the exposition of 9:1-10:18, Hebrews maintains that the NC blessings of 8:10-12 are present realities for the people of God. The *quod erat demonstrandum* of 10:16-17 indicates that they are important aspects of the writer's exposition.[5] This point is also supported in the exhortation that immediately follows in 10:19-25: access to God and the exhortation to love and good works are the practical effects of the theological truths of the forgiveness of sins and the internalized and transformed law. Forgiveness and cleansing of sin and the inward renewal for the purpose of obedience are the two chief subjective benefits of the NC.[6]

The chapter will therefore proceed in three movements. First will be an overview of the contents and flow of 9:1-10:18. This will be followed by the essential discussion of the law's "having a shadow." Third will be a theological consideration of the role of the NC blessings in the exposition. This will then be followed by a conclusion.

Exegetical Overview of 9:1-10:18

Structurally, Hebrews 9:1-10:18 can be divided into three main sections: 9:1-10, 9:11-28, and 10:1-18.[7] This is part of a larger section beginning with the hinge verses of 8:1-2, and thus there is a significant connection to Hebrews 8, structurally speaking. Contextually speaking, this is especially true when considering that 9:1-10:18 is bordered by the inclusio of Jeremiah 31 (8:8-12; 10:16-17). The Jeremiah text serves as a broad framework for the whole of the present section which answers questions that the Jeremiah text raises. Thus,

---

[5]Rightly, Peterson avers that the oracle is "vital to our writer's thinking." See David Peterson, *Hebrews and Perfection: An Examination of the Concept of Perfection in the "Epistle to the Hebrews,"* SNTSMS 47 (Cambridge: Cambridge University Press, 1982), 132.

[6]W. G. Johnsson, "Defilement and Purgation in the Book of Hebrews" (Ph.D. diss., Vanderbilt University, 1973), 338. See also William L. Lane, *Call to Commitment: Responding to the Message of Hebrews* (Nashville: Thomas Nelson, 1985), 131; idem, *Hebrews*, WBC, vol. 47b (Nashville: Thomas Nelson, 1991), 2:258; Peterson, *Perfection*, 138.

[7]See above, chapter 3 regarding specifics of structure.

9:1-10:18 are an explanation of Jeremiah's prophecy.[8]

France avers that the Jeremiah text forms an obvious basis for the writer's ensuing argument.[9] However, Jeremiah makes no mention of the means and manner by which his prophecy would be fulfilled, how the NC would be established or how its blessings would take effect. Answers to such fundamental questions lie with the writer of Hebrews in his Christological exposition of Jeremiah through the hermeneutical lens of the "latter day" revelation of the son (1:1-2). It is only now, in light of final revelation from God, that what Jeremiah foretold can be explained with such clarity and force. Such an explanation in light of the present voice of God in Christ is in keeping with the writer's hermeneutic.[10] A covenant must be inaugurated with blood, and if there is to be sacrifice then there must be blood as well. In short, Jeremiah's prophecy of a new covenantal arrangement cannot be understood except in terms of OC cultic practices. They were a parable and shadow of what is now present (9:9; 10:1).

Hebrews 9:1-10

This brief section is set apart by the inclusio regarding "regulations" (δικαιώματα) in 9:1 and 10, establishes the cultic character and tone so explicit in Hebrews 9.[11] Verse 1 announces two topics that verses 2-10 take up in reverse order: the earthly sanctuary (9:2-5) and regulations for worship (9:6-10).[12]

In verses 2-5 the writer stresses the earthly nature of the tabernacle, which will soon be contrasted to the heavenly sanctuary (9:11). The tabernacle, with

---

[8]G. B. Caird, "The Exegetical Method of the Epistle to the Hebrews," *CJT* 5 (1959): 44-51; Richard N. Longenecker, *Biblical Exegesis in the Apostolic Period*, 2nd ed. (Grand Rapids: Eerdmans, 1999), 163-64; R. T. France, "The Writer of Hebrews as a Biblical Expositor," *TynBul* 47 (1996): 245-76; J. Walters, "The Rhetorical Arrangement of Hebrews," *AsTJ* 51 (1996): 59-70. See also Barry C. Joslin, "Christ Bore the Sins of Many: Substitution and the Atonement in Hebrews," *SBJT*, 11:2 (2007): 74-103, esp. 81-83.

[9]France, "Biblical Expositor," 264.

[10]France agrees. He writes, "The means by which the problem of sin is finally dealt with may not have been specifically present in Jeremiah's mind, but it involves no distortion of the significance of his words to identify it in the single sacrifice of Christ to take away sins once for all" (France, "Biblical Expositor," 265).

[11]George H. Guthrie, *The Structure of Hebrews: A Text-Linguistic Approach* [Grand Rapids: Baker, 1998], 86; Hans-Friedrich Weiß, *Der Brief an die Hebräer*, 15th ed., KEKNT, vol. 13 (Göttingen: Vandenhoeck & Ruprecht, 1991), 449.

[12]Peterson, *Perfection*, 132; Otfried Hofius, "Das 'erste' und das 'zweite' Zelt: Ein Beitrag zur Auslegung von Hbr 9:1-10," *ZNW* 61 (1970): 271; Harold Attridge, *The Epistle to the Hebrews*, Hermeneia (Philadelphia: Fortress, 1989), 231; Lane, *Hebrews*, 2:217.

its two divisions and strict regulations, were a continual reminder of the holiness of God and the ritual impurity of the people. There was no direct access to God for the people in the earthly tent. Only priests were allowed to serve the outer tent, and the inner tent, the Holy of Holies (῞Αγια ῾Αγίων), could only be penetrated by the high priest once a year.[13]

In verses 6-10, the writer of Hebrews draws from the Day of Atonement ritual and brings out its unique character in verses 6-7.[14] The μεν...δε construction in 6b-7 contrasts the priests who continually serve in the outer tent with the high priest who has the specific duty to enter the holy place once per year. Blood (αἷμα) is mentioned for the first time in this section (9:7), and anticipates 9:18 and 9:22.[15] In Hebrews' theology, it is only by blood that cleansing from sin can occur in both the OC and NC, and blood (i.e., the pouring out of the victim's life) must therefore play a central role in his explanation of Jeremiah 31. Blood, in this respect, is seen as the medium of cleansing (9:21),[16] and is found throughout Hebrews 9 (7, 12, 13, 14, 18, 19, 20, 21, 22, and 25).

Verses 8-10 give the writer's evaluation of the tent (9:8) and the sacrifices (9:9-10). The structure and regulations of the sanctuary have a profound meaning that is now only shown via the Holy Spirit in the present. In the tabernacle there was a lack of access to God, and its very structure and regulations kept the worshipper at a distance. The cultic regulations had a symbolic significance that is only now understood in the time of reformation (9:10).[17] The point is that while there is a sacrificial system (carried out in the outer compartment of the tabernacle), there is no real access to God in the true,

---

[13]Riggenbach notes that 9:2-5 stress the significance between the inner and outer tents of the tabernacle, and such emphasis sets up the distinctions in 6-10 (Eduard Riggenbach, *Die Brief and die Hebräer*, KNT 14 [Leipzig: Deichert, 1922], 238-39). See also Hofius ("Das 'erste' und das 'zweite,' 274-75), who notes the parallels in Josephus in which τὸ ἱερόν refers to the whole of the temple area, and τὸ δεύτερον ἱερόν refers to the inner sanctuary reserved for Jews only.

[14]Albert Vanhoye, *Old Testament Priests and the New Priest According to the New Testament*, trans. J. Bernard Orchard (Petersham, MA: St. Bede's Publications, 1986), 184-85; Dunnill, *Covenant and Sacrifice*, 139-41. Dunnill states unequivocally that Hebrews "straightforwardly expounds the death and exaltation of Jesus as fulfillment of the Day of Atonement ritual" (140).

[15]Lane, *Hebrews*, 2:223.

[16]On the importance of blood in Heb 9, see Johnsson, "Defilement and Purgation," 152-61; 306-39. Johnsson points to the importance of blood in Lev 16, and of sin as defilement and ritual impurity that can only be cleansed with blood. See Joslin, "Christ Bore the Sins of Many," 75-79.

[17]There is no element of gnosticism here. Contra Otto Michel, *Der Brief an die Hebräer*, KEKNT (Göttingen: Vandenhoeck & Ruprecht, 1966), 306.

heavenly sanctuary (τὴν τῶν ἁγίων ὁδόν; see 8:2).[18] The parenthetical comment of verse 9a (ἥτις παραβολὴ εἰς τὸν καιρὸν τὸν ἐνεστηκότα) indicates that the first tent (τῆς πρώτης σκηνῆς) was a parable (παραβολὴ) that "symbolizes the total first covenant order with its daily and annual cultic ritual."[19] External washings and regulations do nothing for the heart/conscience,[20] and thus stand in contrast to the internal work that is at the heart of the NC blessings.

Now that the time of reformation has arrived (9:10), such symbols are no longer operative, having been superseded by what has arrived in the ministry of the new high priest.[21] Now the meaning and purpose of the cultus is clear: there is no access to God while the sacrificial cult is in practice.[22] Such sacrifices cannot perfect the worshipper in his or her conscience (συνείδησιν τελειῶσαι).[23] Peterson rightly notes that such perfection involves being in a right relationship with God, and while defilement of conscience persists, only distance and imperfection mark the relationship between God and worshipper.[24] Only the NC promises of cleansing from sin and the internalization of the fulfilled law can satisfy the uneasy heart and mind. Such OC regulations were

---

[18]B. F. Westcott, *The Epistle to the Hebrews*, 2nd ed. (Grand Rapids: Eerdmans, 1950), 252. Attridge, *Hebrews*, 240; Westcott, *Hebrews*, 252; Hugh Montefiore, *The Epistle to the Hebrews*, BNTC (London: Adam & Charles Black, 1964), 149; David DeSilva, *Perseverance in Gratitude: A Socio-Rhetorical Commentary on the Epistle "to the Hebrews"* (Grand Rapids: Eerdmans, 2000), 300; Craig Koester, AB, vol. 36a (New York: Doubleday, 2001), 397; Ceslas Spicq, *L'Épître aux Hébreux* (Paris: Gabalda, 1953), 2:253-54; Peterson, *Perfection*, 133; Lindars, *Theology*, 87; Dunnill, *Covenant and Sacrifice*, 233-34; Johnsson, "Defilement and Purgation," 281.

[19]Lane, *Hebrews*, 2:224. On the matter of the Spirit's disclosure in 9:8, see below.

[20]F. F. Bruce, *The Epistle to the Hebrews*, rev. ed., NICNT (Grand Rapids: Eerdmans, 1990), 206.

[21]See F. C. Synge, *Hebrews and the Scriptures* (London: SPCK, 1959), 26; Hofius, "Das 'erste' und das 'zweite' Zelt," 276; N. H. Young, "The Gospel According to Hebrews 9," *NTS* 27 (1980-81): 201-02.

[22]Michel, *Der Brief*, 306; Otfried Hofius, *Der Vorhang vor dem Thron Gottes* (Tübingen, Mohr, 1972), 61-65.

[23]"Conscience" must take into account the OT view of man in general, and of the 'heart' in particular. See Christian Maurer, "σύνοιδα, συνείδησις," in TDNT, ed. G. Kittel, trans. G. W. Bromiley (Grand Rapids: Eerdmans, 1971), 7:908-19. Cf. C. A. Pierce, *Conscience in the New Testament* (Chicago: Allenson, 1955), 21-59. Pierce notes that the starting point for Hebrews' view of the conscience is the fact that man cannot worship God with a guilty conscience (100). Lane agrees and affirms that συνείδησις is typically used in the negative sense of a conscience that is plagued by guilt that is an "internal witness that defilement extends to the heart and mind" (Lane, *Hebrews*, 2:225). It is telling, therefore, that the heart and mind are precisely in view when one considers that the NC's better promises specifically address the heart and mind of the people.

[24]Peterson, *Perfection*, 126-67.

external and could not penetrate to the conscience and heart. If a right relationship is to exist between God and creature, a purging of the conscience must occur (cf. 9:14). This relationship is not based on external regulations, but by Christ and the NC.[25] Verse 10 establishes the main thrust of 11-28, viz., external regulations for worship could not cleanse the defiled conscience nor effectively atone for sin. They pointed to something further that is now present in the "time of reformation" (καιροῦ διορθώσεως). The cultic ministry was a temporary parable that has been fulfilled in the work of the new high priest who brings about true cleansing which leads to obedient service (9:11-14).

Hebrews 9:11-28

The writer of Hebrews' theological aim of verses 11-28 is to demonstrate that Christ fulfills the Day of Atonement ritual in his death and self-offering as the new high priest. His sacrifice both permanently atones for sin as well as inaugurates the promised NC of Jeremiah 31, announced in Hebrews 8:8-12.

HEBREWS 9:11-14[26]

Whereas 1-10 are largely negative, verses 11-14 are positive and set forth the matters for discussion in 9:15-28. By means of Christ's entering the holy place in heaven by having offered his own blood, he has secured the transformation of the worshipper guaranteed in 8:10-12. Peterson asserts that the writer of Hebrews makes use of the positive promises of the Jeremiah text at this point, in that both cleansing from sin and the promise of obedience are in view in verses 11-14.[27] Likewise, Martin-Achard asserts that while the NC is based upon forgiveness of sins, it continues via the transformation of the covenant people.[28] Forgiveness of sins and obedient service are the effects assured to the believer by means of Christ's work. The NC assures the readers that forgiveness of sin and an obedient heart are part of the one act of God the end of which is obedient service to God (9:14).

In 9:11, Christ (Χριστὸς δὲ)[29] has appeared as the high priest (ἀρχιερεὺς),

---

[25]Michel, *Der Brief*, 308.

[26]For text critical questions in 9:11 and 9:14, see Appendix 8. This section is vital for understanding Hebrews' theology. It is so essential in fact, that for Vanhoye, the priestly work of Christ described in 9:11-14 is the literal center of the entire epistle to the Hebrews. See chapter 3, above.

[27]David Peterson, "The Prophecy of the New Covenant in the Argument of Hebrews," *RTR* 38 (1979): 76-77; idem, *Perfection*, 129.

[28]He writes, "une transformation profonde des membres du peuple élu." See Robert Martin-Achard, "Quelques remarques sur la nouvelle alliance chez Jérémie (jer 31, 31-34)," in *Questions disputées d'Ancien Testament*, ed. C. Brekelmans (Louvain: Leuven University Press, 1974), 154.

[29]The δέ should be given full adversative force. There is a distinct temporal contrast between two stages of redemptive history.

which reinforces the idea that the event in mind is specifically the Day of Atonement (9:7). Grammatically, the main clause of 9:11-12 is "Christ entered the holy place" (Χριστὸς...εἰσῆλθεν...εἰς τὰ ἅγια) via the heavenly counterpart to the σκηνή,[30] and has done so once and for all (ἐφάπαξ) in contrast to the high priest who entered year after year.[31] Christ entered the "holy place" (τὰ ἅγια) which is synonymous with the right hand of God.[32] He enters through his own blood, but not *with* his own blood. Hebrews nowhere states that Christ carries his own blood into the presence of God.[33] Through his

---

[30]On the varied interpretations of this verse and especially the meaning of σκηνή, see Albert Vanhoye, "Par la tente plus grande et plus parfait...(Heb 9,11)," *Bib* 46 (1965): 1-28. See also P. E. Hughes, *A Commentary on the Epistle to the Hebrews* (Grand Rapids: Eerdmans, 1977), 283-90. The issues surround the grammatical usage of διά, as well as the meaning of σκηνή, and decisions for each are related. Interpretations of σκηνή in v. 11 include Christ's resurrected body, Christ's incarnate body, the church, a cosmic passageway, or heaven itself (G. Guthrie, *Hebrews*, 310; see also Paul Ellingworth, *The Epistle to the Hebrews*, NIGTC [Grand Rapids: Eerdmans, 1993], 446-48, 450). A close examination of the text of 11-12 indicates that the destination is the very presence of God (τὰ ἅγια) that is reached by Christ's passage "διὰ τῆς μείζονος καὶ τελειοτέρας σκηνῆς," which refers to the "true tent" that God pitched (8:2). Such an interpretation presumes a local (and not instrumental) sense of διά in 9:11, and an instrumental sense in 9:12. This is the view taken here. On the benefits of such an approach, see Ellingworth, *Hebrews*, 450-51; Jean Héring, *L'Épître aux Hébreux* (Neuchâtel: Delachaux & Niestlé, 1954), 84; Spicq, *L'Épître aux Hébreux*, 2:256; Michel, *Der Brief*, 310-11; Gräßer, *An die Hebräer*, 2:145-46; Helmut Koester, "'Outside the Camp': Hebrews 13:9-14," *HTR* 55 (1962): 309-10; and Lane, *Hebrews*, 2:236-38. Lane concludes, "The way into the presence of God was through the heavenly counterpart to the front compartment of the earthly tabernacle" (238). For the view that σκηνή is the whole sanctuary, see William Loader, *Sohn und Hoherpriester*, WMANT 53 (Neukirchen: Neukirchener, 1981), 166-67; Koester, *Hebrews*, 409; P. E. Hughes, "The Blood of Jesus and His Heavenly Priesthood in Hebrews," *BibSac* 130 (1973): 313-14; idem, *Hebrews*, 288-90.

This understanding relinquishes the highly metaphorical interpretations of σκηνή (see Paul Andriessen, "Das grössere und vollkommenere Zelt (Heb 9:1)," *BZ* 15 [1971]: 86). Andriessen is correct in criticizing the many creative interpretations of σκηνή (82), which are offered often as a result of interpreting διά in 9:11 instrumentally. Such views cloud the clear Day of Atonement imagery being exploited by the writer of Hebrews (Attridge, *Hebrews*, 246). Contra James Swetnam, "Greater and More Perfect Tent: A Contribution to the Discussion of Hebrews 9:11," *Bib* 47 (1966): 91-106.

[31]Spicq, *L'Épître aux Hébreux*, 2:256-58. On the chiasm in 9:11-12, see Hofius, *Vorhang*, 66.

[32]Shinya Nomoto, "Herkunft und Struktur der Hohenpriestervorstellung im Hebräerbrief," *NovT* 10 (1968): 17. Similarly Hofius, *Vorhang*, 65-66; and Andriessen, "Das grössere," 84-85.

[33]See esp. F. F. Bruce on 9:12. See also Mark A. Seifrid, "Death of Christ," in *Dictionary of Later New Testament and Its Developments*, eds. R. P. Martin and Peter H.

appearance as high priest, the good things have now come (τῶν γενομένων ἀγαθῶν). The phrase τῶν ἀγαθῶν is comprehensive, referring to the NC promises as well as to the fulfillment of what the OC cultus foreshadowed. Purgation from sin, access to God, and the better promises are in view and flow from the atoning work of Christ.[34] The result is eternal redemption via the non-repeatable sacrifice of Christ, and not by the medium of the blood of goats and calves and ashes of a heifer.[35] Windisch rightly concludes, "Das einmalige wirksame Opfer Christi hat die nutzlosen Häufungen von Tieropfern zum Stillstand gebracht."[36]

The *a fortiori* argument of verses 13-14 offer proof in the form of a first class condition (εἰ...ἁγιάζει). If animal sacrifices can sanctify on some external level, how much more cleansing is there by the blood of Christ? In the OC sacrificial system, there was an element of cleansing that occurred each Yom Kippur, yet it was merely external, cleansing the flesh only.[37] This is in contrast to the internal cleansing that is assured in the NC (9:14). Christ effects in reality what the cultus could only provide symbolically and in seminal form. The self-offering of Christ procures the internal cleansing of the conscience, *from* dead works and *to* obedient service to God. Hughes, Lane, Cody, and Peterson rightly connect this to the promise of the law on the heart in 8:10/10:16.[38] Those who draw near to God through Christ's sacrifice *are*

Davids (Downers Grove, IL: Intervarsity, 1997), 274-75; P. E. Hughes, "The Blood of Jesus and His Heavenly Priesthood in Hebrews Part II: The High-Priestly Sacrifice of Christ," *BibSac* 130 (1973): 210-11. His work was completed on the cross. Hebrews 9:12 should be translated as "*after* he obtained eternal redemption, he entered the Holy Place once for all," where he *sat down* as ruler and Lord (Ps. 110:1).

[34]P. E. Hughes, *Hebrews*, 327.

[35]See Numbers 19 and the account of the red heifer.

[36]Hans Windisch, *Der Hebräerbrief*, HNT 14 (Tübingen: J. C. B. Mohr, 1931), 87.

[37]Bruce states that "flesh" here refers to the "physical element of the human make-up...in contrast to one's inner being, or conscience" (Bruce, *Hebrews*, 215 n. 87). Cf. James W. Thompson, *The Beginnings of Christian Philosophy: The Epistle to the Hebrews*, CBQMS 13 (Washington, DC: Catholic Biblical Association, 1982), 108-09.

In addition, Ware is correct in his assertion that "it would be wrong and completely unfair to an Old Testament understanding to conclude from the promise of forgiveness in Jer 31:34 that forgiveness per se would be new" (Bruce A. Ware, "The New Covenant and the People[s] of God," in *Dispensationalism, Israel and the Church: the Search for Definition*, ed. Craig A. Blaising and Darrell L. Bock [Grand Rapids: Zondervan, 1992], 81.)

[38]P. E. Hughes, *Hebrews*, 397, see also 300-01; Lane, *Hebrews*, 2:268; Aelred Cody, *Heavenly Sanctuary and Liturgy* (St. Meinrad, IN: Grail Publications, 1960), 134; Peterson, *Perfection*, 134-40, 150. These scholars rightly connect the NC promises of 8:10-12 and 10:16-17 to the obedient service to God in 9:14, 10:10, and 10:14. See also Peterson (*Perfection*, 135) in which he links the heart and conscience.

perfected,[39] which is in direct contrast to 9:9.[40] Christ willingly offered himself through the Holy Spirit to God, and in doing so assures a clean conscience and life of service to God for the people.[41] Verse 14 summarizes the Christian benefits and "describes a definitive consecration to God through a cleansing that fulfills the promises of Jeremiah 31:31-4."[42] Peterson adds, "[The] conscience must be cleansed to empower the believer to serve God in this way," and "this has its proper outworking in a life of obedience to God's will and perseverance in hope."[43] There is no more guilt from sin that keeps man at a distance from God when the accusing conscience has been perfected.[44]

Such cleansing in 9:14 leads to a change of heart and generates service to God. The result is worship expressed in a life that acknowledges the name of God (13:15) and is pleasing to God by means of obedience (13:16). The effective purgation of the conscience and its orientation to obedient service is the epitome of the NC promises in 8:10-12, and draws attention to the specific matter of διαθήκη taken up in 9:15-22.[45]

HEBREWS 9:15-22[46]

Logically and grammatically speaking, verse 15 is the climax of 11-14 and 16-

---

[39]Peterson, *Perfection*, 129 n 17. On the cleansing here Spicq avers, "C'est une *sanctification*, et si complète qu'elle est synoyme de perfection" (Spicq, *L'Épître aux Hébreux*, 2:282).

[40]F. F. Bruce astutely observes that the real barrier between God and the people was not an external cultus. The cultus only represented symbolically the barrier within the conscience of the individual. The tabernacle and its restrictions were in place due to the *internal* impurities of the people. Once there is an *internal change*, the tabernacle and its rituals are no longer necessary. "It is only when the conscience is purified that one is set free to approach God without reservation and offer him acceptable service and worship" (Bruce, *Hebrews*, 209). The "good things to come/that have come," among other things, involve removal of sin and a change of nature, to a clean conscience which produces service to God. This is the fulfillment of Jer 31:33-34.

[41]There is a textual issue here ("*eternal* spirit" vs. "*holy* spirit"), but most modern scholarship affirms πνεύματος αἰωνίου as the original, and conclude with the scribes that the reference is in fact to the Holy Spirit. See Metzger, *Textual Commentary*, 598-99.

[42]Peterson, *Perfection*, 150.

[43]Ibid., 140.

[44]Lindars, *Theology*, 4-15, passim.

[45]Lane writes, "The blood of Christ achieves what had been promised through Jer 31:31-34 and demonstrates that Jesus is διαθήκης καινῆς μεσίτη" (Lane, *Hebrews*, 241). He adds, "As the priestly mediator of a new covenant, he is able to administer the eschatological blessings that specify the newness of the διαθήκης καινῆς" (242).

[46]For text-critical matters, see Appendix 8.

22 are a parenthetical explanation of verse 15.[47] Though there remains substantial debate concerning the translation of διαθήκη in 9:16-17,[48] the fundamental point of these verses is less debated: they are argumentative support for the necessity of Christ's death if the NC is to be inaugurated and its

---

[47]Lane, *Hebrews*, 2:234. Attridge rightly avers that 9:15 is the thesis underlying the whole of 15-22 (Attridge, *Hebrews*, 254).

[48]Within current Hebrews scholarship, there is still considerable debate over the matter of the translation of διαθήκη in 9:16-17 as "will/testament" (and thus a play on the term's secular meaning), or "covenant," as it is uniformly translated in vv. 15 and 18 as well as the rest of Hebrews. There is no consensus in either scholarship or translation, and those who maintain either "will/testament" or "covenant" each typically conclude that the passage is confusing if taken the other way. Though not an unimportant matter, neither view affects the present study to any significant degree given that the overall point of 9:15-22 is not obscured: they are argumentative support for the necessity of Christ's death if the NC is to be inaugurated and its blessings realized, and covenant requires death. For references and discussion, see Koester, *Hebrews*, 417-18, 424-26; Attridge, *Hebrews*, 255-56; Ellingworth, *Hebrews*, 462-64; DeSilva, *Perseverance in Gratitude*, 308-09; P. E. Hughes, *Hebrews*, 368; Gräßer, *An die Hebräer*, 2:172-73; Michel, *Der Brief*, 315-22; Montefiore, *Hebrews*, 156-57; Moffatt, *Hebrews*, 127-28; Spicq, *L'Épître aux Hébreux*, 2:60-65, 285-99; F. F. Bruce, *Hebrews*, 221-22; Lindars, *Theology*, 95-96; Dunnill, *Covenant and Sacrifice*, 250-51; Vanhoye, *Old Testament Priests*, 203; G. Vos, "Hebrews, the Epistle of the Διαθήκη," *PTR* 13 (1915): 587-632; and J. Swetnam, "Suggested Interpretation of Hebrews 9:15-18," *CBQ* 27 (1965): 373-90. Each of these maintains, for various reasons and with varying levels of certainty, that διαθήκη in Heb 9:16-17 should be rendered as "testament."

Though the translation of διαθήκη as "testament/will" has enjoyed significant support, others maintain that διαθήκη should be consistently rendered by "covenant" throughout 9:15-18. For example, see Westcott, *Hebrews*, 265; Lane, *Hebrews*, 2:231, 242-43; George H. Guthrie, *Hebrews*, NIVAC (Grand Rapids: Zondervan, 1998), 313; Alexander Nairne, *The Epistle of Priesthood* (Edinburgh: T & T Clark, 1913), 140, 364-66; K. M. Campbell, "Covenant or Testament? Heb. 9:16, 17 Reconsidered," *EvQ* 44 (1972): 106-11; G. D. Kilpatrick, "Diatheke in Hebrews." *ZNW* 68 (1977): 263-65; Johnsson, "Defilement and Purgation," 308-18; John J. Hughes, "Hebrews 9:15ff and Galatians 3:15ff: A Study in Covenant Practice and Procedure," *NTS* 21 (1979): 27-96; and Scott Hahn, "A Broken Covenant and the Curse of Death: A Study of Hebrews 9:15-22," *CBQ* 66 (2004): 416-36. Hahn and J. Hughes soundly demonstrate on lexical, syntactical, semantic, and contextual levels why "testament" is inconsistent in these verses. They also argue that the "testament" rendering has no real basis in Greco-Roman legal practice.

In sum, though for much of the twentieth century there was a near consensus that διαθήκη ought be rendered "testament" or "will" in 9:16-17, the more recent efforts of J. J. Hughes, Lane, and Hahn make a compelling case for a consistent translation of διαθήκη as "covenant." The focus of these verses seems to be on death more as it inaugurates a covenant via the priestly mediator, rather than on death as a prerequisite for an inheritance (J. Hughes, "Hebrews 9:15ff," 38-39). Such is the understanding here.

blessings realized.[49] Blood is required for a new covenantal arrangement, and is necessary if the better promises of the NC (8:6) and its blessings are to be actualized.[50] This dictum reinforces the point that for Hebrews, there must be death if there is to be a new covenantal arrangement, even though Jeremiah did not specify how the new arrangement would be enacted. Since Christ is mediator (μεσίτης) of the NC (9:15; cf. 7:22; 8:6), there must be blood, since even the Sinai covenant was marked by blood (9:18-22). The NC has a new foundation, and is therefore a decidedly *new* work.[51] Vanhoye rightly observes that Christ's blood at once fully atones for sin (under both covenants) as well as inaugurates the NC, and concludes that such is an "astonishing coalescence."[52] Jesus died and in his death assured the blessings of forgiveness and obedience. Lane reasons that Christ's death was "a representative death as the cursed one so that those whom he represents may receive the blessings of the covenant promised to those who obey its mandates."[53]

Verse 18 continues the argument (ὅθεν), stating that the first covenant "was ratified with blood," again marking the importance of blood in the covenant procedure.[54] Verses 19-22 support and explain this statement (γὰρ). After

---

[49]The thesis for 9:15 (supported by 16-22) is: "any covenant requires a death" (Attridge, *Hebrews*, 253; see also Dunnill, *Covenant and Sacrifice*, 250; Cody, *Heavenly Sanctuary*, 183-84). For further references see Leonhard Goppelt, *Typos: The Typological Interpretation of the Old Testament in the New*, trans. D. H. Madvig (Grand Rapids: Eerdmans, 1982), 168; and Hahn, "A Broken Covenant," 431. Concerning these verses Vanhoye states, "according to the Old Testament, a covenant between God and mankind is based on a bloody sacrifice. He observes that the event of Calvary has fulfilled this requirement" (Vanhoye, *Old Testament Priests*, 201). The NC has a better foundation, being founded upon the bloody sacrifice of Christ, and thus is different from and superior to the OC. Therefore, it is not a mere "prolongation" of the OC or even its perfect restoration in contrast to Qumran thought.

[50]The promise (τὴν ἐπαγγελίαν) here refers to eternal salvation and the assurance of the NC blessings. See Cody, *Heavenly Sanctuary*, 136; G. Guthrie, *Hebrews*, 309-10.

[51]For the difficulties of considering the 'new covenant' as a second, different covenant, see Annie Jaubert, *La notion d' alliance dans le Judaïsme aux abords de l'ère chrétienne*, PatS 6 (Paris: Éditions du Seuil, 1963), 222.

[52]Vanhoye, *Old Testament Priests*, 204; see also Attridge, *Hebrews*, 253. Attridge is helpful here, asserting that under the OC sins could not be expiated, and thus Christ's work had a "retrospective" effect (Attridge, *Hebrews*, 255), though it is not as though the idea of forgiveness is new to the NC (see Ware, "New Covenant," 81). Cf. 11:40 and the "perfection" of the OT faithful. The unique substantival use of the perfect passive participle in 9:15 (οἱ κεκλημένοι) refers to "the called" under both OC and NC.

[53]Lane, *Hebrews*, 2:242. He adds, "From the perspective of covenant practice, Christ's death was a covenant sacrifice, which consummated the old order and inaugurated the new order. As the priestly mediator of a new covenant, he is able to administer the eschatological blessings that specify the newness of the διαθήκης καινῆς."

[54]Johnsson, "Defilement and Purgation," 306-07.

Moses gave every commandment of the law (πάσης ἐντολῆς κατὰ τὸν νόμον), he sprinkled (ἐρράντισεν) the book of the law as well as the people with blood, thus inaugurating the OC with blood.[55] For Hebrews, since the OC had blood, Jeremiah's NC must have blood as well. That blood has a cleansing function is clear from verses 21-22 which concludes with the summary statement that according to the law (κατὰ τὸν νόμον) almost everything is cleansed (καθαρίζεται) by means of blood.[56] The pericope concludes with the maxim that there is no forgiveness without bloodletting (9:22). Such is a statement with which none in Judaism would argue. It is the author's theological purpose to affirm this fundamental truth, as well as to argue that it is Christ's blood, and not that of animals, that effects true forgiveness (ἄφεσις) and internal cleansing from the defilement of sin. Far from canceling the rubric of the cultus, the writer of Hebrews takes pains to show that the OC cult has met its end and goal in the NC cult, which is better in every way.

HEBREWS 9:23-28

The verb καθαρίζω serves as a catchword that forms a link between verses 15-22 and the final pericope of Hebrews 9. Logically, 9:23 concludes what has come before (οὖν), and recalls the contents of 9:11-14.[57] The emphasis in these verses is on the definitive character and finality of the work of Christ accomplished in the true tabernacle of heaven.[58] Verse 23 has elicited not a few interpretations with its claim that the heavenly things themselves are in need of cleansing.[59] The cleansing occurs in heaven itself (αὐτὸν τὸν οὐρανόν) where

---

[55]The two aspects of blood (medium of purity and covenant inauguration) coalesce in the citation from Exod 24:8 in Heb 9:20. For a concise treatment and explanation of the variations from the OT ritual, see Lane, *Hebrews*, 244. Contra Attridge who asserts that the writer of Hebrews simply conflated a number of Pentateuchal rituals (Attridge, *Hebrews*, 257-58). For the connection to Lev 17:11 see Joslin, "Christ Bore the Sins of Many," 79-81.

[56]On the importance of blood in Heb 9, see especially Johnsson, "Defilement and Purgation," 152-61; 306-39; Gräßer, *An die Hebräer*, 2:149-51; and Dunnill, *Covenant and Sacrifice*, 100-03. Dunnill writes that "*defilement* is the fundamental religious problem, which sacrifice confronts by providing *purgation* by means of *blood*" (121, emphasis his). See also 9:14 and the blood of Christ which cleanses (καθαρίζω) the conscience.

[57]Harold Attridge, "Use of Antithesis in Hebrews 8-10," *HTR* 79 (1986): 7; Lane, *Hebrews*, 2:247.

[58]Koester, *Hebrews*, 427; Johnsson, "Defilement and Purgation," 336.

[59]For a list of nine suggested interpretations of this *crux interpretum*, see David J. MacLeod's helpful article, "The Cleansing of the True Tabernacle," *BibSac* 152 (1995): 60-71. None of the views of 9:23 is without its problems, but the most viable interpretation in light of the context of covenant and sanctuary inauguration in 9:18-23 is the view that suggests that what needs cleansing is not heaven itself, but the "sphere of

the exalted high priest enters the very presence of God and appears there on behalf of his people (9:24). Verses 25-26 make the point clear that Christ is not like the Levitical priests who repeatedly offer sacrifice. If his offering were like that of the sacrificial system, then Christ would have to be offered continually from the beginning of time.[60] His sacrifice is superior to the animal sacrifices, will not be repeated, and has been offered at the consummation of the ages (συντελείᾳ τῶν αἰώνων)[61] to put away sin (ἀθέτησιν [τῆς] ἁμαρτίας). The repeated sacrifices were displaced by one that fully atoned for sin. This action involves a change in the human condition which is guaranteed in 8:10 and 10:16.[62]

The final sentence of Hebrews 9 (vv. 27-28) asserts the axiom that men die once, thus Christ could only offer himself once "to bear the sins of many"[63] (briefly citing Is 53:12). Judgment follows death, yet salvation awaits those who await the return of Christ. Christ entered the holy place and will return from that holy place, appearing a second time (δευτέρου ὀφθήσεται). The second appearance (9:28) that is anxiously anticipated by his people (τοῖς αὐτὸν ἀπεκδεχομένοις) is likely analogous to the Yom Kippur ritual when the priest returned from offering the sacrifice for the people.[64]

---

communion" between God and man. Just as in the OC, the presence of sinful worshippers defiled the tabernacle, so also the continued approach of NC worshippers "defiles" the heavenly tabernacle. This "defilement" stems from the fact that believers are not yet glorified and are still to seek forgiveness and help from their exalted high priest due to sin and weakness. MacLeod writes, "The implication of 9:23 is that the 'heavenly things' are defiled by this constant process of forgiving believers who sin" (70). Yet he warns that Hebrews' language should not be pressed, and should be understood to be speaking relationally and not locally (i.e., heaven itself is not defiled). The "sphere and all means of their relations to God...must be sanctified by the blood of the New Covenant" (ibid.). For a list of scholars holding this view, see MacLeod, "Cleansing of the True Tabernacle," 69 n. 41. See also Dunnill, *Covenant and Sacrifice*, 232-33.

[60]This *reductio ad absurdum* assumes that the listeners grasp the preexistence of Christ (Koester, *Hebrews*, 428).

[61]Bruce rightly notes that it is the manifestation of Christ (πεφανέρωται) that makes "now" (νυνὶ) the time of fulfillment (Bruce, *Hebrews*, 231).

[62]Koester, *Hebrews*, 429.

[63]προσενεχθεὶς εἰς τὸ πολλῶν ἀνενεγκεῖν ἁμαρτίας. Many scholars agree that this is a citation of Isaiah 53:12 (LXX) which reads, αὐτὸς ἁμαρτίας πολλῶν ἀνήνεγκεν. For the implications this text has on understanding the atonement in Hebrews, see Joslin, "Christ Bore the Sins of Many," 88-95.

[64]See Sirach 50:5-10; see also C. K. Barrett, "The Christology of Hebrews," in *Who Do You Say That I Am? Essays on Christology*, ed. Mark Allan Powell and David R. Bauer (Louisville: Westminster John Knox, 1999), 124-25.

Hebrews 10:1-18

Structurally, 10:1-18 is connected to 9:1-28, and carries on the theme of NC sacrifice vis-à-vis the OC.[65] The content as well as structural parallels indicate continuity from 9:1-10:18.[66] The whole of 8:3-10:18 centers around the NC's inauguration and precisely how its "better promises" can be assured. The inclusio that opened in 8:8-12 does not close until 10:16-17, thus providing a helpful framework for understanding the whole of this section. Though verses 1-18 round out what began at 9:1, they also conclude the larger section begun at 8:3.[67] The discussion of the new and eternal sacrifice is made in the context of the new and eternal covenant that is announced in the Jeremiah text. The final verses of the central section of exposition further describe Hebrews' understanding of the employment of Jeremiah 31 and the superiority of the NC offering.

The burden of 10:1-18 is to demonstrate that the one-time obedient sacrifice of Christ has positive effects on the NC people, is superior to the animal sacrifices of the OC, and is therefore an appropriate climax to the central section of Hebrews. There is a decidedly positive tone in this final section. The positive NC effects were promised in 8:10-12 and are repeated in 10:16-17. The writer asserts that fulfillment of the NC's better promises is present in light of Christ's accomplished work and ongoing priestly mediation. The effects of Christ's decisive action extend to the lives of all his people.[68]

HEBREWS 10:1-4

Verse 1 asserts that the law possesses a shadow (Σκιὰν γὰρ ἔχων ὁ νόμος) of the good things to come.[69] In context, the "shadow/foreshadowing" here is the

---

[65]For text-critical matters in this section, see Appendix 8.

[66]See above, chapter 3.

[67]Recall from chapter 3 that 8:1-2 operates as a "hinge" of sorts and thus belongs to both what comes before as well as what comes after. Regarding Heb 10, Guthrie observes four inclusions that open in 10:1 and close in 10:14, thus subdividing 10:1-18 into vv.1-14 and 15-18 (G. Guthrie, *The Structure of Hebrews*, 87). Yet it is also true, given the content of 10:15-18, that the writer of Hebrews, in his masterful way, has crafted 10:15-18 not simply to conclude 10:1-18 (though it does), nor simply to conclude 9:1-10:18 (though it does), nor simply to conclude 8:3-10:18 (though it does), but also to round out the entire central section of 7:1-10:18.

[68]Vanhoye, *Old Testament Priests*, 213. Lane argues that 10:1-18 focuses on the "subjective benefits" of the NC surveyed in 9:13-14 (where emphasis was placed on the experience of Christian salvation), whereas 9:11-28 focused on the "objective benefits" (William Lane, *Call to Commitment: Responding to the Message of Hebrews* [Nashville: Thomas Nelson, 1985], 131).

[69]Gräßer (*An die Hebräer*, 2:49) notes that the law's prescribed cultus points to the eschatological Christ-service that is foreshadowed in it. Hofius agrees on this point, stating that according to God's decree, it is the cultic law that is specifically the shadow

sacrificial system with its tabernacle, priests, and animal sacrifices, all of which were insufficient and temporary.[70] Their shadowy nature attests to the sacrifices' limitations and stands in contrast to the effectual one-time offering of Christ (9:28). Christ has overtaken and fulfilled the sacrificial system, procuring clean consciences and the covenant blessings for his people.[71] The law, no matter how closely followed, could not perfect the worshipper since its sacrifices were divinely anticipatory. Distance and guilt were the results due to the limitations built into the sacrificial system that only now are understood in the time of reformation (9:10). In these verses, the contrast lies between the adequacy of Christ's blood (recall 9:11-14, 23-28) and the inadequacy of animal blood for purgation of sin.[72]

The parenthesis of verses 2-3 drives home the point in logical fashion in the form of a rhetorical question: if the cultic sacrifices indeed took away sin and made the worshipper perfect, why were they repeated? The verdict comes in verse 3, viz., that there is a reminder of sins in their repetition and could not unburden the sinful, accusing conscience (συνείδησιν ἁμαρτιῶν).[73] Such a reminder (ἀνάμνησις) of sins (Lev 16:21; cf. Num 5:15) stands in juxtaposition to the NC promise that sins would no longer be remembered by God (8:12, 10:17).[74] There could be no effective, obedient service to God (9:14) unless the worshipper were effectively changed and the "burdened, smitten heart" made right with God.[75] This issues in another axiomatic statement (10:4, cf. 9:13-14) assuring the audience that in the sacrificial system, there is no full and final forgiveness, the logical corollary to the claim in 10:1 that the sacrificial system was a σκιὰν.[76]

(Otfried Hofius, "Biblische Theologie im Lichte des Hebräerbriefes," in *New Directions in Biblical Theology*, ed. Sigfred Pederson, NovTSup 76 [Leiden: E. J. Brill, 1994], 119).

[70]Johnsson, "Defilement and Purgation," 338-40.

[71]Michel, *Der Brief*, 331; Cody, *Heavenly Sanctuary*, 137-38.

[72]Johnsson, "Defilement and Purgation," 341-42.

[73]Peterson, *Perfection*, 135; Pierce, *Conscience*, 99-102.

[74]Gräßer observes that in the present speaking of the son, something new has occurred that was never before achieved, viz., the eschatological forgiveness of sins (Erich Gräßer, *Der Alte Bund im Neuen* [Tübingen: Mohr, 1985], 113). There is a fullness and finality to the forgiveness procured by Christ in the NC.

[75]Lane, *Hebrews*, 2:261. A decisive cleansing from sin and heart put right with God is thus needed and promised in the NC (10:16-17).

[76]The term is not used here in a Platonic sense ("unreal," "deceptive") but rather means "imperfect" or "incomplete" (MacLeod, "Cleansing," 60-63; Lane *Hebrews*, 2:259). See comments on 8:5 concerning Platonism and Hebrews. The cultus pointed forward (eschatologically) to what was to come in Christ, and not upward to a Platonic ideal. See also C. K. Barrett, "The Eschatology of the Epistle to the Hebrews," in *The Background*

HEBREWS 10:5-10

The facts established in verses 1-4 are elaborated in light of Christ, who is not mentioned in verses 1-4. The many sacrifices were ineffective and ultimately insufficient as an appropriate means of atonement. Further, such divine rejection of these sacrifices is an OT idea, demonstrated in the writer's use of Psalm 40:6-8 in verses 5-7.[77] Koester notes that by appealing to the OT for such a critique of the sacrificial system, the writer of Hebrews avoids the appearance that such a conclusion regarding them is not merely his opinion, but comes from God himself.[78] Hebrews puts these words into the mouth of Christ, who summarily "confesses" in 10:7 (via Ps 40) that the fundamental purpose of his self-offering is to do the will of God (ἥκω...τοῦ ποιῆσαι ὁ θεὸς τὸ θέλημά σου). In doing so, his human body becomes the effective sacrifice that bulls and goats only foreshadowed (10:4).

Such obedience to the will of God operates as an example for all NC

---

of the New Testament and its Eschatology, ed. W. D. Davies and D. Daube (Cambridge: University Press, 1956), 363-93, esp. 386. Recall Heb 9:15; cf. Rom 3:21-26.

[77]For a helpful treatment of Ps 40 in the context of Heb 10:1-18, and especially how "laws on the heart" factors into the exposition, see Simon Kistemaker, *The Psalm Citations in the Epistle to the Hebrews* (Amsterdam: Van Soest, 1961), 124-33.

[78]Koester, *Hebrews*, 436. It is God who announces that the very sacrifices he prescribed are unsatisfying to him. Further, the psalms were understood to postdate the book of the law, and βιβλίου here (10:7) likely refers to the book of the written law of Moses (see 9:19). But see K. T. Schäfer, "ΚΕΦΑΛΙΣ ΒΙΒΛΙΟΥ," in *Weg zur Buchwissenschaft*, ed. O. Wenig (Bonn: Bouvier, 1966), 1-10, who leaves the exact referent undecided (1). The point is that the son obeys the written will of God. See also Johnsson, "Defilement and Purgation," 341-44. If the Psalm text is Davidic and a unity (see especially Walter Kaiser, "The Abolition of the Old Order and the Establishment of the New: Psalm 40:6-8 and Hebrews 10:5-10," in *Tradition and Testament: Essays in Honor of Charles Lee Feinberg*, ed. John S. Feinberg and Paul D. Feinberg [Chicago: Moody Press, 1981], 21-23), then the possibilities of exactly which book is referred to is reduced to the Pentateuch, part of Samuel's work, possibly Joshua, Judges and perhaps Ruth (Kaiser, "Abolition," 30).

Concerning 10:5b, the LXX's reading, "a body you have prepared for me," varies from the MT's "an ear you have dug for me," which is possibly an interpretive rendering on the part of the LXX translators. Jobes argues that the changes were purposeful on the part of the writer of Hebrews and are phonetically related (Karen Jobes, "The Function of Paronomasia in Hebrews 10:5-7," *TJ* 13 [1992]: 181-91), expanding her earlier argument that the writer of Hebrews is actually responsible for the LXX reading of Ps 40. She argues from first century rhetorical principles that all changes to Ps 40 in Heb 10 are not from any Greek translation, and that all extant LXX MSS of Ps 40 were "corrected" in order to conform to the reading of Hebrews (Karen Jobes, "Rhetorical Achievement in the Hebrews 10 'Misquote' of Psalm 40," *Bib* 72 [1991]: 387-96, esp. 388).

believers who have the law internalized in their hearts and minds.[79] On 10:5-10 Lane observes, "The basis for consecrating the new covenant community to the service of God is the unrepeatable offering of the body of Jesus on the cross in fulfillment of the will of God."[80] The ritual sacrifices cannot merely be rejected without a substitute; what must be offered is an efficacious sacrifice in the place of the former offerings. In Christ, the law's demand for sacrificial mediation is fulfilled.[81] Sacrifices that are offered without a corresponding obedient and devoted heart do not please God. Rather, devotion and obedience from the heart please God, and such are found in Christ's obedience and self-offering.[82] In this self-offering, he effectively removes the first covenant with its animal sacrifices and establishes the second, which is based on the offering of his body which inaugurates the NC (9:11-28).[83] This also procures the sanctification of God's people.[84] The manner in which believers relate to God has changed in the NC; they have been transformed and set apart for service to God (10:10; cf. 9:9, 14; 10:16-18, 19-25).

HEBREWS 10:11-14

Verse 11 parallels verse 1, in that both state the point that the repeated OC sacrifices cannot purge or decisively remove the defilement of sin. The willing and single sacrifice of Christ is superior to those offered by the many priests who are perpetually in motion, carrying out their duties. Such "motion" stands in contrast to Christ who is seated in the presence of God (10:12b; see Ps

---

[79]Peterson repeatedly makes the connection between the heart-obedience of Christ to the NC promise of Heb 8:10 and 10:16 (Peterson, *Perfection*, 148, passim), though he does not make explicit exactly what he means when he refers to the law "on the heart." He is not to be criticized here, however, given that such a question is not fundamental to his thesis which is solely concerned with the concept of perfection, though it is clear that at this point the present thesis intersects with Peterson's work in a complementary fashion.

[80]Lane, *Call to Commitment*, 133; see also 134, 135.

[81]Vanhoye, *Old Testament Priests*, 218.

[82]The main idea in Ps 40:6-8 is also found in other OT literature; see 1 Sam 15:22; Ps 50:8-10; 51:16-17; Isa 1:10-17; 66:2-4; Jer 7:21-24; Hos 6:6; Amos 5:21-27; Mic 6:6-8. The verb ἁγιάζω in 10:10 points to this positive purification, cleansing, and consecration to God and his service.

[83]Susanne Lehne, *The New Covenant in Hebrews*, JSNTSS 44 (Sheffield: JSOT Press, 1990), 31. See also Peterson, *Perfection*, 147.

[84]It is noteworthy that the writer of Hebrews momentarily shifts to the first person, "*We* have been sanctified" (ἡγιασμένοι ἐσμὲν) in 10:10 and anticipates τοὺς ἁγιαζομένους in v. 14. As a result of Christ's obedience and sacrifice there is a radical transformation in the people and a consecration to the service of God. Heretofore in the covenant people there had been a lack of correspondence between sacrifice and heart obedience, yet now such disparity has been erased. The verb ἁγιάζω refers to a "definitive consecration expressed in heart-obedience toward God." See Lane, *Hebrews*, 2:265.

110:1),[85] indicating that his offering is acceptable in the holy place. His one sacrifice stands in contrast to their many, his being seated is in contrast to their standing, and their place in the earthly tabernacle contrasts to his place at the right hand of God.[86] Given that Jesus is seated in heaven he is able to administrate the NC perpetually since his offering has perfected his people for all time (τετελείωκεν εἰς τὸ διηνεκὲς). His enthronement in heaven ensures that the benefits of his new and eternal covenant (13:20) are granted to his people.

In 10:5-10 the contrast lies with the death of an animal (10:1-4) and the perfect obedience of Christ (10:5-10).[87] Such obedience of Christ to the will of God brings about sanctification and perfection (10:10, 14) in God's people and assures the NC blessings of verses 15-18. The obedience described via Psalm 40 establishes an example of perfect obedience to the written law of God (10:16).[88] Bruce writes, "the will of God is recorded in two forms: externally,

---

[85]David M. Hay, *Glory at the Right Hand: Psalm 110 in Early Christianity*, SBLMS 18 (Nashville: Abingdon, 1973), 150-52. Hay avers that Christ's being seated means that he is essentially idle at the present time (87-88, 125). However, it is more correct in the context of Hebrews that he is in that exalted position in order to mediate and intercede, and is thus *not idle* in his exaltation. Christ's position at God's right hand (10:12b) elicits a confidence in the people that the way to the presence of God is no longer fettered (note 4:14-16; see Michel Gourgues, *A la Droite de Dieu: Résurrection de Jésus et actualisation du psaume 110:1 dans le Nouveau Testament* [Paris: J. Gabalda, 1978], 110-19).

[86]This is highlighted grammatically by the writer's use of a μὲν-δέ construction.

[87]Kaiser, "Abolition," 34.

[88]Attridge observes the omission of the phrase, "your law is in my heart" from the Ps 40 citation and argues, with no discussion, that the reason for its omission is "obvious" (Attridge, *Hebrews*, 274 n. 84). However, Bayes (Jonathan F. Bayes, *The Weakness of the Law: God's Law and the Christian in New Testament Perspective* [Carlisle, England: Paternoster Press, 2000], 201-03) and Malone (Fred A. Malone, "A Critical Evaluation of the Use of Jeremiah 31:31-34 in the Letter to the Hebrews" [Ph.D. diss., Southwestern Baptist Theological Seminary, 1989], 192-94) independently of one another make persuasive cases that such an observation in no way diminishes the aspect of the law on the heart. Malone argues correctly that if this was truly the writer's purpose then it would have been eliminated from 10:16 as well (Malone, "A Critical Evaluation," 193), and Bayes argues that Ps 40 was called to mind *because* of the reference to the law whose thought is completed by the Jeremiah citation immediately following (Bayes, *Weakness*, 201). He rightly argues that for the writer of Hebrews to include the first part of Ps 40 ("I delight to do Thy will") *means* that the written law is in his heart (ibid.). This "delight" is "tantamount to loving righteousness and hating lawlessness" (cf. 1:9). Further, the omission of the phrase "is not to be read as indicating that the sentiment of the phrase is alien to the writer's purpose" and the phrase's "assonance with Jeremiah 31:33 was...the reason for the inclusion of this quotation at this point" (ibid.). Further, Peterson has asserted that both aspects of the NC ("my laws

'in the scroll of the book,' and inwardly in his servant's heart, so that his life is the translation into practice of the written law."[89] The desire of God is not sacrifice per se, but rather obedience that comes from the heart. "He is claiming their whole being, for they are called to do God's will,"[90] (10:36; 13:21). The action of Christ's perfect heart-obedience establishes the NC, and this obedience is representative of the kind of heart-obedience provided for in the NC in which the law is internalized.

HEBREWS 10:15-18

The writer of Hebrews concludes his argument by ending where he began: Jeremiah 31.[91] The present tense in verse 15 (μαρτυρεῖ) assures the readers of the point that the prophecy of Jeremiah is being fulfilled in the present lives of the people. Yet here he has condensed the NC prophecy down to its two essential elements: internalization of the law and the forgiveness of sins.[92] As argued above, both aspects are essential for an effective change in the people. Forgiveness alone is not enough, since the complaint with the people (and the root of their sin) is their disobeying the law; defilement from sin (and thus separation from God) is the *result* of disobeying the law.

Therefore, while cleansing from sin is imperative, for Hebrews it is not enough. Such forgiveness must be accompanied by an internal change that

---

on the heart" and "I will remember their sins no more") are essential to the writer's understanding of the NC (Peterson, *Perfection*, 148, passim).

[89]F. F. Bruce, *The Time is Fulfilled: Five Aspects of the Fulfillment of the Old Testament in the New* (Exeter: Paternoster Press, 1978), 83.

[90]Kistemaker, *Psalm Citations*, 129.

[91]Peterson correctly asserts that the repetition of Jer 31 in 8:8-12 and 10:16-17 makes it clear that Jeremiah's prophecy is "vital to our author's thinking" (Peterson, *Perfection*, 132).

[92]Lane argues that of these two fundamental aspects of the NC, the "central affirmation of the new covenant is the pledge of the presence of the law in the hearts of believers as the gift of God," and asserts that there is no change in the content of the law between the old and new (Lane, *Hebrews*, 1:cxxxii). The content of the law across the covenants is for Lane the same; what is altered is the human heart (see also 209). While the present writer largely agrees with Lane's assertions on this point, it was argued in chapter 5 that this view does not appear to take into consideration the matter of fulfillment and how Christ's fulfillment affects how the NC worshipper presently relates to the law. This is precisely why the thesis was put forward that the law has been transformed in Christ's coming, and this is defined by fulfillment in Christ and its internalization in the people. Thus, the NC people can obey the law and keep the will of God as his covenant people. In one sense Lane and this writer are in harmony—the people are transformed, yet what has been argued here is that what is internalized is a "Christologized law," and not simply the Mosaic law in toto without *some* kind of alteration. This writer reasons that what is internalized is what is to be obeyed, and thus that which has been cancelled via fulfillment in Christ (the cultus, for example) is not to be practiced any longer.

produces obedience to the law from the heart, and this obedience is made possible only through Christ's fulfillment of the law and its transformation and internalization in the NC people. Thus God has taken it upon himself to decisively cleanse the people and engrave the "Christologized law" (the νόμους viewed through the lens of Christ's work, as argued here) on their hearts and minds such that the NC people will obey him, in contrast to the OC people as a whole (3:7-4:13; 8:8a).

Precisely how this epochal change has occurred has been the burden of the writer of Hebrews since he cited Jeremiah in Hebrews 8. The "inward writing" of what was formerly external is simple enough to understand for a (likely) Jewish audience,[93] but how can sin truly be effectively forgiven and the accusing conscience made perfect? The answer comes in 9:1-10:18 where Hebrews labors to show the insufficiency of the OC sacrifices, and how the NC has a better priest and a better cultus that not only purges sin from the heart but also transforms the worshipper into an obedient servant of God. With such exposition accomplished, the writer of Hebrews then exhorts them to obedient NC living and perseverance in 10:19ff.

The Law Possesses a Shadow

Having articulated the present writer's understanding of the argument and theology of 9:1-10:18, the task remains to discuss the importance of 10:1 and the assertion that the law "possessed a shadow of the good things to come." It should be noted that Hebrews does not say that the law *is* the shadow, but rather that the law has/possesses a shadow (Σκιὰν γὰρ ἔχων ὁ νόμος).

For the identical form of the verb, see Hebrews 7:3 in which the clear meaning is that of "having" or "possessing." See also Heb 2:14; 4:14; 5:12, 14; 6:9; 7:6, 28; 9:4, 8; 10:19; 11:10 and 12:1. In short, whenever the participle of ἔχω is used in Hebrews, it never means "is" and most naturally carries the normal meaning of "having" or "possessing" or some other synonym. Thus, though one must consider contextual and theological matters in addition to lexical meanings of terms in the task of exegesis, one must *begin* with the range of possible meanings for a term in a given text by a given biblical author. The argument here (that ἔχων is best translated with "having" or "possessing") does justice to each of these categories (lexical, contextual, exegetical, theological) and makes good sense without attempting to use the term differently than its

---

[93]See Rolf Rendtorff, "Was ist neu am neuen Bund (Jer 31)?" in *Lernen in Jerusalem—Lernen mit Israel*, ed. Martin Stöhr, Veröffentlichungen aus dem Institut Kirche und Judentum 20 (Berlin: Institut Kirche und Judentum, 1993), 27. Rendtorff notes that the concept of law (by which he means Mosaic Torah) on the heart goes back to at least Deuteronomy, and would therefore have been a well-known idea to the original audience.

usage elsewhere in Hebrews.[94]

Thus, it is not Hebrews' point to suggest and defend the idea that the whole Mosaic law was a shadow, and thus it has been abrogated in its entirety.[95] Rather, he envisions the cultus to be the shadow that outlines and prefigures the priestly ministry of Christ. From the context of 9:1-28 it is clear that the "shadow" is the cultus, with its tabernacle, priests, and sacrifices each receiving treatment in 9:1-10:18 as "shadowy outlines" of Christ's ministry. These categories belong most explicitly to the Day of Atonement ritual, and as such become the paradigm for understanding Christ's work.[96] Therefore, the content of σκιὰν in 10:1 is most particularly the tabernacle, the priesthood, and the sacrifices.[97] To these matters the discussion will now turn.

The point of the following section is first to demonstrate that eschatology and not Platonism is in view in this context. Subsequently, the tabernacle, priesthood and sacrifices will be explored as to how Hebrews views them as shadows of the ministry of Christ. When understood in this light, Hebrews' theology of the law comes more clearly into view.

Εἰκών and Σκιά

The matter of the writer's philosophical perspective has been articulated at various points already,[98] thus what remains here is to assert the present writer's

---

[94]A survey of scholarship (as well as modern English translations, compare the NASB, ESV, RSV, NKJV, NRSV, and NET translations with the NIV) reinforces the point made here that 10:1 is translated (and interpreted) in different ways, yet there is little dialogue concerning this matter.

[95]Such an understanding as the whole law being a shadow (rather than possessing a shadow) leads some scholars such as Attridge to the understandable conclusion that the whole law has therefore been abrogated in full (Attridge, *Hebrews*, 269-72). Yet the writer of Hebrews says that that the law "has" or "possesses" a shadow (using the participle ἔχων) of the "good things," which are defined here as the NC blessings and all they entail. Bayes makes this same observation (Bayes, *Weakness*, 186). Should Hebrews have wanted to say that the law itself in its entirety *is* the shadow, then such would have been easy to do. Yet as has been argued in the present study, Hebrews' theology of the law is more complex than mere discontinuity. In contrast to scholars such as Attridge, Hughes' line of argumentation follows the distinction made here— specifically for the writer of Hebrews the *cultus* is the shadow in the law, and thus the law as a whole is not the shadow (see also P. E. Hughes, *Hebrews*, 389-404, esp. 393).

[96]John M. Scholer, *Proleptic Priests: Priesthood in the Epistle to the Hebrews*, JSNTSS 49 (Sheffield: JSOT, 1991), 95.

[97]Lindars rightly asserts that the earthly phenomena of the sacrificial system are "temporary manifestations of God's *intentions*," and that Hebrews treats the cultus seriously as God's preparatory revelation that "gives a proper basis for understanding the nature of sacrifice" (Lindars, *Theology*, 51).

[98]See above, chapters 4 and 5.

understanding of these terms in 10:1. Fundamentally, the question is whether or not the writer of Hebrews envisions the cultus as the "shadows" that dance on the wall of the cave as seen in Plato's *Republic*. If true, then the meaning would be that the heavenly realities give the shadows their form, and that the shadows merely correspond to the heavenly liturgy.[99] Thus the main idea would be a "below" and "above" and not "first" and "second," the latter being more historically and eschatologically focused. However, for Hebrews, the contrast between εἰκών and σκιά is not the *higher* and *lower* Platonic forms and particulars, but rather between the *old* and the *new* (eschatology).

Though the terms themselves εἰκών and σκιά can have Platonic overtones,[100] the outlook here is one of primitive Jewish Christian eschatology; the writer of Hebrews seems to be using such terms without the philosophical baggage of Platonism.[101] Such an understanding concludes that the σκιά points *historically forward* toward the εἰκών, but the shadow is not the actual form itself (10:1).[102] Lane notes that σκιά is the foreshadowing of the good things to come, signifying something that is incomplete, and that the relationship is one of anticipation and fulfillment.[103] The cultus therefore points forward to its εἰκών in Christ's work. McComisky rightly observes that the sacrifices have

---

[99]See especially the aforementioned works of Ronald Williamson and L. D. Hurst, who convincingly deny the long-held Platonic position defended and most identified with Ceslas Spicq, Ernst Käsemann, and more recently Erich Gräßer and Gerd Schunack. This understanding significantly colors one's interpretation of 10:1. Though such a view has its modern supporters, it is becoming less accepted due to ongoing research. See George H. Guthrie, "Hebrews in its First-Century Contexts: Recent Research," in *The Face of New Testament Studies*, ed. Scot McKnight and Grant Osborne (Grand Rapids: Baker, 2004): 425-29. MacRae argues for *both* vertical as well as horizontal categories in Hebrews (George W. MacRae, "Heavenly Temple and Eschatology in the Letter to the Hebrews," *Semeia* 12 [1978]: 179-99), as does G. Vos (*The Teaching of the Epistle to the Hebrews* [Grand Rapids: Eerdmans, 1956], 55-58).

[100]See pp. 224-26 above. See also Philo, *Allegorical Interpretation*, 3.96, 99; idem, *Dreams* 1.206; idem, *On the Confusion of Tongues*, 69; idem, *That God is Unchangeable*, 177; idem, *On the Decalogue*, 82; idem, *On the Migration of Abraham*, 12. See Siegfried Schulz, "σκιά," in TDNT, ed. G. Kittel, trans. G. W. Bromiley (Grand Rapids: Eerdmans, 1972), 7:396.

[101]Williamson, *Philo*, 566-70; F. F. Bruce, *Time Is Fulfilled*, 81; Goppelt, *Typos*, 166-67; Barrett, "Eschatology of the Epistle to the Hebrews," 363-93, esp. 386; idem, "Christology of Hebrews," 110-27. Though Barrett has demonstrated that Jewish eschatology better represents Hebrews' background of thought, he still maintains that at times Hebrews is still "quasi-Platonic" (Barrett, "Christology of Hebrews," 123-25).

[102]Kittel notes that in Heb 10:1 εἰκών and σκιά are sharply distinguished. See Gerhard Kittel, "εἰκών," in TDNT, ed. G. Kittel, trans. G. W. Bromiley (Grand Rapids: Eerdmans, 1972), 2:395.

[103]Lane, *Hebrews*, 2:259-60.

"faded into the realities that they represented."[104] It is Christ's NC ministry and all that it entails that is the εἰκών; the cultus was in outline form what Christ is in reality, and it is only in the eschatological latter days (1:2; 9:10) that the outlines are understood. Thus, when "the good things to come" have arrived in the person and work of Christ, God fills up the shadowy outline of such things. "Such an interpretation would mean that the heavenly things do not cast their outline *beneath* them (the Platonic model), but that future events and entities cast their outline *ahead of* them (the apocalyptic model)."[105] Thus Christ "fills out" and completes the shadows of the OT cultus that is outlined in the law.

The Tabernacle as Shadow

Though the tabernacle itself is not a shadow in the same manner as the priesthood and the sacrifices (see below), attention should be given to the statement made in 9:9, "ἥτις παραβολὴ εἰς τὸν καιρὸν τὸν ἐνεστηκότα,"[106] and how it contributes to the overall discussion.[107] It was noted above that in 9:1-10 Hebrews focuses on the tabernacle (2-5) and the cultus of the tabernacle (6-10), and that these verses serve to put the discussion into a cultic framework. The priests enter into the tabernacle's first section (τὴν πρώτην σκηνήν), and the high priest into the second (τὴν δευτέρα) once per year according to the Day of Atonement ritual. Such divisions were designed to

---

[104]Thomas E. McComiskey, *The Covenants of Promise: A Theology of the Old Testament Covenants* (Grand Rapids: Baker, 1985), 85.

[105]Hurst, "How 'Platonic,'" 163. See also Vanhoye, *Old Testament Priests*, 208-09.

[106]An important matter is the antecedent for the feminine nominative singular pronoun ἥτις. The most natural referent is to σκηνῆς in v. 8, which many scholars affirm (see Moffatt, *Hebrews*, 118; Lane, *Hebrews*, 2:223-24; Attridge, *Hebrews*, 241; Ellingworth, *Hebrews*, 439). However, some have understood the antecedent of ἥτις to be the whole of what is described in vv. 6-8, its gender being attracted to the feminine παραβολὴ (Windisch, *Der Hebräerbrief*, 77; Bruce, *Hebrews*, 208; Michel, *Der Brief*, 307; Loader, *Sohn und Hoherpriester*, 164). The former view is more likely given that elsewhere in Hebrews the pronoun has a specific antecedent (see 2:3; 8:6; 9:2; 10:9, 11, 35; 12:5). Young is persuasive ("Gospel According," 201). Additionally, the grammatical referent for καθ' ἣν can either be παραβολη (in 9:9a, see Attridge, *Hebrews*, 241; F. F. Bruce, *Hebrews*, 206; Franz Delitzsch, *Commentary on the Epistle to the Hebrews*, trans. Thomas L. Kingsbury [Grand Rapids: Eerdmans, 1952, 2:70; Steve Stanley, "Hebrews 9:6-10: the 'Parable' of the Tabernacle," *NovT* 37 [1995]: 397), or σκηνῆς (9:8b; see Lane, *Hebrews*, 2:224; Peterson, *Perfection*, 258 n. 52), with no real difference in meaning.

[107]To the degree that there is historical correspondence between the earthly tabernacle and what it points to, there is a strong element of typology present. Ellingworth states that Hebrews seems to make no significant distinction between παραβολή, ὑπόδειγμα, and σκία (Ellingworth, *Hebrews*, 440). This then reinforces the point made here that in the theology of Hebrews, the tabernacle (and thus what takes place in the tabernacle) serves as a παραβολή or σκία of the better things now realized in Christ.

keep worshippers (and even priests) at a distance from the presence of God, due
to defilement.

Verse 8 begins the sentence which culminates in ἥτις παραβολὴ in 9:9a,
and states that the Holy Spirit makes known something that was previously
hidden concerning the tabernacle (τοῦτο δηλοῦντος τοῦ πνεύματος τοῦ
ἁγίου). The pronoun τοῦτο points forward to the content of 9:8b. The
tabernacle's divisions are now made clear in light of Christ's fulfillment of the
OT cultus. Further revelation in the son (1:2) has revealed something about the
construction of the tent itself previously hidden, and special insight concerning
the tabernacle is now available.[108] Michel notes that the entire arrangement has
meaning (Absicht und Kundgebung) that is assigned to it by the Spirit, and that
the word of the law, by the Spirit, speaks to us.[109] Lane summarizes the
meaning of the Spirit's disclosure when he states, "The Holy Spirit disclosed to
the writer that, so long as the front compartment of the tabernacle enjoyed
cultic status, access to the presence of God was not yet available to the
congregation."[110] While (ἔτι) the outer compartment had a valid status
(ἐχούσης στάσιν), access by the people to the Holy of Holies (the presence of
God) was not made known or evident (μήπω πεφανερῶσθαι), and access was
denied.[111] While the outer tent had standing, the time of reformation (9:11) and
the good things (9:11; 10:1) had not yet come. The time of correction (καιροῦ
διορθώσεως) has broken into the present age (τὸν καιρὸν τὸν ἐνεστηκότα),
and thus the NC has been inaugurated.[112]

---

[108]Hofius comments, "So lange dieses irdische Heilige im Unterschied zum
Allerheiligsten hat, 'als die von Gott geordnete Kultusstätte Bestand und Geltung hat,'
ist die himmlische Wohnung Gottes verschlossen" (Hofius, *Vorhang*, 62-63) and affirms
Riggenbach's thoughts on this point (see Riggenbach, *Die Brief*, 249). See also Michel
(*Der Brief*, 306) who writes concerning 9:8a, "Dies Zugeständnis gibt aber nicht der
Alte Bund von sich aus, sondern der Heilige Geist, der den Alten Bund recht zu
verstehen lehrt."

[109]Michel writes, "In dieser ganzen Anordnung des Kultus und Priesterdienstes liegt eine
Absicht und Kundgebung des Heiligen Geistes, der in Zeichen und Gleichnissen, und
doch anders, als die Juden das Wort des Gesetzes verstehen, zu uns redet" (Michel, *Der
Brief*, 306). He adds, "Der Heilige Geist ist also das lebendige Gotteswort, das auch
durch das Wort des Gesetzes zu uns reden kann." See also Gräßer, *An die Hebräer*,
2:132-33.

[110]Lane, *Hebrews*, 2:223. In addition, the meaning of σκηνή in v. 8 is identical to vv. 2,
6 which clearly refers to the "outer tent" of the two-part tabernacle. Contra Spicq,
L'Épître aux Hébreux, 2:253; Bruce, *Hebrews*, 208. On this question Young agrees and
observes, "The spatial reference in vv. 2 and 6 is incontestable and a shift to a temporal
idea in v. 8 would be unnecessarily harsh" (Young, "Gospel According," 200).

[111]Synge, *Hebrews and the Scriptures*, 27; Peterson, "The Prophecy of the New
Covenant," 76; Attridge, *Hebrews*, 240.

[112]Hofius, "Das 'erste' und das 'zweite,'" 276; Koester, *Hebrews*, 398; DeSilva,
Perseverance in Gratitude, 302. The two phrases are virtually synonymous, giving full

The tabernacle as a whole, with its divisions and especially the outer compartment, symbolized the cultus with its sacrifices that could not remove sin. It also acted to conceal the way into the inner sanctuary.[113] The first compartment symbolizes the OC and its institutions, while the second symbolizes the Holy of Holies, made accessible in the New (second) Covenant. Thus, the terms "first" and "second" here are eschatological as well as spatial.[114] The tabernacle was a παραβολή in that it pictured separation and segregation from the divine.[115] The worshipper who draws near to God is prohibited from acquiring the cleansing that is required (10:1). Distance—the result of ritual impurity from sin—is maintained in the tabernacle. Yet that distance has been erased in Christ (4:16), and thus all may draw near and receive cleansing and thus perfection.[116] As Isaacs notes, the destiny of the people of God is his presence,[117] yet such a destiny cannot be attained in the imperfect παραβολή, and as such the parable foreshadows the perfection that has come.[118]

As a result of the author's usage of the tabernacle and its divisions (both of compartments and sacrifices),[119] he is able to teach his readers about the heavenly sanctuary and to establish the framework for explicating Christ's offering which begins in force at 9:11. Given this pedagogical function, it stands as a type and comparison that points toward something eschatologically later and better, which, for the writer of Hebrews, is found in the priestly work of Christ.[120] There is something new to be learned about God's new work in

---

scope to the element of foreshadowing in παραβολή. See Ellingworth (*Hebrews*, 440-41; also Attridge, *Hebrews*, 241), who explains the interpretive options as well as the reasons for seeing τὸν καιρὸν τὸν ἐνεστηκότα and καιροῦ διορθώσεως as both referring to the Christian dispensation.

[113]H. Koester, "Outside the Camp," 310; Stanley, "'Parable' of the Tabernacle," 385-99.
[114]Young, "Gospel According," 201-02; Synge, *Hebrews and the Scriptures*, 26; Craig. R. Koester, *The Dwelling of God: The Tabernacle in the Old Testament, Intertestamental Jewish Literature, and the New Testament*, CBQMS 22 (Washington, DC: Catholic Biblical Association, 1989), 158.
[115]Spicq, *L'Épître aux Hébreux*, 2:254.
[116]Cleansing is essential to the writer of Hebrews' notion of the conscience, yet does not exhaust the idea. More is involved—such as the promise of 8:10 and 10:16 promised in the NC, as Peterson argues (Peterson, *Perfection*, 116, 132-40, 148, 150).
[117]Marie Isaacs, *Sacred Space: An Approach to the Theology of the Epistle to the Hebrews*, JSNTSS 73 (Sheffield: Academic Press, 1992), 205-19.
[118]John. H. Davies, *A Letter to Hebrews* (London: Cambridge University Press, 1967), 86.
[119]Stanley, "'Parable' of the Tabernacle," 395-99.
[120]Ibid., 390-91; see also Delitzsch, *Hebrews*, 2:66-67; Friedrich Hauck, "παραβολή," in TDNT, ed. G. Friedrich, trans. G. W. Bromiley (Grand Rapids: Eerdmans, 1967), 5:572; Goppelt, *Typos*, 176-77.

Christ, in light of the illumination granted by the Holy Spirit (9:8). It is by looking at the tabernacle with such Spirit-endowed illumination and understanding that one gains this insight, and as such, the tabernacle is rightly referred to as a παραβολή in 9:9. With such understanding, the writer of Hebrews explores the correspondence between the old and the new and uses the tabernacle to teach his audience about what God has done in the son in the present time of reformation (9:10).[121] The tabernacle corresponds to the "greater and more perfect tabernacle" (9:11) through which Christ entered into heaven itself (9:24) as the high priest of the NC.[122] This emphasis on using the old to teach about the new (the pedagogical function of the cultus) plays an essential role in 9:1-10:18, and such is no more evident than in the expression, "ἥτις παραβολὴ εἰς τὸν καιρὸν τὸν ἐνεστηκότα."

The Priests and Sacrifices as Shadow

The Levitical priesthood and the sacrifices foreshadowed the good things that have come in Christ. The concept of the priesthood and sacrifice issues from the outset of the epistle (1:3), and plays a central role throughout the exposition of 7:1-10:18.[123] The former priests are compared and contrasted to Christ the high priest, yet there is a new form of comparison in Hebrews 9 that was anticipated in 5:1, 7:27, and 8:3. Utilizing the Day of Atonement ritual (9:7, 11-14) as well as the covenant-inauguration ritual (9:15-22),[124] the writer of Hebrews sees in the former priests (especially the high priest) and sacrifices a correspondence in shadow form of the priestly activities of Christ. There is thus an instructive connection and correspondence (as well as escalation) between the old and new.[125] The priestly duties pointed forward to the true and eternal priest whose ministry of mediation and (self) sacrifice (10:5-10) would ultimately be what theirs was only in outline form. Therefore, there is both correspondence and contrast.

The good things (τῶν ἀγαθῶν) in 10:1 are outlined in the priestly cultic ministry, and consist of the full salvation and all of the blessings of the new age as prefigured in the earthly tabernacle and its priests and sacrifices. What Christ

---

[121]Stanley, "'Parable' of the Tabernacle," 391, 394, 399. He concludes that there are two levels of correspondence in the παραβολή: the outer tent is to the Holy of Holies what the earthly tent is to the heavenly tent, and the daily sacrifices are to the Yom Kippur sacrifices as the Levitical sacrifices are to the sacrifice of Christ (398).

[122]For the several exegetical difficulties in 9:11-12 and 9:23-24, see the exegetical overview section above.

[123]Recall the point made in chapters 3 and 5 concerning Heb 8:1, viz., that priesthood is "the main point" or "the main thing" (κεφάλαιον).

[124]See Joslin, "Christ Bore the Sins of Many," 82.

[125]In a very real sense, παραβολή in 9:9 applies to the priests as well as the sacrifices by extension, since it is not just the construction of the tabernacle that is symbolic (though it is), but also what occurs within the tabernacle (i.e., the priestly sacrificial service).

accomplished as the high priest (9:11-12, 14, 23-24, 26) and covenant mediator (7:22; 8:6; 9:15) was outlined in the old cultus (9:15-22), and it is in and through the cultus that the writer of Hebrews and his audience can ascertain the NC's "good things" and how they have been procured by Christ. For Hebrews, the most direct route for understanding the work of Christ is to see him as the consummation and fulfillment of what the old cultus represented and anticipated. Redemption, forgiveness, unimpeded access to the divine, sanctification, purification, and perfection of the conscience (etc.) all have the common denominator that they were foreshadowed long before the high priestly work of Christ was accomplished in the time of reformation (9:10).[126] Thus 10:1 asserts a certain level of anticipation and expectation of something more and something future from the perspective of the OC priestly service. What the OC high priests and sacrifices were symbolically and temporarily, Christ *is*. They prefigured his ministry and its enduring effects.

In 9:11-12 Hebrews views the act of the Yom Kippur high priest (9:7) as establishing the basis for understanding Christ's sacrifice. For Hebrews, Leviticus 16 serves as the formal backdrop for understanding and expressing the meaning of Christ's death. Vanhoye notes that this day was the "supreme moment toward which the whole ancient worship was tending and...reached its climax."[127] It was necessary for the people to have a single mediator and representative from among them to go before the presence of God in order to procure cleansing and forgiveness on behalf of the people.[128] Yet whereas the Levitical high priest only entered the earthly tabernacle (itself a shadow), Christ enters the actual presence of God (9:12, 23) and procures that which only the former priests could obtain in shadow form.[129] The means by which this is procured is his own blood (9:12, 14, 23, 26) from his own self-offering on the cross (9:25; 10:5-10). This denotes a radical departure from the former priests on the Day of Atonement, in that Christ is both high priest *and* sacrifice (9:12, 26). Thus sacrifice and priesthood are joined uniquely in the ministry of Christ.

Verse 15 concludes that even though blood was offered for sin by the high priest (9:7, 13), that blood could not produce the eternal redemption (αἰωνίαν

---

[126]Cody, *Heavenly Sanctuary*, 139-41; Michel, *Der Brief*, 331; Lane, *Hebrews*, 2:260. This again highlights the horizontal (historical and eschatological) orientation of the writer of Hebrews.

[127]Vanhoye, *Old Testament Priests*, 185.

[128]Vos pointedly observes that by means of the Levitical high priest and its mediatory role, the people understand the need for priestly mediation. This mediatory role is central for priesthood; the people are identified with their priest since he comes from among them. The matter of identification with the people stresses Christ's incarnation being joined together with his priesthood (2:17; 4:14-15). See Vos, *Teaching*, 94-95.

[129]Young, "Gospel According," 204-05. Not only did the office of the high priest foreshadow the office of Christ's high priesthood, but the (incomplete) effects of this office foreshadowed the (completed) effects of Christ's high priesthood as well.

λύτρωσιν) lacking under the old and gained by Christ in the new (9:13-14, 22; 10:4). However, there is an external cleansing procured (9:13) in the OC sacrifice.[130] Yet such an external cleansing (ἀγιάζει πρὸς τὴν τῆς σαρκὸς καθαρότητα) merely foreshadows the internal cleansing that penetrates to the heart, mind, and conscience of the NC believer (8:10-12; 9:14; 10:16-17). As such, that which was external could not quiet the accusing conscience.[131] There was atonement in the Yom Kippur sacrifice, but due to the fact that it was that of an animal, human sin could not be effectively forgiven (10:4). Thus, forgiveness and cleansing from sin's impurity was foreshadowed but not effectively obtained in the priesthood and sacrifices. Since he has obtained such an effective cleansing and eternal redemption by his sacrifice, Christ is therefore the priest and mediator of the NC that is inaugurated on the basis of his blood (9:16-22).[132]

Conclusion

The point concerning the "shadow possessed by the law" in 10:1 affirms that God's purposes for the law were never frustrated.[133] To be sure, the law was insufficient to bring about perfection and salvation for the people of God, but nowhere in Hebrews is it stated that this was understood to be the law's purpose. Rather, in 10:1, the thesis put forth here is that the sacrificial system

---

[130]Cody, *Heavenly Sanctuary*, 170-80. F. F. Bruce is correct in his assertion that in Hebrews, the idea of "flesh" is non-Pauline, but rather "denotes the outer and physical element of the human make-up in contrast to one's inner being, or conscience" (F. F. Bruce, *Hebrews*, 215). Note the usage of σάρξ in 5:7 (ἐν ταῖς ἡμέραις τῆς σαρκὸς αὐτοῦ), referring to Jesus.

[131]Peterson, *Perfection*, 135. This is essentially the basis for the negative comments concerning the law in Hebrews. The cultus inevitably left the OC worshipper wanting and could not affect the heart.

[132]Lindars avers, "He will use the laws of the Day of Atonement to prove that the death of Jesus is rightly to be understood as a sacrifice for sin, and the account of the inauguration of the Sinai covenant to prove that it brings into effect the new covenant" (Lindars, *Theology*, 82; see also 84). See also Francis M. Young, "Temple Cult and Law in early Christianity," *NTS* 19 (1973): 330; and Lane, *Hebrews*, 2:241-43. Attridge states that the writer of Hebrews has blended Yom Kippur with the covenant-inaugurating event at Sinai, and calls this "theological chemistry" (Attridge, "Use of Antithesis," 9). What is clear is that Christ's solitary sacrifice becomes both the sacrificial blood-offering for atonement for sin (9:11-14, 15) as well as the blood that accompanies covenant inauguration (9:16-22).

[133]Frank Thielman, *The Law and the New Testament: The Question of Continuity* (New York: Crossroad, 1999), 125; R. A. Harrisville, *The Concept of Newness in the New Testament* (Minneapolis: Augsburg, 1960), 48-57; Simon J. Kistemaker, *Exposition of the Epistle to the Hebrews*, NTC (Grand Rapids: Baker, 1984), 272; Moises Silva, "Perfection and Eschatology in Hebrews," *WTJ* 39 (1976): 68; Lindars, *Theology*, 51-52; P. E. Hughes, *Hebrews*, 393.

prescribed by the law served as a parable and shadow of the work of Christ that is now made clear in light of the new revelation in the son (1:2) and by the Holy Spirit (9:8-9), and the limitations of the cultus now make sense in light of new revelation. It is self-evident that the outline is inferior to the form itself, and consequently the writer of Hebrews argues on the one hand for the insufficiency of the OC sacrifices while at the same time using those same sacrifices as the basis for his argument concerning the work of Christ.

Thus the conclusion drawn here can be simply stated: While the law-prescribed sacrificial system is insufficient to atone permanently for sins (negative statement), it serves as the fundamental mode of expression for understanding Christ's work since it foreshadows his ministry (positive statement).[134] The tabernacle, priesthood, and sacrifices were given as good gifts by God. They had both cleansing and atoning functions (9:9-10, 21-22), but were never designed to make the worshipper perfect, and this is the basis for the writer's negative evaluation. The cultic aspects in the spotlight of this section of Hebrews thus serve as a foil for the writer.[135] The old priests mediated, but were faulty and limited due to their own mortality and sinfulness. The sacrifices procured purgation, but not a decisive purgation that could reach to the conscience. They were repeated; Christ's is not repeated due to its sufficiency. The priests offered the blood of animals, while he offered his own blood for cleansing. They both mediate a covenant by means of blood. They entered the earthly holy of holies, yet Christ enters heaven itself. The people were brought to God only symbolically in the OC priesthood, but in the NC priesthood of Christ, there is the exhortation (based on theological exposition) to *actually* approach God and to do so with boldness and without fear (4:16;

---

[134]Contra Stylianopoulos (Theodore G. Stylianopoulos, "Shadow and Reality: Reflections on Hebrews 10:1-18," *GOTR* 17 [1972]: 215-30), who argues for a Platonic model for understanding 10:1 (as well as 8:5 and 9:23-24), and thus what is in view is not an eschatological foreshadowing in the cultus, but rather is "the true reality itself in the Platonic sense of an archetype or incorporeal model" (217, see also 218, 221, passim). Stylianopoulos contends with the findings of C. K. Barrett ("Eschatology of the Epistle to the Hebrews," 363-93), who, in the mind of Stylianopoulos, should be criticized for not giving enough recognition to the Platonic schema that Stylianopoulos feels is at work (Stylianopoulos, "Shadow and Reality," 218 n. 9).

Given such Platonic conclusions, and therefore "radical difference and separation" (218), it is no surprise that Stylianopoulos says not a single word about "laws on the hearts" in 10:16 in his article. This is a consistent trait of those scholars who maintain a Platonic/Philonic background for Hebrews, since such a view all but renders continuity impossible. If the Platonic dichotomy for which Stylianopoulos argues is indeed present in Hebrews, then the only conclusion can be a "sharp devaluation of the Law," since it is merely part of the Platonic particulars of old (Stylianopoulos, "Shadow and Reality," 228).

[135]Thompson, *Beginnings*, 104.

10:19). In short, they outlined and Christ fulfilled. Lindars summarizes the matter well when he writes, "everything that belongs to the Jewish sacrificial system for removing the barrier of sin has been done by Jesus in a way that makes access to God permanent."[136] Christ has thus procured the good things to come (τῶν μελλόντων ἀγαθῶν).

It is true that both the priesthood and its sacrifices foreshadowed Christ and the good things to come. Yet it is also true that the *effects* of the sacrificial system foreshadowed the good things to come. Though a true statement, it is not enough to say that the cultus was a shadow of the good things that have now come. One needs to be more specific—the good things that are now present are not only the NC cult prefigured in the OC, but also the *effects* of the new cultus outlined in the old. Just as the OC cult had effects, the NC cult has better and lasting effects. These effects (forgiveness, access to God, cleansing, etc.) were prefigured in the OC, being given in limited measure, and it is these effects that are essential in the writer's understanding of the good things that have now come in Christ.

Being that the tabernacle and its various cultic activities served as a παραβολή that has now been brought to light (9:8-10), there is therefore a positive assessment latent in 10:1. Without the cultus, Hebrews would not have a canvas on which to paint the portrait of Christ—the eternal high priest who has sacrificed himself for the forgiveness and cleansing of God's covenant people. The writer extrapolates from the OT the doctrine that is latent within the cultic symbols. Thus, the shadow that Christ casts back into the OT is seen most clearly in the cultus for the writer of Hebrews. Since the true form has come, the shadows have faded into the reality of Christ, and his superior work serves as a witness to Christian salvation.[137] Accordingly, Vanhoye is correct in his assessment of 10:1 when he asserts that the sacrificial system has a prophetic function, noting that the Levitical system is preparatory for the "definitive design."[138] Christ has fulfilled the sacrificial system. Thus, the pedagogical (and typological) function of the cultus is not only fundamental to

---

[136]Lindars, *Theology*, 60-61.

[137]William Manson, *The Epistle to the Hebrews: An Historical and Theological Reconsideration* (London: Hodder & Stoughton, 1951), 184; Peterson, *Perfection*, 145; Michel, *Der Brief*, 330-31; contra Moffatt, *Hebrews*, 135; Spicq, *L'Épître aux Hébreux*, 1:75, 2:301-02.

[138]Vanhoye, *Old Testament Priests*, 181. See also Stanley, "'Parable' of the Tabernacle," 389. Stanley argues that not only does the old teach about the new, but also that the new teaches much about the old as well (391). Therefore he asserts that though there is typological correspondence at work, there is more in the continuity between those things that correspond. The readers gain a better understanding of both the old and the new due to the close relationship between the two.

9:1-10:18; it is essential.[139] Therefore, 10:1 demonstrates both positive and negative aspects concerning the law.

Final Comments on 10:16-17

Before the present chapter is concluded, final attention should be given to the writer's use of Jeremiah 31:33-34 in 10:16-17. Both Jeremiah's and Hebrews' meaning of these verses were argued in chapter 5, therefore what remains is to draw conclusions based upon the reiteration of the Jeremiah text and to discuss two final points: the exegetical and theological importance of the repetition of Jeremiah 31:33-34 in Hebrews 10:16-17, and the alterations to the Jeremiah text in its recapitulation at 10:15-17.

Exegetical and Theological Importance of Hebrews 10:16-17

Though some have suggested that the Jeremiah text plays little or no key role in 9:1-10:18,[140] the opposite has been argued here. Though such an assertion perhaps (but not necessarily) might have more merit were there no repetition of Jeremiah 31 in 10:16-17, the fact of the repetition of Jeremiah 31 necessitates that the exegete not be satisfied with such dismissal.[141] The *fact* of the NC cannot be kept distinct from the *blessings* of the NC. Rather, as Lane writes, "the writer makes it clear that the preceding discussion of sacrifice and

---

[139]The present writer sees "typological function" and "pedagogical function" as having a fundamental relation. That which points forward typologically (the cultus) does so in a way that is pedagogically instructive. P. E. Hughes asserts, "The Mosaic [sacrificial] system was divinely instituted (3:2ff.; 8:5; 12:18ff.) and accordingly within the scope of God's beneficent purposes for mankind. But it was by nature preparatory, or propaedeutic, showing in particular the seriousness of sin, the reality of the righteousness of God, and the necessity of atonement" (P. E. Hughes, *Hebrews*, 393). See also Peterson, "The Prophecy of the New Covenant," 77; and Goppelt, *Typos*, 161-78. Contra Gerd Schunack, *Der Hebräerbrief* (Zürich: Theologischer Verlag, 2002), 135.

[140]See chapter 5 above. Recall, for example, the views of Schunack, Weiß, Frey, Gräßer, and Rendtorff, who maintain the view that essentially the Jer 31 text has little meaning for the writer of Hebrews, and is largely irrelevant to the discussion. This is squarely in contrast to the views put forward here as well as by Peterson, Kistemaker, Malone, Caird, Walters, France, Lane, McCullough, G. Hughes, and Longenecker, each for various reasons.

[141]Therefore the repetition of Jer 31 has *both* structural and exegetical/theological importance. It closes out the present section, and also reinforces the importance of Jer 31 for the author's exegesis and theology. See Spicq, *L'Épître aux Hébreux*, 2:310; Malone, "Critical Evaluation," 191.

priesthood is to be related to the prophecy of the new covenant,"[142] including the "subjective benefits" articulated by Johnsson and Lane. Rather than dismissing it as little more than a proof text, the NC text from Jeremiah 31 actually establishes the content of 9:1-10:18.

Though there is no mention of cultic activities in Jeremiah 31, it can be argued that no Jewish understanding of a covenant with God would omit cultic ideas. As such, in explaining what Jeremiah means and how such a new covenant is inaugurated, the writer of Hebrews expounds Jeremiah in terms of the cultus. Peterson ties Jeremiah and the cult together when he states that Hebrews "views the Old Covenant in those [cultic] terms and sees the work of Christ as *the reality towards which the cult and the prophecy were both pointing*."[143] In covenantal terms, there is no way that forgiveness of sins can be procured (8:12; 10:17-18) without the shedding of blood (9:22). Given such an axiomatic statement as that of 9:22, there seems to be little doubt that if Hebrews is to explain how sins are forgiven (as that which is promised in Jeremiah's prophecy), then he must do so in terms of sacrifice and cultus.[144] Thus, the writer of Hebrews explains Jeremiah 31 in these terms, which involves the tabernacle, priesthood, and sacrifice (9:1-10:14). The promised forgiveness is assured only since an eternal sacrifice (9:12, 14, 26) has been offered once and for all time (9:12, 26, 28; 10:10, 12).

Yet forgiveness of sin is not alone. Forgiveness of sins is granted to the individual, putting the person in a right relation with God; internalization of the laws produces obedience so that the person may *remain* in right relation to God. This is the full meaning of "I will be their God and they will be my people" (Heb 8:10). Thus, forgiveness of sin and obedience from a changed heart both form the foundation of the NC. Jeremiah first announces that it *will* happen; Hebrews announces that it *has* happened and precisely *how* it has come to fruition in 9:1-10:18.

---

[142]Lane, *Hebrews*, 2:268.

[143]Peterson, "Prophecy of the New Covenant," 77 (emphasis his). After the first citation of Jer 31 in Heb 8, Hebrews does not immediately address the positive promises within the NC (9:1-10 first establish the cultic context). However, the "fundamental point is made that the covenant that Jesus institutes and maintains is based on better promises and these are listed" (Peterson, *Perfection*, 132). He adds, "When a second, abbreviated citation from the same prophecy concludes the central exposition of the work of Christ (10:15-18), it is clear that the oracle is vital to our writer's thinking" (ibid.). See also McKnight (Edgar V. McKnight, *Hebrews-James* [Macon, GA: Smyth & Helwys, 2004], 186), who also notes that the repetition of the Jeremiah text makes it clear that both of the "better promises" of the NC are "foremost in the author's mind." Malone concludes, "The double use of Jer 31:31-34 in Heb 8:1-10:18 supports the view that 9:1-10:15 is an exposition and application of how the new covenant is fulfilled in Jesus Christ and is presently in effect" (Malone, "Critical Evaluation," 270).

[144]Contra Rendtorff, "Was ist neu am neuen Bund (Jer 31)?," 34.

Therefore, any mention of a covenant between God and people implies the notion of sacrifice and thus priestly mediation. This is exactly what is discovered in Hebrews' explanation of Jeremiah 31 and thus it is central to the discussion of 9:1-10:18. The shadow that the law possesses (10:1) comes into full view when Jeremiah 31 is illuminated in the light of Christ's NC work. The dual promises of the internalized law and forgiveness of sins enclose the whole of this section and are the essence of what it means to be part of the NC people.

Alterations to the Jeremiah Text:
Hebrews 8:8b-12 and 10:15-17

Finally, the importance of the Jeremiah text can be seen in the alterations made to the text for the sake of summary and emphasis.[145] Were its repetition merely a structural marker (indicating the close of an inclusio), then one would not expect to find alterations to the text. In addition, its repetition and the intentional alterations affirm the text's importance to the writer. From the initial quotation in 8:8-12, the author restates what amounts to an excerpt from 8:10, skips verse 11, and alters verse 12. Due to this summarizing of the NC promises, it is unconvincing to suggest that only 10:17 (forgiveness of sins) is important to the writer.[146] Concluding this section without the promise of the law on the heart in 10:16 was certainly possible for the writer, if indeed the initial promise of the law on the heart was as unimportant as Schunack suggests.

When comparing 8:8 with 10:15, one finds several changes.[147] First, when speaking of the new covenantal arrangement, 8:8 uses the term καινήν while 10:15 does not. Second, in 8:8 it is the Lord that speaks (λέγει κύριος), whereas in 10:15-16 it is the Holy Spirit who testifies to the Lord's speaking (Μαρτυρεῖ...τὸ πνεῦμα τὸ ἅγιον...λέγει κύριος). Third, whereas in 8:8 and 10 the covenant will be made with the house of Israel and Judah (τὸν οἶκον Ἰσραὴλ καὶ ἐπὶ τὸν οἶκον Ἰούδα...τῷ οἴκῳ Ἰσραήλ), in 10:15 it is made to the Christian community (ἡμῖν) and all for whom Christ has been sacrificed in 10:16 (πρὸς αὐτούς).[148] Fourth, in 10:16, the phrase "upon their hearts"

---

[145]See Kenneth J. Thomas, "The Old Testament Citations in Hebrews," *NTS* 11 (1965): 310. Additionally, Kistemaker notes that the reiteration of Jer 31:33-34 represents a summarization of and integration of the primary truths, and is characteristic of the author's exegetical method (Kistemaker, *Psalm Citations*, 129).

[146]So Schunack, *Der Hebräerbrief*, 112.

[147]See Appendix 9.

[148]Moffatt, *Hebrews*, 141. P. E. Hughes adds that the writer of Hebrews "is intent on emphasizing particular aspects of that prophecy for the benefit of those to whom he is writing" (P. E. Hughes, *Hebrews*, 403). For a helpful explanation of this expansion from Israel and Judah to the wider Christian Church, see Ware, "New Covenant," 68-97; esp. 91-97. See also Homer Kent Jr., "The New Covenant and the Church," *GTJ* 6 (1985):

(ἐπὶ καρδίας αὐτῶν) has been moved forward in the clause from 8:10 and the phrase τὴν διάνοιαν αὐτῶν has been moved to second in the order ("heart and mind" versus "mind and heart") in 10:16. Finally, in 10:17 the writer of Hebrews has added the phrase "and their lawless deeds" (καὶ τῶν ἀνομιῶν αὐτῶν). If the Jeremiah text were unimportant to Hebrews, it seems rather unlikely that (1) it would be repeated to begin with, and (2) that its recapitulation would be marked so many changes that round out the writer's argument.

Continuing, the repetition of the Jeremiah text in Hebrews 10 is much more positive in focus, omitting the statements concerning the sins of the Exodus generation. Rather, the two better promises (8:6) of the internalized law and the forgiveness of sins are distilled and crystallized in Hebrews 10. Kistemaker and Malone are helpful when they note the alterations in the text and argue that such changes are purposeful. In his lengthy study, Malone concludes that the editorial addition of the phrase καὶ τῶν ἀνομιῶν αὐτῶν in 10:17 "calls the reader to interpret the forgiveness of ἀνομιῶν...in terms of forgiveness from actual transgressions" of the same laws as those inscribed on the heart and mind in 10:16 (νόμους).[149] It is not merely sin (ἁμαρτιῶν), but disobedience to the laws (ἀνομιῶν) that God hates[150] (cf. 1:9) and will no longer "remember."

Therefore in Hebrews the idea of forgiveness also entails a positive inward change that produces obedience. The point is well made by McKnight that "lawless deeds" (ἀνομιῶν) is added in verse 17 in order to reinforce the promise just made in verse 16.[151] There is a connection between ἀνομιῶν and ἄφεσις in 10:18 that "prevents the elimination of obedience to God's laws following forgiveness."[152] "Lawless deeds" (ἀνομιῶν) are those that violate the Mosaic law, and as such it is transgressions of the Mosaic law that are forgiven,[153] which, as Malone rightly argues, has a direct correspondence to the νόμους that are internalized as an essential part of the NC. In other words, that which has been transgressed is now internalized on the hearts and minds of the NC people; there is a specific (and Christological) correspondence between the laws that are broken and those that are internalized in the NC (recall chapter 5).

Further, in his *Academisch Proefschrift*, Kistemaker asserts that the

---

289-98; Vanhoye, *Old Testament Priests*, 221; Koester, *Hebrews*, 435; DeSilva, *Perseverance in Gratitude*, 325. Rissi notes that one aspect of continuity is due to the fact that both covenant peoples comprise the "house of God" (Mathias Rissi, *Die Theologie des Hebräerbriefs: ihre Verankerung in der Situation des Verfassers und seiner Leser* [Tübingen: J. C. B. Mohr [Paul Siebeck], 1987], 122).

[149]Malone, "Critical Evaluation," 193.

[150]On the matter of God's wrath in Hebrews, and especially how it intersects with the atonement, see Joslin, "Christ Bore the Sins of Many," esp. 91-95.

[151]E. V. McKnight, *Hebrews-James* (Macon, GA: Smyth & Helwys, 2004), 233.

[152]Malone, "Critical Evaluation," 193-94.

[153]See for example the use of ἀνομία in Matt 5:21-22; 7:23; 23:23, 28.

rearrangement of καρδίας and διάνοιαν in 10:16-17 is not to be attributed to carelessness or a faulty memory on the part of the writer of Hebrews.[154] Carelessness and inattention are not attributes of the writer of Hebrews. Rather, Kistemaker avers that such a rearrangement of καρδίας and διάνοιαν points to "the importance of the word *law* and the word *heart* in the earlier part of the discourse. *Law*...signifies the inexorable pentateuchal law, which was given to the people on tables of stone." He adds, "If they who are sanctified have the laws put on their heart, and written upon their mind, they are bent on doing God's will. They are manifesting active obedience, for the law (i.e., the will) of God has become an internal entity."[155] Such a conclusion is in concert with the thesis presented here, though with the modification of "transformation" as detailed in chapter 5.

What is noteworthy is that Kistemaker does not attempt to redefine νόμος either as "covenant," or a generic idea of "God's will." Where he falls short is in his lack of comment concerning the NC people's new relation to the law since Christ has fulfilled it. Malone also bypasses this question largely by asserting that only the Decalogue is in view, and then discusses the matter of the Sabbath in an appendix. The question has been advanced here, it is hoped, by suggesting that for the writer of Hebrews the Mosaic law must now be viewed through the lens of Christ when speaking of the NC internalized laws, and as such there is continuity and discontinuity regarding specific νόμους, and this accounts for the balance of Hebrews' statements regarding the law. This is the Christological principle at work—yet precisely *how* this fleshes out in every matter of life is not explicitly stated in Hebrews.[156] However, DeSilva may be

---

[154]Kistemaker, *Psalm Citations*, 129. See also E. McKnight, *Hebrews-James*, 232-33.

[155]Kistemaker, *Psalm Citations*, 129.

[156]The most obvious reason is simply that the matter of the law is not the chief concern for the writer of Hebrews. It is enough that the general principle can be elucidated in these terms; he is clearly not concerned with fleshing out all of these specifics since his main concern is to demonstrate that Jesus Christ is the new and eternal high priest who has inaugurated a new and eternal covenant based on better promises, and who has offered a new and eternal sacrifice that is acceptable to God. To go back to the OC way of life is to regard Christ and his work as irrelevant. To convince his readers of this is his foremost pastoral concern.

Yet one does see hints of this in the practical exhortations in Heb 13. In his arguments for a third use of the law, Bayes finds evidence in Heb 13 for such an ongoing use of the law in the life of the Christian (Bayes, *Weakness*, 205). He writes that Hebrews "makes use of the law in instructing his readers about life in Christ," and finds numerous allusions to OT laws in this chapter (see also DeSilva, *Perseverance in Gratitude*, 285). See too the older work of Pink (Arthur W. Pink, *An Exposition of Hebrews* [Grand Rapids: Baker, 1954], 1105-07), as well as the more recent commentary of Kistemaker, each of whom assert essentially the same conclusions about Heb 13. Beneath the exhortations lies the law, the will of God, which is still relevant for

correct in his suggestion that the promise of the commandments on the heart of the people specifically resonates with the practical exhortations found throughout the epistle.[157]

Conclusion

These final two points reiterate the importance of the Jeremiah text in Hebrews, seen both in its recapitulation as well as the alterations made to the text. Since the author has distilled the NC text into two main features, it seems apparent that these encapsulate the "better promises" assured in 8:6 and are thus essential to the writer of Hebrews' understanding. Additionally, it has been demonstrated that the blessings of the law on the heart and divine forgiveness are inseparable. The worshipper is put into a right relationship with God by the sinner being forgiven for his disobedience to the law. Tethered to the assurance of forgiveness is the inward writing of the transformed law (as defined here) and renewal of the heart in order that obedience becomes the mark of the NC in contrast to the OC. When the law is understood in such a Christological manner, it is seen to play a positive role in the NC people and as such in Hebrews.

Conclusion

The emphasis in 9:1-10:18 is on Christ's *fulfillment* of the Mosaic law.[158] He has filled out the shadow of what the tabernacle, priesthood, and sacrifices outlined. In Hebrews' theology of the law, this fulfillment of the law now makes its "Christological internalization" a blessing of the NC people. Therefore, God's people are no longer under the law, rather the law, the written expression of God's will for his covenant people, is *within* them. This change

---

the NC believer. As was asserted above, the NC people should still look to the law as a signpost for the will of God, viewing it *through the lens of Christ's work* as God's will for his people in the NC age. An example of this is illuminated by Filson (Floyd V. Filson, *'Yesterday': A Study of Hebrews in the Light of Chapter 13*, SBT 2:4 [Naperville, IL: Allenson, 1967], 81), who contends that in 13:1-6 the animal sacrifices have been overtaken in the NC by sacrifices of praise.

[157]DeSilva, *Perseverance in Gratitude*, 285. See also p. 326 where he emphasizes the fact that "law on the heart obedience" is immediately demonstrated in 10:19-25. See also Lindars, *Theology of Hebrews*, 100, 101, 103.

[158]The conclusion must be stated this way since Hebrews does not differentiate between various parts of the law. When he refers to "law," what is in view is the whole law and how Christ has affected it. Therefore it is argued here that suggestions of Christ's fulfillment of the "ceremonial law" in contrast to "civil" or "moral" would be foreign to the writer of Hebrews. Rather, it is more accurate to assert that the writer of Hebrews sees the whole law through the lens of Christ, and such a "view" of the law entails discontinuity as well as continuity. In Heb 7-10 the focus is on the fulfilled cultus.

of preposition ("under" vs. "within") is one essential difference between OC and NC people and is the most important change regarding how the people relate to the divine law. In Christ's new and eternal covenant, this guarantees the obedience to God that never marked the OC people.

Nόμος in 9:1-10:18 is again a set of commands (9:1, 10, 22; 10:1, 8, 16) written in a book by Moses (9:19), and there is a distinct emphasis on that which governs the cultus.[159] Therefore, given the writer's focus on the sacrificial system and its inefficacy, the accent concerning the law is largely negative in 9:1-28. This is due to the writer's argumentation that the sacrificial system is insufficient to remove sin effectively. Therefore, for one to live again under the law and its cultus is to ignore what Christ has accomplished and to settle for that which neither satisfies the requirements of God nor the heart of man. Under the law, the worshipper is left in his impurity (10:4) and God still remembers sin. He is therefore left with an accusing conscience and smitten heart when the promise of obedient service through the NC's high priest and mediator is offered (8:10-12; 9:10, 14; 10:10, 14, 16). Man is left under the law and there is no solution to his plight if Christ is rejected. Thus the writer of Hebrews is understandably forceful in his argumentation.

Yet all is not negative, and in 10:1 and 10:16 positive elements were found. Regarding 10:1, the law's cultus foreshadowed and prepared the people for understanding the good things to come (τῶν μελλόντων ἀγαθῶν) that are now present in Christ (9:11-14; 10:10, 14, 15-18), who is the reality (εἰκόνα) to which they pointed and anticipated. As such, the cultus was never designed by God to deal effectively with sin and was thus always anticipatory and pedagogical. It was designed to stir the people to anticipate the actual form that would come in time, and to establish a framework for understanding the Messiah's work. Thus, the sacrificial system foreshadowed the cross of Christ, and was fulfilled in Christ.

Likewise, since there is fulfillment and completion in Christ, the writer reinforces the NC blessing in 10:16-18 that true forgiveness has been obtained. The promise of forgiveness is the basis that ensures that the law is no longer exterior to them, producing the heart-obedience seen in the obedience of Christ to the will of God (10:5-10). In its Christological fulfillment the law is transformed and engraved on the mind and heart producing obedience to God. Now the covenant people have both a new relation to God (forgiveness and cleansing resulting in unfettered approach), as well as a new relation to the law (transformed and internalized). Cleansing alone is insufficient; it must be accompanied by the positive act of the internalized law procuring the obedience of the NC people. Christ is the lens through which the law must be viewed and understood. Therefore, in 9:1-10:18 one sees Hebrews' complex understanding of the law that entails both negative and positive elements that yield both

---

[159]Windisch, *Der Hebräerbrief*, 66.

discontinuity and continuity.

CHAPTER 7

Conclusion

Introduction and Summary

At this point all that remains is to summarize the conclusions of the arguments put forward in these pages and to offer a few implications for the NC believer, as well as to posit future areas of possible research.

Chapter 1 explained the thesis of this monograph and the method for its development. Further, though too little has been said with regards to the law in Hebrews, several scholars from the past 150 years were cited that have in some fashion articulated their view of Hebrews and the law. Two broad categories could be identified: those who maintained that the law has no ongoing validity in the NC era, and those who maintain that there is ongoing validity for the law in the NC era.

Chapter 2 reviews five of the most important and relevant Jewish works of the period: the OT Apocrypha, the OT Pseudepigrapha, Josephus, Philo, and the Dead Sea Scrolls (1QS and CD) and then offers several conclusions concerning the law in Second Temple Judaism. First, the ancient literature demonstrates a high view of, and a high regard for, the law of Moses. Indeed, the law of Moses was consistently elevated to an elite status in the Judaism of the period. Second, νόμος overwhelmingly referred to the written law of Moses, the Pentateuch. More specifically, νόμος generally tended to refer specifically to the collection of commandments found in the Pentateuch, those given at Sinai. Third, the literature clearly indicates that the Mosaic law had inherent authority because of the common belief that God himself was its author and that he had given his law to the people of Israel through his servant Moses. His commandments were divinely authoritative and were thus to be obeyed. Fourth, evidence from the apologists and several Maccabean texts indicates that the commandments were authoritative in the day-to-day lives of Jewish laity. This observation does not suggest that all Jews were pious and law-keeping, but one has no reason to assume that Philo and Josephus willfully misled their readers or to assume that none or only a few were pious and law-keeping. In such ancient writings, the written law of Moses was regarded as the highest standard of ethics and central to life. In such writings, this expectation extended to the whole of the people. Fifth, Jewish piety of the period was directly connected to the law. If one were pious, then by definition he or she kept the commands of the law, even if at times doing so meant the penalty of death. The righteous (i.e., those who kept the law) could expect blessings, while those who were unfaithful to the law of God would reap judgment either in this life, in the eschaton, or both. Sixth, a common refrain in these writings indicates that the law of Moses was associated and even equated with wisdom. Finally, one should note that these ancient texts offer no identifiable parallels to the book of Hebrews regarding the cessation of the practice of any laws. (Even when the Qumranites could not or would not go to Jerusalem, they reinterpreted various "Jerusalem-specific" and/or "temple-specific" commandments, and thus did not regard those commandments as having ceased.) In contrast, the writer of Hebrews clearly believes that certain commands of the Mosaic law are no longer valid, in light of the Christ event. Conversely, in the ancient literature under investigation, the near-unanimous view is that the law was to be obeyed fully in all of its parts.

Chapter 3 focused on the matter of the literary structure of Hebrews with specific attention given to 7:1-10:18. After the proposals of Albert Vanhoye, Leon Vaganay, Ceslas Spicq, Wolfgang Nauck, Donald Guthrie, Harold Attridge, F. F. Bruce, and George Guthrie were put forward, this writer concluded for several reasons that of these scholarly offerings, the more recent proposal of George Guthrie provides the most persuasive approach to viewing the structure of Hebrews. It is Guthrie's emphasis on visually identifying, within his outline, the movement back and forth between exposition and parenesis that makes his work most helpful. The divisions of 7:1-10:18 found in chapters 4, 5, and 6 are thus mostly based on the divisions set forth by Guthrie and Lane, which in turn are quite similar to and largely proceed from the Vaganay-Vanhoye school of thought. Yet, it is George Guthrie who stands on the shoulders of both Vanhoye and Nauck, and his eclectic approach to the structure of Hebrews remains persuasive to the present writer.

Chapters 4, 5, and 6 are the exegetical and theological heart of the monograph, and there it was argued that the work of Christ has transformed the law, and this transformation involves both its internalization and fulfillment in the NC. In short, the law has forever been affected Christologically. When taken as a whole, what the writer of Hebrews envisions for the law in the NC is its transformation, and not simply its abrogation in full. It is now viewed through the lens of Christ, and as such there is transformation that involves fulfillment and internalization. There are continuous and discontinuous aspects of the law, and this continuity and discontinuity turns on the hinge of Christ.

Specifically, the fourth chapter (7:1-28) argued that the writer of Hebrews envisions a "change in the law" in the sense of "transformation." First, it was put forward that what the writer of Hebrews means in the axiomatic statement of 7:12 is that the law has been *transformed* in light of Christ. The phrase νόμου μετάθεσις does not mean "abrogation of the law in full," but "transformation of the law." Such a conclusion was based on lexical, exegetical, and theological considerations. This transformation involves the cessation of the priestly lineage requirement, and by extension the whole of the

Levitical priesthood. Thus, both priesthood and law are transformed in Christ. When Christ and the law intersect, radical changes occur that do involve cessation and abrogation, to be sure, but are not limited to or merely defined as such. Regarding the element of fulfillment, Christ has fulfilled what the office of priesthood always aimed to be. This was due to the fact that the priesthood, as a divinely-appointed office, has been overtaken and filled up by the new Melchizedekian priesthood of Christ.

Second, in Hebrews' argumentation of 7:1-28, one ascertains a certain level of dissatisfaction with the externality and weakness of the law and what it produces (an imperfect people). There is a latent need for something better. Third, in the context of Hebrews 7 it was shown that the meaning of μετάθεσις contains a strong element of cessation to go along with its primary element of transformation. The Levitical priesthood (and by implication its sacrificial system) has been fulfilled and thus has ended in Christ. Fourth, it was also asserted that the writer of Hebrews does not view the law merely and simply in negative terms, although the accent in Hebrews 7 is more negative than positive. When dealing with external matters of lineage requirements and the Levitical priesthood, there is an incompleteness and dissatisfaction rooted in the inability to produce perfection. Hebrews can, on the one hand, be critical of the law's inabilities to perfect the people (negative), yet on the other hand state that in the NC the law is transformed (positive), which entails its internalization (Heb 8) and fulfillment (Heb 9-10). Fifth, it was demonstrated that apart from Christ, the law itself was insufficient to perfect the covenant people and was external only, even though it was given to the people as a divine gift. In Christ, it has been transformed, with the emphasis in Hebrews 7 falling on cessation of the Levitical priesthood due to the presence of the new Melchizedekian priest. Yet the statement of 7:12 prompts the reader to the reality that more will be said concerning the law. The theme of perfection is linked only to the NC, in which νόμος plays a role in the changed hearts and cleansed consciences as the "Christologized law." Finally, if the law has been transformed in such a manner, then it opens the door to the law's playing a role in the NC believer such as its internalization in the NC believer, which produces an obedient people who have a true knowledge of God (8:10-12; 10:16-17). Such is the basis for chapter five.

Chapter 5 (8:1-13) argued that the νόμοι internalized in the heart is this transformed NC law. There seems to be nothing negative about the promise of "laws on the heart" and such having significant correspondence to the OC law in Hebrews 8. In these latter days, the law and how God's people relate to it has changed. As such, NC people should still look to the law as a signpost for the will of God and as a shadow that points to the reality that has come in Christ. Such a view does justice to the original intent of Jeremiah, as well as acknowledges the reality of the new and transformative work of Christ that the writer of Hebrews describes. In addition, this view understands νόμος to refer to the Mosaic commands divinely given to God's people, and therefore does not suddenly redefine νόμος in abstract terms. An original audience of converted Jewish Christians would have easily understood the promise of "I will write My laws on your hearts" to have an intimate connection to the OC commands, yet the writer of Hebrews views such commands as having been transformed by Christ's work. This explains how he can, on the one hand, refer to abrogation and on the other refer to internalization—Christ is the "filter" or "hinge," so to speak. Further, to sever the term "νόμους" in 8:10 from its most common referent with no explanation was argued in chapter 5 to be quite unlikely. Redefining it as "God's will" or "instruction" apart from any connection to the law's specific commandments is untenable and out of step with the term's usage in Hebrews (and Second Temple Judaism; see ch. 2). Again, the view here is consistent with the writer's hermeneutic in his appropriation of OT texts, and as such does no violence to the original meaning of Jeremiah 31, yet at the same time escalates all elements of the Jeremiah prophecy, including (even *especially*) the promise of the internalized laws. To use a musical turn of phrase, Hebrews 8 is Jeremiah 31 in a higher, Christological "key." The melody and harmonies are still there, but the "key" has changed. This therefore illumines the fact that the NC people are fundamentally different from the OC people. Whereas they were generally without faith and disobedient, even provoking YHWH to wrath, the NC people are transformed in heart and mind by the work of God in Christ.

Further, in Jeremiah, the law was promised "in those days" to be on the hearts of the NC people, yet the application of such a "better promise" (8:6; cf. 9:11; 10:1) could not be made without the fulfillment and transformation brought about in Christ. The law is no longer seen as a set of external regulations, but has been internalized as a blessing of God that renews and changes the heart. By viewing the law through the person and work of Christ, the law becomes an effective signpost for the NC people to know the will of their covenant-making and covenant-keeping God. It is no longer ruling *over* the covenant people, but through Christ it becomes an internal blessing and delight that evokes obedience from the heart. Such an idea is quite continuous with and flows from OT theology and is embodied in the perfect example of Christ, the one who obeys, delights in, and fulfills the law. Thus, the writer of Hebrews could speak of the law's inabilities to bring about perfection and the limits of its cultic requirements (external), and at the same time could affirm with Jeremiah 31 that in the NC there is a positive value ascribed to the law (fulfilled and internalized). These positive statements and the positive affirmations of 8:10 (10:16) occur when the law is seen in its relation to Christ and the NC. Christ (and his work) is the *hermeneutical principle for how NC believers understand and obey the commandments of God in these "latter days."* Thus, Hebrews' theology of the law turns on the hinge of Christ. The law could not produce perfection due to the weakness of the people and the OC arrangement. In keeping with Jeremiah's prophecy, a new and eternal covenantal arrangement was inaugurated that would not be deficient (8:10-13;

13:20). Yet in the NC the law is granted a positive function in that it is transformed, and this involves both its internalization in the believer and its fulfillment by Christ. Therefore, that which is internalized has significant correspondence to the Mosaic commandments, yet not direct (i.e., one-to-one) correspondence due to the fulfillment and cessation/annulment of such specifics as the cultus. The end and goal of the cultus is found in Christ.

Chapter 6 (9:1-10:18) focused on this matter of Christ's fulfillment of the cultus which itself foreshadowed the good things that have come now that the NC has been inaugurated by the eternal Melchizedekian high priest. He has filled out the shadow of what the tabernacle, priesthood, and sacrifices outlined. Given the writer's focus on the sacrificial system and its inefficacy, the accent concerning the law is largely negative in 9:1-28. This is due to the writer's argumentation that the law's sacrificial system was insufficient to remove sin effectively: for one to live again under the law and its cultus is to ignore what Christ has accomplished. If this is the case, then man is left under the law where there is no solution to his plight if Christ is rejected. Thus the writer of Hebrews is understandably forceful about the law in his argumentation of 9:1-28.

Yet all was not negative in this section. In 10:1 and 10:16 positive elements were found. The law's cultus foreshadowed and prepared the people for understanding the good things to come that are now present in Christ, who is the reality to which they pointed and anticipated. As such, the cultus was never designed by God to deal fully and finally with sin and thus was always anticipatory and pedagogical. Thus, the sacrificial system foreshadowed the cross of Christ, and was fulfilled in Christ. Since there has been fulfillment and completion in Christ, the writer reinforces the NC blessings in 10:16-17 that true forgiveness has been obtained. The promise of forgiveness is the basis that ensures that the law is no longer exterior to the covenant people. Now the exemplary obedience from the heart that was seen in the perfect example of Christ (10:5-10) can be duplicated in each member of the NC.[1] Christ is the example of obedience to follow; his indestructible life of heart-obedience to the will of God serves as an abiding example to the covenant people. The law is now transformed and engraved on the mind and heart, working to produce the kind of obedience to God seen in the life of Christ. The NC people have both a new relation to God (forgiveness and cleansing resulting in an unfettered approach to God as well as perfection/completion) as well as a new relation to the law (transformed and internalized). Cleansing alone is insufficient; it must be accompanied by the positive act of the internalized law such that the covenantal people of God live in obedience to him (ct. Heb 3-4). Therefore, in 9:1-10:18 one sees Hebrews' complex understanding of the law that entails

[1]Recall that this is not to suggest that what is in view is "sinless perfectionism," viz., that the NC believer would never again sin. See chapter 5, page 221.

both negative and positive elements that yield both discontinuity and continuity.

Contemporary Issues and
Further Research Possibilities

If the view of Hebrews and the law argued above is correct, then it provides plausible answers to a few matters that this writer has pondered for quite some time. First, for the NC believer, the OC revelation still has significant *practical* worth. Perhaps it merely has been a long-held misunderstanding of this writer, but the manner in which the OC commandments (and sometimes the whole of the OT) are spoken of at times today inevitably has led to an unspoken denigration of the OT revelation, which the writer of Hebrews would surely never endorse.[2] The law (and the entirety of the Hebrew Scriptures) is the revelation from God and thus still speaks to his NC people, yet it must be interpreted and applied via the NC revelation in Christ (Heb 1:1-4). He is the interpretive principle for how a NC believer reads the whole of the OT and applies the commandments in the present NC era. Now that the law is internalized, the NC believer can say along with the OC believer, "I love thy law! I delight in it!" (Ps 119, for example).

Second, if the view here is correct, then one of the litmus tests for those scholars who maintain some kind of continuity with the OC commands can be answered. Specifically, views (such as that which is presented here) that maintain some level of continuity are often challenged by the application of specific commands such as wearing of clothing comprised of more than one thread (Deut 22:11), or commands that regulate one's diet. In brief, this writer would suggest the following: based on the epistle to the Hebrews, *all* matters of purity have been fulfilled in Christ, and as such these requirements are no longer binding on the NC believer. This would include food requirements as well (cp. Acts 10:9-16). Such were given for the people's purity, yet Hebrews maintains that such purity requirements never yielded *true* purity, and thus drawing near to the presence of God was prohibited except by means of priestly representation, and then but once per year. Approaching the presence of God demands purity, and the purity that food and clothing requirements (etc.) pointed towards has come in the NC to all covenant members.

Third is the matter of the familiar three-fold division of the law (moral, civil, and ceremonial). Hebrews does not make such distinctions, although there is a specific emphasis on cultic matters in 7:1-10:18, to be sure. But rather than

---

[2]For example, when asked recently his view on the OT and specifically why he never taught it, a well-known and influential American pastor and author replied, "We are the New Testament Church, not Old Covenant Israel. I mainly use the Old Testament as illustration." This view of the Hebrew Scriptures is often, sadly, all too familiar.

attempting the unenviable (and impossible!) task of dividing out all OC laws into one of three categories, this writer suggests that all commandments (the law as a whole) be viewed Christologically (what is meant by "the lens of Christ's person and work"). Such a view then produces cessation of some of the commandments, a one-to-one trans-covenantal carrying over of others, and reinterpretation of still others such as the NC offering of sacrifices of praise and good works (13:15-16). The writer of Hebrews does not answer all such questions the reader might raise, rather he is content to leave his readers with a framework from which they can operate (again, the law and how it relates to the NC believer is not his central concern). This seems to be a plausible explanation and application of the data. In the greater picture of the whole Bible, love for God and neighbor (Deut 6:5; Lev 19:18—the basis for all biblical commands in both OC and NC), is still the heart of how the covenant people relate to God the covenant-maker, as well as to one another (Matt 22:37-40).

Fourth, the research here perhaps can be helpful in offering a new manner of understanding the difficult warnings of Hebrews 6:4-6 and 10:26-31. If it is true that the main purpose of the internalization of the νόμοι in the NC is the obedience of the people, and it is true that this NC blessing is a *divine* work accomplished by the covenant-maker himself, then is true apostasy and loss of salvation a viable interpretive option for the warning texts? Can human sin nullify the divine works of internalization of the νόμοι and the assurance of forgiveness (and the "divine forgetting" that accompanies forgiveness of sin in the NC)? In Hebrews 8:8-12 (10:16-17, cf. 18) there is a distinct emphasis on the work accomplished by God on behalf of the NC people which leads to obedience, in contrast to the OC people who did not continue/remain in the covenant and whom God rejected (8:9). Further, one must consider how the "indicative" informs the "imperative" of Hebrews' warnings. If "all sins and lawless deeds" have been forgiven and "forgotten" (and surely this means sins committed both before and after conversion) then does this mean "all sins *except one*" (viz., apostasy)? In short, if this NC work is a distinctly divine work, then the question is raised as to whether human sinfulness can finally and fully overturn and undo it. At minimum, the question of the NC blessings ought to be considered when addressing the question of the warning texts.

Finally, this view (and what is learned from Hebrews as a whole) is relevant for the Christian Church and for preaching. The Church should drink deep from the well of the תּוֹרָה (cf. CD 6:3-4) finding there the eternal wisdom of God. The OT is, to be sure, relegated to a secondary status in far too many of our modern churches, and the view put forward here has practical relevance for the preaching and teaching of the OT (even Leviticus!) in a modern NC context.[3]

---

[3]Thus, Hebrews is extremely helpful to the discipline of Biblical Theology in that it demonstrates *how* a true "Christotelic" biblical theology is possible. Hebrews ties

When Christ becomes the set of lenses, the NC people can then look to the OC for instruction on how to conduct their lives in conformity to God's unchanging standards of holiness. Such an understanding produces worship and exaltation in the covenant people that is continuous with the praises that resound throughout the OT and across the covenants (cf. Heb 11:39-40; 12:1).

A Personal Word

Given that this monograph is the first extensive study on this topic (as far as I have been able to ascertain from my research), a final personal word is offered here. Though I am confident in my work, I do think that the arguments made in these 270 pages will, on some matters, need emendation and/or refinement. In fact, I am fairly certain that further research, interaction, and theological musing will lead to enhancements of the present thesis. Even if the thesis put forward in this monograph is indeed refined in the future, I am fairly certain that the present study raises good questions that are rarely, if ever, addressed in Hebrews studies. If such questions lead to enhanced clarity of Hebrews' theology and thus New Testament theology, then these pages and years of work will have served their foremost purpose—to explain the words that have been spoken by God in these latter days in his Son, and therefore further the understanding of God's word by God's covenant people, the Church.

---

together the Old and the New as much or more than any other New Testament document, and does so in such a manner that the peaks and valleys of what God has spoken across the testaments are not planed and pressed. Rather, such contours are allowed to contribute to the complex texture of biblical revelation—a chorus in which both the melody and harmonies can be heard.

Appendix 1

Jewish Law-Obedience in the
Second Temple Period

On the whole, the average Jew of the Second Temple period did indeed seek to adhere to the commandments of the law.[1] Sanders avers that Jews in Palestine believed that they were to obey the law of Moses, and that "there was a world-wide feeling of solidarity among Jews" both in Palestine and the Diaspora regarding this issue.[2] Sanders states that this is a fact that is easily proved and argues persuasively. While he acknowledges that Diaspora Jews could not fully participate in temple worship, he asserts that they largely obeyed law commands such as to pay the temple tax and to come to the Jerusalem temple from abroad. Sanders also goes on to describe the "daily life of the ordinary Jew,"[3] their observance of the law of God[4] and how the cultus was both "simple and straightforward" for the average Jew.[5] Sanders' conclusions regarding daily obedience to the law are worth stating verbatim. He writes,

> [Laity] could study laws of sacrifice and develop theories about them, and some did so. . . . The laity could also study aspects of divine law that they themselves could control: prayer, sabbath, some of the subcategories of purity, planting, sexual relations and the like. Priests were the official authorities on even these domestic rules, but they could not *do* anything about the way most people kept them . . . . Just now I want to emphasize the degree to which ordinary people were responsible for knowing and observing the law in their private lives . . . it is . . . important that the Jewish law was internalized and individualized to a degree that sets Judaism apart from Graeco-Roman paganism.[6]

The particular issue of Diaspora Jews and law-keeping is taken up in Sanders' *Jewish Law from Jesus to the Mishnah*.[7] Here he explains how

---

[1]See E. P. Sanders, *Judaism: Practice and Belief 63 BCE-66CE* (Philadelphia: Trinity Press International, 1992), 47-51.

[2]Ibid., 47.

[3]Ibid., 119-45.

[4]Ibid., 190-240.

[5]Ibid., 191.

[6]Ibid., 191-92.

Diaspora Jews did in fact keep the law regarding purity, food, and offerings. Logically, therefore, *how* they kept these laws necessitates *that* they kept (or at least sought to keep) these particular laws articulated by Moses in the Pentateuchal law.

The point that the average Jew, both in Palestine and in the Diaspora, largely observed the Mosaic law is contested by W. D. Davies who states precisely the opposite. For Davies, the religious leaders adhered to the laws, but "The rest of the population was likely ignorant of the law and even indifferent to rules of cleanness and uncleanness."[8] This is also the view of Jacob Neusner in his *Reading and Believing: Ancient Judaism and Contemporary Gullibility.*[9] Neusner asserts that the masses typically did *not* keep the purity laws.

This claim of Davies' has also been assumed by Eduard Lohse in his work *The New Testament Environment,*[10] as well as that of David M. Rhoads in his *Israel in Revolution 6-74 C.E.*[11] However, what Davies lacks is evidence for this claim (Lohse and Rhoads offer none to speak of either). Sanders argues that the only evidence that could be used from this period to support this claim is found in the Gospel of John 7:47-49.[12] It states, "The Pharisees then answered them, 'You have not also been led astray, have you? No one of the rulers or Pharisees has believed in Him, has he? But this crowd which does not know the law is accursed."[13] Sanders correctly argues that it is difficult to build such a case on this singular statement. Sanders' evidence is much more persuasive to this writer, and it seems difficult to maintain the conclusions argued for by Davies, et al., especially given the absence of substantive counter-evidence.

Sanders contends, "No opinion could less well reflect the overwhelming impression given by ancient literature, both Jewish and pagan, than the view that ordinary Jews neither knew nor observed the law."[14] His view of the common Jew is persuasive and is based on primary sources from Judaism of the Second Temple period. He argues for a general Jewish observance and

---

[7]E. P. Sanders, *Jewish Law from Jesus to the Mishnah: Five Studies* (Philadelphia: Trinity Press International, 1990). See 255-308.

[8]W. D. Davies, *Jewish and Pauline Studies* (Philadelphia: Fortress, 1984), 3-26.

[9]Jacob Neusner, *Reading and Believing: Ancient Judaism and Contemporary Gullibility*, Brown Judaic Studies 113 (Atlanta: Scholars Press, 1986), 54-56.

[10]Eduard Lohse, *The New Testament Environment*, trans. John. E. Steely (Nashville: Abingdon, 1976), 80.

[11]David M. Rhoads, *Israel in Revolution 6-74 C.E.: A Political History Based on the Writings of Josephus* (Philadelphia: Fortress, 1976), 33.

[12]Sanders, "Law in Judaism of the New Testament Period," 263.

[13]On this text from the Gospel of John, see the comments of Leon Morris, *The Gospel According to John*, rev. ed., NICNT (Grand Rapids: Eerdmans, 1995), 383.

[14]Sanders, "Law in Judaism of the New Testament Period," 263.

reverence for the Mosaic law, and his thesis seems to be properly supported if even a bit *understated* at times due to the evidence he has marshaled in support of his claim.

In keeping the big picture in mind, it seems relevant to mention that the audience of Hebrews appears to be very interested in the law and its observance given that they wanted to return to Judaism and its laws and religious observances, if the prevailing understanding of Hebrews' audience and purpose is close to correct. Additionally, if the view here concerning the recipients of Hebrews is indeed correct, then Sanders' position is at least tacitly supported by Hebrews itself: if the readers of Hebrews were Jewish Christians, then it is logical that they would have had to know the law on some level, and to have embraced it as authoritative (at least on some level and at some point) *prior* to their turning to Christ. This is likely the case *if* it holds true that they are now in danger of returning to it for atonement and assurance.[15] The present work contends that the average Jew venerated the Mosaic law and in general followed *at least* the main aspects of the Mosaic law. Whether all did is unknowable, but from the present research it is concluded that there was a recognition of the validity of the Mosaic law for the Jewish people, even those in the Diaspora. This point permeates the literature of the Second Temple period.

---

[15]See chapter 1 for a brief discussion concerning the audience to whom Hebrews was written, as well as a list of scholars who maintain this widely-held view. See especially the argument of Lindars (Barnabas Lindars. *Theology of the Letter to the Hebrews* [Cambridge: University Press, 1991], 4-15), who asserts that the very reason Hebrews was written was so as to assure the readers that their sins had indeed been atoned for in Christ, and not in and by the sacrificial system.

Appendix 2

Evidence from Judith and
Wisdom of Solomon

In Judith, there is somewhat of an emphasis on the temple. Carey Moore notes that there is also a strong emphasis on Jerusalem, and it is assumed that the Jerusalem cultus is in full operation including the priests, altars, and sacrifices.[1] He notes, "In short, except for almsgiving and the baptism of Gentile converts to Judaism, virtually all the traditional Jewish practices of both the cultus and individuals are mentioned.[2] From the evidence at hand it seems safe to suggest that Judith assumes the practice of specific laws. Νόμος only occurs in 11:11-12 in which Judith is speaking: "Sin has them (the Jewish people) in its power, and they are about to enrage their God when they commit a sacrilege . . . they have decided to consume all that God in his laws [τοῖς νόμοις αὐτοῦ] has forbidden them to eat."[3] The people are said to be planning to eat their cattle, and Moore assumes that they will also drink the blood of the animals given that both their food and water supplies are exhausted. This appears to be a clear reference to the specific laws of cleanness found in Leviticus 3:16-17 and 17:10-14.[4]

P. R. Davies states that law-keeping is both for the nation (so that Israel would not be invaded) as well as for the individual (such as Judith) and gains divine favor.[5] He concludes that the necessity of strict obedience to the law is found in the tale of Judith. Davies writes, "The secret of national survival is rigid adherence to the divine laws, particularly the cultic laws."[6] Thus for Davies, law-keeping is for the good of the individual as well as the nation. Writing from a different perspective, E. P. Sanders would likely not dispute this general statement, since in his understanding of Second Temple Judaism, law-

---

[1]Carey Moore, *Judith*, AB, vol. 40 (New York: Double Day, 1987), 60.

[2]Ibid., 60-61.

[3]Ibid., 206. Moore's translation.

[4]Ibid., 210.

[5]P. R. Davies, "Didactic Stories," in *Justification and Variegated Nomism*, vol. 1, *The Complexities of Second Temple Judaism*, ed. D. A. Carson, Peter T. O'Brien, and Mark A. Seifrid (Grand Rapids: Baker, 2001), 118.

[6]Ibid., 117.

keeping has both individual and national components.[7]

In Wisdom of Solomon, there is little with regards to the law. There is no specific focus on the law, and it is mentioned only in passing (2:12; 6:4; 16:6).[8] The Mosaic law is not specifically mentioned in 6:17-20, but the love of wisdom is seen in obedience to "*her* laws." This, Blenkinsopp maintains, would have certainly included the stipulations of the Torah, but also finds a close correlation to Stoic moral philosophy.[9] Jack Sanders notes the elevation of the Torah in Wisdom of Solomon, citing 18:4, 9, in which the law is described as an "imperishable light," and that the people "with one accord agreed to the divine law"[10] as written in the Pentateuch. Here the reference is to the Mosaic laws of the Pentateuch, and as in other wisdom literature of the period the Pentateuchal law is associated with wisdom. David DeSilva agrees, noting that Wisdom of Solomon "promotes the wholehearted pursuit of that wisdom which begins with the reverence for God and for God's law, to which all are accountable."[11]

[7]For example, see E. P. Sanders, *Paul and Palestinian Judaism: A Comparison of Patterns of Religion* (Philadelphia: Fortress, 1977), 419-23.
[8]See Donald E. Gowan, "Wisdom," in *Justification and Variegated Nomism*, vol. 1, *The Complexities of Second Temple Judaism*, ed. D. A. Carson, Peter T. O'Brien, and Mark A. Seifrid (Grand Rapids: Baker, 2001), 224-25.
[9]Joseph Blenkinsopp, *Wisdom and Law in the Old Testament and in Early Judaism* (Oxford: University Press, 1984), 147.
[10]Jack Sanders, "When Sacred Canopies Collide: the Reception of the Torah of Moses in the Wisdom Literature of the Second-Temple Period," *JSJ* 32 (2001): 128.
[11]David DeSilva, *Introducing the Apocrypha: Message, Context, and Significance* (Grand Rapids: Baker, 2002), 127.

Evidence from Psalms of Solomon and Testament of the Twelve Patriarchs

Psalms of Solomon

According to R. B. Wright, *Psalms of Solomon* was written in the first century BC and consists of eighteen Psalms.[1] Concerning the usage and meaning of νόμος, the term occurs only three times (4:8; 10:4; 14:2) and reinforces certain findings in chapter 2.[2] E. P. Sanders notes that *Psalms of Solomon* does not specify commandments that are to be followed (in contrast to Jubilees), though law-keeping is certainly presumed.[3] *Psalms of Solomon* 14 makes this last point clear. It states that the Lord is faithful to "those who live in the righteousness of his commandments, in the law, which he has commanded for our life" (14:2). Note also Sanders' treatment of the *Psalms of Solomon* in his *Judaism: Practice and Belief*, where he argues that in the *Psalms* (along with *T. Mos.*) the Jewish people are expected to obey the law as the covenant people of God.[4] For Sanders, *Psalms of Solomon* (as well as *T. Mos.*) demonstrates "how passionately some Jews held these views: how fiercely they loved God" and how God "punishes sinners severely and chastises the righteous for their transgressions."[5]

Seifrid notes that salvation is granted to those who are pious (i.e., those who keep the law). He writes, "the behavior of the 'pious' is accorded a saving significance."[6] In short, the obedience of the 'pious' is said to bring blessing (see 2:33-37; 3:11, 12; 4:23-25; 5:18; 7:9, 10; 8:33, 34; 9:3-5; 10:5-8; 12:4-6;

---

[1]R. B. Wright, "Psalms of Solomon," in *OTP*, ed. James Charlesworth (New York: Doubleday, 1983), 2:639-70. Citations are from his translation. Evans suggests a date of 50 BC (Craig A. Evans, *Noncanonical Writings and New Testament Interpretation* [Peabody, MA: Hendrickson, 1992], 38).

[2]The original language was likely Hebrew. See Wright, "Psalms of Solomon," 640.

[3]E. P. Sanders, *Paul and Palestinian Judaism: A Comparison of Patterns of Religion* (Philadelphia: Fortress, 1977), 390.

[4]E. P. Sanders, *Judaism: Practice and Belief 63 BCE-66CE* (Philadelphia: Trinity Press International, 1992), 452-55, 57.

[5]Ibid., 457.

[6]Mark A. Seifrid, *Justification by Faith: The Origin and Development of a Central Pauline Theme*, NovTSup 68 (New York: E. J. Brill, 1992), 109-10.

13:6-12; 14; 15; 16:15). Yet the pious are not without sin. What sets them apart from the wicked, Seifrid avers, is the "discipline by God, which preserves them for salvation, rather than destroying them along with 'sinners.'"[7] For those who live in obedience to the law, it "can be regarded as the source of life."[8] Seifrid criticizes Sanders' use of *Psalms of Solomon,*[9] arguing that the covenantal nomistic ideas of "getting in" and "staying in" the covenant are absent, and that even the term "covenant" is rare. The dichotomy, Seifrid argues, is not covenantal people vs. non-covenantal people (Israel versus Gentiles). Rather, the contrast lies between the "pious versus the sinner,"[10] and finds this dichotomy throughout the *Psalms of Solomon.*[11] Seifrid concludes that being "pious" is directly connected with one's fidelity to the law (also in 1QS), and that eschatological blessing is "contingent upon personal righteousness."[12]

Similarly, Gathercole avers, "There is . . . a fairly consistent picture of a definite period or day of judgment at which the righteous will be vindicated with resurrection to eternal life."[13] Like Seifrid, he defines those that are righteous as those who live in obedience to the commandments of the Torah, citing 14:2.[14] This, too, is concluded by Winninge, even though such a statement stands in contrast to the overall thesis of his book.[15] In his comments on 14:2-3 Winninge writes, "The devout are firmly rooted and shall live by means of the Torah. Thus they will inherit everlasting life . . . righteousness is connected with the demand of living according to the Torah."[16]

Psalms of Solomon 14:3 is important, in that those who are righteous are said to live by the law forever, an apparent allusion to Leviticus 18:5. Such statements lead Gathercole to surmise that in *Psalms of Solomon* future life comes by the law and that "it is dependent upon obedience to the Torah . . . doing Torah is the precondition of future life."[17] He concludes, "God is portrayed as saving his people at the eschaton on the basis of their obedience" to the law.[18] There is a confidence for those who live in obedience to the

---

[7]Ibid., 121.

[8]Ibid., 122.

[9]See Sanders, *Paul and Palestinian Judaism,* 404-09.

[10]Seifrid, *Justification by Faith,* 129.

[11]Ibid., 122, 131.

[12]Ibid., 132.

[13]Simon J. Gathercole, *Where is Boasting? Early Jewish Soteriology and Paul's Response in Romans 1-5* (Grand Rapids: Eerdmans, 2002), 63.

[14]Ibid., 66.

[15]Mikael Winninge, *Sinners and the Righteous,* ConBNT 26 (Stockholm: Almqvist & Wiksell International, 1995), 119-20.

[16]Ibid., 119.

[17]Gathercole, *Where is Boasting?,* 67.

demands of the law. They "will be prepared for the restoration which is yet to come."[19] In addition to these, Elliott observes merit theology in 14:1-2 and makes the statement that on a fundamental level, mercy is legalistic for the writer of *Psalms of Solomon*.[20] He observes "a rather legalistic understanding of the purpose of God's law . . . one fulfills God's commandments in order to find life."[21]

Testament of the Twelve Patriarchs

Additionally, the *Testament of the Twelve Patriarchs* should briefly be mentioned. Bockmuehl notes that these writings have an explicit concern for Torah piety, including matters of the ritual law. The *Testament of Naphtali* 3:2-5 commands that one should not alter the law of God by the disorder of one's actions. Bockmuehl states, "The natural order, perceived in creation, calls for certain orderly patterns of human behaviour, which are also in keeping with the Law of God."[22] In slight contrast, H. C. Kee comments that in *Testaments* the law is seen as a virtual synonym for wisdom (citing *TLevi* 13:1-9), and that the idea of "law" moves more toward the ideas of conscience and moral ideals evident from nature. For example, note the condemnation of homosexuality in *Testament of Naphtali* 3:3-4.[23]

---

[18]Ibid., 90. Contra James D. G. Dunn, *The Theology of Paul the Apostle* (Grand Rapids: Eerdmans, 1998), 152-53.

[19]Mark A. Seifrid, *Christ, Our Righteousness: Paul's Theology of Justification*, NSBT 9 (Downers Grove, IL: Intervarsity, 2000), 23; idem, *Justification by Faith*, 61.

[20]Mark A. Elliott, *The Survivors of Israel: A Reconsideration of the Theology of Pre-Christian Judaism* (Grand Rapids: Eerdmans, 2000), 184.

[21]Ibid., 184 n. 211. For a discussion of the exclusivist soteriology found in the *Psalms of Solomon*, see 140-43.

[22]Markus Bockmuehl, *Jewish Law in Gentile Churches: Halakhah and the Beginning of Christian Public Ethics* (Edinburgh: T & T Clark, 2000), 102.

[23]H. C. Kee, "Testaments of the Twelve Patriarchs," in *OTP*, ed. James H. Charlesworth (New York: Doubleday, 1983), 1:775-828, esp. 779-80.

Appendix 4

Further Evidence from Josephus for
Jewish Obedience to the Law

In his essay, "The Law in the NT Period," E. P. Sanders argues that for Josephus, Jewish law covered all aspects of life (recall the citation above from *Against Apion* 2.174 [see also *Antiquities* 4.209-210]).[1] Concerning the overall objective of the *Antiquities* Sanders writes, "The moral of Josephus's Jewish Antiquities was to teach that people prosper who conform to the will God, by which he meant the law."[2] There are several lines of evidence that illustrate that by and large the Jewish people showed concern for following the law. Four are mentioned here in brief.

First, in his record of the appeal of Titus in *Jewish Wars* 6.126, Josephus notes that Rome allowed the Jews to execute Gentiles who ventured beyond the Court of the Gentiles. Rome knew of the temple laws that guarded its purity, and capitulated to the demands of the Jews that they be allowed to carry out the law which demanded the deaths of Gentiles who went beyond the proper boundaries, even if they were Roman citizens.

Second, in *Antiquities* 13.372-74, Josephus records the account of how one year at the Feast of Tabernacles the common people attacked Alexander the priest who was considered by them to be "unworthy." They shouted at him that he was not of fit lineage and that he was unfit to sacrifice or even hold the office. As a result the priest had six thousand of them killed.[3]

Third, during the pilgrimage festivals, scores of Jews came to the temple from all over Palestine and the Roman world (*Wars* 6.423-38).

Fourth, the Jews were well-known for their unique religious practices, commanded in the Mosaic law. For instance, the temple tax poured in from all over the Diaspora (*Antiquities* 16.172; 18.312-13).[4] Smallwood notes that even after the war the Jews were allowed to practice their Judaism, however, the

---

[1] E. P. Sanders, "Law in Judaism of the New Testament Period," in *ABD*, ed. David Noel Freedman (New York: Doubleday, 1992), 257-58.

[2] Ibid. 255.

[3] See also *Jewish Wars*, 2.7.

[4] See also E. Mary Smallwood, *The Jews Under Roman Rule from Pompey to Diocletian: A Study in Political Relations*, 2nd ed. (Boston: Brill, 2001), 344-45, 371-76.

temple tax was no longer collected given the destruction of Jerusalem.[5] To this could be added the practices of circumcision, Sabbath, food laws, and monotheism.

In short, the Jews were known for their practice of at least some of the specific laws (quantification is impossible), and thus this writer agrees with Sanders, "No opinion could less-well reflect the overwhelming impression given by ancient literature, both Jewish and pagan, than the view that ordinary Jews neither knew nor observed the law."[6]

---

[5]Ibid., 345.
[6]Sanders, "Law in the NT Period," 263.

Leon Vaganay's Structural Outline of Hebrews[1]

Introduction (1:1-4)

I. 1st Theme in One Section: Jesus Superior to the Angels (1:5-2:18)

II. 2nd Theme in Two Sections: Jesus, Compassionate and Faithful High Priest (3:1-5:10)
   A. 1st Section: Jesus Faithful High Priest (3:1-4.16)
   B. 2nd Section: Jesus Compassionate High Priest (5:1-10)

III. 3rd Theme in Three Sections: Jesus Author of Eternal Salvation, Perfect Pontiff, Great Priest According to the Order of Melchizedek (5:11-10:39)
   Oratorical precautions before embarking on the main subject (5:11-6:20)
   A. 1st Section: Jesus Great Priest According to the Order of Melchizedek (7:1-28)
   B. 2nd Section: Jesus Perfect Pontif (8:1-9:28)
   C. 3rd Section: Jesus Author of Eternal Salvation (10:1-39)

IV. 4th Theme in Two Sections: Perseverance in the Faith (11:1-12:13)
   A. First Section: Faith (11:1-12:2)
   B. Second Section: Perseverance (12:3-13)

V. 5th Theme in One Section: The Great Duty of Holiness with Peace (12:14-13:21)

Conclusion: Final Recommendations (13:22-25)

---

[1]See Leon Vaganay, "La Plan de L'Épître aux Hébreux," in *Memorial Lagrange*, ed. L. –H. Vincent (Paris: J. Gabalda et Cie, 1940), 269-77.

Albert Vanhoye's Structural
Outline of Hebrews[1]

1:1-4 – Exordium Introduction de l'Épître

(first announcement: 1:4)

I. 1:5-2:18 **Première Partie** (Situation of Christ)
1:5-14 (exposition): Son of God Superior to the Angels
2:1-4 (exhortation): Need to take seriously the message
2:5-18 (exposition): Brother of men

(second announcement: 2:17)

II. 3:1-5:10 **Deuxième Partie** (High Priest Worthy of
  Faith and Merciful)
A. Worthy of Faith (3:1-4:14)
  3:1-6 (exposition): Jesus worthy of faith,
  superior to Moses
  3:7-4:14 (exhortation): We should give him our faith

B. Merciful (4:15-5:1-10)
  4:15-16 (exhortation): Let us go to obtain mercy
  5:1-10 (exposition): He has shared our sufferings

(third announcement: 5:9-10)

---

[1]See Albert Vanhoye, *Structure and Message of the Epistle to the Hebrews*, SubBi 12, trans. J. Swetnam (Rome: Editrice Pontifico Istituto Biblico, 1989), 40a-40b; idem, *La structure littéraire de l'Épître aux Hébreux* (Paris: Desclée de Brouwer, 1963), 59; see also 283-85.

III. 5:11-10:39   **Troisième Partie** (Unique Value of the Priesthood
and of the Sacrifice of Christ)

   Preamble: 5:11-6:20 (exhortation)

  A. 7:1-28 (exposition): High Priest According to the order of
Melchizedek

  B. 8:1-9:28 (exposition): Made Perfect by His Sacrifice

  C. 10:1-18 (exposition): Cause of Eternal Salvation

   Exhortation finale: 10:19-39 (exhortation)

          (fourth announcement 10:36-39)

IV. 11:1-12:13   **Quatrième Partie** (Faith and Endurance)

  A. 11:1-40 (exposition): Faith of the Ancestors

  B. 12:1-13 (exhortation): Necessary Endurance

          (fifth announcement 12:13)

V. 12:14-13:18   **Cinquième Partie**   (The Straight Paths)
(exhortation)

13:20-21 – Conclusion de l'Épître

13:19, 22-25 – Mot d'envoi

George Guthrie's Structural Assessment of Hebrews[1]

As noted, the value of Guthrie's structure of Hebrews becomes more apparent when visualized. Due to the type of image file, the reproduction of Guthrie's structural outline is found on the following page. The writer apologizes for any lack of sharpness in the printed image.

---

[1]See George Guthrie, *The Structure of Hebrews: A Text-Linguistic Analysis* (Grand Rapids: Baker, 1998), 144. The depiction on page 285 is Dr. Guthrie's most recent (Autumn 2008) visualization of the structure of Hebrews. I would like to express my gratitude to Dr. Guthrie for his allowing me to reproduce his work here.

The Structure of the Book of Hebrews

INTRODUCTION: GOD HAS SPOKEN TO US IN A SON (1:1-4)

I. THE POSITION OF THE SON, OUR MESSENGER, IN RELATION
   TO THE ANGELS (1:5-2:18)

   A. The Son Superior to the Angels (1:5-14)

   ab. The Superior Son, to Whom all things are Submitted,
       for a Time Became Lower than the Angels (2:5-9)

   B. The Son Lower than the Angels (i.e., among humans) to
      Suffer for the "sons" (i.e. heirs) (2:10-18)

Warning: *Pay Attention to What We Have
Heard Through God's Superior Son (2:1-4)*

Jesus, the Supreme Example of a Faithful Son (3:1-6)

A Series of Exhortations on "The Rest":
   *The Negative Example of Those Who Did Not Listen to
      His Voice" (3:7-19)*
   The Promise of Rest for Those Who Hear His Voice (4:1-10)
   Warning: *Strive to Enter God's Rest or Face the Word of
      Judgment (4:11-13)*

II. THE POSITION OF THE SON, OUR HIGH PRIEST, IN
    RELATION TO THE EARTHLY SACRIFICIAL
    SYSTEM (4:14-10:25)

OPENING: HAVING A GREAT HIGH PRIEST,
Hold Fast and Draw Near
(4:14-16)

   A. The Appointment of the Son as a Superior High Priest
      (5:1-10, 7:1-28)

      1. Introduction: The Son Taken from Among
         Humans and Appointed According to the Order
         of Melchizedek (5:1-10)

A Powerful, Strategic Pause in the Treatment of Christ's
Melchizedekan Priesthood:
   *The Difficulty in Giving Advanced Teaching on the Subject: Their
      Immaturity (5:11-6:3)*
   Warning: *The Danger of Falling Away from Christian Faith (6:4-8)*
   The Author's Confidence in and Desire for the Hearers (6:9-12)

Transition: God's Oath, Our Basis of Hope (6:13-20)

      2. The Superiority of Melchizedek (7:1-10)

      3. The Superiority of Our Eternal, Melchizedekan
         High Priest, Found in the Oath of Ps. 110:4
         (7:11-28)

   ab. We Have Such a High Priest Who is a Minister in Heaven (8:1-2)

   B. The Superior Offering of the Appointed High Priest (8:3-10:18)

      1. Introduction: The More Excellent Ministry of the
         Heavenly High Priest (8:3-6)

      2. The Superiority of the New Covenant (8:7-13)

      3. The Superior New Covenant Offering (9:1-10:18)

         a. The Place and Practice of Old Covenant
            Offerings (9:1-10)

         b. The New Covenant Offering Superior as to
            Blood, Place, and Eternality (9:11-10:18)

CLOSING: SINCE WE HAVE A GREAT PRIEST,
Draw Near, Hold Fast, Consider (10:19-25)

Warning: *The Danger of Rejecting God's Word and God's Son (10:26-31)*
A Series of Exhortations on Endurance:
   *The Positive Example of the Hearer's Past and Encouragement to
      Endure to Receive the Promise (10:32-39)*
   The Positive Example of the Old Testament Faithful who Endured (11:1-40)
   Jesus, the Supreme Example of Endurance (12:1-2)
   Endure Discipline as Sons (12:3-17)
The Blessings of the New Covenant (12:18-24)
Warning: *Do Not Reject God's Word! (12:25-27)*
Practical Exhortations (12:28-13:19)
Benediction (13:20-21)
Conclusion (13:22-25)

Appendix 8

Text Critical Matters for
Hebrews 7:1-10:18

Hebrews 8:8

An interesting textual variant is found in 8:8. The question concerns the case of the pronoun αὐτός, whether the dative αὐτοῖς or the accusative αὐτούς is the original. Ellingworth rightly observes that the external evidence is rather evenly divided.[1] ℵ*, A, D*, I, K, P, Y, 33, 81, 326, 365, 1505, 2464, *al* latt co; and Cyr have the accusative (which could be taken grammatically with the participle μεμφόμενος), while 𝔓[46], ℵ[2], B, D[2], 0278, 1739, 1881, and 𝔐 have the dative (which could grammatically go with either μεμφόμενος or λέγει). Commentators and translators are divided, and the UBS[4] committee gives the accusative a rating of {B}.[2] Metzger and Ellingworth each note that in the immediate context the meaning is changed very little, since in the passage it seems clear that *both* the OC itself and the people are faulty. The people were faulty due to their consistent rebellion against God, and the covenant was faulty, not because of any failure on its part, but because it was always intended to be provisional. The citation of the *new* covenantal arrangement immediately following makes this point clear.

Reasonable arguments could be made for either reading to be original. For instance, given that the two pronouns vary only in one letter (υ vs. ι, or Y vs. I), it is conceivable that either could have been corrupted unintentionally by an error of eyesight.[3] Likewise, the text could have been altered intentionally due to grammatical or doctrinal reasons.[4] Therefore, should the reading be (1) "for finding fault with *them* he says" (accusative direct object of the participle), (2) "for finding fault with *them* he says" (dative direct object of the participle),[5] or

---

[1]Ellingworth, *Hebrews*, 415.
[2]Bruce Metzger, *A Textual Commentary on the Greek New Testament*, 2nd ed. (Stuttgart: United Bible Societies, 1994), 597.
[3]See for example Bruce M. Metzger and Bart D. Ehrman, *The Text of the New Testament: Its Transmission, Corruption, and Restoration*, 4th ed. (New York: Oxford University Press, 2005), 251-59.
[4]Ibid., 261-62, 265-68.
[5]BDAG, s.v. "μεμφόμαι."

(3) "for finding fault he says *to them*" (dative taken with the indicative verb)?

The reading preferred here is the accusative αὐτούς. Ellingworth notes, "The tendency to take αὐτοῖς with λέγει would have been an influence towards the dative, so αὐτούς is probably to be preferred."[6] In contrast, Lane argues for the dative on contextual and syntactical reasons. He writes, "If αὐτοῖς is taken with the verb λέγει, 'he says,' instead of with μεμφόμενος, 'finding fault,' the logical connection with the preceding verse is sustained."[7] Yet this is precisely the point. The dative does make very good sense—too much sense, in fact, and this writer suggests that it is not the harder reading. Lane is correct in that his interpretation of the data makes good sense, yet for that very reason could well be why a scribe would have changed it. The dative with the indicative verb is an easier reading.

Further, added weight for the accusative (*txt*) reading is merited when it is discovered that in Hebrews the specific verb form λέγει is never accompanied by a dative. Also, λέγει *without* an expressed object is not unusual (see 1:6, 7; 3:7; 5:6; 8:9, 10; 10:5, and 10:16). In short, if the dative going with λέγει were the original reading, this would be the only verse in Hebrews that uses λέγει with a dative. As such, translations (such as Lane's; cf. NET translation) that take it in this manner ("he says *to them*") are out of step with the writer's usual usage of λέγει. In contrast, the phrase "he says," "the Holy Spirit says," or "the Lord says" is fairly common and is the manner in which OT quotations are typically cited in Hebrews, and never with "he says *to them*" (neither λέγει αὐτοῖς nor αὐτοῖς λέγει as it would be here). As such, option #3 above is less likely.

Yet technically speaking, the dative is still textually possible, but grammatically speaking would go with the participle rather than the indicative verb (option #2 above). As noted above, the meaning and translation would be unchanged since the verb μεμφόμαι can take either a dative or accusative direct object. But as Metzger and committee concluded, "Observing the direction in which scribal corrections moved, a majority of the Committee preferred the reading αὐτούς."[8] Taking into account the comments of Ellingworth as well as Attridge,[9] the view here is that it is best to see it as functioning as the accusative direct object of the participle μεμφόμενος. Therefore it should be translated, "For finding fault *with them*, he says . . ." Contextually as well, the accusative seems likely, with God finding fault with "them" (αὐτούς), i.e., the people who were disobedient to the law and broke the covenant, having been led out of the land of Egypt by the hand of God (8:9; see 3:7-4:13). Thus, God takes it upon himself to remedy the chief problem of the people's disobedience

---

[6]Ellingworth, *Hebrews*, 415.

[7]Lane, *Hebrews*, 1:202.

[8]Metzger, *Textual Commentary*, 597.

[9]Attridge, *Hebrews*, 225.

by establishing another and better covenant based upon the better promises in verses 10-12.[10]

Hebrews 9:11

There are two textual matters worth noting in verses 11-14. The first is in verse 11, and concerns the *txt* reading γενομένων ("the good things *that have come*") and the variant reading μελλόντων ("the good things *about to come*"). The MSS are fairly evenly balanced. The *txt* reading is attested by ($\mathfrak{P}^{46}$), B, D*, 1739, it^d, syr$^{p, h, pal}$, Origen, *al*. The variant is found in ℵ, A, D^2, I^{vid}, 0278, 33, 1881, 𝔐, lat, sy^{hmg}, co, Eus. Modern scholarship tilts in favor of the *txt* reading, and Metzger and committee are fairly certain, giving it a {B} rating.[11]

Metzger suggests that the variant can be explained as an assimilation to the similar phrase found in 10:1. Modern English translations and many commentators are split on the matter. For the *txt* reading ("good things *that have come*") see NIV, RSV, NRSV, NEB, ESV; Westcott,[12] Attridge,[13] Weiß,[14] Lane,[15] and Gräßer.[16] For the variant reading ("good things *about to come*") see NASB, NASU, NKJV, ASV, KJV, NET; Moffatt,[17] Hegermann,[18] and Montefiore.[19] Given the likelihood of an assimilation to 10:1, γενομένων is preferable and fits well with the context and flow of the chapter.

Hebrews 9:14

In 9:14, the variants in question concern the *txt* reading ἡμῶν versus the variant ὑμῶν. Metzger and committee give the *txt* reading a rating of {C},[20] indicating uncertainty. The MSS are mixed and balanced: the *txt* reading is attested by A, D*, K, P, 365, 1739*, *al*, vg^{cl}, sy^p, bo^{pt}, Ambr. The variant by ℵ, D^2, 0278, 33, 1739^c, 1881, 𝔐, lat, sy^h, sa. In this instance, either reading yields an acceptable meaning to the verse. Metzger suggests that since the writer reserves direct address for the hortatory sections of the epistle, the balance tips in favor of the first plural (ἡμῶν). Thus internal evidence tips the balance in favor of the *txt* reading. The translations are split here as well. For ἡμῶν see NRSV, NIV,

---

[10]Westcott, *Hebrews*, 2nd ed., 220.
[11]Metzger, *Textual Commentary*, 598.
[12]Westcott, *Hebrews*, 256.
[13]Attridge, *Hebrews*, 244.
[14]Weiß, *Der Brief*, 15th ed., 464.
[15]Lane, *Hebrews*, 2:228-29.
[16]Gräßer, *An die Hebräer*, 2:143.
[17]Moffatt, *Hebrews*, 120.
[18]Hegermann, *Der Brief*, 177.
[19]Montefiore, *Hebrews*, 151.
[20]Metzger, *Textual Commentary*, 599.

ESV; for ὑμῶν see ASV, RSV, NKJV, NASB, NASU.

Hebrews 9:19

The question in 9:19 surrounds the phrase, μόσχων καὶ τῶν τράγων. NA[27] encloses καὶ τῶν τράγων in brackets, "indicating a certain doubt that they belong there,"[21] and thus the committee's {C} rating. All available MSS contain μόσχων, while others either lack καὶ τῶν τράγων ($\mathfrak{P}^{46}$, ℵ[2], K, L, Ψ, 0278, 1241, 1505, 1739, 1881, *al*, sy[(p)]), rearrange the order of μόσχων καὶ τῶν τράγων ([4, 2, 3, 1] D, 365, sa[ms]), or rearrange the order omitting the article ([1, 2, 4] 33, 𝔐, bo). The *txt* reading is well attested by external evidence (ℵ*, A, C, 81, 326, 629, 2464, *al*, lat, sa[mss]), but external evidence cannot answer the question. Internally, homoeoteleuton could account for the omission of the bracketed καὶ τῶν τράγων, or perhaps scribes sought to conform the phrase to that found in Exodus 24:5. The text is simply uncertain, and many scholars opt for the shortest reading. For μόσχων only see the works of Attridge,[22] Lane,[23] Bruce,[24] and Koester.[25] See also the REB and NIV translations (against most English translations). Ellingworth is noncommittal.[26]

Westcott suggests that the addition of καὶ τῶν τράγων is problematic due to the fact that goats are not mentioned directly in the OT account.[27] The offering of a goat is never prescribed by the cultic commandments. Thus, I suggest that perhaps the shorter reading preferred by many might in fact *not* be the harder reading, since it would be easier to see why a scribe would omit a reference to goats, rather than including it since it is not found in the cultic prescriptions. However, an assimilation to 9:12 is still possible.[28]

Hebrews 10:1

The textual issue in 10:1 deserves a brief comment. $\mathfrak{P}^{46}$, standing alone, offers a creative reading that exchanges καὶ for οὐκ αὐτήν, which is most certainly not the original reading. The variant therefore reads, "the law, possessing a shadow of the good things to come *and* the image of the things," and identifies εἰκών and σκιά, as virtual synonyms rather than contrasting the two terms.[29]

---

[21]Ibid.
[22]Attridge, *Hebrews*, 253.
[23]Lane, *Hebrews*, 2:229, 232.
[24]F. F. Bruce, *Hebrews*, 219.
[25]Koester, *Hebrews*, 419.
[26]Ellingworth, *Hebrews*, 468.
[27]Westcott, *Hebrews*, 267.
[28]Metzger, *Textual Commentary*, 599.
[29]See Metzger, *Commentary*, 599-600; Lane, *Hebrews*, 2:254; and F. F. Bruce, *The Time is Fulfilled*, 78-80.

Metzger (et al.) rightly observes that the construction of the sentence mitigates against seeing the terms as synonymous. Lane suggests that the variant arose from a scribe who saw Platonism at work in the passage, in which εἰκών and σκιά are contrasted to reality and not to one another.[30]

---

[30]Lane, *Hebrews*, 2:254.

Appendix 9

A Comparison of Hebrews 8:8b-12 and 10:15-17[1]

Hebrews 8:8b-12	Hebrews 10:15-17
8 μεμφόμενος γὰρ αὐτοὺς λέγει· ἰδοὺ ἡμέραι ἔρχονται, λέγει κύριος, καὶ συντελέσω ἐπὶ τὸν οἶκον Ἰσραὴλ καὶ ἐπὶ τὸν οἶκον Ἰούδα διαθήκην καινήν,	15 Μαρτυρεῖ δὲ ἡμῖν καὶ τὸ πνεῦμα τὸ ἅγιον· μετὰ γὰρ τὸ εἰρηκέναι·
9 οὐ κατὰ τὴν διαθήκην, ἣν ἐποίησα τοῖς πατράσιν αὐτῶν ἐν ἡμέρᾳ ἐπιλαβομένου μου τῆς χειρὸς αὐτῶν ἐξαγαγεῖν αὐτοὺς ἐκ γῆς Αἰγύπτου, ὅτι αὐτοὶ οὐκ ἐνέμειναν ἐν τῇ διαθήκῃ μου, κἀγὼ ἠμέλησα αὐτῶν, λέγει κύριος·	
10 ὅτι αὕτη ἡ διαθήκη, ἣν διαθήσομαι τῷ οἴκῳ Ἰσραὴλ μετὰ τὰς ἡμέρας ἐκείνας, λέγει κύριος· διδοὺς νόμους μου εἰς τὴν διάνοιαν αὐτῶν καὶ ἐπὶ καρδίας αὐτῶν ἐπιγράψω αὐτούς, καὶ ἔσομαι αὐτοῖς εἰς θεόν, καὶ αὐτοὶ ἔσονταί μοι εἰς λαόν·	16 αὕτη ἡ διαθήκη ἣν διαθήσομαι πρὸς αὐτοὺς μετὰ τὰς ἡμέρας ἐκείνας, λέγει κύριος· διδοὺς νόμους μου ἐπὶ καρδίας αὐτῶν καὶ ἐπὶ τὴν διάνοιαν αὐτῶν ἐπιγράψω αὐτούς,

---

[1]The text is that of NA[27] (*Novum Testamentum Graece*, ed. Eberhard Nestle, Barbara Aland, Kurt Aland, Johannes Karavidopoulos, Carlo M. Martini, and Bruce M. Metzger, 27th ed. [Stuttgart: Deutsche Bibelgesellschaft, 1993]).

11 καὶ οὐ μὴ διδάξωσιν ἕκαστος τὸν πολίτην αὐτοῦ καὶ ἕκαστος τὸν ἀδελφὸν αὐτοῦ λέγων· γνῶθι τὸν κύριον, ὅτι πάντες εἰδήσουσίν με ἀπὸ μικροῦ ἕως μεγάλου αὐτῶν,	.·.
12 ὅτι ἵλεως ἔσομαι ταῖς ἀδικίαις αὐτῶν <u>καὶ τῶν ἁμαρτιῶν αὐτῶν οὐ μὴ μνησθῶ ἔτι.</u>	17 <u>καὶ τῶν ἁμαρτιῶν αὐτῶν καὶ τῶν ἀνομιῶν αὐτῶν οὐ μὴ μνησθήσομαι ἔτι.</u>

Bibliography

Commentaries

Avigliano, Don. *Clarifying Hebrews: A Commentary from Old Covenant Law to New Covenant Grace*. Modesto, CA: Oasis Publications, 1998.

Attridge, Harold. *The Epistle to the Hebrews*. Hermeneia. Philadelphia: Fortress, 1989.

Bénétreau, Samuel. *L'èpître aux Hébreux*. 2 vols. Vaux-sur-Seine: Edifac, 1989-90.

Black, Matthew. *The Book of Enoch or 1 Enoch: A New English Edition with Commentary and Textual Notes*. Leiden: E. J. Brill, 1985.

Bright, John. *Jeremiah*. Anchor Bible. Garden City, NY: Doubleday, 1965.

Brown, Raymond. *Christ Above All: The Message of Hebrews*. Downers Grove, IL: Intervarsity, 1982.

Bruce, Alexander. *The Epistle to the Hebrews: The First Apology for Christianity*. 2nd ed. Edinburgh: T & T Clark, 1908.

Bruce, Frederick F. *The Epistle to the Hebrews*. Rev. ed. New International Commentary on the New Testament. Grand Rapids: Eerdmans, 1990.

Brueggemann, Walter. *To Build, To Plant: A Commentary on Jeremiah 26-52*. Grand Rapids: Eerdmans, 1991.

Buchanan, George Wesley. *To the Hebrews*. Anchor Bible, vol. 36. Garden City, NY: Doubleday, 1972.

Calvin, John. *Commentaries on the Epistle to the Hebrews*. Edited and translated by John Owen. Reprint, Grand Rapids: Eerdmans, 1949.

Davies, John. H. *A Letter to Hebrews*. London: Cambridge University Press, 1967.

Delitzsch, Franz. *Commentary on the Epistle to the Hebrews*. 2 vols. Translated by Thomas L. Kingsbury. Grand Rapids: Eerdmans, 1952.

DeSilva, David A. *Perseverance in Gratitude: A Socio-Rhetorical Commentary on the Epistle "to the Hebrews."* Grand Rapids: Eerdmans, 2000.

Duhm, Bernhard. *Das Buch Jeremia*. Hanndkommentar zum Alten Testament. Tübingen and Leipzig: J. C. B. Mohr, 1901.

Edwards, Thomas. *The Epistle to the Hebrews*. New York: A. C. Armstrong, 1888.

Ellingworth, Paul. *The Epistle to the Hebrews*. Epworth Commentary Series. London: Epworth, 1991.

—— *The Epistle to the Hebrews*. The New International Greek Testament Commentary. Grand Rapids: Eerdmans, 1993.

Farrar, F. W. *The Epistle of Paul the Apostle to the Hebrews*. Cambridge: University Press, 1888.

Fitzmyer, Joseph A. *Tobit*. Commentaries on Early Jewish Literature. New York: Walter de Gruyter, 2003.

Goldstein, Jonathan A. *1 Maccabees: A New Translation with Introduction and Commentary.* Anchor Bible, vol. 41. Garden City, NY: Doubleday, 1976.

— *2 Maccabees: A New Translation with Introduction and Commentary.* Anchor Bible, vol. 41a. Garden City, NY: Doubleday, 1983.

Gordon, Robert P. *Hebrews.* Sheffield: Sheffield Academic Press, 2000.

Gräßer, Erich. *An die Hebräer.* 3 vols. Evangelisch-Katholischer Kommentar zum Neuen Testament. Zürich: Neukirchen, 1990-97.

Guthrie, Donald. *Hebrews.* Tyndale New Testament Commentaries. Grand Rapids: Eerdmans, 1983.

Guthrie, George. *Hebrews.* New International Version Application Commentary. Grand Rapids: Zondervan, 1998.

Hagner, Donald A. *Encountering the Book of Hebrews.* Grand Rapids: Baker, 2002.

— *Hebrews.* Good News Commentary. San Francisco: Harper and Row, 1983.

— *Hebrews.* New International Biblical Commentary 14. Peabody, MA: Hendrickson, 1995.

Haldane, James A. *Notes Intended for an Exposition of the Epistle to the Hebrews.* 2nd ed. Newport Commentary Series. Springfield, MO: Particular Baptist Press, 1860. Reprint 2002.

Hegermann, Harald. *Der Brief an die Hebräer.* Theologischer Handkommentar zum Neuen Testament 16. Berlin: Evangelische Verlagsanstalt, 1988.

Héring, Jean. *L'Épître aux Hébreux.* Neuchâtel: Delachaux & Niestlé, 1954.

Holladay, William L. *Jeremiah: A Commentary on the Book of the Prophet Jeremiah, Chapters 26-52.* Hermeneia. Minneapolis: Fortress, 1989.

Huey, F. B. Jr. *Jeremiah, Lamentations.* New American Commentary, vol. 16. Nashville: Broadman, 1993.

Hughes, Philip E. *A Commentary on the Epistle to the Hebrews.* Grand Rapids: Eerdmans, 1977.

Isaacs, Marie E. *Reading Hebrews and James: A Literary and Theological Commentary.* Macon, GA: Smyth & Helwys, 2002.

Kent, Homer. *The Epistle to the Hebrews: A Commentary.* Grand Rapids: Baker, 1972.

Keown, Gerald, Pamela J. Scalise, and Thomas G. Smothers. *Jeremiah 26-52.* Word Biblical Commentary, vol. 27. Dallas: Word, 1995.

Kistemaker, Simon J. *Exposition of the Epistle to the Hebrews.* New Testament Commentary. Grand Rapids: Baker, 1984.

Koester, Craig. *Hebrews.* Anchor Bible, vol. 36a. New York: Doubleday, 2001.

Kuss, Otto. *Der Brief and die Hebräer.* Regensberg: Friedrich Pustet, 1966.

Lane, William L. *Hebrews.* 2 vols. Word Biblical Commentary, vol. 47a. Nashville: Thomas Nelson, 1991.

Lenski, R. C. H. *The Interpretation of the Epistle to the Hebrews and of the Epistle of James.* Columbus, OH: Wartburg, 1937.

Lofthouse, W. F. *Jeremiah and the New Covenant.* London: SCM Press, 1925.

Longenecker, Bruce W. *2 Esdras.* Sheffield: Sheffield Academic Press, 1995.

Mackay, John L. *Jeremiah.* 2 vols. Mentor Commentary. Fearn, Ross-shire, Scotland: Christian Focus, 2004.

Manson, William. *The Epistle to the Hebrews: An Historical and Theological Reconsideration.* London: Hodder & Stoughton, 1951.

McKane, William. *A Critical and Exegetical Commentary on Jeremiah.* 2 vols. International Critical Commentary. Edinburgh: T & T Clark, 1986-96.

McKnight, Edgar V. *Hebrews-James.* Macon, GA: Smyth & Helwys, 2004.

Michel, Otto. *Der Brief an die Hebräer.* Kritisch-exegegetischer Kommentar über das Neue Testament 13. Göttingen: Vandenhoeck & Ruprecht, 1966.

Milligan, Robert. *A Commentary on the Epistle to the Hebrews.* Nashville: Gospel Advocate, 1975.

Moffatt, James. *A Critical and Exegetical Commentary on the Epistle to the Hebrews.* International Critical Commentary. Edinburgh: T & T Clark, 1924. Reprint 1952.

Montefiore, Hugh. *The Epistle to the Hebrews.* Harper's New Testament Commentaries. New York: Harper and Row, 1964.

Moore, Carey A. *Judith: A New Translation with Introduction and Commentary.* Anchor Bible, vol. 40. Garden City, NY: Doubleday, 1985.

— *Tobit: A New Translation with Introduction and Commentary.* Anchor Bible, vol. 40a. New York: Doubleday, 1996.

Morris, Leon. *The Gospel According to John.* Rev. ed. The New International Commentary on the New Testament. Grand Rapids: Eerdmans, 1995.

— *Hebrews.* Bible Study Commentary. Grand Rapids: Zondervan, 1983.

Murray, Andrew. *Holiest of All: An Exposition of the Epistle to the Hebrews.* Chicago: Fleming H. Revell, 1894.

Myers, Jacob M. *1 and 2 Esdras: Introduction, Translation and Commentary.* Anchor Bible, vol. 42. Garden City, NY: Doubleday, 1974.

Nicholson, Ernest W. *The Book of the Prophet Jeremiah.* Vol. 2. Cambridge: University Press, 1975.

Owen, John. *An Exposition of the Epistle to the Hebrews.* Rev. and abridged. 4 vols. Boston: Samuel T. Armstrong, 1811-12.

— *Hebrews.* Crossway Classic Commentaries. Wheaton: Crossway, 1998.

Phillips, Richard D. *Hebrews.* Reformed Expository Commentary. Phillipsburg, NJ: P & R Publishing, 2006.

Pink, Arthur W. *An Exposition of Hebrews.* Grand Rapids: Baker, 1954.

Plumer, William S. *Commentary on the Epistle of Paul, the Apostle, to the Hebrews.* New York: Anson D. F. Randolph, 1872. Reprint, Grand Rapids: Baker, 1980.

Riggenbach, Eduard. *Die Brief and die Hebräer.* Kommentar zum Neuen Testament 14. Leipzig: Deichert, 1922.

Schlatter, Adolf. *Die Briefe des Petrus, Judas, Jakobus, der Brief an die Hebräer.* Stuttgart: Calmer Verlag, 1950.

Schunack, Gerd. *Der Hebräerbrief.* Zürich: Theologischer Verlag, 2002.

Skehan, Patrick W., and Alexander A. Di Lella. *The Wisdom of Ben Sira: A New Translation with Notes.* Anchor Bible, vol. 39. New York: Doubleday, 1987.

Smith, Robert H. *Hebrews.* Augsburg Commentary on the New Testament. Minneapolis: Augsburg, 1984.

Spicq, Ceslas. *L'Épître aux Hébreux.* 2 vols. Paris: Gabalda, 1952-53.

Stone, Michael E. *Fourth Ezra*. Hermeneia. Minneapolis: Fortress, 1990.

Tasker, R. V. G. *The Gospel in the Epistle to the Hebrews*. London: Tyndale, 1950.

Tholuck, August. *A Commentary on the Epistle to the Hebrews*. 2 vols. Translated by James Hamilton. Edinburgh: Thomas Clark, 1842.

Thompson, J. A. *The Book of Jeremiah*. New International Commentary on the Old Testament. Grand Rapids: Eerdmans, 1980.

Weiß, Hans-Friedrich. *Der Brief an die Hebräer*. 15th ed. Kritisch-Exegetischer Kommentar über das Neue Testament, vol. 13. Göttingen: Vandenhoeck & Ruprecht, 1991.

Wenham, Gordon J. *The Book of Leviticus*. New International Commentary on the Old Testament. Grand Rapids: Eerdmans, 1979.

— *Genesis 1-15*. Word Biblical Commentary, vol. 1. Waco, TX: Word, 1987.

Westcott, Brooke Foss. *The Epistle to the Hebrews: The Greek Text with Notes and Essays*. 2nd ed. New York: Macmillan and Co., 1892.

Windisch, Hans. *Der Hebräerbrief*. Handbuch zum Neuen Testament 14. Tübingen: J. C. B. Mohr, 1931.

Winston, David. *The Wisdom of Solomon: A New Translation with Introduction and Commentary*. Anchor Bible, vol. 43. Garden City, NY: Doubleday 1979.

Books and Monographs

Albani, Matthias, Jörg Frey and Armin Lange, eds. *Studies in the Book of Jubilees*. Texts und Studien zum Antiken Judentum 65. Tübingen: Mohr Siebeck, 1997.

Anderson, David R. *The King-Priest of Psalm 110 in Hebrews*. Studies in Biblical Literature 21. New York: Peter Lang, 2001.

Aquinas, Thomas. *In Omnes S. Pauli Apostoli Epistolas Commentaria*. Taurini, Italy: Petri Marietti, 1917.

Arenhoevel, Diego. *Die Theokratie nach dem 1. und 2. Makkabäerbuch*. Walberberger Studien der Albertus-Magnus-Akademie 3. Mainz: Matthias-Grünewald-Verlag, 1967.

Aune, David. *The New Testament in its Literary Environment*. Library of Early Christianity 8. Philadelphia: Westminster, 1987.

Avemarie, Friedrich, and Hermann Lichtenberger, eds. *Bund und Tora: Zur theologischen Begriffsgeschichte in alttestamentlicher, frühjüdischer und urchristlicher Tradition*. Tübingen: J. C. B. Mohr, 1996.

Barr, James. *Old and New in Interpretation: A Study of the Two Testaments*. New York: Harper and Row, 1966.

Bartlett, John R. *1 Maccabees*. Sheffield: Academic Press, 1998.

Bateman, Herbert W. IV. *Early Jewish Hermeneutics and Hebrews 1:5-13*. American University Studies. Series VII, Theology and Religion 193. New York: Peter Lang, 1997.

Bayes, Jonathan F. *The Weakness of the Law: God's Law and the Christian in New Testament Perspective*. Carlisle, England: Paternoster Press, 2000.

Becker, Jürgen. *Das Heil Gottes. Heils- und Sündenbegriffe in den Qumrantexten und im Neuen Testament*. Studien zur Umwelt des Neuen Testaments 3. Göttingen, Vandenhoeck & Ruprecht, 1964.

Bilde, P. *Flavius Josephus Between Jerusalem and Rome. His Life, His Works, and Their Importance*. Journal for the Study of the Pseudepigrapha Supplement Series 2. Sheffield: JSOT Press, 1988.

Blenkinsopp, Joseph. *Wisdom and Law in the Old Testament and in Early Judaism*. Oxford: University Press, 1984.

Bockmuehl, Markus. *Jewish Law in Gentile Churches: Halakhah and the Beginning of Christian Public Ethics*. Edinburgh: T & T Clark, 2000.

Borgen, Peder. *Philo of Alexandria: An Exegete for His Time*. Supplements to Novum Testamentum 86. New York: Brill, 1997.

Borgen, Peder, Kåre Fuglseth, and Roald Skarsten. *The Philo Index: A Complete Greek Word Index to the Writings of Philo of Alexandria*. Grand Rapids: Eerdmans, 2000.

Broshi, Magen, ed. *The Damascus Document Reconsidered*. Jerusalem: Israel Exploration Society, 1992.

Bruce, Frederick F. *The Time is Fulfilled: Five Aspects of the Fulfillment of the Old Testament in the New*. Exeter: Paternoster Press, 1978.

Brueggemann, Walter. *An Introduction to the Old Testament*. Louisville: John Knox, 2003.

Carroll, Robert P. *From Chaos to Covenant: Uses of Prophecy in the Book of Jeremiah*. London: SCM Press, 1981.

Carson, D. A. *Divine Sovereignty and Human Responsibility: Biblical Perspectives in Tension*. Atlanta: John Knox Press, 1981.

Carson, D. A., Peter T. O'Brien and Mark A. Seifrid, eds. *Justification and Variegated Nomism*. Vol. 1, *The Complexities of Second Temple Judaism*. Grand Rapids: Baker, 2001.

Charlesworth, James H., ed. *The Old Testament Pseudepigrapha*. 2 vols. New York: Doubleday, 1983, 1985.

Childs, Brevard. *Biblical Theology in Crisis*. Philadelphia: Westminster, 1970.

— *Biblical Theology of the Old and New Testaments*. Minneapolis: Fortress, 1992.

Clements, Ronald E. *Old Testament Theology: A Fresh Approach*. Atlanta: John Knox Press, 1978.

Cody, Aelred. *Heavenly Sanctuary and Liturgy*. St. Meinrad, IN: Grail Publications, 1960.

Cohen, Boaz. *Law and Tradition in Judaism*. New York: Jewish Theological Seminary of America, 1959.

Cohen, Naomi G. *Philo Judaeus: His Universe of Discourse*. New York: Peter Lang, 1995.

Cullman, Oscar. *Christ and Time: the Primitive Christian Conception of Time and History*. Translated by Floyd V. Filson. Philadelphia: Westminster, 1950.

Danby, Herbert. *The Mishnah*. London: Oxford University Press, 1933.

D'Angelo, Marie R. *Moses in the Letter to the Hebrews*. Society of Biblical Literature Dissertation Series 42. Missoula, MT: Scholars, 1979.

Davies, W. D. *Jewish and Pauline Studies*. Philadelphia: Fortress, 1984.

— *Paul and Rabbinic Judaism: Some Rabbinic Elements in Pauline Theology*. 4th ed. Philadelphia: Fortress, 1980.

— *Torah in the Messianic Age and/or the Age to Come*. Journal of Biblical Literature Monograph Series 7. Philadelphia: Society of Biblical Literature, 1952.

Dawson, David. *Allegorical Readers and Cultural Revision in Ancient Alexandria*. Berkeley: University of California Press, 1992.

Demarest, Bruce. *A History of Interpretation of Hebrews 7,1-10 from the Reformation to the Present*. Beiträge zur Geschichte der biblischen Exegese 19. Tübingen, J. C. B. Mohr, 1976.

DeSilva, David Arthur. *Despising Shame: Honor Discourse and Community Maintenance in the Epistle to the Hebrews*. Society of Biblical Literature Dissertation Series 152. Atlanta: Scholars, 1995.

— *Introducing the Apocrypha*. Grand Rapids: Baker, 2002.

Dodd, C. H. *According to the Scriptures*. New York: Scribner, 1953.

— *The Bible and the Greeks*. London: Hoddard & Stoughton, 1935.

— *Gospel and Law: The Relation of Faith and Ethics in Early Christianity*. Cambridge: University Press, 1951.

Dunn, James D. G. *The Theology of the Apostle Paul*. Grand Rapids: Eerdmans, 1998.

Dunnill, J. *Covenant and Sacrifice in the Letter to the Hebrews*. Society for New Testament Studies Monograph Series 75. Cambridge: University Press, 1992.

Dussaut, Louis. *Synopse structurelle de l'èpître aux Hébreux*. Paris: Éditions du Cerf, 1981.

Elliott, Mark Adam. *Survivors of Israel: A Reconsideration of the Theology of Pre-Christian Judaism*. Grand Rapids: Eerdmans, 2000.

Ellis, E. E. *The Old Testament in Early Christianity*. Tübingen: J. C. B. Mohr, 1991.

— *Prophecy and Hermeneutic in Early Christianity*. Wissenschaftliche Untersuchungen zum Neuen Testament 18. Tübingen: J. C. B. Mohr, 1978.

Endres, John C. *Biblical Interpretation in the Book of Jubilees*. The Catholic Biblical Quarterly Monograph Series 18. Washington, DC: Catholic Biblical Association of America, 1987.

Evans, Craig A. *Noncanonical Writings and New Testament Interpretation*. Peabody, MA: Hendrickson, 1992.

Feinberg, John S., ed. *Continuity and Discontinuity: Perspectives on the Relationship Between the Old and New Testaments*. Wheaton: Crossway, 1988.

Feld, H. *Der Hebräerbrief*. Erträge der Forshung 228. Darmstadt: Wissenschaftliche Buchgesellschaft, 1985.

Feldman, Louis H. *Josephus's Interpretation of the Bible*. Los Angeles: University of California Press, 1998.

Filson, Floyd V. *'Yesterday': A Study of Hebrews in the Light of Chapter 13*. Studies in Biblical Theology 2:4. Naperville, IL: Allenson, 1967.

Fitzmyer, Joseph A. *The Dead Sea Scrolls: Major Publications and Tools for Study*. Rev. ed. Society of Biblical Literature Resources for Biblical Study 20. Atlanta: Scholars Press, 1990.

— *The Dead Sea Scrolls and Christian Origins.* Grand Rapids: Eerdmans, 2000.

Funk, Robert W. *Language, Hermeneutic, and Word of God: the Problem of Language in the New Testament and Contemporary Theology.* New York: Harper and Row, 1966.

Gathercole, Simon J. *Where Is Boasting? Early Jewish Soteriology and Paul's Response in Romans 1-5.* Grand Rapids: Eerdmans, 2002.

Gench, Frances Taylor. *Hebrews and James.* Westminster Bible Companion. Louisville: Westminster John Knox, 1996.

Goodenough, E. R. *By Light, Light: The Mystic Gospel of Hellenistic Judaism.* New Haven, CT: Yale University Press, 1935.

Goppelt, Leonhard. *Theology of the New Testament.* Vol. 2. Edited by Jürgen Roloff. Translated by John E. Alsup. Grand Rapids: Eerdmans, 1982.

Gourgues, Michel. *A la Droite de Dieu: Résurrection de Jésus et actualisation du psaume 110:1 dans le Nouveau Testament.* Paris: J. Gabalda, 1978.

Gräßer, Erich. *Aufbruch und Verheißung: Gesammelte Aufsätze zum Hebräerbriefe.* Beihefte zur Zeitschrift für die neutestamentliche Wissenschaft 65. New York: Walter de Gruyter, 1992.

— *Der Alte Bund im Neuen.* Tübingen: Mohr, 1985.

Gundry, Stanley, ed. *Five Views on Law and Gospel.* Grand Rapids: Zondervan, 1996.

Guthrie, Donald. *New Testament Introduction.* Rev. ed. Downers Grove, IL: Intervarsity, 1990.

Guthrie, George H. *The Structure of Hebrews: A Text-Linguistic Analysis.* Grand Rapids: Baker, 1998.

— *The Structure of Hebrews: A Text-Linguistic Analysis.* Novum Testamentum Supplements 73. New York: E. J. Brill, 1994.

Hagen, Kenneth. *A Theology of Testament in the Young Luther: the Lectures on Hebrews.* Studies in Medieval and Reformation Thought 12. Leiden: E. J. Brill, 1974.

Hanson, Anthony T. *Jesus Christ in the Old Testament.* London: SPCK, 1965.

— *The Living Utterances of God: The New Testament Exegesis of the Old Testament.* London: Darton, Longmann & Todd, 1983.

Harnisch, Wolfgang. *Verhängnis und Verheißung der Geschichte: Untersuchungen zum Zeit- und Geschichtsverständnis im 4. Buch Esra und un der syr. Baruchapokalypse.* Göttingen: Vandenhoeck & Ruprecht, 1969.

Harrington, D. J. *Invitation to the Apocrypha.* Grand Rapids: Eerdmans, 1999.

Harrisville, Roy A. *The Concept of Newness in the New Testament.* Minneapolis: Augsburg, 1960.

Hay, David M. *Glory at the Right Hand: Psalm 110 in Early Christianity.* Society of Biblical Literature Monograph Series 18. Nashville: Abingdon, 1973.

Hempel, Charlotte. *The Damascus Texts.* Companion to the Qumran Scrolls 1. Sheffield: Academic Press, 2000.

Hengel, Martin. *Judaism and Hellenism: Studies in Their Encounter in Palestine during the Early Hellenistic Period.* 2nd ed. Translated by John Bowden. Minneapolis: Fortress, 1981.

— *Judentum und Hellenismus: Studien zu ihrer Begegnung unter besonderer Berücksichtigung Palästinas bis zur Mitte des 2 Jh. v. Chr.* Wissenschaftliche Untersuchungen Zum Neuen Testament 10. Tübingen: J. C. B. Mohr, 1969.

— *The Son of God: the Origin of Christology and the History of Jewish-Hellenistic Religion.* Translated by John Bowden. Philadelphia: Fortress, 1976.

Hiebert, Edmond. *An Introduction to the New Testament.* Vol. 3. Chicago: Moody, 1977.

Hofius, Otfried. *Der Vorhang vor dem Thron Gottes.* Tübingen, Mohr, 1972.

Holwerda, David E. *Jesus and Israel One Covenant or Two?* Grand Rapids: Eerdmans, 1995.

Horbury, William, ed. *Templum Amicitiae: Essays on the Second Temple Presented to Ernst Bammel.* Journal for the Study of the New Testament Supplement Series 48. Sheffield: JSOT Press, 1991.

House, Paul R. *Old Testament Theology.* Downers Grove, IL: Intervarsity, 1998.

Hughes, Graham. *Hebrews and Hermeneutics: The Epistle to the Hebrews as a New Testament Example of Biblical Interpretation.* Society for New Testament Studies Monograph Series 36. Cambridge: University Press, 1979.

Hurst, L. D. *The Epistle to the Hebrews: Its Background of Thought.* Society for New Testament Studies Monograph Series 65. Cambridge: University Press, 1990.

Isaacs, M. *Sacred Space: An Approach to the Theology of the Epistle to the Hebrews.* Journal for the Study of the New Testament Supplement Series 73. Sheffield: Academic Press, 1992.

Jaubert, Annie. *La notion d' alliance dans le Judaïsme aux abords de l'ère chrétienne.* Patristica Sorbonensia 6. Paris: Éditions du Seuil, 1963.

Jeremias, Joachim. *Jerusalem in the Time of Jesus: An Investigation into Economic and Social Conditions During the New Testament Period.* Translated by F. H. and C. H. Cave. London: SCM Press, 1969.

Kaiser, Walter. *Toward an Old Testament Theology.* Grand Rapids: Zondervan, 1978.

Käsemann, Ernst. *Das wandernde Gottesvolk.* Göttingen: Vandenhoeck & Ruprecht, 1939.

— *The Wandering People of God.* Minneapolis: Augsburg, 1984.

Kistemaker, Simon. *The Psalm Citations in the Epistle to the Hebrews.* Amsterdam: Van Soest, 1961.

Kobelski, Paul. *Melchizedek and Melchireša^c.* Catholic Biblical Quarterly Monograph Series 10. Washington, DC: Catholic Biblical Association, 1981.

Köberle, Justus. *Sünde und Gnade im religiösen Leben des Volkes Israel bis auf Christum.* München: C. Beck, 1905.

Koester, Craig. R. *The Dwelling of God: The Tabernacle in the Old Testament, Intertestamental Jewish Literature, and the New Testament.* Catholic Biblical Quarterly Monograph Series 22. Washington, DC: Catholic Biblical Association, 1989.

Kümmel, Werner Georg. *Einleitung in das neue Testament.* Heidelberg: Quelle & Meyer, 1963.

Laansma, Jon. *"I Will Give You Rest': The 'Rest' Motif in the New Testament with Special Reference to Mt. 11 and Heb. 3-4*. Wissenschaftliche Untersuchungen zum Neuen Testament 98. Tübingen, Mohr Seibeck, 1997.

Lane, William. *Call to Commitment: Responding to the Message of Hebrews*. Nashville: Thomas Nelson, 1985.

Lausberg, Heinrich. *Handbuch der literarischen Rhetorik: Eine Grundlegung der Literaturwissenschaft*. München: Max Hueber, 1960.

Leeser, Isaac. *The Jews and the Mosaic Law*. Philadelphia: E. L. Carey and A. Hart, 1834.

Lehne, Susanne. *The New Covenant in Hebrews*. Journal for the Study of the New Testament Supplement Series 44. Sheffield: JSOT, 1990.

Levenson, Jon D. *Sinai and Zion: An Entry into the Jewish Bible*. Chicago: Winston Press, 1985.

Levin, Christoph. *Die Verheissung des neuen Bundes in ihrem theologiegeschichtliche Zusammenhang ausgelegt*. Forschungen zur Religion und Literatur des Alten und Neuen Testaments 137. Göttingen: Vandenhoeck & Ruprecht, 1985.

Limbeck, Meinrad. *Das Gesetz im Alten und Neuen Testament*. Darmstadt: Wissenschaftliche Buchgesellschaft, 1997.

Lindars, Barnabas. *Theology of the Letter to the Hebrews*. Cambridge: University Press, 1991.

Loader, William R. G. *Sohn und Hoherpriester*. Wissenschaftliche Monographien zum Alten und Neuen Testament 53. Neukirchen: Neukirchener, 1981.

Lohse, Eduard. *The New Testament Environment*. Translated by John. E. Steely. Nashville: Abingdon, 1976.

Longenecker, Richard N. *Biblical Exegesis in the Apostolic Period*. 2nd ed. Grand Rapids: Eerdmans, 1999.

Marcus, Ralph. *Law in the Apocrypha*. Columbia University Oriental Studies 26. New York: Columbia University Press, 1927.

Martínez, Florentino García, and Eibert J. C. Tigchelaar, eds. *The Dead Sea Scrolls Study Edition*. 2 vols. Boston: Brill, 1997, 1998.

McComiskey, Thomas E. *The Covenants of Promise: A Theology of the Old Testament Covenants*. Grand Rapids: Baker, 1985.

Ménégoz, E. *La théologie de l'Épître aux Hébreux*. Paris: Fischbacher, 1894.

Meyer, F. B. *The Way into the Holiest*. Grand Rapids: Zondervan, 1950.

Milligan, George. *The Theology of the Epistle to the Hebrews*. Edinburgh: T & T Clark, 1899.

Moore, George F. *Judaism in the First Centuries of the Christian Era*. Vol. 1, *The Age of the Tannaim*. Cambridge: Harvard University Press, 1927.

Morris, Leon. *New Testament Theology*. Grand Rapids: Zondervan, 1986.

Müller, Klaus. *Tora für die Völker*. Studien zu Kirche und Israel 15. Berlin: Inst. Kirche und Judentum, 1994.

Murphy, Frederick James. *The Structure and Meaning of Second Baruch*. Society of Biblical Literature Dissertation Series 78. Atlanta: Scholars Press, 1985.

Murray, Scott R. *Law, Life, and the Living God: The Third Use of the Law in Modern American Lutheranism.* St. Louis: Concordia, 2002.

Nairne, Alexander. *The Epistle of Priesthood.* Edinburgh: T & T Clark, 1913.

Neusner, Jacob. *First Century Judaism in Crisis.* Nashville: Abingdon, 1975.

— *Jewish Law from Moses to the Mishnah: The Hiram College Lectures on Religion for 1999 and Other Papers.* South Florida Studies in the History of Judaism 187. Atlanta: Scholars, 1998.

— *Judaic Law from Jesus to the Mishnah: A Systematic Reply to Professor E. P. Sanders.* South Florida Studies in the History of Judaism 84. Atlanta: Scholars, 1993.

— *Mishnah: Introduction and Reader.* Philadelphia: Trinity Press, 1992.

— *The Reader's Guide to the Talmud.* The Brill Reference Library of Ancient Judaism 5. Boston: Brill, 2001.

— *Reading and Believing: Ancient Judaism and Contemporary Gullibility.* Brown Judaic Studies 113. Atlanta: Scholars Press, 1986.

— *The Theology of the Oral Torah: Revealing the Justice of God.* London: McGill-Queen's University Press, 1999.

— *Torah from Scroll to Symbol in Formative Judaism.* Brown Judaic Studies 136. Atlanta: Scholars, 1988.

Nicholson, Ernest W. *God and His People: Covenant Theology in the Old Testament.* Oxford: Clarendon Press, 1986.

Nickelsburg, George W. E. *Jewish Literature Between the Bible and the Mishnah.* Philadelphia: Fortress, 1981.

— *Resurrection, Immortality, and Eternal Life in Intertestamental Judaism.* Harvard Theological Studies 26. Cambridge: Harvard University Press, 1972.

Nickelsburg, George W. E., and Michael E. Stone. *Faith and Piety in Early Judaism: Texts and Documents.* Philadelphia: Fortress, 1983.

Nikiprowetzky, Valentin. *Commentaire de l'Écriture chez Philon d'Alexandrie.* Arbeiten zur Literatur und Geschichte des Hellenistischen Judentums 11. Leiden: Brill, 1977.

Noth, Martin. *The Laws in the Pentateuch and Other Studies.* London: Oliver & Boyd, 1966.

Novak, David. *Law and Theology in Judaism.* New York: Ktav Publishing, 1974.

O'Conner, Michael Patrick, and David Noel Freedman, eds. *Backgrounds for the Bible.* Winona Lake, IN: Eisenbrauns, 1987.

O'Hare, Padraic. *The Enduring Covenant.* Valley Forge, PA: Trinity Press, 1997.

Östborn, Gunnar. *Torah in the Old Testament.* Translated by Cedric Hentschel. Lund: Hakan Ohlssons Koktryckeri, 1945.

Palmer, Earl F. *Old Law-New Life: The Ten Commandments and New Testament Faith.* Nashville: Abingdon, 1984.

Pentecost, J. Dwight. *Thy Kingdom Come.* Wheaton: Victor Books, 1990.

Peterson, David. *Hebrews and Perfection: An Examination of the Concept of Perfection in the 'Epistle to the Hebrews.'* Society for New Testament Studies Monograph Series 47. New York: Cambridge University Press, 1982.

Pierce, C. A. *Conscience in the New Testament.* Chicago: Allenson, 1955.

Reisinger, Ernest C. *The Law and the Gospel*. Phillipsburg, NJ: P & R Publishing, 1997.

Rhoads, David M. *Israel in Revolution 6-74 C.E.: A Political History Based on the Writings of Josephus*. Philadelphia: Fortress, 1976.

Richardson, Peter, and Stephen Westerholm. *Law in Religious Communities in the Roman Period: The Debate over* Torah *and* Nomos *in Post-Biblical Judaism and Early Christianity*. Studies in Christianity and Judaism 4. Ontario: Wilfrid Laurier University Press, 1991.

Rissi, Mathias. *Die Theologie des Hebräerbriefs: ihre Verankerung in der Situation des Verfassers und seiner Leser*. Tübingen: J. C. B. Mohr (Paul Siebeck), 1987.

Robertson, O. Palmer. *The Christ of the Covenants*. Phillipsburg, NJ: Presbyterian and Reformed, 1980.

Rosenthal, Erwin I. J., ed. *Judaism and Christianity*. Vol. 3, *Law and Religion*. New York: Macmillan, 1938.

Sanders, E. P. *Jesus and Judaism*. Philadelphia: Fortress, 1985.

— *Jewish Law from Jesus to the Mishnah*. Philadelphia: Trinity Press, 1990.

— *Judaism: Practice and Belief 63 BCE–66 CE*. Philadelphia: Trinity Press, 1992.

— *Paul and Palestinian Judaism: A Comparison of Patterns of Religion*. Philadelphia: Fortress, 1977.

Sandmel, Samuel. *The Genius of Paul: A Study in History*. Philadelphia: Fortress, 1979.

Sayler, Gwendolyn B. *Have the Promises Failed? A Literary Analysis of 2 Baruch*. Society of Biblical Literature Dissertation Series 72. Atlanta: Scholars Press 1984.

Schechter, Solomon. *Some Aspects of Rabbinic Theology*. New York: Macmillan, 1923.

Schenck, Kenneth. *Understanding the Book of Hebrews: The Story Behind the Sermon*. Louisville: John Knox, 2003.

Schiffman, Lawrence H. *Sectarian Law in the Dead Sea Scrolls: Courts, Testimony, and the Penal Code*. Brown Judaic Studies 33. Chico, CA: Scholars Press, 1983.

Schnabel, Eckhard J. *Law and Wisdom from Ben Sira to Paul: A Tradition Historical Enquiry Into the Relation of Law, Wisdom, and Ethics*. Tübingen: J. C. B. Mohr, 1985.

Scholer, John M. *Proleptic Priests: Priesthood in the Epistle to the Hebrews*. Journal for the Study of the New Testament Supplement Series 49. Sheffield: JSOT, 1991.

Schreiner, Thomas R. *The Law and Its Fulfillment*. Grand Rapids: Baker, 1993.

Schröder, Bernd. *Die ‚väterlichen Gesetze'–Flavius Josephus als Vermittler von Halachah an Griechen und Römer*. Tübingen: J. C. B. Mohr (Paul Siebeck), 1996.

Schröger, Friedrich. *Der Verfasser des Hebraerbriefes*. Biblische Untersuchungen 4. Regensburg: F. Pustet, 1968.

Schwenk-Bressler, Udo. *Sapientia Salomonis als ein Beispiel frühjüdischer Textauslegung*. Beiträge zur Erforschung des Alten Testaments und des antiken Judentums 32. Frankfurt: Peter Lang, 1993.

Scott, E. F. *The epistle to the Hebrews: Its Doctrine and Significance*. Edinburgh: T & T Clark, 1923.

Seifrid, Mark A. *Justification by Faith: The Origin and Development of a Central Pauline Theme*. Novum Testamentum Supplement Series 68. New York: E. J. Brill, 1992.

Smallwood, E. Mary. *The Jews Under Roman Rule From Pompey to Diocletian: A Study in Political Relations.* 2nd ed. Boston: Brill, 2001.

Smend, Rudolph, and Ulrich Luz. *Gesetz.* Biblische Konfrontationen 1015. Stüttgart: Kohlhammer, 1981.

Sowers, Sidney G. *The Hermeneutics of Philo and Hebrews: A Comparison of the Interpretation of the Old Testament in Philo Judaeus and the Epistle to the Hebrews.* Richmond: Knox, 1965.

Stone, Michael E. *Features of the Eschatology of IV Ezra.* Harvard Semitic Studies 35. Atlanta: Scholars Press, 1989.

—, ed. *Jewish Writings of the Second Temple Period: Apocrypha, Pseudepigrapha, Qumran Sectarian Writings, Philo, Josephus.* The Literature of the Jewish People in the Period of the Second Temple Period and the Talmud 2. Philadelphia: Fortress, 1984.

Strack, H. L. and G. Stemberger. *Introduction to the Talmud and Midrash.* Translated by Markus Bockmuehl. Minneapolis: Fortress, 1992.

Synge, F. C. *Hebrews and the Scriptures.* London: SPCK, 1959.

Thielman, Frank. *The Law and the New Testament: The Question of Continuity.* New York: Crossroad, 1999.

Thompson, James W. *The Beginnings of Christian Philosophy: The Epistle to the Hebrews.* Catholic Biblical Quarterly Monograph Series 13. Washington, DC: Catholic Biblical Association, 1982.

Thurén, Jukka. *Das Lobopfer der Hebräer: Studien zum Aufbau und Anliegen von Hebräerbrief 13.* Åbo, Finland: Åbo Akademi, 1973.

Trotter, Andrew. *Interpreting the Book of Hebrews.* Grand Rapids: Baker, 1997.

Van Groningen, Gerard. *Messianic Revelation in the Old Testament.* Grand Rapids: Baker, 1990.

VanderKam, James C. *The Book of Jubilees.* Sheffield: Academic Press, 2001.

Vanhoye, Albert. *La structure litteraire de L'Épître aux Hébreux.* Paris: Desclée de Brouwer, 1963.

— *La structure littéraire de l'Épître aux Hébreux.* 2nd ed. Paris: Desclée de Brouwer, 1976.

— *Old Testament Priests and the New Priest According to the New Testament.* Translated by J. Bernard Orchard. Petersham, MA: St. Bede's Publications, 1986.

— *Our Priest in God: The Doctrine of the Epistle to the Hebrews.* Rome: Pontificio Instituto Biblico, 1977.

— *Structure and Message of the Epistle to the Hebrews.* Rome: Pontificio Instituto Biblico, 1989.

Vermes, Geza. *The Dead Sea Scrolls–Qumran in Perspective.* London: William Collins and Sons, 1977.

Vogelsang, Erich. *Luthers Hebräerbrief-Vorlesung von 1517/18.* Berlin und Leipzig: Walter de Gruyter, 1930.

Volkmann, Richard. *Die Rhetorik der Griechen und Römer in Systematischer Übersicht.* Leipzig: B. G. Teubner, 1885.

Von Campenhausen, Hans. *The Formation of the Christian Bible.* Translated by J. A. Baker. Philadelphia: Fortress, 1972.

Von Rad, Gerhard. *Old Testament Theology.* 2 vols. Translated by D. M. G. Stalker. Edinburgh: Oliver and Boyd, 1965.

Von Soden, Hermann. *Urchristliche Literaturgeschichte: die Schriften des Neuen Testaments.* Berlin: Dunker, 1905.

Vos, Geerhardus. *Biblical Theology: Old and New Testaments.* Grand Rapids: Eerdmans, 1948. Reprint, Carlisle, PA: Banner of Truth, 1996.

— *The Teaching of the Epistle to the Hebrews.* Grand Rapids: Eerdmans, 1956.

Westfall, Cynthia. *A Discourse Analysis of the Structure of Hebrews: the Relationship Between Form and Meaning.* Library of New Testament Studies 297. New York: T&T Clark, 2005.

Whiston, William, ed. *The Works of Josephus: Complete and Unabridged.* Peabody, MA: Hendrickson, 1987.

Whittaker, Molly. *Jews and Christians: Graeco-Roman Views.* Cambridge Commentaries on Writings of the Jewish and Christian World 200 B.C. to A.D. 200, vol 6. New York: Cambridge University Press, 1984.

Williamson, Ronald. *Philo and the Epistle to the Hebrews.* Leiden: E. J. Brill, 1970.

Winninge, Mikael. *Sinner and the Righteous: A Comparative Study of the Psalms of Solomon and Paul's Letters.* Coniectanea Biblica New Testament Series 26. Stockholm: Almqvist & Wiksell International, 1995.

Winston, *Philo of Alexandria: The Contemplative Life, the Giants, and Selections.* New York: Paulist Press, 1981.

Yadin, Yigael. *The Temple Scroll.* Vol. 1. Jerusalem: Ben Zvi, 1983.

Yahuda, Joseph. *Law and Life According to Hebrew Thought.* London: Oxford, 1932.

Yinger, Kent L. *Paul, Judaism, and Judgment According to Deeds.* Society for New Testament Studies Monograph Series 105. Cambridge: University Press, 1999.

Yonge, C. D., ed. *The Works of Philo: Complete and Unabridged.* Peabody, MA: Hendrickson, 1993.

Zimmerli, Walther. *The Law and Prophets: A Study of the Meaning of the Old Testament.* Translated by R. E. Clements. Oxford: Basil Blackwell, 1965.

Zimmerman, Hans. *Das Bekenntnis der Hoffnung: Tradition und Redaktion im Hebräerbrief.* Köln: Peter Hanstein Verlag, 1977.

Articles and Essays

Andriessen, Paul. "Das grössere und vollkommenere Zelt (Heb 9:1)." *Biblische Zeitschrift* 15 (1971): 76-92.

Anderson, H. "4 Maccabees." In *The Old Testament Pseudepigrapha.* Vol. 2, *Expansions of the "Old Testament" and Legends, Wisdom and Philosophical Literature, Prayers, Psalms, and Odes, Fragments of Lost Judeo-Hellenistic Works.* Edited by James H. Charlesworth, 531-64. New York: Doubleday, 1985.

Attridge, Harold. "New Covenant Christology in an Early Christian Homily." *Quarterly Review* 8 (1988): 89-108.

— "The Uses of Antithesis in Hebrews 8-10." *Harvard Theological Review* 79 (1986): 1-9.

Bandstra, A. J. "Heilgeschichte and Melchizedek in Hebrews." *Calvin Theological Journal* 3 (1968): 36-41.

Banks, Robert. "The Eschatological Role of the Law in Pre- and Post-Christian Jewish Thought." In *Reconciliation and Hope: New Testament Essays on Atonement and Eschatology Presented to L. L. Morris on His 60th Birthday*, ed. Robert Banks, 173-85. Exeter: Paternoster Press, 1974.

Barrett, C. K. "The Christology of Hebrews." In *Who Do You Say That I Am? Essays on Christology*, ed. Mark Allan Powell and David R. Bauer, 110-27. Louisville: Westminster John Knox, 1999.

— "The Eschatology of the Epistle to the Hebrews." In *The Background of the New Testament and Its Eschatology*, ed. W. D. Davies and D. Daube, 363-93. Cambridge: University Press, 1956.

Bartels, Robert A. "Law and Sin in Fourth Esdras and St. Paul." *Lutheran Quarterly* 1 (1949): 319-29.

Barth, M. "The Old Testament in Hebrews: An Essay in Biblical Hermeneutics." In *Issues in New Testament Interpretation*, ed. W. Klassen and G. F. Snyder, 53-78. New York: Harper & Row, 1962.

Bauckham, Richard. "Apocalypses." In *Justification and Variegated Nomism*. Vol. 1, *The Complexities of Second Temple Judaism*, eds. D. A. Carson, Peter T. O'Brien, and Mark A. Seifrid, 135-88. Grand Rapids: Baker, 2001.

Baumgarten, A. I. "The Torah as a Public Document in Judaism." *Studies in Religion/Sciences Religieuses* 14.1 (1985): 17-24.

Baumgarten, Joseph M. "Damascus Document." In *Encyclopedia of the Dead Sea Scrolls*. Edited by Lawrence H. Schiffman and James C. VanderKam. Oxford: University Press, 2000.

— "Sadducean Elements in Qumran Law." In *The Community of the Renewed Covenant: The Notre Dame Symposium on the Dead Sea Scrolls*. ed. Eugene Ulrich and James VanderKam, 27-36. Christianity and Judaism in Antiquity Series 10. Notre Dame, IN: University of Notre Dame Press, 1994.

Beckwith, Roger T. "Christ as Sacrifice in Paul and Hebrews." In *Sacrifice in the Bible*, ed. Roger T. Beckwith and Martin J. Selman, 130-35. Grand Rapids: Baker, 1995.

— "The Unity and Diversity of God's Covenants." *Tyndale Bulletin* 38 (1987): 93-118.

Bird, C. L. "Typological Interpretation within the Old Testament: Melchizedekian Typology." *Concordia Journal* 26 (2000): 36-52.

Black, David Alan. "The Problem of the Literary Structure of Hebrews: An Evaluation and a Proposal." *Grace Theological Journal* 7.2 (1986): 163-77.

Black, Matthew. "The Christological Use of the Old Testament in the New Testament." *New Testament Studies* 18 (1971-72): 1-14.

Blank, Sheldon H. "LXX Renderings of Old Testament Terms for Law." *Hebrew Union College Annual* 7 (1930): 259-83.

Bligh, John. "The Structure of Hebrews." *Heythrop Journal* 5 (1964): 170-77.

Bockmuehl, Markus. "1QS and Salvation at Qumran." In *Justification and Variegated Nomism.* Vol. 1, *The Complexities of Second Temple Judaism,* eds. D. A. Carson, Peter T. O'Brien, and Mark A. Seifrid, 381-414. Grand Rapids: Baker, 2001.

Borgen, Peder. "Heavenly Ascent in Philo." In *The Pseudepigrapha and Early Biblical Interpretation,* ed. James H. Charlesworth and Craig A. Evans, 246-68. Journal for the Study of the Pseudepigrapha Supplement Series 14. Sheffield: Sheffield Press, 1993.

Bowley, James E. "Moses in the Dead Sea Scrolls: Living in the Shadow of God's Anointed." In *The Bible at Qumran: Text, Shape, and Interpretation,* ed. Peter W. Flint, 159-81. Grand Rapids: Eerdmans, 2001.

Bright, John. "An Exercise in Hermeneutics: Jeremiah 31:31-34." *Interpretation* 20 (1966): 188-210.

Brooke, George. "Torah in the Qumran Scrolls." In *Bibel in jüdischer und christlicher Tradition – Festschrift für Johann Maier zum 60. Geburtstag,* ed. Helmut Merklein, Karlheinz Müller und Günter Stemberger, 97-120. Theologie Bonner Biblische Beiträge 88. Frankfurt: Anton Hain, 1993.

Bruce, F. F. "The Structure and Argument of Hebrews." *Southwestern Journal of Theology* 28 (1985): 6-12.

Buchanan, G. W. "The Present State of Scholarship in Hebrews." In *Christianity, Judaism and Other Greco-Roman Cults: I Festschrift Morton Smith,* ed. J. Neusner, 299-330. Leiden: Brill, 1975.

Büchler, A. "Ben Sira's Conception of Sin and Atonement." *Jewish Quarterly Review* 14.1 (1923): 53-83.

Büchsel, F. "Hebräerbriefe." In *Religion in Geschichte und Gegenwart.* Edited by Hermann Gunkel and Leopold Ascharnack. Tübingen: J. C. B. Mohr [Paul Seibeck], 1928.

Burkes, Shannon. "'Life' Redefined: Wisdom and Law in Fourth Ezra and Second Baruch." *Catholic Bible Quarterly* 63.1 (2001) 55-71.

Burns, Lanier. "Hermeneutical Issues and Principles in Hebrews As Exemplified in the Second Chapter." *Journal of the Evangelical Theological Society* 39 (1996): 587-607.

Caird, G. B. "The Exegetical Method of the Epistle to the Hebrews." *Canadian Journal of Theology* 5 (1959): 44-51.

Carson, D. A. "Summaries and Conclusions." In *Justification and Variegated Nomism.* Vol. 1, *The Complexities of Second Temple Judaism,* eds. D. A. Carson, Peter T. O'Brien, and Mark A. Seifrid, 505-48. Grand Rapids: Baker, 2001.

Clements, R. E. "The Use of the Old Testament in Hebrews." *Southwestern Journal of Theology* 28 (1985): 36-45.

Cockerill, Gareth L. "Between Sinai and Zion: The Biblical Theology of Hebrews." Paper presented at the annual meeting of the Evangelical Theological Society, Philadelphia, PA, 16-18 November 1995.

Collins, J. J. "Sibylline Oracles." In *The Old Testament Pseudepigrapha.* Vol. 1, *Apocalyptic Literature and Testaments.* Edited by James H. Charlesworth, 317-472. New York: Doubleday, 1983.

Collins, Raymond F. "New." In *The Anchor Bible Dictionary*. Edited by David Noel Freedman. New York: Doubleday, 1992.

Coppens, J. "La nouvelle alliance en Jérémie 31, 31-34." *Catholic Biblical Quarterly* 25 (1963): 12-21.

Crawford, Sidnie White. "Lady Wisdom and Dame Folly at Qumran." *Dead Sea Discoveries* 5 (1993): 355-65.

Daniels, Richard. "How Does the Church Relate to the New Covenant? or, Whose New Covenant is it, Anyway?" *Faith and Mission* 16 (1999): 64-98.

Davies, Philip R. "Didactic Stories." In *Justification and Variegated Nomism*. Vol. 1, *The Complexities of Second Temple Judaism*, eds. D. A. Carson, Peter T. O'Brien, and Mark A. Seifrid, 99-134. Grand Rapids: Baker, 2001.

— "Who Can Join the 'Damascus Covenant'?" *Journal of Jewish Studies* 46 (1995): 134-142.

Davies, W. D. "Law in First Century Judaism." In *The Interpreter's Dictionary of the Bible*. Edited by George Arthur Buttrick. New York: Abingdon Press, 1962.

— "Law in the New Testament." In *The Interpreter's Dictionary of the Bible*. Edited by George Arthur Buttrick. New York: Abingdon Press, 1962.

— "The Moral Teaching of the Early Church." In *The Use of the Old Testament in the New and Other Essays: Studies in Honor of William Franklin Stinespring*, ed. James A. Efrid, 310-32. Durham, NC: Duke University Press, 1972.

Descamps, Albert. "La structure de l'Épître aux Hébreux." *Revue Diocésaine de Tournai* 9 (1954): 251-58.

— "La structure de l'Épître aux Hébreux." *Revue Diocésaine de Tournai* 9 (1954): 333-38.

DeSilva, D. "The Epistle to the Hebrews in Social-Scientific Perspective." *Restoration Quarterly* 36 (1994): 1-21.

Desjardins, Michel. "Law in *2 Baruch* and *4 Ezra*." *Studies in Religion/Sciences Religieuses* 14.1 (1985): 25-37.

Dohmen, Christoph. "Zur Gründung der Gemeinde von Qumran (1QS 8-9)." *Revue de Qumran* 11.1 (1982): 81-96.

Ellingworth, P. "Hebrews." In *New Dictionary of Biblical Theology*. Edited by T. D. Alexander and B. S. Rosner. Downers Grove, IL: Intervarsity, 2000.

— "'Like the Son of God': Form and Content in Hebrews 7, 1-10." *Biblica* 64 (1983): 255-62.

Emerton, J. A. "The Riddle of Genesis 14." *Vestus Testamentum* 21 (1971): 403-39.

Enns, Peter. "Expansions of Scripture." In *Justification and Variegated Nomism*. Vol. 1, *The Complexities of Second Temple Judaism*. Edited by D. A. Carson, Peter T. O'Brien, and Mark A. Seifrid, 73-98. Grand Rapids: Baker, 2001.

Evans, Craig. "Scripture-Based Stories in the Pseudepigrapha." In *Justification and Variegated Nomism*. Vol. 1, *The Complexities of Second Temple Judaism*. Edited by D. A. Carson, Peter T. O'Brien, and Mark A. Seifrid, 57-72. Grand Rapids: Baker, 2001.

Fabry, Heinz-Josef. "Der Begriff 'Tora' in der Tempelrolle." *Revue de Qumran* 18.1 (1997): 63-72.

Feldman, Louis. "Torah and Greek Culture in Josephus." *Torah U-Maddah Journal* 7 (1997): 41-87.

Filson, F. V. *'Yesterday': A Study of Hebrews in the Light of Chapter 13.* Studies in Biblical Theology 2:4. Naperville, IL: Allenson, 1967.

Fischer, John. "Covenant, Fulfillment and Judaism in Hebrews." *Evangelical Review of Theology* 13 (1989): 175-87.

Fitzmyer, J. A. "Further Light on Melchizedek from Qumran Cave 11." *Journal of Biblical Literature* 86 (1967): 25-41.

— "Melchizedek in the MT, LXX, and the NT." *Biblica* 81 (2000): 63-69.

— "'Now This Melchizedek' . . . (Heb 7:1)." *Catholic Biblical Quarterly* 25 (1963): 305-21.

France, R. T. "The Writer of Hebrews as a Biblical Expositor." *Tyndale Bulletin* 47 (1996): 245-76.

Frey, Jörg, "Die alte und die neue διαθήκη nach dem Hebräerbrief." In *Bund und Tora: Zur theologischen Begriffsgeschichte in alttestamentlicher, frühjüdischer und urchristlicher Tradition*, ed. Friedrich Avemarie and Hermann Lichtenberger, 263-310. Tübingen, J. C. B. Mohr, 1996.

Gamberoni, Johannes. "Das 'Gesetz des Mose' im Buch Tobias." In *Studien zum Pentateuch*, ed. G. Braulik, 227-42. Vienna: Herder, 1977.

Gammie, John G. "Loci of the Melchizedek Tradition of Genesis 14:18-20." *Journal of Biblical Literature* 90 (1971): 385-96.

Gilbert, M. "Wisdom Literature." In *Jewish Writings of the Second Temple Period: Apocrypha, Pseudepigrapha, Qumran Sectarian Writings, Philo, Josephus*, ed. Michael E. Stone, 283-324. Philadelphia: Fortress Press, 1984.

Gordon, Robert P. "Better Promises: Two Passages in Hebrews against the Background of the Old Testament Cultus." In *Temple Amicitiae: Essays in the Second Temple presented to Ernst Bammel*, ed. William Horbury, 434-49. Journal for the Study of the New Testament Supplement Series 48. Sheffield: JSOT, 1991.

Gowan, Donald E. "Wisdom." In *Justification and Variegated Nomism*. Vol. 1, *The Complexities of Second Temple Judaism*, eds. D. A. Carson, Peter T. O'Brien, and Mark A. Seifrid, 215-40. Grand Rapids: Baker, 2001.

Greenberg, Moshe. "Was ist neu am neuen Bund (Jer 31)?" In *Lernen in Jerusalem – Lernen mit Israel*, ed. Martin Stöhr, 14-25. Veröffentlichungen aus dem Institut Kirche und Judentum 20. Berlin: Institut Kirche und Judentum, 1993.

Greengus, Samuel. "Biblical and ANE Law." In *The Anchor Bible Dictionary*. Edited by David Noel Freedman. New York: Doubleday, 1992.

Guhrt, J. "Covenant." In *New International Dictionary of New Testament Theology*. Edited by Colin Brown. Grand Rapids: Zondervan, 1975.

Gutbrod, W. "Νόμος." In *Theological Dictionary of the New Testament*. Edited by Gerhard Kittle. Edited and translated by Geoffrey W. Bromily. Grand Rapids: Eerdmans, 1967.

Guthrie, George H. "Hebrews in Its First-Century Contexts: Recent Research." In *The Face of New Testament Studies*, ed. Scot McKnight and Grant Osborne, 414-43. Grand Rapids: Baker, 2004.

310 *Bibliography*

— "Hebrews' Use of the Old Testament: Recent Trends in Research." *Currents in Biblical Research* 1 (2003): 271-94.

Gyllenberg, Rafael. "Die Komposition des Hebräerbriefs." *Svensk Exegetisk Årsbok* 22-23 (1957-58): 137-47.

Hafemann, Scott. "Moses in the Apocrypha and Pseudepigrapha." *Journal for the Study of the Pseudepigrapha* 7 (1990): 79-104.

Hagner, D. A. "Interpreting the Epistle to the Hebrews." In *The Literature and Meaning of Scripture*, ed. M. A. Inch and C. H. Bullock, 217-33. Grand Rapids: Baker, 1981.

— "Old Testament in Hebrews." In *Dictionary of Later New Testament and Its Developments*. Edited by R. P. Martin and Peter H. Davids. Downers Grove, IL: Intervarsity, 1997.

Hahn, Scott. "A Broken Covenant and the Curse of Death: A Study of Hebrews 9:15-22." *Catholic Biblical Quarterly* 66 (2004): 416-36.

Hallbäck, Geert. "The Fall of Zion and the Revelation of the Law: An Interpretation of 4 Ezra." *Scandinavian Journal of Theology* 2 (1992): 263-92.

Harrelson, W. J. "Law in the Old Testament." In *The Interpreter's Dictionary of the Bible*. Edited by George Arthur Buttrick. New York: Abingdon Press, 1962.

Hay, David M. "Philo of Alexandria." In *Justification and Variegated Nomism*. Vol. 1, *The Complexities of Second Temple Judaism*, eds. D. A. Carson, Peter T. O'Brien, and Mark A. Seifrid, 357-80. Grand Rapids: Baker, 2001.

— "Putting Extremism in Context: The Case of Philo, *De Migratione* 89-93." *Studia Philonica Annual* 9 (1997): 126-42.

Hellerman, Joseph. "Purity and Nationalism in Second Temple Literature: 1-2 Maccabees and *Jubilees*." *Journal of the Evangelical Theological Society* 46.3 (2003): 401-22.

Himmelfarb, Martha. "Torah, Testimony, and Heavenly Tablets: the Claim to Authority of the *Book of Jubilees*." In *A Multiform Heritage: Studies on Early Judaism and Christianity in Honor of Robert A. Kraft*, ed. Benjamin G. Wright, 19-29. Scholars Press Homage Series 24. Atlanta: Scholars, 1999.

Hofius, Otfried. "Biblische Theologie im Lichte des Hebräerbriefes." In *New Directions in Biblical Theology*, ed. Sigfred Pederson, 108-25. Supplements to Novum Testamentum 76. Leiden: E. J. Brill, 1994.

— "Das 'erste' und das 'zweite' Zelt: Ein Beitrag zur Auslegung von Hbr 9:1-10." *Zeitschrift für die Neutestamentliche Wissenschaft* 61 (1970): 271-77.

Horbury, W. "The Aaronic Priesthood in the Epistle to the Hebrews." *Journal for the Study of the New Testament* 19 (1983): 43-71.

Hübner, Hans. "Νόμος." In *Exegetical Dictionary of the New Testament*. Edited by Horst Balz and Gerhard Schneider. Grand Rapids: Eerdmans, 1981.

Hughes, John J. "Hebrews 9:15ff and Galatians 3:15ff: A Study in Covenant Practice and Procedure." *Novum Testamentum* 21 (1979): 27-96.

Hughes, Philip E. "The Blood of Jesus and His Heavenly Priesthood in Hebrews." *Bibliotheca Sacra* 130 (1973): 305-14.

— "The Christology of Hebrews." *Southwestern Journal of Theology* 28 (1985): 19-27.

— "Epistle to the Hebrews." In *The New Testament and Its Modern Interpreters*, ed. E. E. Epp and G. W. MacRae, 351-70. Philadelphia: Fortress, 1989.

Huntjens, Johannes. "Contrasting Notions of Covenant and Law in the Texts From Qumran." *Revue de Qumran* 8.3 (1974): 361-80.

Hunzinger, Claus-Hunno. "Beobachtung zur Erwicklung der Disziplinarordnung der Gemeinde von Qumran." In *Qumran-Probleme*, ed. Hans Bardtke, 231-45. Deutsche Akademie der Wissenschaften Zu Berlin 42. Berlin: Akademie, 1963.

Hurst, Lincoln D. "Eschatology and 'Platonism' in the Epistle to the Hebrews." *Society of Biblical Literature Seminar Papers* 23 (1984): 41-74.

— "How 'Platonic' Are Heb. 8:5 and 9:23f.?" *Journal of Theological Studies* 34 (1983): 156-68.

Hyatt, J. Philip. "Torah in the Book of Jeremiah." *Journal of Biblical Literature* 60 (1941): 381-96.

Isaac, E. "1 Enoch." In *The Old Testament Pseudepigrapha.* Vol. 1, *Apocalyptic Literature and Testaments*. Edited by James H. Charlesworth, 5-90. New York: Doubleday, 1983.

Isaacs, Marie. "Why Bother with Hebrews?" *Heythrop Journal* 43 (2002): 60-72.

Janowitz, Naomi. "The Rhetoric of Translation: Three Early Perspectives on Translating Torah." *Harvard Theological Review* 84 (1991): 129-40.

Jobes, Karen. "The Function of Paronomasia in Hebrews 10:5-7." *Trinity Journal* 13 (1992): 181-91.

— "Rhetorical Achievement in the Hebrews 10 'Misquote' of Psalm 40." *Biblica* 72 (1991): 387-96.

Johnson, Luke Timothy. "The Scriptural World of Hebrews." *Interpretation* 57 (2003): 237-50.

Johnsson, W. G. "The Cultus of Hebrews in Twentieth-Century Scholarship." *Expository Times* 89 (1978): 104-08.

Kaiser, Walter C. "The Abolition of the Old Order and the Establishment of the New: Psalm 40:6-8 and Hebrews 10:5-10." In *Tradition and Testament: Essays in Honor of Charles Lee Feinberg*, ed. John S. Feinberg and Paul D. Feinberg, 19-37. Chicago: Moody Press, 1981.

— "The Old Promise and the New Covenant: Jeremiah 31:31-34." *Journal of the Evangelical Theological Society* 15 (1972): 11-23.

Kamlah, E. "Frömmigkeit und Tugend: Die Gesetzesapologie des Josephus in c Ap 2,145-295." In *Josephus-Studien: Untersuchungen zu Josephus, dem antiken Judentum und dem Neuen Testament*, ed. Otto Betz, Klaus Haacker, and Martin Hengel, 220-32. Göttingen: Vandenhoeck & Ruprecht, 1974.

Karlberg, Mark. "Legitimate Discontinuities Between the Testaments." *Journal of the Evangelical Theological Society* 28.1 (1985): 9-20.

Kee, H. C. "Testaments of the Twelve Patriarchs." In *The Old Testament Pseudepigrapha.* Vol. 1, *Apocalyptic Literature and Testaments*. Edited by James H. Charlesworth, 775-828. New York: Doubleday, 1983.

Kent, Homer Jr. "The New Covenant and the Church." *Grace Theological Journal* 6.2 (1985): 289-98.

Kilpatrick, G. D. "Diatheke in Hebrews." *Zeitschrift für die neutestamentliche Wissenschaft* 68 (1977): 263-65.

Klijn, A. F. J. "2 Baruch." In *The Old Testament Pseudepigrapha.* Vol. 1, *Apocalyptic Literature and Testaments.* Edited by James H. Charlesworth, 615-52. New York: Doubleday, 1983.

Knowles, Michael. "Moses, the Law, and the Unity of 4 Ezra." *Novum Testamentum* 31.3 (1989): 257-74.

Koester, Craig R. "The Epistle to the Hebrews in Recent Study." *Currents in Research* 2 (1994): 123-45.

Koester, Helmut. "'Outside the Camp': Hebrews 13:9-14." *Harvard Theological Review* 55 (1962): 299-315.

Kögel, Julius. "De Begriff τελειοῦν im Hebräerbrief im Zusammenhang mit dem neutestamentichen Sprachgebrach." In *Theologische Studien für M. Kähler,* ed. Friedrich Giesebrecht, 37-68. Leipzig: Deichert, 1905.

Konkel, August. "The Sacrifice of Obedience." *Didaskalia* 2 (1991): 2-11.

Kugler, Robert A. "Testaments." In *Justification and Variegated Nomism.* Vol. 1, *The Complexities of Second Temple Judaism,* eds. D. A. Carson, Peter T. O'Brien, and Mark A. Seifrid, 189-214. Grand Rapids: Baker, 2001.

Ladd, G. E. "Hebrews." In *A Theology of the New Testament,* ed. D. A. Hagner, 617-33. Rev. ed. Grand Rapids: Eerdmans, 1994.

Lane, William L. "Hebrews." In *Dictionary of Later New Testament and its Developments.* Edited by Ralph. P. Martin and Peter H. Davids. Downers Grove, IL: Intervarsity, 1997.

— "Hebrews: A Sermon in Search of a Setting." *Southwestern Journal of Theology* 28 (1985): 13-18.

Lee, E. Kenneth. "Words Denoting 'Pattern' in the New Testament." *New Testament Studies* 8 (1962): 166-73.

Lightstone, Jack. "Torah is *Nomos*—Except When it is Not: Prolegomena to the Study of the Law in Late Antique Judaism." *Studies in Religion/Sciences Religieuses* 13.1 (1984): 29-37.

Lindars, Barnabas. "Hebrews and the Second Temple." In *Temple Amicitiae: Essays in the Second Temple Presented to Ernst Bammel,* ed. William Horbury, 410-33. Journal for the Study of the New Testament Supplement Series 48. Sheffield: JSOT, 1991.

— "The Rhetorical Structure of Hebrews." *New Testament Studies* 35 (1989): 382-406.

Longenecker, R. N. "The Melchizedek Argument of Hebrews: A Study in the Development and Circumstantial Expression of New Testament Thought." In *Unity and Diversity in New Testament Theology,* FS G. E. Ladd, ed. Robert Guelich, 161-85. Grand Rapids: Eerdmans, 1978.

Lundbom, Jack. "New Covenant." In *The Anchor Bible Dictionary.* Edited by David Noel Freedman. New York: Doubleday, 1992.

Luz, Ulrich. "Der alte und der neue Bund bei Paulus und im Hebräerbriefe." *Evangelische Theologie* 27 (1967): 318-36.

MacLeod, David J. "The Cleansing of the True Tabernacle." *Bibliotheca Sacra* 152 (1995): 60-71.

MacRae, George W. "Heavenly Temple and Eschatology in the Letter to the Hebrews." *Semeia* 12 (1978): 179-99.

Marböck, Johannes. "Gesetz und Weisheit: zum Verständnis des Gesetzes bei Jesus ben Sira." *Biblische Zeitschrift* 20.1 (1976): 1-21.

Marshall, I. Howard. "Church and Temple in the New Testament." *Tyndale Bulletin* 40.2 (1989): 203-22.

Martens, John W. "Philo and the 'Higher' Law." *Society of Biblical Literature 1991 Seminar Papers* 30 (1991): 309-22.

Martin-Achard, Robert. "Quelques remarques sur la nouvelle alliance chez Jérémie (jer 31, 31-34)." In *Questions disputées d'Ancien Testament*, ed. C. Brekelmans, 141-64. Louvain: Leuven University Press, 1974.

McConville, J. Gordon. "Jeremiah: Prophet and Book." *Tyndale Bulletin* 42 (1991): 80-95.

McCready, Wayne. "A Second Torah at Qumran?" *Studies in Religion/Sciences Religieuses* 14.1 (1985): 5-16.

McCullough, J. C. "Hebrews in Recent Scholarship." *Irish Biblical Studies* 16.2 (1994): 66-86.

— "Hebrews in Recent Scholarship (Part 2)." *Irish Biblical Studies* 16.3 (1994): 108-20.

— "The Old Testament Quotations in Hebrews." *New Testament Studies* 26 (1980): 363-79.

— "Some Recent Developments in Research on the Epistle to the Hebrews." *Irish Biblical Studies* 2 (1980): 141-65.

— "Some Recent Developments in Research on the Epistle to the Hebrews." *Irish Biblical Studies* 3 (1981): 28-43.

McKnight, Scot. "The Warning Passages of Hebrews: A Formal Analysis and Theological Conclusions." *Trinity Journal* 13.1 (1992): 21-59.

McLeod, David J. "The Doctrinal Center of the Book of Hebrews." *Bibliotheca Sacra* 146 (1989): 291-300.

Mendenhall, G. E., and Gary Herion. "Covenant." In *The Anchor Bible Dictionary.* Edited by David Noel Freedman. New York: Doubleday, 1992.

Metzger, Bruce M. "The Fourth Book of Ezra." In *The Old Testament Pseudepigrapha.* Vol. 1, *Apocalyptic Literature and Testaments.* Edited by James H. Charlesworth, 517-60. New York: Doubleday, 1983.

Moo, Douglas J. "The Law of Christ as the Fulfillment of the Law of Moses: A Modified Lutheran View." In *Five Views on Law and Gospel*, ed. Stanley Gundry, 319-76. Grand Rapids: Zondervan, 1993.

Motyer, Stephen. "The Psalm Quotations of Hebrews 1: A Hermeneutic-Free Zone?" *Tyndale Bulletin* 50.1 (1999): 3-22.

Müller, Karlheinz. "Gesetz und Gesetzeserfüllung im Frühjudentum." In *Das Gesetz im Neuen Testament*, ed. Karl Kertelge, 11-27. Freiburg: Herder, 1986.

Murphy-O'Conner, Jérôme. "La genèse littéraire de la Regle de la Communauté." *Revue Biblique* 76 (1969): 528-49.

Myre, Andre. "La Loi de la Nature et la Loi Mosaique selon Philon d' Alexandrie." *Science et Esprit* 28.2 (1976): 163-81.

Nauck, Wolfgang. "Zum Aufbau des Hebräerbriefes." In *Judentum-Urchristentum-Kirche: Festschrift für Joachim Jeremias*, ed. W. Eltester, 199-206. Beihefte zur Zeitschrift für die neutestamentliche Wissenschaft und die Kunde der älteren Kirche 26. Berlin: Töpelmann, 1960.

Neeley, Linda. "A Discourse Analysis of Hebrews." In *Occasional Papers in Translation and Linguistics* 3-4 (1987): 1-146.

Nitzan, Bilhah. "The Concept of the Covenant in Qumran Literature." In *Historical Perpsectives: From the Hasmoneans to Bar Kokhba In Light of the Dead Sea Scrolls: Proceedings of the Fourth International Symposium of the Orion Center for the Study of the Dead Sea Scrolls and Associated Literature, 27-31 January, 1999*, ed. David Goodblatt, Avital Pinnick, and Daniel R. Schwartz, 85-104. Studies on the Texts of the Deserts of Judah 37. Boston: Brill, 2001.

Nomoto, Shinya. "Herkunft und Struktur der Hohenpriestervorstellung im Hebräerbrief," *Novum Testamentum* 10 (1968): 10-25.

Omanson, Roger. "A Superior Covenant: Hebrews 8:1-10:18." *Review and Expositor* 82 (1985): 361-73.

Osborne, Grant R. "The Christ of Hebrews and Other Religions." *Journal of the Evangelical Theological Society* 46.2 (2003): 249-67.

Peterson, David. "Biblical Theology and the Argument of Hebrews." In *In the Fullness of Time*, ed. David Peterson and John Pryor, 219-35. Homebush West, Australia: Lancer, 1992.

— "God and Scripture in Hebrews." In *Trustworthiness of God*, ed. Paul Helm and Carl R. Trueman, 118-38. Grand Rapids: Eerdmans, 2002.

— "The Prophecy of the New Covenant in the Argument of Hebrews." *Reformed Theological Review* 38 (1979): 74-81.

Pouilly, Jean. "Evolution de la legislation pénale dans la communauté de Qumrân." *Revue Biblique* 82 (1975): 522-51.

Pretorius, E. A. C. "*Diatheke* in the Epistle to the Hebrews." *Neotestamentica* 5 (1971): 37-50.

Rajak, Tessa. "Dying for the Law: The Martyr's Portrait in Jewish-Greek Literature." In *Portraits-Biographical Representation in the Greek and Latin Literature of the Roman Empire*, ed. M. J. Edwards and Simon Swain, 39-67. Oxford: Clarendon Press, 1997.

Redditt, Paul L. "The Concept of Nomos in Fourth Maccabees." *Catholic Bible Quarterly* 45 (1983): 249-70.

Reinhartz, Adele. "The Meaning of Nomos in Philo's Exposition of the Law." *Studies in Religion/Sciences Religieuses* 15.3 (1986): 337-45.

Remus, Harold E. "Authority, Consent, and Law: *Nomos, Physis,* and the Striving for a 'Given.'" *Studies in Religion/Sciences Religieuses* 13.1 (1984): 5-18.

Renaud, B. "La Loi et les Lois dans les Livres des Maccabées." *Revue Biblique* 68 (1961): 39-67.

Rendtorff, Rolf. "Was ist neu am neuen Bund (Jer 31)?" In *Lernen in Jerusalem–Lernen mit Israel*, ed. Martin Stöhr, Veröffentlichungen aus dem Institut Kirche und Judentum 20, 26-37. Berlin: Institut Kirche und Judentum, 1993.

Richardson, Peter. "When is Torah Nomos?" *Studies in Religion/Sciences Religieuses* 15.3 (1986): 275-76.

Rooke, D. W. "Jesus as Royal Priest: Reflections on the Interpretation of the Melchizedek Tradition in Heb 7." *Biblica* 81 (2000): 81-94.

Sanders, E. P. "Law in Judaism of the New Testament Period." In *The Anchor Bible Dictionary*. Edited by David Noel Freedman. New York: Doubleday, 1992.

Sanders, Jack. "When Sacred Canopies Collide: the Reception of the Torah of Moses in the Wisdom Literature of the Second-Temple Period." *Journal for the Study of Judaism in the Persian, Hellenistic and Roman Period* 32.3 (2001): 121-36.

Schäfer, K. T. "ΚΕΦΑΛΙΣ ΒΙΒΛΙΟΥ." In *Weg zur Buchwissenschaft*, ed. O. Wenig, 1-10. Bonn: Bouvier, 1966.

Segal, Alan F. "Torah and *Nomos* in Recent Scholarly Discussion." *Studies in Religion/Sciences Religieuses* 13.1 (1984):19-27.

Seifrid, Mark A. "Righteousness Language in the Hebrew Scriptures and Early Judaism." In *Justification and Variegated Nomism*. Vol. 1, *The Complexities of Second Temple Judaism*, eds. D. A. Carson, Peter T. O'Brien, and Mark A. Seifrid, 415-42. Grand Rapids: Baker, 2001.

Shutt, R. J. H. "Letter of Aristeas." In *The Old Testament Pseudepigrapha*. Vol. 2, *Expansions of the "Old Testament" and Legends, Wisdom and Philosophical Literature, Prayers, Psalms, and Odes, Fragments of Lost Judeo-Hellenistic Works*. Edited by James H. Charlesworth, 7-34. New York: Doubleday, 1985.

Silva, Moises. "Perfection and Eschatology in Hebrews." *Westminster Theological Journal* 39 (1976): 60-71.

Smith, Robert H. "Abram and Melchizedek." *Zeitschrift für die alttestamentliche Wissenschaft* 77 (1965): 129-53.

Songer, Harold. "A Superior Priesthood: Hebrews 4:14-7:28." *Review and Expositor* 82 (1985): 345-59.

Spicq, Ceslas. "Alexandrinismes dans l'Epitre aux Hebreux." *Recherches de science religieuse* 39 (1951): 481-502.

—— "L'authenticitié du chapitre XIII de L'épître aux Hébreux." *Coniectanea Neotestamentica* 11 (1947): 226-36.

—— "Le Philonisme de l'Epitre aux Hebreux." *Revue Biblique* 56 (1949): 542-72.

—— "Le Philonisme de l'Epitre aux Hebreux." *Revue Biblique* 57 (1950): 212-42.

Spilsbury, Paul. "Josephus." In *Justification and Variegated Nomism*. Vol. 1, *The Complexities of Second Temple Judaism*, eds. D. A. Carson, Peter T. O'Brien, and Mark A. Seifrid, 241-60. Grand Rapids: Baker, 2001.

Stanley, Steve. "Hebrews 9:6-10: the 'Parable' of the Tabernacle." *Novum Testamentum* 37 (1995): 385-99.

—— "The Structure of Hebrews from Three Perspectives." *Tyndale Bulletin* 45.2 (1994): 245-71.

Stegemann, Wolfgang. "Tora—Nomos—Gesetz." In *Lernen in Jerusalem–Lernen mit Israel*, ed. Martin Stöhr, Veröffentlichungen aus dem Institut Kirche und Judentum 20, 148-68. Berlin: Institut Kirche und Judentum, 1993.

Stylianopoulos, Theodore G. "Shadow and Reality: Reflections on Hebrews 10:1-18." *Greek Orthodox Theological Review* 17.2 (1972): 215-30.

Swetnam, James. "Christology and the Eucharist in the Epistle to the Hebrews." *Biblica* 70 (1989): 74-95.

— "Form and Content in Hebrews 1-6." *Biblica* 53 (1972): 368-85.

— "Form and Content in Hebrews 7-13." *Biblica* 55 (1974): 333-48.

— "Greater and More Perfect Tent: A Contribution to the Discussion of Hebrews 9:11." *Biblica* 47 (1966): 91-106.

— "The Structure of Hebrews: A Fresh Look." *Melita Theologica* 41.1 (1990): 25-46.

— "Suggested Interpretation of Hebrews 9:15-18." *Catholic Biblical Quarterly* 27 (1965): 373-390.

Thien, F. "Analyse de L'Épître aux Hébreux." *Revue Biblique* 11 (1902): 74-86.

Thomas, Kenneth J. "The Old Testament Citations in Hebrews." *New Testament Studies* 11 (1965): 303-25.

Thompson, James W. "Hebrews 9 and the Hellenistic Concepts of Sacrifice." *Journal of Biblical Literature* 98 (1979): 567-78.

Toussaint, S. D. "The Eschatology of the Warning Passages in the Book of Hebrews." *Grace Theological Journal* 3 (1982): 67-80.

Tromp, Johann. "Taxo, the Messenger of the Lord." *Journal for the Study of Judiaism in the Persian, Hellenistic, and Roman Period* 21 (1990): 200-09.

Vaganay, Leon. "La Plan de L'Épître aux Hébreux." In *Memorial Lagrange*. Edited L. – H. Vincent, 269-77. Paris: J. Gabalda, 1940.

Vanhoye, Albert. "Discussions sur la structure de l'Épître Hébreux." *Biblica* 55 (1974): 349-80.

— "Literarische Struktur und theologische Botschaft des Hebräerbriefs (1. Teil)." *Studien für die Neue Testament Umwelt* 4 (1979): 119-47.

— "Literarische Struktur und theologische Botschaft des Hebräerbriefs (2. Teil)." *Studien für die Neue Testament Umwelt* 5 (1980): 18-49.

van Unnik, W. C. "'Η καινὴ διαθήκη—a Problem in the Early History of the Canon." In *Sparsa Collecta: The Collected Essays of W. C. van Unnik*, ed. C. K. Barrett, 157-71. Supplements to Novum Testamentum 30. Leiden: Brill, 1980.

— "Par la tente plus grande et plus parfait . . . (Heb 9,11)." *Biblica* 46 (1965): 1-28.

Vermes, Geza. "A Summary of the Law by Flavius Josephus." *Novum Testamentum* 24 (1982): 289-303.

— "Torah is Light." *Vetus Testamentum* 8 (1958): 436-38.

Vos, G. "Hebrews, the Epistle of the Διαθήκη." *Princeton Theological Review* 13 (1915): 587-632.

— "Hebrews, the Epistle of the Διαθήκη." *Princeton Theological Review* 14 (1916): 1-61.

Walters, J. "The Rhetorical Arrangement of Hebrews." *Asbury Theological Journal* 51 (1996): 59-70.

Ware, Bruce A. "The New Covenant and the People(s) of God." In *Dispensationalism, Israel and the Church: the Search for Definition*, ed. Craig A. Blaising and Darrell L. Bock, 68-97. Grand Rapids: Zondervan, 1992.

Weinfeld, Moshe. "Jeremiah and the Spiritual Metamorphosis of Israel." *Zeitschrift für die alttestamentliche Wissenschaft* 88 (1976): 17-56.

Wenham, Gordon J. "The Theology of Old Testament Sacrifice." In *Sacrifice in the Bible*, ed. Roger T. Beckwith and Martin J. Selman, 75-87. Grand Rapids: Baker, 1995.

Westerholm, Stephen. "Torah, Nomos, and Law: A Question of Meaning." *Studies in Religion/Sciences Religieuses* 15.3 (1986): 327-36.

Williamson, Ronald. "The Eucharist and the Epistle to the Hebrews." *New Testament Studies* 21 (1975): 300-12.

Wintermute, O. S. "Jubilees." In *The Old Testament Pseudepigrapha*. Vol. 2, *Expansions of the "Old Testament" and Legends, Wisdom and Philosophical Literature, Prayers, Psalms, and Odes, Fragments of Lost Judeo-Hellenistic Works*. Edited by James H. Charlesworth, 35-142. New York: Doubleday, 1985.

Witherington, Ben III. "The Influence of Galatians on Hebrews." *New Testament Studies* 37 (1991): 146-52.

Wright, R. B. "Psalms of Solomon." In *The Old Testament Pseudepigrapha*. Vol. 2, *Expansions of the "Old Testament" and Legends, Wisdom and Philosophical Literature, Prayers, Psalms, and Odes, Fragments of Lost Judeo-Hellenistic Works*. Edited by James H. Charlesworth, 639-70. New York: Doubleday, 1985.

Yadin, Yigael. "The Dead Sea Scrolls and the Epistle to the Hebrews." In *Aspects of the Dead Sea Scrolls*, ed. Chaim Rabin and Yigael Yadin, Scripta Hierosolymitana 4, 36-55. Jerusalem: Central Press, 1958.

Young, Francis. "Temple Cult and Law in Early Christianity." *New Testament Studies* 19 (1973): 325-38.

Young, Norman H. "The Gospel According to Hebrews 9." *New Testament Studies* 27 (1980-81): 198-210.

Theses and Dissertations

Bell, William E. Jr. "The New Covenant." Th.M. thesis, Dallas Theological Seminary, 1963.

Cockerill, Gareth L. "The Melchizedek Christology in Heb 7:1-28." Th.D. diss., Union Theological Seminary, 1976.

Dunn, Laura A. "The Law in Hebrews and Paul: A Comparison of Select Passages in Hebrews and Galatians 3:19-25." M.A. thesis, Trinity Evangelical Divinity School, 1991.

Hamilton, James Merrill, Jr. "He Is with You and He Will Be in You: The Spirit, the Believer, and the Glorification of Jesus." Ph.D diss., Southern Baptist Theological Seminary, 2003.

Johnsson, W. G. "Defilement and Purgation in the Book of Hebrews." Ph.D. diss., Vanderbilt University, 1973.

Lloyd, Linda Kathryn. "A Discourse Analysis of Hebrews." M.A. thesis, University of Texas at Arlington, 1976.

MacLeod, David J. "The Theology of the Epistle to the Hebrews: Introduction, Prolegomena, and Doctrinal Center." Th.D. diss., Dallas Theological Seminary, 1987.

Malone, Fred A. "A Critical Evaluation of the Use of Jeremiah 31:31-34 in the Letter to the Hebrews." Ph.D. diss., Southwestern Baptist Theological Seminary, 1989.

McCullough, J. C. "Hebrews and the Old Testament." Ph.D. diss., Queen's University, Belfast, 1971.

Miller, Chris A. "The Relationship of Jewish and Gentile Believers to the Law between A.D. 30 and 70 in the Scripture." Ph.D. diss., Dallas Theological Seminary, 1994.

Tetley, Joy D. "The Priesthood of Christ as the Controlling Theme of the Epistle to the Hebrews." Ph.D. diss., University of Durham, 1987.

Lexicons, Grammars and Textual Works

Bauer, Walter. *A Greek-English Lexicon of the New Testament and Other Early Christian Literature.* 3rd ed. Revised and edited by Frederick William Danker, William F. Arndt, and F. Wilbur Gingrich. Chicago: University of Chicago Press, 2000.

Blass, F., and Debrunner, A. *A Greek Grammar of the New Testament and Other Early Christian Literature.* Translated and revised by Robert W. Funk. Chicago: University of Chicago Press, 1961.

Liddell, Henry George, and Robert Scott, eds. *A Greek-English Lexicon with a Revised Supplement.* 9th ed. Revised and augmented by Sir Henry Stuart Jones. Oxford: Clarendon Press. New York: Oxford University Press, 1996.

Louw, Johannes P., and Eugene A. Nida, eds. *Greek-English Lexicon of the New Testament Based on Semantic Domains.* 2 vols. New York: United Bible Societies, 1988.

Metzger, Bruce M. *A Textual Commentary on the Greek New Testament.* 2nd ed. Stuttgart: United Bible Societies, 1994.

— *The Text of the New Testament: Its Transmission, Corruption, and Restoration.* 3rd edition. New York: Oxford University Press, 1992.

Robertson, A. T. *A Grammar of the Greek New Testament in the Light of Historical Research.* 4th ed. Nashville: Broadman Press, 1934.

Smyth, Herbert Weir. *Greek Grammar.* Revised by Gordon M. Messing. Rev. ed. Cambridge, MA: Harvard University Press, 1956.

Wallace, Daniel B. *Greek Grammar Beyond the Basics: An Exegetical Syntax of the New Testament.* Grand Rapids: Zondervan, 1996.

Index of Scripture and
Extrabiblical Literature

Genesis
6:18 161
14 120, 123, 135, 136,
    137, 138, 141, 142
14:17-20 126, 135, 136,
    137
14:18 136
14:18-20 142
14:20b 139
17 162
17:4 51
18:13 189
21:22-24 161
26:26-29 161

Exodus
3:5 151
15:9 180
16:18 146
18:21 33
19:1-24:11 194
20:17 56
20:25 33
23:14-17 38
24:1-8 162
24:3 162
24:5 289
24:8 236
24:12 146, 163, 216
25-31 180
25:40 179
29:38-42 33
31:18 216
32:15 216
32:19 196
34:1 216

Leviticus
3:16-17 274
10:3 151

11:1-31 56
16 228
16:21 239
17-26 84
17:10-14 274
17:11 236
18:5 83, 277
19:9-10 56
19:18 73, 268
23:22 56
25:35-55 56, 58

Numbers
5:15, 239
18:21-32, 139
19, 232
36, 39
36:5-12 38

Deuteronomy
4:1 41
4:8 197
4:13 216
5:22 216
6 198
6:5 73, 268
6:6 198
6:6-9 15
9:10 216
9:17 196
10:2-4 216
10:12-13 29
10:16 198
11 198
11:18 198
11:32 197
14:28-29 38
15:7-11 56, 58
17:19-20 198
20:1-9 33

22:11 268
23:19-20 56, 58
24:19-21 56
25 39
25:5-10 38
27:6 33
27-30 41
30 198
30:5 198
30:6 198
30:14 184
30:11-14 40, 198
30:16 29
32:45-46 198
33:19-20 47

Joshua
1:8 198
8:32 162
8:34 162
15:9 161
22:5 146, 198

1 Samuel
11:1 161
18:3 161

2 Samuel
3:12-13 161
7 162

1 Kings
5:12 161
9:6 197
20:34 161

2 Kings
11:4 161
13:23 162
14:6 199

22:8 196
23:1-3 162
23:3 193

1 Chronicles
5:1 139

Ezra
9-10 162

Nehemiah
9-13 162
9:29 41

Esther
1:6 100

Psalms
1:2 198
8:1-2 119
8:4-6 203
31:6 151
33:19 151
37:31 198, 240
40 203, 207, 242
40:6-8 203, 240
40:8 198
50:8-10 241
51:16-17 241
95:7-11 121, 203
110 114, 120, 123, 138,
    148, 151, 178
110:1 177, 232, 241-42
110:4 4, 10, 123, 126,
    133, 134, 135, 136,
    138, 140, 142, 144,
    145, 150, 153, 154,
    157, 158 165, 170,
    203
119 268
144:18 151

Proverbs
3:11-12 221
8:22 27

Isaiah
1:10-17 241

51:7 198
53:12 237
66:2-4 241

Jeremiah
1-29 200
3:10 193
3:17 193
4:4 193
4:14 193
4:18 193
5:23-24 193
6:19 196
7:21-24 241
7:23 193
7:24 193, 205
9:12 193, 205
9:13 197
9:13-14 196
9:14 193
9:26 193
11:6 193
11:8 193
11:10 193
11:20 193
12:11 193
13:22 194
13:23 194
16:11 193, 196
16:12 193
17:1 193, 194, 205
17:5 193
17:9 193, 194, 205
17:10 193
18:12 193
20:12 193
22:17 193
23:17 193
23:26-27 193
24:7 193
26:4 196, 199
30:8 194
30-33 194, 200
31 14, 15, 16, 19, 20, 22,
    127, 128, 148, 152,
    160, 162, 169, 176,
    185, 190, 193, 196,
    198, 200, 201, 203,

204, 205, 206, 213,
217, 220, 225, 226,
228, 230, 238, 243,
255, 256, 257, 266
31:12 195
31:31 219
31:31-32 218
31:31-34 19, 20, 22,
    127, 155, 162, 168,
    173, 176, 177, 183,
    185, 187, 188, 192,
    193, 194, 195, 200,
    204, 219, 220, 233,
    256
31:33 191, 192, 193,
    194, 195, 196, 198,
    199, 200, 206, 207,
    211, 213, 216, 242
31:33a 196, 218, 219
31:33b 218, 220
31:33c 219
31:33-34 233, 255, 257
31:33-34a 192
31:33c-34 218
31:34 195, 207
31:34a 219
31:34b 192, 219
31:40 195
32:33 196
32:40 15
33:21 162
34:8 161
34:8-22 162
36:23 196
41:18 186
44:10 196
44:23 196
51:63 196

Ezekiel
11:19-20 198
20:11 41
36 196, 198
36:25-27 198
36:27 198

Daniel
3:30, 146

Hosea
6:6 241
12:6 151

Amos
5:21-27 241

Micah
6:6-8, 241

Habakkuk
2:3 75
2:4 75

Zephaniah
3:2 151

Matthew
5-7 218
5:21-22 258
7:23 258
11 181
12:11 78
22:37-40 269
23:23 258
23:28 258
26:28 219

Luke
10:26 216
22:20 219

John
7:47-49 272
8:35 156
12:34 156
21:18 189

Romans
3:21-26 240
7:12 216
7:14 216
13:8-10 216

1 Corinthians
3:3 147
9:21 218

Galatians
3:19, 53

Hebrews
1 97, 202
1-2 97
1:1 201
1:1-2 88, 174, 179, 227
1:1-4 3, 98, 99, 100,
    114, 119, 121, 268,
    281, 282, 285
1:1-2:18 110
1:1-4:13 102
1:1-10:18 95, 101
1:2 2, 5, 158, 204, 247,
    248, 253
1:2b-3 103, 104
1:3 218, 250
1:3b 132
1:4 98, 100, 282
1:4-2:18 95
1:4-6:9 111
1:5 98, 100, 114, 158,
    183
1:5-14 119, 123, 282,
    285
1:5-2:18 100, 119, 281,
    282
1:6 183, 287
1:7 183, 287
1:8 158
1:9 139, 242
1:11 189
1:13 183
2 97
2:1-4 53, 95, 96, 100,
    119, 121, 282, 285
2:1-19 119
2:3 247
2:3-4 2
2:5-9 119, 123, 285
2:5-18 282
2:9 108
2:10 119, 221
2:10-18 119, 123, 285
2:14 244
2:14-18 121
2:17 98, 119, 120, 156,

    251, 282
2:17-18 119, 120
2:18 98, 112, 114, 119
3-4 89, 181, 183, 215,
    267
3:1 98, 120, 121, 156
3:1-6 110, 121, 282, 285
3:1-4:13 110, 121
3:1-4:14 120, 282
3:1-4:16 281
3:1-5:10 97, 100, 114,
    281, 282
3:2 255
3:6 158, 189, 219
3:7 287
3:7-19 110, 121, 205,
    285
3:7-4:6 183
3:7-4:11 96
3:7-4:13 174, 183, 186,
    188, 190, 194, 224,
    244, 287
3:7-4:14 282
3:10 190
3:12 183, 190
3:12-13 215
3:19 188
4:1 121, 155
4:1-2 121, 285
4:1-10 120
4:1-13 110
4:2 188
4:3 183
4:3-11 121, 285
4:4 183
4:6 188
4:7 18
4:10 120
4:11 120, 215
4:11-13 103
4:11-16 120
4:11-10:25 120
4:12 205
4:12-13 103, 104, 121,
    285
4:13 102, 112, 118
4:14 109, 120, 121, 124,
    158, 244

4:14-15 251
4:14-16 93, 94, 96, 103,
    104, 108, 110, 114,
    118, 119, 120, 124,
    285
4:14-6:20 110
4:14-10:18 120
4:14-10:25 119
4:14-10:31 103
4:15-16 282
4:15-5:1-10 282
4:16 124, 249, 253
5 110, 122
5:1 179, 250
5:1-3 126, 157
5:1-10 110, 119, 122,
    123, 157, 281, 282,
    285
5:1-10:18 118
5:1-10:39 120
5:3 158
5:5 158
5:6 114, 126, 134, 142,
    154, 183, 287
5:7 156, 252
5:8 158
5:9 98, 100
5:9-10 98, 282
5:10 98, 121, 126, 154
5:11 98, 121, 122
5:11-14 110, 221
5:11-6:3, 121, 285
5:11-6:8 110
5:11-6:12 96
5:11-6:20 97, 98, 108,
    114, 118, 119, 121,
    122, 123, 134, 281,
    283
5:11-10:25 114
5:11-10:39 101, 281,
    283
5:12 244
5:14 244
6 122
6:1-8 110
6:4-6 269
6:4-8 122, 123, 285
6:6 158

6:9 244
6:9-12 110, 122, 215,
    285
6:11 155
6:13 155
6:13-20 110, 122, 285
6:13-7:3 122, 123
6:14 139, 183
6:16 155
6:19-20 122
6:20 98, 112, 122, 123,
    126, 134, 142
7 110, 126, 127, 128,
    133, 134, 141, 142,
    149, 157, 158, 159,
    166, 171, 172, 175,
    177, 265
7-10 18, 260
7:1 98, 114, 122, 126,
    134, 135
7:1-2a 136
7:1-3 98, 122, 135, 138
7:1-10 10, 22, 110, 126,
    134, 135, 137, 141,
    285
7:1-25 157
7:1-28 2, 22, 100, 108,
    114, 119, 120, 123,
    126, 127, 129, 130,
    131, 132, 134, 135,
    177, 264, 265, 281,
    283
7:1-10:18 1, 2, 8, 20, 21,
    22, 87, 89, 93, 100,
    102, 122, 123, 124,
    125, 126, 129, 131,
    132, 138, 141-42,
    148, 150, 176, 224,
    238, 250, 264, 269,
    286
7:1-10:39 97
7:2 135, 139
7:2b 136
7:2b-c 136
7:2b-3 136
7:2c 136
7:3 135, 136, 137, 138,
    140, 154, 158, 244

7:3c 137
7:4 135, 139
7:4-10 98, 135, 138
7:5 5, 139, 140, 146,
    163, 164, 179
7:6 135, 244
7:6b 139
7:7 139, 140
7:8 140
7:8b 140
7:9 140, 164
7:9b 141
7:10 126, 135, 136, 140,
    141
7:11 5, 9, 126, 141, 142,
    144, 147, 148, 155,
    170
7:11b 143
7:11-12 7, 14, 168-69
7:11-12a 166
7:11-14 110, 140
7:11-19 6, 10, 17, 18,
    22, 126, 134, 141,
    152, 153
7:11-25 98
7:11-28 126, 134, 138,
    142, 285
7:12 4, 5, 9, 10, 11, 13,
    14, 16, 20, 22, 133,
    134, 141, 143, 144,
    146, 148, 150, 151,
    158, 159, 163, 164,
    166, 167, 168, 171,
    172, 173, 215, 264,
    265
7:13-14 139, 143, 144,
    154, 158, 165
7:13-16 179
7:14 110, 111
7:15 111
7:15a 145
7:15b 145
7:15-17 144
7:15-28 110
7:16 5, 137, 143, 145,
    146, 150, 151, 152,
    154, 156, 158, 163,
    164, 165

7:16a 145
7:16b 145
7:17 145, 149, 154
7:18 146, 150, 151, 152, 153, 165, 166, 167
7:18-19 126, 149, 152, 154, 164, 166
7:19 5, 126, 141, 148, 156, 165, 170, 173
7:19a 147, 149, 151, 163, 224
7:19b 151
7:20 126
7:20-21 126, 154
7:20-22 154, 182
7:20-25 154
7:20-28 22, 126, 134, 141, 154, 157
7:20b-21 154
7:21 126, 154, 155, 183
7:22 155, 163, 182, 235, 251
7:23 151, 156
7:23-24 145, 156
7:23-25 156
7:24 154, 156, 158
7:25 126, 156
7:26 157
7:26-28 98, 126, 157, 177
7:27 151, 156, 157, 179, 250
7:28 5, 112, 126, 142, 154, 158, 164, 165, 244
8 1, 22, 67, 89, 127, 128, 130, 134, 155, 159, 163, 166, 172, 173, 174, 176, 177, 187, 189, 192, 200, 205, 210, 218, 226, 244, 256, 265, 266
8-10 157, 179, 187, 203
8:1 108, 121, 127, 132, 150, 250
8:1-2 119, 120, 121, 127, 128, 129, 130, 131, 177, 226, 238,

285
8:1-5 182
8:1-6 22, 176, 177-78
8:1-7 111
8:1-13 2, 22, 120, 123, 127, 128, 129, 130, 176, 265
8:1-9:28 98, 100, 102, 106, 281, 283
8:1-10:18 111, 114, 127, 129, 131, 177, 186, 204, 256
8:2 120, 178, 208, 229, 231
8:3 120, 127, 156, 178, 238, 250
8:3-4 179
8:3-6 120, 285
8:3-13 130
8:3-10:18 119, 120, 123, 129, 130, 177, 238
8:4 5, 164, 178
8:4-5 182
8:5 178, 179, 180, 239, 253, 255
8:6 5, 14, 128, 155, 163, 182, 183, 190, 207, 225, 235, 247, 251, 258, 260, 266
8:6-13 6, 7, 13
8:7 128, 164, 182, 183, 184
8:7-13 22, 120, 128, 176, 182, 285
8:8 15, 164, 176, 183, 189, 257, 286, 291
8:8-9 174, 183
8:8-12 127, 160, 177, 184, 215, 225, 226, 230, 238, 243, 257, 269
8:8-13 111, 225
8:8a 244
8:8b-9 186
8:8b-12 185, 257, 291
8:9 182, 186, 269, 287, 291
8:9a 229

8:10 5, 7, 9, 10, 11, 12, 14, 15, 16, 17, 20, 22, 144, 150, 152, 159, 163, 166, 171, 173, 175, 176, 182, 184, 185, 186, 187, 188, 190, 191, 192, 199, 200, 206, 207, 208, 209, 210, 211, 212, 213, 214, 215, 216, 218, 222, 224, 232, 237, 241, 249, 256, 257, 258, 266, 287, 291
8:10-11 191, 192
8:10-12 128, 155, 172, 183, 188, 189, 191, 225, 226, 230, 232, 233, 238, 252, 261, 265
8:10b 220
8:11 176, 188, 192, 257, 292
8:11-12 288
8:12 188, 189, 191, 192, 207, 218, 239, 256, 257, 292
8:13 9, 10, 128, 129, 164, 169, 182, 183, 189
8:13a 17
9 133, 142, 178, 180, 227, 228, 236, 237, 250
9-10 153, 207, 265
9:1 128, 129, 164, 207, 227, 238, 261
9:1-10 22, 111, 128, 190, 226, 230
9:1-28 129, 131, 226, 245, 261, 267
9:1-10:14 138, 194, 247, 256
9:1-10:15 256
9:1-10:18 2, 22, 120, 124, 127, 128, 129, 130, 132, 152, 153, 157, 171, 172, 182,

183, 189, 190, 191,
221, 223, 224, 225,
226, 227, 238, 244,
245, 250, 255, 256,
257, 260, 261, 267,
268, 285
9:2 247, 248
9:2-3 239
9:2-5 227, 228, 247
9:2-10 227
9:3 239
9:4 244
9:6 248
9:6-7 228
9:6-8 247
9:6-10 227, 228, 247
9:6b-7 228
9:7 228, 231, 250, 251
9:8 228, 229, 244, 247,
248, 250
9:8-9 253
9:8-10 228, 254
9:8a 248
9:8b 247, 248
9:9 143, 148, 225, 227,
233, 241, 247, 250
9:9-10 165, 228, 253
9:9a 247, 248
9:10 89, 128, 174, 175,
190, 205, 227, 228,
229, 230, 239, 247,
250, 251, 261
9:11 107, 109, 128, 190,
227, 230, 231, 248,
249, 250, 266, 288
9:11-12 231, 250, 251
9:11-14 111, 190, 230,
233, 236, 239, 250,
252, 261, 288
9:11-28 22, 129, 226,
230, 238, 241
9:12 228, 231, 232, 251,
256, 289
9:13 143, 228, 251, 252
9:13-14 232, 238, 239,
252
9:14 143, 148, 165, 175,
190, 205, 225, 228,

230, 232, 233, 236,
239, 241, 251, 252,
261, 288
9:15 155, 164, 182, 233,
234, 235, 240, 251,
252
9:15-18 234
9:15-22 111, 233, 234,
236, 250, 251
9:15-28 230
9:16 164
9:16-17 7, 234
9:16-22 233-34, 235,
252
9:18 156, 164, 228, 234,
235
9:18-22 235
9:18-23 236
9:19 5, 164, 179, 228,
261, 289
9:19-22 235
9:20 228, 236
9:21 228
9:21-22 236, 253
9:22 5, 164, 179, 228,
236, 252, 256, 261
9:23 236, 237, 251
9:23-24 250, 251, 253
9:23-28 111, 236, 239
9:24 237, 250
9:25 228, 251
9:25-26 237
9:26 251, 256
9:27-28 237
9:28 143, 237, 239, 256
10 67, 89, 112, 129, 133,
179, 180, 210, 217,
218, 238, 240, 258
10:1 5, 10, 12, 14, 16,
18, 20, 22, 128, 130,
144, 148, 153, 178,
179, 190, 215, 225,
226, 227, 238, 239,
241, 244, 245, 246,
248, 249, 250, 251,
252, 253, 254, 255,
257, 261, 266, 267,
288, 289

10:1-4 6, 129, 143, 238,
240, 242
10:1-10 111, 240
10:1-14 238
10:1-18 22, 100, 129,
131, 207, 226, 238,
240, 283
10:1-39 98, 281
10:1b 224
10:2 164, 165
10:4 165, 240, 252, 261
10:5-7 240
10:5-10 157, 217, 225,
240, 241, 242, 250,
251, 261, 267
10:5b 240
10:7 240
10:8 5, 164, 179, 261
10:9 164, 247
10:11 130, 241, 247
10:10 129, 143, 232,
241, 242, 256, 261
10:11-14 241
10:11-18 111, 129, 13
10:12 25
10:12b 241
10:13 191
10:14 130, 143, 190,
232, 238, 241, 242,
261
10:15 190, 243, 257,
291
10:15-16 257
10:15-17 127, 186, 191,
255, 257, 291
10:15-18 131, 238, 242,
243, 261
10:16 5, 7, 9, 11, 12, 14,
16, 17, 20, 22, 144,
150, 152, 159, 163,
166, 171, 173, 175,
176, 185, 187, 191,
200, 206, 207, 208,
209, 210, 212, 213,
214, 218, 222, 224,
232, 237, 241, 242,
253, 254, 257, 258,
261, 266, 267, 287,

291
10:16-17 22, 128, 160,
 172, 177, 185, 191,
 207, 225, 226, 232,
 238, 239, 243, 249,
 252, 255, 259, 265,
 269
10:16-18 6, 155, 241,
 261
10:17 9, 131, 139, 191,
 207, 239, 257, 258,
 292
10:17-18 256
10:18 101, 102, 103,
 104, 112, 118, 127,
 258, 269
10:19 101, 108, 109,
 124, 127, 244
10:19-23 108, 124
10:19-25 93, 94, 103,
 104, 110, 111, 114,
 118, 119, 120, 123,
 124, 127, 207, 226,
 241, 285, 260
10:19-31 118
10:19-39 96, 104
10:19-12:29 95, 101,
 102, 111
10:19-13:17 95
10:20 124
10:21 124
10:22 124, 175, 190,
 198, 205, 207, 221,
 225
10:23 124
10:24-25 215
10:25 104, 114
10:26-31 103, 123, 269,
 284
10:26-32 284, 285
10:26-38 114
10:26-12:13 114
10:28 5
10:29 210
10:30 183
10:31 103, 104, 118,
 124
10:32 103

10:32-36 215
10:32-39 123, 284
10:32-13:17 103
10:33-39 285
10:35 103, 247
10:36 155
10:36-39 98, 283
10:39 100, 104, 114
11 89, 112, 188, 189,
 195, 221
11:1 112
11:1-2 123
11:1-3 89
11:1-40 108, 114, 123,
 125, 283, 285
11:1-12:2 98, 281
11:1-12:13 98, 101, 281,
 283
11:1-12:29 97
11:5 4, 166
11:6 89
11:10 244
11:19 156
11:36-39 89
11:39-40 123, 269
11:40 235
12:1 244, 269
12:1-2 98, 123, 285
12:1-13 114, 283
12:1-17 221
12:1-13:7 96
12:3-13 98, 281
12:3-17 123, 285
12:4 221
12:4-13 221
12:5 247
12:10-11 98
12:12 155, 283
12:14 98-99, 215, 221
12:14-13:18 107, 283
12:14-13:21 98, 101,
 114, 281
12:16-17 215
12:18 255
12:18-24 143, 285
12:18-25 123
12:18-29 114
12:22-24 189, 219

12:24 182, 189
12:25-29 123, 285
12:26 183
12:27 108
12:28 215
12:29 112
13 97, 102, 171, 259
13:1 221
13:1-3 215
13:1-6 260
13:1-8 111
13:1-19 100, 101, 102,
 123, 285
13:1-21 111, 114
13:4-5 210
13:7 103
13:9 103, 215
13:9-16 111
13:15 233
13:15-16 215, 221, 268
13:16 233
13:17-21 111
13:18-25 103
13:19 107, 283
13:20 138, 152, 163,
 170, 242, 266
13:20-21 123, 221, 283,
 285
13:20-25 101, 114
13:22 3, 96
13:22-25 99, 107, 111,
 123, 281, 283, 285
13:25 103

James
2:8 218
2:11 218
2:12 218

Jude
4, 166

APOCRYPHA
Baruch
1:1-14 39
1:15-22 41
1:15-3:8 39
1:22 41

2:1-10 41
2:2 39, 40, 41
2:28 39, 40
3:12 41
3:13-14 41
3:15-23 40
3:27-28 40
3:31 40
3:36 40
3:9-37 40
3:9-4:4 40
4:1 39, 40, 41
4:1-5 41
4:3 40
4:4 40, 42
4:5-5:9 40
4:12 39
4:12-13 41

Judith
8:27 151
11:11-12 275

1 Maccabees
1:10-15 32
1:14 32
1:44-64 33, 35
1:49 35
1:54-57 32
1:56 32, 33
1:60-61 32
1:62-63 32
2 32
2:17-25 32
2:26 32
2:26-27 35
2:27 32
2:29-38 32
2:34 32
2:37-38 2
2:41 33
2:48 33
2:50 35
2:58 35
2:64 33
2:67 33
2:68 33
2:70 33

3:48 33
3:56 33
4:42 33
4:47 33
4:53 33
10:14 33
13:4 33
13:48 33
14:14 33
14:29 33
15:21 33

2 Maccabees
1:3-4 34
2:2 34
2:3 34
2:19-32 34
2:22a 34
2:22b 34
3:1 34, 35
3:3-40 36
4:2 35
4:11 35
4:12 35
5:15 35
5:16 35
6:1 35
6:5 35
6:18-31 35
6:23 37
6:28 35
6-7 56
7 35
7:1 36
7:2 35, 37
7:3-5 35
7:9 35, 37
7:11, 35, 37
7:13-40 35
7:23 37
7:30 36, 37
7:37 36, 37
7:40 36
7:42 35
8:21 36
8:36 36
10:26 36
10:28 155

11:31 36
12:40 36
13:10 36
13:14 36
15:9 36

4 Maccabees
1:7 55
1:9 55
1:13 55
1:17a 58
1:19 55
1:30 55
1:34 56
2:5-6 56
2:6 55
2:8 56, 58
2:9, 56
2:24 55
4:24 57
5:16 57
5:18 57
5:25 57
5:29 57
5:1-17:6 56
6 57
6:18-7:20 55
6:21 57
6:27-29 57
7:9 57
7:16 55
9:1-12 56
9:2 57
9:15 57
11:27 57
12:11 57
12:14 57
13:1 55
13:22 57
15:2 57
15:9-10 57
16:1 55
17:1 57
17:18 57
18:2 55
18:4 57
18:6-19 56
18:10 56

Sirach
1:26 28
2:16 29
3:1 30
3:6 30
15:1 28
17:11-14 29, 31
17:14 31
18:4 28
18:9 28
19:20 28
23:27 29
24 27, 29, 31, 40, 46
24:22 29
24:23 29
24:23a 29
24:28a 30
24:28b 30
25:8 30
28:1 30
29:15 155
30:14-20 30
32:15 29
34:20-26, 31
35:1-5 30, 31
35:4 30
35:5 30
35:24 146
38:24-39:11 28
38:34 28
41:8 29
45:4-5 30
45:5 146
50:5-10 237
51:13-30 30
51:25-26 31
51:30 30

Tobit
1:3 38
1:6 38
1:8 37, 38
1:16-17 38
3:15 38
3:17 38
6:12-13 38
6:13 37
7:1-17 38

7:11 38
7:11-13 37
7:12-14 38
7:13 37
7:14 37
14:9 37, 38, 39

Wisdom of Solomon
2:12 275
6:4 275
16:6 275
18:4 275
18:9 275

PSEUDEPIGRAPHA
2 Baruch
14:5 47
14:11 46, 47
18:2 47
19:1-3 45
21:9 47
21:11 47
24:1 46, 47
29:2 47
30:1-2 47
32:1 46, 47
32:42 46
32:44 46
38:1 47
38:2 47
38:4 47
41-42 45
41:1 46
41:3 46
41:6 47
42:4 47
44:3 47
44:7 47
44:14 46, 47
45:2 47
46:1-5 46
46:3 47
46:4-5 46
48:22 46, 47
48:24 46
48:27 46
48:40 47
51:3 47

51:4-7 47
51:7 47
54:4 47
54:5 47
54:13-14 46
54:14 47
54:15 47
54:15-19 47
54:17 47
54:19 47
57:1-2 46
57:2 47
59:2 46
66:1 47
75:7 47
77:14 43
77:16 43
78:7 47
84:1-6 46
84:2 46
84:2-11 46
85:3 46
85:3-5 48
85:7 47

4 Ezra
3:21-22 49
3:22-26 49
6:32 51
7:19-25 50
7:20 49
7:21-24 50
7:45-48 50
7:53 51
7:60-61 51
7:72 48, 50
7:77 51
7:83 51
7:88-89 50
7:89 51
7:91 50
7:94 51
7:96 50
7:98 51
7:105 50
7:127-31 50
8:3 49
8:32-33 51

8:33 51
8:36 50, 51
8:39 51
9:26-37 48
9:36 48
9:37 48
14:21-22 48
14:29-34 51

Jubilees
1:1-4 52
1:26-27 53
2:18 54
3:8 53
3:8-11 54
3:31 53, 54
6:10 54
6:17 53, 54
6:20-21 53
6:22 52
7:20-25 53
7:20-39 52
7:21 53
7:34 53
16:5-9 53
16:29 54
17:17-18 53
18:14-19 53
20:2-13 53
20:6-8 53
20:9-10 53
21:4-20 55
23:16-21 53
23:26 53
30:9 53
30:10 53
30:17-23 53
30:21-22 53
33:10 54
33:10-15 53
33:16 55
39:6 53
40:8-11 53
50:12 61

Psalms of Solomon
2:33-37 276
3:11 276

3:12 276
4:8 276
4:23-25 276
5:18 276
7:9 276
7:10 276
8:33 276
8:34 276
9:3-5 276
10:4 276
10:5-8 276
12:4-6 276
13:6-12 277
14 276, 277
14:1-2 278
14:2 276
14:2-3 277
14:3 277
15 277
16:15 277

T. Benj.
10:3-4 146

T. Dan
5:1 146

T. Levi
13:1-9 278

T. Naph.
3:2-5 278
3:3-4 278

**QUMRAN
LITERATURE**
1 QH
6 74
7 74
13 74
15 74
16 74

1QpHab
2:4 75
7:9 75
8:1 75
8:1-3 74

8:10-11 74
8:18 74

1 QS
75, 77, 78, 79, 80, 81, 82,
   83, 86, 88
1:1ff. 74
1:1-3a 77
3-4 78
4 79
4:2-14 81
5:1-2 75-76
5:7-11 75, 76
5:7-12 77
5:8 79
5:8-9 76
5:10-11 81
6:6-8 79
6:24-7:25 84
6:24b-7:25 79
8:5-17 76
8:10-12 77
8:14-16 85
8:15 77, 79
8:20-23 76
8:24-26 76
9:1ff, 79
9:23-26 74
10:18 78
10:25 74
13:19 79

1QSb
2:23 78

CD
1:3-4:9 77
1:14 82
1:18-2:1 82
3:12 82
3:14 82, 83
3:14-16 82-83
3:15 84
3:17 83
3:20 83
5:7-9 78
6:3-4 83
6:11-7:10 84

6:14 83
6:15-21 83
7:4b-6a 84
10:10 84
10:14 84
11:13-14 78
16:10 84

CD-B
9b-10a 84
10b 84
19:29-35 84
19:33b-20:1a 84
20:1b-8a 84
20:8b-13a 84

4QMMT
75, 82, 85, 86
C 23-35, 78

4Q418
103:6-9 75

4Q419
1:1-2 75

4Q525 (4QBeat)
86
2:3-4 75

11QTemple
85

JOSEPHUS
33, 87, 88

Life
9 62
135 61
198 62

Against Apion
1.285-86 166
2.18 61
2.26 167
2.82 61
2.164-219 65
2.174 62

2.174-78 62
2.175 62
2.178 62, 63, 64
2.181 63
2.182-83 67
2.190-217 60
2.217-18 65
2.217-19 65
2.276 143

Jewish Antiquities
Preface 3 61
1.181 139
3 61
4 61
3.90-286 65
3.223 65
3.224-86 60
4.8.3 60
4.190-301 60, 65
4.209-210 63
4.212 66
4.218-19 64
18.57 166
20.263 62

Jewish Wars
2.19 33, 61
3.374 65
3.374-75 65
6.99 157

PHILO
180-81

On Abraham
1 67
3 71
4 72
5 71, 72
6 71, 72
18 166
81 166
276 71

On the Confusion of Tongues
69 246

On the Decalogue
1.1 69
132 69
82 246

That God is Unchangeable
177 246

On Drunkenness
141 69

On Flight
118 157

On Giants
66 166

Who is Heir of Divine Things
168-73 73

Hypothetica
7.1 68
7.12 68
7.14 68

On the Life of Joseph
42 72
63 67

Allegorical Interpretation
3:96 99

On the Embassy to Gaius
210 72

On the Migration of Abraham
12 246
89 68

On the Life of Moses
2.13 72
2.14 71
2.216 68

On the Creation
3 69, 71
61 68
170-72 71

Every Good Man is Free
62 71

On Dreams
1.206 246

*On the Special
  Legislation*
1.1-10 68
1.4 68
1.5 68
1.66-345 73
1.76 73
1.113 157
1.141-4 72
1.154 72
1.155 72

1.235 143
2.13 69
2.35 143
2.62 68
2.63 73
3.51 68
4.143 73

On the Virtues
134 71

Index of Modern Authors

Anderson, Hugh 57
Andriessen, Paul 231
Arenhoevel, Diego 34
Attridge, Harold 3, 10, 11, 12, 14, 93,
    104, 109, 110, 111, 113, 114, 115,
    121, 128, 129, 136, 142, 146, 147,
    152, 159, 169, 179, 198, 211, 212,
    213, 234, 235, 236, 242, 245, 252,
    287
Aune, David 91, 92

Barrett, C. K. 181, 202, 237, 239, 246,
    253
Bartels, Robert 49
Bauckham, Richard 43, 44, 45, 46, 47
    48, 49, 50, 51
Baumgarten, A. I. 25, 64, 68, 81
Bayes, Jonathan 146, 148, 159, 199,
    242, 245, 259
Becker, Jürgen 80
Behm, J., 160
Bénétreau, Samuel 109
Black, David A. 92, 95, 96, 105, 107,
    112, 112-113
Blank, Sheldon H. 199
Blenkinsopp, Joseph 29, 30, 58, 60, 76,
    77-78, 79, 275
Bligh, John 99
Block, Daniel 149
Bockmuehl, Markus 28, 69, 71, 79, 80,
    278
Borgen, Peder 69, 70
Bright, John 193
Brown, Colin 162, 197
Bruce, F. F. 15, 16, 93, 94, 109, 110,
    111, 112, 113, 122, 138, 148, 215,
    232, 233, 237, 242-43, 252
Buchanan, G. W. 109, 120, 146, 147,
    215
Büchler, A. 30
Büchsel, F. 106, 116
Burkes, Shannon 47-48

Caird, G. B. 203, 204
Calvin, John 215
Carroll, Robert 196-97
Carson, D. A. 44
Childs, Brevard 161
Cockerill, Gareth L. 146, 157, 158
Cody, Aelred 178, 232
Cohen, Naomi 72

D'Angelo, Marie 175, 204
Davies, Philip 37, 39, 55, 57, 274
Davies, W. D. 24, 26, 60, 82, 193, 198,
    199, 211, 224, 272
Delitzsch, Franz 8, 9
Demarest, Bruce 136, 136-37, 139, 140,
    146
Descamps, Albert 106
DeSilva, David 28, 122, 215, 259, 260,
    275
Desjardins, Michel 43, 46, 47, 48, 50
Di Lella, A. 27, 29
Dodd, C. H. 23, 24, 25, 26, 202
Duhm, Bernhard 193, 197
Dunn, James 40
Dunnill, J. 149, 154, 168, 168-69, 225,
    228
Dussaut, Louis 94, 109, 113

Ellingworth, Paul 16, 17, 99, 109, 111,
    112, 128, 135, 136, 140, 147, 147-48,
    153, 154, 159, 166, 179, 182, 189,
    192, 199, 209, 247, 286, 287, 289
Elliot, Mark 26, 45, 48, 50, 55, 58, 59,
    78, 79, 83, 85, 86, 278
Ellis, E. E. 215
Endres, John 52
Enns, Peter 54
Esser, H. 161
Evans, Craig 57

Fabry, Heinz-Josef 75
Feldman, Louis 61, 65, 65-66, 66

Filson, Floyd V. 92, 96, 107, 260
Fischer, John 19
Fitzmyer, J. A. 37, 38, 86, 139, 142
France, R. T. 203, 204, 227
Frey, Jörg 191, 212

Gamberoni, Johannes 38, 39
Gathercole, Simon 26, 33, 36, 40, 41,
    45, 47, 53, 54, 57, 58, 58-59, 60, 62,
    64, 65, 75, 78, 79, 81, 82, 83, 86, 277
Gench, Frances 209
Gilbert, M. 56
Goldstein, Jonathan 31, 33, 34, 35, 36
Goodenough, E. 69, 70
Goppelt, Leonhard 17
Gordon, Robert P. 209
Gourgues, Michel 178
Gowan, Donald 28, 29, 30, 31, 40, 41
Gräßer, Erich 12, 16, 17, 18, 19, 20,
    125, 142, 144, 145, 152, 153, 156,
    169, 170, 181, 187, 188, 191, 197-98,
    208, 212, 213, 238, 239, 246
Greengus, Samuel 162
Guhrt, J. 161
Gutbrod, W. 60-61, 70, 73
Guthrie, Donald 93, 94, 95, 96, 101,
    112, 192, 215
Guthrie, George 6, 91, 93, 94, 96, 104-
    05, 108, 110, 115, 116, 117, 118, 119,
    120, 121, 122, 123, 124, 125, 126,
    127, 128, 129, 131, 149, 154, 172,
    181, 201, 205, 238, 264, 284
Gyllenberg, Rafael 105, 106, 116

Hafemann, Scott 52
Hagner, Donald 1, 209
Hahn, Scott 234
Haldane, James 209
Hallbäck, Geert 48
Hanson, Anthony 136, 181
Harrington, D. J. 36
Harrisville, Roy 15, 19, 180, 184
Hay, David 68, 70, 72, 177, 178, 242
Hegermann, Harald 15, 210
Hellerman, Joseph 37, 53
Hengel, Martin 24, 152, 181
Hofius, Otfried 174, 228, 238, 248
House, Paul 196

Huey, F. B. 194, 195, 198
Hughes, Graham 4, 5, 140, 149, 153,
    154, 174, 185, 203, 204
Hughes, John 234
Hughes, P. E. 11, 14, 15, 94, 108, 216,
    232, 245, 255, 257
Huntjens, Johannes 74, 75, 79, 85
Hurst, L. D. 146-47, 147, 152, 181, 182,
    185, 202, 246, 247
Hyatt, J. Philip 197

Isaacs, Marie 1, 10, 12, 161, 165-66,
    169, 170, 212

Jaubert, Annie 80
Johnsson, W. G. 228, 256
Joslin, Barry 128

Kaiser, Walter 19, 197
Käsemann, Ernst 152, 181, 208, 246
Kee, H. C. 278
Keown, Gerald 196, 198
Kistemaker, Simon 95, 185, 203, 207,
    215, 243, 257, 258, 259
Kittel, Gerhard 246
Klijn, A. F. J. 47
Köberle, Justus. 44
Koester, Craig 11, 12, 17, 92, 94, 108,
    109, 122, 138, 139, 144, 148, 153,
    186, 210, 240
Kümmel, Werver G. 96, 101, 103, 108,
    118
Kuss, Otto 107, 108

Laansma, Jon 181
Lane, William 3 17, 18, 103-04, 109,
    117, 118, 120, 121, 122, 125, 126,
    129, 137, 138, 139, 141, 145, 146,
    147, 154, 165, 166, 177, 180, 184,
    188, 214, 220, 229, 231, 232, 233,
    234, 235, 238, 241, 243, 256, 287,
    290
Lee, E. Kenneth 179
Lehne, Susanne 5, 12, 13, 150, 154-55,
    169, 173, 184, 187, 198, 205, 211,
    212
Levin, Christoph 18, 19, 20, 168, 169,
    187, 188

Lindars, Barnabas 7, 8, 17, 92, 92-93, 93, 215, 225, 245, 252, 254, 273
Loader, William 156
Lofthouse, W. F. 216
Lohse, Eduard 272
Longenecker, Richard 50, 203, 204
Louw, Johannes 128
Lundbom, Jack 197, 209, 210
Luz, Ulrich 14, 198, 212

Mackay, John 197
MacLeod, David 132, 180, 236, 237
MacRae, George W. 246
Malone, Fred A. 160, 177, 187, 188, 190, 199, 205, 216, 242, 256, 258, 259
Manson, William 209
Marböck, Johannes 29
Marcus, Ralph 25, 26
Martens, John 70, 71, 72, 73
Maurer, Christian 166
McComiskey, Thomas 195, 196, 247
McConville, Gordon 160
McCready, Wayne 77, 79
McCullough, J. C. 1, 6, 176, 180, 185, 186, 203
McKane, William 197
McKnight, Edgar 191, 209, 258
Mendenhall, G. E. 161
Ménégoz, E., 7
Metzger, Bruce 48, 154, 286, 287, 288, 290
Michel, Otto 96, 97, 99, 102, 103, 108, 114, 118, 122, 141, 156, 157, 228, 248
Milligan, George 7
Moffatt, James 93-94, 114, 157, 209
Montefiore, Hugh 9, 10, 109, 147, 215
Moore, Carey 38, 274
Moore, George 25, 26
Morris, Leon 210, 215
Motyer, Stephen 202

Nairne, Alexander 7
Nauck, Wolfgang 92, 93, 94, 96, 102, 103, 104, 108, 113, 114, 117, 118, 119, 124, 125, 131
Neeley, Linda 94, 120, 122

Neusner, Jacob 272
Nicholson, Ernest 161, 195, 196, 198
Nickelsburg, George W. 37, 40-41, 57, 81, 83, 86
Nida, Eugene 128
Nikiprowetzky, Valentin 70

Osborne, Grant 178, 212
Östborn, Gunnar 190, 211

Peterson, David 150, 175, 190, 191, 211, 212, 226, 229, 232, 241, 243, 256
Pierce, C. A. 229
Pink, A. W. 259

Redditt, Paul 56
Reinhartz, Adele 71
Renaud, B. 32, 34
Rendtorff, Rolf 197, 197-98, 212, 244
Rhoads, David 272
Riggenbach, Eduard 228, 248
Rissi, Mathias 160, 258
Robertson, O. Palmer 200

Sanders, E. P. 25, 26, 32, 33, 44, 45, 49, 50, 51, 52, 54, 58, 59, 60, 61, 65, 67, 72, 73, 78-79, 83, 85, 162, 163, 271, 274, 276, 277, 279, 280
Sanders, Jack 28, 29-30, 40, 75, 275
Sandmel, Samuel 24, 69, 70
Scalise, Pamela J. 196, 198
Schäfer, K. T. 240
Schechter, Solomon 24, 25, 26
Schenck, Kenneth 10, 12
Schrenk, Gottlob 146
Schunack, Gerd 11, 149, 187, 191, 212, 246, 257
Segal, Alan 33-34, 36, 68
Seifrid, Mark 51, 276, 277, 278
Silva, Moises 147, 148
Smallwood, E. Mary 279-80
Smend, Rudolph 14, 198, 212
Smothers, Thomas 196, 198
Spicq, Ceslas 9, 93, 100, 101, 102, 103, 104, 107, 110, 113, 114, 128, 137, 157, 159-60, 181, 202, 214, 233, 246
Splisbury, Paul 60, 62, 63, 64, 66-67

Stanley, Steve 201, 202, 250, 254
Stone, Michael 57
Stylianopoulos, Theodore 253
Swetnam, James 94, 99, 107, 108, 113,
   114, 115
Synge, F. C. 116

Theissen, Gerd 208
Thielman, Frank 12, 13, 14, 148, 152,
   159, 169
Thien, F. 97, 97-98, 100, 105, 106
Thomas, Kenneth 185, 186
Thompson, James 193

Vaganay, Leon 93, 97, 98, 99, 100, 101,
   102, 104, 105, 108, 110, 113, 114,
   118, 131, 281
Van Groningen, Gerard 194
VanderKam, James 54
Vanhoye, Albert 92, 93, 94, 104, 105,
   106, 107, 109, 110, 112, 113, 114,
   115, 116, 118, 119, 120, 122, 124,
   125, 126, 131, 161, 214, 235, 251,
   254, 282
Vermes, Geza 64, 65, 66, 75, 77, 85, 86
Von Campenhausen, Hans 16
Von Rad, Gerhard 195, 196
Von Soden, Hermann 105
Vos, Geerhardus 7, 251

Walters, J. 203, 204
Ware, Bruce 196, 198, 232
Weinfeld, Moshe 198
Weiß, H-F 12, 16, 17, 103, 143, 151,
   165, 183, 202
Westcott, B. F. 179, 185, 210, 289
Westfall, Cynthia 116, 117, 119, 120,
   121, 122, 122-23, 126, 127, 128, 129
Williamson, Ronald 9, 100, 181, 202,
   246
Windisch, Hans 96, 150, 232
Winninge, Mikael 277
Wintermute,O. S. 52
Wright, R. B. 276

Young, Norman 247, 248

Paternoster Biblical Monographs

(All titles uniform with this volume)
Dates in bold are of projected publication

Joseph Abraham
Eve: Accused or Acquitted?
A Reconsideration of Feminist Readings of the Creation Narrative Texts in Genesis 1–3

Two contrary views dominate contemporary feminist biblical scholarship. One finds in the Bible an unequivocal equality between the sexes from the very creation of humanity, whilst the other sees the biblical text as irredeemably patriarchal and androcentric. Dr Abraham enters into dialogue with both camps as well as introducing his own method of approach. An invaluable tool for any one who is interested in this contemporary debate.

2002 / 0-85364-971-5 / xxiv + 272pp

Octavian D. Baban
Mimesis and Luke's on the Road Encounters in Luke-Acts
Luke's Theology of the Way and its Literary Representation

The book argues on theological and literary (mimetic) grounds that Luke's on-the-road encounters, especially those belonging to the post-Easter period, are part of his complex theology of the Way. Jesus' teaching and that of the apostles is presented by Luke as a challenging answer to the Hellenistic reader's thirst for adventure, good literature, and existential paradigms.

2005 / 1-84227-253-5 / approx. 374pp

Paul Barker
The Triumph of Grace in Deuteronomy

This book is a textual and theological analysis of the interaction between the sin and faithlessness of Israel and the grace of Yahweh in response, looking especially at Deuteronomy chapters 1–3, 8–10 and 29–30. The author argues that the grace of Yahweh is determinative for the ongoing relationship between Yahweh and Israel and that Deuteronomy anticipates and fully expects Israel to be faithless.

2004 / 1-84227-226-8 / xxii + 270pp

Jonathan F. Bayes
The Weakness of the Law
God's Law and the Christian in New Testament Perspective

A study of the four New Testament books which refer to the law as weak (Acts, Romans, Galatians, Hebrews) leads to a defence of the third use in the Reformed debate about the law in the life of the believer.

2000 / 0-85364-957-X / xii + 244pp

Mark Bonnington
The Antioch Episode of Galatians 2:11-14 in Historical and Cultural Context
The Galatians 2 'incident' in Antioch over table-fellowship suggests significant disagreement between the leading apostles. This book analyses the background to the disagreement by locating the incident within the dynamics of social interaction between Jews and Gentiles. It proposes a new way of understanding the relationship between the individuals and issues involved.

2005 / 1-84227-050-8 / approx. 350pp

David Bostock
A Portrayal of Trust
The Theme of Faith in the Hezekiah Narratives
This study provides detailed and sensitive readings of the Hezekiah narratives (2 Kings 18–20 and Isaiah 36–39) from a theological perspective. It concentrates on the theme of faith, using narrative criticism as its methodology. Attention is paid especially to setting, plot, point of view and characterization within the narratives. A largely positive portrayal of Hezekiah emerges that underlines the importance and relevance of scripture.

2005 / 1-84227-314-0 / approx. 300pp

Mark Bredin
Jesus, Revolutionary of Peace
A Non-violent Christology in the Book of Revelation
This book aims to demonstrate that the figure of Jesus in the Book of Revelation can best be understood as an active non-violent revolutionary.

2003 / 1-84227-153-9 / xviii + 262pp

Robinson Butarbutar
Paul and Conflict Resolution
An Exegetical Study of Paul's Apostolic Paradigm in 1 Corinthians 9
The author sees the apostolic paradigm in 1 Corinthians 9 as part of Paul's unified arguments in 1 Corinthians 8–10 in which he seeks to mediate in the dispute over the issue of food offered to idols. The book also sees its relevance for dispute-resolution today, taking the conflict within the author's church as an example.

2006 / 1-84227-315-9 / approx. 280pp

Daniel J-S Chae
Paul as Apostle to the Gentiles
*His Apostolic Self-awareness and its Influence on the Soteriological Argument
in Romans*
Opposing 'the post-Holocaust interpretation of Romans', Daniel Chae competently demonstrates that Paul argues for the equality of Jew and Gentile in Romans. Chae's fresh exegetical interpretation is academically outstanding and spiritually encouraging.
1997 / 0-85364-829-8 / xiv + 378pp

Luke L. Cheung
The Genre, Composition and Hermeneutics of the Epistle of James
The present work examines the employment of the wisdom genre with a certain compositional structure and the interpretation of the law through the Jesus tradition of the double love command by the author of the Epistle of James to serve his purpose in promoting perfection and warning against doubleness among the eschatologically renewed people of God in the Diaspora.
2003 / 1-84227-062-1 / xvi + 372pp

Youngmo Cho
Spirit and Kingdom in the Writings of Luke and Paul
The relationship between Spirit and Kingdom is a relatively unexplored area in Lukan and Pauline studies. This book offers a fresh perspective of two biblical writers on the subject. It explores the difference between Luke's and Paul's understanding of the Spirit by examining the specific question of the relationship of the concept of the Spirit to the concept of the Kingdom of God in each writer.
2005 / 1-84227-316-7 / approx. 270pp

Andrew C. Clark
Parallel Lives
The Relation of Paul to the Apostles in the Lucan Perspective
This study of the Peter-Paul parallels in Acts argues that their purpose was to emphasize the themes of continuity in salvation history and the unity of the Jewish and Gentile missions. New light is shed on Luke's literary techniques, partly through a comparison with Plutarch.
2001 / 1-84227-035-4 / xviii + 386pp

Andrew D. Clarke
Secular and Christian Leadership in Corinth
A Socio-Historical and Exegetical Study of 1 Corinthians 1–6
This volume is an investigation into the leadership structures and dynamics of first-century Roman Corinth. These are compared with the practice of leadership in the Corinthian Christian community which are reflected in 1 Corinthians 1–6, and contrasted with Paul's own principles of Christian leadership.

2005 / 1-84227-229-2 / 200pp

Stephen Finamore
God, Order and Chaos
René Girard and the Apocalypse
Readers are often disturbed by the images of destruction in the book of Revelation and unsure why they are unleashed after the exaltation of Jesus. This book examines past approaches to these texts and uses René Girard's theories to revive some old ideas and propose some new ones.

2005 / 1-84227-197-0 / approx. 344pp

David G. Firth
Surrendering Retribution in the Psalms
Responses to Violence in the Individual Complaints
In *Surrendering Retribution in the Psalms*, David Firth examines the ways in which the book of Psalms inculcates a model response to violence through the repetition of standard patterns of prayer. Rather than seeking justification for retributive violence, Psalms encourages not only a surrender of the right of retribution to Yahweh, but also sets limits on the retribution that can be sought in imprecations. Arising initially from the author's experience in South Africa, the possibilities of this model to a particular context of violence is then briefly explored.

2005 / 1-84227-337-X / xviii + 154pp

Scott J. Hafemann
Suffering and Ministry in the Spirit
Paul's Defence of His Ministry in II Corinthians 2:14–3:3
Shedding new light on the way Paul defended his apostleship, the author offers a careful, detailed study of 2 Corinthians 2:14–3:3 linked with other key passages throughout 1 and 2 Corinthians. Demonstrating the unity and coherence of Paul's argument in this passage, the author shows that Paul's suffering served as the vehicle for revealing God's power and glory through the Spirit.

2000 / 0-85364-967-7 / xiv + 262pp

Scott J. Hafemann
Paul, Moses and the History of Israel
The Letter/Spirit Contrast and the Argument from Scripture in 2 Corinthians 3
An exegetical study of the call of Moses, the second giving of the Law (Exodus 32–34), the new covenant, and the prophetic understanding of the history of Israel in 2 Corinthians 3. Hafemann's work demonstrates Paul's contextual use of the Old Testament and the essential unity between the Law and the Gospel within the context of the distinctive ministries of Moses and Paul.
2005 / 1-84227-317-5 / xii + 498pp

Douglas S. McComiskey
Lukan Theology in the Light of the Gospel's Literary Structure
Luke's Gospel was purposefully written with theology embedded in its patterned literary structure. A critical analysis of this cyclical structure provides new windows into Luke's interpretation of the individual pericopes comprising the Gospel and illuminates several of his theological interests.
2004 / 1-84227-148-2 / xviii + 388pp

Stephen Motyer
Your Father the Devil?
A New Approach to John and 'The Jews'
Who are 'the Jews' in John's Gospel? Defending John against the charge of antisemitism, Motyer argues that, far from demonising the Jews, the Gospel seeks to present Jesus as 'Good News for Jews' in a late first century setting.
1997 / 0-85364-832-8 / xiv + 260pp

Esther Ng
Reconstructing Christian Origins?
The Feminist Theology of Elizabeth Schüssler Fiorenza: An Evaluation
In a detailed evaluation, the author challenges Elizabeth Schüssler Fiorenza's reconstruction of early Christian origins and her underlying presuppositions. The author also presents her own views on women's roles both then and now.
2002 / 1-84227-055-9 / xxiv + 468pp

Robin Parry

Old Testament Story and Christian Ethics

The Rape of Dinah as a Case Study

What is the role of story in ethics and, more particularly, what is the role of Old Testament story in Christian ethics? This book, drawing on the work of contemporary philosophers, argues that narrative is crucial in the ethical shaping of people and, drawing on the work of contemporary Old Testament scholars, that story plays a key role in Old Testament ethics. Parry then argues that when situated in canonical context Old Testament stories can be reappropriated by Christian readers in their own ethical formation. The shocking story of the rape of Dinah and the massacre of the Shechemites provides a fascinating case study for exploring the parameters within which Christian ethical appropriations of Old Testament stories can live.

2004 / 1-84227-210-1 / xx + 350pp

Ian Paul

Power to See the World Anew

The Value of Paul Ricoeur's Hermeneutic of Metaphor in Interpreting the Symbolism of Revelation 12 and 13

This book is a study of the hermeneutics of metaphor of Paul Ricoeur, one of the most important writers on hermeneutics and metaphor of the last century. It sets out the key points of his theory, important criticisms of his work, and how his approach, modified in the light of these criticisms, offers a methodological framework for reading apocalyptic texts.

2006 / 1-84227-056-7 / approx. 350pp

Robert L. Plummer

Paul's Understanding of the Church's Mission

Did the Apostle Paul Expect the Early Christian Communities to Evangelize?

This book engages in a careful study of Paul's letters to determine if the apostle expected the communities to which he wrote to engage in missionary activity. It helpfully summarizes the discussion on this debated issue, judiciously handling contested texts, and provides a way forward in addressing this critical question. While admitting that Paul rarely explicitly commands the communities he founded to evangelize, Plummer amasses significant incidental data to provide a convincing case that Paul did indeed expect his churches to engage in mission activity. Throughout the study, Plummer progressively builds a theological basis for the church's mission that is both distinctively Pauline and compelling.

2006 / 1-84227-333-7 / approx. 324pp

David Powys
'Hell': A Hard Look at a Hard Question
The Fate of the Unrighteous in New Testament Thought
This comprehensive treatment seeks to unlock the original meaning of terms and phrases long thought to support the traditional doctrine of hell. It concludes that there is an alternative—one which is more biblical, and which can positively revive the rationale for Christian mission.

1997 / 0-85364-831-X / xxii + 478pp

Sorin Sabou
Between Horror and Hope
Paul's Metaphorical Language of Death in Romans 6.1-11
This book argues that Paul's metaphorical language of death in Romans 6.1-11 conveys two aspects: horror and hope. The 'horror' aspect is conveyed by the 'crucifixion' language, and the 'hope' aspect by 'burial' language. The life of the Christian believer is understood, as relationship with sin is concerned ('death to sin'), between these two realities: horror and hope.

2005 / 1-84227-322-1 / approx. 224pp

Rosalind Selby
The Comical Doctrine
The Epistemology of New Testament Hermeneutics
This book argues that the gospel breaks through postmodernity's critique of truth and the referential possibilities of textuality with its gift of grace. With a rigorous, philosophical challenge to modernist and postmodernist assumptions, Selby offers an alternative epistemology to all who would still read with faith *and* with academic credibility.

2005 / 1-84227-212-8 / approx. 350pp

Kiwoong Son
Zion Symbolism in Hebrews
Hebrews 12.18-24 as a Hermeneutical Key to the Epistle
This book challenges the general tendency of understanding the Epistle to the Hebrews against a Hellenistic background and suggests that the Epistle should be understood in the light of the Jewish apocalyptic tradition. The author especially argues for the importance of the theological symbolism of Sinai and Zion (Heb. 12:18-24) as it provides the Epistle's theological background as well as the rhetorical basis of the superiority motif of Jesus throughout the Epistle.

2005 / 1-84227-368-X / approx. 280pp

Kevin Walton
Thou Traveller Unknown
The Presence and Absence of God in the Jacob Narrative
The author offers a fresh reading of the story of Jacob in the book of Genesis through the paradox of divine presence and absence. The work also seeks to make a contribution to Pentateuchal studies by bringing together a close reading of the final text with historical critical insights, doing justice to the text's historical depth, final form and canonical status.
2003 / 1-84227-059-1 / xvi + 238pp

George M. Wieland
The Significance of Salvation
A Study of Salvation Language in the Pastoral Epistles
The language and ideas of salvation pervade the three Pastoral Epistles. This study offers a close examination of their soteriological statements. In all three letters the idea of salvation is found to play a vital paraenetic role, but each also exhibits distinctive soteriological emphases. The results challenge common assumptions about the Pastoral Epistles as a corpus.
2005 / 1-84227-257-8 / approx. 324pp

Alistair Wilson
When Will These Things Happen?
A Study of Jesus as Judge in Matthew 21–25
This study seeks to allow Matthew's carefully constructed presentation of Jesus to be given full weight in the modern evaluation of Jesus' eschatology. Careful analysis of the text of Matthew 21–25 reveals Jesus to be standing firmly in the Jewish prophetic and wisdom traditions as he proclaims and enacts imminent judgement on the Jewish authorities then boldly claims the central role in the final and universal judgement.
2004 / 1-84227-146-6 / xxii + 272pp

Lindsay Wilson
Joseph Wise and Otherwise
The Intersection of Covenant and Wisdom in Genesis 37–50
This book offers a careful literary reading of Genesis 37–50 that argues that the Joseph story contains both strong covenant themes and many wisdom-like elements. The connections between the two helps to explore how covenant and wisdom might intersect in an integrated biblical theology.
2004 / 1-84227-140-7 / xvi + 340pp

Stephen I. Wright
The Voice of Jesus
Studies in the Interpretation of Six Gospel Parables
This literary study considers how the 'voice' of Jesus has been heard in different
periods of parable interpretation, and how the categories of figure and trope may
help us towards a sensitive reading of the parables today.
2000 / 0-85364-975-8 / xiv + 280pp

Paternoster Theological Monographs

Emil Bartos
Deification in Eastern Orthodox Theology
An Evaluation and Critique of the Theology of Dumitru Staniloae
Bartos studies a fundamental yet neglected aspect of Orthodox theology:
deification. By examining the doctrines of anthropology, christology, soteriology and ecclesiology as they relate to deification, he provides an important
contribution to contemporary dialogue between Eastern and Western
theologians.
1999 / 0-85364-956-1 / xii + 370pp

Graham Buxton
The Trinity, Creation and Pastoral Ministry
Imaging the Perichoretic God
In this book the author proposes a three-way conversation between theology,
science and pastoral ministry. His approach draws on a Trinitarian
understanding of God as a relational being of love, whose life 'spills over' into
all created reality, human and non-human. By locating human meaning and
purpose within God's 'creation-community' this book offers the possibility of a
transforming engagement between those in pastoral ministry and the scientific
community.
***2005** / 1-84227-369-8 / approx. 380 pp*

Iain D. Campbell
Fixing the Indemnity
The Life and Work of George Adam Smith
When Old Testament scholar George Adam Smith (1856–1942) delivered the
Lyman Beecher lectures at Yale University in 1899, he confidently declared that
'modern criticism has won its war against traditional theories. It only remains to
fix the amount of the indemnity.' In this biography, Iain D. Campbell assesses
Smith's critical approach to the Old Testament and evaluates its consequences,
showing that Smith's life and work still raises questions about the relationship
between biblical scholarship and evangelical faith.
***2004** / 1-84227-228-4 / xx + 256pp*

Tim Chester
Mission and the Coming of God
Eschatology, the Trinity and Mission in the Theology of Jürgen Moltmann
This book explores the theology and missiology of the influential contemporary
theologian, Jürgen Moltmann. It highlights the important contribution Moltmann
has made while offering a critique of his thought from an evangelical
perspective. In so doing, it touches on pertinent issues for evangelical
missiology. The conclusion takes Calvin as a starting point, proposing 'an
eschatology of the cross' which offers a critique of the over-realised
eschatologies in liberation theology and certain forms of evangelicalism.
2006 / 1-84227-320-5 / approx. 224pp

Sylvia Wilkey Collinson
Making Disciples
The Significance of Jesus' Educational Strategy for Today's Church
This study examines the biblical practice of discipling, formulates a definition,
and makes comparisons with modern models of education. A recommendation is
made for greater attention to its practice today.
2004 / 1-84227-116-4 / xiv + 278pp

Darrell Cosden
A Theology of Work
Work and the New Creation
Through dialogue with Moltmann, Pope John Paul II and others, this book
develops a genitive 'theology of work', presenting a theological definition of
work and a model for a theological ethics of work that shows work's nature,
value and meaning now and eschatologically. Work is shown to be a
transformative activity consisting of three dynamically inter-related dimensions:
the instrumental, relational and ontological.
2005 / 1-84227-332-9 / xvi + 208pp

Stephen M. Dunning
The Crisis and the Quest
A Kierkegaardian Reading of Charles Williams
Employing Kierkegaardian categories and analysis, this study investigates both
the central crisis in Charles Williams's authorship between hermetism and
Christianity (Kierkegaard's Religions A and B), and the quest to resolve this
crisis, a quest that ultimately presses the bounds of orthodoxy.
2000 / 0-85364-985-5 / xxiv + 254pp

Keith Ferdinando
The Triumph of Christ in African Perspective
A Study of Demonology and Redemption in the African Context
The book explores the implications of the gospel for traditional African fears of
occult aggression. It analyses such traditional approaches to suffering and
biblical responses to fears of demonic evil, concluding with an evaluation of
African beliefs from the perspective of the gospel.
1999 / 0-85364-830-1 / xviii + 450pp

Andrew Goddard
Living the Word, Resisting the World
The Life and Thought of Jacques Ellul
This work offers a definitive study of both the life and thought of the French
Reformed thinker Jacques Ellul (1912-1994). It will prove an indispensable
resource for those interested in this influential theologian and sociologist and for
Christian ethics and political thought generally.
2002 / 1-84227-053-2 / xxiv + 378pp

David Hilborn
The Words of our Lips
Language-Use in Free Church Worship
Studies of liturgical language have tended to focus on the written canons of
Roman Catholic and Anglican communities. By contrast, David Hilborn
analyses the more extemporary approach of English Nonconformity. Drawing
on recent developments in linguistic pragmatics, he explores similarities and
differences between 'fixed' and 'free' worship, and argues for the
interdependence of each.
2006 / 0-85364-977-4 / approx. 350pp

Roger Hitching
The Church and Deaf People
*A Study of Identity, Communication and Relationships with Special Reference to
the Ecclesiology of Jürgen Moltmann*
In *The Church and Deaf People* Roger Hitching sensitively examines the history
and present experience of deaf people and finds similarities between aspects of
sign language and Moltmann's theological method that 'open up' new ways of
understanding theological concepts.
2003 / 1-84227-222-5 / xxii + 236pp

John G. Kelly
One God, One People
The Differentiated Unity of the People of God in the Theology of
Jürgen Moltmann
The author expounds and critiques Moltmann's doctrine of God and highlights the systematic connections between it and Moltmann's influential discussion of Israel. He then proposes a fresh approach to Jewish–Christian relations building on Moltmann's work using insights from Habermas and Rawls.
2005 / 0-85346-969-3 / approx. 350pp

Mark F.W. Lovatt
Confronting the Will-to-Power
A Reconsideration of the Theology of Reinhold Niebuhr
Confronting the Will-to-Power is an analysis of the theology of Reinhold Niebuhr, arguing that his work is an attempt to identify, and provide a practical theological answer to, the existence and nature of human evil.
2001 / 1-84227-054-0 / xviii + 216pp

Neil B. MacDonald
Karl Barth and the Strange New World within the Bible
Barth, Wittgenstein, and the Metadilemmas of the Enlightenment
Barth's discovery of the strange new world within the Bible is examined in the context of Kant, Hume, Overbeck, and, most importantly, Wittgenstein. MacDonald covers some fundamental issues in theology today: epistemology, the final form of the text and biblical truth-claims.
2000 / 0-85364-970-7 / xxvi + 374pp

Keith A. Mascord
Alvin Plantinga and Christian Apologetics
This book draws together the contributions of the philosopher Alvin Plantinga to the major contemporary challenges to Christian belief, highlighting in particular his ground-breaking work in epistemology and the problem of evil. Plantinga's theory that both theistic and Christian belief is warrantedly basic is explored and critiqued, and an assessment offered as to the significance of his work for apologetic theory and practice.
2005 / 1-84227-256-X / approx. 304pp

Gillian McCulloch
The Deconstruction of Dualism in Theology
With Reference to Ecofeminist Theology and New Age Spirituality
This book challenges eco-theological anti-dualism in Christian theology, arguing that dualism has a twofold function in Christian religious discourse. Firstly, it enables us to express the discontinuities and divisions that are part of the process of reality. Secondly, dualistic language allows us to express the mysteries of divine transcendence/immanence and the survival of the soul without collapsing into monism and materialism, both of which are problematic for Christian epistemology.
2002 / 1-84227-044-3 / xii + 282pp

Leslie McCurdy
Attributes and Atonement
The Holy Love of God in the Theology of P.T. Forsyth
Attributes and Atonement is an intriguing full-length study of P.T. Forsyth's doctrine of the cross as it relates particularly to God's holy love. It includes an unparalleled bibliography of both primary and secondary material relating to Forsyth.
1999 / 0-85364-833-6 / xiv + 328pp

Nozomu Miyahira
Towards a Theology of the Concord of God
A Japanese Perspective on the Trinity
This book introduces a new Japanese theology and a unique Trinitarian formula based on the Japanese intellectual climate: three betweennesses and one concord. It also presents a new interpretation of the Trinity, a co-subordinationism, which is in line with orthodox Trinitarianism; each single person of the Trinity is eternally and equally subordinate (or serviceable) to the other persons, so that they retain the mutual dynamic equality.
2000 / 0-85364-863-8 / xiv + 256pp

Eddy José Muskus
The Origins and Early Development of Liberation Theology in Latin America
With Particular Reference to Gustavo Gutiérrez
This work challenges the fundamental premise of Liberation Theology, 'opting for the poor', and its claim that Christ is found in them. It also argues that Liberation Theology emerged as a direct result of the failure of the Roman Catholic Church in Latin America.
2002 / 0-85364-974-X / xiv + 296pp

Jim Purves
The Triune God and the Charismatic Movement
A Critical Appraisal from a Scottish Perspective
All emotion and no theology? Or a fundamental challenge to reappraise and
realign our trinitarian theology in the light of Christian experience? This study
of charismatic renewal as it found expression within Scotland at the end of the
twentieth century evaluates the use of Patristic, Reformed and contemporary
models of the Trinity in explaining the workings of the Holy Spirit.
2004 / 1-84227-321-3 / xxiv + 246pp

Anna Robbins
Methods in the Madness
Diversity in Twentieth-Century Christian Social Ethics
The author compares the ethical methods of Walter Rauschenbusch, Reinhold
Niebuhr and others. She argues that unless Christians are clear about the ways
that theology and philosophy are expressed practically they may lose the ability
to discuss social ethics across contexts, let alone reach effective agreements.
2004 / 1-84227-211-X / xx + 294pp

Ed Rybarczyk
Beyond Salvation
Eastern Orthodoxy and Classical Pentecostalism on Becoming Like Christ
At first glance eastern Orthodoxy and classical Pentecostalism seem quite
distinct. This ground-breaking study shows they share much in common,
especially as it concerns the experiential elements of following Christ. Both
traditions assert that authentic Christianity transcends the wooden categories of
modernism.
2004 / 1-84227-144-X / xii + 356pp

Signe Sandsmark
Is World View Neutral Education Possible and Desirable?
A Christian Response to Liberal Arguments
(Published jointly with The Stapleford Centre)
This book discusses reasons for belief in world view neutrality, and argues that
'neutral' education will have a hidden, but strong world view influence. It
discusses the place for Christian education in the common school.
2000 / 0-85364-973-1 / xiv + 182pp

Hazel Sherman
Reading Zechariah
The Allegorical Tradition of Biblical Interpretation through the Commentary of
Didymus the Blind and Theodore of Mopsuestia
A close reading of the commentary on Zechariah by Didymus the Blind
alongside that of Theodore of Mopsuestia suggests that popular categorising of
Antiochene and Alexandrian biblical exegesis as 'historical' or 'allegorical' is
inadequate and misleading.
2005 / 1-84227-213-6 / approx. 280pp

Andrew Sloane
On Being a Christian in the Academy
Nicholas Wolterstorff and the Practice of Christian Scholarship
An exposition and critical appraisal of Nicholas Wolterstorff's epistemology in
the light of the philosophy of science, and an application of his thought to the
practice of Christian scholarship.
2003 / 1-84227-058-3 / xvi + 274pp

Damon W.K. So
Jesus' Revelation of His Father
A Narrative-Conceptual Study of the Trinity with Special Reference to
Karl Barth
This book explores the trinitarian dynamics in the context of Jesus' revelation of
his Father in his earthly ministry with references to key passages in Matthew's
Gospel. It develops from the exegeses of these passages a non-linear concept of
revelation which links Jesus' communion with his Father to his revelatory words
and actions through a nuanced understanding of the Holy Spirit, with references
to K. Barth, G.W.H. Lampe, J.D.G. Dunn and E. Irving.
2005 / 1-84227-323-X / approx. 380pp

Daniel Strange
The Possibility of Salvation Among the Unevangelised
An Analysis of Inclusivism in Recent Evangelical Theology
For evangelical theologians the 'fate of the unevangelised' impinges upon
fundamental tenets of evangelical identity. The position known as 'inclusivism',
defined by the belief that the unevangelised can be ontologically saved by Christ
whilst being epistemologically unaware of him, has been defended most
vigorously by the Canadian evangelical Clark H. Pinnock. Through a detailed
analysis and critique of Pinnock's work, this book examines a cluster of issues
surrounding the unevangelised and its implications for christology, soteriology
and the doctrine of revelation.
2002 / 1-84227-047-8 / xviii + 362pp

Scott Swain
God According to the Gospel
Biblical Narrative and the Identity of God in the Theology of Robert W. Jenson
Robert W. Jenson is one of the leading voices in contemporary Trinitarian theology. His boldest contribution in this area concerns his use of biblical narrative both to ground and explicate the Christian doctrine of God. *God According to the Gospel* critically examines Jenson's proposal and suggests an alternative way of reading the biblical portrayal of the triune God.
2006 / 1-84227-258-6 / approx. 180pp

Justyn Terry
The Justifying Judgement of God
A Reassessment of the Place of Judgement in the Saving Work of Christ
The argument of this book is that judgement, understood as the whole process of bringing justice, is the primary metaphor of atonement, with others, such as victory, redemption and sacrifice, subordinate to it. Judgement also provides the proper context for understanding penal substitution and the call to repentance, baptism, eucharist and holiness.
2005 / 1-84227-370-1 / approx. 274 pp

Graham Tomlin
The Power of the Cross
Theology and the Death of Christ in Paul, Luther and Pascal
This book explores the theology of the cross in St Paul, Luther and Pascal. It offers new perspectives on the theology of each, and some implications for the nature of power, apologetics, theology and church life in a postmodern context.
1999 / 0-85364-984-7 / xiv + 344pp

Adonis Vidu
Postliberal Theological Method
A Critical Study
The postliberal theology of Hans Frei, George Lindbeck, Ronald Thiemann, John Milbank and others is one of the more influential contemporary options. This book focuses on several aspects pertaining to its theological method, specifically its understanding of background, hermeneutics, epistemic justification, ontology, the nature of doctrine and, finally, Christological method.
2005 / 1-84227-395-7 / approx. 324pp

July 2005

Graham J. Watts
Revelation and the Spirit
*A Comparative Study of the Relationship between the Doctrine of Revelation
and Pneumatology in the Theology of Eberhard Jüngel and of
Wolfhart Pannenberg*
The relationship between revelation and pneumatology is relatively unexplored.
This approach offers a fresh angle on two important twentieth century
theologians and raises pneumatological questions which are theologically crucial
and relevant to mission in a postmodern culture.
2005 / 1-84227-104-0 / xxii + 232pp

Nigel G. Wright
Disavowing Constantine
*Mission, Church and the Social Order in the Theologies of John Howard Yoder
and Jürgen Moltmann*
This book is a timely restatement of a radical theology of church and state in the
Anabaptist and Baptist tradition. Dr Wright constructs his argument in dialogue
and debate with Yoder and Moltmann, major contributors to a free church
perspective.
2000 / 0-85364-978-2 / xvi + 252pp